THE REMINISCENCES OF
Rear Admiral Wayne E. Meyer
U.S. Navy (Retired)

INTERVIEWED BY
Paul Stillwell

U.S. Naval Institute • Annapolis, Maryland

Copyright © 2012

Preface

Few technological innovations in naval warfare can be described as revolutionary. Among those that qualified for the U.S. Navy in the 20th century were nuclear power and the Aegis combat system. The officer who headed the nuclear power program for many years was Admiral Hyman Rickover. For Aegis—in impact though not in longevity—the comparable individual was Rear Admiral Wayne Meyer. I first became acquainted with Admiral Meyer in 1991 when we sat next to each other at the decommissioning of the battleship *New Jersey* (BB-62). As we chatted, I invited him to take part in the Naval Institute's oral history program.

It took a long time for that planted seed to bear fruit. Five years ago, Troy Kimmel, who for many years worked for Meyer, twisted the admiral's arm and got him to agree to a series of interviews in the office suite where they worked in Crystal City, Arlington, Virginia. The admiral and I met periodically in a conference room that was adorned with various illustrations, plaques, and models that depicted aspects of the Aegis program. On a large bulletin board was a series of progress photos of his namesake destroyer *Wayne E. Meyer* (DDG-108), then under construction at Bath Iron Works in Maine. The photos were updated regularly as we proceeded through an interview process that lasted nearly a year and a half and covered the period from his boyhood until his retirement from active duty. Unfortunately, the admiral's health was declining during that same period, with the result that our plans to discuss his post-active duty years were never fulfilled. He died a few months later.

Admiral Meyer's boyhood in Missouri was a touchstone to which he referred often during the course of our visits. He grew up in severe poverty during the Depression of the 1930s, a situation he described in considerable detail. From his parents he received a strong work ethic and apparently a gene that involved leadership and organizational ability. Interestingly, Meyer and all his siblings got into occupations that involved running large, complex organizations. Another factor to which the admiral referred frequently was the education he received in Catholic schools in Brunswick, Missouri. The sticky farm soil from which Meyer sprang was called "gumbo," and he often used that one word as a shorthand reference to his Missouri experience. In one particularly touching scene in Meyer's narrative, he recalled talking to his father about his plans to become a farmer after he had received Navy education and training during World War II. His father responded by saying that the education was a precious asset to be used in a broader arena than the family farm. Young Meyer turned that admonition into a long and productive naval career.

One of the benefits of a career-length oral history is the opportunity to view, one at a time, how the building blocks of that career came together. In part, it is a matter of timing and opportunities and in part the ability to produce when the opportunities present themselves and to create further opportunities. Meyer began his commissioned service shortly after World War II as electronics were playing an ever-larger role in the operation of the fleet. After getting some sea duty under his belt—including, as he recalled playfully, learning port from starboard—he attended guided missile school at a time when that discipline was young. He pushed for postgraduate education and acquired knowledge of fire control that he put to use with an assignment to one of the Navy's first guided missile cruisers, the USS *Galveston* (CLG-3) in that early 1960s.

In that same period, the Navy's surface-to-air guided missiles produced a series of poor performances. For all the hype that the new weapon systems were receiving, they did not live up to it in reality. Captain Eli Reich, documented the failures with a series of tests while commanding the cruiser *Canberra* (CAG-2). As a result, in 1962, soon after Reich was promoted to rear admiral, he was put in charge of the Special Navy Task Force for Surface Missile Systems. Meyer entered the project as one of Reich's staff members the following year and essentially remained as part of it for almost all of the remainder of his career. It was as part of the program that Meyer, soon after his own selection to be a flag officer, was put in charge of the Aegis Shipbuilding Project. From reading his recollections of his long span of time in command, one learns a lot about his philosophy, his leadership and management techniques, and his personality. He liked to be in charge, and in doing so he produced a revolutionary system and a loyal band of followers. His legacy remains in many ships in the fleet of the 21st century.

John Maloney produced the superb original transcript of the interview recordings. Because Admiral Meyer died without having an opportunity to review the transcript, two of his long-time associates, Troy Kimmel and Robert Gray, undertook that project on his behalf. I am grateful to both of them for their many suggestions and corrections. Even with the editing that they and I have done, the admiral's style of speaking was largely untouched. I did reorganize the transcript for the sake of continuity, and I eliminated some of the repetition. When I asked Admiral Meyer questions, sometimes he would provide a direct answer; sometimes he would recall background that related to the question; and sometimes he would go off on unrelated digressions and even digressions from the digressions. The revised sequence provides more continuity than the original.

Two publications were particularly helpful in the editing process. Ms. Adelaide Madsen produced a history of the Aegis program and its predecessors. It was consistently helpful in checking dates and names. A comprehensive publication useful for anyone tracing the history of Meyer's program is "The Story of Aegis," a special one-topic edition of *Naval Engineers Journal*, Volume 121, Number 3, produced in 2009 for distribution at the commissioning of the USS *Wayne E. Meyer*. I also recommend the article "Acquisition Reform the Meyer Way," by Robert Gray, Troy Kimmel, and Sam Tangredi, published in the December 2010 issue of *Naval Institute Proceedings*.

In winding up this project, I thank Deborah Geanuleas and Charlene Yang, who worked in Admiral Meyer's office during the course of the interviews. Meyer's wife Anna Mae was invariably supportive. All three were consistently helpful. As mentioned, Troy Kimmel and Bob Gray were an indispensable part of editing the transcript. Janis Jorgensen of the Naval Institute staff has been a friend of long-standing. It was she who coordinated the printing and binding of the finished history.

In completing this volume, the Naval Institute expresses its gratitude to the Tawani Foundation and the Pritzker Military Library of Chicago for their generous financial support of the oral history program that produced this memoir.

Paul Stillwell
U.S. Naval Institute
December 2012

REAR ADMIRAL WAYNE EUGENE MEYER
UNITED STATES NAVY (RETIRED)

Born: 21 April 1926, Brunswick, Missouri

Died, 1 September 2009, Washington, D.C.

Chronological Record of Service:

13 May 1943	Enlisted in the U.S. Naval Reserve
1 July 1943	Reported for active duty
8 February 1946	Commissioned ensign, U.S. Naval Reserve
Mar 1946-Feb 1947	Massachusetts Institute of Technology, Cambridge, Massachusetts, Student (Electronic Engineering)
21 May 1947	Appointment, U.S. Naval Reserve, terminated
22 May 1947	Augmented to regular commission, U.S. Navy
Feb 1947-Jul 1948	USS *Goodrich* (DD-831), Electronics Officer
Jul 1948-Dec 1949	USS *Springfield* (CL-66), Electronics Officer
Dec 1949-Jul 1951	USS *Sierra* (AD-18), ASW/CIC officer
Jul 1951-Apr 1952	Naval Administrative Unit, Antiaircraft and Guided Missiles Branch, Fort Bliss, Texas, Student
Apr 1952-Sep 1954	Fleet Training Center Norfolk, Virginia, Instructor in Nuclear Weapons
Sep 1954-May 1955	General Line School, Monterey, California, Student
May 1955-Dec 1956	USS *Strickland* (DER-333), Executive Officer
Dec 1956-Jun 1958	Staff, Commander Destroyer Force Atlantic Fleet, Assistant Plans and Operations Officer
Jun 1958-Jul 1960	Naval Postgraduate School, Monterey, California, Student
Jul 1960-Jun 1961	Massachusetts Institute of Technology, Cambridge, Massachusetts, Student

Jun 1961-Jul 1963	USS *Galveston* (CLG-3), Fire Control Officer, Weapons Officer
Jul 1963-Sep 1965	Bureau of Naval Weapons, Terrier Fire Control System Manager, Special Navy Task Force for Surface Missile Systems/Member, Surface Missile Systems Project
Sep 1965-Jul 1966	Office of Naval Material, Surface Missile Systems Project, Fire Control Systems Manager, Terrier System Project
Jul 1966-Jan 1967	Naval Ordnance Systems Command, Terrier Weapons System Fire Control Manager, Anti-Air Warfare Systems Directorate
Jan 1967-Jun 1970	Naval Ship Missile Systems Engineering Station, Port Hueneme, California, Director, Engineering Directorate/Acting Executive Officer
Jun 1970-Jul 1974	Naval Ordnance Systems Command, Weapon Systems Manager, Advanced Surface Missile System (Aegis), Surface Missile Systems Directorate; Additional Duty: Aegis Project Office Project Manager, Surface Missile Systems Project
Jul 1974-May 1975	Naval Sea Systems Command, Project Manager, Aegis.SM-2, Director, Surface Warfare Systems, Group 3
May 1975-Oct 1976	Naval Sea Systems Command, Director for Combat Systems
Oct 1976-Aug 1983	Naval Sea Systems Command, Project Manager, Aegis Shipbuilding Project
Aug 1983-Nov 1985	Naval Sea Systems Command, Deputy Commander for Combat Systems; Additional Duty: Office of the Chief of Naval Operations (Executive Manager for Explosive Ordnance Disposal and Technology Training)
1 December 1985	Retired from active duty

Dates of Rank:

Ensign: 8 February 1946
Lieutenant (junior grade): 8 February 1949
Lieutenant: 1 May 1952
Lieutenant Commander: 1 November 1957
Commander: 1 July 1962
Captain: 1 July 1967
Rear Admiral: 1 July 1975

Deed of Gift

The U.S. Naval Institute is hereby authorized to make available to individuals, libraries, and other repositories of its choosing the tapes and/or transcripts of 18 oral history interviews concerning the life and naval career of the late Rear Admiral Wayne E. Meyer. The Naval Institute may also, at its discretion, use the material in electronic/digital format, including posting on the Internet. The interviews were recorded in the period from October 2007 to March 2009 by Admiral Meyer in collaboration with Paul Stillwell for the U.S. Naval Institute.

The undersigned does hereby release and assign to the U.S. Naval Institute the rights and title to these interviews, with the exception that the undersigned retains the right to use the material for her own purposes and to designate others to use it, as she sees fit. The copyright in both the oral and transcribed versions shall be the property of the U.S. Naval Institute. The tape recordings of the interviews are and will remain the property of the U.S. Naval Institute.

Signed and sealed this 20th day of August 2011.

[signature]
Anna Mae Meyer
on behalf of Wayne E. Meyer

*The United States Naval Institute
gratefully acknowledges*

**Mr. Peter M. Edmondo
Vice Admiral John W. Nyquist, USN (Ret.)
Rear Admiral Kathleen K. Paige, USN (Ret.)
Vice Admiral J. Theodore Parker, USN (Ret.)
Vice Admiral William H. Rowden, USN (Ret.)
Lockheed Martin Corporation**

*for their generosity in
underwriting the oral history of*

Rear Admiral Wayne E. Meyer
U.S. Navy (Retired)

Interview Number 1 with Rear Admiral Wayne E. Meyer, U.S. Navy (Retired)
Place: Admiral Meyer's office in Arlington, Virginia
Date: Monday, 29 October 2007

Paul Stillwell: Good morning, Admiral. We're ready to get started on the story of your life, born in Brunswick, Missouri. But before we turned on the tape recorder you mentioned something about your ancestors and the background in that county in Missouri that would be useful to put on the record.

Admiral Meyer: Well, I was born in what's called the gumbo, the Missouri River bottom.* Brunswick is at the confluence of the Grand River, which flows down out of Nebraska to Chillicothe, Missouri, and the Missouri, which we called "The River." Then it wanders around eventually through Jeff City and on down near Columbia, and then on into St. Louis.†

Paul Stillwell: And Brunswick's somewhat northwest of Columbia.

Admiral Meyer: It is, about 60 or 70 miles. Many, many kids from Brunswick, Missouri, nowadays attend college or some part of college at Columbia.

Paul Stillwell: That's one of my alma maters also.

Admiral Meyer: Oh, right. Well, you didn't have journalism there, though.

Paul Stillwell: Yes, I did.

Admiral Meyer: Did you? All right. Well, I see. When I was a boy, only the well to do were able to go. People of my ilk were not members, nor in that era were there many scholarships lying around.

---
* "Gumbo" is a type of heavy, sticky mud. Throughout the remainder of the oral history, Admiral Meyer often used the word as a metaphor for his humble origins on farms in Missouri.
† Jefferson City is the state capital; Columbia is the site of the University of Missouri.

I don't know that it ever became an alma mater for me or anyone in my family. I was born on the 21st day of April in 1926. I enlisted in the United States Navy on the 12th day of May 1943. I believe the correct date when I graduated from high school was the 24th of May of 1943. It was approximately that. So a couple weeks after turning 17, I entered the Navy, and I've been there ever since. I was called up in June of that year, and I reported in July.

Paul Stillwell: Could we go back and get some of the background?

Admiral Meyer: I am. That's what I want for an anchor point there. All right?

Paul Stillwell: Okay.

Admiral Meyer: That's when my life underwent what I suppose you'd call an irreversible or an adiabatic change.

Brunswick, Missouri, was a town roughly of 1,600 people at the time, today about 950. The learned people were Father John Joseph Groetsch, pastor of St. Boniface Catholic Church; Reverend W. J. Bainey, pastor of St. John's Lutheran Church; Mr. Merrill, the lawyer in town; and Mr. McKinney, the president of Chariton County National Bank. They were looked upon as knowledgeable people, plus we had two doctors everybody adored. One was Dr. Wilson, one was Dr. Tatum. People went to them when they needed to ask somebody something, because they were thought to know all things. Which, of course, they did not, but they were thought to know it.

My daddy went to sixth grade. My mother had graduated from Brunswick High School through a quirk of some sort. She had a mother who was a farm woman, and her mother, my granny, was Lizzie Gunn, G-U-N-N. In my earlier days, I always told people that I'm a son of a gun because that's my origin. She became a widow woman before I was born, so I never knew her husband, or my grandpa. He had had several women, a couple of which we were told were squaws, but my granny was our granny, and in general when I was a boy she lived with us.

She had three sons. And, of course, you get their nicknames. My Uncle Frank was known as "Pistol:" "Uncle Pistol" or "Uncle Shot." They were not on the highest social level. As a matter of fact, they loved to drink, and they did drink. None of them that I can remember ever held a job permanently. One was a barber. My "Uncle Gat" was the third one. He was a damned good carpenter; he worked in a sawmill. Whenever they'd work, they were very, very good in their dexterity. It's just that you couldn't count on them to work.

She also had two girls, my Aunt Jessie and my mother, Nettie. Nettie was the baby of the family. My Uncle Gat was the oldest one, and his wife died in childbirth in her second child, and it kind of fell somehow to my mother, who was still at home, to raise those two boys they had. One was Jackie Boy and the other was Ray Boy. Jackie Boy was with us the rest of his life, off and on, as was my grandmother. Ray broke away and started wandering the country. He married a red-haired woman, which was kind of out of order where we come from; she was always suspect.

Paul Stillwell: Just because she had red hair?

Admiral Meyer: Yes. On my father's side there was one girl born in the whole group. My Aunt Roberta was her name. As soon as she reached age, she left for Dayton, Ohio, and she never returned. She had red hair. No one knows why she had red hair, but she was just about shamed out of town. So we talk about this bullshit of segregation and tormenting of people. Well, you can get it just as much with red hair as you can with the color of your face.

Paul Stillwell: Did you have any siblings per se, other than these two cousins who were raised with you?

Admiral Meyer: Yes. I was born as the oldest, and then the next year was my sister, Rose Ellen, whose nickname was Oodie. I don't know why. It was said that I couldn't pronounce her name and that I called her Oodie, and that stuck. Then the next year there was a third one, William Jewell, and he, interestingly enough, took on the nickname of

Bill. And then there was a fourth one a couple years after that, Margie Jean. My name is Wayne Eugene, and this was an era—and it may be before your time—but in that part of the country most children were given two names, and the older people called them by their two names. And anything official, those two names were used. Their baptism or on any kind of records those names were used. So I'm Wayne Eugene.

Paul Stillwell: There's a William Jewell College in western Missouri. Was there a connection in that name?

Admiral Meyer: None. But my grandpa on my dad's side, his name was Julius. My mother's mother really was a river rat. My mother grew up on an island in the river, and she was put ashore with some relatives to go to school, which was one of the reasons she got through school. My dad got to the sixth grade, which was about an ordinary level reached in that time by people of the dirt, farm people. They hardly ever got to high school. Later we'll come to the matter of how *I* ended up in high school, because of the progressive and changing nature of the state of Missouri.

Paul Stillwell: So you had a crowded household growing up.

Admiral Meyer: We did.

My dad's youngest brother had the given name of Vernon, but he was called Wienie because he was a skinny little thing. His older brothers, of which there were four, all referred to him as Wienie. Today, as we speak, you and I, this October, I have only one of that whole crew that's still alive, and that's my Uncle Wienie. He's about 94 or so. He's very, very active, and we can talk about him another time if need be. This is a man that you cannot get to on Saturday night. He is a widower. He raised children. But he's a man that loves to dance, and he goes dancing every, every Saturday night. Then Friday nights, these days, he and his girlfriend usually go gambling someplace, because he likes to roll the dice.

He took over what is known as the Brunswick Community Sale from the Spence boys, who were losing it. Now, that was an era in the 1930s associated not only with the drought but also the Depression.* Today we'd call them farm sales. There became so many of them that community sales grew up, and the whole matter of shipping cattle and hogs was a challenge in the Midwest. St. Louis was a market, Kansas City was a market, St. Joe was a market. And, of course, Chicago was too far, and Quincy was too far. They generally had to go by rail, and not only was that not cheap, but it also was not very livestock-friendly. I mean, the livestock underwent a lot of abuse to go to St. Louis, which was 200 miles, and Kansas City, which was 100 miles, so they lost a lot of weight in the process.

Paul Stillwell: How close did the railroad come to Brunswick?

Admiral Meyer: It ran right through the middle of Brunswick. There would be no Brunswick without the railroad. I own right now what was my mother's house.† It's roughly 300 yards from the railroad. So when Anna Mae and I visited there a few weeks ago, the first thing that happens when you get there is the goddamn trains just drive you crazy.‡ Just freight train after freight train after freight train going down. But after you're there about half a day, you don't even hear them. They just come right straight through town. There were about eight or nine crossings in town. Today there may be three of them left. They've been blocked up for safety reasons. A number of years ago one of my cousins was killed on one of the crossings, which resulted in that closing. Life just keeps going on. It goes on all night, as long as we're on the subject.

    Moberly, which is north of Columbia, is about 40 miles from Brunswick. When I was a boy, it was a really, really big deal to go to Moberly. I was in Moberly maybe three times in my life, because that's where the big stores were.

Paul Stillwell: That's where Omar Bradley came from.

---

* Following the crash of the New York Stock Exchange in late October 1929, the United States was plunged into the Great Depression, from which it did not recover until the nation geared up for World War II. The Depression was marked by high unemployment and many business failures.
† Meyer bought his mother's home in Brunswick after her death.
‡ Anne Mae Meyer was the admiral's second wife. His first wife died, as related later in this oral history.

Admiral Meyer: That's where Omar Bradley came from, you're right.* Maxwell Taylor came from Keytesville, which is the county seat, 12 miles away.† So I'm right up there with the biggies. [Chuckle]

The railroad roundhouse used to be at Brunswick, and we had what is known as a high line. You may be acquainted with the expression. High lines are spurs that come off the main road, and the main road across that part of the country was the Wabash, which ran to Detroit. Of course, the Wabash was everything in people's lives. Again, when we lived in the gumbo, we were maybe two miles down in the mud below the railroad when the first streamliner came through.‡ Kids all over the county walked out and got up there in the field to stand there and watch that amazing, beautiful streamliner come rolling across the fields for the first time. It was a passenger train, of course.

Paul Stillwell: It's in Chicago now, at the Museum of Science and Industry.

Admiral Meyer: Right. It, of course, was on a show-and-tell mission around the country, and people turned out everyplace to see the beauty of the thing.

Well, a bunch of my uncles worked on the railroad, and one of them worked in the roundhouse. Today the roundhouse, of course, is no more. The roundhouse that exists is in Moberly, and all the main switching generally has been moved to Moberly. The railroad's now Norfolk Southern; it's not any longer Wabash. But they're making up trains and switching to building these 100-car trains, 110-car trains, all night long. They originate in Moberly, which is 40 miles away.

Paul Stillwell: Do you remember having a legacy of the Civil War in that area when you were growing up? Were there any veterans still around?

---

* General of the Army Omar N. Bradley, USA, served as Chairman of the Joint Chiefs of Staff from 16 August 1949 to 14 August 1953.
† General Maxwell D. Taylor, USA, served as Chairman of the Joint Chiefs of Staff from 1 October 1962 to 3 July 1964.
‡ In 1934 the Burlington Zephyr went into commercial service. The engine ran on diesel-electric power, rather than the steam typical of the period. It had a streamlined design that featured a silver-colored outer skin of the lightweight alloy Duralumin used for aircraft.

Admiral Meyer: Well, my granny was a girl. I can't honestly remember an adult or a soldier. Now, we have an old cemetery in Brunswick which has a problem getting a claimant, and generally the city takes care of the cemetery when the weeds get so bad, or a bunch of people make a donation to go clean it up. Most of the stones have been turned over, tipped over, or become unreadable. And so there's information exists, I'm sure, around in the various files and historical places, but the general knowledge doesn't exist on any veterans.

In my growing-up years, the veterans were from World War I.[*] The soldiers that went from where I came from were all farm boys. They ended up going over in the expeditionary force as privates, and they came back as privates. I don't know what the percentage was that got gassed, but it was a very high number.[†] Many of my friends that I grew up with, their fathers had been gassed. Now, interestingly enough, my dad and his brothers were all too young for the First World War and too old for the Second World War.

Paul Stillwell: When was your dad born?

Admiral Meyer: He was born in 1903, I believe.

Paul Stillwell: So he was a teenager during the war.

Admiral Meyer: He was a teenager, right. Those two wars teach you something, and you already know this, I'm sure, but what happens in wars—I digress here a minute now—is that wars follow year groups, and one of the popular ones, of course, for World War II is the year the stars shined on all the generals that were created to fight the war.

---

[*] Meeting in joint session on 6 April 1917, Congress overwhelmingly approved President Woodrow Wilson's request for a declaration of war on Germany, thus bringing the United States into World War I on the side of the Allies. The war ended in armistice on 11 November 1918.

[†] Poison gas was among the weapons used in World War I, with the result that some soldiers wound up with damaged lungs. In the Geneva Gas Protocol, signed in 1925, a number of nations pledged not to use poison as in the future.

Paul Stillwell: Eisenhower's class.*

Admiral Meyer: Eisenhower's, you got it.

Paul Stillwell: Nineteen fifteen.†

Admiral Meyer: And it's a lesson that I'm not sure you writers keep reminding the public enough about. I *know* we don't. I mean, we can raise generals and admirals; we can just raise them every year. But they grow old, and they may put a whole tour in and never be needed for anything, but the month you need them you need them. And that gets swept aside in America. We tend to think that we can just simply go out in the countryside with a truck and round up whomever we need. Well, to a degree you can, for soldiers and sailors, but you can't do that for your leaders. You've got to grow those leaders.

Paul Stillwell: You can't hire them from a Fortune 500 company.

Admiral Meyer: You cannot get them from that; it won't happen. One of my sayings in my many speeches is that I keep reminding people in Aegis, it takes 25 years to make an Aegis cruiser skipper.‡ Just in the Navy. This is before he got to us. So he's had 25 years of service by the time he gets command of that cruiser. And we ain't found no shortcuts. There's just no easy way out. God created the ability to parent a lot different than the ability to produce leadership. The two don't sync up at all.

Now, you can get a lot of heroics at 18. It occurs all the time. Even at 17. So there are men, mostly dead, who are awarded the Medal of Honor and such. So heroism

---

* Dwight D. Eisenhower served as President of the United States from 20 January 1953 to 20 January 1961. During World War II he had been Supreme Commander of the Allied Expeditionary Force for the invasion of Europe. In the early 1950s, as a five-star general, he served as Supreme Allied Commander in Europe when the military portion of the North Atlantic Treaty Organization (NATO) was established.

† The West Point class of 1915 was known as "the class the stars fell on." Of the 164 graduates, 59 reached the rank of general officer.

‡ The Aegis air defense system, which involves the use of computers and phased-array radars, is installed in the cruisers of the *Ticonderoga* (CG-47) class and destroyers of the *Arleigh Burke* (DDG-51) class, as well as in warships of a number of allied navies.

is not consigned just to older people. Leadership generally is. You can't get many 19-year-old generals. And I shall talk about the meaning of that subject if we survive long enough, because I was commissioned at 19.

Paul Stillwell: Could we talk some about your father, what sort of work he did, and the background that he brought to it?

Admiral Meyer: My daddy was an ordinary farmer. His nickname was Boob, and, of course, most people look at that as derogatory. Today you wouldn't dare use it. He was called Boob all his life.

Paul Stillwell: Where did that come from?

Admiral Meyer: His nephews and nieces called him "Uncle Boob." I don't know. He and his brothers all had nicknames. I told you one was Wienie. That was the youngest. Uncle Beef, whose name was Julius Herman, was a big fellow, easily 6-foot-2 or 6-foot-3. A really muscular-type guy, drove a truck. Frosty was one that worked on the railroad. His name was Louis. He got the name Frosty because he ran away from home when he was in the eighth grade or thereabouts with the boy next door. They hopped a freight at Brunswick, and hoboes hit them over the head and threw them out by DeWitt because they had no money on them. Later, as the story goes, that night my grandpa got a call by the sheriff that they had these two boys in the hospital at Carrollton, Missouri, near death. As a result of that experience, he lost some toes. They got frostbitten. So he had the name "Frosty" the rest of his life. And then the other one, the oldest one, his name was Andrew, but his nickname was Jeff. I think I was in the Navy before I ever knew that he even had a name other than Jeff. He was always our Uncle Jeff. He drove a truck, worked on the railroad some.

Paul Stillwell: Did you know your grandfather on that side?

Admiral Meyer: Yes. Grandpa, or popularly known as "J. O." I don't know his middle name; I think it was Otis. Julius, "J. O." Meyer. He was called "J. O." by everybody. His wife's name was Sophie, and they were both German, but I can't remember whether they immigrated or not. They may have been children when they came from Germany. Because I knew my great grandpa, who lived down the road, and I can remember him—I've said this to Anna Mae—when I was a little bitty boy, and he died when he was, like, I don't know, 97-98, a little bitty shriveled-up man. And he's buried out there in a graveyard. I can't say I identified with him, but he was my ancestor. And he was married to a little bitty shriveled-up woman.

Well, their name was Meyer, as I said. Her name was Straub. The Straubs and Meyers intermarried over time, and, God, if you went to sort out my structure today it would just wear you out. It wears me out. I'm the only one left alive that could even attempt to sort it out.

In the main, they immigrated just like they were, so half of my family are Catholic, and half of them are Lutheran, and that's how they came. And they came generally as farmers. As kids we'd gather around my grandpa, J. O., and ask, "Grandpa, what are we? What are we?"

He'd say, "You're the Low Dutch." That'd be his answer. We never knew what it meant, but it shut us up. [Chuckle] But he meant Dutch in the Deutsch spelling of it. He spoke a few words of German, as did she, but not enough. They would use a phrase now and then around us kids, but otherwise they didn't speak it.

When I was a boy, Father Meinhardt was a pastor of St. Boniface, but it wasn't that I was in the church. We had quit going to church. Meinhardt was a German, and he spoke German very fluently and was sent there for that reason. As a matter of fact, Reverend Bainey spoke German; he was the Lutheran pastor. So that they could communicate; it was really just that simple. That generation's all died out now and gone.

Paul Stillwell: Well, did you wind up in one church or the other during your boyhood?

Admiral Meyer: In 1935 farmer after farmer after farmer was displaced, and Eugene Clarence, known as Boob Meyer, was also displaced. His wife, four kids, and his mother-in-law, and a big dog named Cicero. And in March of 1935 we moved 13 miles. We didn't have much left. We had one old truck with hard rubber tires on it. We had a Rumely tractor.* We had four horses left, out of, I don't know, hell, 30 horses; a few hogs; 12 head of milk cows. We moved to clay country. As I say, it was 13 miles. It was like moving to the other side of the moon. In the bottom you had cattle, horses, hogs, barley and oats, and corn. In the hills all you had was goddamn rocks and clay. Sheep, goats, smelly creatures, terrible. It was a whole change of life.

It took a number of years for me to truly feel my dad's pain and my mother's pain. We saw it off and on. We'd see them cry, and the suffering that they were going through, of what they had lost. They had moved and had no money.

Paul Stillwell: How big a farm did you have before you moved?

Admiral Meyer: About 800 acres. You want to ask me after we moved?

Paul Stillwell: After you moved?

Admiral Meyer: A hundred and twenty, all rocks and brush. Big change. They had no money. Farmer after farmer had just mortgaged himself and mortgaged himself away. He needed $400.00 to buy this no-good piece of dirt from a bank out in the hills. He borrowed the money from his brother, Louis, named Uncle Frosty, worked on the railroad. One of the worst mistakes he ever made in his life. It took him a long time to get over it. He borrowed the money and gave a quarter of the farm to his brother in return. I was the oldest. I could not understand the seriousness of it, but I knew it was serious, whatever it was. I could tell it was, because I would hear the adults talk about it, my mother and my dad, and what were they going to do.

At that time we had a 1926 Chevrolet that was about to fall apart. And so my Uncle Frosty, who was a pretty good carpenter, made a deal with my dad. In return for no money my Uncle Frosty would do carpentry work. And all good Germans, the first

---

* The Rumely Company was founded in 1853 in La Porte, Indiana, and manufactured tractors until it was purchased by Allis-Chalmers in 1931.

building they work on is their barn. The last building they work on is their house, because livestock is more important to Germans than house. I'm sure you've traveled some in Germany in your time.

Paul Stillwell: Very little.

Admiral Meyer: Yes. Well, if you go around you'll find it even today. You get out in the countryside. A lot of them still live with their livestock and they have their livestock just in a barn attachment right alongside their house, and they look after them very, very well, because livestock are important to Germans of the dirt. Or, as my grandpa said, "Low Dutch."

Paul Stillwell: So was there a house on this second farm when you moved to it?

Admiral Meyer: It was a house that had papers to 1810. The first two rooms had been erected out of hewn walnut logs that had been felled on that farm, and they were roughly 6 inches thick and roughly 8 to 9 inches wide. They'd been put together with wooden pegs. Then, as time went on and the house turned over and turned over and turned over, a porch was added. And they had porches on porches. The house was surrounded with porches. It had an upstairs where the main walnut logs were, upstairs on each room, so one room upstairs was the boys' room, my brother and I, and the other was the girls' room.

Now, the heating stove was in the front room, and the pipe ran through the upstairs room of the girls, so they were right above the living room. There was a heating stove, a small one, in my parents' bedroom alongside. But, of course, normally they never lit it off. It had to really be bad. Well, whenever you'd try to get some heat you'd scurry into the girls' room to get close to that pipe. And the next thing you'd have was all this wailing and flailing going on. "Mama—these boys are in our room! They're in our room! These boys are in our room! Get them out of our room!" So that flail would go on, and they'd make a firm vow, to restore peace, that on cold nights they'd build a fire. But that never really happened much.

On the other hand, the big heating stove, when winter would come, particularly, say, from early January on into March, my dad generally never went to bed. He'd sit up all night—he had a big chair in the front room—and he'd make sure that there was wood in the stove, and stoked the stove. Well, to pacify my brother and I, there was a duofold downstairs, and so we were allowed to sleep in the front room on those really cold nights in the duofold. And just, you know, so many things change in one person's life. This has always been true. I mean, to wake up with snow drifting atop your bed in the front room, and it doesn't register on you till much later in life how bad that really was. How leaky the windows were that it came pouring through.

Everything we had, of course, were comforters, and all homemade, and those damned comforters, they could be warm but, boy oh boy, you were tired when you got up. [Chuckle] Man, those comforters were heavy. Because all through my life, both up in the hills and in the bottom, more in the hills than the bottom, were quilting bees, so the women all traded off and in a spare room someplace they usually had their frame set up and they'd rotate around working on each others' quilts. Virtually nothing was ever thrown away. Every single rag was kept. And, I mean, they were plenty raggy by the time they were rags. But they were kept because they went into quilts. Those women were just incredible, given a pair of scissors and some pretty heavy needles, in what they could cut and shape. And the materials they could use. They could mix any materials. The sewing that they could do was just amazing.

Paul Stillwell: Would your house accurately be described as a log cabin?

Admiral Meyer: It might be a little dramatic to describe it that way, because it had been structured originally by a pretty well-to-do person. A 120-acre farm, someplace on that farm there were maybe at least a dozen wells on that little farm, and four or five ponds, and the water for our house was a cistern. And we had an unusual setup because we had a hand pump. In the kitchen was a basin that we could pump and draw water out of the cistern in the house. I mean, that's unusual, really unusual.

It didn't help for the toilet, because the toilet was maybe 150 feet or so from the house. Well, interestingly enough, when we moved out there my dad and uncle built a new toilet, and they built this toilet atop an old well. And [chuckle] we never did know how deep it was, but you would always listen for the sound.

Paul Stillwell: The splash?

Admiral Meyer: The plop, right. (Laughter) That toilet never filled up. It *never* filled up. That toilet never had to be emptied. So it was a marvelous farmer-type innovation. It really was an incredible thing. So we never ever worried about a toilet again. Had to worry about flies, but we had a good toilet.

Paul Stillwell: How was the food supply during those Depression years?

Admiral Meyer: Well, I'd say we never bitched or moaned. You knew you were poor and, I mean, you just accepted it. Everybody was poor, and being poor was a way of life. Dealing with the drought was maybe harder than the other, because how to make your little garden grow? Because a garden is absolutely vital. So how well you ate was dependent on your vegetable gardens; your tater patch, both white taters and sweet taters; the canning of corn; and things of that nature. Grew a lot of beets, a lot of turnips—ate a lot of turnips—because beets and turnips can take the drought. You didn't have to like them, but you'd start liking them come about February.

Paul Stillwell: They'd fill you up.

Admiral Meyer: Yes. So then there was the problem, of course, of keeping wood for the cook stove besides the heating stoves. Splitting wood for the damned cook stove was a tiresome thing. And we two boys were still a little light in the pants to be able to split wood, so generally my dad had to do that. When we got a little older, before I left home, well, we took on the chores of splitting wood. Man, that stuff was hard to split, in particular while it was green.

All our wood came off that farm. We felled it all there, and we sawed it up on the buzz saw. And the buzz saw was operated by our Rumely Oil Pull tractor. Have you ever seen a Rumely Oil Pull tractor?

Paul Stillwell: I've seen pictures of these big steam-operated tractors.

Admiral Meyer: Well, the Rumely Oil Pull was kind of the first derivative after steam. I mean, it came directly from steam design. So it looked just like it was a boiler mounted there. There was a big stack. But in there were two big pistons. The pistons were about 12 inches each, and these pistons operated horizontally, and that gave it its signature when you could hear it. Allis-Chalmers had a lot to do with the design of that Rumely Oil Pull. My dad had the Rumely Oil Pull long after I'd gone to the Navy.

You stood up to drive this tractor. Its rear wheels were lugs – I mean, like big lugs—and its front wheels were two wheels far apart. It took a man to steer this tractor. So you couldn't use it in a little bitty field. This tractor was a great tractor in the gumbo. It would pull three 16-inch plows. No other tractor could challenge it in that gumbo. Do a beautiful job just putt-putt-putt going right along.

Paul Stillwell: Did it have metal wheels?

Admiral Meyer: Yes, all metal. *All* metal. No such thing as rubber tires.

Well, out in the hills he somehow came by a plow that was three 12-inch plows. You couldn't use the three even 12-inch many places out there; the places weren't big enough. And you had to have roughly a five-acre field or it wasn't worth trying to plow with a tractor because you couldn't turn it around. It took a lot of distance to turn it around. Your dad would learn how to turn it around, but, boy, it was a chore. So usually a field smaller than that, particularly cornfields, either walking cultivators or riding ones. We had one riding cultivator, which nobody liked to plow with, my dad or my grandpa, and the reason was the riding cultivator just did too much damage to the cornstalks. So the walking cultivators were the in things.

Interesting enough, my mother—I'm jumping around on you now—she, having been her mother's daughter, she loved to farm, and so she loved to get in the field. And she had a way of getting rid of her kids, and that was turn them over to Granny, who was in the house. So Granny would find herself getting dinner—we called it dinner, which you call lunch—and doing generally the chores in the kitchen while my mother was out in the field. She loved to be in the field. Granny loved to be in the field, but she was getting just a little bit too old.

Paul Stillwell: Was corn the cash crop?

Admiral Meyer: In the hills it was problematical. We sold almost no grain. We tried to raise hay, and the grain we raised went into our steers; our cash crop was steers. And if my dad could get enough dollars together he'd buy a steer at the time the steer was a calf. We still had usually about 12 or 13 head of milk cows which, of course, would only produce a dozen calves a year, and statistically half of them were heifers. So you'd only end up with six or seven steers that way. So you'd have to either find a way to trade off or go find a way to buy some to get up to maybe—he'd try to get 15 to 20 steers in the feed lot, and the mud was damn deep.

So now let me jump a hoop a minute, to come back. My youngest uncle liked to take chances. He had a flair, was a good-looking boy. He ran with good-looking women. When I was a little boy, he owned a Whippet roadster with the top down, red, and he was the baron's son. This was the mid-'30s. Well, he ended up taking possession of the Brunswick sale barn. I mentioned community sales that were getting their startup in that era. The Spence brothers had started it in the early '30s, and they couldn't make a go of it. They didn't have, first of all, business sense, but second of all they just didn't know how to run something like that. My Uncle Wienie took it over, and in that era there wasn't anything the community sale didn't sell. It'd sell anything.

There was Monday sale. His slogan for the next 50 years became "Sale Every Monday." "Sale Every Monday." So usually they would open at noon with fence posts, so men who had cut fence posts and felled them would bring in fence posts on a wagon or something, 12 posts, something like that. So they'd sell fence posts. And then they'd sell what we called junk, so if you had stuff you wanted to get rid of you brought it in to be sold. That would take about an hour, hour and a half, so by 2:00 o'clock was when the livestock sale would start. The first to be sold were the damned, stinking sheep, followed by hogs, followed by calves, followed by cows and a couple bulls. And later at night would be what was known as the fat cattle. They'd be sold, and they'd go on a truck immediately to go to market.

It was a shaky business, but he was good at it.

Paul Stillwell: Was he the auctioneer?

Admiral Meyer: No. Hired an auctioneer. Mr. Garner, from Mendon, Missouri, was his auctioneer for almost a half a century. Getting an auctioneer who had a reputation for honesty was very, very difficult. Mr. Garner had a lot of flaws, but he was dead honest. And so, in later years, my uncle always attributed that to the reason for survival of his sale. Brunswick Sale Company is the oldest surviving sale company that ever existed in Missouri. He went out of the junk business, and then eventually he even stopped dealing hogs because MFA, the Missouri Farmers Association, started dealing hogs, buying them on a commission straight from the farms and sent them straight to the butcher.[*] So he stopped dealing hogs; it was strictly cattle. He bought and sold cattle for himself all his life. The sale barn was a worn-out building that at one time was known as the Brunswick Brick and Tile Company on the bank of the Grand River. He created that sale barn out of whole cloth, right 100 feet from the railroad.

He convinced my dad to operate the back end for him, so my dad was the foreman all those years. You would bring your hog in or whatever else you wanted, and they'd check them in and they'd get marketed and then go out that night. So my dad was what you'd call the manager of the whole back end of moving the livestock, because my uncle would be preoccupied all day in the ring. He'd be running the sale and seeing that the sale was moving along. My dad was in charge of all the people behind the auction block, and it's pretty tricky keeping the stock lined up and in a smooth flow, because a good

---

[*] The Missouri Farmers Association was founded in Brunswick in 1914.

sale, just like so many other things, once the crowd loses attention it's really, really hard to get it back.

You get a crowd, they set up on these goddamn cottonwood hard bleachers, and they look like they don't have any money, but that fools you; they've got plenty of money. It's that they're pretty shrewd. They may sit there all afternoon and never buy anything. Then wow, all of a sudden one will be there and he'll just [snap, snap, snap] buy, buy, buy, buy. Because they get orders. These guys travel around, and they get orders for feedlots, so they're looking for cows for feedlots. They'd have what are called cow/calf sales in the wintertime because they got orders for them someplace. So it didn't take many people to run a sale. Fifteen, twenty, is all you need as bidders.

Well, his wife, my aunt Madeleine, and my mother, Nettie, set up a lunch stand and ran it. On Mondays people would start coming to Brunswick in order to eat their lunch at the Brunswick Sale Company. They weren't going to buy anything; they came there to eat lunch. Sit on a hard bench to get a decent hamburger and hot dog or, what they called, get a wienie.

Time passed. Bookkeeping became harder and harder, like everything else with our government over the years. So my mother became one of the bookkeepers, and she got out of the restaurant business and my aunt then, she decided they were making enough money that somebody else could run it.

In their early days they made pies and ice cream. Every Saturday in that era was preoccupied, the whole damned house. They'd make 25-30 pies—be on every place you could set one down. My sisters would turn to, and you couldn't walk in the kitchen. I mean, you risked your life if you went in the kitchen [laughter] while they were making these damned pies. And my dad loved coconut cream pies, his favorite pie. And so, to pacify him, they made two coconut cream pies early on so whenever things got out of hand they'd just serve him a piece of pie, and he'd walk off and eat it someplace. [Chuckle]

Then on Sundays, in season, is when we'd make ice cream. All hand cranked. Put it together and crank it and repack it into five-gallon cans. People would come from everywhere just to eat our ice cream and our pies. The place would be jammed for a couple hours because they loved to come and eat that stuff. Then they'd say, "Oh, well, it looks like they're having a sale here too." They didn't come to buy anything except to eat.

Paul Stillwell: They put ice and rock salt around the can of cream?

Admiral Meyer: You got it. That's affirmative. Make it on Sunday, so you start selling on Monday she'd be frozen pretty darn hard in that container.

Paul Stillwell: So the farming took place between Tuesday and Friday, apparently?

Admiral Meyer: [Laughter] Right.

Paul Stillwell: How soon did you start driving the tractor?

Admiral Meyer: I can't remember when I started driving the tractor. I think I was probably driving the car under limited conditions even before that. I think I was driving a car probably about 12. Somewhere in that era, I forget what year now, Missouri, being a very enlightened state amongst others, put through a law that you had to have a license at 12 to drive, but in the farm country boys learned to drive much sooner than that, as they did on machinery.

My driving the Rumely Oil Pull tractor was very limited. That was usually my dad or a hired hand. It took a lot of muscle to wrestle that tractor and how you dealt with that tractor, and he didn't cotton to either my brother Bill or me operating that tractor. Because, again, as I've said, I left home when I turned 17. So I only had a couple years there to really do that.

Paul Stillwell: Did you have electricity in your house?

Admiral Meyer: Oh, what questions you ask. We had no electricity.

My mother and dad were fallen-away Catholics. My mother was a convert. Her family had been terribly upset about it. She was a Baptist. And when they married, they had a fit. But they had been married by the pastor, married by a priest, and I was baptized. And my sister Rose Ellen, one year after me, she was baptized. But by then they quit going to church. One of the reasons was it was just too hard. You were six miles out of town down in the gumbo. When you had to do that, it's easy to understand why we have so many country churches around through the Midwest. It's hard to get there, and driving a wagon six miles is just pretty demanding. It was all mud roads, and a muddy road, once you got past the Model T, you just couldn't. Early Model A's could handle some mud, but you just couldn't deal with the mud.*

When we moved to the hills in March of 1935—I have not covered this subject, but I'd like to cover it another time—I was enrolled in the Warden School in the bottom. That's a one-room schoolhouse with eight grades in it. Miss Helen Duncan was the teacher. She was about this tall.

Paul Stillwell: Five feet, maybe?

Admiral Meyer: When she started, she'd never set foot in a teachers' college. She did make teaching her career. She spent her whole life taking a six-week course every summer till she finally got a degree. And she became a well-honored and devoted teacher in Brunswick, Missouri. She still lives today. Anna Mae and I visit her when we're there. I think she's 94 now and a widow woman now; she never had any children. But she remembers us just like that, and Wayne, or more properly, Wayne Eugene.

In Warden School I was the only one in the third grade. George Fromm, my neighbor, was in the fourth grade. He was the oldest boy but he had two older sisters, and they were in the upper grades, seventh and eighth grades. So George and I studied a lot together. When you've got eight grades in one room, the teacher's an incredible person. I mean, it's just absolutely incredible when you reflect back on it, of their ability to lead and to handle things. So you helped each other, and the seventh and eighth grade kids helped the kids below that. So it's all a help outfit.

Recess? Everybody played. Under Miss Helen it didn't matter whether you were first grade or eighth grade. Everybody was in the ball game. Everybody played. Little

---

* The Model T and Model A were early automobiles mass-produced by the Ford Motor Company.

kids couldn't handle it, an older kid batted for them and the little kid did the running. But everybody played. You didn't have an option of sitting it out unless you were a cripple. You didn't have the option of going and doing something else or piddling around with a dice game. That teaches you a lot. She's a wonderful woman.

Well, in the middle of the year she had run out of materials, so she petitioned the school board as to whether she could advance me and George one grade. That's how I got in the 17-year-old syndrome. The school board endorsed it, so I was advanced to the fourth grade, George was advanced to the fifth grade, and we just kept going.

Also that was when disaster was ready to strike. So March 1935, we were on the road. The Fromm family, by the way, who lived right down there, maybe a half-mile from us, they were also on the road, so they were moved out in the hills too. I think there were six in their family. They were a bigger family than we were.

Well, I don't know why they decided to go back to church. But about a quarter mile from our house—and boy, we thought this was going to be great—Allega School was located. We'd been walking a mile and a half to school on a mud road except when we could ride the pony. I had Old Cap, and I could ride Old Cap. And we had a hitching rail at the school the kids; the older kids had ponies to ride. But Allega School was almost across the street.

Paul Stillwell: How do you spell the name of that new school?

Admiral Meyer: Allega. A-L-L-E-G-A. Named after a family. Miss Louise Hanna was the teacher. And she had a nice reputation.

Someplace there they had decided to enroll us in the Catholic school—or the popular expression of the day, the derogatory expression, was the "Catholicker" school. We didn't have a vote on it; they decided to do that. I don't know how they decided it. And, of course, the Catholicker school is downtown. We were now on a gravel road when we moved out in the hills. That was a big breakthrough too. Ironically, the school bus turned around right out there in front of our yard on its route, but parochial kids couldn't ride the bus. Neither could Episcopalians or Lutherans, for that matter, but someplace in that era their schools closed, so it became irrelevant in their case.

That poor couple. They figured out a way, in 1935—and I was in the fifth grade—to take us to school each day and pick us up and bring us home. Six miles. How in the world they afforded it I'll never know, but they were determined they were going to do it. It was ironic, because St. Boniface School was a two-room schoolhouse, so I'd already upgraded from one room to two. Grades 1 through 4 and 5 through 8.

Sister Mary Albertina from Austria—she was about four foot tall—had the lower grades. Sister Mary Joanne, born and raised in Canada, had the upper grades. I was in the fifth grade. Well, it didn't take them but a half a day to figure out that when it came to religion I was a misfit in the upper room. So I underwent the ignominy that every day for religion I had to go to the lower room—I think it was about 10:00 o'clock or 10:30—and sit with the little snot-nosed kids in grades three and four.

An incident happened to me that year that has affected my entire life. I don't know whether you've ever been associated with parochial schools.

Paul Stillwell: No.

Admiral Meyer: Well, their discipline is wonderful. It's well to behold, and it never leaves you. These were Order of St. Francis sisters, and if you were going to ask a question the first thing you did was you get your hand up and your mouth shut until Sister recognized you. Then you got up on your feet and you asked the question. And if she didn't understand the question, either you reframed it or she reframed it. And then you sat back down. And then she figured out how we were going to answer the question. Was it going to be a student, or was it going to be her? Really well run.

I finally got up enough nerve after a couple of months over there to ask a question. So I went through the process, and what I'm about to say to you brings tears to my eyes yet today. I stood up and I asked her, "Sister, do cattle have souls?" The whole room broke out giggling and carrying on and everything, and I really felt it. It hurt something fearful. She carried her basic shillelagh; it was a 12-inch ruler. She ran 30 kids with a ruler, and they damned well knew the purpose of the ruler.

Paul Stillwell: On your hand.

Admiral Meyer: Yes. Right on your fingers. It got your attention. And first she'd snap it on the desk or the table. If that wasn't enough, then them boys pretty soon learned to pay attention. As far as I know, she never hurt anybody, but I don't think it ever mattered, because that was an era where the parents thought if you got whacked you rated being whacked. You didn't have a right. There were no rights. [Chuckle]

Paul Stillwell: Did you get the ruler for that question?

Admiral Meyer: No. She whacked the ruler and called the class to order. She looked around to all of them and glared at them through her glasses, this little short woman. Then she looked back at me and she said, "Well, of course cattle have souls." She put the whole class down. She said, "Their souls are physical souls. Your soul is a spiritual soul." What a beautiful answer. I've never forgotten that answer. She shut that entire room up. From then on I was king of the walk too. [Laughter] Never again did anybody challenge me. Because I'd asked a question that was far above their intellect. [Laughter]

Paul Stillwell: Did you have to learn the catechism?

Admiral Meyer: Oh, yes. The Baltimore Catechism was our basic catechism. I had to learn that to get out of the little room. I was in the fifth grade, but it took me all year to learn that catechism so that I could get back to the big kids. The big kids never abused me. As a matter of fact, in my class there were four kids and three were girls, two of whom were our cousins.

So, because of my wise-ass question and how it ripped around the school it wasn't long before I was widely respected in the upper grades too, for my superior knowledge [chuckle]. And by now I could recognize a girl from a boy.

Paul Stillwell: Your education was growing by leaps and bounds.

Admiral Meyer: It was, but I had to use a little care because, you see, by now I was a grade ahead of my sister. In fact, two grades ahead because she did not skip a grade. So by the time I got over into the seventh grade she was now in the fifth grade. So I had a squealer at home if I wasn't careful.

But what I was going to say is that in 1935 to '36, somehow they drove us to school. The Moser kids, who lived over on the next hill, were a big family. They were enrolled in that school, and the Moser girls were really good-looking girls. One of them in my class was Mary Ann; she was the older girl in school. The really oldest one in the family was Eulalia; she'd already graduated out. She was in high school, and she had a license, so she drove that family back and forth to school every day, the Catholic school, and she went to high school.

Time passed, and we went along. Nineteen thirty-six came around, and a couple things started happening. One was related to electricity, which you brought up earlier. But another thing happened in that school, and it was that somehow Father John Joseph Groetsch from Pittsburgh had managed to retain the Order of St. Francis. He had two teachers and a cook. They lived in a convent next door. So the school was nailed down, and the school was widely thought of because the Episcopalian had closed and the Lutheran had closed. We did get a handful of kids from those schools that were negotiated by the pastor. I don't know; they paid some kind of fee to be able to attend in the Catholic school. But time passed on.

Sister Mary Joanne had a degree. She at that time was 27-28 years old. She died this past year in a retirement home at Parkville, Missouri. She was a wonderful woman, a wonderful teacher, and I had her all four grades. When I entered Brunswick High School, I had only had two teachers in my life up to then, Miss Helen and Sister Mary Joanne. And up until this past year we regularly visited both of them. This past spring we flew out to the burial of Sister Joan. They call her Joan now; she was always Joanne then.

Those two women—I wouldn't say they were wise in the ways of the world or any of those things, and they weren't smart-alecky or any of those things, and they had no children. They were just first-class women.

Paul Stillwell: Very devoted to the students.

Admiral Meyer: They were devoted to the students. And they were *their* students. They were determined that you were going to do the best you knew how to do, and if they didn't think you were doing the best you could do, little sessions occurred. It'd start with Father Groetsch. Then it would start with the mother, that Wayne is not doing as well as he could be doing. So you couldn't do anything but admire them.

Nineteen thirty-seven. Father Groetsch was a tinkerer of sorts. He considered himself knowledgeable in things of electricity and those mechanical things. He, of course, was not, [chuckle] but he thought he was. Well, he'd make periodic trips to St. Louis, and one of the reasons was he would do all the buying for the bazaar and for the picnic each summer of the prizes to be given away. He loved to go do that. And he loved to get these bargains at a big discount store or someplace in St. Louis, and have them all shipped to little old Brunswick. And people would come for miles to buy a ten-cent ticket on the drawings to get one of these prizes. That's how he financed the school. Brilliant. Only someone from Pittsburgh would have that wisdom.

By the way, in the years that followed, till 1939, he taught civics and he taught health in the school, but he taught us what a Jew was. Where I come from we didn't have the foggiest idea what a Jew was except the reference to it in the Bible. He taught us what a Jew was.

I'm jumping a little ahead here a minute—1939 I believe it was, a little old man by the name of Fritz Drueppel, a displaced person, came wandering somehow into Brunswick, Missouri. Spoke no English. He was an escapee somehow from Germany.* Father Groetsch spoke German fluently, and so he befriended this little man. He had no place to stay, so Father Groetsch created a little place for him in the back of the furnace room in the church basement, because our church basement, interestingly enough, had a toilet in it and everything because that's where a lot of social life occurred.

Fritz Drueppel was a potter; that was his trade. And in return Father started teaching him different words of English and introducing him to the older kids to help him with his English, and he in turn made pottery. To this day if you went to visit St.

---

* Adolf Hitler became Chancellor of Germany in 1933. As his power increased during the 1930s, he instituted more and more offensive actions against Jewish citizens in Germany, leading a number of them to seek refuge in other countries.

Boniface Church at Brunswick, Missouri, you'll find pieces of pottery around on the stone walls and around the church and outside the church, which were made—I don't think anyone any longer remembers—by Fritz Drueppel in that era as his return.

Paul Stillwell: Was there any positive or negative connotation in teaching you about who Jews were?

Admiral Meyer: No, it was just kind of a ho-hum thing. We didn't measure it one way or another. We knew the Jews around the Old Testament and we, once he taught it to us that it was the Jews who were the predominant people, we never—I don't think we really understood from the pulpit what he was telling us in the years '37, '38, '39, of what was going on in Germany. We didn't get it. He'd talk to us about it, but we didn't get it, because it was just far above our pay grade. I mean, the *Capper's Weekly* was our newspaper. But he would tell us what was happening to the Jews every Sunday. We never missed a single Sunday praying for the Jews because of their treatment in Germany and what was going on. Insofar as I know, none of my family structure were Jewish-related. They were either Lutheran or Catholic, as they had moved out of Germany. And there were no other Jew in Brunswick, Missouri. We just didn't know what one was.

Paul Stillwell: Well, did that raise your consciousness when Drueppel showed up?

Admiral Meyer: I'd say it raised our curiosity. It raised our curiosity because Father Groetsch was much admired, as was Reverend Bainey, who was the Lutheran pastor. And by the way, Bainey also talked to his congregations a lot about this subject, and half my family were Lutherans. So they raised their consciousness of it, but the seriousness never registered. It didn't register. They talked about it, and I think they were as descriptive as they knew how.

Fritz Drueppel never got over being grateful for what was done for him by the people of Brunswick, Missouri. Really, all they knew was that he was a displaced person. The idea that he was a Jew didn't mean very much to them. By the time I left home, his language wasn't bad. You could hold a little conversation with him. He was a smart guy. When I left for the Navy, I went to say goodbye to him, and that of itself is a long, windy story.

In 1937, on one of his trips to St. Louis, Reverend Bainey bought a little table model Emerson radio, one of the very first ones ever made. And with great flair he had it installed on a little shelf up high, that Sister had to stand on a stool to tune it, in the classroom of the upper grades. He and two of us boys helped him construct the aerial. We had an aerial that ran all the way around the school and back in through one of the rooms to come in to hook to this little radio. And out of there is how we were going to learn civics.

Well, if you'll reflect for a minute on '37 it was quite a year of things going on. Ethiopia, Mussolini, and the behaviors of Hitler.[*] So there were all kinds of worldly events. Sister would have us listen to these events for 15 minutes from whatever was being broadcast, and then on the blackboard we'd have to outline what we heard, or sometimes we'd have to write a little paper on it. Sometimes he would come and talk to us about what these events were, and what was going on around us, and that was our civics.

Paul Stillwell: Who did the disciplining in your family?

Admiral Meyer: I'd say my mother. My mother kept whatever books had to be kept, whatever records had to be kept, and she operated whatever discipline had to be operated.

Another big thing happened—I think it was 1937. The two younger Meyer kids were baptized. But also, in the Catholic Church the bishop administers the sacrament of confirmation, and out in that part of the country it's pretty rare. It's every maybe five years or so that it's administered because there's so many parishes that the bishop has trouble, at least then. Well, we were in the Diocese of St. Joseph, so now in '37 the bishop was going to come to administer confirmation. That's where we made the papers, both the *Kansas City Star* and the *Catholic Register*, which was, I think, printed out of Denver. And it was because a mother and her four children were all confirmed at once.

---

[*] Benito Mussolini organized the Fascists in Italy in the 1920s and ruled as dictator in that country until he was executed in 1945.

So that was our big star in the sun that year. And that was the end of that. It didn't ever happen again.

Back to the discipline. The physical discipline was rare. My mother would get a little upset and send you a-running someplace. My dad never laid a hand on me.

Interesting enough—let me step forward a minute. The time is February 1946. I'm home on leave a few days. I have now been commissioned. I now have a degree. I am 19 years old. I'm in the milking barn with my dad on Sunday evening, and we were talking as we were sitting there milking cows. The stalls could accommodate ten cows; we had ten stalls. He asked me what I was going to do. I said, "Well, I've been thinking a lot about it, and I thought I really would like to come back home and go into farming with you." He jumped up, he slammed his bucket down in the trough, he walked over to me and he grabbed me by my shirt and jerked me off the stool. He came the closest ever, ever, to hitting me in his whole life. All he did was say to me, "How could you be so goddamn stupid?" That was his statement. It took a while for that to sink into me, some weeks. I'd never appreciated how much that man had suffered and stored up for me.

Paul Stillwell: Sacrifice.

Admiral Meyer: Yes. Yes. And here he was about to see me throw it away, in his eyes. I thought farming is a wonderful vocation, a wonderful profession. He was a farmer when he was born, he was a farmer when he died, and that was pretty damned good to me. But it had been such a life that, certainly in real time he had trouble seeing the joys. The children were his joy, and their success was extraordinarily important to him.

Paul Stillwell: Their success, your success, was his success.

Admiral Meyer: Exactly. Exactly. And he almost invariably gave that credit, said or unsaid, to my mother. Those two teachers had a lot of effect on it. Father Groetsch had a lot of effect on her, in hindsight. But how your life gets affected, as the old saying goes on TV, there are a million stories in the city, and every human has a lot of stories of what made him or her what they are, and some of those are impossible stories.* Some of them are unbelievable stories. And some of them are just really routine. They vary all over the place. Many times you'd think that perhaps you had the roughest time of all. But in hindsight that Sunday evening in the milking barn was a turning point for me [chuckle]. It did change me, and it took me a long time to appreciate that it was a turning point.

Paul Stillwell: In other words he was saying: "Take advantage of this precious opportunity that you've been given."

Admiral Meyer: Yes. He was telling me that. In a way, the hurtful thing about it is he was saying to me, "Why would you want to put up with what I've put up with?" And yet I felt that we'd had some wonderful times. It was true that we had a lot of hard times, but I could wear you out from now until dark on the things we did as a family that were, to me, extraordinary things. They're just little things, like going to South Missouri and picking fruit in late August and bringing it all back, and all hands turning to, to preserve it. The mother and the two girls in the kitchen, the daddy and the boys outside, amongst other things, keeping the water boiling in the two black pots we had, 20-gallon cauldrons.

We had what was known as a—the commercial name of it at the time was Warm Morning cook stove. My dad had somehow convinced my mother, I'd say again about 1936 or '37 when they had no money, he wanted her to have a new stove, and they ordered this stove. I don't know how many years it took them to pay for it. New cook stove. It was a wonderful stove: four burners, big reservoir for warm water, big oven down below, warming ovens atop it. It was a wonderful stove. It really took a lot of work off of my mother and her sisters.

Paul Stillwell: What was the fuel?

Admiral Meyer: Wood. But you had grates in it that you could use coal. In, like about 1937, the Blount boys, who were creative people but never worked a job in their life,

---

* Admiral Meyer was referring to a television program called "Naked City" that ran from 1958 to 1963. It involved crime solving by New York City Police detectives. The tagline at the end of each episode was, "There are eight million stories in the naked city. This has been one of them."

lived on their dad's farm after he died, about two miles up the road from us. They were roustabouts of one kind or another. Anyhow, there was quite a bit of soft coal in our part of the country in the hills there, and it was in a layer that was not very thick, maybe 20 inches, 30 inches. They were big dragline operators, so they decided they were going to start mining coal. They started right on their own farms, and they ended up destroying them. So they took the draglines, and they started pulling the dirt and clay off of them, and the brush, and then about 12 or 14 feet they'd be down to the seam of coal. By your measure, real soft coal. But they had a rule for their neighbors. You could have a load of coal, all the coal you could get in a wagon bed, for a dollar.

It was about a mile and a half, two miles, over to where the mines were. We boys and Daddy would take the team and head out on a Saturday morning to get a load of coal. We'd put that coal on there by hand, very carefully. Every piece was on there for the road back, because we were going to come around the back way, which was dirt and gravel and a field. But all the coal we could get on there, every bit of it, for a dollar.

Paul Stillwell: Didn't want any bouncing out.

Admiral Meyer: We'd bring that coal back, and we'd off-load it right there by the well in the backyard. The girls would come out and admire what we had done, and my mother would look at it, and right away she'd start out. Instead of biscuits, she'd make what are called light rolls, which she made in a pan from yeast. It was our favorite food, including my dad, so our reward that night would be, with these new grates we could do this coal now. In the beginning we'd not predicted how you don't get something for nothing. You'd get more goddamn ashes and dirt and stuff [chuckle] out of coal, so a dollar's worth of coal produces about $30.00 worth of work in moving the ashes and cleaning up behind it. But it was quicker than wood, and it substituted for wood when you needed a little fire. So we burned it off and on for several years, actually till I went to the Navy. Because these Warm Morning stoves could accommodate wood or coal. By then we had electricity. I think it was '36; it may have been '37.

Father John Joseph Groetsch loved to play cards. His favorite game was bridge. And he started teaching me, in grade school now, how to do the church books and the work. And one of the things that he wanted set up was a program to recopy and certify baptismal certificates. As you can appreciate, for that whole part of the country, for enlisting in the Navy—or doing anything, as a matter of fact—a baptismal certificate was used in lieu of a birth certificate, which a lot of people didn't have. They had baptismal certificates, but those had reached the point where many of them were unreadable. They were endangered, and they had names you couldn't pronounce, so forth and so on. So he set up a two-year program to re-transcribe them in a spare room at the rectory, because we'd get in the older people to go over them and look at them and check the spelling and stuff. The old papers, as far as I know, are still on preservation someplace, but they were recopied, redone, and certified to be the best you could, though some had faded. And a lot of people had died, and there weren't any ongoing survivors. So that was one of my early tasks, to take that on. I was kind of the chief of that.

Paul Stillwell: You must have had good penmanship.

Admiral Meyer: No, I did not. But, now that you bring it up, my grammar and my writing were totally unacceptable when I got to St. Boniface School. And Sister Mary Joanne and Father Groetsch, it turns out, had a number of conversations about me and what they were going to do about it, because they weren't about to have a kid in the upper grades as bad as I was. So I got an assignment from the sixth grade through the eighth grade, three years. Every week I had to give Sister Mary Joanne a composition. One page was enough, any subject I wanted, but I had to use ten new words. Well, that sounds real easy, but after a couple months that really gets hard. [Laughter] And so she started relenting on me because she had inculcated the habit in me by then where she was teaching me vocabulary and teaching me grammar. And she, of course, as a good nun will, particularly a Franciscan, she would faithfully grade those papers and every curlicue and every misspelled word would get marked. To this day I'm that way. My officers at times would get really pissed off at me because punctuation, spelling, and grammar, would really cost you if I were running you, if you worked for me. It would really cost you. And some I don't know how they even got to be officers, it's so poor. Well, I don't want to imply that I'm perfect or any of those things, but I know what perfection is. I may not be as good at practicing it, but I know what it is, and I do it right now. I'm that way right now. If the chief of staff brings me up a piece of paper, I'll tell right this afternoon and wants me to sign it I can guarantee you there'll be some corrections I'll put in it. It'll be grammatical or be punctuation. So that part worked out pretty good. So they taught me religion, and they got me over the hump on that.

Well, now we had the problem of writing. Penmanship. I could do Palmer Method till you'd scream. I don't know whether you know Palmer Method. Palmer Method was the style of penmanship in that era, just as Gregg was the style for shorthand. So all girls learned Gregg shorthand, but everybody in Catholic school got the Palmer Method, and you'd do ovals, ovals, ovals, ovals, ovals, till you could scream. You'd do the marks, page after page after page. She'd mark them up, and you'd get the message. Well, after a couple of years I got so I could write pretty well. I mean, that woman really taught me something. She taught me those fundamentals.

I generally could handle math. I don't want to say that I was a whiz by myself at math, because she taught me a lot about that. But grammar, penmanship. And she had, of course, a beautiful hand. Her writing was just beautiful. So you asked me, and that's where it came from, right there.

Paul Stillwell: Did you do your homework by lamplight before the electricity came in?

Admiral Meyer: As I got into grade school, we came by what was known as an Aladdin lamp. You may not have heard of an Aladdin lamp. It was a lamp which the coal oil operated under pressure and had a mantle instead of a wick, so it got white light. Well, it's a beautiful lamp. As a matter of fact, it was a decorative thing, beautiful. Cost a little money. You'd get it for, I don't know, 25 cents a week or whatever it was till you got it paid for. Anyhow, My mother bought one. No one was allowed to touch that but my mother, not even my dad, because the mantle was very fragile. Poof, it'd go to dust if you weren't careful. Not even Granny would touch it. So the only way it got turned on was my mother. You could turn it off, but my mother turned it on.

Well, up till then I used coal oil lamps. And I was born to read. I don't know who taught me reading. I don't know whether it started with my mother or Miss Helen or how, but I was born to read. And I've always asked God to preserve my eyesight because as long as I can read I'm going to be a happy person. That's my wish, my spiritual wish.

It was around 1936 or so, about the time that I started Catholic school, someone—I think it was in the parish but I'm not sure, but some person died and left in the will a significant amount of books to the Catholic school. And they were just mostly ordinary books, but one piece of it was the Horatio Alger series.[*] And, man, I started on them. I read one every night. When I finally finished them after a couple months, I started over again. I loved those books.

Well, I can hear my mother now. I was in the front room, my mother and dad had gone to bed in their bedroom, my brother had gone to bed, Granny was in bed, and I was still up sitting under that lamp, later the Aladdin lamp. I mean, I was the only one privileged to have the Aladdin lamp left on. The other kids didn't have that privilege. I would be sitting there reading that book, and I'd hear my mother. "Wayne, go to bed; Wayne, go to bed."

"I'm going in a minute, Mom, just as soon as I finish this chapter."

Pretty soon, "Wayne, go to bed. Well, I never worried too much about it till she said, "Wayne Eugene, go to bed!" I went to bed. [Laughter] It's that simple. I stumbled through the dark and wandered upstairs to my bed. But I loved to read.

Well, of course, I didn't like to get up in the morning, which meant my brother rawhided me. Because we slept in a double bed, and of course we had to be in that milking barn at 5:30. My dad didn't care how late you stayed up, but you'd better have your ass in that milking barn at 5:30. It comes pretty early, and Wayne was often not there on time, and my stinking-ass little brother was. And that always created strife. And my retort was: "Yeah, but I'm going to be somebody." I don't know whether that was true or not, but that's what my answer was, and that's what kept sending me on this road. I can't say I had the foggiest idea where I was going. From the time that I was in kindergarten till I was a junior in high school, I didn't have any idea.

---

[*] Horatio Alger Jr. (1832-1899) was an American novelist whose stories often portrayed boys from humble backgrounds who achieved success—often described as "rags-to-riches" stories.

Paul Stillwell: That's not uncommon.

Admiral Meyer: No, it's not. But I just had no idea what was going to happen. Actually, what I was going to do was farm. So time wore on and having said that, that's what I was going to do.

During my upper grades, Father Groetsch considered me material fit for the ministry, and he, I believe, solicited Joanne to help him. So they kept subtly exposing me, never twisted my arm—and later I appreciated and understood—but subtly exposing or preparing me just by where they took me to and what they showed me to.

By the seventh grade, my sweetheart was Mary Ann Moser. God, she was a beautiful woman. She was so pretty in the seventh grade. She was one of the Moser girls that I mentioned to you. Well, amongst other things they believed that they had to make sure that Mary Ann and I never got very close together. So we would meet occasionally in the furnace room. I would be there for duty reasons, because I'd have to be dumping ashes or something or other, and she'd come by and we'd use a pencil to pass kisses. [Chuckle] But time came they solved that. Mary Ann was smart as a whip, and they ended up getting a scholarship for her in Loretto Academy in Kansas City. So she got sent away to the academy while Wayne went to high school. They got me separated real quick. [Laughter]

Paul Stillwell: Have to keep you pure for the priesthood.

Admiral Meyer: You got it. They were keeping me pure.

Paul Stillwell: What became of your siblings?

Admiral Meyer: Something that I never expected. They're all in the graveyard. Someplace in the 1950s, my mother was struck down by cancer of the uterus. And I'm the only one in my family, this whole generation, who ever got a degree, except my sister Rose Ellen, who was brilliant. She was right behind me, as I say, but she was a year apart because I skipped a grade. But she was awarded a scholarship from the school of nursing at Washington University in St. Louis. It was a full scholarship, and she took that scholarship. I was really, really, really proud of her. So instead of going in the service, she chose to take that scholarship with the intention of entering the service after she went through nursing school. She became a registered nurse when the war was over, and she did become associated with the military and she attended many, many, many soldiers at the famed Jefferson Barracks at St. Louis that you've probably heard about.

Paul Stillwell: Yes.

Admiral Meyer: Because it's a big receiving point, a big receiving station, and particularly in World War II. So she got to be quite well known through that structure and, over time, she married a schoolteacher who taught biology in high school. And then she became chief of nursing at the big St. Elizabeth's Hospital in Belleville, Illinois, and she had 800 or 900 nurses under her. She had that for several years. And she became quite, I guess you'd say noted or admired.

I went to her funeral to, amongst other things to speak at her funeral. But what was stunning about her funeral is the number of religious people who turned out to her funeral. Because St. Elizabeth's was a hospital that, like all those hospitals, didn't have enough nuns to operate it anymore, but it had quite a few of them, which were nursing nuns. I think every single one attended and every single one associated. It bowled me over, the number that turned out. So it was an extraordinary tribute to her as I watched that. And the United States Army granted a waiver so that she could be buried in the cemetery at Jefferson Barracks at St. Louis, which is where she is today. She died of a cancer.

My youngest sister, Margie Jean, was interesting. She was born 1931, so she's the baby of us. Here we were. She became the pet. I mean, I left home immediately, my brother went into the Army Air Corps, my sister went to Washington University. So Margie Jean was attending some kind of school of nursing in Kansas City, I forget the name of it. Anyhow she was on scholarship. She got to running around with a boy who it turned out, amongst other things, was in the Episcopalian seminary, in a town out in Kansas. She had met him, it turned out on New Year's Eve. She and her girlfriend had broken out, and they had, like, orders to be back at 1:00 o'clock or something like that on New Year's Eve. They come strolling in about 3:00 o'clock, and the head nun met them and told them to get their gear packed. Later my mother and dad went back up and talked to the mother superior. She relented, but by then the girls had taken the attitude, "The hell with you; we're not going back, we don't want any of it."

So my younger sister broke off and she married this boy, and they moved to Manhattan, Kansas, and later Topeka. And their employment was a mixed thing, like he finally ended up in Medicare. He started in insurance, and then he became a pretty big state wheel, in Medicare and the operation of the medical system in Kansas. But most important they started raising babies.

Well, my dad and mother kind of didn't really have a problem with it, but his dad and mother never got over it, that this guy had gone off and married a Catholic. By the time they got to about the fourth baby, they had made up and decided, "Well, maybe that wasn't the most important thing after all." But when they finished they had, I think I'm right, 13 kids. They lived in a big old house in Topeka. I don't know; I think it had 50 rooms in it, kids everyplace. None of them had a nickel. Clothes were handed from one to the other. They were generally healthy kids, about half and half boys and girls, one kind or another.

He continued his business. She decided that she was going to feed the world's poor, so she went to work and managed to become an agent of the bishop out there, along with the state. The next thing you knew, she had warehouses setting up and a big food distribution system and resales going on to look after the poor. She harnessed everybody she could get her hands on; she was very persuasive. She had a big territory, so she posted watches at the truck terminal and she'd have goods that she wanted to get delivered over to Colorado. So she had a watch posted to just go nab a driver, and before he could get away he had agreed to move the goods, three boxes full or whatever it was, to Colorado. It's really quite an impressive business.

She became cancerous. She was the first one to die. She kept going downhill, going downhill. Just an aside: I had never been to a funeral before hers where a cardinal and a bishop came to officiate. And they had more religious—well, they had as many as they had civilian for her. The state legislature issued a big piece of paper in recognition of her contributions to the state, her contributions to the poor. So she had lived a really fulfilled life. Today I don't know where her kids are, scattered everyplace. They've all got kids. They may even have grandkids of their own.

Uncle Jack is still alive. He's the same age I am and lives in Topeka. I'm sure he keeps track of them, but my guess is that—I just smell this; Alzheimer's has overtaken him. He has retired. I don't believe there's a single kid that completed any college at all.

My older sister had five kids; she's got one daughter in Texas that's going to contribute to tending the poor. She's down there teaching English as a second language stuff. I'm estranged from her because I don't like that expression. I've told her repeatedly that English should be taught as the first language, not the second language. So I don't speak to her. One of her sons went in the Navy, retired as a chief petty officer, radar. So they all clippety-clopped along.

My brother Bill took after a couple of his uncles. He came out of the Army Air Corps. He had gone into medical, and he was very good as a corpsman. He was stationed at San Antone and the big Brooks Hospital down there. He was doing quite well, but he decided he was going to do better. He also liked "iced tea" quite a bit.[*] So he liked to drink. Well, you know, in the Air Force it takes you about 90 days to make sergeant.

He married a young girl from down in Louisiana, a really nice woman, very quiet, sheltered. He liked to gamble. Well, he got out of the Air force. This guy knows how to make money. And he was going to get into the dispensing and selling of medical devices, when they were becoming really something. So he got in with a couple people, he packed up his little wife and shipped her to Missouri for my mother and dad to take care of her, and he started out in that.

Well, that wasn't fast enough. Signed an agreement with the now United States Air Force. He was going to do research work with them, related to acceleration in space. Amongst other things he signed up to ride the sleds out at Holloman Air Force Base.[†] In one of the firings, it somehow failed to properly secure one of his hands. And in the firing his arm was severely damaged. He didn't lose it or anything, but it had finished

---

[*] "Iced tea" was a term Admiral Meyer used for liquor.
[†] Holloman Air Force Base is near Albuquerque, New Mexico.

that. Besides, the Air Force had now decided that they didn't think they ought to be using people for these tests anymore anyhow. Instead they were going to use chimpanzees. My brother sent for his wife, Nancy. She came out to Edwards Air Force Base and they opened up a business.* He started procuring monkeys for the United States Air Force. And Nancy had to piddle ass around changing the diapers on these goddamn chimpanzees and raising them. I don't know whether they ever made any money or not. He was in that business about three years or so, and I guess Nancy blew up. He took off to Alaska. Nancy came back to Missouri. My brother gambled and drank up there till he ran out of money; then he came back.

But he had an association with an old man in Biloxi, Mississippi, in a place known as Alto Trailer Sales, and he decided he was going into the trailer business. You and I call them mobile homes—or *he* does; we call them trailers. He started out selling them. He made a fortune. He didn't only make a fortune, he made about four fortunes. He made fortunes right and left. He was repeatedly elected as an official, one kind or another, in all the associations. He was successful at putting legislation through the Congress on moving 14-wides over the highways. They could only be moved at off-rush-hours and stuff, but they could move them. He's done a lot of things for the mobile home business. He made a *lot* of money. And then when gambling moved in to Mississippi and such he was now big time. So not only did he have a built-in clientele, but he had a built-in hobby.

So he called me up and asked me if I could come down to see him. I was leaving the Navy. I got down there and he said, "I've just bought a bank, and I've decided that I'll make a lot more money by doing my own financing than I will having others handle it." By now Nancy had pulled the plug, shoved off. He had kids scattered all over. And he just had a general mess of his life.

Ocean Springs is a pretty big town between Biloxi and Pascagoula. A lot of people from the shipyard live there.† Well, the Catholic church had a big fire down there,

---

* Edwards Air Force Base is on the border of Kern County and Los Angeles County, California, about seven miles east of Rosamond. It is located next to a dry lake that provides an extension of the base's runways. Edwards has long been used for experimental flight testing.
† The shipyard in Pascagoula, established in 1938, has been under a variety of ownership over the years. It is now part of Huntington Ingalls Industries. At the time of this interview it was part of Northrop Grumman Corporation.

and the church burned to the ground. In the meantime my brother had won a pretty good-sized building in a crap game. So he went to see the bishop and he said, "Look, I'm going to give that church this building for them to operate their services for as long as they need it." Well. And he did. They needed it about four years, as I recollect.

Right after that, one of those big hurricanes and floods swept up through West Virginia. It destroyed trailers all over the place up there. He and his two sons took their tractors and they drove to West Virginia. Well, the feds—the forerunner of FEMA—were up there and had to get everything done by Wednesday, get the people housed and everything.[*] So they were just throwing away trailer after trailer: Write them off, zero, no value, pulling in other housing for them. Much of this housing, all that happened to it is it had gotten a little water in it. My brother and his boys could buy those for $20.00, $50.00 apiece, just to get them out of the way. So they took their trailers and pulled several hundred of them off to high ground and stored them.

Well, it so happened he went over to Atlanta, because he was pretty well known over there, and there was an outfit over there, supplier, that was going out of business, that furnished materials, including appliances and stuff, for mobile homes. He bought the whole damned thing. The church gave him his building back. He took one of his sons and set him up in business and he created an overhaul and repair place right on the spot. So now he had a bank and an overhaul and repair spot. He pulled these damned trailers in, they'd strip them down, put this new gear in them, because all that was wrong with them, really, was the smell. And he'd resell them with a guarantee, and he had a finance plan for them. Making money like no tomorrow.

He said, "Wayne, I need somebody to run this bank." He really wanted me to come down and run a bank.

I said, "Bill, I don't know anything whatsoever about it."

He said, "You don't have to know anything about it. I'll teach you."

"Bill, I don't want anything to do with it. We wouldn't get along. We'd end up fighting sooner or later."

So he married his new wife, who had a daughter, and she started out running the business for him. Naomi is her name; she's a wonderful woman. And time wore on. He

---

[*] FEMA – Federal Emergency Management Agency.

was such a big customer, whenever he wanted to gamble all he had to do was pick up the phone, and the next thing you knew a big car would appear. It would haul him wherever he wanted to go. When he finished, they'd bring him home.

His new wife set up a pretty good plan with him. The agreement was that she'd be in charge of the money, and he could gamble all he wanted, but all he could gamble was ever how much money she let him have. So he'd have an allotment, and when he'd spent that he was out of money. She'd put it in her sock and she'd store it. She was a wonderful woman. She saved money and saved money.

Then cancer struck him down. So he died of a heart attack. I think about five years ago now. His widow lives there. Anna Mae and I associate with her a great deal, like she goes on cruises with us, and we keep track of her. She's just a wonderful woman.

So that's a long shaggy-dog story that I had never predicted two sisters, my brother, all younger, they're all dead.

Paul Stillwell: But there's a common thread that you have with the three of them—organizational and management skills—because each one of them was running an enterprise.

Admiral Meyer: You know, Paul, that is a penetrating observation, because I've thought about that often. As I said, one sister had got a degree in nursing. I eulogized every one of them. I went and eulogized them. And so it caused me to have to sum up my thinking. And I've thought about those three people and the skills they exhibited. You called them enterprise—a lot of it was their leadership skills. Where did this come from? Did this come out of the mother? Did it come out of the father? They didn't have Miss Helen; they were too young. But they did have the sisters; they did go to Brunswick High School. They did have the influence of Father Groetsch, not nearly the amount that he had on me because about then—this was long after I was in the Navy—he was transferred to someplace else, and he died. So I don't know why, but you've got an important observation. It's an important observation.

Another thing happened in that sense. They had extraordinary admiration for me. Because here I had gone in the Navy and I had been, in their mind, and correctly so actually, specially selected. I was enlisted in the Navy, and I had gotten a degree in engineering, which they weren't sure what it meant, but they knew it was significant, and I had been commissioned. So they were really, really, always, all their life, a lot more respectful of me, I believe, than I of them. And yet their children had all asked me to eulogize them. These dyings, they and my mother, all happened in about a two-year period or so, so I was pretty damned busy there for a couple years delivering eulogies.

I don't have that answer.

Paul Stillwell: Well, maybe it's just a combination of the way all your brains are wired and then the example that you set.

Admiral Meyer: Sometimes I think that maybe my old granny affected it. She couldn't write. Missouri was a very progressive state. In 1937, Missouri had the first old-age pension. My granny was not eligible for any Social Security at that moment. I remember—I can see it plain as day in our big kitchen—when Granny's first check came. She was a-tremble because she never got a piece of mail. We all gathered around this big kitchen table while my mother helped Granny open this to look at it, and all of us stood there and looked at it. Oh, Granny. And she got this $7.00 check. My dad and one of her sons had enclosed one of these mini-porches, and so that was her room. We called that Granny's room. They had a little heater in there and had an oil stove and stuff.

Well, it's funny. She started getting that $7.00 check. She made her daughter write her out a budget. I don't know how many she got before she died—but every month the first dollar went to her burial. Her orders were that she was not going to be a burden on my dad. So she'd save one dollar, and I can tell you right where it went. It went right into the stand of the table in her room, that's where she stored it, to bury her with. That left $6.00. Well, then she loved Post's 40% Bran Flakes. To this day that's what I eat. She loved those. Buy two boxes full. And we milked cows, but she wouldn't drink a drop of it. Instead she had the luxury of canned Pet Milk. So Pet Milk went on her cereal with a little bit of water on it to make it more liquid. And then there would be a couple little things. Pulp Western novels were 25 cents apiece. Have you ever seen one of them? They're about that thick.

Paul Stillwell: Half an inch, maybe.

Admiral Meyer: Yeah. Right. She'd buy two. Well, they had to be bought at the liquor store, so my dad had to go buy them. My mother wasn't about to set foot in the liquor store, and Granny certainly wasn't. So every month she'd get two of those. Fifty cents of it would go to those Westerns. That's how she split up that pension. Did she make us that way? I don't know.

Paul Stillwell: Well, she certainly had her things organized.

Admiral Meyer: She did, there's no doubt about it. There's no doubt about it. From the day I knew her, she had no teeth. She had shrunk. She wore a dust cover over her head all the time, and she always wore two aprons so if company came she could whip off one apron, and she'd have a clean apron on. And she wore a long dress, as farm women did in those days, and cotton socks. It's amazing.

    I don't know whether she had that effect on those kids or not. She did have a pretty good hand in our raising. My mother and dad never felt any constraints as we were growing up in high school about leaving us with Granny. We were big enough to do the chores, and Granny was agile enough to oversee it.

    I remember later on, checking ahead into the '50s, my grandpa, J. O.—I remember being stationed in Norfolk at the time, and Grandpa died. And so we made the decision to take leave—we had one baby—and we'd drive to Brunswick for the funeral. It was going to be nip or tuck to get there. I was stationed aboard USS *Sierra*, a destroyer tender.[*] I was the radio officer, the CIC officer, and the ASW officer; I was all of them. As a matter of fact, I was the only unrestricted line officer in the ship, a lieutenant (junior

---

[*] Meyer served in the USS *Sierra* (AD-18) from 1949 to 1951.

grade), except for the XO and the captain. We had LDOs, staff corps, Marines, dentists, and doctors running out your ears.*

Paul Stillwell: That's an LDO heaven, a ship like that.

Admiral Meyer: Right. Exactly. So I was getting ready to head out. It was 1,200-and-some-odd miles, and I was going to have to drive it in one sitting. My wife didn't drive. So I went to Doc, and I said to him, "Is there something you can help me with, on this driving?"

He pondered it. He said, "I know you very well, and yes, I can." And he said, "I'm going to give you these, and you have to agree that you're going to be very, very cautious with how you use them, because you'll think that you're OK and you're not." Well, it turned out what he was giving me, and this is well over 50 years ago, were amphetamines, which were brand new in that era. This was an amphetamine of a really very small size. I don't know whether it mixes different or not today. Of course they're now really, really harshly controlled. But it turned out that they're pretty goddamn good. We got to Brunswick, Missouri, and we pulled in about an hour before the funeral was due in our home. There was a neighbor lady there looking after a couple of children. And she said, "Well, you all are too late. They're already all gathered downtown." Because in those days he was waked in their front room. She said, "I think he's still being waked, because you've got about 40 minutes or so." So we changed our clothes, jumped in the car, and drove right down to the wake and right on in to the church.

Well, the daughters-in-law of those brothers I mentioned to you earlier had taken steps to prepare appropriate meals post-funeral. My grandma was called "Maw," "Maw Meyer," and she was a sharp little dumpy Deutsch-speaking woman. She really was. We just didn't appreciate how broken up she was. So we came from the funeral, from the cemetery, went in there, and someone said, "Maw Meyer, why don't you go in and lie down for a minute?" She went in on the sofa in her front room and lay down there. She never walked again. She refused to get up. I think it took her about six years to die.

---

* LDO – limited duty officer, a former enlisted man whose duties were limited to the area of his enlisted rating specialty.

We got through that day and went on back, but I visited a couple times in the ensuing years, and that's what I'm winding this piece up with. My mother and dad, these two sainted people, chose to take care of his mother and take care of her mother simultaneously, one well up in her 90s, the other in her 80s. And I remember twice, but particularly I remember the first time, coming home to this big old house built in 1810. It was in the summer, and it was like coming into a deserted place. It really hit me hard. There are two souls living here, two of them, two separate rooms. They cleaned them every day, they turned their bodies, they rubbed them down with oils and greases and tried to spoon-feed them whatever they'd take. These two hardy old women just wouldn't die. I would say that they finally starved themselves to death, probably. But they spent three years, as I remember, taking care of those two old women.

Now, each of them had siblings, but not a one helped them. They never expressed any concern whatsoever. It was their duty and their joy to do so. And I wasn't home at either one of the funerals. They just died one day, and they buried them. Those two old women went along on their way to wherever they went, for eternity. One's in the Evergreen Cemetery, DeWitt, Missouri, and the other's in the Catholic cemetery at Brunswick, Missouri. There you are.

Paul Stillwell: I wonder if the two sisters, both going into nursing, was the result of some kind of sense of compassion or humanity that they got from your parents.

Admiral Meyer: Well, it's perplexing. I don't know how they got that. I don't ever remember my mother being a nut on this or anything. Matter of fact, when my mother was younger, she was pretty happy-go-lucky. My mother very rarely had anything to drink, but she was a joy girl. I mean, she loved to dance; she was the life of a party. And in Prohibition and even while my others were alive, we could remember plain as day.[*] Saturday nights, usually we had a cousin or two that came to stay with us, but all of them were gathering to go to a dance, because you'd usually have to drive 15-20 miles to get to

---

[*] The 18th Amendment to the Constitution was ratified in 1919 and went into effect in 1920, prohibiting the consumption of alcoholic beverages in the United States. The Volstead Act, enacted by Congress in 1919, spelled out the penalties for violations. In December 1933 the ratification of the 21st Amendment to the Constitution repealed the 18th Amendment and thus ended national prohibition.

a dance. They wouldn't go to the dance till 9:30-10:00 ten o'clock, so they'd all gather around in the kitchen and have a few drinks before they left. And us kids would all sit there google-eyed watching it and thinking we were going to join in and such as they got all ready to head on down the road. And they'd get in, there were maybe three carloads of them, head off someplace to the dance. Next morning we'd be up, we'd be in the milking barn taking care—my granny's running around—and said, "Where's Mama?" "Shhh. Your dad and your mother are resting." [Laughter] They were drinking that green whiskey. Although one of the favorite whiskeys then was Old Crow, once they got out of Prohibition.

Paul Stillwell: What values would you say you got from your parents?

Admiral Meyer: Some of it may be a point of weakness. I can't pass up a cripple. I can't pass up a person that is in need of some kind of help. My late wife would say—and she never said it derogatorily, but she'd say to me, "I don't know where you find them, but they seem to collect for you."

In the coming years I went to work leading, just the way I learned in the gumbo and at home. I mean, I was the oldest on that farm. My granny never let the other three forget that, "Out in the field, Wayne is in charge, and if you've got something to complain about, you come see me, but you're to do what Wayne says." So that was just the way I was raised.

Paul Stillwell: You were a foreman early on.

Admiral Meyer: I was, real early on. In the Aegis program, I was able to get results from people that others had rejected. And, as you appreciate, it's a rewarding thing to have had a hand in it, to see it happen. But I don't know why that is, and I don't want to sound stuck up or too persnickety or something. I just don't know why. I know it's so, I know it is, but I don't know why. And I don't know who it came out of. It came, as a matter of fact, I guess, in a backhanded way, your probing here and thinking, where secretly I was kind of hoping that somehow out of here you'd figure it out, out of that array of people. And we haven't even got to high school yet. [Chuckle]

You know the old saw: Everything I learned I learned in kindergarten, or whatever it was.* Well, I don't agree with that, but somehow I learned, and somehow lessons were taught.

I recall an incident when I was still in Warden School, and I was maybe either third or fourth grade, and I've never forgotten it. You know how things stick in your mind one time. And I've told you it was about a mile and a half or so from our house to school. Along the way there was a couple who everybody said were not married, and they had these kids. They had two girls in Warden School. They were about mid-grade or so. Their name was Pippin. Nadine Pippin and her sister—I'll say the name of her little sister in a minute. But Nadine was the bigger one. She was maybe sixth grade or so. And, of course, all they ever wore was whatever dress their mother or grandmother sewed for them.

One afternoon we were all walking home down the dirt road headed home. Our house was the farthest one along, and we were really pouring it on these girls. We were stoning them with hedges and clods and everything. They'd run and hidden in a ditch, and we really had them on the run, particularly me and my brother and one of the Fromm kids. Coming down the road was a man whom we knew. His name was John Brown. He was sitting on a wagon with a load of wood poles that he had cut in a pasture. It was alleged that he was one of the live-ins associated with the Pippins. I don't know whether it was ever true or not. But, anyhow, John Brown saw what was happening. We all stood there and looked and watched. He stopped his team. He got out his hatchet and he cut two big switches off the lumber in his wagon and he called these two Pippin girls over, and he gave them to them. He said, "Now, tell the boys to come on if they want to." We never bothered the Pippin girls again. That never happened again.

Well, people say that those little kinds of things don't affect you. They do. They do affect children. You just don't know it for a long, long time that they really did amount to some bend in the road as you were going along. They really did have an effect on you. And your code of conduct is affected by it.

---

* Robert Fulghum, *All I Really Need to Know I learned in Kindergarten* (New York: Villard Books, 1990).

Paul Stillwell: Well, we're right near the end of the tape. That's an intriguing story to finish up on for today. Thank you.

Admiral Meyer: Do you think so? Well, that would be good, because you about drained me there.

Interview Number 2 with Rear Admiral Wayne E. Meyer, U.S. Navy (Retired)
Place: Admiral Meyer's office in Arlington, Virginia
Date: Monday, 12 November 2007

Admiral Meyer: Where should we pick up?

Paul Stillwell: When we talked the last time, we covered your boyhood, growing up on the farm, and going to the Catholic school, where you got both discipline and education. You talked about your parents, the Depression, your siblings, and I think we were about to embark on your high school time.

Admiral Meyer: We eventually reached the eighth grade and graduated. By then the Lutherans and the Catholics had pretty good-sized graduations, even though the Lutherans had had to close their school. They still taught them a day a week or so. At the graduation Mass in May, I was awarded the medal of excellence and the medal of religion and the medal of math. And there was a medal for—I want to say scholastics, but that may be the wrong name, and Mary Ann Moser received that medal. Patricia Manson, my cousin, and Marian Strube, my other cousin, didn't receive medals.

Paul Stillwell: Did students come in from other areas to join the high school class?

Admiral Meyer: Well, it was called a consolidated school, but what it really was in those years was that the various district schools were closing down kind of one at a time, so whoever graduated out of those district schools came to the high school. Our high school usually numbered around 140 to 150 in the four grades, which in fact was a pretty good-sized high school.

Paul Stillwell: This was a public high school?

Admiral Meyer: Yes, a public high school. And Father Groetsch, St. Boniface pastor, and Reverend Bainey, St. John's pastor, Lutheran, spent a lot of time paying attention to what was being taught. Well, no one thought of that because they were learned men, they were educated men, and two of the few, as I mentioned earlier, so they generally participated in the school board, made suggestions and recommendations. We didn't teach any religion per se in high school, but in fact we participated in all the appropriate holy days and such that are generally recognized across the fruited plain, as Rush would say.[*]

Paul Stillwell: Were there any African Americans in Brunswick or the surrounding area?

Admiral Meyer: At that time we had the colored school, which was known as B. K. Bruce, named after a famous Negro there.[†] I have trouble recalling how high school was handled. Before I went in the Navy I don't remember any blacks in high school. There surely were some, because there were some pretty savvy girls, particularly, out of B. K. Bruce. They went on to become teachers and such.

We were a border state during the Civil War, and in fact the dividing line of the war went right through Chariton County, which was the county I was born and raised in. Brunswick was on the North. The county seat, Keytesville, 12 miles away, was on the South.

Paul Stillwell: What was the dividing line for loyalties during the war?

Admiral Meyer: I think it's probably just what the elders recommended. I don't recall anyone within my family who'd served in that war, and I think that was generally true. We had a lot of raiders, as you know in the history books, that went on in that part of the country, and a lot of skirmishes. The big claim to fame for Hannibal, Missouri, which is right up the river from Brunswick, is it's got a cannon ball lodged up in the courthouse, and everybody comes to look at it. But the story as to how it got there varies a good deal. But mostly you had raiders that swept through, stole food, stuff like that, animals.

---

[*] This is presumably a reference to radio commentator Rush Limbaugh.
[†] Blanche K. Bruce (1841-1898), a Republican, represented Mississippi in the U.S. Senate from 1875 to 1881. He was the first elected African American to serve a full term.

Paul Stillwell: But, in any event, then, you have no strong memories of black students or being associated with black contemporaries.

Admiral Meyer: Before we lost everything in the bottom, two black men worked for my dad, and he housed them. I don't recall the first, but the other one's name was Bill Miller, a giant of a man. What was so great about him was he could pick all four of us kids up in his two big arms. "Hey, Bill, take us for a ride. Bill, pick us up, take us for a ride." And he'd grab us all up and laugh and carry on, and he'd carry us around. Well, they, in essence, boarded with us. I don't know what they got paid—not much. Of course, didn't anybody get paid anything, so that was not unusual. That was in the bottom. But they mostly milked cows, because we had a 100 head of milk cows. And they worked their ass off all day long taking care of that.

My dad had to let them go once we moved to the clay country. And so there we were, from '35 to '43, when I went in the Navy. We had one that was with us almost all the time by the name of Wimpy Anderson. It was hard to know what his pedigree was, and he was technically an illiterate. He couldn't write and he couldn't read. But he was beautiful on the guitar. In our front room there were four steps exposed which went upstairs from the living room to the girls' room, and at night he'd come in and sit on those steps and take my dad's old guitar, and play and sing for us. In some ways we started to lose interest in that once we got electricity in '37, and then that begot a radio. And so we tended to drift away. But I think most of them, Wimpy just kind of made them up as he went, or he heard them someplace in his upbringing. Wimpy was killed in the war in the Pacific. I believe he was older than I was, and he was drafted in '42 or something like that, and he never came back.

Those people had a real cultural effect on me. You learn more about sex and life on a farm than any other place. It is a natural exposure. It's not unusual. One year my uncle, who showed red hogs, had one that broke her leg at the state fair, and so he gave her to me. We had a little A-frame to put her in. We bred her, and we watched her deliver six pigs, stroked those pigs and took care of them. Same way with lambs, horses, cows.

A cow who gets disturbed often has a great deal of trouble completing the birth. If the calf is half emerged or something and she is scared or gets disturbed, the fright, she has trouble returning. We had the expression when we were little, was "Find the calf." So when a cow was going to calve, my dad's practice was turn her loose in the pasture and leave her there till she showed up. And she'd show up with her calf, her little calf. In later years, particularly the milk cows, we tended to pen them up to calve, and there it's easy for them to get disturbed, perturbed, whatever, trying to calve.

Wimpy was a wonderful person. My mother would do anything for him, and he would do anything for my mother. She's patch his clothes and wash his clothes and stuff like that.

So about 1937 or '38, someplace in there, out in the clay country the blacks had thinned out. We still had the B. K. Bruce School in Brunswick, but they tended towards the bottom land, or what is known in our context as Dalton, Missouri, which is in the river bottom. And they tended to have shacks down there of one kind or another where they lived and dwelt. I just can't remember when, because I don't remember blacks in our high school, but someplace in there B. K. Bruce was closed, and they were brought under the public school system. They were already under the public school system; they were just separate.

Paul Stillwell: Do you remember cases of discrimination or prejudice in Brunswick?

Admiral Meyer: I think people would probably dispute me, but if there ever was a racial problem in my whole life in Brunswick, Missouri, I don't know where or how it occurred. As I said, I left home at 17, but I think I was exposed to about everything. Father Groetsch introduced me to an awful lot of things about people in that town, and if there was, I never saw it. Now, they had their ways and we had our ways.

I can't say we ever thought a lot about it one way or another. It was what it was, and that's just the way it was. Nobody argued or fought, nor did they socialize. As far as I know, none starved. They didn't live a very good life, but there wasn't anybody living a good life in Brunswick, Missouri, I'm here to tell you. You read now in later years that the researchers say the real Depression was '37. In '37 I was in the upper grades, and I'm here to tell you that we were poor. We knew we were poor, but nobody resented that. It was just poor.

Paul Stillwell: It was the norm.

Admiral Meyer: It was a hell of a lot different pattern of behavior than the pattern of behavior we have today, particularly in the urban areas. We knew we were poor, but we didn't go out and start a riot or start an argument or start a fight or anything else. We just accepted it for what it was. It was the norm.

Paul Stillwell: Well, getting on to your formal education in high school, did you have some kind of a career goal or objective that you were shooting for at that point?

Admiral Meyer: The answer is no. Nobody counseled me. I believe that, as I said to you earlier, Father Groetsch and Sister Mary Joanne thought that I was good material for the priesthood, and so they were laying the groundwork to have me enter what was known as the junior seminary, in Conception, Missouri, during the high school period. That never panned out. Victor Moser was a fellow over on the hills once removed from us. He was the older brother of my friends. Victor went to the junior seminary and then to the seminary in Conception and eventually was ordained. As a matter of fact, he's retired today. He's a monsignor, and he dwells in St. Joseph and serves as help for different parishes. I'd say he's got to be pushing 90. He's older than I am.

Paul Stillwell: Did you have any expectation or hope at that point of getting into a non-religious-type college?

Admiral Meyer: Zero. Zero.

Paul Stillwell: How was the curriculum laid out? It sounds as if it was not a college preparatory course.

Admiral Meyer: The two most important things in high schools then were home economics for girls and agriculture and shop for boys. Our school had a big building that was shop and agriculture for the boys. It had an attached building for home economics for the girls, which was sewing and cooking and typing and the care of children. In my day Dr. Boucher was the teacher for agriculture, and Miss Stella Locke was the teacher associated with home ec. Her husband was Ralph Locke, and he was the music teacher. I'd say the expectation was to get through life, is what it amounted to. There was no road or vision up ahead anyplace. And it's hard to describe the impact of war on the Midwest and the part of the country where you came from.

Paul Stillwell: There was a lot of isolationist sentiment there.

Admiral Meyer: Yes. But they also had trouble knowing who to believe. I brought that up before. So they tended to believe their pastor or their associate pastors, or the doctor or the banker or the lawyer. They had no one else to believe. Our major communication was the *Capper's Weekly*. The Capper family published a paper. It started back about the turn of the century and all in my era published it, a wonderful paper, once a week. Farmers would scratch and scratch and scratch to get the subscription, which was, I think, about 25 cents a month or something, so that they could read the *Capper's Weekly*. But outside of that there wasn't any long-range objective except to survive.

Now, the war brought about this dramatic change, which at the time wasn't necessarily comprehended. I remember Sunday, December 7, but I also remember the winds of war in the five years or seven years building up to then.[*] But in 1941 I was almost the number-one aide to Father Groetsch. Father Groetsch had me doing everything: keeping the books, redoing things in the records of the church. We had a mission church also. St. Raphael's was at Indian Grove, Missouri, which is about 12 miles away. In the early days Father Groetsch would go there to say Mass about once a month. A man in town by the name of Dick Smith ran a little taxi service and also a little

---

[*] On Sunday, 7 December 1941, Japanese carrier planes attacked and heavily damaged American warships at the naval base at Pearl Harbor, Hawaii. The U.S. Congress declared war on Japan the following day.

café. So he usually drove, because in that era the priests had to fast until they had completed their Masses. And often that Mass would be at 11:00 o'clock. So Dick Smith would fetch Father out in his taxi to the Grove, he'd say Mass, and the ladies' altar sodality would prepare him a scrumptious breakfast afterwards, and then Dick would fetch him home.

When I got licensed and was big enough, he gave me that assignment with *his* car. I don't know why he was a Studebaker man but he was, before we ever even heard of Studebakers. Had the only Studebaker in town, a big one, a Commander size. And so in 1941 I was now 15, turning 16. So I had a license part of that year, and I started driving him to the Grove on Sunday and bringing him back. And I think I mentioned earlier that he loved to play cards on Sunday, and particularly bridge, and taught my folks how to play bridge. They never cared for it, but they learned to just appease the pastor.

Well, we had this big corner out on our farm. It was where the Allega School used to be, and that was a ball diamond. And so almost every Sunday we had a ball game there of kids that would come from all the hills around and walk over. Sometimes Father Groetsch would bring the sisters out, and he would come and they'd all have a big ball game that afternoon followed by ice cream. Father Groetsch taught me bridge, and I've loved bridge ever since. I don't get to play anymore, but I love bridge.

He also was an entrepreneur of sorts. Once I started driving him, he required St. Raphael's to pay me to do the driving, including the assessment for the mileage on his car. So he was a straightforward businessman. And these old codgers out in Indian Grove, no one ever knew how much money they had, because they never put any money in the bank. They always just kept it someplace at home, but they had money, earned the hard way.

Paul Stillwell: Back to the high school, what did you have in the way of academic subjects, besides the agriculture and shop?

Admiral Meyer: Algebra, followed by plane geometry. Two kinds of English. Latin for two years, at the insistence of Father Groetsch and Reverend Bainey. And the reason that they could teach Latin is Miss Marston had studied Latin when she went to teachers' college. Miss Sorensen taught civics and government, and much of our civics was reading the paper and reading magazines and writing an assessment of what we took out of them. That was how we were appraising civic affairs and what was going on in the world, and how we developed a consciousness of what was happening. In hindsight, it was pretty damned smart by these old ladies in what they did with nothing. They just taught us that we had to read, read, read, and in return for reading we had to write a report. I mean, we wrote jillions of reports. And if you've ever been a teacher, you know those teachers can go through a report once a minute and find the crux of it and decide how to mark it, which they were expert on. They'd spent all their lives as professional teachers.

Paul Stillwell: What were your individual strengths academically?

Admiral Meyer: Math and whatever sciences I could get. We had physics, and we had a chemistry course. They were going to try to teach advanced math, but it just didn't go over well. By my junior year, Miss Edith Marston had become the principal in the school. All the men were gone to war, and so she took over. She took seven of us boys and took away all our freedom and she started teaching us, whether we wanted it or not [chuckle], math, physics, chemistry, or whatever she could get out of a book.

I had that curiosity. I had a good memory. And the other thing I had was that I grew up on a farm. In that era survival in the country on a farm called for creativeness. You heard it said, "Give a farmer a baling wire and he can fix anything." And that's true. Nothing ever breaks as far as you're concerned. Or if some bar has broken, you've somehow got to get it to town to get Jim Spencer to weld the damned thing back together. Or you've got to convince Jim Spencer to come out and weld it for you.

Paul Stillwell: Did you have natural abilities in manual dexterity and mechanics?

Admiral Meyer: None in dexterity, none. I don't have any to this day. Zero. My sisters weren't bad. I was not good at sports of any kind. I didn't particularly dislike them; I just had no interest in them because I just wasn't good. But [chuckle] I can say this—I was always number one in class through all of grade school, and I was number one in class through all of high school. Well, you can look at it in one sense—that there wasn't any competition either.

Paul Stillwell: How many in your graduating class?

Admiral Meyer: I think there were 18 or 20 of us. See, in grade school we always got out of school in April. In high school it started being early May, and eventually later May, once the school bus system came in. In grade school in those earlier years, you had to go farm, so the schools would close. And some years schools would start in August in the country, but they would close in the first part of October for two to four weeks for harvest, and then resume. They don't do any of that kind of thing anymore. It was just a life that was really oriented to survival, to growing up, to thinking in terms of farming or a little business.

Virtually no one in my class aspired to the university. I think at one time there were about 30 in my class. There aren't dropouts. I'm the first person ever in my generation in my family who got a college degree. In fact, I literally didn't even know what the hell one was. And I believe I mentioned to you that my sister got a scholarship in the admired school of nursing at Washington University, and she got a degree out of that. We're the only ones in the whole family. You go through the Meyer family, the Straub family, the Gunn family, which are all the backgrounds—no one.

Well, I think if we were to go through my class today, there are two people still alive who went in the Navy, Carlisle Berry and Wayne Meyer, and each of us got a degree. I can't think of a single woman in my class that got a degree at university. I don't think there's another boy. There may be. Now, some of them earned some pretty good livings. Except for one or two, they left Brunswick, Missouri. That's the problem in that part of the country.

If you look at the upcoming class of '08 in Brunswick next May of what they plan to do, there may be 30 left in the class. It may drop below 30. And their aspirations are to attend a beauty school or attend the matter of medical, handling people. I've got a mental blank on this. Help me here. How to take care of people, attend people.

Paul Stillwell: Like physicians' assistants?

Admiral Meyer: Well, that's pretty high level. Like every town has an exercise place nowadays where we're going to teach you the latest things and how you stay in condition.

Paul Stillwell: Personal trainers?

Admiral Meyer: Right, stuff like that. Nurses' aides, things like that. Not nurses—nurses' aides. A couple of the men may go to the school of agriculture at the university. If an engineer comes out, it will be rare indeed.

Paul Stillwell: You mentioned December 7, 1941. What are your specific memories of that day?

Admiral Meyer: We had no Mass at the Grove on that Sunday, so there were two Masses at Brunswick. Miss Margaret, Father Groetsch's housekeeper, had prepared his breakfast. The collection had been sacked up and brought over, and probably the envelopes wouldn't get opened for some time that week. The church would be tidied down. It would be kind of cold outside, the furnace would be all set, and things like that. And so it was time to go out to my folks' place. My mother had invited him out to have a late dinner and to play bridge. We lived six miles out of town. By now we were on a gravel road. So we got everything all neatened up and tidied up. Father told Miss Margaret that she could go take the rest of the day off, and she said, "Well, I'll leave you a piece of cake for when you come home," or something.

Went down and got in the Studebaker, Wayne the driver, to drive out to the farm. Turned on the radio. All of a sudden, started hearing these newscasts about how some place called Pearl Harbor, which we had no acquaintance with at all, had been struck. Well, once it became Hawaii we knew what Hawaii was; we didn't know what Pearl Harbor was. We didn't know what it meant.

Out to the farm, radio on, listened. People hurt, damage, ships sunk, broadcasting. No one was prepared to do the broadcasting. The whole thing was a total shock to the nation. We didn't know what it meant. We listened off and on all afternoon. Father Groetsch had more insight than anybody else. He knew that this would be all-out war, because I think I told you before, Father Groetsch gave us—every Sunday we had sermons on what was being done to the Jews in Germany. We mostly shrugged our shoulders. We didn't know what he meant. He told us about the camps, he told us what was happening. But this, of course, started happening in '41, '42, but it was also happening in the '30s.

I think I mentioned to you Father Groetsch was a tinkerer. He bought a little kitchen model Emerson radio. With two of us boys to help him, he took great effort to install it up on the shelf in the upper classroom, and we ran an aerial. The aerial went all the way around the room. And it was how we were going to get our civics. Well, we got a hell of a lot of civics in the late '30s out of that little radio. For example, in those years the Pope was always in trouble.* Secondly, we had the invasion, particularly Ethiopia, and the occupation of the other countries.† So every day we were tuning those in, or Sister was, of what it was we were to listen to and take notes on of what was going on. We learned a lot. We didn't have a book, only old geography books. All they needed was a little imagination.

Well, time wore on. We couldn't play bridge that afternoon, December 7. We were in some form of shock—shocked, but we just didn't know what it meant. We didn't understand it, couldn't comprehend it. How were our big ships attacked, and where did these people come from? How did this happen? It was about Tuesday before Roosevelt recovered.‡ I can't remember now whether it was Tuesday or Wednesday.

Paul Stillwell: Well, he made a speech to Congress on Monday, the eighth of December. That's when he talked about the "date which will live in infamy."

Admiral Meyer: Live in infamy, right. I think he made an announcement that afternoon,

---

* Pius XI was Pope from 1922 to 1939. Pius XII was Pope from 1939 to 1958.
† In the Indo-Ethiopian War of 1935-36, the Italian military forces sent by dictator Benito Mussolini were victorious, resulting in Italian occupation of Ethiopia. Ethiopia was annexed into a new colony known as Italian East Africa.
‡ Franklin D. Roosevelt was President of the United States from 4 March 1933 to 12 April 1945.

Sunday, but I think he spoke to the people later that week. I just don't recall.

Paul Stillwell: Did you hear his speech to Congress when you were in school?

Admiral Meyer: I don't know whether I did or not, because in 1941 I was in high school. I can't even remember whether we went to high school Monday or not. I don't know.

Paul Stillwell: There was a lot of patriotic fervor in the wake of that. Did you start thinking toward going into the service very soon after that?

Admiral Meyer: No. We didn't know what any of that meant. As a junior in 1942, I can't say that I was yet thinking about it, but as I think I had said to you, in 1942 we had no men left in school; they'd all gone to war. Miss Marston was elderly. She had agreed with the school board that, if they wanted, her contribution to the war would be to be the principal. Which she did. She served till the end of the war. She was probably the most learned, certainly the most educated, teacher we had. But by 1942, she was just simply drawing on her experience as a young girl in the First War. That's when she took everything away from us. She didn't know where it was going to lead to, but one thing she did know is that the boys who knew the most were the boys that were going to come out on top. That much she knew. So she set that course of action, and then presumably she told the school board what she was doing.

Paul Stillwell: What do you mean, she took everything away from you?

Admiral Meyer: All sports. She took all study halls. I don't think she took away drama. I was the editor in chief of the paper, the *Brunswick Wildcat*, and as I remember, that remained. But we had no time to piddle. She outlined what we were to study. She personally supervised the seven of us. Instead of a study hall, we got Miss Marston. She'd start teaching something that we were not really overjoyed on, something about algebra or geometry or something we didn't give a damn whether we ever learned. But she knew where she was going. We had no idea what was going to happen to us.

I believe I'm right, that the first boy that was killed, at least the first boy that I knew, that I could remember, was Eugene Moser, and he was a younger brother of Victor Moser that I just mentioned a moment ago. Eugene Moser, I think, was in the class of 1940 or '41. When the war broke out, almost immediately he enlisted in the Marines. He shipped out, and he was killed in the taking of Guadalcanal.[*] We never knew anything about him, how he was killed. Neither did his folks. They didn't whine. They properly mourned and thought of him, because his daddy had been in the First War, and his daddy had been gassed and two or three of his uncles had been gassed, so these men kind of knew the nature of war.

I don't know where Gene Moser's body is today. I think it's someplace in Guadalcanal. In the context of Brunswick, Missouri, he was never mentioned particularly again. I don't believe his youngest brothers even much remember him, because they were pre-school almost when he was killed. But my age and his cousins were the right age to know him pretty well, so that was, I'd say, the first personal touch that we felt from the war.

Now, did I describe the whole V-12 effort to you or not?[†]

Paul Stillwell: Not yet.

Admiral Meyer: Well, maybe I'll leap ahead to the moment and start talking about that. I've described it to a number of people.

Roosevelt had determined that the war was going to last a very long time, and he had a significant and major concern about—I'll use the word "intellect;" it may be the wrong word—about the intellect of the nation. Because the faculties were drained, the universities were being drained, men were all going in one way or another into

---

[*] On 7 August 1942, U.S. Marines invaded the islands of Guadalcanal and Tulagi in the Solomons chain as part of the first U.S. counteroffensive in the Pacific War. The primary purpose was to gain control of an airstrip on Guadalcanal and thus to prevent the Japanese from achieving control of the surrounding air and sea regions. The campaign was long and difficult before organized Japanese resistance finally ended on 9 February 1943.

[†] During World War II, V-12 was a Naval Reserve officer training program in which individuals received naval instruction at the same time they worked toward bachelor's degrees. The program, which was held at civilian colleges and universities, took about two years. See James G. Schneider, *The Navy V-12 Program: Leadership for a Lifetime* (Boston: Houghton Mifflin, 1987).

something. And he was concerned how to arrest that. Well, in 1942 his advisers, which emerged in the beginning of 1943, cobbled up school programs. In the Navy they became known as the V-series programs. In the Army they were the A-series, and in the Marines they were the M-series. And if I, just for the moment, talk about the Navy, I ended up in the V-12 program—there was a V-5 program and a V-7 program, which took men who were partway through school, completed them to a certain level, nominally at least four terms, and then took them into a commissioning process.* The Army and the Marines had similar programs.

So this was Roosevelt's personal scheme. It is alleged that he personally supervised the planning and how it was all put together. I've got a book in there on it; I don't know whether this is true or not. But he was going to take men on a competitive basis, both physically and intellectually, and furthermore they would be on a continuing competitive basis while in the program, and they would be on active duty. And the idea was then, he was going to neutralize them from assault and attack from all of those who were going and tromping in the mud.

The program was pretty damned effective. Just for the record, as far as I know, I was the last person on active duty in our Navy of the V-12 program. I believe I'm correct that Earl Fowler was the next to last, and the third to last was the communications guy, made flag.† He was in NavElex a lot and such. I just almost said it. He was a good sailor. He was a good sailor. My year group and Fowler's year group. We were all commissioned in February of 1946. We were the first and the last.

The V-12 involved competitive exams, and you applied for them. I think they were sent to you by the Department of War. I received an application in January of 1943. The form had three blocks of what your preference was. One was V-12 for Navy, one was A-12 for Army, and one was M-12 for Marines. I checked V-12, and another time I'll tell you why.

---

* The V-7 Naval Reserve Midshipmen's School program began in 1940 for men who were college juniors or seniors. In 1941 the entry requirement was changed to include a college degree and some courses in mathematics. The purpose was to train individuals to become officers in surface warships.
V-5 was a naval aviation cadet program that procured and trained officer pilots. At the end of the six-stage program, individuals were commissioned as Naval Reserve ensigns or Marine Corps Reserve second lieutenants.
† Vice Admiral Earl B. Fowler, Jr., USN, served as Commander Naval Sea Systems Command from 1980 to 1985, when he retired. He died 2 March 2008.

Well, early February the exams were sent to our school. We all checked V-12. Matter of fact there were four of us. The fourth one, Paul Allen, wanted to fly so bad he could taste it. His daddy had been in the First War. He managed by hook or crook to get himself into the V-5 program. Anyhow, those exams were three days long, and they were supervised locally by the school officials. It was revealed in March that all four of us had passed the exam, and subsequently it was determined that the Navy was concerned that the exams had been compromised, because no one else had.

But it also turned out to have a very simple explanation, and it was Miss Edith Marston that made the difference. She didn't know how it was going to happen or where it was going to come from, but she knew what she had to teach her boys, and she was on the money. It wasn't that we were smarter; it was that we were oriented to what the subject was. They sent a petty officer to Brunswick to examine and audit the administration of the exams. She took a little offense at it, but I believe that Navy man was really happy when he got out of there [laughter], because she showed him no mercy about questioning the integrity of Brunswick High School.

We were called to Kansas City a second time in March. Accompanying getting the exam, now that I think about it, we had to take a preliminary physical in January. We were 100 miles from Kansas City. Father Groetsch had gas, Reverend Bainey had gas. Most of the farmers had tractor gas.

Paul Stillwell: This was during an era of rationing.

Admiral Meyer: Oh, yeah. I mean, 1943 was at the peak of rationing. I don't know whether the town convened or what it did, but it was decided that Father Groetsch would drive two of us and Reverend Bainey would drive two of us, and they'd take us to Kansas City and see to our safety. Therefore their parents felt okay, and Miss Marston felt okay because these two men were going to do this.

Paul Stillwell: Had you discussed with your parents the business of going into the Navy at a young age?

Admiral Meyer: We discussed it as much as we knew about it. We didn't know anything about it. I was only 16. The others were 17. They didn't know what to do. I was the oldest in our family. The kids in my family were 16, 15, 14, and 12.

We got up there, and the first thing they really wanted to find out in January was whether we could pass the visual and the audio, particularly the Doppler.* Otherwise we were just going to be rejected out of hand. Well, we went back again in, I believe it was March or April to be examined for real. But this preliminary was to be sure we could, because otherwise they weren't going to spend any time on us.

Time wore on. There were several letters exchanged and papers of one kind or another. My dad and mother signed whatever Father Groetsch said they should sign. I mean, they had no other advice.

I turned 17 on the 21st of April. Got called up again the 11th day of May. The two ministers drove us to Kansas City, and they said if we got through everything that day we'd be allowed to go to the big Forum Cafeteria in Kansas City and have a nice supper. On the 12th day of May we were sworn in.

Now, during the war you could only be sworn in to the United States Naval Reserve. In fact, if you had an enlistment before the war and that enlistment expired, you could do one of two things. By the fiat that had been created, your enlistment could be automatically extended until six months after the war, so you remained a regular. Or I think there were some things you could collect if you reenlisted. I don't remember, because it never came up in my case. In any event, it didn't matter. Everybody was in the Naval Reserve. Once you reenlisted you were in the reserves, and you remained that way until the war was over.

Since I was 17, my folks had to sign minority papers for me. I didn't know what they meant one way or another, but they were plenty scared. I couldn't explain it very well, and neither could Father Groetsch, but he signed. So we came back home. We graduated from high school the night of the 22nd of May. I was the valedictorian. Carlisle Berry, one who had enlisted with me, was salutatorian. And Denny Grojohn

---

* The Doppler effect is an apparent change in the pitch—that is, frequency—of sound or a radio wave caused by relative motion between the source and the listener.

wasn't any of those, but he could play the snare drums in the band. Paul Allen was an incredible triple-tongued trumpet player.

The Allens lived about four miles as the crow flies from us over on the hill. His dad was a mail carrier. Lived on a little farm. His dad was in the drum and bugle corps for many a year, including in the First War. But in the summer in the evening you could go out in our front yard, and you'd hear Paul Allen practicing on his trumpet four miles away. It was such a beautiful sound coming across the hillsides, just incredible, for us people who weren't anybody and didn't know anything, but there was talent.

Paul Stillwell: Why had you picked the Navy rather than the Army or the Marine Corps?

Admiral Meyer: It's a shaggy dog story. [Laughter]

There was a boy in our town older than us by the name of Bobby Jones. He may not have graduated from high school, I don't know; I want to say he did—about '37, '38. In any event, Bobby Jones was something else. He had curly black hair, he was a wiry type, he was an incredible dancer, and all of that begot girls, and it begot them in a string. Every mother in the country and town was nervous every time Bobby Jones came around, with good reason. And Bobby Jones was full of mischief. He managed to get a scrape here and a scrape there, some bootleg liquor and stuff like that.

Well, in '38 or thereabouts Bobby Jones was in one scrape too many, and he went before the magistrate. The magistrate said to his dad, "Look, I'll give you a choice. I can't stretch it any more, Mr. Jones. Either he's going to have to do time, or he can enlist in the Navy." Because in those days it's how we got rid of troublemakers all across the country in these little towns, and the Navy accepted that. Bobby Jones went to Great Lakes and enlisted.[*] Boot camp was 26 weeks long then.

Time passed. Hardly anybody gave it any thought, it was so long. Here, all of a sudden, in the spring—it may have been about '38; I remember still being in grade school—Bobby Jones came home on boot leave, 14 days, as I recollect. He had his Dixie

---

[*] Great Lakes, Illinois, a town on the shore of Lake Michigan, about 30 miles north of downtown Chicago, was the site of a large naval training station that included recruit training and a number of specialized schools. It is now known as Great Lakes Naval Station.

cup on the back of his head, his hair growing back. He was dressed in whites and stuff. I mean, he was just right out of the photograph gallery. They couldn't believe it. They threw fronds in his path [chuckle] as he came. "Our boy Bobby. He's back from the Navy." I mean, everybody loved Bobby, everybody. It was incredible. And I remember saying at that time to Carlisle Berry, my very close friend, "You know, if we ever have to do that, we ought to get some of that. That's what we ought to get."

Well, Bobby Jones became a sonarman. He was killed in the war because his destroyer was sunk on him. But when we got to January of 1943 and had to check a block, that's the only thing we had to go on. We didn't have any other measure. We knew a couple of the older boys who had been drafted. Some were drafted and then released before the war. They went through Selective Service, I think it was for like a year or something or other and allowed to come back. Well, as soon as the war started, as soon as Pearl Harbor, man, [slap] they were gone like that. But we just weren't old enough to think very deep about it at all. And that's how it happened. That's how we checked the block, the V block. All of us checked the V.

Time wore on. We got out of high school in May. There was a lot of parties. All the mothers were really, really proud of us. The whole town was proud of us. We received orders in June for us to report to the naval air station at Olathe, Kansas, for further assignment, and on 1 July we did. The orders told us to bring only a small duffel bag and the clothes we had on, because we would be immediately outfitted. I mean, there were only just a couple pages of instructions. It turned out that two of the parents who drove the four of us over there weren't allowed on the base; we were let out at the gate. We waved goodbye, and that was it.

Well, the people running the air station didn't have the foggiest damned idea what to do with us or why we were there. After they had pondered for a day, they understood that we were to be reassigned to the University of Kansas.[*] The reason we were ordered to the air station was that it was an official naval institution. Within the next two or three days or something, we got over to KU. It turned out that there already was a naval installation, disconnected, at the University of Kansas. The university had built a big

---

[*] Olathe is in the eastern part of Kansas, not far from Kansas City. Lawrence, site of the University of Kansas, is about 30 miles west of Olathe.

new academic building there. In '41, maybe '42, the Navy walked in and took it over and turned it into a electrician's mate school. The Navy requisitioned all the machine shops—overnight—for a machinist's mate school. They moved in a number of teachers but appropriated the faculty members too. They started what we would call today a Class A machinist's mate school and a Class A electrician's mate school.* So they were in the process of forming an administrative unit on the campus to deal in these. Hell, they just sent them in. I think each one of those schools had about 400 students in it. They were just building all over the place. And here we were.

Paul Stillwell: You had been told to show up only with the ditty bags and the clothes on your back. When did you get outfitted?

Admiral Meyer: Olathe had no uniforms and, of course, the University of Kansas had none at all, and there we were. So the month of July was genuine hell. It was incredible, because some 500 sailors had been ordered in. I don't know how we got outfitted. Somehow pieces of uniform came in the next few days, and we just somehow got through July. We fumbled and wandered through it. Of course, it was hotter than hell, really hot. But it didn't take me, or the other two, long to realize that we had made the right choice with the Navy.

Paul Stillwell: Why do you say that?

Admiral Meyer: The Navy came in there for this new thing called the V-12, and it staffed it in our case with eight officers. The senior one was a lieutenant commander. All reserves. And they were schoolteachers, school professors. They didn't know anything except they were of age. So they were to be our unit. That was one thing. The other thing the Navy did was go out and start requisitioning fraternity houses. Just took them. My fraternity house was one on West Hill Avenue, and they were going to name

---

* The basic A School is a level of Navy training that provides specialized instruction that will enable enlisted personnel to strike for a given occupational rating.

our barracks PTs. I was in PT-3. There would be nine barracks, nine houses requisitioned. Took them over.

Paul Stillwell: Was there any ROTC structure on the campus? You're shaking your head "no."*

Admiral Meyer: No. Nothing. So almost simultaneously—you may have heard of this earlier in your investigative work—in the war the Navy created a rating called the Diamond A rating. The Diamond A rating was a right-arm rating, and it was a diamond with an "A" in the middle of it, meaning athlete. And it was mostly the jocks of the country. The coaches from all the high schools, the universities and all this, they were mostly jocks, one kind or another.

Paul Stillwell: Gene Tunney ran that program, the boxer.†

Admiral Meyer: Did he? Well, they really were able to get some monsters in that program, I mean just out and outright evil people. [Chuckle] But the way that they had in my PT, there were about 70 of us that I recollect, something in that neighborhood, and every two-man room was now a three-man room, and every one-man room was now a two-man room, whatever it could take. They'd assign one of these Diamond A's as the "house mother," and they were to put it on a Navy discipline footing. Nobody knew what that was except what they read in a book. But, anyhow, one of the good things they did was set up a fire-alarm system, because we had them jammed full of men. We were maybe a mile to a mile and a half from campus. Well, a big donor in the late '30s had given money for a new student union building, a thing of beauty. It had just been completed, with a big ballroom and stuff like that. Well, the Navy solved that; they requisitioned it and turned it into a mess hall.

---

* ROTC – reserve officers' training corps.
† Lieutenant Commander James J. "Gene" Tunney, USNR, had been the heavyweight boxing champion from 1926 to 1928. During World War II, he was in charge of the Navy's program of athletic instruction. The men he recruited as assistants were given direct appointments as chief petty officer specialists.

Well, the next thing they had a problem with is how are they going to feed us? Navy solved that. They opened a cooks and bakers school. All this done in a month. Well, of course, the people who populated the cooks and bakers school were all these gangly farm kids like ourselves, who came walking in and they went, "Hmm, I guess, well, yes sir, no, I've never done any cooking, but I've watched my mother." [Laughter] And so they were going to school. They got assigned to be the people to feed us. And still at that time the Navy had an incredible mobilization and storage type structure, they really did. I mean, the Navy's been beat up on things, like a 2,000-year supply of battleship anchors and stuff like that, but the Navy did have a lot of things ready for war. An example here was the whole matter of galley gear. They requisitioned all this, pots and stuff. It didn't take them long to get this kitchen and galley into operation and such. It took them about a year, though, before they could get anybody who knew how to cook anything [chuckle]. I mean, it was really, really awful. But the Navy solved the problems. And that's why I'm glad I chose the Navy.

Now, the same month the ASTP, Army Specialized Training Program, I believe—ordered in 500 soldiers. They did have uniforms. But they billeted them underneath the stadium and decided to set up field kitchens to feed them from. So they would live there.

The Marine Corps ordered in 200 Marines. Around 15 miles outside of Lawrence, Kansas, is a big Indian school for advanced education. I think it was maybe the first one in the United States. It was a nice, big campus and everything. The Marines went out there and occupied a sward at Haskell Institute and set up their field kitchens and set out their tents, and they got ready to go to school from there.[*] The Army got ready to go to school from the stadium. In the meantime, we Navy were going to school out of these fraternity houses.

Well, the rules and regulations, of course, were just piling up that high as fast as you could go. The summer was wearing on. We finally got fitted a piece at a time. By September we had mostly a full seabag, or if you didn't have, you got your ass repeatedly chewed out because somebody would be inspecting your seabag every Saturday morning.

---

[*] This was the Haskell Institute, founded in 1884 and renamed in 1887 to honor Dudley Haskell, the U.S. Representative who was responsible for the school being at Lawrence.

Time wore on. First term started. They were four-month terms. Moved into second term. Thanksgiving came, and it was getting cold in Kansas. The Army took one look at this and decided they weren't going to make it where they had their men billeted, and the whole damned unit disbanded and folded.

Christmas came. Like it got *really* cold in Kansas. The Marines decided they couldn't make it. Besides, they had a lot of other pressures. They were needed for the war, so their presence at Haskell folded. So now the Navy was the survivor. That's the reason I'm glad I checked it, because the Navy had the imagination and structure. I was 17 years old, and I learned all those lessons right there, of how to do things and do them with aplomb.

Well, to drag that story on a little bit further, in February 1944 or so, the Navy had decided that it was going to have to do something about how to staff the V-12 programs. It was running out of professors, and they were going to have to turn to specialties of some kind. So it was decided various universities would take on a specialty. By then, at the end of two terms, we were asked to check our likes and dislikes of what course we wanted to take. We weren't guaranteed we'd get it, but nevertheless the Navy gave us the option.

I chose electrical engineering. It was called communications and pre-radar. Now, mind you, I had not the foggiest idea the previous year what an engineer was. I had two uncles that worked on the Wabash Railroad, and I knew what an engineer was in that context. I had not the foggiest idea, so help me, what an engineer was all about. I surmised, from talking to another guy, that, well, they built bridges and dams and that kind of thing. So I chose communications and pre-radar, electrical engineering. It was pre-radar that caused me to do it. There was another choice, and it was electrical engineering—power.

In February we decided we were going to rearrange the whole United States. We had, of course, like the other units, we'd lost a number. The attrition rate wasn't good, for either misfits or couldn't cut the grades or any number of things. A few cheaters and a few running over the hill. So two things happened. Roosevelt said we've got to be fair, so the whole fleet was allowed to take the exam for the replenishment people. Well, don't you know that every sailor in the Pacific that could write his name took the examination, because there were a hell of a lot of smart sailors in the Pacific, sonarmen in particular, and radiomen. And many, many of them got on a list to be selected. They had to take an officers' physical—that knocked a lot of them out—to be considered to bring in to the V-12 unit. They couldn't cut it. First of all, they chose the school as a lark to get out of the Pacific, and they got selected as a lark. The way the school was operated, you could get two terms. In the first term you went on probation, and if you were still on it in the second term: "Goodbye, hello boot camp at Great Lakes for retraining," in my own case. So you could get two terms, which is what they were looking for.

Paul Stillwell: Then, presumably, if they couldn't hack it they'd go back to the fleet.

Admiral Meyer: They'd go back. Interesting thing. They lost their rating while they were in the V-12, because everybody was an apprentice seaman. But their rating was preserved. If they returned to the fleet, they got their rating back, they didn't lose it. They just lost their money; their money got suspended. When they came, of course, they had a pretty good potful of money because they had been saving money for quite a while there, and they literally practiced the art of the drunken sailor. So almost all of them left the V-12 for disciplinary reasons. Hell, bed check meant nothing to them. Hours meant nothing to them. They just did what they pleased, and they got tolerated for two terms.

Well, in the rebuilding in February, they were confronted with this whole professor issue that I mentioned in schools. Well, when all the dust settled, unbeknownst to me—I just was stunned and shocked—the University of Kansas was selected to be what today we'd call a center of excellence, the center of excellence for electrical engineering—communications and pre-radar. The way it got selected is the head of the department was Dr. V. P. Hessler, in that era quite well known throughout government for some of his electromagnetic contributions. And, in fact, during my time—I only met him once—during my era he was mostly up in Alaska working on something. But he was a nationally respected person, and particularly in the armed forces.

Boulder, Colorado, was selected, the University of Colorado, for power. And there's about six or eight others. Well, all these people got orders. Wayne stayed right where he was. So if you had selected power, (poof) you went to Boulder, Colorado.

Well, the unit was rebuilt by the first of March, and it was rebuilt by the leftovers from other places. In that rebuilding, which, again, was, I think, part of my good fortune, a lot of the students who came in to rebuild—sailors, actually, students secondarily—they came in. They had been to Stevens Institute in New Jersey, top institute in the nation. A number of them from the University of Oregon, University of Washington. So here all of a sudden, my God, we were meeting strangers. I mean, we were meeting other tribes, people who couldn't even speak our language. And I ended up with two new roommates, one of which came out of Hoboken, and I spent the next year trying to just be able to speak to the man. And every other word was "Fuck this," or "Fuck that." That was the only language they knew. My other one, Paul Leonard, was from Snoqualmie Falls, Washington. He had been a ranger before he enlisted in the Navy. Well, about six words a day was the limit of what you could get out of him. Those were my two roommates.

Paul Stillwell: Did any of these sailors who came from the fleet see this was an educational opportunity and work at it?

Admiral Meyer: I can't name you a single one. There surely were some, but not in my acquaintance. I've often thought about that, and how they must have later regretted their behavior, of this wonderful education.

Well, we were rebuilt to 400 and something. By late '44 or so, our unit was shrinking and shrinking, shrinking dropouts, for one reason or another. We were going to have eight terms, 32 months. And we would complete one term Friday afternoon, we'd draw books Monday for the next term. So I was in school 32 months, continually. Well, I don't give a damn what age you are or how smart you are or any of those things, it's tiring. It grows on you. And while some would be motivated by what they read about the war, that of itself was not compelling. I can't name a single one of my associates who were motivated to stay in the school to avoid the Pacific. I think that they were praising God that they had not yet gone to the Pacific, but there was no doubt in their mind that they were going to the Pacific.

Paul Stillwell: Was that your expectation as well?

Admiral Meyer: Oh, yeah, no doubt. I mean there was no doubt. Roosevelt thought this was going to be a very long war, and there was no doubt in his mind it was a long war, and it was his idea was to make sure the nation wasn't wiped out. He thought it was going to be long enough that he'd even need officers to replenish with in the middle of the war, which was the fundamental purpose of this program. Plus get schooled people and not have the universities lapse. There's any number of good reasons for it. I mean, it was a marvelously conjured program, which neither of the other services accomplished. The Marines and the Army did not accomplish it. Now, it was true that their pressures were a lot different in many ways, but this 17-year-old kid didn't forget it that when the Navy set its mind to do something it *did* it, and it put its best effort forward to do it.

And you know something? I've spent the last 20 years working in ballistic-missile defense and its ancestors, and I've got to tell you, the Navy can't be touched in leadership. I just watched it. I spent 20 years serving on those panels, serving on those staffs over there, and I'm just bowled over at—I'd hesitate to call it ineptness, but the lack of ability, imagination, creativity, and such in the officers of the Air Force and the officers of the Army, as contrasted to naval officers. I'll take a naval officer anytime, sight unseen. I don't know why that is, but it's true.

Paul Stillwell: And it all goes back to Bobby Jones.

Admiral Meyer: [Chuckle] In my case it goes back to Bobby Jones, you know, a good point. But, while I'm not the oldest naval officer you know, I nevertheless am one of the oldest active naval officers you are aware of. But you're right; it goes back to Bobby.

Paul Stillwell: How competitive was the academic atmosphere? Was there an emphasis on class standing?

Admiral Meyer: Well, there's no one in your class but you. There were virtually no 4-F people in the university, at least in this part of engineering.[*] They were smart. Now, I started in, I said, in July of '43. If I ratchet ahead—I'm getting slower on you all the

---

[*] 4-F was the designation for men who were not drafted because of physical problems.

time, but I'll come back and fill in some of the blanks, hopefully. Went through '45, going to school five days a week, and on Saturdays we drilled. So, except for short holiday periods, the thing never shut down. And I was building up. When I was a junior and a senior, in that era, even KU's faculty got in a situation where virtually every teacher I had in electrical engineering were two men that whole time. They taught the courses, both of them fairly young fellows. They were both 4-F. And I've never forgotten them to this day. Glenn Richardson and Irving Robb. Irving Robb was crippled. I don't know why Glenn was—I think it was probably hearing in his case. And I've often thought about those two men and what the nation owes those men, which nothing ever came to them that I'm aware of, nothing. No recognition in any way, shape, or form. And they were dedicated night and day, constantly harassed by the students, in the sense of their workload. Every night.

One of my terms as a junior I had seven three-hour labs. Because the Navy determined the curriculum; we didn't determine it. You could add on a couple of electives if you thought you could handle it. Well, when I graduated after eight terms I had 164 college hours. I carried a minimum of 20 hours every term, as did others, so I'm not some unusual bird. That's just the way it was. And in the end the problem was rest, because we'd drill, drill, drill, on Saturday. Finally about 1400 the Diamond A's would release you for liberty till Sunday night if you weren't on restriction. If you had a D you'd be on restriction so you could only have Saturday off. You had to be back studying on Sunday till you got rid of your D. Because the Navy determined your grades, determined what you did and how you were doing. I didn't know any better, but it was a military/non-military thing, I guess you would say. We practiced military behavior; we were led by the military.

One of the interesting things is we did a lot of drilling. In all that time I never carried a rifle. I carried a wooden rifle. In all that time they had no rifles; there weren't any. Never carried a pistol in all that time. We didn't even have wooden pistols, but we had wooden rifles, I guess so you could get used to the weight of them.

There came February of 1946. The war was over. Because we got a half a day off on V-E Day but we were allowed a day and a half off on V-J Day.[*] We had no goddamn idea what the atom bomb meant, none at all. It had no meaning to us.[†] So time wore on, the war was over. There was created nationally a point system, I don't know whether you're acquainted with it or not.[‡]

Paul Stillwell: Yes, I am.

Admiral Meyer: That's how people were separated. The demobilization was by points, and if you served so much time in the Pacific you got so many points, if you were in combat you got so many, and on and on and on and on. Well, going to school you didn't amass very many points. You did amass points, but you were at the low end of the totem pole. So on 1 February the university announced to the Navy that they had now completed the academic curriculum. Not only that, another piece of the Navy had come in and said, well, we're going to set up an NROTC, and a lieutenant (senior grade) was ordered in to get that started.[§] Now, where he got all his brilliance beats the hell out of me, but that's who came in to do it. He was really high on the totem pole at that time. Today he'd be a nothing.

So when the university announced that, we were now just adrift. Nobody knew what to do. There were 34 left, starting with on the order of 400. Fussed around, fussed around. One day BuPers sent out an order—you would get this with your experience, years in the Navy—and the order was to commission us.[**] Well, only this lieutenant

---

[*] V-E Day – Victory in Europe Day, 8 May 1945, when the German surrender was ratified in Berlin. V-J Day – Victory over Japan Day, marked the end of the war in the Pacific on 15 August 1945. Because of the time difference it was 14 August in the United States when combat ended.

[†] In the first combat use of atomic bombs, U.S. B-29 bombers hit Hiroshima, on the island of Honshu, on 6 August 1945 and Nagasaki, on Kyushu, on 9 August.

[‡] For the demobilization of the U.S. armed forces after World War II, the services had a point system to determine individual priorities for leaving the service. Points were awarded for length of service, overseas service, battle stars, decorations, and dependent children. Those with the highest number of points were the earliest discharged.

[§] NROTC – Naval Reserve Officers' Training Corps.

[**] BuPers – Bureau of Naval Personnel.

(senior grade) had the foggiest idea what that meant. Our OinC was a lieutenant commander (reserve).*

So they got the book out, the forerunner of the appendices to the BuPers Manual and stuff, and first they found we rated a uniform allowance. Second, we needed uniforms, so the Navy said it would solve that. The 34 of us were loaded on a bus and transported to Kansas City, Missouri, 70 miles away. We were taken to the big Wolf Brothers men's clothing store, and there we were outfitted in a seabag of as much as could be available. And the Wolf Brothers did a fantastic job at outfitting us. I can't any longer remember the prices, but I think our clothing allowance was about $300.00 or something like that. They did a fantastic job, except—one of the national crises at the time were white shirts, and you could only be issued two white shirts no matter what. Later, my mother managed to take two white shirts away from my dad's youngest brother and send them to me, that I deserved them for the nation and he didn't. [Laughter] So I had four white shirts.

But this wore on and the next week or so, ten days, we'd piddle, piddle, piddle, got all shaped up to do this commissioning ceremony. It was February and colder than hell. So they were going to commission us, and the university had agreed to award our degrees in the same ceremonies, 34 of us. Well, of course, I told my folks, who lived out in Missouri, and away from Kansas they lived roughly 170 miles, 180 miles.

In 1939 my dad, in a moment of weakness while drinking Old Crow whiskey, had traded from one of his buddies, the Wolf brothers, who had opened a new agency in Brunswick, Missouri, that nobody understood, to sell Studebakers. None of them in that part of the country. The next thing is, my dad owned one, and it was fortuitous in a way, because whatever you went into the war with, that's what you came out of the war with.

My brother, two years younger than I, had managed to enlist in the Army Air Corps by 1946, but during that era he was the big man in the house, even though my sister was older, but she was away at Washington University. He was out with that Studebaker one night with a girl, driving down through the bottom, and as you know our part of the country is all levees, so you've got to be careful how you go over those levees. So he went over one of them about half drunk and went airborne, managed to roll it over

---

* OinC – officer in charge.

and bang it up. Well, they didn't get hurt, but that didn't help, because there wasn't any way to fix the damned thing except with a hammer in the way a farmer does it. So they banged it back in shape, but the window was busted on the right hand side up front and they couldn't get a window. So, as a farmer would do, they put a piece of plywood in there, and that fixed that. And it had a few other dents. You could tie the doors shut, so you could make it work.

It now came February, and there were going to be these ceremonies. I want to say they were on the eighth of February. My folks didn't have the foggiest idea what this meant, but one thing they knew, it was big, and they were going to see their boy, Wayne. They had no idea what it meant, but it was good. And so they'd use tractor gas, and they were going to drive to Kansas for this graduation.

They came through Kansas on Highway 40 where 24 intersects, and they passed a big state-line liquor store which we all frequented quite well because Kansas was dry. My dad convinced my mother they were going to stop there at the state-line liquor store, and they bought a case of Three Feathers whiskey, which was a really popular cheap whiskey in that day. So they bought 12 bottles of it. They didn't know what they were going to, but they knew it was something big and it was dry in Kansas.

So they got out there. Well, they didn't have any idea what to do except they wanted to do what Wayne wanted them to do. It turned out they were the only parents that showed up, the only ones that could make it.

Paul Stillwell: That had to be a big day in your life.

Admiral Meyer: The day was so big that it overwhelmed me. It took me a long time after that to really appreciate the significance and seriousness of it.

I mentioned the Haskell Indian Institute out at the edge of town. See, you could drink liquor anyplace in Kansas as long as you weren't creating a disturbance; you just couldn't buy it. So occasionally we sailors had gotten out there, because it was too damned hard to get there—a place called The Tepee, which was a joint. My dad offered to take us all to supper and stuff. Hell, they had a giant crowd. He didn't have any money. But by the time he started with us, I mean he must have had about 60 or 70 people. So they drove us out. Plus the lieutenant got a bus and a bus took everybody out, and we went out to The Tepee. And that night we drank that case of Three Feathers whiskey. [Laughter] We, of course, were all underage.

I was an ensign in the United States Navy, and I held a degree of bachelor of science in electrical engineering, and I was 19 years old. Now, afterwards I really got stuck with myself on that because I got to thinking about being 19 years old and those things, and that's kind of right up there, you know, with Newton or somebody, when you think about the distance I had come from nothing.[*] That I'd come from *nothing* in 32 months. From nothing.

Well, the next day here we were. What were we going to do next? We had no orders. Nobody knew what to do with us. There we were.

Paul Stillwell: Typically the V-12 program included midshipman school training in addition to the academic. Was that just skipped for you?

Admiral Meyer: Well, the war was over. They were trying to figure out how in the hell to get rid of us. And the answer to your question is yes. I'd now been in the Navy three years, and I'd never had a single day of naval training, not a one. But I learned it all the hard way, primarily under these damned Diamond A's, and they learned it out of a book.

So each morning we were lying around, and this lieutenant was trying to shape up the NROTC spaces. We were hanging out, and now there's a fairly good crowd of us with nothing to do. I don't know, several days later an AlNav came in.[†] This AlNav was soliciting applications to attend graduate training in electrical engineering to study the new science of electronics at the Massachusetts Institute of Technology for five terms. Of course, where I came from, you just would salivate at that. And we pondered it and pondered it. We didn't know what to do, so we talked to this lieutenant (senior grade). I took some advice. He said, "Look, officers, the Navy doesn't do stupid things. The Navy knows you've been going to school the last 32 months, and they're not about to

---

[*] Isaac Newton (1642-1727) was a British physicist, mathematician, and astronomer who postulated the law of gravity and the laws of motion.
[†] AlNav is a type of message put out to all the Navy.

order you back to school right now. This program will come around again, take my word for it. This is a postwar program being started. It's going to be needed in the Navy, and it will be back around. So what you should do is apply. By application you show interest and you'll be on the record, so when it comes around again you'll go to the head of the line." Sounded pretty damned logical. Sounded pretty good. We never thought anything more about it. We put it in.

Another week or so passed. We got orders. [Laughter] My orders were to board a personnel transport at San Francisco for further transfer in the Pacific. One of my mates got orders to Guantanamo. The other got orders down into Charleston, South Carolina.

So we took off. I got out there. The first time in my life I'd been on an airplane. Flew to San Francisco. I was billeted at an officers' barracks on Buchanan Street. They didn't know where my ship was, but I was to report in each day till they found it. This went on for several days, and now we were into March. Finally, one morning I was mustered and ordered to report to the Army Air Forces base at Oakland, which is where the airport is right now, for further transport to the Pacific.

So, as was the style in those days, you had to be out there, like, at 11:00 o'clock in the morning to be ready for takeoff at 1600 or something. So got out there, spent the whole damned afternoon sitting around. Gear was all loaded, everything was all buttoned up, and so 25 or 30 of us were waiting to be loaded onto this plane. First stop Hawaii.

A WAVE came running out.* She was paging Ensign Meyer. I accosted her. She said, "Ensign, you have a change of orders here. I'm looking at these; they're message orders. Let's see, you're to report to a place called MIT [laughter] in Massachusetts."† She was reading on, and she said, "You're supposed to be there by the 20th of February."

I said, "What? It's now the 15th of March." [Chuckle]

"Well," she said, "I'm just telling you what it says."

---

* WAVES—Women Accepted for Voluntary Emergency Service. Until the 1970s, when women ceased to have a separate organization within the Navy, the term WAVE was used to refer to a Navy woman.
† As Admiral Meyer related the story, the WAVE pronounced MIT like the word "mitt." The abbreviation, of course, stands for Massachusetts Institute of Technology.

So I pondered that. Of course, now the ground crew was really pissed at me, because they had to go find my gear. They finally got it. She said, "You've got a Pri 3 to fly with," which didn't mean anything to me at the time. It turned out later it was pretty damned important.

So got my gear out, got to the airport. Now, with a Pri 3 it turned out I could be a big wheel and walk right up there. I got on an airplane to Kansas City. I called my girl and I told her, "I'm just passing through. I'm under orders. I've got to go and I'm going to catch a plane and I'm going to Boston, Massachusetts, wherever the hell that is."

"Okay," she said, "goodbye."

On the 17th of March I landed at about 4:00 o'clock in the afternoon in Boston, Massachusetts. I didn't know what to do. I got my gear. I went out to get a taxicab, because I was green, I didn't know anything. Besides, I was wearing a money belt. I said to him, "I've got these orders to get over to this place called the Graduate House in Cambridge. Can you get me there?"

He looked at me and he said, "Yes, but that's going to cost you a lot of money. You got enough money?"

I said, "Well, what do you mean, a lot of money?" And he finally told me, I don't know, $25.00 or something. I said, "Well, I've got no other way to get there. I don't know how to get there."

"Well," he said, "you could take the subway."

I said, "I'm not taking the subway."

So he said, "I'll take you over there.

So he did. During the ride, I said to the taxi driver, "I don't understand all this population. You always have this kind of jam-up around here and everything?"

He looked at me again in the back seat and he said, "Don't you know what day this is?"

"Well, I don't know. It's the 17th of March."

"Well," he said, "the 17th of March is St. Patrick's Day." [Chuckle] Oh. Except on the church calendar we never paid any attention to it.

Anyway, he took me over there, and I got there and I reported in to this place on Memorial Drive and Massachusetts Avenue. I went in there and saw a rather short black man by the name of Andy behind the counter. I was in uniform, and he looked at me. He didn't even ask who I was. He said, "Ensign Meyer, we've been waiting for you." [Laughter]

"Really?"

He said, "Yes, your roommate has already been here, Ensign Talago.[*] You're pretty lucky, because he's already rented quarters and everything and set up a graduate apartment for you and he and, let's see, another one—Ensign Strider."

I said, "Well, I'll be damned. That's all three of us."

"Well," he said, "Ensign Strider is not here. I don't think Ensign Talago is here. I'll take you up to the third deck to the quarters."

It turned out he became a hell of a good friend to us later on, and his friendship started as time wore on, but it really, really developed by Thanksgiving of that year. With Thanksgiving now approaching I recall Andy, because he said, "Look, you officers don't have anything to do. Why don't you come to our house? My wife will cook us a turkey." Well, that sounded pretty good, and we did, we went over to Andy's and we just had a wonderful day with her cooking.

Anyhow, that night Red Rider Strider came in as I was standing there, because up here on the mantle Joe Talago had a bottle of Seven Crown whiskey setting there with a note on it. It turned out it had been there for about two weeks. He'd predicted my arrival any day. But we were now a month late for school.

After we had had a couple drinks, Joe said, "Look, why don't we go out tonight? I want to show you all around. Either one of you ever been on a subway?" Well, of course, we never had. He said, "I'm going to show you around. We're going to take the subway and go to Boston." All right.

So we got on the subway, and we went over there. We got off at Copley Square and came up to the surface. We were standing there just kind of gawking around and talking and looking. It was just now about dark. A car pulled up, and it had two girls in it. One of them leaned out the window and said, "You officers interested in a party?" What are we going to do?

The answer was, "Well, I guess so; we're from the country."

---

[*] Ensign Joseph Talago Jr., USN.

"Well, you all get in." The three of us hopped in this car, without any sense.

Well, it turned out that the parents of one of them were off visiting someplace for the weekend, and so they decided they were going to have a party at their house. I mean, we had a wonderful time all night for the party. Summed up, four months went by before we ever met another woman. [Laughter] No one ever spoke to us the next four months. But they did that night. And that was my introduction to MIT, and I was supposed to go for some 20 months.

Joe had said, "You know, I don't think we can handle this. You're going to be stunned at how hard this is." Well, it was. I mean, they had 300-350 students, and every room was standup. They all stood up. And they ran in age all the way from 65 back to our age. I mean, it was back to school, postwar, and there's where we started studying atomic physics and all these things. We couldn't cut it. There were no books. We couldn't understand the language most of the time. You just stood up, you couldn't even take a note. I mean, it just was horrible.

We weren't doing very well. At MIT you can be on probation for up to two terms. MIT, in those days at least, graded on a numbering system of 5, unlike any in the entire United States. Three was probation. Well, we were already late for the first term; we didn't make that one, so we were already down to, like, a 2. Started going through the summer. Things looked grim, really grim.

God is good. It turned out the Navy was running out of money. Mind you, this was the year 1946 we're talking about. We were commissioned in February of '46. Now we were down to that end of the year in '46, out of money. We were going to be cut back to three terms. It saved our ass. They were going to give us a consolation prize of a BS degree, not a master's degree. So came the subsequent February 1947, not only did I make the cut for a degree, but I was under orders to report to Newport, Rhode Island, to USS *Goodrich*, and that started my life at sea.

Paul Stillwell: Did the classes get easier when you got switched to this bachelor's program?

Admiral Meyer: No, not a damned bit. [Chuckle] They didn't change at all. They didn't change a bit. As I say, I think it was just a consolation prize. I mean, the head of the electrical engineering department was kind of embarrassed because he hadn't been too prepared for what the Navy was getting ready to do. He was trying to accommodate the Navy, and he felt that we'd been taken advantage of. And we had people way above our stature. I mean, you had people in 1946 and '47 trying to catch up on four years' loss in education. So, I mean, you'd have a classroom, half of them would be PhDs. They were coming back to take these courses as a revisit. And no books. Dr. Müller of the Müller-Geiger counter was one of our professors.* He was an American, but he was a German-American. His English was incomprehensible. And he was only about this tall. I mean, what oddball people.

In those days, they had these big classrooms surrounded by four blackboards. Every bulkhead had a blackboard. So Dr. Müller would come walking in that door, pick up the chalk, and he'd start writing there. He'd start writing up as far as he could reach, which would be about two-thirds up on the blackboard, start writing. Mumble mumble mumble, write, mumble mumble. Mumble mumble mumble—little-bitty print. Mumble mumble. He'd go around, around, around, around and around, around, around, around. Wham!—out the door he'd go when he hit the door again. [Laughter] He had it down pretty pat; it was about a 50-minute hour. I mean, I took that goddamn course on X-rays for three terms. I guess I really learned a lot, but I never understood it. I took two terms of atomic physics.

One thing did happen to me. One term I took a graduate course called "Vibration and Sound," and it was acoustics. The author of the textbook was Dr. Morris, who was the professor. Unfortunately Dr. Morris for that whole year was out at Bikini.† So he would have some graduate student come sashay in and teach to you, or one of his assistants would walk in, and she'd have one of these carts pushing piled high and she'd say, "I regret to tell you that Dr. Morris is not here today, but these materials are for you to study and such, and so each of you take a set. Goodbye."

---

* In the 1920s, Walther Müller worked with Hans Geiger to improve the original Geiger counter.
† In July 1946 a joint Army-Navy task force conducted tests at Bikini Atoll in the Marshall Islands to determine the effects of atomic bombs on moored warships.

I couldn't cut it. I couldn't cut it. And we were still doing equations in the time domain. The frequency domain was not being taught, so Fourier analysis was not yet being taught.* So you'd write one of these equations for these atonal notes, like related to a bass horn or something. That equation would run all the way across this room and back around. And if you made a mistake someplace over here, you'd spend the rest of the day trying to find the error. One thing we learned as Navy people was that it took group work. Without group work you'd never make it. But it was awful.

Paul Stillwell: Were you administered through the NROTC unit there?

Admiral Meyer: I think administratively we were, but I cannot remember ever seeing that CO or anything like it.

Paul Stillwell: Well, you must have gone somewhere to get your pay on a regular basis.

Admiral Meyer: Well, the checks came to us. They were loose; they weren't in an envelope. But I think about that, and part of my time was spent in the sonar school, which was located in a building on the Institute campus but operated by Harvard. Then we had another school, which was the radar school. It was located in the Harbor Building over on Atlantic Avenue in the city. That's how I learned to ride the subway. They gave us free passes to do it, and we'd go over there usually a day and a half a week, sometimes two days. That's where the labs were. And the teachers there were busy trying to complete their books. That school is where the great book, "Principles of Radar," came from, which is about that thick, which is a classic book. Today I think it's about third or fourth edition. But we as students got the task—how we passed that was as proofreaders, which in those days became, you know, a pretty good approach. Professors needed help, and they had no way to get help except from students. And in return, if you were a halfway decent person, you'd pass the course. So it was a tradeoff. He'd teach you all he

---

* Joseph Fourier devised a system by which general mathematical functions could be simplified by a trigonometric series.

could teach you, and in return you had to help him with his book. So I had quite a bit to do with that book originally. And, again, it isn't clear to me at all how I did that.

Paul Stillwell: Did you get exposed at all to Dr. Stark Draper, who was there?[*] He was big in fire control.

Admiral Meyer: Well, good question. I'll come back to it in a minute.

I left in February 1947, and I started sailing, and we'll talk about that another day. Years later I did get returned to PG school at Monterey.[†] They put me in a guided-missile course. I couldn't get a master's degree out of it. It came at the end of two years. Well, they had a mandatory quota of six officers at MIT in aeronautics and astronautics. And the officers that they had picked who had been trained to go there, five accepted and the other would not accept it. The next thing I knew, I was drafted to go. So, the third year I was ordered to MIT and returned in the instrumentation lab under Dr. Draper and Dr. Wrigley.[‡] So I spent another year at MIT, so I've been there twice. And, by golly, I finally got the degree. [Chuckle] I finally got it.

The short answer is that I didn't spend a lot of time with Draper, but I spent a lot of sessions with Dr. Wrigley, who was his deputy in essence, spent a lot of time with Wrigley. And now another Dr. Mueller, a different one than I mentioned earlier, who was the inventor of a device called microsyn, which is a high-impedance transfer device off of a rotating commutator.[§] He was the inventor of that, and I wrote my thesis under him.

Paul Stillwell: Well, we can get to that in due course. I want to go back to the University of Kansas. Did that fraternity-house setup stay the whole time you were there?

---

[*] Dr. Charles Stark Draper of the Massachusetts Institute of Technology had an important role in the development of the inertial navigation systems used in Polaris missiles and later in the space missions sent to the moon.
[†] Naval Postgraduate School, Monterey, California.
[‡] Walter Wrigley was a student of Draper's, later worked at the university.
[§] Robert K. Mueller.

Admiral Meyer: The short answer is yes. One group of sailors enlisted in the Navy and entered V-12 in July of 1943. That group of sailors eventually became a very small number and graduated around the United States in February of 1946—32 months. That's the only class that started and finished V-12. Now, a lot of people cycled in and out of V-12, and more cycled in and out of various V's which offered degrees in one form or another. But there's only one year group that started and finished. In February of '46 V-12 was terminated, and the people who were behind us in V-12 were forced into ROTC or—I think I'm right—they could opt out of the Navy. But the V-12 was terminated. So God was good.

Paul Stillwell: Well, a lot of the V-12 people got commissions but not degrees, just because of the way the timing worked. They got maybe two years of college and then got a commission, but didn't have a degree yet. Admiral Gravely would be an example; he didn't get his degree before he got commissioned.[*]

Admiral Meyer: Now, I don't know about Sam Gravely. In other words, it's true that there's an optional-type behavior there. I don't ever remember being offered the option of opting out of V-12, but I think I had it in the last year of it. Now, the people behind me, as I say, they had no choice. They either went ROTC or "Goodbye."

There were a number of people, of course, in school in some form or another in July of '43 already. How those all got accounted for, damned if I know. There were V's all over the place where they got credits of one kind or another. Whether groups of them went into the V-12—at least it wasn't in any V-12 that I was associated with. Our V-12 was kind of a purer-type structure.

Paul Stillwell: How much contact did you have with the civilian students when you were there at the University of Kansas?

---

[*] Ensign Samuel L. Gravely Jr., USNR, was commissioned through the V-12 program in December 1944, served on active duty until 1946, then completed his college degree. Samuel L. Gravely with Paul Stillwell, *Trailblazer: the U.S. Navy's First Black Admiral* (Annapolis: Naval Institute Press, 2010).

Admiral Meyer: Zero. Except the girls.

Paul Stillwell: Oh, please tell me about that.

Admiral Meyer: Well, the girls. Of course, men got really, really, really scarce, so the girls, the sorority houses and the halls, would throw dances or socials to try to attract the sailors to come to their affairs. Well, even though in the beginning there were 400 or 500 of us, it still was not an overwhelming number in the university as a whole. And I remember in the beginning, as a country boy, I went into them off and on to just see what was up.

The other thing that we did, which I've never seen any serious publicity on it because no one ever paid attention to it—you could bootleg and get away with it. See, when I enlisted in the Navy you were paid $35.00 a month. Shortly after that pay went to $50.00 and stayed at that the rest of the time I was an enlisted man. Well, you couldn't be much of a wheel on $50.00 a month. Now, if you played your cards right, you could do okay, but out of $50.00 a month I bought a $6.25 savings bond, and I bought life insurance, so I had some $13.00 coming out of my paycheck before I ever saw it.

But you had to live by your wits. So to go to Kansas City, which was incredible, you would hitchhike. The book said you shouldn't hitchhike, but everybody did it during the war. All you had to do was go out and stand on the roadside in your uniform. Anybody would stop and pick you up. Some would go out of their way to deliver you. It would take you maybe a little longer, a couple hours, to get to Kansas City, but it didn't cost you anything. Sunday night, now, became another matter. So what you did was you made sure that you bought a furlough ticket, on the 8:00 o'clock train, because you had to be in for bed check at 11:00, and there was too much risk of hitchhiking after dark.

I went to Kansas City a number of times with nothing more than a few coins in my pocket, and I came home with all of them, because Saturday night the problem was where are you going to stay? And traveling became, as a sailor, your whole life was in your Dopp kit.*

---

* The Dopp kit is a small case that holds shaving materials and other accessories.

There's a place on Highway 40 outside of Kansas City called Mary's. It had started during bootleg times, and it was amongst other things a girl place. But Mary's was a big place, and Saturday nights they'd have band after band after band. And, as was the style in that part of the country in those places, it had big, long mess-hall-like tables. Well, the girls were working in the bomber plants, and the girls had plenty of money. Well, a place like Mary's can't operate without a cover charge, so they had to charge three or four bucks, except no serviceman ever paid. No sailor ever paid anything; he just got his hand stamped and walked in. But the girls paid, and they'd buy the liquor.

So you'd come out here, and you'd drink all you could drink, you'd eat all you could eat, and you could dance all you could dance, and whatever girl you could find that wanted to go with you, you could go home with her. The problem was, when you got to where you were going, most of those girls were living anywhere from three to six of them per apartment, so by Sunday morning the apartment got pretty damned crowded. [Laughter] It got pretty full. It's as simple as no housing, it's just that simple. So sex was a challenge, a real challenge: first of all without a great deal of experience, and second of all the working conditions weren't ideal.

Paul Stillwell: Not much privacy.

Admiral Meyer: Not a bit. Not a bit. And you'd have to sometimes be a little alert, because it would go on right in Mary's. They were pretty clever at getting it done on a chair, because it was really dark. But always treated respectfully in those days.

Also, there was a big Forum Cafeteria—I don't know whether you've ever heard of it—in Kansas City. It was in its heyday well known, a wonderful feeder. All you'd do on a Sunday was just walk up there and stand there. You'd never pay. Somebody in line would come up and say, "Sailor, are you going to have breakfast here?"

"Yes, ma'am."

"Come right in, be my guest." So you'd go to Kansas City and come back with the same coins in your pocket.

And times were right. I mean, girls everyplace. The bomber factories were full of them. And these young girls, of course, were away from home the first time in their life, and they were living wherever they could. They were right from out of the Midwest. They were surrounded in military, but there's no doubt that sailors were their preference. It was quite an era for a couple years, really. It was something. It was amazing.

Paul Stillwell: Well, let's get the *Goodrich* next time.

Interview Number 3 with Rear Admiral Wayne E. Meyer, U.S. Navy (Retired)
Place: Admiral Meyer's office in Arlington, Virginia
Date: Monday, 3 December 2007

Paul Stillwell: Admiral, great to see you again. This is shortly after Thanksgiving and looking forward to Christmas. We talked last time about your commissioning through the V-12 Program.

Admiral Meyer: As I mentioned, I arrived at MIT St. Patrick's Day, 1946, and Boston was still a very active sailor town. Although you were allowed to go ashore now without your uniform, most people did not. Most people chose to wear their uniforms, because there was far more attraction to wearing the uniform than not wearing it. It set you aside from the common people.

Paul Stillwell: Was this still a time when civilians were buying drinks for servicemen and so forth?

Admiral Meyer: Yes, it was. And girls came up and sat down by you on both sides if you weren't careful.

Paul Stillwell: Were bartenders not too diligent about checking ID cards?

Admiral Meyer: You know, I can't ever remember mine being checked. From the day I was 17 years old and I entered the Navy, I can't ever remember it being checked.

Paul Stillwell: So it would have been counterproductive to go in civilian clothes.

Admiral Meyer: [Chuckle] That's true. But nobody ever worried about it. The shore patrol, if they had a sailor problem they nominally handled it, and that was the end of that. I just don't ever remember any brawls.

I want to cycle ahead a couple of years to when my ship was ported in San Francisco and also being decommissioned there. The United States Air Force had been created as an independent entity.* This might have been 1949 or '50. I'm trying to think when I was married. I know the month but I don't know the year. But I've jumped ahead here. We were given quarters in half of a Quonset hut at $35.00 a month.† But the city was in turmoil. The OSD had now taken over, and the OSD decided it was going to reform those services and square them away, don't you know?‡ They were businessmen, and they were in charge.

Paul Stillwell: Well, Louis Johnson was also cutting the budgets dramatically in that era.§

Admiral Meyer: That's why I was in that shipyard at Hunters Point that year, having returned from mainland China.** That's the reason we were sent home, and we were ordered in to be decommissioned after we got there. But what the hell point was I going to hit?

Paul Stillwell: You were over 21 by that time.

Admiral Meyer: Well, by that time I was, and I had just made lieutenant (junior grade).†† I was more than three years a lieutenant (junior grade), and we'll dwell on that another time if we're going to go chronologically. But the problem was, the MP structure and the SP structure—and the SP structure was operated with the Marine Corps—was taken over

---

* On 20 June 1941 the U.S. Army Air Corps was officially redesignated the U.S. Army Air Forces and retained that title until the establishment of the U.S. Air Force as a separate service on 17 September 1947.
† A Quonset hut is a semi-cylindrical metal building that can be shipped to an advance base area and erected quickly.
‡ OSD – Office of the Secretary of Defense.
§ Louis A. Johnson served as Secretary of Defense from April 1949 until September 1950. He cut back substantially on defense expenditures, a program that had to be reversed with the beginning of the Korean War in June 1950. He was removed as SecDef a few months after the war started.
** Hunters Point Naval Shipyard, San Francisco, California. The ship he referred to here was the light cruiser *Springfield* (CL-66), in which Meyer served from July 1948 to December 1949.
†† Meyer's date of rank as lieutenant (junior grade) was 8 February 1949, three years to the day after he was commissioned an ensign on 8 February 1946.

by the geniuses of the staff of OSD.* That was my first introduction as a JO into OSD.†
And they decided that, well, in big cities there's no need for all this waste. And so big
cities like San Francisco and such had semi-permanent patrols in those days. You'd go
there, and you'd be there maybe for six months or 12 months on duty, and so you
reported to somebody else. Well, after OSD took over, you reported to OSD.

Paul Stillwell: Was the naval district running it up till then? Com 12 was in San Francisco.

Admiral Meyer: That's affirmative, and nominally the district saw to the shore patrol, and the military districts saw to the MPs, the military police. But they took them over and turned them into policemen, and every night was a goddamned brawl, every bloody night in that city was a brawl. And the brawls broke out between sailors and primarily Air Force people. And here was a peaceable place, never been any trouble, always lovable, sailors were thought of as great. And now, thanks to OSD, we had created a place that there'd be a brawl every night. Well, that continued on through later years into the Vietnam War, because the attitude of that city changed and became not only anti-Vietnam, it became almost anti-everything. And in those years I dreaded to go there.

But back to where we were.

Paul Stillwell: You were reporting aboard *Goodrich*.‡

Admiral Meyer: Well, I reported aboard on George Washington's Birthday in 1947. For our historian, that's February 22. [Laughter]

Paul Stillwell: It was back then.

---

* MP – military police; SP – shore patrol.
† JO – junior officer.
‡ USS *Goodrich* (DD-831) was a *Gearing*-class destroyer commissioned 24 April 1945. She had a standard displacement of 2,425 tons, was 390 feet long, 41 feet in the beam, and had a maximum draft of 18 feet, 6 inches. Her top speed was 35 knots. She was armed with six 5-inch guns, and ten 21-inch torpedo tubes. She had a long career of naval service before being decommissioned in 1969.

Admiral Meyer: Right. Now, Lord knows what it falls on. Whatever Monday comes up, I guess.

We were moored at Buoy Mike-1, along with *Everett F. Larson.* The two other ships of the division, which were the Dirty Herbie, *Thomas*, and *Hanson*, were moored at the next buoy.* So we were at the farthest buoy at sea. I told you before in the record that my experience at sailing was in a rowboat and a couple of times in a motorboat on the Grand River and the Missouri River. That was my experience. So I didn't know what the hell a storm was, in that context.

I got on a bus in Boston, and it followed a snowplow to Newport. We debarked there down at the bus station, and it was a pretty good distance to walk to what was labeled the fleet landing, but there didn't seem to be any other way to get there. I had my gear, and in those days officers had a big Val-Pak.† Enlisted only could have seabags; officers could have a Val-Pak because they had uniforms that they allegedly couldn't roll. Well, it turns out you can roll officers' uniforms pretty good. In fact, you can wash them if you're a little careful, and they won't run.

So I got on this motor whaleboat. It was a holiday, but it was on a guard mail run simply because there was due to be a guard mail run. They made me put on a life jacket and took me out, headed to the buoy. I didn't think we'd ever get there. That buoy was a long ways out, and it was just storming like hell. Got up, finally, on the ship—they did have an accommodation ladder down—and it was iced all over. I asked the petty officer who the officer of the deck was. He said, "Well, the officer of the deck is Ensign Atkinson."

I said, "Well, maybe you could tell him that Ensign Meyer has now reported." So Eddie "Dumbo" Atkinson came up to the quarterdeck rubbing his eyes and such, and I greeted him.‡ They were expecting me to show up sometime. That night I learned how to steam at the buoy, my first experience ever.

Paul Stillwell: Who taught you?

---

* USS *Everett F. Larson DD-830);* USS *Herbert J. Thomas* (DD-833); USS *Hanson* (DD-832). The ships were home-ported at Newport, Rhode Island.
† Val-Pak is a brand of folding garment bag.
‡ Ensign Edward C. Atkinson, USN.

Admiral Meyer: Ensign Dumbo Atkinson and the duty engineering chief, who was a boilerman. He was also duty engineering officer. They taught me how to stand a watch on the bridge and steam at the buoy. You'd steam three to six knots, depending on the surge that you were taking. The trick to it was to not pull the damned buoy out of the water. That was the alleged fear, that you would unearth the buoy. So the idea was to try to take the pressure off of the chain, or relieve the pressure somewhat.

Paul Stillwell: So you would counteract the current.

Admiral Meyer: Yes. Now, whether that's true or not, I don't know. At least it certainly was a sailor's lot to do so then. We did it almost till daylight with no thought of going to bed.

Paul Stillwell: How did Dumbo get his nickname?

Admiral Meyer: He had big ears. [Chuckle] Dumbo eventually went to aviation, and I guess had a full life in the Navy, I don't know. I lost track of him.*

Paul Stillwell: How soon did you get into the routine of duty section, and what was your billet initially?

Admiral Meyer: My orders read to be the electronic repair officer for the division. However, there was no such billet in the fleet. That was a billet in the eyes of the Bureau of Personnel that was just newly created.

Paul Stillwell: Was the commodore on board your ship?

Admiral Meyer: No. I had no idea what my posting was, none at all. The next day, after the storm abated, I went to lunch in the wardroom. I'd never been in a wardroom in my

---

* Atkinson retired in 1971 as a commander.

life. The captain was back aboard, the XO was back aboard.* In those days the captain and the XO hardly ever worried about their ship in port. They trusted their OODs, and that was it.† A storm just kind of ran off their back. And generally, as I remember, they were married, and Lieutenant (j.g.) Rawls was married, and that was the end of married officers.‡ All the rest of them were ensigns. One lieutenant (j.g.). So he chatted me up a little bit. I met him at lunch and such. And in that ship, a *Sumner*-class long-hull, as you walked forward from the wardroom, the XO cabin was immediately on the right hand and the CO cabin was immediately on the port hand. There was also a sea cabin, but the sea cabin was not too far away so the captain could interchange pretty well as he chose. He had sailed in the old cruiser *Helena* and he had been the assistant gun boss, and he had spent several days in the water when she was sunk.§

Paul Stillwell: That was in the summer of '43.

Admiral Meyer: Right. Well, his memories did not leave him. And I believe the XO had spent a day in the water too, in a destroyer.

Paul Stillwell: Can we get their names on the tape, please?

Admiral Meyer: Well, I'll try. I'd better get them while I'm thinking. Commander—we called him "Jungle Jim"—Leonard J. Baird was the CO, and he was a Naval Academy graduate.** Lieutenant Commander Phil Teeter was the XO.†† He was not a reserve at the time, but he had not come out of the Naval Academy either. Then there was Lieutenant (j.g.) E. S. Rawls; he was out of the Naval Academy. And that was it. Most of them were out of the Naval Academy; they were all ensigns. It turned out I was destined to be an ensign for 36 months before I was ever promoted.

---

* XO – executive officer.
† OODs – officers of the deck.
‡ Lieutenant (junior grade) Elbert S. Rawls Jr., USN.
§ USS *Helena* (CL-50) was torpedoed in the early morning hours of 6 July 1943 near the island of New Georgia in the Solomons. Of her crew of nearly 900 men, 168 died in the action.
** Commander Leonard J. Baird, USN, Naval Academy class of 1935, commanded the USS *Goodrich* from September 1946 to June 1948.
†† Lieutenant Commander Phillip H. Teeter, USN.

But we got to talking, and he asked me this question at lunch. They'd put me down at the end of the table because everybody assumed I was George.* And the fiddle boards had been rigged on the table.† I didn't know what the hell a fiddle board was, but I learned pretty quick. But at Buoy One there was actually that much rolling and pitching that fiddle boards were normally put out on a winter day. I doubt you ever sailed in one of those ships, but if you ever did, the biggest goddamned board in the ship is kind of built right over the wardroom, so it's really, really noisy. Anyhow, the captain in the middle of it said, "Ensign, Meyer, let me ask you a question."

Way down at the end of the table, I said, "Yes, sir, Captain."

"Which light is the green light and which light is the red light?"

I stumbled, and finally I said, "Well, Captain, would you repeat the question? I can't hear down here."

"Well," he said, "we have two running lights. One running light is red and one running light is green. Which is which?" It got deadly silent. Even the stewards made sure they got far away.

Finally I confessed, "Captain, I don't know." Not a word was said the rest of the lunch. Nothing. Stone quiet.

Afterwards the XO called me into his cabin and he said, "Meyer, the way I remember this is: Think of port wine. Port wine's red, and the port light is red." And that's the way I've always remembered it. I've never forgotten it to this day. I didn't know enough to be embarrassed. He couldn't embarrass me, because I didn't know anything about it.

Then, I think it was a Thursday, my ass was off to emergency ship-handling school at the fleet training center at Newport for the next two days. That was in February. In July, I was the senior watch officer in the ship.

Paul Stillwell: So you were not really George, because you had gotten commissioned in February 1946.

---

* "George" is the traditional nickname given to the most junior ensign serving in a ship.
† A fiddle board is a wooden device put on a shipboard table to keep plates and silverware from sliding off in rough weather.

Admiral Meyer: That's right. Well, I was really not George, but I didn't know what George was, so it didn't make a damned bit of difference to me. It was just assumed. But it teaches you something about assumptions. You need to be careful what you assume.

So the CO and the XO apparently had a discussion that afternoon and decided they were going to straighten me out and see what they could do with me. Well, I never realized what you could learn and learn so fast. I had no midshipman school. I was destined to go to boot camp, and it was terminated because in the middle of the war it was decided there was no need to expend the resources to send us V-12s to boot camp, that "We'd get them later."

Now, many came out of the V-12 program in different ways. Some, depending on where you were, in an ROTC or what else you were, you entered in the middle of it, and you might transition three terms or four terms. You were just a roustabout. You weren't recognized as a bona fide, disciplined, V-12-er. And then the ones that were behind us—because they had full classes behind us—they were dribbled out in different ways. They were dribbled out into ROTC, or they could be discharged if they had enough points.[*] The issue, then, was whether you had to have points for discharge. No issue about being discharged if you had enough points. But if you were in my case, and 19 years old and gone to school, you didn't accumulate very many points compared to somebody out of the South Pacific who'd accumulated a hell of a lot of points. So the whole matter of getting discharged was just unknown.

Paul Stillwell: Did you have any sense at that point that you wanted to make a career of the Navy?

Admiral Meyer: No. None at all. As I've told you, bred in the gumbo, the idea of school and learning had been pounded into me, by my mother; by Father Groestch, the pastor of St. Boniface; Sister Mary Joanne; and not Miss Helen so much, although she was in my

---

[*] For the demobilization of the U.S. armed forces after World War II, the services had a point system to determine individual priorities for leaving the service. Points were awarded for length of service, overseas service, battle stars, decorations, and dependent children. Those with the highest number of points were the earliest discharged.

country school, one-room schoolhouse, but I was little bitty then, I was in up to grade four. But she must have pounded it into me.

Paul Stillwell: Sometimes literally [chuckle].

Admiral Meyer: Literally.

Paul Stillwell: Well, I think we covered that one pretty well. Can we into your watch standing on board the *Goodrich*?

Admiral Meyer: I'm pretty slow today. In those months, since I had no baseline, I had no real feel for the condition of the ship. All I know is that that squadron had left Tsingtao the previous fall.[*] They were to be home-ported, one division in Norfolk and one in Newport, and they broke down every place they went. So they had just arrived the week before George Washington's Birthday. So it took them three months to make the voyage. They were 600-pound steam with superheat, and they could really run well through the water once you got it up and if you had crews that knew how to get it up.[†] They were amazing.

When I reported on board, we were a radar picket destroyer.[‡] I knew what one was only from what I read and also listening to the big boys speak, of what the role was of radar pickets in the islands in the Pacific, and particularly Okinawa, which these ships had been in. There was so much gear rushed onto these ships. The gear was rushed on on weekends, installed as best as could be done, and the spare parts were all in boxes. So in the ship I reported to, USS *Goodrich*, and her sisters, every passageway was filled with boxes, metal boxes. Particularly obnoxious was the main passageway through the ship.

---

[*] The *Goodrich* was involved in supporting the postwar occupation of Japan until October 1946, when she was sent to Tsingtao, China, and patrolled along the coast of Korea. She arrived in San Francisco on 21 December 1946 and then departed on 7 January 1947 for her new homeport of Newport, Rhode Island.

[†] This is a reference to the steam pressure of 600 pounds per square inch.

[‡] The conversion to radar picket destroyer, a reaction to the Japanese kamikazes of World War II, involved the removal of torpedo tubes and the addition of a tripod mainmast forward of the number-two smokestack; the mast carried the SP pencil-beam early-warning radar. The ship's formal designation later changed to DDR-831 on 18 March 1949, several months after Meyer left..

You could not go from forward to aft in the ship without going out in the weather because you had to go through midships, cross passageway.

Well, these spare parts boxes, it turned out, all belonged to me. They were brought aboard, and none of them were in the custody of the supply officer. In fact, in those days, the supply officer had custody of virtually no electronics. Didn't have the structure, we didn't know what to do with them. They were bought on the spot in the factories that were making them, and they were really guesswork. And they were packed by women into metal boxes, and a list of what was in there was included.

Paul Stillwell: Were you essentially the electronics material officer?

Admiral Meyer: That's what you'd call it today. Originally I was called a radio repair officer. I don't remember the word "electronics" emerging until I reported to the cruiser *Springfield*. But I would be what the electronics material officer is today. Plus I was also the CIC officer, which as far as the captain was concerned was the same ball of wax.[*]

But these spare parts—I want to not understate that. It turned out that there were several thousand boxes of them around the ship, because the yards had just stuck them wherever they could find a place to stick them, and the inventory was terrible. The custody of them belonged to whatever—what today would be called electronics technician was then called a radio technician.[†]

Paul Stillwell: Were you able gradually to get these into storerooms and inventoried?

Admiral Meyer: No. I finally had it out with the XO one day about what to do with the damned things. I thought somebody ought to be worried about them just from a stability viewpoint, there were so many of them. And we didn't know what they were. When you had something that failed, you kind of went on a search, and if you searched long enough you might run across it. Virtually all the boxes had a label on the outside of them of what piece they went with, like the SP radar.

---

[*] CIC – combat information center.
[†] The enlisted rating of radio technician was established in 1942. In 1945 the designation was changed to electronics technician's mate. Since 1948 it has been electronics technician.

The reason these pickets were converted was the big SP-1M radar, which had a spark-gap generator. It was a parabolic dish, and it was the reason that a big tripod was put aft in these ships. It had to be stabilized. Well, it was stabilized with the only thing that we knew of in those days as the Mark 16 stable element that was on the guns. But it had a tumble capacity of around 20 degrees. So when you started wanting to stabilize something way up there, it would tumble all the time on you. You couldn't keep it stabilized. And the issue was avoiding damage with it. So nominally when you'd go to sea with that radar we had big chains, and we chained that antenna down to the platform and kept it chained there until there really, really was a use for it. So it never got used unless you were really going to exercise.

Well, I'd heard old folks talk about a spark-gap generator, but I'd never seen one. The gaps in this modulator were good for a day or so. It was a Westinghouse, it was a beautiful design for its day, and if you changed the points on these sparks every day she'd run pretty damned good. And one thing, you could find a goddamned target with her. But her beam was very, very narrow, and trying to get stability to go with the beam did not work too well.

Paul Stillwell: Did the ship's rolling affect the ability to pick up targets?

Admiral Meyer: Oh, yeah. Yeah. [Interruption]
This was my first ship ever, even close, going aboard one. I was a reserve, and we should make no bones about the difference between reserves and regulars. There was like a big difference. In hindsight I don't know that it was devastating, but it had a certain amount of cruelty in it in real time, as there always is in human beings starting right in school in first grade.

Paul Stillwell: How did the regulars treat you?

Admiral Meyer: Well, in what now would be called the operations department they came to have great respect for me, particularly when we sailed in the Mediterranean. I had the radarmen, the sonarmen, the radio technicians, the postal clerks, and a couple other ratings in there as well.

Paul Stillwell: So you were the division officer?

Admiral Meyer: I was the officer, period. I was the officer, and the senior petty officer was a third-class radarman by the name of DuBois.

Paul Stillwell: That's not very much horsepower.

Admiral Meyer: My salvation and my teacher was a little round chief petty officer by the name of McAllister. He was about 5-foot-1 or 5-foot-2. He was a Scotsman, of course, and he was a reserve. He had been called up during the war to teach school. He taught at the radio school here in Washington, D.C., what would now be called the electronics school, and he must have been a hell of a professor. He finally had convinced the Navy to let him go to sea before he was released. Chief McAllister was my assistant and the chief petty officer for the division.

Paul Stillwell: What was his rating?

Admiral Meyer: I believe it was radio technician.

Paul Stillwell: So he had some professional background in this area.

Admiral Meyer: Well, but it was all civilian.
　　　　Another little sea story. He started out teaching me. He told me that I could never, never work in this kind of business and be a professional without mastering the Morse code. He made me start learning the Morse code, which I never did really master, but I got through it to where he was proud of me after a year. But that was important to him, and little bitty things were important to him. He gave me as a precious gift, maybe four months or so after I was working with him on this ship, a set of jeweler's

screwdrivers. Now, I don't know whether you know what a set of jeweler's screwdrivers are. I don't even know whether they're even used anymore. They're a set of little screwdrivers about this long.

Paul Stillwell: Three or four inches.

Admiral Meyer: Yeah. And there's maybe eight of them in the set. They literally were jewelers' screwdrivers of the day. Mac said, "Every good technician, Ensign, has to carry a set of screwdrivers." So he taught me a lot of basics. He didn't take a lot of guff off anybody else. That also went backwards; I kind of protected him, because in the chiefs' mess, he being one of those "girls" in what we now call electronics, he had no respect at all.

Paul Stillwell: And a reserve on top of that.

Admiral Meyer: Right. All of that, and they were all snipes and gunners, and who in the hell are these people?[*] The best they could tolerate was a radioman. And the reason they tolerated radiomen was so you'd get the ball scores.

So I guess he and I were respected, but we weren't honored.

Let me skip ahead to the summer of 1947. Not only was I standing watches, I was one of two officers standing watches, Eddie Dumbo and I. Well, like all his other mates, every regular officer kept applying for whatever there was to be applied for.

Paul Stillwell: Aviation, submarines.

Admiral Meyer: Or anything. The guy who was the chief engineer, who I always thought was a wonderful officer—he was academy class of '46—was Johnny Collins.[†] He was later the founder of the project for the *Spruance* destroyer, 963.[‡] Collins, I thought, a top officer. After he left the ship, he went to graduate school at MIT in marine

---

[*] "Snipes" is a nickname for personnel in a ship's engineering department.
[†] Lieutenant (junior grade) John T. Collins, USN, later captain.
[‡] USS *Spruance* (DD-963), lead ship of the class, was commissioned 20 September 1975.

engineering and naval architecture, and he became an EDO.* So his whole career was an EDO and he retired from being the manager for *Spruance*. He's the one that first introduced me to *Spruance* as a possible candidate for the Aegis ship.†

Paul Stillwell: Interesting how these ties go way back.

Admiral Meyer: You're just reading my forehead. When you reflect on your life, and you can do it, you will find that there's item after item that comes up that has a personal relationship in some manner of how you ended up doing something or connecting to somebody. That is astounding.

Paul Stillwell: Well, back to the *Goodrich*. You talked about this division between the regulars and the reserves. Was there hazing? Was there animosity?

Admiral Meyer: I wouldn't say it was particularly hard over either way. It wasn't animosity, but at the same time it wasn't particularly brotherhood. It was just kind of different.

Paul Stillwell: Did some of that difference fade away as you got to know them better?

Admiral Meyer: In my case it faded away more than any other when I was transferred to the cruiser *Springfield*. I was 18 months in *Goodrich*, and it seemed like in many respects I was ten years there. I mean, my learning was equivalent to ten years. When I left *Goodrich*, there wasn't anything I didn't know how to do in ship handling and ship keeping, because it turned out we were assigned to the attack carriers. Normally we sailed with the brand-new *Midway* and the brand-new *Coral Sea*, and later the *FDR*, so wherever they went we went.‡ We were key to not only their successful plane guarding

---

* EDO – an officer designated for engineering duty only.
† Later interviews in the oral history cover the Aegis program in great detail.
‡ USS *Midway* (CVB-41), the name ship of her class, was commissioned 10 September 1945. USS *Franklin D. Roosevelt* (CVB-42) was commissioned 27 October 1945. USS *Coral Sea* (CVB-43) was commissioned 1 October 1947.

but also their fighter direction.* They had more fighters than they had qualified fighter-director officers, and so they were always looking for a way to hand off their airplanes once they came off the catapult because they just couldn't handle them. So you had some degree of intimacy with the carriers. You didn't know who the hell they were, but you still had intimacy with them. You got to know them by their radio voices.

I said we had gear scattered all over that ship. Because we were hurried up and turned into a picket and the handling of airplanes, we had installed in the ship AN/ARC-4 radios. The AN/ARC radios were the VHF prime radios in airplanes at that time, and damn good ones.† Damn good ones. They came in a box about this long, about this high, about that thick.

Paul Stillwell: Maybe three feet long and six inches high?

Admiral Meyer: Yeah. And they had four preset channels in them. And they used 28 volts for a power supply, which was a big drawback aboard ship because we had no 28-volt DC in the ship.‡ The power supplies in our ship were installed from Allied [phonetic] aviation somewhere, and the maintenance for them, and also for the AN/ARCs, in my time, was either the carrier or Quonset Naval Air Station whenever we were home. Quonset Naval Air Station had a big facility.§ But it would take a whole day to go over there and come back, by boat, to get your radio or power supply looked at. But they were highly reliable; we liked them. TBS was our main radio, 72.1 megacycles.

Paul Stillwell: What kind of range could you get on the UHFs?

Admiral Meyer: Well, I'd have to bluff you here, but I'd say we got all the range we needed.

Paul Stillwell: Like 100 miles?

---

* A plane-guard destroyer steams astern—or off on one quarter—of an aircraft carrier in order to recover aircraft crew members who go into the water.
† VHF – very high frequency.
‡ DC – direct current.
§ Quonset Point, Rhode Island, was the site of a naval air station until the mid-1970s.

Admiral Meyer: Yeah. They'd just get up to altitude. We used our fighters out 75 miles or so, and we never worried as long as we had them in radio range and as long as *they* didn't get worried. If they got worried about themselves, then we'd try to watch after them radar-wise, but we never worried so much about radar contact with them as with radio contact.

Paul Stillwell: Well, you could get greater range with IFF if you needed to.[*]

Admiral Meyer: You could. Although it of itself gave you a few challenges too. So all those things were challenges, but at the same time you didn't know they were challenges. I mean, they were what they were.

I was moving up to an incident where, by July of 1947, Ensign Eddie "Dumbo" Atkinson had been accepted for flight school, and Ensign Johnny T. Collins had been accepted to go to MIT. And those, as far as I was concerned, were the two most knowledgeable officers on there, although we had another pretty knowledgeable officer. He was a gunnery officer, Ensign Soupy Campbell, who was a Naval Academy graduate.[†] His problem was he could not get along with the captain. The captain had grown up in gunnery so he, the captain, knew a hell of a lot about gunnery. And in those ships the way you communicated was out on the wing of the bridge. Now, you're supposed to communicate with sound-powered phones, but you didn't do that in those destroyers. Instead, if you wanted to talk to the director officer you'd turn to your talker and you'd say, "Tell the director officer to stick his head outside so I can talk to him." [Laughter] So he'd get out there and the wind flying by, and the old man started yelling at him about how to handle the guns. Campbell was a smallish fellow, and so he'd just shrink down in there. Pretty soon the captain would get pissed and send word that he wanted him to get up out of there so he could see him, because he kept telling him how to do the exercises. So he never got along at all with the captain, and the rest of us didn't mind that because that switched the—

---

[*] IFF – identification, friend or foe. This was an electronic feature that allowed friendly aircraft to have an additional identifying signature when they showed up on radar screens.
[†] Ensign William R. Campbell Jr., USN, Naval Academy class of 1945.

Paul Stillwell: The heat went elsewhere. [Chuckle]

Admiral Meyer: Right, you got it. But that summer both those officers got transferred, and it turned out [chuckle] that I was now the senior watch officer.

Paul Stillwell: With what, five, six months of experience?

Admiral Meyer: You got it. You got it. But it didn't matter, because by September we reached the point where we couldn't get under way. We still sailed in the daytime out of Newport. In the daytime the old man and a chief quartermaster stood the watch on the bridge. Nighttime, Dumbo and I split the watch. But, you know, it not only was very primitive, but we didn't kill anybody either. Usually we had two ships, and if you had a submarine it would be rare, so you were just operating for the hell of operating. Which you did a lot of in those days out in the Newport area.

Paul Stillwell: Who broke you in to train you to stand these underway watches?

Admiral Meyer: I don't know. I guess just one day the XO told me that I was going to stand watches. Those two officers spent a little time in instruction, a couple hours, and I read and read and read, and I listened, listened, listened.

One of the things that always bothered me about learning to stand a watch on the bridge—I may have told you this before; if I did wave your hand. When I was mastering the bridge at that time, I was told by a senior—Lieutenant Rawls, actually, before he left the ship—those officers who came out of the Naval Academy had been developed and trained that they were to be better on the bridge than the enlisted crew. And that used to piss me off. So the OODs would spend their time reading the semaphore, reading the flag hoist, watching for contact, doing the lookout duties, and see if they could beat the lookout at spotting a ship, or see if they could beat the signalman. It always pissed me off. So that summer I called the enlisted bridge watch standers together, and I changed that: "As long as I'm the officer of the deck, I'm important to you to do my duties and you're important to me. I'm not going to do your duties! I'm *not* going to read semaphore, I'm *not* going to read flashing lights, and I'm *not* going to spend my time scanning the horizon, because there are other things I'm supposed to do as the officer of the deck." It probably was a turning point, really, in my life there, because from then on they'd do almost anything I wanted. I don't know, I suppose there was some risk to it, but there was nobody to argue with me. Because, come September we were immobilized. So we reported to Davisville, Rhode Island. Now, I don't know if you know Davisville.

Paul Stillwell: It's a Seabee base.

Admiral Meyer: Well, yes and no. It was abutting the air station, but it also is a big ammo depot. It's a Seabee base secondarily. It was ammo before that. And it had a number of schools over there. Like my first training in fighter direction was at the radar stations at Beavertail Point which were located—it's so far that you stayed all week over there, because you couldn't go back and forth; it took you too long to get over there. Which is where I guess you'd say I qualified as a fighter director. They were training squadrons at Quonset, because it hadn't turned into almost exclusively an ASW outfit as it did in later years. Any fighters and things like that were moved out of there.[*]

Anyhow, if you're an ensign and you're floating around in the system and you're in a new world, you're just constantly learning and constantly trying to understand one outfit from another outfit, how they're connected, how they link, and so forth and so on. So I guess what that reaffirmed in my mind in that era is: Never take no for an answer. I had gotten that way; at least my mother used to say I was. And so I learned that.

I mean, that's how Aegis made it. The world was against Aegis, and it started right with Arleigh Burke.[†] The world was against it. Too big, too expensive, too complicated, take too many men. Too everything. So we just had to adopt a determination that, "Well, that ain't the way it's going to be. We're going to make it different than that." And we won. We really genuinely, bona fidely won. We're running

---

[*] In later years, when the Navy had specialized antisubmarine aircraft carriers, Quonset Naval Air Station was the base for the planes and the carriers.
[†] Admiral Arleigh A. Burke, USN, served as Chief of Naval Operations from 17 August 1955 to 1 August 1961. His oral history is in the Naval Institute collection.

those ships today with a qualified level that submariners and aviators wouldn't entertain for one minute. Now, neither will the father of Aegis entertain it, [chuckle] but he has nothing to say about it.* Because I patterned them all after the submariners, and particularly nuclear power, in qualifications.

So that summer was scary. We were moored at the big ammunition-handling pier at Davisville, which in essence was immobilized, and it was like the end of the world. It was going no place to no place. And it was decided to send the Acey-Deucy squadron there to immobilize them too, DesRon 12.† So there were eight ships there, and there was DesDiv 142—that's me—four more ships, so 12 destroyers were immobilized at that pier. We were in nests of four, so we were three nests. That was September and October, before bad weather struck. And we tried to exchange steam in the nests, with only modest success. But we fell down to 100 men and six to seven officers.

I want to say it was two weeks before Christmas—my date may be wrong but my memory is about that—and, of course the weather is always bad there. When you're in Quonset, the only worse place you could be is at Davisville. And the only way you got out of there was by boat or by bus. Well, the only way that Admiral Johnson would let boats run after dark was a Mike boat.‡ A Mike boat would leave before dark over to Newport side, and it would leave the next morning to come back. So it was just for, you might say, commuters, of which there weren't very many, a handful.

Paul Stillwell: What was Admiral Johnson's billet?

Admiral Meyer: He was not only SOPA, he was ComDesLant.§ Note I didn't say CruDesLant, I said ComDesLant. And that, of course, was a very important and key billet in those days. I mean, you were the king in New England, and you dare not make a move without clearing through that admiral.

---

* Admiral Meyer himself was known as the "Father of Aegis."
† Acey-deucy is a variation of the board game backgammon. In this case, however, the Destroyer Squadron 12 nickname derived from the cards representing the numbers one and two in a suit.
‡ Mike boat is the nickname for an LCM, a landing craft mechanized, because Mike is the word for the letter M in the phonetic alphabet.
§ SOPA – senior officer present afloat. Rear Admiral Felix L. Johnson, USN, commanded Destroyer Force Atlantic Fleet from 21 April 1948 to 25 August 1949. His oral history is in the Naval Institute collection.

Well, to tell you the truth, we didn't understand it too well. We were mobilized those three weeks before Christmas, and we received orders from the CNO to sail on the sixth of January to the Mediterranean, to Gibraltar. Those were our mobilization orders. Well, we had to be rebuilt, so how are they going to rebuild us is really the first test of the reserve structure. So, man, recall orders went out all over New England for officers and sailors to report aboard immediately, that week, into these ships.

Paul Stillwell: This would be December 1947.

Admiral Meyer: Yes. The Acey-Deucy squadron wasn't activated; it was just us, DesDiv 142. And I believe the reason we were activated was that they were straight stick, and we were radar ships, and they wanted the radar ships over there with the carriers.

Well, we were all scared. We had virtually no information. I believe the captain knew, and I think our division commodore knew, but I can't remember now whether he sailed with us or not. But our captain said, "Wait a minute; I'm not going to sail without an availability at the tender." So I think it was around New Year's Eve—it was roughly a week—we were moved down to Yoyo, *Yosemite*. Amongst other things, that was the flagship at Melville, and we had this availability alongside.

We had a secret piece of gear installed, of which I became the custodian. It turned out to be the Navy's new bathythermograph machine. And so one of our extra duties in these four ships was under the Hydrographic Office we were going to be collecting data wherever we sailed. Well, by then we knew we were going to be doing a lot of sailing in the eastern Mediterranean. And I think *Maury* was the hydrographic ship that ran around over there; there's a lot of big, big holes in what those waters were. The Germans didn't provide a hell of a lot of anything for them.

So the purpose was to measure temperature differences for sonar effects. Of course, the whole thing was to prove whether we could collect these gradients and therefore predict the sonar range. And, hell, I think 50 years later they're still arguing on whether you can do it or not. I don't know even whether ships use bathythermographs anymore. I guess they do. But it was a new toy. We were given three, and we managed to lose two of them on the deployment, because of not knowing what speed to run. And the kind of winch and stuff we had was just something put on by the tender. You just lowered the thing away, and it was easy to rupture.

Paul Stillwell: Did you pick up any extra officers for the deployment?

Admiral Meyer: Only the officers that were ordered in related to what I said a moment ago, that BuPers ordered men and officers.

On the fifth of January the captain insisted we were going to have a one-day sea trial before he would get under way. So we got under way, and of course we just had this crazy Popeye Navy, catch as catch can. We got out to sea and milled around and had a couple man-overboard drills and stuff, and we were to come back in that evening, due to sail the next morning. We headed back in. The weather deteriorated, and deteriorated fast. Eventually we reached the lee of Prudence Island, which was the ammunition magazine in those days, and we finally got permission that we could take a buoy that was located there, really for ammunition use. The other two destroyers had made it back into port. We put a motor whaleboat in the water, and the whaleboat managed to have its engine crap out trying to get the buoy. Put the other whaleboat in. We had such a mess that finally, about dark, the captain ordered us to anchor, and then he reported to SOPA that we had anchored. Finally he was told to stay there till he got under way, that he would sail from there.

We recovered the whaleboats, managed to limp them back, and we managed to put a couple men in the water in the process. It was my first experience associated with trying the snatch a buoy. In those days we didn't know how to snatch buoys very easily. So we managed to spill a couple men into the water, and that was my first experience on the breakout of whiskey. Because the XO solicited the captain, and the whiskey was broken out in the wardroom for those who were in the water and who got wet in the whaleboats [chuckle]. It was very carefully limited and measured, how much. That was my first experience. I was in awe when I saw that happen, and that that could be done. Another ceremony.

Somehow the captain and the XO got off that night to say goodbye to their families. They got back at first light, we got under way, and sailed for Gibraltar. We half-assed rendezvoused with *Midway* someplace out in the Atlantic.

In any event, we got to Gibraltar, we started off-loading sailors.* We had, gosh, it just seemed like we had dozens of them, but it must not have been that bad, of chronic seasickness. Reserve after reserve had reasons why they couldn't be on board. Dying children, just one after the other. It was a terrible learning experience.

Paul Stillwell: Some real and some imagined?

Admiral Meyer: Well, right, you don't know. You couldn't figure it out. So the captain ordered them off-loaded. We just dropped them at the station in Gibraltar. By the time we got over in the eastern Med, the crisis wasn't over, but the crisis had calmed down. That was towards the end of January 1948, and a new country was born—Israel.† They have not had a day of peace since, and much of it their own choosing.

One of the things about the Navy, and a good thing about our Navy—over half a century I've been associated—the Navy sails, and worries later. That's the kind of Navy we have. They sail first, and then start worrying about what is it we're sailing for. And invariably it turns out there's a reason why they sailed, even though I'm sure that most of them are different than the reasons that they took in all lines. So, I don't know; that's a strange thing about a navy and its diplomatic application. But as far as I'm concerned, it works.

We went over there and milled around for around a week around Haifa, and the place started calming down. And it was really my first exposure to how you use presence to start calming people down. There's something about a greyhound. The people ashore are never sure what they will do or what they can do. There's something about it.

When we were over in the eastern Mediterranean, I often say when I'm describing it to people that I was in the first war in Israel, in Palestine, and that was the founding of it. I've never been back since, however.

---

* The *Goodrich*'s Mediterranean tour was from 2 February to 22 May 1948.
† The Israeli Declaration of Independence was on 14 May 1948. That same day U.S. President Harry S. Truman recognized Israeli statehood.

Paul Stillwell: Did the ships engage in tactical maneuvers with the carrier over there?

Admiral Meyer: Quite a bit. As a matter of fact, once this calmed down there was a difficulty, I think, in our commanders knowing what to do with us. But it turned out that our nation knew exactly what to do with us, because we were surrounded with crises.

The big crisis was in Trieste. Trieste was left as a tripartite structure between the American and the Brits and the Yugoslavians, and in the second crisis we were going to give the Italians the right to vote. And I think about it, not unlike what we saw going on this past week in Venezuela. So we were split up into divisions, and one division would operate, I'll say, in Grecian islands, and the other division would operate in the Adriatic. We were sent to Venice, and our sister ship was sent to Trieste. The State Department wanted a naval presence but wanted it oh, so easy.

To speed ahead, we were moored right downtown, in the Grand Canal in Venice. I mean, this was a brand-new, scary experience. The year is 1948, and I had progressed all the way to being 22 years old, and I was just about everything on that ship one way or another, including being, as I said, the senior watch officer.

As far as I know, we had very limited instructions. We were there to be alert and to be attentive. The basic reason we were there was evacuation out of Trieste. There were some 1,200, as I remember the number, civilians of one kind or another to be salvaged and evacuated out of Trieste if it had to be abandoned. As we understood, the reason that this destroyer was posted there was to do the evacuation, and also provide gunfire support. There was, I believe, a British frigate located someplace around us too, in my memory. The Yugoslavs were nowhere to be found except out in the damned snow banks and in the woods.

So we rotated after, I want to say a month. We rotated to Trieste, and the Adriatic was still mined, so you had to travel swept routes, very daintily, by the way. I mean, if you could steam normally it might only take you a couple hours, but if you're traveling swept routes you're going to spend the major part of a day getting there.

Paul Stillwell: Where did you get the charts with the swept channels on them?

Admiral Meyer: I don't know. It's a good question. I don't recall how we came by those charts. I don't know whether an officer brought them aboard or not. I'm trying to think how we got mail in that era, and at the moment I just can't say how. I know we didn't get much, but I just can't say how we got it.

One morning at Trieste I went over to be briefed up and prepared on how we could handle the situation over there. Since I was CIC officer, I'd be involved with gunfire support and such. A British officer was in charge. We kept asking him how we were going to get 1,200 people aboard the ship. The answer generally was, "Well, let's just hope we don't have to do that."

Paul Stillwell: [Laughter] Contingency planning.

Admiral Meyer: Right, exactly. But I'm sure we'd have found a way if we'd have had to do it. Again, it was in my young mind that this was another example of presence, particularly in keeping the Yugoslavians cooled down. There were a lot of roustabouts because Trieste was an open port and a free port.[*] The argument at that time was whether it was going to be deeded to Italy or Yugoslavia, and neither one wanted to revert back to the prewar status, so therefore neither one could be satisfied.

Several things stick in my mind about Venice. I once said, though I changed my mind later in life, that if I ever needed another wife I was going to go to northern Italy to get one. But it turned out I got a sailor's good choice, and I didn't have to go to northern Italy at all to overcome it. But the first thing that strikes you as a sailor is how many beautiful women there were. There are more blonde than there are black-haired women in northern Italy, a mixture of Scandinavian-type blood and such. And these were some pretty wise women, pretty smart women, at least from a viewpoint of 22 years old.

In another aspect of the situation, I believe I'm correct in saying that the Italians were to be allowed to cast their first postwar vote on Easter Sunday.[†] It may not have been Easter Sunday, but I distinctly remember it. There was plenty of nervousness about

---

[*] From 1947 to 1954 Trieste was an independent city-state, run by an Allied military government. In 1954 it was ceded to Italy.
[†] The Italian general elections were on 18 April 1948, amid U.S. and Soviet Cold War wrangling. The Christian Democracy Party won, defeating the Soviet-backed leftists. Easter was on 28 March.

the rebellious behavior, of course, going on, of what we'd today call Communists milling around, with their own socialistic government. So the election was counting down. We were moored at Venice at that time.

We were concerned about our security—now, I'm talking about the second incident; I mentioned one of them related to Venice, I'll come to the third in a minute— and how we were going to protect ourselves if we had to. No one seemed very nervous about it. No one in Washington, D.C., seemed bothered by it. But our State Department announced the previous week that if Italy went socialist, the American aid would be terminated. It just seemed like to me it was overnight. In two days the whole behavior pattern shifted. Italy voted democratic, and it's been democratic ever since. Now, its form might be different than you and I would think of it, but generally for those people over there it's been pretty good. But, again, it was something that impressed me. Here I was, just brand spanking new, and I had these three big things happen to me in a year's time of what naval power meant. And while the ship was there it just was there, the sailors were all drinking Cinzano champagne. God, it was the only thing to drink. It was wonderful.

That brings me to my third part, which was gonorrhea. Gonorrhea was rampant and runaway in Italy. When we got to northern Italy, we were too young to really seriously appreciate the seriousness of it. But the prefects said every woman from seven to 65, I think it was, had to be photographed and labeled. I want to say the prefect of Venice, but it doesn't sound right to me. We had an independent corpsman aboard ship, a first-class petty officer. We didn't have a hell of a lot of knowledge on these subjects. So we had what appeared to be a lot of gonorrhea, or the slang expression for it, the clap. The standard practice for the Navy in those days, for gonorrhea, was, if the doctor stated you had it, we now had penicillin, which was generally effective. And between the XO and the doc, they determined how long you were to be restricted aboard ship. Nominally it could be up to three weeks. Well, three weeks' restriction, of course, would really ruin your life in Venice.

And I mean those women were everyplace. They would come over to the ship. I don't know how many times they came; not often. But the local officials had these big wooden suitcases filled with framed photographs. They'd lay them out on the wardroom table, and our sailors who appeared to have gonorrhea were all lined in, and they went through and they were to finger those women that they'd been associated with. Well, of course, after two or three hours of this, all those sailors would have as many as a half a dozen women each, the pictures they'd picked out, that they had had intercourse with. Which was not, I guess, too unusual. But the prefect wasn't going to put up with this. They just left the ship, got the gendarmes rounded up, and went over and arrested all those women, because they were all registered. And they'd take them all down to the station. They all had to be tested and examined.

Well, it would be suppertime before they got back out and got released as not having gonorrhea. But by that time they were ready to visit the ship. So these women were ganging up around the ship, and what they wanted to see was Johnny or Jimmy or whoever his name was, they wanted to see him, like, right now. In their Italian voices they were screaming at you. I remember we brought armed people to the quarterdeck because we just weren't sure we could handle these people. But all they were was Italian frustration of these women having been fingered and having been designated as diseased when they weren't.

We learned three months or four months later, down from off of the carrier, it was believed to be a strain that was not contagious. The XO just decided that it occurred from people screwing too much, but I don't think that was the reason. It just finally passed. It just went by. It was just an incident that went by in my young life.

Paul Stillwell: A lot of facets to naval presence.

Admiral Meyer: Yeah, right. [Chuckle] Right. But God, were those women pissed. Oh, they were pissed. [Chuckle] And those sailors, of course, were all hunkered down aboard ship. Old Johnny wouldn't stick his head out.

Paul Stillwell: I wonder if Secretary Forrestal was involved in this.[*] He was very stridently anti-Communist.

---

[*] James V. Forrestal served as Secretary of Defense from 17 September 1947 to 27 March 1949.

Admiral Meyer: By God, you're coming in here. Okay. Thank you. When I was moored in Trieste, Forrestal was coming for a visit, and for safety reasons he wanted to be in the ship. Well, he was going to stay in the sea cabin of our ship. That's where he was going to be. I thank you for reminding me of that very important fact. So he came overnight or something, some kind of big visit or some such.

In any event, out of politeness more than anything else, I think, he the next morning wanted to understand the bombardment plan and the evacuation plan. Of course, I was in charge of that bombardment and stuff, so Ensign Meyer was given the assignment to orient Forrestal down in the CIC.

See, when the first CICs were built in those ships, there were three of them built that were contiguous. One was the air CIC, one was surface CIC, and one was underseas CIC, and all three of them were right together. I was the CIC officer for all three of them there so I could flip back and forth between them. There's something to be said for the arrangement, frankly. And it was right underneath the bridge, underneath the pilothouse. That was some problem because the captain on the bridge had no communications—we had voice tubes— and so he'd start yelling down through the voice tubes to keep wanting to know what was going on. Naturally, pretty soon the radarmen would stuff shirts into the voice tube [chuckle], and the old man would get pissed off and he would send the quartermaster down. He'd come down to CIC and pull all those shirts out. He'd never say a word; just pull them all out and walk back up so that the old man could talk to us.

Paul Stillwell: Did he have some kind of aversion to sound-powered telephones.

Admiral Meyer: Well, we had sound-powered phones; he just didn't like them. As I told you, he yelled to the gunnery officer. He didn't like them. I don't know why he didn't like them. I think *Helena* somehow taught him that. He didn't like them.

So I was to explain to Forrestal what our plan was. The only thing I remember him saying to me was, "Mr. Meyer, that seems like to me a pretty ambitious plan." [Chuckle] Then he left. That was it.

A lot of those people to be evacuated were British dependents. I never appreciated till later that the British army had dependents all over that part of the globe who stayed through the war. I mean, their families grew up during the war in Greece and parts of southern Italy.

I was constantly amazed at what I did not know about geography, and still don't know. My geography consisted of which ones were the mountain states and which ones were the middle states. It's quite a difference. So in that year and a half, I mean, I really learned a lot about geography.

But that point about that announcement that came out of the United States on that election—I couldn't believe the effect it had on those people. Now, I was thinking only this morning: What if Bush would have made that announcement in the case of Venezuela?[*] I doubt it had any effect at all. That's what's changed in 50 years. Everybody thinks that it's their own right to be whatever they want to be under whatever circumstances they want it to be. But the Italians, even though they behaved in a mob-like way, they still were civilized people. They were still nice people. Gosh, I loved that northern Italy. What a wonderful place.

One other incident happened to me there. The supply officer at that time was Ensign E. B. Longmuir.[†] He was a Naval Academy graduate, and the reason he was a Supply Corps officer was his eyesight. It had always pissed him off that he was bilged from being a line officer. But he and I became pretty good chums. So there was a trip to be made up to a place in the mountains. It was a German officers' rest camp up there, a noted vacation spot, ski resort. Only officers could frequent it.

Well, the Allies took that all over, of course, and turned it into a place to be frequented by all people. Here was a rare incidence where our sailors could frequent it, but they had to have two officers for escorts. So we somehow came by bus. The paymaster and I opted to volunteer for the bus, and it took most of the day for the bus to take us all to hell up into the mountains up there to visit this place for three days and come back. That was the only time I've ever had a pair of skis on in my life. I put them on up there on that trip, and I took them off and I've never put them on since. [Laughter]

Paul Stillwell: Was that deployment your first exposure to underway replenishment?

---

[*] George W. Bush was President at the time of this interview.
[†] Ensign Edward B. Longmuir, Supply Corps, USN. He was a member of the Naval Academy class of 1947, which graduated in 1946.

Admiral Meyer: It was my first exposure, and this could be in error, but I can't recall replenishing from anything but the aircraft carrier. We were the aircraft carrier's chicken. And from ice cream to mail to everything we got from the aircraft carrier. And depending what the aircraft carrier did determined how many high lines we did every day or every week, because any mail that would come to us—the mail would eventually get routed to the carrier and get re-sorted out to her chickens. As a matter of fact, in that era the reason you learned how to fuel is you plane guarded every day or part of a day; you or your sister ship did the plane guarding. But the leaders in those days directed that you topped off every bloody day, weather permitting. They were of the old school, and if the weather was good you were going to be topped off, for the day when the weather might not be good. They were very sensitive to that, and so we almost always stayed topped off when we were with *Midway*.

Another incident happened to me. I mentioned the AN/ARCs earlier. We were working pretty hard over there in sea exercises, and particularly when we went down into the Grecian islands. The carriers never went up north. I'm not sure there was enough water in those days for them to get there. But anyhow, we were operating with *Midway* one day and, as I said to you before, I had one petty officer and me. We were controlling fighters or something in an exercise, and all of a sudden there was a noise in the headset. I went bananas, and I jerked them off. The radarman's name was DuBois, and I said, "DuBois, come over here and stand with me. I feel something funny." Well, okay, so here I went on back to doing what I was doing, and he was doing as he was doing, and it happened to me again.

Paul Stillwell: It was like a dizzy feeling?

Admiral Meyer: Yeah. Just clear knocked out of balance. This time DuBois saw it and, of course, he got scared. So I pulled them off and shut them down or whatever. Anyhow, DuBois charged off to tell the chief and tell the XO what he had seen. By the next morning the captain was plenty scared. Well, it never happened to me again, whatever went on. So the captain was plenty scared. So he handled his scaredness by getting hold of the XO in *Midway* and get me to the medical department there. As a matter of fact, he decided he was going with me. So we got in a whaleboat and traipsed over there to *Midway*, which of itself was a real challenge, getting over and boarding *Midway* by whaleboat. I think we'd come in to anchor overnight.

Anyhow, we got in and the doctor looked at me. He was a surgeon. And I described what had happened and he said—and he was mostly talking to the captain, not me; I was like the child present. He said, "What I think happened here, you have these balances in your ears and the fluids there, and if you resonate those fluids they'll throw you off balance and you'll lose your sense of balance. Well, hell, I'd never heard of that before, but it made a lot of sense to me. I don't want to say it was fairly common in aviation, but it was understood in aviation what it was. So he said, "I think he's just fine as long as you use caution when he is using the radio and also have somebody around him. Have it examined when you get back to the States, because I don't think there's anything wrong with him. I just think it's just an incident." Which, as far as I know, that's what it was. Never occurred again. So there you are and here I am.

Paul Stillwell: So you had one bout with vertigo and one with skis.

Admiral Meyer: Yeah [laughter]. You got it. Okay, right. Thank you.

Paul Stillwell: Was the captain your teacher for ship handling?

Admiral Meyer: I thought the XO was closer to being the teacher, and the chief quartermaster taught me quite a bit. The XO and the captain would get into it periodically. Generally it would be over what track we were going to follow from Point A to Point B. An example is, we were sent into Long Island Sound for a demonstration off of Port Washington one time. And it was to demonstrate the new F8F fighter.[*] They were going to send out several hundreds of people from Port Washington. They would board by boats, but they could only take a few at a time, and all day. We were going to

---

[*] Grumman F8F Bearcat fighters first entered fleet squadrons in 1945. The Grumman plant was at Bethpage, Long Island.

do this fighter direction demonstration for them to observe how far we had come with this new fighter. F8F was the last propeller-driven fighter.

Paul Stillwell: And built at Grumman, which was nearby.

Admiral Meyer: Exactly. Right. Exactly. And we had them aboard to kind of record and witness what it was we were doing, so we were kind of the actors in a drama. Well, it all went off pretty good, as I recollect. It was three days' worth of operations. So during the nights, a couple nights we just milled around in the Sound.

One night the old man and the XO got in a argument over which hand to leave a buoy. The captain wanted that buoy left to starboard, and the XO wanted it left to port. Well, on the goddamn chart the buoy was, to me, clearly sitting there marking the end of the shoal, and you'd better leave it on the port hand, or you were going to run aground. I was the officer of the deck. So they were pouting back and forth for a while, and it was squalling; that's what made the issue so tense, because squall lines kept coming up. It was raining off and on, and they were locked in the pilothouse trying to stay dry. Finally push came to shove, and the XO came over and whispered in my ear, "Meyer, do you agree with what I am saying?"

I said, "Yes, I do."

He said, "Well, we're not going to run this ship aground." So here we were milling, and the XO shouted out "Officer of the deck, I have the conn."* And the old man walked outside on the wing of the bridge and dogged the door. He issued the rudder orders, and we watched the buoy go right on down our port side, cleared it. The incident was over. Never came up again in any way, shape or form. But it was the pinnacle of their arguments. I don't remember one where the result could have been so bad or so serious as that example.

So actually we never got in trouble in ship keeping in that ship. We were pretty damned good ship-keepers in spite of all the green hands that we had, in spite of all ensigns. It's just incredible. Those two officers—that's why I remember their names to this day: Teeter and Baird. Baird is in the graveyard; I don't know where Teeter is. I

---

* The individual with the conn—normally an officer—directs the ship's movements in course and speed.

imagine he is also in the graveyard. But I remember their names because, in fact, they had a heavy effect on me in mastering what little seamanship I mastered.

The next summer, our ship overhauled in Brooklyn Navy Yard.[*] Now, you're going to walk a long ways to find an officer anymore who overhauled in Brooklyn Navy Yard. And then we had RefTra.[†] I was exposed to about everything you could get exposed to in that ship in that incredible period of 18 months.

All of a sudden, one day when we came back from this deployment message orders appeared on the fox skeds, transferring Ensign Meyer to USS *Springfield* to report no later than such-and-such; it wasn't very much time.[‡] The old man was livid. *Springfield* was in the Pacific and he, having a certain amount of paranoia in him, as all skippers get sooner or later, immediately thought I had something to do with it, which I assured him was totally untrue. Well, what really made it bad is the next day there came a signal over from the flagship, which said that the admiral would like to see Ensign Meyer at his convenience. Now, this really pissed the old man off. I didn't know the admiral from anybody.

So I went over there, got in *Yosemite*, was escorted by a Marine up to the admiral's cabin. He was gracious and thanked me for coming. He said, "I see you have orders to *Springfield*."

"Yes, sir."

He said, "Do you know anything about *Springfield*?"

I said, "Admiral, I'd never even heard of the ship before."

"Well, I want you to know that I put that ship in commission. And under the mast-pole is a coin. I'd like for you to go find that coin and tell me that it's still safe under there when you report to the ship. I hope you have a wonderful cruise on her."[§]

---

[*] The New York Navy Yard, popularly known as the Brooklyn Navy Yard, was established in 1801. In late 1945 it was officially renamed the New York Naval Shipyard. In 1966 the yard was decommissioned as a result of cost-effectiveness initiatives on the part of Secretary of Defense Robert McNamara.
[†] RefTra – refresher training, a period of getting a ship's crew back up to speed after a yard period.
[‡] "Fox" was the word for the letter F in the phonetic alphabet of the day. The fox schedule referred to the messages sent on the fleet broadcast.
[§] Captain Felix L. Johnson, USN, was the first commanding officer when the light cruiser *Springfield* (CL-66) was commissioned on 9 September 1944. She had a standard displacement of 10,000 tons, was 610 feet long, 66 feet in the beam, and had a draft of 25 feet. Her top speed was 33 knots. She was armed with twelve 6-inch main battery guns and twelve 5-inch dual-purpose guns. She served through World War II and was later decommissioned in 1949.

And that was that. [Laughter]

Man, I didn't know what to do with this piece of dynamite. I wasn't sure going back on the whaleboat how to handle this, just how I was going to torture the old man with this. [Laughter] He and the XO were both waiting at the quarterdeck when I got back. [Chuckle] I had to tell them the truth. They looked at me, and I'm not sure to this day that they ever believed me. But that's what it was. It was just a little recall in his young life when he was the captain and he put her in commission.

I went later and I looked for the coin. I couldn't find it. Like the boatswain said to me, "Well, Ensign, you ought to know that you can't find the coin. It's underneath the pole." So I wrote a respectful note back to the admiral and told him that I couldn't find the coin, but I was assured it was still safe there, and that was the end of that.

Paul Stillwell: Well, one other event of 1948 was that you applied to become a regular officer. How did that process work out?

Admiral Meyer: Well, you're reading my forehead, because I was thinking that issue earlier in our conversation. I told you previously about the experience with my dad in the milking barn. I told him I was thinking of leaving the service and coming back to the farm. He looked at me and said, "How can you be so Goddamned stupid?" And I was taken aback. I didn't know what I'd done. He said, "After all the opportunity you have received, are you going to throw that away here?" That's was the only time that I ever heard come out of my dad his feeling that he had spent all his life trying to raise his children. That was his assignment, raising his children.

Now your question was how'd I get to the regular Navy? They weren't begging for applications for the regular Navy, but BuPers was soliciting applications. And it was a brand-new program, it was a brand-new undertaking. I don't believe the Navy had ever, ever before done this since the Navy was structured originally. It was, I'd say, born out of necessity, plus the recognition of the thinking of the new order of officers. I don't want to say that the lock on Naval Academy education had been broken, because where I come from, to have gone to the Naval Academy was extraordinary indeed. But you had to have a certain amount of elitism to do that, because your parents and associates of your parents in political dimensions had to understand what it meant. Where I come from, hell, I didn't understand what going to the Naval Academy meant. It had no real meaning to me at all, none at all.

We had a couple officers that had gone, and one of them was the name of Paul Holmberg; he's in the graveyard now.* And the other was the name of Wayne Merrill, and he's in the graveyard. Well, Paul Holmberg eventually became an aviation engineering duty officer. He was an aviator in World War II and flew a torpedo bomber and managed to survive out of that great battle, but for that he wore the Navy Cross and he was well respected and well thought of. Much of that, including his combat behavior, eventually took him to be an admiral. Well, he was the son of some pretty well-to-do parents who were politically sensitive. They lived in Brunswick, but they were of the upper class.

Wayne Merrill was the son of the town's lawyer, Mr. Louis Merrill, and Wayne Merrill attended the Naval Academy.† Paul Holmberg, I think, came out of the Academy in 1939. Wayne Merrill came out earlier than that, and he was, I'd say, not a naval officer of note.

Paul Stillwell: Was there a direct connection between the milk barn incident and your applying for the regular Navy?

Admiral Meyer: I'm afraid you're right. It made me do a lot of serious thinking that up till then I wasn't doing that much serious thinking about. So I believe you're correct, there was a direct connection. One day it came out, and I talked to the XO, Lieutenant Commander Teeter. He said, "Well, Wayne, I'm not able to really counsel you on that or advise you. Whatever you'd like to do."

I said, "Well, I'm not sure I want any advice from the captain either."

"Well," he said, "I think it's a very noble thing to do, and you should not believe all the things you hear about not being competitive or not being socially acceptable." He

---

* Rear Admiral Paul A. Holmberg, USN, had graduated from the Naval Academy in the class of 1939. He retired in 1971 and died in 1986.
† Wayne R. Merrill graduated from the Naval Academy in 1934 and later resigned from the service. He died in 1991.

said, "I don't believe any of that to be correct, to be true. That's just manufactured things."

Probably that little conversation had more effect on me than anything else, because I was not blessed with the social graces. I didn't know a hell of a lot about social graces. At one time, at least, we thought, well, maybe they'd teach them in midshipman school, but they certainly never did teach us any in midshipman school because we never went. So there you are.

It's kind of like they're raising LDOs today.[*] They take first-class petty officers. I think the Navy's doing some bad things, really bad things on officerships, and one is taking good petty officers and hanging shoulder boards on them. I'll be damned if I would keep doing that if I were running the Navy. Now, I'd give them the opportunity to go to school and become educated and become an officer. Because our whole culture has changed. There's some really good men. I mean, they're really quality men. But I'll be damned if I would fill our Navy up with uneducated officers. And that's what we have done, and we go through these cycles of trying to purge them and try to redeem our errors and we keep salvaging ourselves with LDOs.

You go out and look at an Aegis destroyer today and find out how many LDOs you've got it in. It's goddamn outrageous. I could guarantee you to maybe the 90% level that the Aegis test officer in that ship is an LDO, which in my time was the fire control officer, which also was—I mean, the most prestigious post that a junior officer could get was being fire control officer. You couldn't get a better post than that. That was higher thought of in the junior-officer Navy than gun boss was. So today officers turn up their goddamn nose at it. You have trouble finding an officer who knows a friggin' thing about fire control or who's ever worked at it.

Go with me around at these various committees and meetings that I continue to sit on 25 years after I retired. You'll see how few officers we have who have what I'd say is a technical motivation. Now, what we have done is, we have convinced ourselves that they've got an operational motivation and you don't have to be technical to be operational. Well, Arleigh Burke didn't believe that, and while I'm not a great admirer of

---

[*] LDO – limited duty officer, a former enlisted man or woman whose duties are limited to the area of his/her enlisted rating specialty.

Arleigh Burke, his predecessors didn't believe that either. They believed that officers had to know the techniques of their trade. They believed that.

Paul Stillwell: Well, he had an ordnance PG, and that was the top of the line at that time.

Admiral Meyer: You betcha. I can write the history right now of the Aegis fleet. As a matter of fact, I see it happening. I can write it right now. I've got to tell you, it's going straight to hell. And it will be there before I'm in the graveyard. The whole schoolhouse system has been returned to the training command without so much as bothering to find out: "Well, wait a minute; how did Meyer take it out of the training command? Why was that done in the first place? Why was that done?" You can go into our operating forces today and you'll have officer after officer after officer tell you that the best schools we have in the Navy are the Aegis schoolhouses, the ones at Dahlgren and the ones at Wallops Island and the ones at Moorestown. And yet we've allowed that to be disassembled. Why would you do that? Well, it's pure petty behavior, that's what the hell it is, and not even such a righteous person as Mullen would crack down on it. I mean, I think Mullen is a pretty square person, but he didn't believe in it.[*]

It was a time when you said you went to graduate school we knew what you studied. Today we don't have any idea what you studied.

Paul Stillwell: What were the specific steps you went through to get a regular commission?

Admiral Meyer: I finally sat down one day and wrote out a letter of application to BuPers, citing my bona fides as asked for. I had it looked at by one of the officers as to whether they thought I had it in proper form and correct. I took it up to the XO, who drafted the endorsement that said, "This officer shows by his record that he would be an asset to the regular Navy, and I, the captain, so recommend him." Turned it in. A couple

---

[*] Admiral Michael G. Mullen, USN, served as Chief of Naval Operations from 22 July 2005 to 29 September 2007, and then became Chairman of the Joint Chiefs of Staff on 1 October 2007.

of months or so a letter came back asking me to fill out these papers for regular Navy, and that was that. That's the best I remember about it. It was a kind of non-event.

Paul Stillwell: Did your commission come through while you were still in the *Goodrich*?

Admiral Meyer: I believe that's correct. I left *Goodrich* in July 1948.

Paul Stillwell: And you still weren't married at that point.

Admiral Meyer: No. I think that's 18 months or equivalent thereof. And I reported to Long Beach, California, and found *Springfield* swinging at a buoy inside the breakwater in the harbor. If the SOPA considered you bad enough, you'd be banished to anchor outside the breakwater. And if you were on his privileged list—I can't remember who the SOPA was, but you could get inside the breakwater.

I discovered several things when I reported to that ship. At that time there was no doubt in my mind about how smart I was, because I'd learned ship-keeping, seamanship, operations, sailed with the carriers. I had a lot of experiences in a short period. Not long, but a lot of them. In the weeks ahead, it took a little while for that to sink into me, that it's true, I was pretty damned smart, and there wasn't anything I couldn't do. The problem was, everything I knew how to do was wrong. [Laughter] And that's the worst thing about a destroyer.

I set out years later to try to change that in the Aegis fleet. And it's true that God was with me, because I always say God is good, and the reason I could change it is the Aegis destroyer became a capital ship, and ironically it was something that Arleigh Burke couldn't stand. He couldn't stand the thought of that ship being a capital ship and not being a small boy. So I believe I personally had a great deal of effect on the profiles not only of the officers but also the petty officers that went into that ship.

Interview Number 4 with Rear Admiral Wayne E. Meyer, U.S. Navy [Retired]
Place: Admiral Meyer's office in Crystal City, Arlington, Virginia
Date: Wednesday, 20 February 2008

Paul Stillwell: Admiral, last time we'd just got you transferred from the *Goodrich*. You applied for regular Navy, you reported to the cruiser *Springfield* inside the breakwater at Long Beach, and you found out that the coins were under the mast, but you couldn't see them personally. [Chuckle]

Admiral Meyer: All right. Okay. That would be mid-'48.

Paul Stillwell: What was your billet when you reported to that ship?

Admiral Meyer: It turned out that an officer that I doubt you ever knew by the name of Horace V. Bird—and we all called him "Dickie Bird"—he was the XO on this cruiser, a commander. He was kind of a prima donna and somewhat pompous. But in spite of all that, I think he was a pretty fair officer. The way I got ordered there was that Horace V. "Dickie" Bird was in BuPers, and he had written to the captain—I found this much later—and also the division commander who, by the way, happened to be Herrmann the German, E. E. Herrmann, who was the first superintendent of the graduate school when it was relocated.[*]

Paul Stillwell: In Monterey, right.

Admiral Meyer: He got that assignment to get that done. He was a noted ordnance person. Just as an aside, Herrmann the German had, by hand, calculated the ballistics tables for 6-inch guns. He had done that in the late '30s while he was a lieutenant commander, done them all by hand. They were published out of Dahlgren and had E. E. Herrmann's flag on.

---

[*] Rear Admiral Ernest E. Herrmann, USN, served as Superintendent, Naval Postgraduate School from 1950 until his death on 19 November 1952. In 1948 he was Commander Cruiser Division 17.

Paul Stillwell: How was he connected with your getting the orders?

Admiral Meyer: Well, he was the division commander of *Pasadena* and *Springfield* and *Astoria*. Those were the three cruisers in that division. Bird had written to Herrmann, and he had written to the CO of the *Springfield*. The ship was scheduled to deploy to the Western Pacific in the occupation forces that autumn, of '48, and he asked them what kind of officers they needed. And they had come back, allegedly, and as far as I know this is correct, they'd gone back to him. I think he was the head of officer detailing; I don't know what the hell he was. But they said they needed some officers who knew something about electronics repair. And whambo, that's how I got zapped, strictly that way.

Paul Stillwell: Now, this was a time when a lot of ships were undermanned because of the postwar demobilization.

Admiral Meyer: Oh, grossly.

Paul Stillwell: What happened once you got on board *Springfield*?

Admiral Meyer: Okay, my first skipper was Captain Freddie Moosbrugger, who was famous for the Solomon Islands battles in World War II.[*] So Freddie Moosbrugger was well, well respected around through, and eventually was selected for promotion and retired from being superintendent at the graduate school. His wife was in the process of dying while he was CO. She was back in Pennsylvania someplace, so he had internal struggles going on.

Well, I was ordered there and when I reported—I can't remember now how, but I was assigned as third division officer. That meant I had turret three, I had the catapults, and I had the goddamn boats, because we carried all our boats. So it was a constant fight

---

[*] Captain Frederick Moosbrugger, USN, commanded the light cruiser *Springfield* (CL-66) from October 1948 to December 1949.

on how to get the boats and the airplanes in the hangar, because we had two floatplanes. They got desperate as they were getting ready to sail in the autumn.

Commander Jack Slaughter was operations officer.* I never knew him before, but I came to admire him as one of the greatest officers I've ever known. As far as I know, he still lives over by Annapolis someplace. The gun boss was a commander; his name was Lloyd Hoffman. He had had two ships blown out from under him, and he by now had gotten himself into—the poor son of a bitch wore his life jacket all the time at sea. Never took his life jacket off. All day he had it on. Well, it turned out he didn't last very long in the ship. He got transferred. The chief engineer was Charlie Foster, probably the oldest what today we'd call an LDO.† He was a temp. He was a lieutenant commander, because he had been a warrant officer for 100 years.

Those were the senior officers. So here my ass was thrown in the deck force under Hoffman. Then when Slaughter discovered my background, I found my ass reassigned as electronics repair officer, a billet to be defined. But nevertheless it was going to be in what today is called the operations department. I think it was still called the communications department or the radio department at that time.

Paul Stillwell: It was just evolving at that time.

Admiral Meyer: It was evolving. Every month it was evolving. And the staff had their hands in it, as did CruPac.‡ CruPac had their hands in how electronics were going to get organized. So it was decided that electronics repair belonged in the engineering department, so we were moved to the engineering department. And at that time virtually all the engineering department were USN temps. Senior grade Lieutenant Dick Ploss was there as damage control, and he was a Naval Academy graduate, and warrants.§ See, warrants had their own mess, and there were at least a dozen of them. It turned out that move gave me opportunity; I ended up befriending the warrants and became a friend of their mess. I was invited into their mess all the time. And I think I may have mentioned

---
* Commander John S. Slaughter, USN, served as interim skipper of the *Springfield* from September 1948 to October 1948, when Captain Moosbrugger took over.
† Lieutenant Commander Charles F. Foster, USN.
‡ CruPac – Cruiser Force Pacific Fleet, the type commander.
§ Lieutenant Richard L. Ploss, USN.

this to you, I really thought I knew a lot where I came from a destroyer, and I did. I knew how to sail, boy. Virtually all of it wrong. [Laughter]

Paul Stillwell: You mentioned that.

Admiral Meyer: I mentioned that. Well, those warrant officers started teaching me. And they taught me how to do things and how to get things done, and whom to respect and whom not to respect, and so on and so forth.

Anyhow, I didn't think that I could learn as much as I learned in so few months. The youngest warrant in the whole damned bunch was a fellow by the name of Norman Woods, a radio electrician.* Or, as they were called in those days, sparktricians, nicknames. Norman Woods reported aboard the same day I reported aboard. Because they'd said they needed a new one, well they yanked a new one, and he was a sonar guy. So he and I then ended up as the electron people.

We had aboard the SPS, it was not the -43 radar, it was the forerunner of the -43 search radar, built by Westinghouse. The staff had decided it couldn't be fixed, and the fleet was just bitching like crazy. Well, Norman Woods and I didn't know anything about radar, but we knew a hell of a lot about the theory of electronics, so we sailed and deployed, and every night after supper we studied that goddamn radar. We'd keep trying to figure out why that receiver would not work.

Paul Stillwell: Was this an air-search radar?

Admiral Meyer: It was the long-range air-search radar, bedspring.† Couldn't figure out, why wouldn't it work? And so you'd tune it up, or you'd think you were tuning it up, and for the next hour or so you'd see a target—we'd get the SC out and be able to track

---

* Radio Electrician Norman G. Woods, USN.
† Some early U.S. Navy radars were rectangular in shape, and the assembled components resembled a bedspring.

it—and then the thing would go to hell and you couldn't find a thing.* We spent a couple months on it.

We found it. There had been a new condenser—now, by then being called capacitors—introduced into the design of the receiver, and it was a button type, which was held by a washer, screw, a wing nut, to the chassis, which was its ground. And then it had the wires, the connectors, came off of it. It was already on ground, so the wires came off to connect into the circuit. I remember the night that Norman and I, about 10:00 o'clock at night, we decided those sons of bitches were shorting and that they were defective, which was the reason they were shorting. It was a defective design. And so it would last a little bit and they'd go to ground. Each receiver had four of them.

We quickly, like good little sailors, reported this to CruPac who had a genius lieutenant commander over there who said, "Oh, that couldn't be the problem. That radar is already discounted and no good; we're going to get rid of that radar." Well, we convinced our supply officer—and we told Commander Slaughter we believed we'd solved it—we convinced them both to order every condenser they could order, every one they could get out of the supply system before we sailed. We got boxes full of them. We stripped Oakland.

Well, we were the only ones in WestPac who could find a goddamn target.†

Paul Stillwell: Did you have a way to eliminate the short?

Admiral Meyer: You could not eliminate the short in that design. The thing had to be rebuilt, and it was, in fact, finally redone after these assholes came to believe us, but by that time Norman and I were leaving the ship. We got a temporary design our own selves that would not short, but it wasn't a good design.

So that's the night I remember Commander Jack Slaughter cried, because we found our airplane, we were up plotting that airplane, and he just couldn't handle it. He came to pieces, that that radar was finding the target. That's just a sidebar story that's worth nothing.

---

* The Curtiss SC-1 Seahawk was a monoplane that first went into fleet service in October 1944 to perform observation and scouting missions for battleships and cruisers.
† WestPac – Western Pacific.

Paul Stillwell: Were you a division officer in that capacity?

Admiral Meyer: I was not only a division officer, I was the electronics repair officer and I was an ensign, United States Navy.

Paul Stillwell: Did you have a separate electronics materiel officer?

Admiral Meyer: No.

Paul Stillwell: So you were probably that also, or else the warrant was.

Admiral Meyer: Right. He and I were all of it. The word "electronics" was coming into just limited use, just some people used it, some wouldn't. Because Norman had been an RT. And then they kind of started making RT mean radar technician rather than radio technician. But technically I don't think "radar technician" was ever approved as a bona fide name.

Paul Stillwell: Did you still stay in the engineering department as time passed?

Admiral Meyer: We stayed there the whole time, and we were belittled constantly. The chief engineer had zero use for us. All he knew is that we just dragged the department down.

Paul Stillwell: But he probably left you alone a lot too.

Admiral Meyer: Oh, he did that, he did that. [Chuckle] As a matter of fact, that's what he told me the first day. "That's how I'll measure you, Ensign Meyer, is how much trouble you cause." I never had any trouble finding him, because he was always in the wardroom at the coffee table. Any time I needed to talk to the chief I'd just go there.

Well, the lesser officers came to think a great deal of me. I guess they decided I was pretty smart, because they weren't used to smartass JOs. All they were used to was having officers down in training in the engineering department.

Paul Stillwell: Did you stand watches?

Admiral Meyer: Oh, yes. As a matter of fact, there was a big argument on how I would stand watches, because the chief engineer was insisting that I would stand engineering watches. The XO was insisting that I'd stand bridge watches. Slaughter was insisting that I'd stand CIC watches.

Paul Stillwell: The latter probably would have made the most sense.

Admiral Meyer: And he's the one that won, right. [Laughter] He won the bidding. So I technically never qualified as engineering officer of the watch, never did. Never stood the watches. And I never qualified as an officer of the deck in that ship. Never stood enough watches. Because once we sailed, the CIC need became so great you were just constantly on watch in CIC. That was where I got all my learning. The tradeoff was that Norman wouldn't have to stand watch, so that meant that I'd stand my eight hours a day, but I could count on him being available in my place around the clock.

Paul Stillwell: So he was probably Mr. Fix-It.

Admiral Meyer: That's right.

Paul Stillwell: How many technicians did you have?

Admiral Meyer: Had one second class, and then before we sailed another second class was ordered. And the rest of them were strikers or third class.* About half the strikers

---

* A striker is a non-rated enlisted man or woman officially designated as being in training for a specific petty officer rating.

just got out of the deck force; they hadn't been to school or anything. We didn't have any. Right before we sailed, from somewhere, a chief radio technician was ordered. It turned out that he knew zero about electronics and radar, and furthermore he didn't want to learn. It was late in life; he was a radioman, pure and simple. But he was a very good leader, so he took the chiefly duties of the division and took that off my back and took it off Norman's back. And then we went all the way down to these young petty officers. But they were so lovable. God, they were lovable. The problem was they didn't know anything.

Paul Stillwell: Were they willing to learn?

Admiral Meyer: Well, Norman Woods taught me that. So we got a couple little blackboards and put them in our spaces, and every time a question would come up we'd get on the blackboard and we'd beat that question to pieces, what the answer was. We started $V=IR$ every time.* And that's where my success came from later in my life when I was ordered to USS *Galveston* as fire control officer for her conversion for the first Talos ship. I was fire control officer. I was a lieutenant commander. And one of the first things I'd ordered was a blackboard put in every one of my radar spaces, fire control spaces, so that I could, when I walked in and talked to these technicians and asked them about their problems, I could get on the blackboard. I couldn't fix it, but I could get on the blackboard and start talking to them and start sketching to them, and I could see the light come on. They'd suddenly start seeing answers. Well, they got so they'd follow me around, because every night they wanted me to teach, because they were so anxious to learn. In those days there just wasn't much official learning opportunity.

Paul Stillwell: Did you get that same eagerness when you were in the *Springfield*?

Admiral Meyer: We developed it. Later in life, I referred to it as a lifeboat approach: We were all in the lifeboat here, and we had to worry about it because we're in the engineering department [chuckle] and there wasn't anybody who liked you. If you were

---

* This equation is known as Ohm's Law and deals with the flow of electrical current through a conductor.

a technician nobody liked you. The snipes didn't like you at all, because you had clean clothes on all the time.

Paul Stillwell: Well, did radiomen and radar operators appreciate the contribution?

Admiral Meyer: I think in later life they did. They were in another department, so little intimacy developed except in the working structure. My technicians did not stand watch, except I created the watch station that exists today in Aegis, and that is that a technician will be on watch. So I started in *Springfield* that one was on watch along with the radarmen and the radiomen, and what in the hell were their problems. Well, that created a pretty upbeat attitude.

Paul Stillwell: Well, not only that; it gave the technicians appreciation for what the operators were dealing with.

Admiral Meyer: Well, it gave them an appreciation for how hard some things were. Plus that technician, they knew, had access to the chief and access to Norman, and if they needed access to me they'd get it. So it was a good enough system that I put it into practice in Aegis later.

Paul Stillwell: What do you remember about Moosbrugger as a leader?

Admiral Meyer: Well, I recall a number of incidents about him. Actually, he was a wonderful leader. It was opportunistically that I got to stand watches on the bridge. He was a very good seaman. But his wife was dying, and he had trouble dealing with that—the poor man. Then eventually we went into Hunters Point for decommissioning, in some four months or so. It was Jack Slaughter that had called us all in as watch officers, duty officers, that we were to keep our eye on the captain for his safety. Not to worry about him except for his safety. Because the officers' club was right on the hill, and he could walk up there and he'd go up there and drink till they closed.

One of the incidents, of course, made the rounds of the ship. The captain would come back when the club closed. He'd come aboard, and the JO and the petty officer of the watch would all make sure that the captain got in to his bunk by following at a judicious distance and watching him. And one night, the incident that I've spent a lot of time building up to is, he came aboard and he turned forward instead of turning aft. The JOOD—which, by the way, we had two officers on watch and a petty officer on watch— JOOD said, "Captain, can I help you? Did you want to go to your cabin and such?"

Moosbrugger stopped and he looked at him, he glared at him. He said, "You go tell Commander Slaughter that whenever I want to inspect my ship I'll inspect it." And he turned around and walked on off to his cabin. [Laughter] But he was eight sheets to the wind. But that little incident sobered him up enough to figure out he'd gone the wrong direction.

Well, it really entwined him to the crew, interestingly enough. He was a lonely man and a man that was at a distance. He had his own mess, his own independent quarters. They were flag quarters. The president of the wardroom was the XO. And so he was not a mixer. That was my association with him.

Paul Stillwell: Well, and that's just the way it was designed. That wouldn't necessarily be his personality.

Admiral Meyer: Exactly. Exactly.

Paul Stillwell: Was he the skipper during the deployment to the Western Pacific?

Admiral Meyer: I think he became skipper right before we deployed, and he took it all the way through almost to decommissioning, when it was brought down to a commander. I think Slaughter was kept as the officer when she was decommissioned.[*] We're still in that category; I want to talk a little bit more about that deployment.

---

[*] Commander Slaughter was commanding officer of the *Springfield* from December 1949 to January 1950. The ship was decommissioned 30 January 1950.

Anyhow, I decided that I was going to get married if the woman I wanted to marry would be willing to get married. The woman I was going with was Margaret Garvey, whom I had met when I was at MIT in earlier years. She was Irish, born and raised in Dorchester, Massachusetts. Her father was a Scotsman who came to this country, and he drove a milk wagon. Her mother was Irish; she had worked as a maid. They lived in Dorchester, which, depending on who you are, is South Boston or not; just borders on Southie.[*]

As I was fond of saying, she grew up on the blacktop; she never knew any different. She was what you would describe as an ordinary person of Dorchester. During World War II, she was a solderer at SubSig, Submarine Signal Company. Then after the war she had gotten posted in training as an operator at AT&T, the telephone company.[†] In those days it took you a long, long time to qualify as an operator. By the time that I married her, not only had she qualified but she had to resign.

I got permission from the captain to get married. You had to have permission if you were less than a lieutenant or less than a second-class petty officer. The hard part was getting leave in the middle of decommissioning, but Commander Slaughter decided that I could have enough leave to go get married. We were in Hunters Point; she was in Boston. Two weeks was all he'd give me. He said, "I just am not willing to deal with what we're dealing in around here with you being gone more than two weeks."

I called her. I said, "If you're ready to get married, I'm ready to get married. But it's going to have to be done in two weeks, and you're going to have to marry me, my folks from Missouri sight unseen,." That was a very trembling thing. Her father was dead. Her mother had been a washerwoman; she'd been a maid. Lived in a third-deck flat on Mount Vernon Street in Dorchester. Irish, Italians, and Polacks were the surroundings, and they were generally friendly. They scrapped a lot and argued a lot, but they were generally friendly.

Paul Stillwell: Can we back up a little? How did you meet her and get on the road to marriage?

---

[*] Dorchester, Massachusetts was formerly a municipality, later became a neighborhood of Boston.
[†] AT&T – American Telephone and Telegraph Company.

Admiral Meyer: I think I met her in a gin mill in Boston that year I was going to school.

Paul Stillwell: So, again, the uniform helped.

Admiral Meyer: The uniform helped. Because in those days—this would be '46—the women had money but no men, so a uniform really helped on that. My schoolmates and I frequented a dive called "Cave" downtown, and I think that's where I probably ran into her first. She would come there with her girlfriend, who was the wife of a guy who drove a truck. Her girlfriend was going with one of the classmates that I was going to school with, an officer, which is how I ended up with that interception.

Paul Stillwell: What was included in the courtship? What kinds of things did you do together?

Admiral Meyer: Not much. Go to supper. And we'd go out to the bar and listen to music. She could dance; I couldn't dance, at least not the way she danced, so in that sense it was just a social life. I was 19 years old and ran across her, and that was that.

Paul Stillwell: What qualities in her appealed to you?

Admiral Meyer: Well, I don't know—I've got another one here now; I don't know that I want to discuss all that.* [Laughter]

Paul Stillwell: So you're saying that's classified?

Admiral Meyer: Yeah, it might be, right. [Chuckle] I'd better be careful about that.

Paul Stillwell: What was the date of your wedding?

---

* Admiral Meyer remarried after his first wife died.

Admiral Meyer: We got married the 17th of September 1949 in St. Margaret's Church in Dorchester,

Well, I had a problem. I didn't have any money. I was a lieutenant (junior grade). She didn't have any money. She brought to the marriage one share of AT&T stock and about $90.00 cash for the second share, and that was a hell of a lot more than I brought to the marriage. So we babied that share of stock all of our life, and I finally disposed of it after she died. But different women had told her she'd be terrified about the manners she had to have and the Navy culture she had to follow and stuff like that, and I kept saying, "Don't worry about it. Look at me. [Chuckle] All you've got to do is pay attention to me. Don't pay any attention to them." Well, it's true that the culture was a shock. It was a shock to *me*, but eventually I outlived it. It turned me into a shy person.[*]

Paul Stillwell: Oh, right. [Laughter]

Admiral Meyer: It did, and a withdrawn person, and it took me some time to come back out of it.

Paul Stillwell: Well, I'm glad you recovered from that.

Admiral Meyer: Yeah, well, thank you. I am too.

Anyway, we decided that after the wedding we would fly to Kansas City, and my mother and dad would drive there to meet us and drive us to their home 100 miles out of Kansas City, down Highway 24, and there we would spend a half a dozen days. Then our plan was to buy a car and drive to San Francisco. Well, I don't know. People, it seemed to me, did a lot gutsier or braver things than sailors would do today. But we started carrying out the plan.

We got on TWA and got to Kansas City and there, they, for the first time, saw the woman I had married. She met the parents at the airport. There wasn't much of a conversation for the next two and a half hours as we drove to Brunswick. Got there. Of

---

[*] Very few people would agree with that description of Admiral Meyer's personality.

course, we lived six miles out of town. I remember the second night we were there, I had already even gone to bed, and Margaret decided she'd go to the toilet before she went. Well, our toilet was the outhouse maybe 150 feet from the house, and my mother had shown her. My sister was not there—she was off in nursing school—but my young sister had shown her. "Here's the flashlight. Use the flashlight to go out to the toilet."

She did. Pretty soon she came tearing back. I didn't see her, but I could hear the racket because I was upstairs. She came tearing back. I went hauling ass downstairs, and she was like a sheet. She had been scared to death. Some animal had come across the yard someplace. Lord knows what it was. I don't know whether it was their dog or whether it was a fox or what it was. Anyhow, it terrified her. She would not go to the head after dark from then on, while we were there, unless I went with her, because she was terrified.

But then we had to get to San Francisco, and we had these big debates. We were going to buy this car. Margaret couldn't drive. We were going to buy a new Champion Studebaker from my dad's friend Carl Wolf, who sold them. Then we were going to drive this thing to California. Well, you sit down and calculate it, and you just virtually have to drive straight through. I didn't have any more time. My mother was having kittens. This could not be done. My uncle was having triple kittens. So it was decided that my dad would go with us. After we got out there, we would load him on a plane and they would go to Kansas City and retrieve him on the other end.

Now, this poor man had never been on an airplane in his life. But anyhow, we drove like hell, two days and two nights, all the way across Kansas, New Mexico, beating our way out there. We finally got to San Francisco. And one of the things that the Navy had permitted me to do, or I'd been able to make arrangements for, was—the junior officers and the warrants could live in a Quonset.* Well, half a Quonset. So I was able to reserve a half a Quonset, and it was right by the filling station, and the warrants and a couple of JOs, because in those days most JOs weren't married. It was rare to have three of them married in a cruiser. It would be one in a destroyer, if any. The warrants would all be married. So we got in this thing, and we had an icebox.

---

* A Quonset hut is a semi-cylindrical metal building that can be shipped to an advance base area and erected quickly.

The first thing we had to do, I said I believe we'd just better get my dad back on a plane. He would just worry himself to death about his cows and such. And my brother by then was in the Air Force, so he was not home. My sister was in nursing school. All that was home was my baby sister. So we did that, we got him on there, the poor man. I don't know how he didn't die of fright. But it turned out he made it fine, and he told the story all his life about his first ride.

We moved into in a little Navy-furnished Quonset, and it had a spring bed, and it had an icebox. Well, after we'd lived there about a week, in discussing it with her I said to Margaret, "I just don't think you're ever going to get by with an icebox. I found out today at ship's service that for $5.00 a month we can rent a Frigidaire." We were paying $30.00 rent, so that would make the payment $35.00. So we decided to do that. Got them to come out, bring out and put in a Frigidaire. I mean, it was really a breakthrough, except the problem of ice. And being around those JOs and those warrant officers the only thing you had to do was drink after you came off the ship, so you would drink constantly.

So that's where we lived for three months and, bless Bess, not only did I get orders, but I was ordered to report to USS *Sierra*, and I was ordered to be on board by 1 January 1950

Paul Stillwell: Well, let's go back and cover the deployment, please.

Admiral Meyer: Okay.

Paul Stillwell: Did the ship go out to WestPac by herself or as part of a task group?

Admiral Meyer: We sailed, and I believe we sailed with *Pasadena*, as best I can remember.[*] I think *Astoria* sailed with a supply ship. It was a hodgepodge. We did not sail with a task force per se, although there was a task force going, but it was scattered to hell and gone.

---

[*] The deployment was from 18 October 1948 to 17 May 1949.

Paul Stillwell: I take it there was not a carrier involved.

Admiral Meyer: I can't remember a carrier. I don't believe there was. I can't remember one. And where we were really going was to the occupation forces, so we sailed into Japan, sailed into Yokosuka. Which, God, I thought I had seen in Greece the horrors of war. I thought I had really seen that. But I couldn't believe what I saw in Yokohama and in that area, courtesy of, amongst others, the United States Army Air Corps. It was hard to believe the devastation. And the people were just in a daze.

Now, mind you, this is the autumn of 1948, so the war had been over for three years. I mean, they were in recovery, and they'd made astounding progress I guess, but this young kid now—by 1948, I was 22. I had come out of the gumbo, and we were poor, really poor, but we weren't dirt. We weren't totally beat into oblivion. And we even understood cleanliness. And here this was the third time in my short life here, my military life, that I'd been subjected to this.

I think it was about December when we were relocated to the Yellow Sea. I think we went to Tsingtao, and then we went to Shanghai. We left Shanghai and went to Tsingtao and went back to Shanghai, but I'm a little foggy on that. Getting to Shanghai is not easy. I don't know whether you've ever sailed up the Delaware to Philadelphia.

Paul Stillwell: No.

Admiral Meyer: Well, it's kind of like that. Going up the Yangtze you fork off and go into the port, and it takes you a couple hours. It's kind of treacherous if you have never done it, and it was really treacherous then because we were moving with the SG radar and visual navigation.* But there wasn't anything else, so people were used to treachery. Nowadays it's nothing; they move right and left and don't even think about it.

We spent some time in northern Japan as part of the occupation forces. We had two destroyers with us, and we went in those northern ports for all the area. One island I never forgot was one called Ruben-shima, "shima" meaning "isle," so it was Ruben Island, way up north. We were up there for the Army CIC, the Counter-Intelligence

---

* SG was a type of surface-search radar.

Corps, I think. So we were hauling Army officers or soldiers and taking them to different places and retrieving them and operating as their communications base, and stuff like that. It seemed like we spent a month at it. The best I recall about it is how goddamn cold it was, how horrible cold it was.

Paul Stillwell: Was this just a show-the-flag mission?

Admiral Meyer: No, this was delivering these guys, taking them for their missions.

Paul Stillwell: A cruiser seems like an unusual type of transport.

Admiral Meyer: Well, I guess it depends. It would appear that they insisted on sending two escorts with us. And what I remember about Ruben-shima is, this is a goddamn island and a rock, almost. It's no place. Just like no place. And here, anchored all around it, must have been, hell I don't know, 50, 75, or 100 freighters of one kind or another. So the whole Soviet smuggling structure was functioning out through here, and this is why the Army intelligence people really were doing this research. I believe that, frankly, we were part of their safety.

Paul Stillwell: I see.

Admiral Meyer: That's what it seems to me, because we stood a lot of Condition III watches up there, and we had 6-inch batteries.

Paul Stillwell: Did you have a flag officer embarked in your ship?

Admiral Meyer: Virtually always, the division commander, almost the whole deployment. Herrmann the German was the division commander. I can't remember the other guy.

Paul Stillwell: I wonder if he had asked for an electronics specialist because he knew he was making that deployment.

Admiral Meyer: Well, I always gave the credit to the XO, but it could have come out of Herrmann, too, I don't know. All I know is my skipper in the destroyer thought I had pulled some strings to get off of his ship [chuckle], and I couldn't convince him. The day I left I think he was confident that I'd pulled strings, and I think when he saw me off at the quarterdeck into the whaleboat I think he was standing there just tickled to death that I was leaving, because he smelled trouble with me, because I'd been over calling on the admiral.

Paul Stillwell: What kind of condition was Shanghai in at that point?

Admiral Meyer: We moored off the Bund in the Whangpoo, and we were not more than 300 or 400 hundred yards from the Bund.[*] And daylight liberty was still being granted, as a matter of fact even pushing it out to 8:00 o'clock or 9:00 o'clock at night. And it was brought clear back to daylight in Tsingtao. But in Shanghai, for this country boy, was just a mess. You just thought you were walking through shantytown someplace. It was just a mess. And my good fortune was that I ran over the Rabinovich sisters, whose ages were 20 and 24.

The warrant officers were determined they were going to properly introduce me to Shanghai. So they were going to take me ashore, and they were going to visit the families and everything that they knew before the war. Well, of course, naturally that didn't work out because they were hard to find. But they did introduce me to the Rabinovich family, whom they knew. They'd known them before the war, and their two young daughters. Well, now the daughters were adults but still lived there, and so the two of them had taken me over to have supper with them, and that's how I came to know this pair of girls. Irena is the one I came to know; she was two or three years older than I.

This woman was an incredible woman. She had a degree out of the University of Shanghai. She was a bona fide White Russian. She had no citizenship. During the war,

---

[*] The Bund was a waterfront commercial center in Shanghai.

she had been raped by the Japanese soldiers in due course, as virtually no woman escaped being raped; it had become a way of life. And while they were alive and in many respects lived pretty good they still, compared to Americans—and certainly Americans in Missouri—were like terrible. Irena worked for a United Nations official, who was a Flemish. And she did one report a week of some kind of, I don't know, a domestic intelligence report or something or other. Anyhow, this guy dictated this report to her each week, and he dictated to her in Flemish, but she transcribed in French. She recorded in French. Then she transcribed into English, and this report went to San Francisco. She was paid pretty well. But that was her job. She spent maybe three days of the week at it.

Paul Stillwell: Did you have any contact with Japanese or Chinese people directly?

Admiral Meyer: Almost none with the Japanese. Almost none. We were actually not allowed to fraternize with them. And so the Army and the Navy had opened up their own clubs and their own entertainment, and all the women in these places were all cleared women. They had all been examined, cleared, and authorized. As a matter of fact, Shanghai had a club and this club—both of these girls were members of this club. Sailors could go there. They could dance, they could fraternize, and be entertained. But they had almost no other life in the city of Shanghai. As a matter of fact, I was scared to death to go into the city.

But I was never scared with Irena. Transportation was in rickshaws. She spoke the street talk well. She handled it well. She was respected by the coolies. And once I had met her, by the second night I never really socialized with any other person.

Paul Stillwell: How conscious were you of the Chinese push and Mao Tse-tung at that time?[*] The Communists were taking over and pushing out Chiang Kai-shek.[†]

---

[*] Mao Tse-tung was head of the Communist Party in the People's Republic of China from the time the Communists seized power in 1949 until his death in 1976.
[†] Generalissimo Chiang Kai-shek served as President of Nationalist China on the mainland from 1943 to 1949 and as President of the Republic of China on Taiwan from 1950 until his death in 1975.

Admiral Meyer: Well, I really became conscious of it in Tsingtao, because my life in Tsingtao was what I described as a life in three. That whole time I was an ensign. As a matter of fact, I was the bull ensign.* We had some 44 ensigns in *Springfield*. On Day One, you stood watch in a 5-inch/38 Mark 37 director.† Day Two you were boat officer. Day Three you were shore patrol officer. Day Four you started over. Because the JOs got no liberty. They got a few daylight hours off whenever the XO could work it in or Commander Slaughter could, but they got no liberty.

It was a city in destruction and a city at war, and the shore patrol was supposed to move in concert with the ChiNats.‡ Well, the ChiNats would have these little companies of men—there might be 12 or 14 of them in there. Following the 12 or 14 would be a couple of gunners, and they would be carrying bandoliers around their necks, a couple of them, and the other two would be carrying a couple machine guns. Because, wait a minute, the theory is here was that we Americans could not be armed ashore. What a hell of a theory.

Even so, Commander Slaughter had allowed us to carry .38s, because we had a number of .38s in the ship, allegedly for the aviators. But a fight broke out outside the USO.§ Lieutenant (j.g.) John Berude, who later became an engineering duty officer, and in fact later became an admiral, was assistant damage control officer in the ship.** He was in this circuit of JOs that I described; the lieutenant (senior grades) were excused from it, as were the warrants. But, anyhow, gunfire broke out, so John Berude, being a little scatterbrained and everything, broke out his pistol and fired a couple rounds. In any event, after the thing was all over, there was a teenage girl who had been hit in one of her legs with a bullet, and it was later determined it was an American bullet. So now it was disclosed that Americans were ashore armed. From then on we had to swear to the officer of the deck that we carried no arms when we went shore to do our duty, for that period of time.

---

* "Bull ensign" is the informal title for the senior ensign in a given ship.
† The Mark 37 director controlled the aiming of the 5-inch guns.
‡ ChiNats – Chinese Nationalists, that is, the forces loyal to Chiang Kai-shek.
§ USO – United Services Organization is a group of U.S. civilians who put on entertainment programs for service personnel and provide hospitality for them in many parts of the world.
** Lieutenant (junior grade) John B. Berude, USN.

It was a bitter-ass winter, a really bitter-ass winter. Then we relocated back to Shanghai. I'd say that Tsingtao was the only city that I was in that was falling, and it wasn't necessarily obvious to you that the city was falling. You only knew it afterwards that it was happening.

Paul Stillwell: Did you go out for ship exercises at sea any time when you were over around China and Japan? Antiair practice or gunnery practice?

Admiral Meyer: I'll tell you a story that will piss you off; at least it pissed me off.

Paul Stillwell: Okay.

Admiral Meyer: It happened while we were in Tsingtao. In those days there was a fairly rigid table of inspections for warships, and the fleet did that themselves. They were referred to as operational readiness inspections, and they had to occur each quarter. And while we were in Shanghai on guard, theoretically we were anchored—and *Pasadena* was with us much—but while we were there, and we were actually pretty far out from the matter of traveling by boat to get ashore, our ORI came due. We were in the middle of this goddamn war. Well, wait a minute. The ORI normally takes three days, but some admiral said we weren't going to spend three days on it. So the division commander, read Herrmann the German, decided it would all be done in one day. So they'd start at 4:00 o'clock and finish up that night.

We did. We started out the check-off lists, went tearing to *Pasadena*, which was the inspector. So *Pasadena*'s officers and chief petty officers and first-class all poured over there, the warrants, to check us out, to make sure we were ready for war. Finally, about 9:00 o'clock or so that night, we were assembled to the wardroom to be debriefed, and the admiral was to get the debrief. So here is the captain of *Pasadena* going through how screwed up we were, all the Irish pennants we had in the ship, and on and on and on and stuff and so forth, saying things that I'm sure were pleasing to the admiral.[*] And it

---

[*] "Irish Pennant" is Navy slang for a loose piece of line left adrift. It can also be used in a figurative sense to refer to something that is sloppy because it hasn't been completed properly.

eventually ground down. The snipes were all in the back part, and naturally we were all in khakis.

Finally the CO, Captain Moosbrugger, turned to the admiral and asked him if he had anything he'd like to say. Herrmann the German stood up and looked around. Every chair in the wardroom was occupied with the officers of *Pasadena* and ourselves, and we stood up. And he looked around and he said, "Yes, I do." As a matter of fact, he was in dress blues. He said, "I note here that all these officers are out of uniform. In my division I expect officers to be in uniform during non-working hours." And sat down. I mean, nobody had anything to say. Well, he walked out. We were just stunned. I mean, I was really having trouble here, at 22, trying to correlate the significance of that and the readiness for war.

Paul Stillwell: Right. [Laughter]

Admiral Meyer: But I did, over due course. [Chuckle] But that was that Navy and how it behaved. And so you asked me if there was an incident, and that's an incident I cite. E. E. Herrmann the German.

Paul Stillwell: So then you came back, and what was your personal role in the inactivation process at Hunters Point?

Admiral Meyer: Well, before that, I'll give another sea story. Of course, we had a Marine detachment, which was commanded by a captain. As a matter of fact, his name was Joe Loprete, and he was later killed in Korea.[*] And the XO was Lieutenant Bill O'Neill. He made it back out of Korea. At Korea is when the Marine detachments from then on started going downhill in our Navy, both in the carriers and in the cruisers, but they were pretty potent forces up till then, when I was a JO.

I ended up befriending O'Neill because I was the senior ensign, and he and I had a room together. So that's how we became friends. Well, the interesting thing was that a jeep was allotted to the admiral, but the admiral never went ashore, so Joe Loprete was in

---

[*] Captain Joseph E. Loprete, USMC.

charge of the jeep. Well, when he was too worn out to go carouse or get drunk, then O'Neill got custody of the jeep, and Ensign Meyer, his friend, got to go with him. So we were much admired for our prowess of having transportation in Yokohama. It's not all it sounds. You had to be careful you didn't get a bucket of slop dumped on you someplace as you were going along. But in that whole period I had not bad transportation around. And the beautiful part was that you could get through all the patrols. The MPs would see you and just wave you on; you'd get through them without any checks or anything else with the goddamn Marines.

Now, next question was, you asked me what my responsibility was.

Paul Stillwell: When you were inactivating the ship at Hunters Point.

Admiral Meyer: Right. We were operating out of a book. A lot of ships had been inactivated by then, and so the process had been pretty well mature, I guess you would say, but also very, very complicated, really complicated. And so it had become mostly—

Paul Stillwell: Just follow the procedures.

Admiral Meyer: Yeah, right. Exactly.

Paul Stillwell: And dehumidification was a big part of that.

Admiral Meyer: It was. Big. Because, in truth, we didn't know how to do dehumidification very well then, and I ain't sure we do yet today, for that matter.

I had the custody of all of these precious electronics tools, test equipment, and all that stuff existed, and the issue with us was what to do with it. It just seemed like a pity to go store it someplace in the ship and abandon it. So we set on a course with a couple of warrants on how to distribute some of it to the shipyard and some to schools in that area. We may have purloined some, but I don't think we did. So I just was the oversight for electronics. And while the chief engineer was in charge, theoretically, he had no interest whatsoever, so Commander Slaughter was the person that I worried about satisfying and trying to preserve the radars. Whether they were ever preserved beats the hell out of me, because to the best of my knowledge they never served any useful purpose again. See, *Springfield*, as you know, was reactivated, but everything was taken off of her when she was converted.[*] She got all new radars, all new everything. And turret three was removed. So I have mixed feeling on that.

Paul Stillwell: Anything else to wrap up *Springfield*?[†]

Admiral Meyer: Well, I guess my closing remark on it would be the one I've said to you before. I thought I knew everything there was to know when I left the destroyer, but it turned out that I really became a Navy person, and I really started understanding the book, when I had a tour in *Springfield*. I'm always grateful that I had this tour, because that's probably what made me a decent naval officer. That's probably what did it, and knocked the corners off of me. And I must give credit to Norman Woods, who lives today in Florida; he's a radio electrician. The boatswain's name was Macmillan; I don't know where he is. He and the gunner spent a lot of time on me. I don't know whether they did it because I was such a nice person or whether they saw extraordinary ability in me, or what. I know one thing, that they were just stunned that I understood something about Ohm's Law and Kirchoff's Laws and fire control loop closures and such. They were stunned that I knew something about all of that, and so I think they always, from the beginning, had great respect for me. So that begot respect.

Paul Stillwell: Well, and you got broadened also in getting some time in the bridge and some time in engineering as well.

Admiral Meyer: I did. I got broadened, you're right, and I learned a lot about CIC because, see *Goodrich* CIC really was still coming out of the larva stage of just being built behind the mast pole, and here it was in *Springfield*, built in, down in the armor belt, and it was pretty fully populated. So it was a big step up for me.

---

[*] The *Springfield* was taken out of mothballs in 1957, converted to a guided missile cruiser, redesignated CLG-7 in 1957, and recommissioned 2 July 1960.
[†] The ship was decommissioned on 30 January 1950.

The other thing I learned a lot about, too, was aviation, and how valuable those two airplanes were. It didn't matter whether you were in port or at sea; if the weather permitted in any way, shape, or form, at least one of those SC airplanes was up. "Man all tracking stations. And be on those directors." Now, the directors for the machine guns were Marines. The other directors were sailors. Every bloody day, every bloody day they had to do that. And I learned that sense of duty of practice. And I learned it about ordnance as I got older and older and older.

Ordnance is a bizarre area that, if you pay attention to it every day it will work when you want it. If you don't, it will be down. I guarantee you it will be broke. I tried to imbue that in there. I tried to later put that sense of duty into the Aegis design.

Paul Stillwell: So you're talking about having both men and material ready when the time comes.

Admiral Meyer: Affirmative. Affirmative.

Paul Stillwell: Well, we can get to that, but you said that you had orders to report on January 1. How did that come about?

Admiral Meyer: Well, it came about just right out of the sky. Now, here we were. It was the beginning of December or so, or the first half of December, and I now had a wife that was pregnant or believed to be pregnant.

Paul Stillwell: That didn't take long.

Admiral Meyer: Didn't take very long. When you're in the goddamn Quonsets and getting drunk every night, it doesn't take long. [Laughter]

Paul Stillwell: So something came out of the sky.

Admiral Meyer: Right. Something came out of the sky. I was to report to Norfolk, Virginia. In trying to get data I had learned en route that my new ship, the *Sierra*, would sail on 6 January. So Margaret and I had a problem. What was I going to do with her? What would be best? We struggled and thought about that and struggled and thought about it, because on the other end there was only going to be a handful of days.

Well, to sum that up, we decided that her mother would welcome her in Dorchester, and she'd go live with her mother. She had three brothers, none of whom were married, two of whom lived at home. So she was comfortable with that, because she had never lived alone in a strange place in her whole life, so she felt very, very queasy about what was going to happen to her. The other was, they had the top-drawer naval hospital at Chelsea, Massachusetts. So she could be well seen to, and that was important to me.

Paul Stillwell: Sure.

Admiral Meyer: I was told I was going to be the *Sierra*'s radio officer.[*] Not at that moment did I figure in that also that meant being the registered pubs officer, because, hell, all I knew about a tender was very, very little indeed as a client for one.[†] I didn't know much about it past that. So we decided that, if we were going to see each other, she'd better go with me to Norfolk. So we went to Norfolk and got a motel, and we spent the next eight days or so. She was in the motel, and her older brother would take a bus down to Norfolk and he would drive her back to Boston. And we put most of what little gear we had in storage, and there we were.

That New Year's Eve I spent aboard ship with this jerk trying to get the registered pubs inventoried. I now started to understand how serious the situation was that I was in.

---

[*] USS *Sierra* (AD-18), a *Dixie*-class destroyer tender, was commissioned 20 March 1944. She displaced 14,037 tons, was 530 feet long, 73 feet in the beam, and had a maximum draft of 26 feet. Her top speed was 20 knots. She was originally armed with four 5-inch guns. She remained in service until decommissioned on 15 October 1993.

[†] Registered publications, as they were then known, required strict accountability in the storage, transfer, and destruction of specific publications, particularly those that involved communication codes.

Paul Stillwell: That inventory was so you knew exactly what you were getting from your predecessor.

Admiral Meyer: Yeah [laughter]. I mean, I started from ground zero. I didn't know a damned thing about registered pubs. As a matter of fact, I had not mastered the crypto machine. Then I started discovering how highly dependent the destroyers were on me, because we carried a lot of reserve pubs for the destroyers. And then, of course, we had the flotilla staff aboard in port. Once on this deployment, they didn't have a flotilla. But when they got back, you had the flotilla constantly bugging you, because you were their comms officer.

So I got Margaret mailed home, and tentatively we were to be back by June. The ship deployed on the sixth of January. And I tell the story that she sailed that day: it was the first deployment that *Sierra* ever made, and she made one more—I was aboard and left her—and she never made another deployment again. But that morning, standing there at the quarterdeck, seeing the chief petty officers come aboard in particular, and then a lot of senior petty officers—in a tender, of course, you have a lot of first-class and second-class that have got mileage on them. You'd hear them dragging these seabags. You'd hear these goddamn bottles rattling [chuckle], one after the other, as they were dragging them all aboard, because they had never deployed in their life and they were getting ready for it.

Margaret made out okay. She got back and forth to Chelsea. She got wonderful treatment there. I have three children. Two of them ended up being born in Chelsea, and one was born in Newport Naval Hospital. So it turned out I had wonderful service out of the U.S. Navy, as far as I'm concerned. When I hear people start bitching and carrying on about it, that ain't been my experience.

So she got by, we got by. We essentially didn't have any money, just didn't have any money. Even deployed and her living there, we were still just poor. I mean, what a struggle to balance. It's amazing that these marriages even last, when you think about the different challenges they're confronted with, then including finance. Just didn't have any money.

So here we were in the ship, and a lieutenant (senior grade), a guy by the name of Cosgrove, left the ship and, not only that, he was retiring from the Navy, because he was a USN-T.[*] That was on the January 5, and I was going to be now in charge and I was going to be the radio officer, registered pubs and comms, CIC officer, believe it or not the ASW officer, and shore bombardment officer, because there was a surface capacity within the ship. The tenders of the AD-16 class were generally thought to have the capacity to act as station ships, or they could act as flagships if they had to. They could only make 17 knots; that was their limitation.

Paul Stillwell: I would think shore bombardment would be well down on the list of priorities of missions.

Admiral Meyer: Well, we wouldn't do it ourselves. We would help formulate it up for the goddamn destroyers to get in line.

Paul Stillwell: I see.

Admiral Meyer: Because we didn't have anything to bombard with except a couple of 5-inch guns. As a matter of fact, I'm trying to think whether our guns were closed-mount or open-mount. I can't remember right now whether they were closed or open. I think they were closed mounts.

Paul Stillwell: I think they were.

Admiral Meyer: So there we are. Well, we were supposed to sail that day at about noon or 1:00 o'clock, and I was up in the radio shack futzing around that morning and stuff. I had asked the navigator what assist he needed to try to get under way and he kept saying, "Well, I don't think we'll need any; I've got it all in hand." So I was futzing around up in the radio shack.

---

[*] Lieutenant Thomas A. Cosgrove, USN.

Finally, the word was passed for Ensign Meyer to report to the captain on the bridge. Well, in truth, in that ship the bridge was only about 30 or 40 feet away. As a matter of fact, I think it was on the same deck, now that I think about it. So I went hauling ass to the bridge to see what the problem was. I got up there, and the XO standing there. He was a surfaced submariner by the name of John Hack, commander.[*] And the captain was there. His name was Rook, Eugene— we later called him "Eugen"— Eugene C. Rook.[†] He was a typical German. He's the only officer I ever served under who wore the World War I victory medal. Actually, I really got so I enjoyed that old man. But I could see that he and the XO had had a warm discussion when I got up there.

So I went up there and said, "Yes, sir, Captain."

Paul Stillwell: Warm in the sense of heated?

Admiral Meyer: Exactly. Right. So the XO turned to me when I got there and he said, "Look, you came out of a destroyer, didn't you?"

I said, "Yes, sir."

He said, "And a cruiser?" I said yes. He said, "Well, you're a qualified officer of the deck, aren't you?"

I said, "Yes, I've stood a number of watches in the destroyer. My watch standing in the cruiser is limited, but, as a matter of fact, I stood as the senior watch officer in the destroyer." They looked at each other, and the captain said, "Get her under way." Just like that.

I subsequently learned that what they were arguing about was how in the hell they were going to get under way. The wardroom was full of officers, but there weren't any line officers. We had all these warrants, we had five dentists, four doctors, three chaplains. You know, we had all these kinds of different officers.

Paul Stillwell: Supply officers.

---

[*] Commander John A. Hack, USN.
[†] Eugen, pronounced oy-gen, is the German equivalent of the name Eugene. Rook commanded the ship from 1 September 1949 to 5 July 1950.

Admiral Meyer: Yeah. You didn't have anybody that worked. I finally learned the first week that there were only two regular officers. One was the XO, and I was the other one. So this turned out to be another incredible situation that God had wrought on me of teaching me about my Navy. They couldn't decide who was qualified. All these officers had turned over at the last minute, and they just couldn't come to any understanding. Well, now here we were, down at the lightship. They were clearing the channel, and they could not come to a decision on my relief. Well finally, about 4:00 o'clock or so [chuckle], the warrant boatswain, the chief boatswain, was assigned as my relief.

We were sailing alone, headed to Gibraltar, and the way it worked out for that nine-day passage was that the watches would be stood by the warrant and myself and the XO. Our job was to get somebody else qualified to stand the watches until the XO and the captain agreed to it.

Now, the captain was a pretty damned good seaman. He was pretty competent. Except there was something I didn't know about him, and it took me a while to discover it, which the XO already knew. It was that he couldn't see, and he particularly couldn't see at night. By the time we had cleared the harbor and on the way over, the XO had talked to me, and any kind of work we did in the Med, entering port, any fleet ops, any association, either he was on the bridge or I was on the bridge, because he said, "The captain just, I'm not confident of his ability to see something when you're telling him about it. So I need you on the bridge, or I'll be on the bridge." And that was the way we worked it out.

Well, my JO was Lieutenant Commander Harry Hickman, the repair officer, and of course he was really, really unhappy about standing a watch. And I said, "Look. I didn't have a goddamn thing to do with putting you on watch. I'm a lieutenant (junior grade). But, by God, if you're going to stand watch under me you're going to get your ass qualified pretty quick, because I ain't standing watches all my life while you all sit on your ass drinking coffee."

Paul Stillwell: [Chuckle] How receptive was he to that speech?

Admiral Meyer: [Laughter] Harry Hickman and I became pretty good friends later in life, but at that moment he wasn't too happy. And he started again—I said, "Wait a minute. You've got a problem? Go see the XO. Don't talk to me. See the XO." That ended it, really. Anyhow, it turned out that Hickman got so he really enjoyed standing watches. And actually he kind of liked my teaching.

So I was a sea detail OOD, I was the maneuvering OOD, any kind of formation stuff I had to be on the bridge, or the XO had to be on the bridge. But, God, the XO wore himself out, because he just was scared to get off the bridge. Because he had this, I don't know whether you'd call it a secret or not, but he really knew deep down here that the captain, while he was determined and everything, he really could not see well. So you'd mention a contact to him: "Captain, there's that contact." The captain really wasn't seeing it. So there was a certain amount of danger to it.

Anyhow, we got through it all. I've often said I became a better seaman in USS *Sierra* than any other ship I ever sailed in.

Paul Stillwell: Few people could probably say that.

Admiral Meyer: You're damned right there's few people could say it. [Laughter] I really did. I became a better seaman there than anyplace.

Paul Stillwell: Well, you were more successful getting that ship out of Norfolk than the *Missouri* was two weeks later. She ran aground [chuckle].[*]

Admiral Meyer: You're damned right I was. You bet your ass. You bet your ass I was. Bet your ass. We kept listening for those reports coming over, and I've got to tell you, the Navy felt a lot of—I don't know whether "shame" may be too strong a word, but—

Paul Stillwell: Embarrassment.

---

[*] The battleship *Missouri* (BB-63) ran aground near Norfolk, Virginia, on 17 January 1950. She was not refloated until 1 February. See Dr. Malcolm Muir, Jr., "Hard Aground on Thimble Shoal," *Naval History*, Fall 1991, pages 30-35.

Admiral Meyer: Embarrassment's the word. I didn't have to do it before that deployment; I had to do it later in my tour in that ship, and that was to go unload ammo and reload. Because in those days the tenders carried a lot of stock, and particularly a lot of 6-inch for the cruisers. So you had that goddamn stuff on there, just baggage.

Paul Stillwell: So you had magazines way down in the ship?

Admiral Meyer: Oh, way down doesn't even describe the goddamn things. [Laughter] *Way* down, and there was no straight shot to the magazines. They were offset, so you had to go a deck at a time, a deck at a time, a deck at a time. And that was for architectural reasons or design reasons, and safety of the ship. But I didn't think much of it. Today, even in the Aegis cruisers, we load storage and go "plunk," straight down the hole. Go straight down. I mean, it only takes about four men to replenish *Ticonderoga* in the designs that were put in. We've got some automation, but also, if you get it down there then you can move it laterally quite easy.

Paul Stillwell: Were there some ammunition hoists in the *Sierra* to aid this process?

Admiral Meyer: Yeah, there were. But [chuckle] they were all like chain falls. I mean, it was a lot of goddamn work. They all went on skip boxes. We had these big hatches. We didn't mind it too much carrying for the destroyers, which was our job, but carrying for the goddamn cruisers really would piss you off. The repair ships were supposed to carry the ammo in those days for the cruisers.

Paul Stillwell: And the 6-inch cruisers were really being phased out about that time too.

Admiral Meyer: They were. They were. You're right. So we were just hauling this crap around.

Well, that was kind of my life.

I'm trying to think why we were headed to Philadelphia the subsequent year. It was in September, and we had to go to the shipyard for, it seems to me it was to change radios or something or other. And so, of course, I was the officer of the deck to go up there. My wife was still in Boston, nine months pregnant.

The old man was in a horrible mood that day, terrible mood. We made the passage up the Delaware River, and he was picking at me and yelling at me all the time about everything I did. By now I thought I understood how to get up that river pretty well. We had a pilot aboard, and I don't think he had a lot of confidence in the pilot, and I wasn't overconfident. I know he had confidence in me because he had sailed with me. But he just really was an asshole.

It was only later that evening, when we got up there, that the telegram had come through from Chelsea Naval that my daughter was born.[*] And, of course, the first one that saw it was the old man. He was so embarrassed. God, he never said a harsh word to me ever again after that.

Paul Stillwell: Now, this was your first child?

Admiral Meyer: Yeah. He had no idea. [Chuckle] And I think he was embarrassed. He blamed it on a reason that was totally wrong, that my poor performance was related to my worry about the baby being born. It wasn't even on my mind. [Chuckle] It just wasn't even on my mind, but that's what he thought it was, my poor performance.

Paul Stillwell: And you're telling me that it wasn't poor performance. [Laughter]

Admiral Meyer: You got it. As a matter of fact, it turned out I was not present for any of my children. So when the doctor said she could move, in about four weeks or so, the captain told me I could take all the leave I wanted. We moved into a hotel in Philadelphia—it was kind of an apartment hotel—for a few months, and lived there with the new baby and Margaret.

Paul Stillwell: We didn't really cover the deployment. What happened when you were over in the Med? You said you left in January to go over there.

---

[*] The daughter is named Paula.

Admiral Meyer: Yeah, and we came back about the end of June, the end of June or early July. I want to say that J. J. Ballentine was the Sixth Fleet commander.[*] Of course, the tender, in those days, played a really big role in support of the flag. So you had these automobiles that were for the flag. He had the extra boats, the barge, besides the gigs, and you were just carrying all this stuff.

Fortunately, we were not carrying the flag. The flag had some quarters taken ashore at La Spezia, Italy, up north of Naples. So we carried all this crap for them, including their food. Mrs. Ballentine was a nut about Virginia cured hams, so all her dinners that she threw, official dinners and everything, were Virginia cured hams, and we carried those goddamn things aboard the tender. So at the last minute you were always rushing over with a goddamn whaleboat to deliver a couple hams for her because they had some party forming up.

Well, that went on, and we got along pretty well. But the thing that pissed you off was, of course, that the admiral and his staff were in a cruiser. The cruiser would go into port first. If you had a carrier, the carrier would be next. Didn't always have a carrier. We would be about fourth in line. And already the goddamn blinking lights were just going like crazy: "Where's the barge? Where's the cars?" On and on and on. Christ, we were still trying to get up the channel. That was a rough undertaking. That was hard work. And, of course, they'd get pissed off at you, figuring you're unresponsive. Staff people can be really snotty. They can really be snotty.

We got through it all, and by then I was applying for about anything that you could apply for. I decided I had to rethink what I was going to do in the Navy, because I just kept seeing this deterioration occurring here. And I loved the Navy. I didn't want to leave the Navy. It wasn't that I didn't want to sail; it was that it was just so damned haphazard. I started thinking about the number of ships I'd already sailed in, as I've recounted to you the number of ships I sailed in in a relatively short period. And here this poor young Irish girl was growing up with this baby, trying to make a go of herself, and not getting any help out of me. Just living almost helter-skelter.

---

[*] Vice Admiral John J. Ballentine, USN, served as Commander Sixth Fleet from 14 November 1949 to 19 March 1951.

I was coming back. I've got to watch my registration. The Korean War broke out.[*]

Paul Stillwell: It was the last week in June in 1950.

Admiral Meyer: Yeah, right. That's when we were returning. I thought sure we'd sail for the war, because we were in a high state of readiness. Our destroyer squadron was in superb condition. No. We didn't sail anyplace. We were moored. They sailed some group that wasn't ready out of Norfolk. That maneuver bothered the hell out of me, too, that the Navy thought that way. Instead of sending ready ships, they sent non-ready ships. I didn't like that. Well, one of the reasons they were non-ready ships was that the Atlantic Fleet wasn't about to give the Pacific Fleet anything in that situation, because all you did was work your ass off to turn the ships over to somebody else.

Well, finally one of the things I'd applied for was to go to guided missile school in Fort Bliss, Texas, wherever the hell that was.

Paul Stillwell: Why did you pick that?

Admiral Meyer: I picked whatever was available to pick. I kept picking and picking. I thought it was a coming thing, and I had an abiding interest in it. I read a lot in magazines. So I applied for it.

My baby was born in September 1950. I was deployed one more time to the Med—I believe I'm correct—in the subsequent winter, and I was notified coming back that I had been selected to go to this guided missile school in August of 1951. And in a way we were tickled, but in another way not. Margaret's family were all over her about she had married this sailor boy, and she was never going to have anything but a haphazard life, and just constantly she'd be traveling. Her brothers didn't care anything

---

[*] The Korean War began on 25 June 1950, when six North Korean infantry division and three border constabulary brigades invaded South Korea. The troops were supported by approximately 100 Russian-made T-34 tanks. In New York that same day the United Nations Security Council adopted a resolution condemning the invasion.

for the service. She had three sisters, and they would gnaw at her. Anyhow, coming back, we took off and headed for Fort Bliss, Texas.[*]

Paul Stillwell: Is there anything about that second deployment to the Med you want to put on the record?

Admiral Meyer: Nothing comes to mind this minute.

Paul Stillwell: So what was your wife's feeling when she was getting this negative talk from her family?

Admiral Meyer: Well, in hindsight I think she was pretty damned strong. She had already come to find out that much of the talk she had heard about the Navy just simply wasn't correct. It was just chatter, chatter, chatter. It was true that she was having a helter-skelter life, but the life did not exceed her capacity to handle it. Granted, she had this little baby, born in September. Well, the subsequent July we got in our car again and headed through Missouri and on down across Oklahoma and eventually into El Paso, Texas, on an August afternoon. It was about 115 degrees outside. We had a bassinet in the back seat with this little baby and two tubs of goddamn diapers. There weren't any paper diapers in that era. Had all these diapers and a squalling baby, trying to maintain our sanity.

Paul Stillwell: And no air-conditioning.

Admiral Meyer: And she detested hot weather. Margaret just couldn't handle hot weather. I kept telling her, "You've got to understand, I've never been there, but I know it's hotter than hell; I'm telling you it's hot, but it's a dry heat." So we headed out of Albuquerque and arrived about 4:00 o'clock in the afternoon.

Here I didn't know what God had wrought. In the next few days we rented a little apartment that was owned by a Baptist preacher as part of his parsonage that we moved

---

[*] Fort Bliss is an Army post partly in west Texas and partly in New Mexico.

into. I suppose it would qualify as two bedrooms if you counted hard enough, but it was adequate. We were going to be there a year. It was on a slab. One slab is all you had down there anyhow. I was still a lieutenant (junior grade). So I felt I was pretty well off.

I reported in to Fort Bliss, Texas, which stunned me. Christ, it's impossible to describe how big Fort Bliss, Texas, is, added on to all the land north of them, Arizona and the missile range. It goes on and on and on and on and on. So we moved into this place in a little town called Ascarate, west of El Paso. And there was a good deal of English spoken, but a lot of Spanish spoken also.

Well, we didn't know what we'd wrought. To shorten that up, we cried when we left a year later. We loved living there. The people were so nice, they were just so nice and so kind.

Paul Stillwell: And she adjusted to the heat somehow, I take it.

Admiral Meyer: Yeah. And, you know, you're in a place where, when the humidity went to 3% people would be carrying an umbrella. [Laughter] I mean, it only rained a couple times a year, and it would be a signal to get out your umbrella. And it was so dry. God, it was dry. Your skin would just peel off of you. So it took a while for your whole sinus to redo itself.

Reported in. Started the school. The commanding general passed a rule that the officers had to join the officers' club. Well, in those days you had to buy a share into the officers' club. We naval officers complained to our authorities back in, I think it was Albuquerque. In any event, we got a one-time waiver to not pay it.

The class consisted of ten naval officers, ten Army officers, ten of the newly minted Air Force, and five Marines. This is in spite of the war; the Marines had five officers there. There were 35 of us.

Paul Stillwell: Were they all about your same rank?

Admiral Meyer: Yeah, right. Lieutenant jaygees and first lieutenants, and there was a captain or two. So they started out teaching us. After seven months they ran out of material. All the data known in the Western world on guided missiles had been taught. They had brought in everyone they could bring in to do this.

In that era the German scientists had now been stationed up at White Sands.[*] We had a number of lectures from them, and we went up to White Sands often, and von Braun taught us.[†] I was on the firing team for the Lark missile, which was a very early Army missile that had a gasoline engine in it. And, of course, it couldn't carburate, and that never got solved. That's why the Lark missile never made it. But what was known as the North McGregor Range, which is the range north of Bliss, headed up to Alamogordo, headed up to Arizona. That's where the missile range is for Fort Bliss, for antiair work. So we got a lot of field experience.

The Navy had built its first SPG-49 radar. It would be the fire control radar for this new thing called the Talos, and they had it in test there.[‡] And so I learned and saw the most powerful shipboard radar that existed in the world, located there on this mount. I got a lot of heady exposure to things. I found out, too, that naval officers were head and shoulders beyond the other officers, and I don't know why. I think it has to do with sailing, and the kind of independence and behavior pattern you develop as a result of going to sea. I don't know what it has to do with, but there's no doubt in my mind. And it's still true. I find it right now in the last few years. I've spent the last ten years with the Missile Defense Agency and its ancestry. There's a difference. There's a real difference in behavior pattern.

But we had a good time. We enjoyed each other. I think there were only about six that were married. It turned out that Juarez was a wonderful place. It cost a nickel to cross the bridge, and when you were there you'd have a wonderful steak and dinner for a dollar. That was when the meat was under embargo for hoof in mouth disease, which did not affect the meat as it was cooked. So virtually all our entertainment was in Juarez. It had some wonderful shows. So my wife and I would go over on Saturday night for a

---

[*] White Sands, New Mexico, Missile Range.
[†] Wernher von Braun was a German-born rocket scientist who helped develop rockets for his country in World War II, then emigrated to the United States in 1945 and began working with the Army. He subsequently played a considerable role in the U.S. space program.
[‡] Talos was a long-range ramjet missile used by surface ships in the antiair mission. It was 33 feet long, 28 inches in diameter, and weighed 7,000 pounds. It had a range of about 75 miles. Its first successful intercept of a drone target was in October 1952. It entered fleet service on board the cruiser *Galveston* (CLG-3) in 1958.

dinner and a show. And one of the fellows in the class with me had gone to school with me at MIT, Dick Stansfield, and he had no wife, so he went with us.* And we'd get a little Spanish girl to look after our little baby, and we never felt any discomfort. We'd get home at 4:00 or 5:00 o'clock in the morning.

And we'd bring back our quota. If you were stationed there, you were allowed one quart a week of whiskey. As I recollect, at that time the price for it was $1.50, so you'd gradually accumulate a pretty good pile of whiskey at home, as a matter of fact more than you'd drink, if you would go very often.

So we cried when we left because we enjoyed the place so much. Our sinuses had adapted, we'd all adjusted to the exposure. Most people don't appreciate that El Paso County was dry then. The interesting thing about it, you could drink anyplace, including sitting on the sidewalk, and people did. As long as you didn't create a disturbance, you could drink wherever you wanted to drink. Your ass would go in if you started creating a disturbance. It was pretty well run. We really enjoyed that year in El Paso.

Paul Stillwell: Well, please tell me more about the substance of the course. And how did you apply what you had learned at MIT to this?

Admiral Meyer: I will do that and then we'll stop.

Understand, in that year there was still a great deal of discussion, and properly so, on the theory related to orbital mechanics, and whether in fact escape could be achieved. You had on the one hand a group who were the Buck Rogers people, who thought it was not an issue, and you had on the other end of the spectrum those who thought that would never be possible.† Von Braun tended to believe that it was possible. He believed the math. But he did not know how we were going to achieve the impulse.

When you enter the White Sands Missile Range from Las Cruces and you come into that gate, all you're doing is still driving across the desert, but you will pass—that's all granite in that country there, which is one of the reasons it was chosen—you will pass yet another granite slab and granite mountain and notice some outcroppings, or people

---
* Lieutenant Richard J. Stansfield, USN.
† A popular comic strip of the era was titled "Buck Rogers in the 25th Century." It featured interplanetary warfare and communications and employed futuristic weapons such as death rays and rocket pistols.

have been chopping on it. That's true all over the range, which is hundreds of miles across. And this particular one was where von Braun convinced the United States Army to set to work on a 500,000-pound test stand. Because of the numbers involved and how hard it would be, it was thought it was going to have to be out of granite, in a granite mountain. There just wasn't anything else hard enough to do it. And they started to work on that. Well, it's long since abandoned. It never reached fruition, although it has produced a number of things, including learning how in the hell to handle granite and how to get through it. But that monument was tried to develop prima facie data that in fact you could handle those kinds of numbers and those kinds of thrusts safely.

When I was going to school, that was a continuing debate. Now, the time we were there was an exciting year. I couldn't say we were overly burdened with home lessons, and we had no textbooks. We learned whatever somebody chose to teach us and whatever we dug up ourselves. But the Korean War was still on the rise and the argument of close air support was a monster. And since we had this class of 35 which was a ready-mixed group of not totally junior officers—I mean while in rank they were junior, in those days you didn't get promoted very fast, so they had a number of years' operating experience. We'd have a lot of discussions on close air support and what the meaning of it was to the Army and the Marines and whether a stand-alone or independent Air Force would ever work and be made to work. And the truth is it never has been made to work; you can't make it work. It has to be some kind of an integral.

But the other question was whether you could escape the earth. And Convair, with the urging of the United States Air Force, had broken out to work on its big undertaking on the mesas in San Diego.[*] Out of there flowed Atlas, primarily, which remains a workhorse to this day.[†] Well over 50 years later, 60 years later, it's a workhorse, such a good engine, such a good rocket. So we'd study those equations, go through those equations, but you still had trouble accepting it. It just was hard to imagine. And it's hard to stand out and glare at the sun and glare at the moon and think that somehow that could be achieved. So the discussions went on and on and on and on

---

[*] Convair was a defense contractor that initially produced aircraft and later got into rockets and spacecraft. The company was formed by the merger in 1953 of Consolidated Aircraft and Vultee Aircraft.
[†] The SM-65 Atlas was the first intercontinental ballistic missile built by the United States. It was done for the U.S. Air Force by the Convair Division of the General Dynamics Corporation. Initial development began in 1951, and the first successful test flight was in 1958.

and on. And some never believed, and others believed so intensely they never bothered to find out the true facts, as we say.

A number of years after that, I was a big wheel in a number of places I went, and particularly when I'd go to Missouri to visit home. "Hey, Wayne, Wayne, Wayne. Talk to us, talk to us about being a space cadet. Tell us how you do that. Tell us how you go about that. Tell us." [Laughter]

"Wait a minute. It's not exactly that."

But the equations of old—most of these equations having evolved in the 1800s, some even in the 1700s—were pretty damned good. They're pretty valid equations. Some of them had truncated terms on them, so to achieve the accuracies being demanded you had to take a lot more terms, because most of these equations are really the product of expanded series. And, of course, series are infinite series, and there's always another term, there's always another term, depending on what degree of accuracy you want.

Paul Stillwell: How demanding was the math in that study? Was your MIT background sufficient?

Admiral Meyer: Well, put another way is, I was more prepared, I'd say, than virtually anybody because, I mean, people thought I was a brain, which I wasn't. It's because I was studying it again. Hell, I was on calculus the third time by then, and so I was starting to understand it. And generally our teachers were visitors, or we had some really skilled Army officers who were specialists—and they were mostly junior officers—who were specialists in the subjects and attempted to teach the subjects. But they had no experience. Experience was very, very limited.

Of course, Army artillery at Fort Sill and the U.S. Navy were the people that understood ballistics better than anybody, with the 16-inch guns. The Air Force never got a grasp of ballistics, and it was a long time before the Marine Corps did. And it was just simply from exposure. And, like everything else, it can become old hat if you're at it long enough. Very soon you forget what other people have put into you and taught you, and you can get persnickety about how those that don't understand are so dumb.

Paul Stillwell: The Navy in the late '40s had tested the German V-1s and V-2s.* Did you have the data from those tests?

Admiral Meyer: Yes.

Paul Stillwell: How useful were those?

Admiral Meyer: Well, in a sense this was all we had. It *was* the data. Of course, they had fired V-2s and were firing them, and we were scheduled to watch one. We saw it from Bliss. We never saw it from the range. The reason they got terminated was that one got out of kilter and landed not too far from Juarez in Old Mexico, on a trajectory that they had not predicted, so they had to kind of cut back in what they were doing. And then the German scientists were losing interest in it. They felt they had gone beyond that and had mastered it all, and through political machinations of one kind or another, I don't know exactly how von Braun got into the Redstone Arsenal, but the artillery people of the Army led them to Huntsville, Alabama. They just completely relocated and abandoned what was a significant undertaking out at White Sands. And still is, for that matter.

Paul Stillwell: Well, did your studies start going beyond the German tests and looking at new potential?

Admiral Meyer: Can you elucidate a little bit more?

Paul Stillwell: Well, you said you had the data from the German tests. Were you then projecting forward on what you could do to get beyond that?

---

* The German V-1 was a pulse-jet flying bomb, also known as a "doodlebug" and "buzz bomb." It was 25 feet long and had a 16-foot wingspan. It carried a one-ton warhead some 150 miles (later increased to 250) at a speed of about 400 miles per hour.
The V-2 rocket bomb was first successfully fired on 3 October 1942 at Peenemünde, Germany. It was a liquid-fuel rocket, 46 feet long and weighing 13 tons. It carried a one-ton warhead. The German V-2 offensive against the Allies began in September 1944 and ended in March 1945.

Admiral Meyer: Well, I don't know that we as students were, but we had people telling us we could. And, of course, von Braun and his people believed very intensely they could go beyond that, and they felt very strongly about being able to accrue enough total impulse to be able to escape earth's gravity. And, parenthetically, that's what this firing that *Lake Erie* was going to do tonight and now is perhaps deferred till tomorrow, is a matter of whether you can amass enough impulse to get to that target.[*] And here we have this little piss-ant, 13½-inch missiles, that's how big it is.

Paul Stillwell: Diameter.

Admiral Meyer: Yeah. That's how big it is. And we get a total impulse out of there that blows your mind, contrasted to what you could get 50 years ago. And in many cases we use a lot of the same materials. So it is a matter of impulse. Specific impulse counts like specific everything counts as the quality of the material you're using, but total matters too [chuckle]. You've got to get so many thousand pounds to get someplace.

Paul Stillwell: You were mentioning the close air support and the applications in Korea. Did that have any connection with what you were doing? I mean, they were using rockets as part of that.

Admiral Meyer: I can't say that it did. The only connection that it had that I recall was officership. Because, interesting enough, we didn't do very much drinking. While the commanding general had let us be members of the officers' club, there still yet was not a great deal of socializing.

But I don't want to overdo that seven months. At the end of seven months you run out of material, and so we were put on the road and we traveled the next five months.

Paul Stillwell: Do tell.

---

[*] On 21 February 2008, the Aegis cruiser *Lake Erie* (CG-70) hit an earth satellite with a modified SM-3 Standard missile. The satellite was by then dead and falling from earth orbit. The interception took place 130 miles above the Pacific Ocean.

Admiral Meyer: Well, we traveled around the United States the next five months. We were just going from lab to lab to company to company. The first one we went to was North American in Lakewood, and we spent a few days there, of those engineers and those scientists talking to us.[*] And that's where we started becoming imbued with the questions that you're asking, of what escape was possible, and the possibility of navigation. Because navigation is dependent on your ability to tell time. Once you know how to tell time, then you can start navigating pretty damn good.

And so this whole world was an awesome world to a young person like myself, who just had no idea that I would ever be a piece of this or part of this. I wasn't any scientist. Or you could not say that I was a great engineer or any of those things. I had gone to school in the subjects, I had studied them. I had practiced only in a limited way. I was a naval officer. And so I was awed at what was happening here in front of me.

Paul Stillwell: Would it be fair to say that it was partly a matter of chance that that's the school you got sent to at that time? You had applied for a number of schools, you said.

Admiral Meyer: I had. I had. And God the Father has been awfully good to me in steering me to the right place at the right time, to the right people at the right time.

So we traveled back and forth from out of Fort Bliss, and I finally took baby and wife back to Boston and left them there till I settled down again.

Paul Stillwell: What were some of the other places you visited besides North American?

Admiral Meyer: Well, the big laboratories. We visited the plant visits, laboratories. We spent two or maybe three weeks at China Lake.[†] Big time in China Lake because China Lake had big aspirations, plus they had Michelson and really impressive scientists. The Michelson Lab was in gestation, they were getting ready to build that. They had big ideas on what the future world was.

---

[*] North American Aviation had a plant on Lakewood Boulevard in Downey, California.
[†] China Lake is another name for the Naval Ordnance Test Station near Inyokern, California.

Paul Stillwell: Well, they were working on Sidewinder.* That came out of there.

Admiral Meyer: The Sidewinder came out of there, but that was their only product I could ever find. [Laughter] The people don't like it when I say that. But it was an impressive product.

Paul Stillwell: Well, that's right.

Admiral Meyer: And an enduring one. It was an enduring product. What some people are not grasping or understanding—Sidewinder is an example, and Standard's the other—is how enduring those programs have been.† How we settled in to those programs as our basic ordnance. I think that that's not talked about enough, not given enough credit, but what the hell. So we've decided we don't have to raise any ordnance people anymore, and we aren't. We aren't schooling ordnance people, we aren't schooling engineers in that. The graduate school's not doing it, and there's no encouragement outside of the services to do it. It's thought to be very, very narrow, narrow field. Well, it's not. It's the most advanced type of engineering you can get yourself into. And without some comprehensive grasp of mathematics you ain't going to do very well.

Paul Stillwell: What about Johns Hopkins APL?‡ What was the contribution there?

Admiral Meyer: APL was working on the three T's, but primarily Terrier. And so APL was joined with Convair in San Diego. The first time I met Alex Kossiakoff, who became the great director of the Applied Physics Laboratory—he's in the graveyard now—was in one of those big hangars out at San Diego, because he was out in Convair

---

* Sidewinder is an air-to-air infrared-homing missile with a speed of approximately Mach 2.5. It has been operational, in various forms, since 1956. It was used extensively in the Vietnam War. For details, see Ron Westrum, *Sidewinder: Creative Missile Development at China Lake* (Annapolis, Maryland: Naval Institute Press, 1999). Dr. W. B. McLean of the Naval Ordnance Test Center at China Lake, California, is generally considered the project's main developer.
† The RIM-66 Standard missile is a medium-range surface-to-air missile developed for the U.S. Navy as a successor to the RIM-2 Terrier and the RIM-24 Tartar. Standard first went into service in 1967.
‡ APL/JHU—Applied Physics Laboratory, Johns Hopkins University.

trying to teach them out there how to do soldering.* The operative word in APL is "A"—Applied. And that's the operative word in Aegis. I have to be careful where I say that because, of course, people's visions get bent.

I always say that the worst thing we have done is let experimentation get into industry. That's what we've done in OSD today. Industry is engineers and builders, not experimenters. So right now, let's just take the DDG-1000.† And we've got all of these incredible programs, some thirteen of them, tied to this one ship. And spending literally billions, billions, in development related to it.

Paul Stillwell: And a lot of time.

Admiral Meyer: Oh, a terrible lot of time. But we've got little assurance that it will come out. Little assurance. How crazy can we get? How crazy can we get? So the idea of development work is of itself significant, not connected or tied to something else. Now we get these efficiency experts: Well, wait a minute; if you don't have it tied to something I ain't going to spend the money. So now you're required to forecast or predict the outcome. Just like, I'll ask you. Who do you think's going to be the next President?

Paul Stillwell: Barack Obama.

Admiral Meyer: Are you sure?

Paul Stillwell: No, of course not. [Laughter]

Admiral Meyer: Exactly. Exactly. You're not sure at all. Hell, he might get hit by a truck next week.

---

* Alexander Ivanovitch Kossiakoff (1914-2005) was born in St. Petersburg, Russia. He immigrated to the United States in 1923. After many years that included missile development work for the Johns Hopkins Applied Physics Laboratory, Dr. Kossiakoff became director in 1969 and remained in that post until his retirement in 1980.
† Guided missile destroyers of the *Zumwalt* (DDG-1000) class are being built to a radical new design that is intended to produce a stealthy, low-profile radar signature. Construction of the *Zumwalt* began in October 2008 at Bath Iron Works, Bath, Maine; the ship is scheduled for delivery to the Navy in 2013.

Paul Stillwell: That could happen.

Admiral Meyer: So that's the situation we're in. We can't be positive on those things.

I happen to believe that the old Navy was not that bad, or for that matter it was pretty damned good.

Paul Stillwell: Well, if you look at the five years from, say '51 to '56, there was a lot of progress in that time in guided missiles in the U.S. Navy.

Admiral Meyer: Oh, yeah, you bet your ass. And I was right in the middle of that. And I think often about how, again, how God the Father had put me in the middle of this.

Paul Stillwell: And BuPers [chuckle].

Admiral Meyer: Right. Right there in that period. Sometimes I get carried away on it, and of course my boys don't even like for me to talk about it. They get tired of hearing from me, because I get rambunctious on it. And Anna Mae doesn't want me to talk about it.[*] "Everybody's heard that." Well, I don't know whether they have or not. It's still pretty damned awesome.

You say to yourself: "How do you get a great fleet? How does a great fleet come about?" This Aegis fleet will go down as perhaps the greatest fleet in several centuries. It'll be a long time before that fleet's replaced. And few appreciate—I mean, I make myself feel bad, today, that that is our fleet. Today it *is* the fleet. I am the designer. It *is* our fleet. Now, did *I* do that? Of course not, but I led it. And you beg the question: Well, could anybody do it? I don't know. I've had officers, say to me, and particularly jealous admirals, "Well, if I'd been given as much money as you've been given, I'd have been good too."

I finally got so my answer to them was, "Well, why didn't you go get the money?" [Laughter] Because that's how I got it. I went and got it.

---

[*] Anna Mae Meyer was the admiral's second wife.

Paul Stillwell: Well, that's a good note to end on, and let's pick up the next chapter next week.

Admiral Meyer: Let's do that, right.

Paul Stillwell: Thank you.

Admiral Meyer: Thank you.

Interview Number 5 with Rear Admiral Wayne E. Meyer, U.S. Navy (Retired)
Place: Admiral Meyer's office in Arlington, Virginia
Date: Friday, 29 February 2008

Paul Stillwell: I wonder, just to start off, since it's fresh in your mind, if you want to talk about the experience last week with the *Lake Erie* and the shoot-down of the satellite.

Admiral Meyer: If you like.

Paul Stillwell: Was it a coincidence that this was the same ship that your wife had sponsored?[*]

Admiral Meyer: Well, some might think it was coincidental, but I pushed from day one that it was determined that we were going to do these early workups on ballistic missilery, and we were going to do it out of Pearl because that was where the range was. And we were going to have to pay a pretty significant amount of money in upgrading the range. The last upgrade of the range occurred by me and an admiral by the name of Fred Backman, who's in the graveyard now.[†] He was an aviator-engineer, and he was the project manager for the Seahawk helo, and eventually had ComNavElex.[‡] But he also commanded the Pacific Missile Range. So he and I always worked together pretty closely about the importance of the range, and we put up a lot of money to modernize the range. The Navy had no planning structure at all. And we had a couple guys over in OSD who didn't stand in our way. If we put up the money they'd let it be done, so the range was living off of that. That's where we did all the Aegis work.

Recall the Aegis ships are the first effort by the Navy where we had some form of free play in evaluating the ships and in qualifying them. For the first time we'd put a ship on the range at Kauai, and she would qualify in surface and she'd qualify in ASW and

---

[*] USS *Lake Erie* (CG-70), a *Ticonderoga*-class guided missile cruiser, was built by Bath Iron Works of Bath, Maine. The ship's keel was laid 6 March 1990, launching on 13 July 1991, and commissioning on 24 July 1993. The sponsor was Mrs. Margaret Meyer, the admiral's first wife.
[†] As a captain, Fred M. Backman, USN, commanded the Pacific Missile Range facility, Barking Sands, Kauai, Hawaii
[‡] ComNavElex – Commander Naval Electronics Systems Command.

she'd qualify in surface-to-air, because we had submarines available that would work with us and we had targets that would work with us. And so we could shake the ship down in a pretty coordinated way. It's true that we did a lot of individual workups of those warfare areas, but there was also a lot of propinquity between those operations when she ran her SQTs.* Well, that still continues insofar as I know in some manner, but thanks to the behavior of an admiral that I won't mention the Navy has lost all of Puerto Rico and all of the Atlantic ranges, and there's going to be a day when we'll sadly regret that, of having let those ranges disappear, slip through our fingers. Because you can't get them back; you won't get them back. I mean, Culebra will be all vacation homes and any number of things.†

Well, so *Lake Erie* seemed to be a logical candidate because of availability, and the timeliness and everything of it, and that's how it kind of worked that way, and I had this soft spot, as you pointed out.

Paul Stillwell: Of course [chuckle].

Admiral Meyer: Captain Mac Grant was the first project manager, and he kind of retained me as his lackey.‡ He said, "Well, I just need you maybe for four or five months, Admiral, to help us get started and get us pointed the right way." Well, here I am, and I think this is the 12th year and we're still pointing them. And I think it's a big piece of the reason for the Navy's success. It wasn't our brilliance of the senior advisory team so much as it was the experience and the effort to use the experience, the effort to use it. I mean, we couldn't apply the experience if the young people didn't want to do it. Well, Mac Grant did want to do it, and so he kind of set it in motion, and he was followed

---
* SQT – ship qualification trials.
† Culebra, an island in the Caribbean, is 17 miles west of Puerto Rico. In 1939, the U.S. Navy began using the island as a target for gunnery and bombing practice. That lasted until 1975, when the target practice moved to the island of Vieques.
‡ Captain Peter McPherson Grant III, USN, program director of the Aegis Ballistic Missile Defense Project.

by Kate Paige.[*] And now this admiral, Brad Hicks, is using us all the time, as though we're kind of part of the project office.[†]

Paul Stillwell: How much involvement did your office have in the event last week?

Admiral Meyer: Well, I personally had none, but several of the members on my team were involved with the admiral, because they were, in a security bight they're wrestling over it. I mean, I don't know, we have to rediscover and rediscover that you can't get anything done without telling people something. You can't just go do it by yourself; it won't work. So I don't want to claim any credit because there's none to be claimed. There are plenty of people already claiming plenty of credit. But that operation was possible for the previous work had been done and associated with the senior advisory team on the test programs that had been established.

So the base was set there, and the base was available for the admiral to adjust and to put the BMD teams to work.[‡] Because most of it involved coefficients changes in the algorithms. And, well, wait a minute, what's the right number? So between the labs and the two industrial bases and also CSEDS—they ran a lot of work at CSEDS at Moorestown, a hell of a lot.[§] It really paid off.

I remember the bitching, the goddamned carrying on, bitching, for—I want to say her name. As far as I know, she's still in charge of radar over in MDA.[**] She's got a PhD. I almost said it then. I wanted to say Sandy, but it's not Sandy. She was dead set against us spending the money upgrading APL on the missile, dead set against it. Well, I finally ended up forcing it down their throats, and we rebuilt the laboratory for missile work at APL in conjunction with Tucson. First of all, it's turned out to work well, but

---

[*] Rear Admiral Kathleen K. Paige, USN, served from 2003 to 2005 as Program Director, Aegis Ballistic Missile Defense.
[†] Rear Admiral Alan B. Hicks, USN, served from 2005 to 2009 as Program Director, Aegis Ballistic Missile Defense.
[‡] BMD – ballistic missile defense.
[§] CSEDS – Combat System Engineering Development Site, Moorestown, New Jersey, an integral part of the Aegis program.
[**] MDA – the Missile Defense Agency, part of the Department of Defense, is charged with protecting the United States against ballistic missile attack.

it's had extraordinary payoff with the lab participation and Raytheon doing the engineering work. Really extraordinary payoff.

We had created in the countdown over the years something called the Three Amigos, so at every program review we had the manager from APL, the manager from Tucson, and the manager from Moorestown. They'd all get up on their feet. The whole half a day would be spent with them making a composite report on how they were doing. So this really was an incredible team-building thing, because people became a part of the team, and they were kind of able to sort out the apportionment of the labor because Admiral Hicks made it clear who was in charge where, and they all accepted that and went to work. And that still goes on.

Paul Stillwell: Was the shot last week the longest range that Aegis has made a hit?

Admiral Meyer: Well, and it exceeded the capability of the missile. It exceeded its capability, which was one of our big concerns. Combined with that, it meant that we had to wait till the last possible instant. This shot window was literally only seconds. Some people could tell you that window was a small as six seconds. I mean, the decision had to be made and had to be made aboard ship, and it had to be made by that crew, because there wasn't time to contemplate it. And they made it. This was made by officers and the petty officers. This was all made by the military crew of the ship. It was all made by them.

We had a number of civilians aboard, and they were there for various reasons, the biggest one being data collection, and also watching after the adequacy of the setup of the data collection and the undertaking. But there was no civilian participation in the conduct of the operation—none.

As a matter of fact, that's been true since day one in Aegis. And you'll find today yet, if there is an exercise to be evaluated at Moorestown at the CSEDS, now called the James Doyle Combat Systems Engineering Development Site, that exercise must include the sailors and the officers.[*] Lockheed now has this habit after all these years, that

---

[*] Vice Admiral James H. Doyle, Jr., USN, served as Deputy Chief of Naval Operations (Surface Warfare) from August 1975 to September 1980. His backing was of great importance in the success of Aegis.

they're not going to waste their time running a demo for the Navy without the sailors in the seats. Contractors don't cut it. So the sailors have developed this relationship and such that they *are* part of the design and they *are* part of the system, and they *do* review it and they *do* comment on it and they *do* participate in it.

And so—I'm digressing again—I was really very pleased, because I was up at Moorestown Tuesday and Admiral Hicks flew up. Of course, he's flying around congratulating everybody, including the speeches he gave up there; it's very nice. But one of them was retiring our super chief.[*] The engineering site up there rates a super chief, not a master chief, and he had retired and a new one's come in. Well, we had a retirement ceremony for him, and the admiral spoke at it, and it was very well done as a retirement ceremony. All the sailors were in attendance and all the civilians who work there. It was quite a nice-size crowd. And you couldn't help but feel, if you were me, this sense of extraordinary pride of all these people who have been involved.

There are virtually no original people left; they've all retired or died or something. But in an undertaking like that normally people—oh, let's see, here's an ad where Moorestown's trying to hire people to work on azimuths; I think I'll go apply for a job. So people take a job not with the idea that it's going to be a career. We have sons now, we may have some grandsons, and we have a lot of daughters who have come into Aegis whose fathers started and retired and brought their kids into it. And these people are dedicated Aegis-philes. I mean, they're just dedicated. That's been their whole career. That's their profession. To me that's just mind-blowing. That's their profession. I mean, it's one of my great unsung accomplishments. Not many people see it, not many people understand it, not many people grasp it. And you get me started on it, I can bore you pretty damn quick on it.

Paul Stillwell: Well, if we could get back to the missile shoot, then, please [chuckle].

Admiral Meyer: Yeah. Well, I'm building up to that.

---

[*] "Super chief" refers to a senior chief petty officer, pay grade E-8; the only higher enlisted pay grade is E-9, master chief petty officer.

Paul Stillwell: I've read several news accounts, and I was curious why there was not a warhead.

Admiral Meyer: Well, the Standard Missile 3 has no warhead. That *is* the warhead.

Paul Stillwell: I see.

Admiral Meyer: That *is* the warhead. I wish we wouldn't say it. I tried, in my early days, to get it squared away. Well, the best I rammed down with my constant nagging with Mac Grant was that it came to be called in the Navy the kinetic warhead. So we got this word that was acceptable to the public. The Air Force didn't know what to do with it. The old ordnance people could finally handle it when it had the word "warhead" in it someplace. [Laughter] So we called it a kinetic warhead. What it really is is the final stage of the missile. Depending how you count it, it's the fourth stage or the fifth stage. And the only way you kill the target is that you've got to hit it.

Well, wait a minute. We even call out where we're going to hit it. And if you go look at the record, it will blow your mind. You're looking at that missile sitting up there, that model, which is an old Terrier model. But today's missile that comes out of that hole is about that long. But hell, it's got two boosters, it's got midcourse—I mean, we've got everything hung on that thing we can hang on it, because in the end how far you can get determines how much poop you've got. So impulse matters, total impulse.

So what happens is, it starts falling away. The first thing that falls away is that one, it starts falling away, falling away. By the time she gets up in the heavens you've only got that one piece left, and it literally is flying of its own self with its own set of engines. And that is what we in the business call the warhead. So it *is* the warhead, kinetic warhead, because that warhead maneuvers. It's got its own engines. And commands to the missile are no longer coming from the ship. The ship has already waved goodbye, and already the commands have been sent that are going to be sent. And now that stage is on its own, and it's its problem to hit the target where we tell it to hit the target.

So if you look at the warhead it's maybe this size. Just say it's this length.

Paul Stillwell: Three or four feet long.

Admiral Meyer: Yeah. It's something of that nature, say. And you want to hit it in, say, about 18 inches from the nose in order to get maximum destruction of it. So you even aim at a point on the damned thing. And we come within centimeters. Our accuracy is phenomenal. It is something that could not be done that's come out of this design.

And so you asked me, and now I'll bore you and wear you out. I'm the founder of the system design which this has to fit into. And as I spent the last two days up there, there's not a person there that's been there longer than I have. Moorestown has had this incredible refresh ability that I've always loved. There is an Italian culture and a Jewish culture within that area, and most of the engineers attended some regional schools, and they get great engineering educations. And they have a work culture and a social culture that I've never met in all my years of working in outfits. They do whatever's got to be done. They just don't worry about the hours; they worry about whether they're doing what's got to be done. And they are very anxious to respond to their Navy leaders and they do it.

And, of course, there's grand elation this week up there from all of them, and rightfully so. They knew in the CSEDS at Moorestown virtually the same instant that the ship knew, because we have devices in the warhead, the final stages, which do transmit back. I don't know whether you've ever seen it. We have some unclassified stuff you might be interested in sometime. But the last, usually I think it's between four and six seconds we get the video that's sent down that shows—we can tell if she's locked on. We see it locked on just a few seconds before. We don't yet know where it's going to hit. And you watch it. If you get it locked on, you're going to do it. You're going to do something. And when that sucker hits, I mean the whole screen just goes kah-plah; there ain't nothing left. It disintegrates.

Paul Stillwell: I saw some video on television and that was dramatic.

Admiral Meyer: Yeah, it is. It is dramatic. You can't help but get chills run up in you, and you can't help but be excited when you see it. It is incredible what it does. You're sitting there watching, and all of a sudden you see this little blinking that starts in the middle of this picture on the screen. You see it blinking and blinking, and it just brings tears to your eyes. It's only a few seconds—pyowk. She goes. So that's our evaluation. So there's no warhead in a traditional sense.

Paul Stillwell: No explosive warhead.

Admiral Meyer: None. Zero. Zero. She homes in, and this is not classified, I'm pretty sure. See, they started about Christmas and gussied up the missile some, because we didn't design the missile to do this. And so we did change some of the homing technique. But it was really down in the noise unless you're an engineer messing around. So we modified the missile for this special undertaking. We did not nullify the missile; we just modified the coefficients in the equations, because we're going to do something that's not part of our repertoire. And as you, I'm sure, read in the paper, we had several backup missiles, and those missiles have been returned to the arsenal. They were brought back to Hawaii and sent to the depot. The modifiers that were put in them have been taken out, and they've been put back in a magazine. So it was relatively modest.

However, neither did we have any, any empirical proof whatsoever. All we had were the simulations. No empirical data at all, and that ain't my style. So that's hard. That's really, really hard. Well, I didn't have anything to do with advising them there. They're all my sons. I raised them all. They knew what the hell to do, and they did it.

Paul Stillwell: Well, they've got the empirical data now [chuckle].

Admiral Meyer: Pisspots full. Today and yesterday, over in Congress, you've got the several geniuses. They want all the fleet modified *now*. Just do it now. Well, that's BS, but they want it done now. Let's get this capability in all ships. Well, our problem—back to your original question—I think technically we went something better than 130 miles. Which really is right on the edge of the poop, right on the edge. And it's really testing the stability of the design. Because our tactical planning does not go that distance; we have not planned that far. Because, as you know, ordnance people are big margin people, so they like to keep margin. So I don't know whether she'd have had any more poop or not. Can't tell.

So they went and counted and counted and counted, counted, until there were only a few seconds—literally. The guy at the console had to make the decision. There was no time for discussion. They rehearsed and practiced this ahead of time. So they counted and counted, and it was a decision, go/no-go. Close the trigger or not close the trigger, because there was no time to have a discussion. And it turned out to be the right way.

Paul Stillwell: Thank you. That was interesting.

Admiral Meyer: Oh, it was tearful. It was tearful. I was over sitting in the MIC at MDA, Anna Mae and I, watching it, and you couldn't help but cry if you were part of it.[*] Just can't.

I want to say a closing word about this firing operation. It came up yesterday when I was talking to some young people about it: "What about the future? What is going to happen, Admiral?" And I got to talking about my being ordered to that school, and how few people there were who believed that you could escape.

Wernher von Braun and his band were located at White Sands, the range, and several lectures we got from him the time I was in that school, for that year—if you could understand them. Their brogue was so tough that it was really hard to hear them. But he felt very, very strongly about the ability to escape earth's gravity. All you had to do was get enough impulse. And I believe down here, and I think you'll find if you read the books enough, discord broke out in the Army. And really, they finally found a scheme to get rid of those guys out of White Sands and shipped them to the Arsenal at Huntsville, because they had so many diversionary things going on the range couldn't focus on what it thought its assignment was.[†]

But if you were to drive into White Sands today from Las Cruces—it would be hard to notice it, because there ain't nothing but desert wherever you're going, so you're

---
[*] MIC – management information center.
[†] The Army's Redstone Arsenal in Huntsville, Alabama.

going down the highway. You go through a modest gate with a couple posts, and you keep on driving because you're still, hell, I don't know, 12-15 miles from headquarters. And you look up on your port hand, and those mountains, the back sides of the Sandias and the mountains down south of there, there's a lot of granite in those mountains, big granites. It's one of the reasons that caused the missile range to land there, the granite.

Paul Stillwell: You mentioned that last time.

Admiral Meyer: And so you'd see up there on the side of a mountain what looks like some abandoned operation, which it is. I mean, they may have reactivated, I haven't been there for a number of years. Finally, to quiet von Braun down, the Army had agreed to undertake, with support from the DoD, to build a 500,000-pound static test stand. This was revolutionary. We had no test stand of even approximately that size. The engine was going to be mounted vertically in the test stand and the issue was how to handle the deflection of the heat and the fire from the engine. And it was going to be blasted out through this granite, which could stand it and handle it and deflect it. And I refer to it—I don't know whether there's anybody else even knows it anymore—as the monument to von Braun. Because in the middle of it was when they all got shipped to Alabama. And I think it got used for two or three things in the ensuing years.

And also, aided by the Army, went to the mountains—I want to say the Santa Susana Mountains, which are north of Los Angeles—and went up in those mountains, and there is a good deal of granite, and the test stands emerged there. This was before they moved up to south of San Francisco and started all the firings up there. In the Santa Susanas it turned out the granite was built in a way that they could put the missile engine in a vertical stand and fire it from that river, whatever the name of that river was—it may be the Santa Susana River. But they could pump massive gobs of water down the mountainside and could carry away this heat that had to get carried away. So that was the undertaking, and I believe North American had been hired as one of the patrons to help the Army do that. So for a number of years—I don't think it's active anymore—but it was very, very active in my time when I was going to that school. And we'd have these discussions on whether you could escape from the earth or not.

Paul Stillwell: Yes, we covered that last time.

Admiral Meyer: Okay, that's good. I mean, the equation says you could. It just defied your imagination. So it that enough on that?

Paul Stillwell: Yes. After Fort Bliss, you received additional training. Please cover that.

Admiral Meyer: When I came out of this school in Fort Bliss, Texas, I had orders to report to Sandia in Albuquerque, and oh, was I depressed.* I'd just made lieutenant, and every friend that I knew, junior officer, petty officers, and warrant officers who had gone into special weapons was never to return. And I knew that my fate was sealed as myself and my partner, Lieutenant Richard Stansfield—now in the graveyard—we were ordered to Sandia Base for special weapons training, and it was depressing.

Well, it turned out that it was just a way stop for a couple, three months, because we were to undergo training on the atomic bomb. And at that time the in-service bomb was rapidly becoming the Mark 6 bomb. The Mark 4 was before that. Recollect, these bombs were 60 inches in diameter, and the Mark 4 weighed 20,000 pounds. The Mark 6, which we were undergoing training on, weighed 10,000 pounds. And we were to train and qualify on that. Because it turned out that we were going to go, and I was going to be in a team of seven officers that were ordered to Norfolk, Virginia, and there we were to open up a new school to train or orient naval officers and civilians in atomic weapons, including weapons employment.

Weapons employment was quite a significant task, because you had to do fuze settings, you had to select ground zero, and select elevations and stuff like that. You got a certificate. You had to have a certificate to be an employment officer in that era when that first started. And our school there, for the employment part, was some eight weeks or nine weeks in duration, wherein we graduated you and certified to the Navy and to an outfit called AFSWP, which is the Armed Forces Special Weapons Project, a DoD outfit, that you had studied and matriculated through the requisite material to be labeled as an employment officer.

---

* Sandia was the site of a nuclear weapons development facility in New Mexico.

Well, and then we put literally thousands through the school in the next three years on orientation, and that orientation was a three-day course on what was an atomic bomb, how did uranium work, and stuff like that. We were opening it up.

The Mark 5 bomb was to be 45 inches in diameter, and the Mark 7 bomb, in development, was going to be 30 inches in diameter. Now, at that time the Navy had built the AJ airplane, contract North American, and the AJ airplane had only one purpose, and that was to deliver the Mark 6 bomb from the deck of an aircraft carrier.[*] Well, wait a minute here. The AJ airplane had a crew of three, one of which was the bomb commander. Well, it so happened that I had on the staff with me Lieutenant Richard DePrez, an aviator who was a qualified bomb commander, one of the very, very few.[†] He had stepped out of an AJ, and he didn't want that experience no more. But they had to make the selections the way they had been made by the two admirals, at the time captains, at the Nagasaki and Hiroshima bomb attacks.

Paul Stillwell: That was Parsons and Ashworth.[‡]

Admiral Meyer: Yeah, Parsons. Thank you.

At that time the Navy had a big station at Port Lyautey in Morocco, and we sortied the bombs from Port Lyautey, because we couldn't handle these AJ airplanes in the attack carriers. The carriers could handle them as visitors, but they couldn't maintain them or take care of them. So the bombs were resident in the carrier, and the AJ would sortie from Port Lyautey. It would land aboard the ship to get the bomb.

Several of my friends ended up in those teams, called SWUs, special weapons units. They were primarily aboard carriers for assembling bombs. And by the way, most

---

[*] The AJ Savage was a propeller-driven carrier-based nuclear strike aircraft built by North American Aviation, Inc. It first entered the fleet in squadron VC-5 in September 1949. It was reclassified A-2 in 1962. The AJ-1 version was 63 feet long; wingspan of 75 feet; gross weight of 52,862 pounds; and top speed of 471 miles per hour. It had a maximum bomb capacity of 12,000 pounds.
[†] Lieutenant Richard J. DePrez, USN.
[‡] Captain William S. Parsons, USN, was involved in the development of the atomic bomb in New Mexico. During the mission of 6 August 1945, Parsons was the weaponeer on board the B-29 named "Enola Gay" that dropped the bomb on Hiroshima, Japan. See Al Christman, *Target Hiroshima: Deak Parsons and the Creation of the Atomic Bomb* (Annapolis: Naval Institute Press, 1998).
Commander Frederick L. Ashworth, USN, was involved in the atomic bomb development. During the mission of 9 August 1945 against Nagasaki, Japan, Ashworth was the weaponeer on board the B-29 "Bocks Car." The oral history of Ashworth, who retired as a vice admiral, is in the Naval Institute collection.

of the team members going to school with me in Fort Bliss ended up in GMUs, guided missile units, and a number of them on patrol planes. The crews didn't assemble those bombs; you had to have special units to do it. Well, I never was part of a unit. I went to this school. It turned out I was there three years.

I enlisted in the United States Navy in 1943. I've told you that. And I was offered the opportunity sometime in 1948 to get transferred to the regular Navy. I applied for it, because I kind of liked it and I thought it was a good deal. I was selected, so I became a regular officer in the United States Navy in 1948. But I was sitting in a wardroom full of Naval Academy graduates. You don't have to be on a turnip truck a long time to understand that you ain't competitive at all. We see this bullshit today about how strife goes on amongst the inside of the Navy, and who's in and who's out, and so forth. I mean, in 1948, in comparison, it was, like, *bad*. A Reserve was nothing.

Well, by the early 1950s I was getting serious about a career. Here I was now in atomic weapons, then called special weapons, and it turned out I was a pretty good teacher. Repeatedly I was complimented on the courses. We ran at least two a month, and they'd be three days long. We'd have anywhere from 60 to 80 people, very senior.

Paul Stillwell: Who were the students?

Admiral Meyer: They were admirals, generals out of the Marine Corps, colonels, captains, GS-16s, some political appointees.[*] They were all senior people. It was strictly for senior officers, and I met ten jillion of them. Well, they kind of liked me, so I decided I knew how to teach pretty well, that I had the ability to do that if I worked on it. I liked the subjects, and I did a lot of research on them. I taught one course 76 times, and I never tired of repeating it. One of the reasons was that I changed it every time. The other was that there wasn't anybody could dispute me. [Laughter] So to some degree you could say what you wanted to say.

Paul Stillwell: What was the classification level in that course?

---

[*] GS, for general schedule, designates a pay grade level within the U.S. Civil Service.

Admiral Meyer: It started out as top secret, and rapidly it changed to secret because it turned out there couldn't be enough. I don't know who changed it, maybe the Secretary, the CNO. The idea was we needed to get a lot of officers oriented, and one of the reasons it was at Norfolk is that spaces were there. We were over at the LantFlt headquarters, and they rebuilt a whole wing for us.* They provided a whole bunch of bombs for us to teach—of course, with no fissile material in them. And the training for the heavy attack squadrons was at Norfolk Naval Air Station, so it was a good choice. Plus, it was close to Washington, D.C. I was there for around three years.

My commanding officer was Commander Harry Marvinsmith. He had been a destroyer captain. I admired him a great deal. But he was an ex-reserve. His buddy was the chief of officer detailing in the Bureau of Personnel at that time, and they had talked about the General Line School because Marvinsmith had gone to it. It was over a year long, and it had started—I believe I'm correct; this might be a little in error—started in Annapolis and they did it at Newport, and it was to train gobs of reserve officers in things of the line.

Paul Stillwell: Well, a lot of it was for aviators who knew how to fly planes but not about the rest of the Navy.

Admiral Meyer: That's correct. So I kept talking to my CO, and I said, "You know, I can't see how I'm competitive in the structure, because there are just so many things I don't know. For example, I'd never had any formal schooling in navigation or any of those kinds of things. Everything I learned I learned myself in the ships.

Well, the school had been moved to Monterey. One of the reasons it was moved out there was to populate the school, to try to ensure that the school was going to survive. It was the goddamn line school, which they tried to cut it to six months. Well, they couldn't get away with that, so technically they were able to retain it, as I recall at the time, something like nine months, so you could have permanent change of orders.

When my time was up there—Calvert was the name of the detailer, Captain Calvert—to cut me a set of orders to send me to the General Line School. And I thought,

---

* LantFlt – Atlantic Fleet.

"Well, you know, I'll be competitive now." And I was also going to get a set of orders, which followed from Calvert later, ordering me as executive officer in a radar destroyer escort, USS *Strickland*, which will be another story where I went on a contiguous line for a year and then I was on the DEW Line for a year.

Well, that's how I ended up in line school. It's the last class. It was an interesting class because, of course, it was full of these aviators you mentioned. Hell, I was a rarity in the class; there weren't any black shoes in the class at all.*

Well, what bothered me that year is the aviators really had trouble, as you point out. They were ordered in gobs to Monterey in what was known at the five-term program, where they took five semesters to get a master's degree. Quite a few of them failed, didn't make it. They had a hard time in line school, and they had a hard time in such things as navigation and a maneuvering board and things like that.† This really bothered me. I mean, how in the hell can an aviator have trouble in those subjects? I mean, I thought that was the very core of what you learned as an aviator.

It turned out that I sailed through line school. I had no problem at all. Hell, I didn't have to study or do anything. As a matter of fact, by the third month or so I was doing a lot of teaching myself. Teaching, examining.

That's how I got there.

Paul Stillwell: Well, was that more of a ticket-punch than really an advancement of your training and education?

Admiral Meyer: That's all, as far as I was concerned. I was a reserve, and I was in trouble, and if I wanted to be in the regular Navy I had to get my ticket punched, and the only way I could get it punched was line school.

Paul Stillwell: What do you remember about the courses you took there?

---

* In the early days of naval aviation, the aviators wore brown shoes with their khaki uniforms and green uniforms. They thus acquired the nickname "brown shoes" to distinguish them from the traditional surface ship officers, who are known as "black shoes."
† A maneuvering board is a sheet of paper containing a compass rose, concentric circles, and logarithmic scales. It is used for working out relative motion problems for ships that are maneuvering.

Admiral Meyer: Probably the ones I enjoyed more than anything were maneuvering board and navigation. I knew a great deal about them from a practical viewpoint, but I had a couple of really good teachers, lieutenant commanders. I ended up kind of leading one of the teams at the time, and I probably enjoyed that. I learned more about it, and I got a better feel for relative motion than I ever thought I'd get. And I learned a hell of a lot about celestial navigation, which I did not heretofore know except what the chief quartermaster taught me. So that's my memory. And we had a good time. We had a really good time while I was there.

Paul Stillwell: Were you able to take your family to Monterey?

Admiral Meyer: I was. My wife was going to have a baby, our second baby, and I had left her with her mother in Boston, just as I had earlier. My first wife had three babies. I never saw any of them born. Two of them were born in Chelsea Navy Hospital, one was born in Newport Naval Hospital. Both were very fine hospitals, and it worked out real well with me not being there anytime.

I got a few days off and was able to go back, and by driving night and day brought her to Monterey. We rented a house up on the mountainside up there.

She couldn't drive, and transportation was not very good in Monterey around through the forest as I took her. I finally made up my mind how I was going to handle her, because she just couldn't stand the thought of not going to church. Finally one morning she got up and got herself all ready for Mass and she said, "Why aren't you getting ready? We've got to be here at 9:00 o'clock Mass. Why aren't you getting ready? I've got the babies ready."

I said, "Well, I've decided I'm not going to go." And we had a fight right there.

"Well, why aren't you going?"

I said, "If you want to go to Mass, you're going to drive yourself. I'll take care of the children." Finally she got so pissed she walked out of that house with her Irish temper, she jumped in the goddamn car and drove off. [Laughter] She went to Mass and came back and she drove ever since. She never missed a day after that.

Paul Stillwell: Well, did you miss church after that?

Admiral Meyer: No. I kept going to church. [Laughter] But really, I had to take her right to the line that morning. That really took her down. It took me several weeks to build up my nerve to do it.

Paul Stillwell: So that was a premeditated plan.

Admiral Meyer: Oh, yeah, it was. Well, to a degree it was premeditated. I couldn't be sure it was going to work, but it turned out it worked. She just had that fright, that little bit of fright.

Paul Stillwell: But you got her mad enough to get her motivated.

Admiral Meyer: I did. Once I got her Irish temper up, that pushed her over the brink. And Mass did it, because that was important enough that she was going to get there somehow, even if she had to call a taxi. And so from then on things were just fine.

Paul Stillwell: That is a beautiful area of the country. Did you get an opportunity to take advantage of that?

Admiral Meyer: We did. We did. I'm trying to figure out where I was transferred to then. It was back East. So we took all the time we could get. We liked to travel, even with the kids, and we'd drive north. One year we drove north—I think it was the second time I was at Monterey—and we spent a few days in Canada. We traveled all over, and we had a wonderful time. Because it turns out—you've probably experienced this—kids see the country as whatever their age is, so you could go take them in two years and they'd see a whole different thing as they're maturing and growing up. So we did a little camping and a little living around, whatever we could afford. We couldn't afford much, but we had a good time. One of the things that forced it into us is my folks lived in Missouri, so that would be the central place that we'd have to stop off at. Then the grandkids could visit and run around out on the farm, and we'd get all the laundry redone and stuff like that.

They were pretty nice years. They were rough years, hard work. She had never been even close to being a Navy wife, but she adapted very well to it. She adapted very well. She wanted to do what her husband wanted to do. She was one of those women.

Paul Stillwell: And that has made a difference in so many careers, whether an individual's wife was willing to do that.

Admiral Meyer: You know, it's interesting you should say that. In my counseling in the Navy I've said, "Look, if your wife doesn't like the Navy, you've either got to get a new wife, or you've got to get out of the Navy, because life is too miserable otherwise. You've got to get an accommodation." Sometimes, as you know, it didn't work out. They could not adapt to it. Because some women just can't. The fear of separation, even for a few days, is too much for them. Others handle it just fine. Others just roll with the punches on their kids, as long as they have a little confidence that they've got a dollar in their pocket and they're secure, they handle it just fine. It varies all over the place.

Paul Stillwell: I was talking to a helicopter pilot's wife yesterday, and she talked about the process of a deployment and how she's in charge then, and when her husband gets back they have to share the responsibility and the kids adjust, and then he goes away again.

Admiral Meyer: Right. Yeah. You know, it gets a little harder when the man tries to issue some guidance. They don't want to pay any attention. [Chuckle] They don't want to pay any attention. I had it happen to me. They go to say, well, "Mama, should I? Should I do what he says?" Because that can happen to you.

Paul Stillwell: Back to the special-weapons school. How much could you teach in a three-day course?

Admiral Meyer: We taught the gamut of whatever the national program was and what was releasable to the secret level. So, of those three days, probably a half a day would be devoted to target selection and employment effort, the way to go about it. A half a day would be devoted to how atomic bombs work and how they're made. Another half a day would be devoted to the national organization, which, of course, was quite large and quite complicated at that time. The Atomic Energy Commission was born and you had, I mentioned, AFSWP. AFSWP was a big outfit, and its field command was located at Sandia Base in Albuquerque. So there was plenty of material to teach to people. And then we had a couple talks that we made our CO give, a commander. He was a senior officer, and we made him talk to the people about tactical situations and what effect was the bomb going to have on behavior patterns.

At that time the so-called lob bombing technique was emerging with the F2H airplane, and an officer by the name of Julian Lake was one of the pioneers in that.[*]

Paul Stillwell: Electronic warfare specialist also.

Admiral Meyer: Yeah. He was going to deliver the Mark 7, which was 30 inches, and it was down to 1,600 pounds, which could be handled by the Banshee.[†]

Paul Stillwell: And the A4D was coming along also.[‡]

Admiral Meyer: Affirmative. Right, the A4D. But the A4D carried it internally; Banshee carried it externally. But you're right. I don't think the A4D ever carried the

---

[*] The loft bombing method was designed as a tactic to prevent airplanes from being damaged by their own nuclear bombs. The method called for the pilot to make a low-altitude approach to the target and pull up into the first part of a Cuban 8. The bomb would be released as the aircraft reached about 45-degree angle during the climb. The pilot then completed the half of the Cuban 8 and flew back in the direction from which he had made his approach. A nickname for the method was "idiot loop." Lieutenant Commander Julian S. Lake, USN.

[†] McDonnell's F2H Banshee was a jet-powered fighter-bomber that first entered the fleet with squadron VF-171 in March 1949. The F2H-2 version was 40 feet long, wingspan of 45 feet, gross weight of 22,312 pounds, and top speed of 532 miles per hour. It had four fixed forward-firing 20-millimeter guns and provision to carry two 500-pound bombs.

[‡] The Douglas A4D Skyhawk attack plane first entered the fleet in October 1956 in squadron VA-72. The A4D was 40 feet, 4 inches long; wingspan of 27 feet, 6 inches; gross weight of 24,500 pounds, and top speed of 670 miles per hour. In 1962 the aircraft was redesignated the A-4.

Mark 6. It carried the Mark 5, which was 40 or 44 inches, and its weight was down to about 3,000 pounds or so.*

Paul Stillwell: Did you have an input in this course from SAC?† Because that was the 800-pound gorilla at that point.

Admiral Meyer: We had whatever relationships we could establish with SAC, and those relations were what they chose them to be. But our executive officer was an aviator, and he was not a close friend, but he was a friend of Dick Ashworth. So he viewed himself kind of as a member of the club with the aura. But Ashworth then was a great deal of help to us in introductions and how we moved around. We developed those relationships out at Albuquerque more than anyplace else. Whenever we weren't teaching, we were generally traveling.

I never got to see a firing. About half of us got to see a firing out in Nevada, and before they got through all of us on the goddamn stuff, it got shut down, and so I got cut out of the pattern. I never saw an atomic explosion. Usually what we were getting was one quota, and a couple of times we'd get two quotas. So our CO got the first one, and he went to Nevada and saw it, and he came back really, really—I mean, like, moved. It's almost like we'd say to him, "Play it again, Daddy; tell us again." [Laughter]

Paul Stillwell: "You were there."

Admiral Meyer: Yeah, right. It was really exciting.

Paul Stillwell: Did you ever meet Dick Ashworth?

Admiral Meyer: I did not. I met Deak Parsons a couple times. Never met Ashworth.

Paul Stillwell: Any memories of Parsons to share?

---

* The Mark 5 nuclear core was 39 inches in diameter and the overall weapon 44 inches.
† SAC – Strategic Air Command, based at Offutt Air Force Base near Omaha, Nebraska. It has since become a joint service command, Strategic Command, rather than Air Force only as it was then.

Admiral Meyer: I didn't know him that well. No, I don't. As you know, he was very admired at the Applied Physics Laboratory, and the auditorium there is named after him. But anybody that knew him is virtually all dead now. I was too young to be in that club, and he died pretty early. I think he was in his 50s, had a heart attack.

Paul Stillwell: Ashworth lived till just a couple years ago. I saw him three years ago out in New Mexico.

Admiral Meyer: Did you? Well, I recall reading in a paper that he died. I believe I met him once.

Paul Stillwell: What was the purpose of your course? The people you were teaching were not going to become weapons specialists. What was this equipping them to do?

Admiral Meyer: No. It was orientation, except for the employment course. There we issued valid certificates, which said, "Lieutenant Paul is qualified." He's had this much study on target selection. And they'd go off to staff someplace.

Paul Stillwell: So that would include probably some intelligence people.

Admiral Meyer: I don't know that we ever had intelligence people in the course. We had a lot of them teaching us. We had very close relationships with them, a lot of them cycling through. We had a steady stream of visitors and interchange, and a steady stream to Washington, D.C. I'm trying to think when's the first time I ever visited the Applied Physics Laboratory, and I think the first time was when I was in the school at Fort Bliss. But then I got to go out there to visit fairly regularly once I was at Norfolk teaching in the special weapons school.

We went through the whole era of pretty tight security, which didn't suddenly disappear. What happened is it just leaked off and leaked off until it was all compromised. As far as I know, we don't have any security in atomic weapons today. Maybe we do, and I don't know. In that era you had to have something called a Queen clearance to work inside atomic weapons. And getting that clearance was exhausting. It was separate from a security clearance, but as far as the AEC was concerned it was the only clearance [chuckle].*

Paul Stillwell: Did you have to undergo an investigation to get the clearance to work?

Admiral Meyer: Affirmative. I think this is correct, what I'm about to say. As a matter of fact, it was the first time I was seriously investigated, and it really stirred up Brunswick, Missouri. [Laughter] Because I had to provide all these character references and my aunts and uncles and my dad. So the next thing I knew, these guys were out asking all these questions about Wayne, and the whole town was getting nervous. What was the problem here with Wayne? Because they didn't know how to answer the questions. [Chuckle] They didn't want to do anything against Wayne, but—yes, I believe that's the first time I underwent a serious investigation, is to get that Queen clearance. It took, I don't know, five or six months to get it. As far as I can remember, it didn't hold us up in school. We went ahead and did what we were going to do anyhow [chuckle].

Paul Stillwell: You talked about the arrangement with Port Lyautey and the planes being there and the weapons on board ship. Was there a counterpart of that in the Pacific?

Admiral Meyer: I don't believe so, at least not in the era that I can recall when I was sailing. This whole thing was directed at the Soviet Union, and the constant struggle with the Air Force and the Navy as to who had the ability to do a deep strike. The idea of in-flight refueling started emerging in that era, for Navy planes. But since I was not intimately connected to it, I don't know. I know that they did attempt to start an atomic weapons school similar to ours in San Diego, but I think it foundered. I was there for two and a half years or so when it stood up. I don't know when it terminated after that. I think it terminated in the next three or four years. It lasted seven or eight years. I can't remember.

---

* AEC – Atomic Energy Commission.

Paul Stillwell: Did you have inputs of information so you could get updated on changes in the various programs so you could teach that material?

Admiral Meyer: Well, we had to get out and hustle ourselves. We were always traveling in order to keep up to date, because it really was fast moving. I mean, it was horrendous going from 60 inches and 20,000 pounds to 10,000 pounds and 60 inches, to 40 inches and 5,000 pounds, and then finally the Mark 7.[*] And they were working on what was called the Betty, which was the atomic depth bomb. As far as I know, we never set one off. And there was the antiair warhead. I finally fell out of the circuit and I don't know whether we—allegedly we had them for Terrier. I know we had them for Talos, because I was the fire control officer in *Galveston* for her conversion, and we had a magazine for atomic heads for the Talos missiles. It was a real, real pain in the ass dealing with the whole security and stuff.

I don't know whether we'll ever go back to atomic weapons in ships. Whether we carry them today in our attack carriers, I don't know. I don't know whether anybody knows.

Paul Stillwell: Well, my understanding is they were taken off the carriers in the early 1990s.[†]

Admiral Meyer: But I think the Navy's official position was that it would neither confirm nor deny that it carries the weapons.

Paul Stillwell: Well, that was it until the early '90s.

Admiral Meyer: I think they must be gone, because the carriers go about into any port they want to go anymore, pretty near, and that was one of the big problems, whether they had atomic bombs aboard or not. As I said, we carried them in the *Galveston*.

---

[*] The Mark 7 nuclear bomb was 15.2 feet long, 2.5 feet in diameter, and weighed 1,680 pounds. The Mark 7 was in service from 1952 to 1968.
[†] On 27 September 1991 President George H. W. Bush announced a unilateral initiative to cease deployment of tactical nuclear weapons on board U.S. Navy surface ships, attack submarines, and land-based aircraft during "normal circumstances."

[Interruption for change of tape]

Paul Stillwell: We'll note for the record that this interview is taking place on Leap Day, and you're ready now to describe your time on board USS *Strickland*.

Admiral Meyer: USS *Strickland*.[*] Let's see, I'm trying to think. I got ordered from line school to there.[†] Okay. So I reported to USS *Strickland* as executive officer. She was in a six-ship squadron, I believe, based at Goat Island.[‡] She was one of the ships the U.S. Navy had converted to sail on the contiguous line on radar patrol. The reason is these ships were diesel ships, Fairbanks Morse. I had never before sailed in a diesel ship, and it turned out that diesel people in that era were not well thought of if you sailed in steam ships.

Paul Stillwell: Had you covered engineering in the line school? Did you get some helpful background in that?

Admiral Meyer: Zero. But when you've sailed in destroyers, you come to love diesels, because you can walk aboard and go. Liberty can be up a quarter to 8:00, and you'd be under way at 8:00 o'clock instead of lighting off at 4:00 o'clock. But there's another thing about sailing in a diesel, and I'll relate it to my early life. You'd go over to the officers' club in Newport; in those days it was the Trident Room. The officers would be sitting there, and they would start turning to each other and saying, "Do you smell something funny in here? [Laughter] Smell something funny in here?" And pretty soon you got so you didn't go to the officers' club, because it was a very subtle reminder that they could smell that diesel on you.

Now, we used to have a saying in Missouri. The farmhouses where I grew up had two porches. You had an outside porch and an inside porch. And you came in from the

---

[*] USS *Strickland* (DE-324) was an *Edsall*-class destroyer escort commissioned 10 January 1944. She had a standard displacement of 1,200 tons, was 306 feet long, 37 feet in the beam, and had a maximum draft of 8 feet, 7 inches. Her design speed was 21 knots. She was armed with three 3-inch guns and antisubmarine weapons. After World War II she was decommissioned. She was later reactivated, converted to a radar picket ship, and recommissioned as DER-333 on 2 February 1952.
[†] Meyer reported to the ship in May 1955.
[‡] Goat Island, in Narragansett Bay, is part of Newport, Rhode Island.

milking barn and the hogs into the outside porch. You changed your clothes. And you went to the inside porch, and you put on other clothes before your momma would let you in the house. Because you didn't have cow manure on you, you had coal oil. But they always had an expression that once you got cow manure on you, you never got it off. You couldn't wash it off. Well, it turns out that's true for diesel. Diesel gets in your shoes; it gets in your clothes.

I'd come off patrol like 2:00 o'clock in the morning or something else, and lived up in Middletown. Go up and beat on the door to wake up my wife to get her to let me in. She would open the door, but she'd never say, "Oh, hello, honey. Hi, husband. I really missed you." The first thing out of her mouth would be, "What's that smell?" [Chuckle]

I said, "I've been in the ship. That's diesel."

"Well," she said, "You'd better go out on the back porch and take you clothes off before you come in. It'll disturb the kids." So that's what living in a diesel ship is.

Paul Stillwell: Well, I've even heard from a submariner that he sent a letter home and the letter smelled like diesel. [Laughter]

Admiral Meyer: Oh, is that right? Well, our support, of course, generally came out of New London, which was a little different.* And actually we got pretty darned good support from them. They had a well-organized structure compared to what we were used to, and they took pretty good care of us, because the Fairbanks Morse diesels were the basic engines in the attack submarines.

It turned out that the objective was to populate the Distant Early Warning line extended. It was called the Atlantic DEW line seaward extension. And the Air Force had thrown all these radars up across the globe from Alaska around, and now we were going to connect into that to complete the nation's ring to detect the Russian bombers. But before that could be done, it was so urgent that we were going to help patrol what was known as the contiguous line, which was the radar line coastal-wise for the eastern United States. And that line commenced right south of Newport and ran all the way

---

* New London, Connecticut, was a base for diesel-powered submarines.

down to the Carolinas. As I recollect now, there were about four patrol stations to cover it.

Well, the reason we were temporary was primarily because the United States Air Force was going to take that over. They were going to build what were called Texas Towers.* These towers were constructed with radar on them, and then they wouldn't need those ships. Then a hurricane came through, wiped the towers out, and that was the end of that. I don't think they were even up a year.

Paul Stillwell: Well, there was one off New Jersey that went down.†

Admiral Meyer: Right. And the other thing, well, we got the idea we'll do this in lesser ships called YAGRs. We'd take some of the ships that were in storage.

Paul Stillwell: They were the old Liberty ships.‡

Admiral Meyer: Right. We put a lieutenant commander and a crew of sailors to start patrolling and sailing on them. And their speed was like a few knots. And in fact it worked pretty well. For the people who did it, it was pretty boring to them and pretty wrung out, but it worked not badly.

So once all that got set up and the surviving Texas Towers were operating, it was decided that, really, we could get on with our major mission. Our mission was to populate the DEW line, and it was going to be done in conjunction with the Super Connie

---

* There were three Texas Towers off the U.S. East Coast. They were equipped with radar to detect approaching Soviet bombers. They were so named because they were modeled after oilrigs off the coast of Texas. The towers went into operation in 1958 and were shut down in 1961 because of a concern for the safety of the crews of the installations.
† Texas Tower Number 4 was in the deepest water, 185 feet, of any of the towers. On the night of 15 January 1961, TT-4 was struck by a storm that included winds up to 85 miles per hour and waves up to 35 feet high. At 7:20 P.M. the first of the three legs broke, followed shortly by the other two. The platform sank to the bottom of the ocean. All on board were lost: 14 Air Force men and 14 civilian repair personnel.
‡ The Liberty ship was a mass-produced cargo ship designed by the U.S. Maritime Commission for use by the Allies in World War II. All told, American shipyards built 2,770 Liberties. A number of them were converted to radar picket ships, YAGRs, in the late 1950s, later redesignated AGRs.

airplane.* Well, I thought I had learned a lot about navigation in line school and it was a damned good thing I did.

I reported to the *Strickland* as executive officer. I was a lieutenant. The captain was a lieutenant commander. I was navigator besides being the executive officer, and just about anything else you could think of. I was senior fighter director; they were still called fighter directors. I think we had four radars; one was a height finder, the SPS-8, and it was installed above the pilothouse. We could make about 16½ to 17 knots, depending on how you went. The big problem we had was making water. It was very, very limited.

Well, eventually we got out of the shipyards and we got sent up for patrol off of Argentia, Newfoundland, first station.

Paul Stillwell: Were you there during the conversion process to DER?

Admiral Meyer: No, they were in commission. They had put them in commission.

Paul Stillwell: Okay. But this was your first patrol out of the yard.

Admiral Meyer: Right. It was my first patrol. *Strickland*, *Otterstetter*, and a couple or three others. And five or six would be nested at a time over there at Goat Island. I mean, it would really just get aggravating if you ended up being the outboard ship. You'd be almost at fleet landing, you were strung out so far. And, of course, the threat of weather was constantly on you. How to safely moor. And invariably the distances that you ran from the DEW line on patrol would bring you home at 2:00 o'clock in the morning. Well, my skipper and other skippers said, "The hell with this noise; we're going to moor. We're going in." So we'd put the goddamn boat in the water and a couple battle lanterns and crew would get up there and search out these buoys, which were unlighted. We'd find the goddamn buoys and maneuver. The ships were really, really highly maneuverable and very adaptable. I mean, after you come from a steam ship they were

---

* The WV Warning Star was a military version of the Constellation commercial aircraft. Lockheed started delivery of the WV-2 model to Navy squadrons in 1954 for use as airborne early warning posts.

surprisingly safe in handling. When you came in, you just had to moor outboard; that was the only choice you had.

Well, the Super Connies were going to fly this racetrack course, and the thing was being set up all the way out down to the Azores.* And we, amongst other things, were station ships. One of our assignments was to assist in safe navigation for the Super Connies, which were based out of Argentia. Well, that turned out to be a backward horse, because first of all Loran ain't worth a damn up in that country.† Wasn't worth anything. And second, you'd go for a week and never even see the sun. You'd finally get so: "How in the world do those fishermen ever find their way home?" [Laughter] The Connies had a super—I think it was called a bubble sextant. And so they would get up and get above all this and be able to shoot sun lines, so they were navigating for *us*. [Laughter]

One of the other interesting things up there is that navigating by the fathometer really, really works well—if you don't ever get lost. But the requirement is you have to know where you started from. And so I learned to navigate a lot by fathometer.

Paul Stillwell: You've got to have good charts too.

Admiral Meyer: Yeah. Exactly. And the charts were pretty damned good. But you had to know which the hell ridge that you were on when you started. I got off station nearly 30 miles once, according to the airplane, and the old man was really, really pissed. And I finally said to him, "Fuck it; if you want to do the navigation you go ahead and take it over." I had an ensign reserve assigned to help me, and I said, "We're doing the best we know how. We don't have any other way to do it." So that calmed him down. It just was embarrassing is all.

Paul Stillwell: Who was the captain?

---

* The Atlantic Barrier (BarLant) was comprised of two squadrons of WV-2 aircraft: VW-13 and VW-15, based at Patuxent River, Maryland, and WV-11 at Argentia, Newfoundland.
† Loran (long-range aid to navigation) is a system of electronic navigation that involves the reception of pulse signals transmitted simultaneously by paired stations ashore.

Admiral Meyer: The first one was Harold R. Youman, in the graveyard now. The second one was Lieutenant Commander Doug Parramore, and I don't know where he is.[*] In that era he was drinking himself to death, and I assume by now he's died. He had no wife, so his wife was a whiskey bottle. I learned a lot from both of them, but I probably learned more from Doug Parramore.

Paul Stillwell: What did you learn?

Admiral Meyer: I learned ship handling, I learned how to run a ship, how to manage a ship, how to lead a ship. The captain just gave it to me. He gave it to me.

Paul Stillwell: Threw you in the briar patch.

Admiral Meyer: When we would come in and start to moor, before number-one line was even doubled up, he would say, "XO, tell me again what time are we getting under way?"

"Well, we're getting under way Tuesday, Captain."

"All right, I'll see you. Goodbye." And he was gone.

Then he'd show up 15-20 minutes before time to get under way [chuckle]. And a lot of times he just ended up at my house. He'd get drunk someplace, and he didn't know where he was going. The next thing we knew, he was up tapping on the door, so my wife would let him in. I'd get up in the morning, and there he was, sleeping on the couch in the front room. [Laughter] So what a world. But he was a good skipper in the sense that he'd just give it to me. I don't even know whether he ever made commander.[†] Because he was not bothersome to me, and at sea he'd just sleep in the chair as long as he could, weather permitting.

Paul Stillwell: Those sound like very boring patrols.

---

[*] Lieutenant Commander Douglas G. Parramore, USN.
[†] Parramore retired as a captain in 1974.

Admiral Meyer: Well, the patrol in the North Atlantic—Goddamn. It's the roughest sailing I've ever, ever done. You never had anything warm to eat, you couldn't stay in your bunk, you couldn't stand up. You spent your whole time struggling.

Paul Stillwell: Holding on.

Admiral Meyer: Holding on. I mean, I never lost anybody. We had lifelines rigged constantly all over that ship. You could not go out of that ship at night without special permission from the officer of the deck. We kept track of every single person. We never lost a man. A lot of the ships did, and some were never found. It was risky in that respect, but it was just so tiring.

In the North Atlantic you would get these rollers. We did a lot of cruising on patrol on one shaft, and you can make about 4 knots to 5 knots, maintain steerageway, with one shaft, to conserve fuel. Our turnaround time on those ships from port to port was something like 27 days, which is unheard of in a steam destroyer. So you'd leave Newport, it would be 27 days before you got back. So it would be three days out, three days back, 21 days on patrol. Naturally, in that kind of weather, conservation of fuel—and all alone—was a significant factor.

You *had* to stay ballasted. It was too heavy topside not to be ballasted. And we had a little 4-inch pipe to handle ballasting so that was a terrible flaw in the conversions that this thing was put on. So you had to de-ballast before you'd get back in port. Well, hell, you had to de-ballast way out off of Cape Georges Bank, or it was invalid. So you had to get yourself de-ballasted a long ways from home. And that wasn't so much that it became rough, it took so damned long to do it. You'd screw around for a day trying to get that all pumped off before you headed finally home. Well, our cruising speed was 12 knots; everybody knows that. Well, 12 times 24 ain't a very big number. It takes a long time to get 500 miles at that rate. At 16 knots you might get a little further. So if you conserve fuel on patrol you might have enough fuel to balance the books out on how in the hell you were sailing for the whole patrol. That's pretty significant to morale.

I didn't do many patrols. I don't remember right now how many patrols I did, but I was damned glad. We did the first patrol on Station One, which was the one right off Argentia.

The other amazing thing about those ships, once you'd sailed in destroyers, is the fuel. Because, you know, in a destroyer your fuel got down to 60%-65%, you started worrying about how you're going to refuel. Hell, on the diesels it could get down to 20, and nobody'd even blink an eye. It'd get down to 10%, and you'd say, "Well, we'd better get a plan in a few days here to get some fuel." It was my first and my last experience in diesel, and I came to have a hell of a lot of respect for diesel because how it reduced the workload. I mean, it really cut the workload. But the problem was you always stunk.

Paul Stillwell: But they were well suited for that role of independent operations.

Admiral Meyer: Oh, whoever decided that in the Navy was a genius. They were well, well suited. A submarine was not suited for it. These ships had been built somehow from the war, and they were just moored someplace in a river, and the Navy got them out and started reworking them. Two of them were steamers; they never made it to the DEW line because they didn't have the legs. I want to say *Vandivier* and *Wagner* were steamers, and we got so we hated them in the goddamn nest. So they were on the contiguous line because they could do a patrol as long as they didn't get too far away, without refueling.

Well, in that era these Connies would fly, as I said, this big horseshoe, big oval, and it would take them about 12 hours. That's about how long they could stay. That was in December, and I don't know whether I could speak the year or not. It was in the middle '50s someplace when we lost one. One of them went around the lower bend, and there you'd lose communications with them from station—I think it was called Station Echo. You'd lose communication for about an hour as they were going around. One went around and never returned. And it so happened that the Navy had a whole flotilla of ships deploying for the Mediterranean in September, including as I recall, an attack carrier. They diverted, they searched and searched and searched. They searched the whole goddamn Atlantic Ocean and they never found the plane. It just disappeared somewhere, and the men with it. So that was kind of sad. Some stations were changed after that so we always tried to have positive communication, but by then I was no longer sailing on the DEW line.

Paul Stillwell: Did you have any special communications gear for this mission?

Admiral Meyer: Aha! We started out on the first mission. The Air Force had these grandiose schemes for communications, and they were headquartered at Rome, New York. And the argument between them and the Navy was: "Who in the hell's in charge of ships at sea?" CinCLantFlt maintained that he was in charge of ships at sea, and by God that was the way it was going to be.[*] Well, it turned out that CinCLantFlt won that argument. So they sent us on patrol, and we were sent three radio operators. In those days a radio operator was among the elite, and he got special pay if he had a speed-key certificate. Because these goddamn reports had to be transmitted by CW, and with a speed key you'd just transmit almost constantly.[†] Without a speed key you'd never get them done.

The first patrol we did was a short one. It was experimental. Couldn't cut it. The communications were too bad. So as we were headed for homeport at Newport, we were diverted en route, ordered to the Philadelphia Naval Shipyard. When we got there, these yahoos came aboard our ship and installed three new transmitter-receivers, called, as I remember, the SRC-16. They were partially digital. They stood, oh, maybe as tall as a man and maybe as wide as this table. They were pretty big suckers; I don't know where they came from. Navy had them somehow, just brand spanking new. We didn't know how to maintain them. They brought aboard boxes of parts.

It turned out they were beautiful. I mean, it turned out that when we went back on patrol it was amazing how we could get through to Norfolk. As far as I know, that transmitter went into service in the Navy. I don't know what ever happened after that to

---

[*] CinCLantFlt – Commander in Chief Atlantic Fleet.
[†] CW, or continuous wave, referred to a type of radio wave interrupted into the dots and dashes of the Morse code for the purpose of communication.

them. But you put your finger right on a serious problem, and the Navy and the Air Force never resolved the tactical structure for homeland defense there.

Paul Stillwell: What do you recall about the internal administration of the *Strickland*, working with the department heads?

Admiral Meyer: Good question. And I'll tell you what. There weren't any sailors that wanted to sail in them damned DERs. [Laughter]

Paul Stillwell: I'm not surprised.

Admiral Meyer: No, they didn't want to be in those things. So what was done? Well, the ships were loaded up with reserves. Wait a minute, they were home-ported out of Newport. What was done? They were reserves out of New England. Wait a minute. Who were these guys? Well, they were out of the ROTC units. Not only were they out of the ROTCs, they were out of the elites: Yale, Harvard, Brown—those universities. That's where they had gone to the ROTC units. So these guys were smarter than God Himself. And here I was, just a can-kicker lieutenant on there and a regular besides. Every one of them was a reserve. And none of them ever wore a uniform, hardly, when they were in the ROTCs because they were reserve ROTCs. They were serving their obligated service.

Well, it turned out I had a pretty good time, because all the leadership I had mastered as I was coming along, including in that ship, I was able to apply. They detested the captain, so in the end they came to respect me and admire me. Some of them would say, "How can you work for that son of a bitch?" They almost had the attitude that, "If you don't like him, why don't you just walk off the ship?"

A couple of them I got so I had great admiration for. One of them went off to teach school in New England as a math teacher. Another went off to law school, and he would glop onto every word I said. He'd listen to me to the point of being tiresome. I've often wondered what ever happened to them all and how they made out. I expect to open up the paper any day now and find them in the Democrat Party or some big wheel or something. They were all rich boys. They were well-to-do boys.

Paul Stillwell: Were they capable at their jobs on board ship?

Admiral Meyer: In the beginning they were totally inept. But, by God, they shaped up as pretty good officers when they got their ass slapped a few times, and they spent a little time on board instead of walking off the ship when the ship moored. They turned out to start to be pretty damned good officers. And I got so I kind of liked them.

Paul Stillwell: Why did they detest the captain?

Admiral Meyer: I think it was elite versus elite. They saw no reason why you should respect the captain the way you were, because they were elitist themselves. They were high and mighty. And yet they had no choice except to pay attention to him. You've got to wonder who in the hell their officers were in the ROTC. Well, the truth is, in those days at least, in the reserve ROTC they virtually saw no officers. Maybe occasionally, once a month or something like that. So they never learned any serious respect. I don't know what happened. I am not in communication with a single one of them anymore. I don't know where they all went. This was many moons ago, 50 years ago.

Paul Stillwell: Were the skippers mustangs?

Admiral Meyer: No, but they had been reserves who transitioned to regular.

Paul Stillwell: Did you provide diversions to the crew to keep the morale up during these patrols?

Admiral Meyer: Well, keeping morale up wasn't that hard, because you were so damned busy, and it was so rough that you didn't have time to worry about morale, really. The watches and the demands on you were such that everybody heaved a sigh of relief when you'd get into port. When we'd get into port, at least in our ship, we kept giving people, the first two days they'd have off. Just go ashore if you want to go ashore. Because all they needed to do was rest, because these ships were not too comfortable. The one good thing about them was that you could get them suckers under way fast. And sometimes maintenance was a challenge, but in hindsight, at least once I got away from there, it turned out I really had enjoyed myself. I really had liked it, and I think I was really loved and respected. And maybe more so than the skippers, because I spent a lot of time with these different guys. I talked to them a lot.

Paul Stillwell: It's usually the other way around. The skipper is the father figure, and the XO's the hard guy.

Admiral Meyer: Exactly. Exactly. But I got so I enjoyed talking to them. Or just, they found they could argue with me, and once they found they could argue with me it gave them some fulfillment. You got the feeling that, well, by God, they're finally beginning to think that I might be as smart as they are, once you could argue with them.

Paul Stillwell: You're talking about the officers.

Admiral Meyer: Yeah, the officers. I can remember there was one lieutenant (j.g.), and the rest were ensigns. They were out of reserve ROTC, so they didn't know a hell of a lot. I had a lot of simpatico to them for the background I described to you, of how I came into the Navy and how I entered and what I knew about ship keeping. So it made me, I hope not an overbearing teacher, but it made me a ship teacher. I had a lot of patience trying to teach them the officer-of-the-deck requirements and other duties, because I learned some of them the hard way.

Paul Stillwell: How did you grow professionally during that tour?

Admiral Meyer: I don't know whether I could say that I did, but the know-how that I had already accumulated was really far above the level of knowhow within those ships. That was true of the skippers, the XOs, and the officers. So, I don't know, I had a pretty good time trying to, I guess you'd say practicing, leading, and such. So I was a little sad when I left.

Mind you, I told you early on that the Navy terminated me in graduate school at MIT because they'd run out of money. So I had this continuing objective in my mind that I was going to get myself a master's degree, because I was the first one ever in my whole generation that had ever gone through school. It was a point of pride with me and that was really, to me, a major, major accomplishment, of coming out of the gumbo and getting done what I got done, and people in Brunswick, Missouri, thought it. They thought it and they felt strong about it. And they were proud I was in the Navy.

So one part of the Bureau of Personnel would keep saying, "Well, you've already been to graduate school; you don't need any more." And the other part would have a reason that, "Well, you've got to do this, you've got to do that if you're going to get promoted."

One day when the ship was in Newport, I was sent for. I was sent for to come over to the flagship, *Yosemite*, to talk to the assistant chief for operations, Captain Nev Shaffer, about assignment on the staff.[*] I knew what it was for, and the captain of the *Strickland* knew, but I wasn't particularly wild about the idea. When I got there, Captain Shaffer interviewed me, then took me up to the chief of staff, who was B. J. Semmes.[†] Admiral Joe Daniel was the type commander.[‡] They wanted me in operations or in plans. When I saw B. J. Semmes, who was a tough sucker, we got to the real nut cutting, and he said, "Well, Lieutenant, would you like to serve on this staff?"

I said, "Well, I'm not sure, Captain. I'll tell you one thing real bluntly. If being on this staff will do anything to get me back in graduate school, I'll take it next week."

He looked at me over his glasses, and he said, "Well, what's your idea of something better to get to graduate school than to serve on this staff?" and just glared.

I finally broke down and said, "Well, I don't have an idea." [Chuckle]

---

[*] Captain John Nevin Shaffer, USN.
[†] Captain Benedict J. Semmes Jr., USN.
[‡] Rear Admiral John C. Daniel, USN, commanded Destroyer Force Atlantic Fleet from 17 June 1955 to 18 January 1958.

"Well," he said, "I'll think about it. Thank you." And he picked me to come over to serve in plans.

We had this tentative agreement that I could get back in graduate school. When I submitted my application, they gave me a flaming endorsement, which I'm sure to this day is what got me there, because I was getting a little old.

Paul Stillwell: Do you have an idea of why the staff called you over to interview for this opening?

Admiral Meyer: Well, I made up one. Commander John Remey Wadleigh was our commodore. Now, I'd never worked for anybody whose name contained the names of two ships, *Remey* and *Wadleigh*. He is from an impressive family in Newport.

Paul Stillwell: He was a good man. I knew him through the *Proceedings*.[*]

Admiral Meyer: He is a wonderful person. Really is a wonderful person. And I feel pretty confident that he's the one that recommended to Semmes that I be interviewed. That's the way I feel. It took me a while to figure it out, of how it happened.

Paul Stillwell: Anything else on Wadleigh from your time in the ship that you remember?

Admiral Meyer: Well, he liked to play cards off and on, and he liked to come and visit the ship and visit with the officers if there were any aboard. Some people would get all nervous because the captain and the XO were ashore; that was not his concern. He just liked to come and visit with them and sit in the wardroom and talk to them. That's the biggest thing I remember about Wadleigh, and the other is periodically you'd get him to start talking about a sea story of his, one or another. You just wanted to gather around and listen to him because he was so calm and straightforward and spoke well.

---

[*] Wadleigh, who became a rear admiral, published a number of articles in the *U.S. Naval Institute Proceedings*. He died in January 1993.

Well, then he ended up over on the staff himself, so darned if I didn't end up being re-associated with him over there, because he became readiness training officer over there.

Paul Stillwell: What did your job involve with the plans?

Admiral Meyer: I had the nuclear weapons, and I had the war plans. Well, I did a lot of current operations, but it also turned out that the chief of staff gave me the extracurricular duty that I was in charge of the goddamn pier at Newport. I'll try to get that story to you, and then we'll close.

Paul Stillwell: Okay.

Admiral Meyer: When I got there, I found out that I was going to take over the job of the shore duty establishment, because they wouldn't get to work on building any piers in Narragansett Bay. So finally the DesLant staff personally took it over and contracted with Raymond Tile to build an el-cheapo pier—$4 million— about as wide as this room, up in the bay. It came to be called Pier 1. Essentially, it was a deck laid on telephone poles—my words—not properly constructed at all. I can't remember the year, but it was in the mid-'50s when a massive hurricane swept through the East Coast.

We were at sea on patrol. We were on the contiguous line at the time, and we were on patrol on a station south of New York. We sat out that hurricane in the mouth of the Delaware River, where we had a pretty good lee, because no one could give us any guidance. That hurricane tore the hell out of Narragansett Bay and the Navy. It holed a lot of ships. Well, the new pier that they had put everybody on it they could, including the flagship, just got ripped asunder and a lot of ships damaged. And when we returned to port there was almost no place to come to. Finally we had to take a buoy. One DER was damaged so badly with her sides stove in that she was towed up through the canal to Boston Naval Shipyard, then we were allowed to come in and berth.

The truth was, that was something through the incompetence of impulsive naval officers doing what they didn't know how to do, and unfortunately not knowing how to go find the right people to do it. And Arleigh Burke was in command of the goddamn place.[*] Now, I happen to not be an idolater of Arleigh Burke's. I can't take from his war record with one of my own.[†] I can punch a lot of holes in his record, though. And Arleigh Burke spent a lot of time of his own, as did his wife, being sure that his image ended up in good shape. So God love him. God save Arleigh Burke. But he never paid one penny of penalty for that disaster.[‡] Except to become the CNO.

When I came on, Shaffer and Semmes both said, "Amongst other things we want you to become the port officer and take charge of the pier effort." Pier 1 was open and a wreck, and Pier 2 was in design. And Pier 2 was going to be an adult pier, twice as wide as this room and be properly built, and was going to cost $20-some million, contrasted to $4 million for this other one.

Paul Stillwell: Built out of something more substantial than telephone poles?

Admiral Meyer: Exactly. You're damn right. You're damn right. Reinforcements of one kind or another. And the Bureau of Yards and Docks made a design and some such. And they bitched and bitched and bitched and bitched, moaned about why should it cost $21 million, whatever it was, and we built this one for four. Right. [Laughter] And they got a pile of telephone poles.

Well, I didn't realize what I was walking into, because I'd had nothing to do with it, knew nothing about it. So there I was up in my spaces in the flagship. Commander Jack Gommengenger, who was the operations officer, reported to Shaffer, and Lieutenant Lee Zeni and Lieutenant Meyer worked for him.[§] Zeni took care of almost all of the maneuvers and assignment of ships and fulfillment of duties and stuff that needed to be done to ships. I worried about the piers.

It turned out another major thing that rained in on me almost instantly was the bomb scare. And so the dispersal of the fleet was born. So while I was there I ended up

---

[*] As a rear admiral, Burke commanded Destroyer Force Atlantic Fleet from January 1955 to June 1955.
[†] Captain Burke was Commander Destroyer Squadron 23 in the Solomons during fighting there in 1943. He also served as chief of staff to Vice Admiral Marc A. Mitscher, Commander Task Force 58, during the latter part of World War II.
[‡] New England was hit by hurricanes in August and September 1955, after Admiral Burke had already left to become Chief of Naval Operations.
[§] Commander John A. Gommengenger, USN; Lieutenant Levio E. Zeni, USN.

put in charge of getting the fleet dispersed. Well, where are you going to disperse it to? We had 120 ships in the place, and we had orders out of Washington to get those ships scattered. So I ended up putting ships in Providence, New Bedford, Boston. Even sent one down to New London. And we had them up to Tiverton. We had them scattered all over New England. We didn't have anything else we could do for them. And, of course, we had no logistics whatsoever.

I don't know whether you knew that area very well in your earlier years. There was—I don't think it's there anymore—the bus transportation system around through Newport was called the Short Line.

Paul Stillwell: No, I had not heard of that.

Admiral Meyer: Well, it was a pretty good outfit. It was very Navy-oriented, and it was very neighborly and stuff. And that bus line supported the Navy as best it could and do whatever it could.

So here I was, reported here, the pier in a goddamn mess, and trying to get the pier back in commission. And all these piles had been taken out. Not only that, the United States Navy received its first new destroyer, USS *Forrest Sherman*.* And so here came USS *Forrest Sherman*, 931 I want to say.

Paul Stillwell: That's correct.

Admiral Meyer: It came down from Boston Naval Shipyard to be our ship, and Commander Rusty Crenshaw, whom we call Crusty Crenshaw, who wrote the book *Naval Shiphandling*, was her skipper.† Well, of course, he was going to be moored right across Pier 1, because he was the pride and joy of the destroyer fleet. He was right across the pier, this little piss-ant pier, almost in the lee of the flagship.

---

* The *Forrest Sherman* (DD-931) class was the Navy's first new destroyer design after World War II. The class eventually comprised 18 ships; commissioning dates ran from November 1955 to August 1959. For details see Daniel G. Felger, "Retrospective: the *Forrest Sherman*s," *U.S. Naval Institute Proceedings,* May 1987, pages 162-175.
† Russell S. Crenshaw Jr., *Naval Shiphandling* (Annapolis: U.S. Naval Institute, 1965). As a commander, Crenshaw was skipper of the *Forrest Sherman* from 9 November 1955 to 20 July 1957.

Paul Stillwell: *Yosemite*.

Admiral Meyer: And he was one of the several officers in that era—they spoke *only* to the admiral. They never spoke to you. You waited for your orders to come down from the front office of what you were to do for them: when they wanted to refuel, when they wanted to get under way, and all those kinds of things. And the goddamn pier was to be cleared of other things when they wanted to load stores.

So I had a chief petty officer assigned to me, a boatswain's mate on shore duty, and he and I were in charge of the whole pier thing, including getting this friggin' pier fixed.

Well, there was another thing. The pier was never going to work unless we did something about a breakwater. So we were in the process of trying to get the shore establishment to not only design but emergency build a breakwater, which did occur. Have you ever sailed out of there? I don't know whether you have or not.

Paul Stillwell: No.

Admiral Meyer: Well, the breakwater ain't bad. It's pretty good. And Pier 2 did get built. While it was operable, it was not completed till after I was transferred, but it got built, and eventually the flagship moved over there. We're all very, very proud of it, and we did get a ways to moor our ships. And then, of course, the goddamn fleet was relocated to other ports down south.

Paul Stillwell: That was a number of years later.[*]

Admiral Meyer: Exactly. [Chuckle] It was. Because there was to be a third pier built too, but it never got under way.

---

[*] Ships home-ported at Newport, Rhode Island, were transferred to ports farther south as part of the Shore Establishment Realignment Program of April 1973.

So I had all these, what some people call SLJs, and I worked on all these things and chased them all all the time, me and the chief. And then—I'm trying to say—I can't remember whether *Barry* was the second ship or *John Paul Jones*. I think it was *Barry*.

Paul Stillwell: Well, *Jones* was 932 and *Barry* 933.

Admiral Meyer: Okay, you've got it. But I can't remember which one got down to Newport first. It's immaterial; they made it approximately the same time. So they were the elitists. Someplace in that time frame I got a phone call at 5:30 in the morning at home, and he said, "Lieutenant, this is the chief. You'd better get down to the pier, and you'd better get down here, like, right now."

I said, "What's the problem?"

He said, "You'd better get down here if you want to see the biggest oil spill you've ever seen. You'd better hurry, because it's really going to blow up any minute." So I jumped in the car and went hauling ass down there. I got down there about 7:00 o'clock. By now things were out of control already.

What had happened was that *Forrest Sherman* had pulled in and moored across the pier. We generally weren't acquainted with the design, had no knowledge of the design, but she did have electric pumps. And the oil king had lined these things all up the night before, because they were going to take on fuel on the morning watch. They had a problem sometime in the middle of the night, believed to be the midwatch.[*] There was kind of an overflow or stripping tank; as I remember the number it was like 11,000 gallons, it wasn't a very big thing. But they'd gotten lined up, and a short had occurred in one of the motors and it started pumping. It started pumping oil through this stripping tank, and the stripping tank started overflowing. And it overflowed and it overflowed. Well, the security watch didn't catch it for quite a while. He was making his walking rounds and looked over the side, and all of a sudden he saw oil everyplace, early in the morning. Quite a few thousand gallons of oil, later it turned out, were pumped over the side.

---

[*] The midwatch runs from midnight to 0400 and the morning watch from 0400 to 0800.

By the time I got down there—I had a lieutenant (j.g.) reserve who was awaiting separation as my assistant, and he was also supposed to be the public affairs guy. He technically worked for Ray Komorowski, who was the public affairs guy.[*] I no more than walked in and saw this guy sitting there with his feet up on my desk. The *Providence Journal* had somehow gotten word of this thing, called up, and this guy answered the phone. The reporter apparently said, "I understand you've got an oil spill down there."

This lieutenant (j.g.) said, "If you want to see the biggest oil spill you've ever seen, you'd better hurry up and get down here." And that's all she took. Man, they came from everyplace. They came pouring down. We didn't know what the hell to do. There was oil every goddamn place.

Rusty Crenshaw knew what to do. He came to his ship at 8:00 o'clock. They took in all lines, they got the hell under way and sailed, and they went to sea and they left the goddamn mess behind them. We didn't have the foggiest idea how to handle this black oil of these quantities. We didn't have any idea.

So we found an outfit in New York City that was going to help us by noon, and they had stuff that you could skim with and stuff you could neutralize it with. So the next three days we worked our ass off trying to clean this stuff, trying to control the press. We put ComDesFlot 6—I forget the name of the admiral—up in one of the new helos and flew him around to look grimly at it.[†] Got Joe Daniel up in the helo and held a press conference, outgrim this thing. We really, really made it. And here was the place where just one goddamn milk carton showed up in Narragansett Bay the Kennedy family would assault the Navy. Now we had oil everyplace. We lived through it, but oh, my God.

Rusty Crenshaw taught me a lesson, how he had no feeling for anybody else except Rusty Crenshaw. I was always tickled to death and delighted that he never got promoted to admiral.

Paul Stillwell: He did make captain.

---

[*] Lieutenant Raymond A. Komorowski, USN.
[†] ComDesFlot 6 – Commander Destroyer Flotilla Six.

Admiral Meyer: Yeah, he made captain, and he was confident he was going to make admiral. There was no doubt in his mind. I don't know who didn't make him an admiral; I don't know if it was from that incident or not. All I know is I inherited the goddamn mess, and it resulted in a frightening amount of rules and regulations and stuff that had to be done. And we handled it. I mean, Captain Semmes and Captain Shaffer went around town and talked to the people. They went on the new television at Providence and talked to them about the situation. And it was serious. We didn't belittle it, we didn't belittle it one bit. It was just a serious situation and a real bust. I mean, we had jillions of sailors out with the goddamn buckets scooping it out of the bay, one after the other. So that was part of my duties.

Also, the war plan was a big part of my duties, and that was having correct ships. The constructive war plan—I don't know whether it even exists anymore, but in those days it existed in Norfolk at headquarters, and there had to be ships stuck in all the holes, that if you were mobilized, where you sailed to. I had to update that every week, what ship went in what hole and what holes were vacant and what ships were crippled, and so on. So that was part of my duties. I have to say I learned a lot.

Then it turned out that the knowledge I had of atomic weapons was pretty valuable indeed, of what I could contribute to the staff. They were in awe of what I knew about these goddamn things that none of them knew anything about. So I became kind of authoritative on that subject, including with Admiral Daniel.

And guess what. By God, I was on the lieutenant commander list. And by God, I got selected to go to graduate school, late in life. So when I went to graduate school I was the section leader. I was a lieutenant commander; everybody else was a lieutenant, so I was senior to everybody, but I got there.

Paul Stillwell: What do you remember about Admiral Joe Daniel and his leadership style?

Admiral Meyer: I remember him as very quiet. From my viewpoint and other junior officers, he had a harpy for a wife, and it made him very, very quiet. I had heard, but I don't know if this is a fact, that they later separated after he left that post, and I think he retired right after that or so, and they separated.* He was kind of, I guess you'd say unremarkable.

Now, look at my good fortune. B. J. Semmes, Nev Shaffer, J. R. Wadleigh—all of these officers were promoted to flag officer, and I had served and worked under all of them. I say that from a different sense than a lot of people would. It is how much I learned from around them, how much they taught me about things I didn't know.

Paul Stillwell: Those were professional destroyer men.

Admiral Meyer: They really were. They really were. They were good. B. J. had a little pomposity in him, but it wasn't overbearing, and they spent a lot of time worrying about their juniors. So I was so fortunate of where I served and how I served. And I remember B. J. sending me a note on the graduate school [chuckle]. It just kind of said, "I told you so." [Laughter] He had gone and Nev Shaffer had fleeted up to be chief of staff by the time I left, but I remember that. But I learned so much from those people. God, I admired them so much.

So Joe Daniel was just kind of in the background. He was still in the shadow of Arleigh Burke, and not much came out of him.

I then became the representative for the staff to all the shore stations, and so I went every week when I was there to the meeting over at the station. Of course, I carried my list of complaints every week, because those captains [chuckle] would give me a list of grievances every week. Never let them get the idea over there that you're satisfied; that was their approach. So that was always my assignment, to be the bad boy. So the captain over there would get so he would laugh whenever he saw me walk into the meeting.

But I enjoyed it. I really liked it. We took off from there and went to Monterey.

Paul Stillwell: Well, we can get that next chapter. Thank you.

Admiral Meyer: At the next chapter. Thank you.

---

* Daniel retired 1 November 1959 with a tombstone promotion to vice admiral. He died in 1992 at age 91.

Interview Number 6 with Rear Admiral Wayne E. Meyer, U.S. Navy (Retired)
Place: Admiral Meyer's office in Arlington, Virginia
Date: Tuesday, 4 March 2008

Paul Stillwell: Admiral, as we start this interview we're getting you out to postgraduate school, which you had laid the foundation for by going to the DesLant staff. When you got to Monterey did you have an option on a major?

Admiral Meyer: Okay. So I finally made it to Monterey, and in many respects I was now over the age line.[*] Earlier in life, usually you had to be a lieutenant commander or so before you got sent to these engineering courses, but now more and more they're dipping down to lieutenant. I think today they have a lot of lieutenants (junior grade), even, and I personally don't like that. Some of them are being taken right out of school. They're commissioned at the Naval Academy or at ROTC, and they go right off to graduate school. I don't agree with that.

Paul Stillwell: Why not?

Admiral Meyer: Because I think that the greatest thing that can happen to a person is that seasoning period. At the time I didn't think much of it. The biggest reason, I think—as I told you, I was kind of obsessed with school. And here I was with these opportunities. But one needs maturity to really take away things from graduate school. And, if you don't mind, maybe we'll go into that a little bit today.

Paul Stillwell: Sure.

Admiral Meyer: I can't right now recall how many we had in the ordnance curriculum, but just to show the difference in construct—this was in the late '50s—Captain Bob

---

[*] Originally established at Annapolis, Maryland, on 9 June 1909, the Naval Postgraduate School was moved to the grounds of the former Hotel Del Monte in Monterey, California, in June 1951.

Odening was the ordnance curriculum OinC.* He had had already what today we call his major command. He had been a destroyer squadron commander, and he had been sent there to see to the education of officers. He oversaw maybe 70 or 80 officers in a couple different year groups. It's not a large number. And then, back in the headquarters here, Commander Mark Woods at that time was stationed in the Bureau of Ordnance, and he was one of our sponsors and a graduate and a noted officer, as you know.† He subsequently not only commanded the Naval Ordnance Systems Command, but he also commanded CruDesPac, and then had a subsequent career at the Applied Physics Laboratory in his twilight zone, and he's now in the graveyard. And Commander Robert Vickery in OpNav was the joint sponsor with him.‡ Vickery was of an intelligence upbringing and stuff, but he was stationed in some operational code. I think it was the OP-30-something in those days.

Paul Stillwell: That was Fleet Operations and Readiness.

Admiral Meyer: Yeah, right Fleet Operations. And every month those two officers visited campus—every single month. They came, and they held interviews with the officers, both as groups and as individuals. They talked to the faculty. They sat in on the classes. They examined the assignments that we were being given, and things like that. I mean, they immersed themselves into it. They were genuinely concerned about our education and what we were being taught.

Paul Stillwell: Was this comparable to the Rickover oversight of nuclear training?§

Admiral Meyer: I wouldn't say it was as rigorous, and it didn't necessarily come from him—I think that it emerged before Rickover even, but it was not unlike it. It was patterned that way.

---

* Captain Robert E. Odening, USN. OinC – officer in charge.
† Commander Mark W. Woods, USN.
‡ Commander Hugh B. Vickery, USN.
§ Hyman G. Rickover was considered the father of the nuclear Navy. He ran the U.S. Navy's nuclear-power program for many years, from 1948 until he eventually left active duty in 1982 with the rank of four-star admiral on the retired list.

Paul Stillwell: But OpNav wasn't leaving it just to the school to say what was taught.

Admiral Meyer: Not by a long shot. The funding for the school—now, I may be off base here—I believe tended to roll through the bureaus in those days. I don't know, because I was younger. I was the only lieutenant commander in my section, by the way, so that made me section leader, although we had a Marine who was a major who at times thought he was section leader. [Chuckle] So there you are.

Paul Stillwell: Was it preordained that you would go into ordnance engineering when you arrived there?

Admiral Meyer: No. We were sent there, and I want to say it tentatively was for two years—I shouldn't say "No" too quickly—and it was a general ordnance curriculum. The first year and a half, which was five terms, I believe, or four terms, we all took generally the same subjects. Then we were branched out. And then, for example, six of us were designated in fire control. Six of us were designated in chemistry, which was warheads, and turning out engines. Six were designated in aerodynamics. And so forth. And then there was kind of a leftover six that weren't quite at the top; they were general purpose. So there was room for everybody. Nobody was bilged out as far as I know, but some didn't get a master's degree either.

Paul Stillwell: What were your responsibilities as section leader?

Admiral Meyer: Well, it was not unlike being a bull ensign in USS *Springfield*, except it was a hell of a lot easier [chuckle], because by then about half of them, or more maybe, had a spouse and many of them had a child. And the school was pretty structured. So I just had to be sure that we got the reports in that we had to get in as the section leader or as the class leader. And when they had to do something or had to be mustered for something, it came through me. It just was more of, I guess you'd say, a prestige post than it was an actual hard-work post. It was simply because of my advanced age or rank. Some of them you may know, or learned about in later life: Jim Morgan, Steve

Hostettler, C. J. Rorie.* That group were all lieutenants when I was there. They were in my section.

So the end of two years had approached, and a decision had been made that some would go to other schools. So I found myself put in that category. It was determined that I did not have enough graduate credits to be awarded a master's degree.

Paul Stillwell: Even though you'd been to MIT earlier.

Admiral Meyer: Yeah, and gone to damned near two years here. So I was really, really irked by now. Of course, what was frightening was the detailer, who said, "You're going to be passed over. You're going to be passed over. You're not going to sea enough." Well, it turned out in my life that I sailed, I believe, I think it was in seven ships or so, so I believe I went to sea my fair share, contrary to what many people thought, who maybe didn't have the moxie to go to graduate school. They instead would talk about not having a desire, but it was a little bit more than that too. Didn't have the moxie. Because I'll tell you, graduate school was hard at Monterey.

Paul Stillwell: Please talk about the course work and the instructors.

Admiral Meyer: Well, they were almost all old-timers. They were civil service, and they were not civil service. They are paid under some kind of an act of Congress that goes back 100 years. They're equivalent in civil service rights and things of that nature, so they have nice pensions, and it ain't a fat paycheck, but they get a nice paycheck.

Paul Stillwell: So they were all civilians?

Admiral Meyer: All civilians. And some had been there quite a number of years. Dr. Wheeler taught me fire control. And Dr. Fowler, who wrote the book, taught—well, I've got a mental blank on what we're taught. It'll come to me in a minute. But I had those,

---

* Lieutenant James E. Morgan, USN; Lieutenant Stephen J. Hostettler, USN; Lieutenant Conrad J. Rorie, USN. All three later became admirals.

most of them, that taught me for about four terms, or five terms. And we did a lot of lab work and a lot of teamwork.

Paul Stillwell: What did the lab work consist of?

Admiral Meyer: It was mostly things electrical. It was bench work of some kind or another. Not very much travel at all, just really straightforward lab work of experiments of one kind or another. And you could pick from a list of what you wanted to work on, some of them.

So the time came when the Navy was again running short of money and deciding that it was going to break up that approach, which by the way developed some really class officers. A lot of those officers went on to serve well.

Paul Stillwell: You mentioned Hostettler and Rorie. They both became flag officers.

Admiral Meyer: They did, right. Quite a few officers in that era became flag officers. And I've always referred to it in later life as the "Arleigh Burke effort." I've given him credit for it, but I'm not sure it was his brains. But he was the person that caused it. And it was very simple. The Navy was transitioning. It was building fleets in eight or ten shipyards all over the place, and all were going to be in guided missilery in some form or another. Flying torpedoes, flying surface-to-air, surface-to-surface, Regulus, Terrier, and such.[*] So it was said that he felt a crisis coming on, and the fact that we just weren't preparing officers.

And I've got to say that the school dragged its feet an awful lot. I remember in the first year I went out there they were teaching the klystron. I later had some run-ins with the faculty out there once I got away from there and got older and I became a commander. That year the klystron was being taught as a low-power tube and a tube used only in receivers.[†] Well, of course, at that very same time the Bureau of Ordnance, which was so unalert as to what was being done out there that the big SPG-49 radar in

---

[*] Regulus was a surface-to-surface missile; Terrier was surface to air.
[†] Klystron is a linear-beam vacuum tube used as an amplifier at microwave and radio frequencies.

Talos and the big SPG-55B radar in Terrier—the most powerful radars ever put to sea until the Aegis radar, several megawatts of power—these radars were powered by klystrons. And those klystrons were designed and built in the great Sperry plant in Clearwater, Florida, the only place we could get them. And these klystrons stood just about as tall as you. They were really monsters. And, of course, they were all on mounts, and they cost an awful lot of money. So getting one up there, and the handling and care and feeding of it, both in storage and also on mount, was dainty.

Paul Stillwell: Were you still studying gun systems and torpedoes at that point?

Admiral Meyer: Affirmative. Affirmative. We were. I thought we were a little bit more advanced in maybe rocket engines, but I was really irked, later in life, with what they were teaching.

Paul Stillwell: Well, the Polaris program was coming along then.[*] Did you get any knowledge on that?

Admiral Meyer: And it was zero, thanks to Polaris. Polaris wanted nothing to do with anybody. Polaris was its own club, and it was like Rickover; you didn't get in either club. In my class, at that time, not a single submariner was there, and that was because Rickover decreed that. And Rickover decreed that putting an attack submarine in commission, or a ballistic missile submarine in commission, was equivalent to postgraduate training. Well, it was, but it wasn't, either. It was as though everybody else was a dummy in the world except his people. His successors finally got around to correcting that, because nuclear underwent a pretty dry spell on officers because no officers were being educated. That education turned out, really, in the end, to be inadequate. Because Rickover had drained the rest of the Navy of officers that had

---

[*] The first test firing of the Polaris AX-1 test vehicle, on 24 September 1958, was unsuccessful. The first successful firing was the AX-6; on 20 April 1959 it was flown 400 nautical miles down the Atlantic Missile Range. A shipboard test of the AX-22 followed on 27 August 1959 from the test ship *Observation Island* (EAG-154).

advanced educations and used them. He never put any back. Rickover was a greedy man, but he got his way.

Paul Stillwell: Did you have any aviators in your course?

Admiral Meyer: A couple. I can't remember whether they couldn't make it in jet training or some transition training; that's why we had them. So they were in essence grounded aviators. And you will recall that right after that is when we started through the turmoil of smashing BuAer and Bu Ord together into BuWeps.* I think that was the second year I was there, when that smash occurred.

The Navy had a quota that they had paid for, for six officers in the fire control curriculum at MIT. And the Navy was getting pig-headed that they could teach us just as well as anybody else. Well, the truth was they couldn't. So it came down to the Institute re-designating its work as aeronautics and astronautics. And the Navy had this quota it had to fill. Well, I wasn't going to fill it because, first of all, I hadn't been designated; I'd already been designated something else. And, second of all, I was too senior. Aha. So they got down to the end, and they only had five officers that met the MIT qualifications. Guess what. Wayne was number six. And so, overnight, I was headed to MIT.

Paul Stillwell: Let me ask you before that, please, how rigorous was the study program at Monterey, in terms of how many hours you had to spend a day and a week?

Admiral Meyer: It was awful. And I've said later—in a minute I'll come back to that. I call that my second tour at MIT. Six of us, and of course all of us had families. I had three children. You couldn't find a place to live. We didn't have any money. Nobody provided for you. Matter of fact, we lived, in my case, most of us did, down on the south shore in a summer house whose heat was not adequate for the winter. We lived in Cohasset, Massachusetts. We got through it, and it was a Navy experience. But the

---

* BuOrd, the Bureau of Ordnance, existed until 1959, when it was combined with the Bureau of Aeronautics to form the Bureau of Naval Weapons (BuWeps). In 1966 there was a split that separated out the former BuOrd as the Naval Ordnance Systems Command (NavOrd). In 1974 NavOrd was merged with the Naval Ship Systems Command to form the Naval Sea Systems Command (NavSea), which exists to the present.

commute to school was hell. Well, five of the six of us commuted in one old station wagon, so we banded together.

The workload. Our professors were—Dr. Draper's name was on many courses, and Dr. Wrigley's name. You think you see them very much? Only at a social—only at a drinkfest would they show up. Otherwise you'd get some graduate student. You think they had any textbooks? Had no textbooks at all. Well, but we had this little brotherhood of the six of us, contrasted to the course we were in, which had maybe, I don't know, 20 civilians and what kind, a collection of people, and even some regular graduate students in with us. They had a hard time. My time at the Institute, the second time, was a snap.

Now, why was it? Well, first of all, I was 35 years old; the others were in their 30s. And we knew how to get organized. So when we got a whole slew of these damned assignments, we parceled them out. Five of us rode back and forth in the truck and parceled them out during the hour-long commuter ride. So you and I would take on this problem, Smith and Jones would take on another problem, and so forth, and then we'd use the telephone. So we'd start exchanging data. It really pissed the whole place off, because they couldn't figure out how the Navy guys kept getting their homework done. [Chuckle]. They couldn't understand it. And, you know, those 22- and 23-year olds just worked their ass off working for their degree, and properly so. Well, we weren't any slugs. I mean, we weren't plagiarizing anything. We just knew how to do the work. And I've got to say I probably learned more that year about teamsmanship than anything else, of how important it was to do that and parcel things out.

So at the end of the year we came out shining. Lieutenant (senior grade) Tommy Noble, a Navy junior—lives down in Annapolis, or used to, I don't know where he lives now—was my mate in that undertaking.* I thought Tommy was pretty smart. I thought he was smarter than I was. But I don't think Tommy was a very good seaman. It appeared to me that his daddy had pushed him into the Navy and here he was. And they lived, you know, right near the circle there down in Annapolis.

Paul Stillwell: There was a chief of the Bureau of Ordnance named Noble. Was that his father?

---

* Lieutenant Thomas I. Noble, USN.

Admiral Meyer: I think it's the same one, right. Right. Went back to that.

Paul Stillwell: Well, you said there were five quotas and you were number six. How did you get in that?

Admiral Meyer: Well, one guy couldn't find any housing—or wouldn't, his wife wouldn't live where we were living—so he ended up on the other side of town. That's up at MIT. So five of us pooled and split the expenses and he traveled separately, so our communication with him was in class or by telephone.

Paul Stillwell: No, but I thought you said there had been five quotas the Navy had to fill through the school.

Admiral Meyer: There were six quotas the Navy had to fill and they only had five to put in them.

Paul Stillwell: Oh, I've got it.

Admiral Meyer: That was the problem. And the one they had picked, Lieutenant Oscar Sanden —the detailer in no way would send him.[*] Decided he *would* go to sea, period. So he was jerked over the objection of the school. And they had the empty quota, and it was paid for, so I was yanked into it in place of Owey. And then the school was so pissed that they created a special undertaking, which at that time was really, really hard, so Owey could get a master's degree in electrical engineering by working overtime and staying four more months at Monterey. So Owey stayed there and he got his degree. And because we'd been picked for this, they wouldn't give us a master's degree. So Owey got his master's degree, and he got it from PG school.

Paul Stillwell: Had you done any thesis work at Monterey?

---

[*] Lieutenant Oscar E. Sanden Jr., USN.

Admiral Meyer: The answer is no. We were awarded a bachelor's as our consolation prize, and that was that.

So we went on. Tommy Noble and I became partners and thesis partners at the Institute. So things were going along pretty good. But school was now easy. I mean, when we figured out how to study, school became a hell of a lot easier. And a point I'm getting slow at making: Monterey really had prepared us. Those kids weren't prepared that were coming out of the regular Institute or were coming from someplace else. Monterey did prepare us for graduate work. So there's no doubt in my mind it was a good school. I got a taste in my mouth, and I've had it ever since, about the quality of Monterey, and its significance and its importance. I'm sorry to say that the inhabitants there never recognized that. They're so haughty. They spend all their time trying to compete that they don't, from an attitude viewpoint, worry about the development and the education of naval officers. But my one-year experience at MIT, I made straight A's. It's the only time in my life I made straight A's. I mean, I've had 18 or 20 semesters; it's the only time I ever made straight A's. And Tommy made straight A.

So it was interesting. We wrote our thesis under Dr. Mueller—not the Dr. Müller of the Geiger counter but another Dr. Mueller who was well known in a couple of his inventions at the time, and he agreed to be our thesis adviser. So we had to come in and tell him the title we had picked. He said, "Well, all right. It's okay." He said, "That sounds good." What we were really going to do—because we didn't think we could get it approved, but we thought that's what a good thing was for naval officers—we're going to do research in the materials that existed and had been researched, and we were going to compile that on fire control and on the matter of servo mechanisms.* Well, Dr. Mueller agreed with that, and so he told us to come see him about every two months.

Paul Stillwell: Did the Navy have any input in that choice? BuWeps?

Admiral Meyer: No. I can't even think where in the hell the O-in-C was for the group. I don't even ever remember seeing him in that time.

---

* A servo a device for controlling action at a remote location.

Paul Stillwell: Did you report administratively to an NROTC unit?

Admiral Meyer: I don't know whether he was called the NROTC guy yet or not, because I can't recall for sure whether NROTC had then been established. They also have had up there since time began the naval architects and marine engineering group which gets postgraduate education at MIT. And I think even they reported separately. The Navy puts a couple engineering duty officers up there, who, amongst other things, do teaching and also oversee the course.

The problem with it was it was in the instrumentation lab. We didn't go in the main building except rarely. We were over in the labs, and those labs were—I think they're all gone now—they were buildings thrown up during World War II by the chocolate factory, and they were just slapped up.

Paul Stillwell: What do you mean, "chocolate factory"?

Admiral Meyer: Well, there's a chocolate factory right nearby, on Mass Avenue, and you could smell that damned thing; wherever you went you smelled that chocolate factory.[*]

Paul Stillwell: Well, that's a pleasant smell.

Admiral Meyer: Well, it was, except pretty soon it would get aggravating because it would get everything rolling in your body. [Laughter] Your body would start responding to it and get upset because you didn't handle it.

So we wandered around. We went in, saw Dr. Mueller every few weeks, told him, "Yeah, we're working on it, we're working on it."

Paul Stillwell: Was your study looking at practical applications?

---

[*] Mass Avenue – Massachusetts Avenue.

Admiral Meyer: That would be a stretch. It was really investigative work. But in that sense it was looking at what could you get out of it to work practically, what was worth saving. You know that great big dome up there. You go up in that dome and you go up there and look around in the archives, and they've got jillions of theses that are stored up there, never get the dust knocked off of them. Which tells you something about how important theses are, from that viewpoint. Occasionally there's a breakthrough but not very often.

So finally the time came for us. We had to go in and present to Dr. Mueller our findings and show him our materials and stuff. So his assistant, she had arranged for us to come in one day and meet with him, in his laboratory, actually. So we were nervous as hell, because we didn't think we were on very solid ground, really. So we reported and she gave us a seat there in the anteroom. She said, "Dr. Mueller is working on something right now, and he'll be with you soon." So we sat there and got nervouser and nervouser.

Finally, after half an hour or so we got brought in, and he was at his desk. He had a couple chairs for us to sit down in. He said, "Well, so you're about to complete school."

"Yes, sir."

He said, "I have looked at your thesis material here and such and your outlines, and what I want to know is whether you learned anything or not."

"Yes, sir. Matter of fact, we're stunned at how much we learned. We really, really learned a lot."

"Well," he said, "I'm pleased to hear that. Thank you very much." [Laughter] And that was it. He gave us an A and we went on.

Paul Stillwell: Had he been helpful in providing inputs as you went along?

Admiral Meyer: I don't know that he was overly helpful. We'd go in and give him these in-flight reports, and he'd make a suggestion where you might go look and find something worth dredging up, including some of his own materials, which we were noble enough to do, Tommy Noble and I, [chuckle] and make sure they got referenced someplace in the appendix, although he was really a chemistry guy. But I learned that he really was a good thesis supervisor. Because we were up in our 30s, he treated us as adults. He didn't treat us as regular students that much. And he was of the view that we were old enough to know what was worthwhile, and whatever we did would turn out to *be* worthwhile. I don't think that he was prepared to devote very much of his time to it trying to teach us that.

Paul Stillwell: Maybe he felt he didn't need to.

Admiral Meyer: Well, that could be too. But he was certainly very kind to us. Anytime we brought something up, he was responsive to us. If we rang her up to talk to him, she'd say, "Well, I can get you such-and-such a time."

"Yes, ma'am." And his own lab was a typical lab like out of a movie. You couldn't get in the damned thing. [Chuckle] So he was kind of honorable, and he is kind of noted. He was a person that couldn't resist things. And I think that he had a lot of students doing research for him, and he didn't particularly need our research. Although my guess is that he took a copy of our paper and saved it. That would be my guess, because it had a pretty damned nice compilation of the things of the day. That itself took a lot of work.

Paul Stillwell: What did the contents include in your thesis?

Admiral Meyer: They included the abstracts, more than anything else, of various masters' degrees; we looked through several doctorals; we created a few things of our own. We decided we were going to kibitz on some of these, based on our own learning. So I like to think that our advisers gave us credit for our originality and our creativity by kibitzing on them. And in later life it turned out for me that was the right thing to do, because the job of an officer is to oversee others. It's not the job of an officer to push everybody out of the way on a bench and start doing research.

I was ordered from there to USS *Galveston*.

Paul Stillwell: I'm still trying to get at the contents. You say you looked at these other theses and so forth. What were the topics of those? Did you do some kind of a synthesis?

Admiral Meyer: No. That's a worthwhile question, and I may just give you a stupid answer, after thinking about this after some 50 years since I did it—I don't even know whether I could even find it now. What we did was a lot of reading. We went through that dome up there. We went through that dome trying to find topics that fit what we thought was fire control and servo mechanisms, and the birthing of servo mechanisms, how they came about. You probably could look at it as—it wouldn't be equivalent to a textbook. It was kind of meant to be a summation of the art. And I think the reason we could get away with it is at that time the world was moving really fast.

Paul Stillwell: It was shortly after Sputnik, for example.[*]

Admiral Meyer: Yes, but I think I told you that the first time I went to MIT we did everything in the time domain in all the courses I took, which were graduate courses. The second time they were all in the frequency domain. And, ironically, the PG school at Monterey was already in the frequency domain in its teachings. That's called, in the jargon, the Laplace transforms.[†] So, instead of doing long exponential equations with the "E's" on them, those equations when they're transformed into the frequency domain under what's known as Laplace's transform—the famous doctor of the century before the 19th century, Laplace created this mechanism where you could transform out of the exponential base into the linear base, and hence start solving the problems in a linear way that the ordinary person could grasp. Plus, way simpler. One of the problems was how to get back. You had to transform back when you were finished. That could be a real bitch to get it done, because you would start losing insight into where you started from.

---

[*] On 4 October 1957, the Soviet Union launched Sputnik I, the first artificial earth satellite. It caused great uproar in the United States, which had expected to be first in space.

[†] In mathematics the Laplace transform is used in solving differential and linear equations. Applications include analysis of such things as electrical circuits, optical devices, and mechanical systems. The transform is named for Pierre-Simon, marquis de Laplace (1749-1827), a French mathematician and astronomer who did work on probability theory.

The other difficulty with exponentials—working in the world of exponentials in advanced work, you'd get partial differential equations, which I've had, I don't know, four courses in. I've had calculus like, I don't know, six times or so. Well, you get those long equations—and sometimes I think that today's world ought to have to work on them. You'd get equations that reach all the way across this room. And if you get an error someplace in the coefficient or in the exponential, just one letter or number, it might take you days or weeks before you ever discovered it or found it. Once you got in the frequency domain, it was relatively easy—I don't want to say it was easy, but it was relatively easy—to capture your error, or conclude, hey, we must have an error in here someplace.

That was the other problem in the time domain. It was hard for you to conclude whether you had an error, because these exponentials, once they started progressing in, I'd say the late '40s and into the '50s—it wasn't that the math didn't exist. Boolean algebra and all that math existed all the way back in the 19th century. The problem was it had no utility and no one used it. And now here, all of a sudden, postwar, this use of it was born in servo-mechanisms, primarily.

What happened, and it's frankly been forgotten today, is almost all the equations in that world are empirical equations, not logical equations, or the other word I'm trying to think of, which I'll think of in a minute here. They are not mathematically derived or discovered. Almost all the big equations—take the radar range equation, or the sonar range equation, all of these important equations. Every one of them has a jock factor in it, because they're not exactly correct.[*] The radar range equation is approximately correct. What's the big jock factor in the radar range equation? Well, it's the target size. And just because the target is this big, or this big, or this big doesn't determine its characteristics, necessarily, from a radar viewpoint, and its behavior.

So the understanding of those jock factors in—when I was much, much younger, and this was still true of Dr. Mueller's labs, by the way—you'd go in to visit your scientist. And I remember how awed I was even with—Dr. Thaler was the head of the department at the University of Kansas, and he was quite well noted in government. He

---

[*] "Jock factor" was a term that Admiral Meyer used to mean "constants" in equations, which often were empirically derived, not mathematically derived.

had done a lot of creative work on bringing electricity into Alaska. But you'd go into their offices or labs, whatever you'd like to call them, but all them in that era, they'd have a suite of rooms like this. And you'd walk around in their rooms, and the rooms would just be full of handbooks. The data in those handbooks came from graduate students. So many, many, many students got direction from their master because the doctor wanted to get some blanks filled in or a table filled in in the handbooks. And if you go down to Dahlgren and start probing deeply into the past at Dahlgren, that was true there in ballistics and ballistic mechanics, that handbooks, one after the other, became very, very important, because that's where the factors were stored, and many of them are still stored today in things like civil engineering and places like that.*

Ah, the digital computer was a godsend, because now you didn't need this handbook. You could store it in the computer, and it would be kept there, providing you could design a system to be able to call out what it is you wanted to call out, or even do research on what to call out. Well, that's not as easy as people think. So now we've raised whole generations who don't connect at all with the two things.

They sophosized Newton's laws, to start with. And then they start flouting the behavior of the universe, because they think they're so goddamn smart. And in the world of the digit—see, there's no inertia in the world of the digit. And so you grow up today in school, and you never learn what inertia means. You just don't learn it. It's my own view—just an old person's view—this is why accidents keep going up in spite of our damnedest effort. We like to blame it on youth and not learning how to drive and all those things. Well, it's because they have no grasp of inertia. Because they start in kindergarten with tools that don't teach them a thing about inertia. It's a little box like that, just tick, tick, tick, tick.

Paul Stillwell: Like a video game.

---

* Naval Surface Warfare Center Dahlgren Division, Dahlgren, Virginia. For many years it was known as the Naval Proving Ground.

Admiral Meyer: It's like a video game. And so there's no time instance or time elapses between the behavior, what it really is, it really is. And therein lies the—my ability to snatch words for you today is not at its usual par.

Paul Stillwell: Did you use digital computers during that course at MIT?

Admiral Meyer: No. No, didn't have any. No, no, no. I never used a digital computer. The second time that I was back to the PG school we had a computer out there. I don't recall its designator right now. But I'm sure you perhaps know, the weather bureau and the Navy aerological service, they've had schools there at Monterey for a number of years, and so they brought a lot of gear in over the years. But they're the first ones that brought in any kind of a computer for number smashing. And it got so bad before we left—certainly, in hindsight, you could see that this big tornado was coming, but the one computer, the designator was like 128 or something. Well, you got time on it as a student, so you would be allowed, like, 30 minutes on Thursday night. They'd run it around the clock. So you'd have to go get yourself in a big queue. For the whole damned school they only had one computer that was going to do some crunching for your particular use. Well, a lot of people, including me, said to hell with this noise; I'm not going to spend my time number crunching. Because the truth is you don't learn anything from number crunching. You don't learn a damn thing, in spite of what people think. All you do is just burn a lot of time.

And the other part is, somebody else will crunch the damned things for you anyhow.

Paul Stillwell: Well, last week, when the tape recorder wasn't running, you told me with some pride that you still don't use computers.

Admiral Meyer: That's true. I still do not. We were not taught them when I went to school, and I never developed the habit afterwards. I don't want to say I have a hate for them; I don't mean that. I don't even have a distaste for them. They frankly don't have any utility to me. Now, I watch Anna Mae. I mean, every night she's on one. But it's mostly playing games with her friends or something like that, is what she's doing. Our daughter came down from Jersey to visit us last night. I get up this morning, there she is out in the front room, our daughter, there she is punching up this—I mean, that thing just couldn't wait, kept calling you all night, that you had to get on there. She said, "Oh, no, no, no; I'm looking up some stuff."

I said. "Yeah, like what?" Well, that stumped her. [Laughter] She couldn't answer that.

I personally, and this is some old man, but I don't believe this is good for our youth. I've given speeches on this at times and may start giving them again, for all I know—the real world is not digital. The real world is analog. So if we're going to deal in the real world, we have to convert and jump over into digital. And, by the way, when you do that, you've got to get back. Now, we've got a bunch of jerks, this new breed, who think they're smarter even than God Himself, who believe that that's not an issue, it's not a problem, that it really is a digital world; you just have to grow up and learn how to operate in it. And they really are jerks.

You have trouble finding people with that behavior that really contribute anything. They make a lot of racket. They make a lot of money. They make piles of money off of that computer. They don't contribute anything.

Now, as a storage mechanism it, of course, has no peer. As a matter of fact, as a calculator it has no peer either. But we keep believing that we can put a brain in the computer that will replace our own. It ain't going to happen in my lifetime. It may happen in yours, but it ain't going to happen in mine.

Does that mean they're useless? No, it doesn't mean they're useless. But it is a sad thing when you find kids 12, 14 years old, 15 years old, who can't even recite the fundamental multiplication tables. I believe that's a sad thing. I believe we're doing a disservice to those people as they grow up, because their daily life will be impacted by that. And I'm sure you've gone into a store and watched these young women at the counter who can't make change. Well, most of the machines now have it designed into them, to do it for them. But they went through the stage where they had this little calculator sitting alongside so that—let's see, two from five's three.

When I grew up, with those beautiful teachers that I mentioned to you, they were all just second thought. Every class that I had, and this was still true in college and even still true in the old-timers in the Institute—your grade in every class was determined by all, by the total performance. A sloppy paper could guarantee you that you'd lose out. You'd get a C at best.

Paul Stillwell: Was there any sense of competition among the Navy students there at MIT at that time?

Admiral Meyer: I can't say that there was, because it was more like a lifeboat approach. And so we just spent our time surviving. We had children, and we did have our families at significant disadvantage. I couldn't say we were in any competition, except that we knew we could beat all those in their 20s, hands down. I mean, there was not even a contest.

Paul Stillwell: Well, it sounds as if you were pooling your knowledge.

Admiral Meyer: We were. And I have to say I enjoyed it. As I say, I made straight A's, and it was an enjoyable year. It was an enjoyable year. It was probably good for me, I know it was good for me, in that I rubbed up against a lot of people not of my class, not of my type, and so had to learn a certain amount of toleration.

Paul Stillwell: What type were they"

Admiral Meyer: Well, there were a lot of smart alecks. There were plenty of smart alecks.

Paul Stillwell: Were there hippies?

Admiral Meyer: I'm not sure they'd meet today's definition necessarily that way because the MIT wasn't all that tolerant of bums. They just wouldn't tolerate bums. The Institute had rules of its own. They used to kid them that you could spot an Institute person against a Harvard person anytime on Mass Avenue just by the way they were dressed. So they weren't hippies. But a lot of them were loners, real loners. Brilliant in their minds, but they weren't very communicative.

Paul Stillwell: Not much on social skills.

Admiral Meyer: No, not a bit. I mean, like a dance at MIT is a very rare thing indeed, really rare. And when I was a student at Kansas University, I mean every weekend there'd be a half dozen dances of one kind or another. Went on all the time. It was very rare at MIT. No, they weren't much on social skills.

Paul Stillwell: Was there any friction with the smart alecks?

Admiral Meyer: I don't think there were enough of us to pose a problem. I think the people who were the graduate students who were subbing as instructors had more of a problem with us than anybody else, because, I mean, we were beyond most of them and they just hadn't caught up with us. It wasn't that they were stupid; they just hadn't caught up with us.

Paul Stillwell: It sounds as if they were not as capable as the instructors at Monterey.

Admiral Meyer: No, they weren't. No, we had seasoned instructors at Monterey. You had a lot of gray hair at Monterey. But they didn't have graduate students either, filling in for the professors. MIT's got a lot of that. You'd have Wrigley's name on the course, but, God, if you saw Wrigley once a month you were doing pretty good. I may have told you about the first time I went to MIT.

Paul Stillwell: You did.

Admiral Meyer: Yeah. It's the only time I ever made an F. In physics. Vibration and sound. I flunked the course that Dr. Morse was supposed to be the professor. It was a Navy-dictated course; it was not my selection. But I still flunked it. I couldn't handle it. And I believe I told you, in that era if you flunked the final you could pay five dollars and take a makeup exam and raise your grade to a D. I did that, and I still flunked it. I never made it. [Chuckle] It's the only F I got in all my keepsakes.

Paul Stillwell: Did you have any contact at all with Dr. Draper?

Admiral Meyer: Yes, we did, but they were usually semi-social things. Doc would be scheduled to give us a little talk at 1700 or 1600. He would talk with students and he was going to talk about some such-and-such subject. Of course, he was a very active inventor his own self at the time, as was Wrigley, both. So they would socialize. And one of the things about MIT, Doc Draper liked to break out the whiskey bottle. And he liked to drink Scotch. So he'd come into the lab at 4:00 o'clock or so, and students would gather around to him and we'd just all listen to him for a couple hours. I'm sure he had something in mind. It would appear that all we were doing was just batting the breeze, but I'm confident he had in mind something. He was getting something out of us, or he wouldn't be doing it.

Paul Stillwell: Well, he'd had a long affiliation with the Navy.

Admiral Meyer: Oh yeah, oh yeah. And he loved youth, he really did. He liked to be around them. And, as I told you that whole thing, my life as it went on and everything, I always thought when I left the Navy I'd be a teacher. It turns out that being associated with youth is pretty darned good. It keeps you alive, keeps you active. And a lot of it is to make sure they stay on the truth line someplace, because they can really drift away.

Well, we got through that year okay. As far as I know, the Navy has no such courses today. I've got to say I believe almost all of them came out of Arleigh Burke or they were initiated by him through all that era, and his predecessors. My original courses—I've told you that, when I went there the first time, you know, you'd have

250-300 people in a class. I mean, they did have people 60 years old. They were back studying subjects trying to catch up. They'd been away working on something for the services and now they were catching up. So we couldn't compete with them. We just couldn't handle it.

I sure don't disregard it as a useless experience. I mean, it was unique, first of all, and second of all it served me well in my life. It took me a while to understand that, and I always think of Commander Robert S. Guy, who was a detailer at the time—that son of a bitch. I'd known him as a commander, because he was on DesLant staff. He was a pompous ass then. Well, he went home. I didn't go home. The Navy was kind enough to promote me.

Paul Stillwell: Now, when you say he went home, that means he didn't make flag?

Admiral Meyer: You got it.* You got it. [Laughter] He started deciding, I think, at lieutenant (j.g.) level that he was going to be admiral. He didn't make it.

Paul Stillwell: Did you have negotiations with BuPers on your next duty after MIT?

Admiral Meyer: No, I didn't, really, because once again the Navy was desperate for officers of my credentials. And, interesting enough, I came out of MIT, and the Navy had created a very early school, at Dam Neck, to orient you on Talos.† I was ordered to all of the school, but it was all cancelled, because it was urgent that I get to the ship. So, once again, I ended up being self-taught. And as I've said to you a couple times now, there ain't nobody dumber than a self-taught person.

---
* Guy retired as a captain in August 1971.
† Fleet Anti-Air Warfare Training Center (FAAWTC), Dam Neck, Virginia Beach, Virginia. Talos was a long-range ramjet missile used by surface ships in the antiair mission. It was 33 feet long, 28 inches in diameter, and weighed 7,000 pounds. It had a range of about 75 miles. Its first successful intercept of a drone target was in October 1952. It entered fleet service on board the cruiser *Galveston* (CLG-3) in 1958.

So I reported in to *Galveston* as fire control officer.* But once I caught onto the Talos lingo, it turned out that my education *had* prepared me to lead petty officers and to lead officers. And I've thought a lot about that, of how the CNO and God somehow created the officers that it needed when it needed them. They somehow get created. Sometimes we bust, but the leadership is more forward-looking than perhaps they get credit for, at times.

I've fired more Talos missiles than any man alive. I don't say that so much in braggadocio, although I'm very proud of it, but it was just something that befell me. It was an opportunity that befell me not only as fire control but then gun boss, in Talos. It was a missile system that the Navy discarded to its loss.

The Navy has been very fortunate in many ways—and part of it is good fortune—that it has not needed these systems, although they provided an extraordinary deterrence, I believe, through the years. But the Talos did, in fact, impact in Korea, and it did, in fact, impact in Vietnam. Now, I say in Korea; this is not during the war in Korea but later in the war, in 1968 I believe is the year—you're really good at this stuff—whenever the EC-121 was shot down.† I participated in that operation. It's another special operation that we may get to one of these days, I don't know.

Paul Stillwell: Yes, we will.

Admiral Meyer: We will? I've been blessed in that there have been a number of operations that I have participated in that were unique, and different things have occurred in my life that were unique, that I was called on to perform or to do. Some of them probably were because I made something of them. You know the expression of making a

---

* The light cruiser *Galveston* (CL-93) was launched 22 April 1945, and her construction was suspended 24 June 1946. After being held in reserve for several years she was reclassified a guided missile light cruiser, CLG-3, on 23 May 1957, converted at the Philadelphia Naval Shipyard, and commissioned on 28 May 1958. She was armed with six 6-inch guns, six 5-inch guns, and was fitted with one twin launcher for Talos surface-to-air missiles. She had a full-load displacement of 14,600 tons, was 608 feet long, 64 feet in the beam, had a maximum draft of 25 feet, and a top speed of 33 knots.
† A U.S. Navy EC-121 electronic reconnaissance aircraft with 31 crewmen on board was shot down 14 April 1969 by North Korean aircraft. The incident took place approximately 90 miles off the coast of North Korea. The entire U.S. crew was lost.

sow's ear out of a pig, or vice versa. And that opportunity ultimately occurred in ASMS, now called Aegis, which was a pig if there ever was one.

Paul Stillwell: Well, we'll get to that, but how far along was *Galveston* in the conversion process when you reported?

Admiral Meyer: She was about half done. She had been taken out of the shipyard at Philadelphia when I reported, to fire a series of missiles—she was only half done—and these were fired down in the Caribbean.* And they were to make a determination whether it was really going to work or not before proceeding any further. After I reported, we went back into the shipyard. It turned out she was in there some 14 or 15 months after that, to finish the job, and then transferred to San Diego. And that's how I ended up firing more missiles.

She was out of the yard when I did report because she was operating in the Caribbean for this stuff, and then we brought her back, and the fire control officer had been an LDO, plus he was also missile officer, and he wanted to retire.† So that's how I ended up being fire control officer. That, plus the admiral had just taken over, Admiral Reich, and he had decreed that the fire control officer for Talos would be a lieutenant commander with a master's degree in ordnance.‡ Well, that put a whole different spin on things. It didn't go very far, either, but it did change the world.

Then we finished this work under my aegis, so to speak, where everybody in the ship every day was PO'd at me because I was the determinant as to when the ship could sail. So every day the captain bugged me, and the truth was I didn't know. And the shipyard would do anything to get rid of us by then. We finally did sail. I'm trying to remember when we sailed. But I recall when we left the yard at Philadelphia the whole yard turned out, including the commanding officer. And they turned out to see us go, not

---

* On 24 February 1959, the *Galveston* made the first successful firing of a Talos missile at sea. Meyer reported to the ship in June 1961. From May through July 1961, the ship did extensive missile testing under the Operational Test and Evaluation Force.
† LDO – limited duty officer, a former enlisted man or woman whose duties are limited to the area of his/her enlisted rating specialty.
‡ In July 1962, Rear Admiral Eli T. Reich, USN, became director of the Special Navy Task Force for Surface Missile Systems. The oral history of Reich, who retired as a vice admiral, is in the Naval Institute collection. Meyer was ordered to the *Galveston* in 1961, the year before Reich took over.

to scratch their back for a job well done but rather: "Thank goodness; we finally got rid of that guy."*

Paul Stillwell: Who was your skipper?

Admiral Meyer: We got a new one at that juncture. He was the new one, though; he wasn't the first one that I had; he was the second.† And he really made my life. He made my life. Because it was interesting. He had no wife, he had no family. We had rented a house that we couldn't afford—it was just an ordinary house, way the hell over in West Berlin, New Jersey—to commute back and forth to that shipyard. So I had my wife and the kids living over there. But the reason I remember this guy is that we invited him out to our house several times during the weekends because he had nowhere to go, so we just invited him to come out, which he took us up on. And he kind of enjoyed the kids and such. He was a very likable person. He was not a mixer, but he was a nice enough person, so my wife and I enjoyed him. He was kind to us in a backhanded way.

Paul Stillwell: What do you mean, "backhanded"?

Admiral Meyer: [Chuckle] He saw that we were watched after. And my word was important to him, because he didn't want to move unless I agreed with it. Well, then right before we sailed we got a new skipper. I can't say that guy's name. And he was one that was really, really pissed off because somebody had assured him that he'd be promoted to admiral—I don't know whether it was, you know, a mess cook or somebody [laughter]—which never happened. And I got an accommodation with him for the next 12 months but it was a tough one.

Paul Stillwell: Please describe some of those missile tests down in the Caribbean.

---

* The *Galveston* was in overhaul at the Philadelphia Naval Shipyard from 30 August 1961 through 23 July 1962. The shipyard period included modifications to the Talos fire control system.
† Captain John H. Cotten, USN, commanded the *Galveston* from 4 February 1961 to 11 April 1962. Captain Gerald P. Joyce, USN, was CO from 11 April 1962 to 1 June 1963.

Admiral Meyer: Well, they were all pretty basic. I'd better describe the tests that we did in the Pacific, because that's where I did most of the firing. Those in the Caribbean were just really kind of proofing that the system would work, and secondly proofing the range. There was no range structure, so we were creating a range at the same time. And so every one of them was a challenge.

Paul Stillwell: Were the target services out of Roosevelt Roads?

Admiral Meyer: Well, we had a number of F6Fs. It took a lot of F6Fs to get one that would fly.[*]

A lieutenant worked for me in *Galveston*, Lieutenant Peyton Randolph Wise II. He reported the same day I did, or the next day, and later he ended up following me to the bureau. And he's the one that made the expression—I may be repeating myself—he said: "The problem with naval officers is every one of them works for himself." You've got to think about the cynicism in that expression. It takes a while before it starts hitting you between the eyes. The way we've raised naval officers and the way we've developed them, they really are odd creatures, because naval officers are at the same time bred to leadership, bred to teamsmanship, bred to care for their crew and such, and yet they work for themselves. There's hardly anybody ever going to send you on a tour of duty if you don't put some time on it yourself. Except those, you know, who are the elevated ones that run around here.

Frankly, I'm pleased to see a whole damn bunch of them being sent home right now. These high fliers who—the reason I know so many of them at my late age is, of course, they got their fame in Aegis cruisers and destroyers. So they took commands in both of them, and it's a rare one indeed that contributed anything long term. And there are many ships that you can walk into a week after the captain left and say, in the wardroom, "By the way, tell me again what was the name of the last captain?" "Hey, John, who was that? I've got it right on the tip of my tongue. I can't say it." Doesn't last very long. And then other captains leave a long, long mark.

---

[*] The F6F Hellcat was the Navy's top carrier fighter plane during World War II. By this time drone versions of the aircraft were used as targets.

Well, I'd hoped that I could raise my officers the second way, to leave a long mark, and so they've gotten a lot of lectures from me in the last 30 years on how important their duties are in this part of our Navy. Because what's in those cruisers is what *they* put in them, not what some passing captain put in them. And it's there forever, and if it's a bummer it's a bummer forever. And if you've got a lousy goddamn design on a coffee pot, you live with it forever. *Hundreds* of people live with it. We hardly ever think about that. And I'm starting to get a little irked with this younger crowd right now because, while they proclaim me the father of Aegis, and they say that in some—I don't want to say a smart-alecky way, but I'm acknowledged as that, but it has no meaning to it. They have no feel whatsoever of how hard it is to get a fleet. Now, I don't want to sound like I'm bemoaning that. But in a way I am, because our officers are not being taught or raised how hard those things are to do.

Interview Number 7 with Rear Admiral Wayne E. Meyer, U.S. Navy (Retired)
Place: Admiral Meyer's office in Arlington, Virginia
Date: Tuesday, 25 March 2008

Paul Stillwell: Admiral, we're ready to resume on USS *Galveston*, and just to recap, she was commissioned in 1958 under Captain John Colwell and did a number of tests.[*] You got there in the summer of 1961, which was maybe two and a half years after she had gone into service. And you told me last time that you were doing some testing down in the Caribbean. What did that involve?

Admiral Meyer: A short preamble. You can shorten it wherever you want. I'm thinking of a cruiser in that era as contrasted to today. First of all, she was a 6-inch cruiser and had three turrets originally. Turret three was removed in order to accommodate the Talos launcher. So in the lingo of the day she became known as a single-ender.[†] And the conversion work had been done in Philadelphia. Certainly in hindsight, it was primitive work. I don't think it was very well supervised. It wasn't very well run, very well put together. But such criticism may not be warranted.

Paul Stillwell: You mentioned previously that you were directed to report to the *Galveston* sooner than planned, so you didn't go to the school at Dam Neck. Was there a perceived shortcoming in the system that somebody in BuPers wanted to fix by sending you with a master's degree?

Admiral Meyer: Well, it wasn't so much that somebody in BuPers wanted to fix it. It was that Admiral Eli Reich, who had just taken the task force, and he and Nitze determined they were going to overhaul the whole Navy on guided missilery.[‡] And as far as I could tell, Arleigh Burke supported it.

---

[*] Captain John B. Colwell, USN, commanded the *Galveston* from the date of her commissioning, 28 May 1958, to 18 November 1958. The oral history of Colwell, who retired as a vice admiral, is in the Naval Institute collection.
[†] Later guided missile ships had missile launchers both forward and aft.
[‡] Paul Nitze did not become the Secretary of the Navy until late 1963, well after Meyer reached the *Galveston*.

Now, what I'm about to say could smack of sour grapes. Arleigh Burke had a great ability to support things that he didn't agree with. When he saw how the tide was swinging, he could switch his—and I frankly believe that he did that in Polaris, and I think he probably did it in guided missilery. But in my association with Arleigh Burke I never saw him support Polaris. I may have mentioned to you that he gave a fire-storming speech out at Monterey shortly after I had arrived. He was the CNO then. And he was talking about naval presence, which was to him the really most significant dimension of a navy, is its presence, and without the presence it would have no meaning. And he used as his examples the Polaris submarine. So he said to all of us, students there, King Auditorium full, "What presence is Polaris going to provide?" The answer, of course, is none. And Arleigh answered the question himself that it was not going to. Well, as you know, even today in some places he's known as the instigator or father of the Polaris and a great booster of it. Well, sometimes things tend to get transposed as time passes.

Paul Stillwell: He does get that credit. Not totally, but certainly for supporting it.

Admiral Meyer: Yeah. Right. Now I say I want to be cautious, because I could see it maybe happening to me right here on this bulletin board [chuckle].* That the reality of life is being transferred to another coordinate system.

Paul Stillwell: But my understanding is that Admiral Reich's task force was set up because there were perceived problems in the surface-to-air missile system, and he was supposed to fix them.

Admiral Meyer: Would you like for me to talk about that a couple minutes?

Paul Stillwell: Sure.

---

* In the conference room where the oral history interviews took place in Admiral Meyer's office complex was a bulletin board that was frequently updated with progress photos of his namesake ship, the guided missile destroyer *Wayne E. Meyer* (DDG-108), which was then being built at Bath Iron Works.

Admiral Meyer: All right. Well. I can't say which year—I think it was '62, but it's approximately then—Eli Reich had command of the cruiser *Canberra*.* And the new young President that we were infatuated with, namely one J. F. Kennedy, had been elected. And very early on he had been attracted by the Navy—I'm not prepared to say which Secretary at the time—but he'd been attracted by the Navy to come to Norfolk on a Saturday for some firepower demos.† And it was to be specifically the cruiser *Boston* and an aircraft carrier. I just can't recall whether she had an angled deck or not. Something significant had been done on the aircraft carrier, either in the catapults or on the decks, and that was to be demonstrated to the President and the Secretary of the Navy.

There was a super-grade civil servant, GS-17 or so, that went with them. He was the Secretary's adviser on the new emerging guided missiles. They took off to go down to Norfolk for this demo. And I think I'm correct in that they heloed out to the Hampton Roads and that that of itself was a little bit gutsy, because helos were kind of in their birthing period as aircraft. And they heloed out—I almost said the name of that aircraft carrier; it's not relevant at the moment—to the aircraft carrier. And amongst other things on here they were going to witness a firing from the *Canberra*—Terrier missiles, BWs, beam-rider missiles, wing-controlled, meaning that those missiles had no tail; they had wings that controlled. And they were advertised at roughly a nominal range, ten miles. And the targets were still very questionable. They were trying to mainly fly an F6F or something of that nature to provide a target.

Well, they went to work to provide this demo, and they watched on the sponson, the story goes. I was in *Galveston*, I think, by that time. And they watched and they watched. They watched almost all of Saturday. And by something like 3:00 o'clock the President apparently said that, "Well, I've got to get home. Jackie's got this big affair tonight and I've got to be at it." Not a shot was fired.

---

* Captain Eli T. Reich, USN, commanded the guided missile cruiser *Canberra* (CAG-2) from 7 November 1960 to 1 December 1961. His Naval Institute oral history is most useful on missile testing.
† Admiral Meyer apparently mixed a couple of stories in his memory. The presidential fleet visit Meyer remembered was from 9 through 14 April 1962. However, the significant missile test failures conducted by Captain Reich in the *Canberra* were in 1960-61. They were the stimulus for the Shaw report, mentioned on page 249, and predated that Kennedy fleet visit. As Adelaide Madsen's history of Aegis indicates, the Shaw report was one of the first items that confronted Fred Korth when he became SecNav on 4 January 1962. Reich soon was put in charge of the missile project. An outgrowth of Kennedy's visit, reports Meyer associate Troy Kimmel, was a directive that guided missile ships had to be equipped with guns also.

Finally they heloed the President off, they returned to Washington, and the Secretary, of course, was just absolutely beside himself, as was the CNO. And this big tall fellow, Milt Shaw, was given an order by the Secretary to conduct an investigation immediately.[*]

In the meantime the *Canberra* sailed for the Caribbean for what we used to call Exercise Springboard. I think she was part of the Springboard operation. She sailed for that, and this guy managed to get an airplane that flew him to Guantanamo Bay, and he went on board and he interviewed the captain about the situation. And this captain unloaded on him. There's a report that's about that thick.

Paul Stillwell: Two inches. Two inches thick.

Admiral Meyer: Yeah. I may have the only copy, I don't know. And I don't even know where the hell it is. It's got a lot of technical babble in it, but it's got some pretty good stuff in it too. But he interviewed and interviewed, and Reich kept bitching about how this had not been engineered, this wasn't going to ever work, couldn't make it go, and so forth. So the Secretary—God, I might be wrong. I've told this story several times; I can't be wrong. But the Secretary sent for Reich. And allegedly the Secretary knew that Reich was on the list to be an admiral. Reich didn't know he was on the list. He interviewed Reich and appointed him on the spot to command this new task force.[†] And this became known as the Special Navy Task Force for Surface Missile Systems.

Reich had had one tour of duty in the Bureau of Ordnance one time in Q, in quality control. He was a surfaced submariner, and he wore the Navy Cross. He had a very striking war record. Not as bombastic as a couple of his close associates like Street and those guys, who are all buried.[‡] But he was a noted submariner. He didn't know his finger from his ass on this subject. [Laughter] And he had a flaw—I think all of us have—but he had a flaw that may be worse than some, and that is he practiced cronyism.

---

[*] Milton Shaw, a senior civilian who had been a pioneer in the nuclear power program, worked from 1961 to 1964 as technical assistant to the Assistant Secretary of the Navy for Research and Development.

[†] In February 1962, Reich became Assistant Chief of BuWeps for Surface Missile Systems; in July 1962, Head of the Special Navy Task Force for Surface Missile Systems, in December 1963 Director, Surface Missile Systems Project. He had already been promoted to rear admiral before the presidential visit.

[‡] During World War II, Commander George L. Street III, USN, was commanding officer of the USS *Tirante* (SS-420). For his exploits Street was awarded the Medal of Honor.

If he believed in you, you were it. So he started ripping officers out of *Canberra* and bringing them up here as his staff to run the task force, starting right with his aides. Commander T. J. Keen, Tim Keen, became his aide.[*] He'd been missile officer in *Canberra*. The subsequent year is when I was ordered back to the task force.

Paul Stillwell: Well, let's cover the *Galveston* first.

Admiral Meyer: I'm trying to make sure I've got myself registered here.

Paul Stillwell: Well, the chronology says that you were in the *Galveston* from June '61 to July '63, and then in July '63 is when you went to the Task Force for Surface Missile Systems.

Admiral Meyer: When does it say I left MIT?

Paul Stillwell: June 1961. So you got just a little time at sea in *Galveston* before she had that long yard period at Philadelphia.

Admiral Meyer: That's affirmative. My schools were all canceled. I was ordered to report immediately to *Galveston*, and I did. And we completed the firing operations, of which really I was kind of a witness, not an active participant, and we off-loaded and we went into the yard at Philadelphia, which was to be, as I recollect, something like nine months long. It turned out to be much longer than that.[†]

Paul Stillwell: What was the purpose of that long yard period?

Admiral Meyer: Well, it was to complete the conversion, and that piece of it came to be known as the LPCW conversion, the long pulse continuous wave. That moved the range Talos could handle from, I want to say 60 miles but it was really about 40, out to 120.

---

[*] Lieutenant Commander Timothy J. Keen, USN.
[†] The *Galveston* was in overhaul at Philadelphia from 30 August 1961 through 23 July 1962.

Paul Stillwell: What made the difference in that boost, doubling it?

Admiral Meyer: It was more the trajectory than anything else. In that fire control equation the launcher always set up at 47 degrees, and so the missile was boosted off and boosted the speed when the booster fell away at, I want to say 60,000 feet. It fell away at 60,000, the missile pitched over and started cruising. This is the only real ramjet we ever flew. It was a ramjet missile with a rocket boost. And it flew at about Mach 2.3.

We haven't really flown any ramjets since then. There's been big movements trying to get back in the ramjet business because ramjets are really reliable and really trustworthy and really provide ranges. But generally the tuning of ramjets is dependent on altitude. So you flew that missile at 60,000 until it went into terminal phase. And terminal, as I recollect, was the last 50 seconds or so. And now it would start looking over, and it'd also start looking for the target. Remember, this is a long-pulse continuous wave. So we had the illuminator in the ship. The illuminator was shining on the target, and the semi-active homing was to be done by the missile. Those are pretty mind-boggling ranges and a lot of people, of course, questioned it—you couldn't do that.

The targets that were selected were the P-2—I forget what letter model but the patrol planes that were in storage at Hawthorne, Nevada.[*] Those airplanes were brought out of there and brought down to Alameda, reconditioned to the point where they would fly, and they'd become the targets. There were, and are, runways out at—not San Clemente Island, whatever the hell the island is down at Mugu range, but I don't think they ever flew from that runway. Lesser planes did, the F6Fs and things like that. But they had to fly from inland. They could fly forever, but they were frighteningly slow, at 110-120 knots.

Paul Stillwell: Not the worst threat that the ship would face, or the fastest, by far.

---

[*] The Lockheed P2V Neptune was a land-based patrol plane that first entered an operational squadron in March 1947 in VP-ML-2. The P2V-3 was 77 feet, 10 inches long; wingspan of 100 feet; gross weight of 64,100 pounds, and top speed of 337 miles per hour. In 1962 the aircraft was redesignated the P-2. By this time, P-3 Orions were replacing P-2s in the fleet.

Admiral Meyer: Right. But it was questionable, though, whether there were any such targets in the world. These were tough targets. Tough, hard targets. The rangers at that time were on the SPG-49 radar, were instrumented to 240,000 yards, which would be 120 miles. Well, that's what we were trying to intercept at. So this was really on the ragged edge, really touch and go.

I don't know how many I fired. My logs someplace showed I fired something like 73 Talos missiles in my life, which I don't think any other person has ever fired that many, so it's one of the not very significant records [chuckle] in ordnance.

Paul Stillwell: Paul Stillwell: Who manufactured the new equipment that came aboard *Galveston* at that point?

Admiral Meyer: Sperry.* The equipment was modernized in place, some was removed, some was taken back, but in the main Sperry did it, and did it *in situ*. And some did not work. Ford Instrument did the computers.† And Sperry.

Paul Stillwell: Ford was a long-established firm in Navy fire control.

Admiral Meyer: Affirmative. And Ford did the computers in Terrier and Tartar, and assisted Sperry in the Mark 111s, which were the computers in *Galveston*. So Ford was a well-respected, well-admired outfit in that area.

Paul Stillwell: Was there any ship's force involvement in this, or was it mainly the contractor and the shipyard?

Admiral Meyer: Ship's force knee deep, day and night.

Well, the time to sail came and, of course, we couldn't sail. We had families, and our homeport had been shifted to San Diego. Families had been scattered everyplace, including my own. But I had moved mine to West Berlin, New Jersey, for right at a year,

---

* Sperry Rand Corporation.
† Ford Instrument Company was a division of Sperry Rand.

so everybody watched me very closely to see when I was packing. And the big thing was shipping cars, because the Navy was going to transfer your car for you. So people every day went out to check to make sure my car was still there. [Laughter] Because they knew they weren't going anyplace till the old fire control officer said they were going.

It wasn't quite twice the amount of time it took, but it took an extraordinary amount of time to get this done. I think the biggest reason was the difficulty of the wiring.

Paul Stillwell: Was it because this was a new system and there hadn't been an established pattern?

Admiral Meyer: Not that so much as that so much more wiring had to be brought in. And the original designs, physical designs, just didn't fit it. So it was constant crowding, constant jamming it up was a problem, constantly trying to get the room. Plus, as you point out, we had very little land-based testing. On the other hand, in hindsight I believe it was adequate. It was just that it was a bitch doing all the cabling that was being introduced into the ship. And particularly get the illuminator in there, illuminator transmitter, which—I believe I'm right—was ten kilowatts, the biggest one ever put aboard ship. And it was, I want to say C-band, but it surely must have been X-band.

That's what we did. The firing results in the Atlantic weren't very good. We finally sailed in *Galveston* after that year and some turmoil. I mentioned the skipper who had no wife and no family, and I think I mentioned to you that he came to our house quite often for the weekends, in New Jersey.

Paul Stillwell: The chronology says that *Galveston* departed Philadelphia on 23 July 1962, transited the Canal, and joined Cruiser Destroyer Flotilla Nine of the Pacific Fleet on 24 August '62.[*] So it took just over a month for leaving the shipyard and then getting set up in California.

---

[*] The commanding officer of the *Galveston* during that period was Captain Gerald P. Joyce, USN.

Admiral Meyer: We did almost nothing en route. I can't remember now how I got my family moved. I didn't move them. They moved with somebody, somebody transported them.

Paul Stillwell: Did you or other parts of the ship's force have to sign off on each hookup and system as it was installed and checked?

Admiral Meyer: [Indicates no]. Just by agreement: "Yes, we're done; no, this part's not done." And factor a number of things not finished that had to be done later. But it wasn't because they were late or any of those things; it was just that's the way it was.

One of the things that drove it was that we were committed to visit our namesake, namely Galveston, and those dates had been set.[*] So we went off to do that. Well, we got virtually no seamanship done before Galveston, and there we had tugs and pilots. But the old man wanted us to go to Acapulco, next stop. We would have to anchor, and we'd have to use our boats, or we'd have to find a way to hire boats. By now I was the gun boss. And at the last minute we finally decided we'd better hire boats. It was just too risky. We had no training; our crews didn't know what to do. We had all the goddamn boats—you know, on those cruisers they were loaded in the hangar deck, so when you sailed someplace you either had to get rid of your airplanes, or you had to get rid of your boats; you couldn't handle them both.

We attempted to use our boats in Acapulco to go ashore. It was a disaster. After a day at it, the captain, the XO, and I decided to go rent some.[†] Couldn't handle it. We didn't have any airplanes aboard.

When we arrived at San Diego, we were all deathly sick.[‡] We arrived there about 9:00 o'clock in the morning. We thought that we were going to moor at State Pier. I remember it was a Friday. State Pier was occupied. Well, we thought *we* were going to occupy State Pier. We didn't have the ship cleaned up or anything. So we had to remain out in the channel, in the stream, which meant we had to moor fore and aft, because the

---

[*] The ship visited Galveston, Texas, on 4 August 1962.
[†] The executive officer was Captain Robert M. Pond, USN.
[‡] The arrival in San Diego was 24 August 1962.

cruiser couldn't swing on a buoy; there wasn't enough room. Well, we had no experience. Hadn't done a bit of it.

We came up. We had our whaleboat in the water. We were trying to take the first buoy. We had the lines over trying to rig the chain. A couple men fell in the water. The first lieutenant, Lieutenant Joe Hunt, was on the forecastle; I was on the bridge with the old man. The next thing we saw, we saw sailors sitting down on the forecastle. At first, we couldn't move, we couldn't understand what the hell was the problem here. It turned out they were all turning sick, and at first we didn't realize it. We finally got help from ashore to help us get moored.

Paul Stillwell: What was the sickness?

Admiral Meyer: Well, nobody knew. And immediately the big problem was trying to figure out what the hell the problem was, because men were going down, just kind of one after the other. Eventually, the following day, after the disease control outfit was called out, the determination was made that it was believed that it came from milk in Galveston, that we got bad milk.

It didn't kill anybody, just rendered them incapacitated. I personally didn't go down. Maybe a third of the officers went down. But one after the other after the other in the crew went down. And they got over it pretty quick. I mean it was like a 20-hour thing or a 24-hour thing for them to get over it. But, God, was it totally disruptive. We didn't know what to do, but it was a hell of an experience of arriving at a new homeport. And by now it was the weekend, and there wasn't anybody in San Diego that cared to have their weekend disrupted just on account of we had one goddamn cruiser sick and adrift out in a channel. I'm trying to think. I think we let go an anchor, which was really, really hazardous to do because of all these cables all over the goddamn place out there. But we started getting scared, and the old man started getting scared. But we pulled out of it. By Monday or so we were all kind of recovered and thanking God for what had happened to us and making us well. That was arrival in San Diego.

Paul Stillwell: Anything you remember specifically about the visit to Galveston, other than the bad milk?

Admiral Meyer: The truth is, the naming of the ship kind of no longer had any meaning to the city. They turned out and handed out free tickets to the sailors and stuff like that, but it was no big deal.

Paul Stillwell: It's interesting that you didn't get much of a reception after that had been the driver on your schedule.

Admiral Meyer: I know. [Laughter] We just kind of felt obligated. We talked later, I remember, the XO and the captain and I, that the best thing we could have done was cancel it. And then we'd look like hell. Here we were changing coasts and go sail right by. So it was a mess. And I remember when the skipper was transferred we had a big party for him at the officers' club, and I was the MC, and we made a lot of jokes about Galveston and about Acapulco and our inability to do basic seamanship, and all falling asleep in this illness. But we didn't kill anybody. Nobody was permanently hurt as far as I know. We transferred a few men to sickbay ashore. But I think at that time we carried two doctors, and we got through it.

In the meantime the pace picked up to take over. We did not get allotted a single day for shakedown or reftra.* We started immediately on the missile development.

Paul Stillwell: Where was your station when the ship was under way?

Admiral Meyer: I was the gun boss—6-inch guns. We must have been in San Diego four or five months before we ever fired them. We had three 5-inch/38s, duals, and two turrets. We finally test fired the 5-inch, but the whole year all we ever did was, I managed to get them test fired, mostly by beating on the captain. But the captain wasn't the problem. The problem was, we weren't given any slack in our schedule. They were demanding that this be done, that these missile firings get conducted. We really had

---

* Reftra – refresher training, a period of getting a ship's crew back up to speed after a yard period.

pressure. And in the middle of them Admiral Reich came out to witness one. Which, as far as I know that's how I got selected and ordered to the task force. He spent the day with us, and he watched the firing. Of course, there wasn't anything to see except blast-off. We compiled a hell of a record. And now we were being allowed to moor at North Island when there was room from the carrier.[*] Which pissed me off.

Paul Stillwell: Why?

Admiral Meyer: Well, the carriers got first priority, and we were just the leftover. No goddamn preparation had been made, really.

(Interruption for change of tape)

Admiral Meyer: I spent a lot of money to be able to accommodate the Aegis fleet starting right with shore power. It was all done out of the project.

I went through, I think, three skippers in *Galveston*.[†] I think I told you before that, and I'll repeat it again, the admiral had established the requirement that the fire control officers in the three Talos ships had to be lieutenant commanders, they had to have a master's degree in ordnance, and they had to have operational experience.[‡] I was ordered to the first one, *Galveston*. My friend, same year group as me, Lieutenant Commander R. W. Anderson was ordered into *Oklahoma City* the same way.[§] By then they had run out of officers that met the requirements, so Lieutenant Commander Jim Campbell was ordered as gun boss of *Little Rock*, and he had no master's degree, he had no anything. He was the senior LDO in the Navy. Well, he was ordered in as fire control, and then he fleeted up. All three of us ultimately were promoted to commanders; we were all fleeted up to gun bosses.

---

[*] North Island Naval Air Station is on the end of the Coronado peninsula, across the harbor from San Diego.
[†] The third was Captain Thomas J. Rudden Jr., USN, who commanded the ship from 1 June 1963 to 19 June 1964. Meyer was detached in July 1963, shortly after Rudden's arrival.
[‡] Admiral Meyer's memory was evidently playing tricks on him because he was ordered to the *Galveston* in 1961, the year before Reich took over the special task force on surface missiles. Reich was still in command of the *Canberra* at the time.
[§] Lieutenant Commander Richard W. Anderson, USN.

Interesting enough, *Oklahoma City* fired a lot of her guns as part of the Vietnam operations, because she was the Seventh Fleet flagship. And that admiral made it mandatory that they participate in the shore bombardments. Hell, we didn't even get to do that. We never had any reftra. Never had anything. It's amazing that we didn't kill somebody. It's amazing that we didn't wreck ourselves. But it was another one of those situations where—you know, the Navy is pretty damned robust. If you've got a few officers and a few petty officers that know a little bit, you can go a pretty long ways. And the more you sail, the more you—see, I sailed approaching 20 years in that effort there in six or seven ships—the more you come to understand how we manned the fleet in World War II, and really more Pacific than anyplace else. You could take a handful of regulars, a few petty officers and a couple officers; it was amazing how much training they could provide to the reserves.

Well, there were a couple things wrong with it. One is, they got a lot of wrong training. I think I mentioned to you, my first destroyer, after I had been aboard a year I was senior watch officer. Man, I could do anything in that ship. We operated out of Newport. I could plane guard all day long. I could make the goddamn oiler just like that. Stores, replenishment. We did a lot of high-lining in those days, a hell of a lot of high-lining. It was a way of life. We had no airplane. And I learned a lot about seamanship, of which I knew nothing. I didn't have a single day of training. And I've often thought about that, of how the Navy did that in the Pacific in manning its destroyers and its cruisers during the great war. It was an amazing thing, really.

Paul Stillwell: Where was your station physically on board *Galveston* during the missile shoots?

Admiral Meyer: That was part of the flaw in the design. It was decided that the conversion would be aft, and it would remove turret three. Okay. So all of the missile battery was aft. Weapons control was in the after superstructure, I want to say the 05 deck.

Paul Stillwell: And the illuminators were aft.

Admiral Meyer: Illuminators were aft. And if you just lay down a line athwartships, amidships, forward on the outside it looked just like it always looked. Well, but if you went underneath, the CIC was buried in the armor, forward. So here was the setup. At general quarters the captain was on the bridge, over yonder. The gun boss was in the after superstructure at the 05 level. I think the bridge is the 05 level; sky forward is 06, as I recall. That's where my assistant would be located during GQ.[*] He would be up there in charge of the guns. And then the ops officer, or what today we call the ops officer, CIC, he was located clear down behind the goddamn armor belt. Communication was a bear, a real bear. You had the 21MC, and you had the sound-powered telephones. If you set out to go talk to each other, you'd never make it. The war would be over before you got there, because you couldn't move in the ship; you were just locked in once you went to general quarters. So that was to me a decided drawback.

The ships never had to engage in battle with that design. *Long Beach* was not built that way; she was built from the ground up.[†] Then the three big CGs, which were double-enders, were not built that way.[‡] It was just those three single-enders that were that way, and so they were unique.[§] It is a credit to naval engineering, frankly. The ship was stable, she sailed well, she did all those things. But they had a design job to do that old business of putting ten pounds in a five-pound bucket.

Paul Stillwell: And limited by the original design and how that could be modified.

Admiral Meyer: Right. And, you know, in those ships that got armor—today we wouldn't even grasp it—but, you know, it really took some pretty amazing engineering and craftsmanship to be on those ships with that armor. I mean, that was hard work.

---

[*] GQ – general quarters, that is, battle stations.
[†] USS *Long Beach* (CGN-9), the Navy's first nuclear-powered cruiser, was the only ship of her class. She was commissioned 9 September 1961.
[‡] The three guided missile cruisers of the *Albany* (CG-10) class were converted from conventional heavy cruisers by the removal of all three 8-inch gun turrets and the construction of towering new superstructures. As converted, each was armed with two twin Tartar missile launchers and two twin Talos launchers, as well as two 5-inch guns, and an ASROC launcher. The other two ships of the new class were the *Chicago* (CG-11) and *Columbus* (CG-12).
[§] The other ships of the *Galveston* class were the *Little Rock* (CLG-4) and *Oklahoma City* (CLG-5). The latter two were also converted to serve as numbered fleet flagships.

In my two years and some odd time on that ship, I was in turret one once. I never went in turret two, and there was no particular need to. As you know, we had turret captains, and their tradition was, they abided in the turret from the day they got selected. Well, that tradition started decaying by the time we got to *Galveston*. But in the old Navy they had petty officers whose entire career was in one turret. They never went anyplace else in the ship. It worked all right. It worked all right. But it was a completely different pace, a different set of demands.

Paul Stillwell: Well, how successful were the missile firings, once you got to the Pacific?

Admiral Meyer: Pretty damned good. I think if you could go back and look at those logs, I think you would find that they had a success rate someplace up in the 70s, which was pretty damned high in those days, pretty high. It was a complicated system, and it was really pioneering in this semi-active homing. I'm a big semi-active homing person, by the way. Every navy in the world that's tried active homing has abandoned it. And I've fought against it and fought against it, because you get these jerks that come along who, "Well, you surface people are so thick-headed. Here we've got this beautiful missile, the AMRAAM, and all those air-to-air missiles, which are really giant-killers are semi-active."[*] Yeah. They shoot from here to your front door, that's how good they are. And they're also plenty vulnerable to jamming. So I'm a believer in semi-active homing. So you don't activate the homer until you command it and you're in terminal phase.

The hardest thing that I had in *Galveston* in my missile experience—I've had nothing like it since, but see, flight times were 260 to 290 seconds. So you'd have three and four minutes' flight time. I smoked in those days—literally myself and the fire control officer and the gunner, I'd light the smoking lamp while the missile was flying out. [Laughter] We had plenty of time to have a smoke. Then you just sat there atremble the whole time because our expectation was that it would make it. And the illuminator, we had really no empirical data, not the kind that we demand today. But the transition to homing was a joy indeed.

---

[*] AIM-9 advanced medium-range air-to-air missile (AMRAAM).

See, those missiles were all proximity-fuze missiles, as you'll recall. Stated in rough terms, the nominal Region R, namely the kill range, was 50 feet, so the idea was to get within 50 feet, and by proximity the fuze would be ignited. And I think I had a target or so, it may have been a couple, that we never killed. We exploded and we didn't kill it. But it's a very small number. We couldn't hit any better than that. I mean, we were ecstatic that we collided with a target, just ecstatic. And when we got better, people started thinking: "You're hoking it up somehow." Well, there wasn't no way you could hoke it up. But the performance, really—it was a Bendix missile, pretty phenomenal. All vacuum tube. That missile was 30 inches in diameter. It was awesome.

Paul Stillwell: So the ship design had to carve room for a missile magazine out of that fantail.

Admiral Meyer: Like a big one. Plus, we carried nuclear heads too. We had nuclear magazines, and we were qualified to change them aboard ship. I'm trying to think. I think that I only oversaw one loading in my time in *Galveston* for a nuclear head, and it was a demo-like thing. I mean, when you looked at it, there was no way for you to easily tell what it was. It was just a warhead.

We had refueling stations, because you'd get evaporation. So if you find a photo of *Galveston* and you look real close, on each side some aft of amidships you see a set of rails and everything that you don't know what the hell they mean. Those were fueling stations. You could back the missile out of the magazine, you could move it into ready service and back it out, to refuel it. Run it back into ready service and put it back in the magazine. I mean, we had about 40-50 men in just the missile crew alone, and it was like *big* work. That son of a bitch would run from here to the end of the building. It was a long, big missile.* And you got over its awesomeness as time passed, but if you were brand new and walked in, you never got over it. But wonderful missile.

Paul Stillwell: Was that time out of San Diego spent in both training and testing?

---

* Talos was 33 feet long, 28 inches in diameter, and weighed 7,000 pounds.

Admiral Meyer: Never did any training.

Paul Stillwell: Well, you get some training just as a byproduct of operating.

Admiral Meyer: I am the first person who ever hit a surface target with a surface-to-air missile. And it was an experiment that was run to find out if we could. We fired against a DE that was adrift, and the first firing missed.* On my word, the admiral back in Washington gave us permission to fire again. So that afternoon we fired again at a range of about 24 miles. It was somewhere in the 20s. And we fired that missile about sunset. We were confident we hit, but we couldn't see, we didn't know. So the old man put on all the speed he could put on, but it still took us an hour to get to the target. And by now dark was approaching. God, what exhilaration. What exhilaration. We saw that son of a bitch afire. It must be the way submariners feel. She was afire, just burning like hell. Well, there wasn't anything in the ship to burn, except it was later determined what was burning was the residual fuel in the missile, because 24 miles was a relatively short range from a fuel viewpoint. There was no warhead in it. It tore the living hell out of the ship.

Paul Stillwell: Just momentum.

Admiral Meyer: Momentum, and loaded with fuel. Seeker brought her in, and she just tore the living hell out of the ship amidships. I was transferred the next day from the ship—that's when I reported back to the task force—with what a joy as my departure. But it burned for something like five days. Didn't exactly know how to put it out and there wasn't anybody that really wanted to put it out. Just let the son of a bitch burn. [Chuckle]

We proved that this capability existed and it ought to be in service, because that distance, pretty damned good shooting, even if you only get a .3 or so. And if you're an old gunnery man, you're ecstatic when you see it, to think that you could hit it that way. But the special service surface mode set up, fired the missile, went into its fire control instrumentation for surface, and there was some question whether you could really do

---

* DE – destroyer escort.

this, and even at the range we did it at, because you got plenty of interference going on with your own ship, and plenty of reflections.

Later, Tartar fired a couple missiles in surface-to-surface, and the Navy abandoned the damned effort. I never understood why. Even though I should have understood why, I never did. I know that a piece of it was so that it did not risk the surface-to-surface development. Regulus was still in motion.*

Paul Stillwell: Well, that had been knocked out to pay for Polaris.

Admiral Meyer: But you're talking about the supersonic Regulus.

Paul Stillwell: Regulus II, yes.

Admiral Meyer: Yeah. I can't remember when we got rid of the regular Reguluses. We had them in cruisers and had them in carriers.

Paul Stillwell: And even a few in submarines.

Admiral Meyer: Yeah, and had a couple submarines, right. *Cusk* and *Carbonero*, I believe. They operated out of Point Mugu in those days, early days.†

I think that Regulus was pretty damned good, although you could make a case that it was kind of vulnerable. But wait a minute. How vulnerable is an attacking missile? We don't know. You don't really know. Mathematically you could make a case that, well, it's an easy target, piece of cake. Well, we've never had to determine that. Although the Brits got so that they could hit the V-1 pretty damned good.‡ But it

---

* Two Regulus missiles were designed to be fired from surface ships or surfaced submarines. Regulus I, which entered the fleet in 1952, was 34 feet long, weighed 12,000 pounds, and had a speed of Mach 0.9 and range of 500 miles; Regulus II, which had its first flight test in 1958, was 57 feet long, weighed 22,000 pounds, and had a speed of Mach 2.0 and range of 1,000 miles. Regulus II did not go into fleet service.
† Point Mugu is located on the California coast, approximately 65 miles northwest of Los Angeles. From January 1959 to April 1975 the facility there was known as the Naval Missile Center.
‡ The German V-1 was a pulse-jet flying bomb, also known as a "doodlebug" and "buzz bomb." It was 25 feet long and had a 16-foot wingspan. It carried a one-ton warhead some 150 miles (later increased to 250) at a speed of about 400 miles per hour. It was first successfully flown in December 1943. The Germans fired more than 13,000 V-1s during the course of World War II.

was a fairly—when you think about Britain compared to, say, a navy, it was a fairly controlled environment, too. Your ability to predict wherever it was going to be and when it was going to be, and the characteristics were pretty well known.

Paul Stillwell: And that didn't have any homing system. It just flew till it ran out of fuel.

Admiral Meyer: That's affirmative.

Now, what would we do today if the Reds decided to activate their missile fields in the Fujian Province. Those, of course, are, well, alleged to be ballistic missiles primarily, although I believe that there are cruise missiles there too, but they'd have to be targeted. Well, they've all got to be targeted. What would happen? I don't know.

Paul Stillwell: Do you remember any impact on the *Galveston* when the Cuban Missile Crisis occurred in '62?[*]

Admiral Meyer: It's something I haven't gotten over to this day. Paul, I never got over this. Our ship sailed from Philadelphia around in the middle of that crisis without a single round of ammunition aboard, gun or missile. Not a single one. In later years I learned that in one of the dustups down in Central America the Navy, in orders from higher authority, sailed a destroyer from Ingalls to the dustup without a single round of ammunition aboard. Got away with it.

Paul Stillwell: So all she could provide was presence.

Admiral Meyer: That's all.

---

[*] The Cuban Missile Crisis was triggered in mid-October 1962, when a U.S. reconnaissance plane photographed a Soviet nuclear missile site in Cuba and the presence of Soviet bombers. On 22 October President John F. Kennedy went on national television to announce a naval quarantine of Cuba, to be implemented on 24 October. On 28 October Premier Nikita Khrushchev of the Soviet Union notified President Kennedy that he was ordering the withdrawal of Soviet bombers and missiles from Cuba.

Paul Stillwell: Well, did you not get ammunition when you got out to San Diego? According to the chronology the Missile Crisis was about two months after you got to San Diego.

Admiral Meyer: Well, it was really occurring while we were on the way.[*] Myself and the assistant gun boss and the XO bet that we would immediately be diverted, be loaded at Yorktown and made ready for the Cuban crisis. It was as though we didn't even exist. We didn't even exist.

Well, then I later learned about this dustup on the destroyer, and I don't know whether what I'm telling you about the destroyer is true or not. I don't know whether it's a true story. But I passed a law on Aegis and—you know, part of the time I was in charge of Aegis I was in charge of SMS Project. My law was: "We're never going to sail a ship without something in her." And it caused a lot of difficulty in *Ticonderoga*, because the bureaucrats had all kinds of rules that, well, Tico could not load ammo at Pascagoula.[†] Well, I said to hell with that noise. If somebody decided it can't be done, then we'll find out who that is, and we will change it. It went on for about two months, the goddamn argument. And my view was, well by God she's going to have 5-inch ammo aboard. And also she's going to have a couple missiles, even though they hadn't been proof fired.

We finally came to an understanding and a reasoning. Jesus. We had to move the ammo and truck it into Gulfport. And the only way we could move that ammo was on Saturday mornings and Sunday, under police escort, everything cordoned off and everything, to move it into the shipyard to load it. Leonard Erb, a retired Navy captain, submariner, was in command of the yard at the time, a hell of a leader.[‡] I'd never gotten it done without his support. As a submariner he knew better.

Well, so I don't know what practice they use today if any. They've probably shit-canned it all. But during my time no ship sailed without ammo. No ship. And we could store ammo over—whatever that Air Force base is there in Florida is one place we

---

[*] The chronology does not support the admiral's memory on this point.
[†] The first of the Aegis cruisers to join the fleet was the USS *Ticonderoga* (CG-47), commissioned 22 January 1983. She was built at the Litton/Ingalls shipyard in Pascagoula, Mississippi.
[‡] Erb was the president of Ingalls Shipbuilding.

could store it. We could also store some temporarily at Gulfport. You could get a waiver to store something.

Paul Stillwell: Well, back to *Galveston*, do you have anything else to recall to finish up with that ship?

Admiral Meyer: I believe the Talos never got the respect it deserves. And I think that one of the reasons was that not many people bothered to learn anything about it. Secondly, the program was not very aggressive in propagating it. And by then, as we moved on in to the '70s we got this idea there was no threat. Threat's abated and it's not there. So, you know, there we had those beautiful cruisers, the three big CGs—*Chicago* and *Columbus* and *Albany*—armed with Talos and armed with Tartar.[*] They were armed with Talos fore and aft, and they had, as I recollect, four batteries, I think, of Tartars. God, what powerful ships! They had no respect. They were just looked at kind of as toys. Just looked at as toys.

I remember that one of my deputies, who was Captain Bill Rowden—you may know Bill Rowden.

Paul Stillwell: Yes.

Admiral Meyer: He was irked and pissed off. He spent a lot of his time worrying about getting command, but I kept telling him, "Better days will come." Well, it turned out for reasons I don't know now that suddenly command of *Columbus* opened up.[†] She was based in Norfolk. We went down and he took over command of *Columbus*, and I was down there with him. And I reminded him that God always looks after people if we give Him a chance. But in those days we always kept three or four officers in reserve in the Naval Ordnance Systems Command, ready to take command instantly. They were part of

---

[*] These three ships had originally been built as heavy cruisers with 8-inch guns. All the large guns were removed during their conversion to guided missile ships. This was different from the converted light cruisers, which retained some of their 6-inch turrets.
[†] Captain William H. Rowden, USN, commanded the USS *Columbus* (CG-12) from 21 August 1973 to 2 August 1974.

the ready force, because you always had somebody break a leg or his wife died, or any number of things would happen. Or, you know, occasionally relieved for cause.

But that fleet never got what it deserved. *Long Beach* did not, and I personally believe the reason *Long Beach* didn't was that the ship was poorly commanded, poorly led, not well designed. I frankly fault the officers involved, because most of them spent their time trying to get in that ship so it was on their record. And there's nothing that will piss me off more than officers spending their time trying to get posted a particular place or trying to get some job for their records. God, it pisses me off. Makes me irate. As you know, you're not rated that way in the gumbo. It's that simple. Instead, you're pleased with what you have. And I feel that way to this day.

Now, I've got to give a speech next Wednesday night for this Reagan Award, this national award, and trying to think about what to say. A lot of people mistake humbleness as an act. But people raised in the gumbo are not acting at all; they're just born that way. And that's probably why they would never succeed to being the Chief of Naval Operations or any other grand undertakings, because they don't have it in them to act. I don't mean to sound pompous about that, but there's a certain amount of pomposity in me on that subject as I've grown up in my life, scared to death in the first destroyer I went into when I did not know port from starboard, as I told you. [Laughter]. It turned out that I'm just as smart as anybody else. Those bastards aren't any smarter at all. As a matter of fact, some of them are pretty damned dumb.

So I looked at that whole matter of leadership and that whole matter of command, and I choose to think in terms of leadership. I don't think I've said this to you, but I've said it to a number of people in my speeches. I've got to tell you, if you're going to run a major project and lead it well, it is 100 times harder than command of a major warship at sea. It is way harder. The number of unknowns, the number of variables, the different kind of peoples, are far different than a ship, where there's a lot of homogeneity in the people, in the gear, and all that stuff.

Naval engineering is a wonderful thing, and I do not welcome it being berated. I class myself as a naval officer, and in recent years I've started to think of myself as a naval engineer too. And it pisses me off with these people who somehow, simply because they wear an officer's uniform, have become so smart in naval engineering and the 200 years of learning behind it. And I have said a number of times in speeches: "The shore establishment doesn't need the fleet to function; the fleet needs the shore establishment, though, to function, and that must never get forgotten."

So what am I going to say next Wednesday night? I've been struggling. The general has given me 15 minutes. Well—I don't think I said this to you last time—I wanted to do a little bit of recall. So I took my team last Wednesday, or a week ago Wednesday, rehearsed them on my recall. And I wanted to start at Fort Bliss, Texas, when I was introduced into guided missilery, in 1951 or whatever the date was on that uncertified piece of paper you have there. [Laughter] And they all pooh-poohed it. They wanted me to give the audience a charge of what they're to do in the future. I don't know that I'm ready to do that, one reason being is, I'm not convinced that they will listen. They will listen maybe to two sentences worth, but that'll be it.

I am a great believer in understanding, or trying to understand, history, whether it's correct or not. That tradition and something about it, I think is important to a human being, and that person's performance and leadership. Reich taught me, and Spreen taught me, in particular, to pay attention to your elders. Listen to your elders. Fundamentally, as they described it, they've screwed up a lot of things, and you ought to try and learn from that and go screw up something of your own. [Chuckle]

Paul Stillwell: Well, we're right near the end of the tape, Admiral, so that's an interesting note to end on.

Admiral Meyer: All right.

Paul Stillwell: Thank you.

Interview Number 8 with Rear Admiral Wayne E. Meyer, U.S. Navy (Retired)
Place: Admiral Meyer's office in Arlington, Virginia
Date: Friday, 4 April 2008

Paul Stillwell: Admiral, last time we were together we talked about your experience in the cruiser *Galveston* as fire control officer and weapons boss. During that tenure you made the rank of commander, and then in July 1963, you moved to the Bureau of Weapons to the Surface Missile Systems Project. What led to that assignment?

Admiral Meyer: It's a good question and I don't want to sound coy, but I believe that Admiral Reich appointed me, because he came out to visit the ship. And most people don't appreciate—and there's no reason they should—that earlier a Tartar missile had fired at a surface ship and almost randomly hit it, a target destroyer. Now I was given my last assignment in that ship, it turned out, to fire a Talos at a destroyer escort.[*]

Paul Stillwell: You mentioned that before.

Admiral Meyer: I mentioned it before, and she was hull down, and my guess is she was some 12 to 14 miles distant, and we hit it for the first time ever. And I'm not sure we ever fired another Talos again at a surface target. But we did it. Admiral Reich had come out to visit the ship, assess the progress, talk to the captain, but more specifically to talk to me. Lieutenant Commander Todd Blades was his own project officer in the ship, and Lieutenant Commander Norman Lemieux was OpTEvFor's project officer.[†] That's how the three of us became good friends, because we served for darn near two years together in the ship. Todd Blades is in the graveyard now, and we in Aegis renamed the computer center down at Dahlgren. He was my rep for a number of years down there, what I called my area commander.

---

[*] An on-line article by Dr. Phillip R. Hays describes an incident involving the guided missile light cruiser *Oklahoma City* (CLG-5), which fired a surface-to-surface Talos shot at a destroyer escort in 1968 off the coast of California. Dr. Hays's description of the event is similar to Admiral Meyer's, that is, no warhead and considerable fuel in the missile. [http://www.okieboat.com/Talos%20firing%20operations.html]
[†] Lieutenant Commander Lawrence Todd Blades, USN; OpTEvFor – Operational Test and Evaluation Force.

Paul Stillwell: We used to work with him at the Naval Institute because he wrote for *Proceedings*. Good man.

Admiral Meyer: Yeah. He was a pretty good writer. He was a pretty good writer. And I think it was through my fitness reports more than any other that he was eventually selected for commander. And he was not displeased with that. He accepted his lot in life. He and Rosemary had, I think, seven children.

Paul Stillwell: He had been with Dennis Wilkinson in the *Long Beach* when she went into service.*

Admiral Meyer: That's correct too. What I'm doing here is testing your own recall. [Laughter] And as a friend and such, I immensely enjoyed him, and I may have told you that he's the one that encouraged my wife and I to come back here with our children—we were transferred here—even though it's the only time I've ever seen BuPers orders warn you to not execute these orders until you have plans for your family, warning you that there is no housing.

Paul Stillwell: Was that when you were reporting to BuWeps in '63?†

Admiral Meyer: Right. And they were correct. There was no housing.

Paul Stillwell: What did you wind up doing?

Admiral Meyer: Well, many people can't believe when I say that, that there was no housing. And Todd Blades and Rosemary Blades had bought a house fairly recently in the sticks, in a place called Springfield, Virginia. Todd said to me, "Look, we've got this massive basement. It's empty and everything. There's no reason that you all can't stay

---

* Captain Eugene P. Wilkinson, USN, commanded the nuclear-powered cruiser *Long Beach* (CGN-9) from September 1961 to September 1963. The oral history of Wilkinson, who retired as a vice admiral, is in the Naval Institute collection.
† BuWeps – Bureau of Naval Weapons.

with us till you find a place to live." And we were going to arrive in June. God was in his heaven, all was right with the world. Well, after about two weeks that was getting a little old, with their kids and our three kids and stuff like. And they were right; you couldn't find a place to live. So we started moving into the motels on Highway 50. A few of them still exist today. This is over half a century later, and they were worn-out motels then. And every week we'd move a little further down the road, a little further down the road, as we were running out of money.

Captain R. P. "Zeke" Foreman was to be my immediate superior and headed what was called the Terrier desk in the Special Navy Task Force.[*] He reported directly to the admiral, and I reported to Captain Foreman. He had orders at the time to become the commissioning commanding officer of *Wainwright*.[†] She was in construction up at Bath, and she would be commissioned in Boston. Dr. Gibson was the director of the laboratory we had at that time.[‡] He was a couple years older than I, and he had managed to get Dr. Gibson to be his speaker at the commissioning, which turned out to be in a snowstorm. But setting that aside, Zeke pretty rapidly taught me a lot of things about how the Bureau of Weapons worked and how the structure worked. And he also taught me how to get things done.

I remember one day an incident when I had the fire control desk. I didn't know Zeke Foreman before that. But once Zeke Foremen had caught me and he had become the captain, he wasn't about to let me slip through his fingers. One day he came back from a staff meeting not in a very good frame of mind. He said, "Commander, come in here. I want to show you how you do things around here."

I said, "Oh?"

He said, "Yes. At the staff meeting this morning the admiral told me that you were going to be reassigned to lead the study work and the subsequent selection for the new Standard missile. Standard missile's the admiral's idea."

---

[*] Terrier was a Navy supersonic surface-to-air, two-stage missile. It was 27 feet long, 12 inches in diameter and weighed 3,000 pounds. It had a range of 15 miles and an operating ceiling of 10 miles. The Terrier first went into fleet use on board the cruiser *Boston* (CAG-1), which was recommissioned on 1 November 1955 after conversion to a guided missile ship.

[†] The guided missile frigate *Wainwright* (DLG-28) was launched 25 April 1965 at Bath Iron Works, Bath, Maine. She was commissioned at the Boston Naval Shipyard 8 January 1966 with Captain Foreman in command.

[‡] Dr. Ralph E. Gibson was director of the Johns Hopkins Applied Physics Laboratory from 1948 to 1969.

I said, "Well, that's the first I've heard of it."

He said, "You're right, but it could be the last you'll hear of it too, because if you're put in that post I'll never see you again. I want to show you how you solve that problem."

He pulled out the phone book and, his glasses down his nose, he started down through there finding names and finding names. Then he made a compilation of the names that he found, right in BuWeps. Well, he homed in eventually on an officer by the name of Commander George Barry Wilson, who was in what I believe was called the RMGA section of the bureau at that time.[*] Foreman wrote a memo up to the admiral, and it said, "Meyer is certainly a superb choice based on his performance here to date with me; he'd be excellent. But, also, as you know, the Terrier is going through a very crucial stage in trying to square away the elevation gear box in the director so that not only can we track at low elevation, but we can also fire at low elevation and we have just recently reengineered USS *Leahy* to do these operations, and Meyer would be a serious loss to that effort. I nominate Commander George Barry Wilson, an officer I've known for a long time, a very high-quality officer and such, and who I believe is capable of doing this job pretty well, and everything. Love, Foreman, or whatever." [Chuckle]

He got a note back in the afternoon; the admiral wrote "Concur. R." And he was right; that's all I ever heard of it.

Well, in about three days George Barry Wilson came up to me, and he was pissed. Oh, he was pissed. Because he knew that I didn't finger him. He knew that the guy that fingered him was Foreman, because he was always arguing with Foreman. And he wanted me to go in and go to battle for him with Foreman. I said, "Well, I don't think I can do that, Barry."

Paul Stillwell: You didn't have much of an incentive to do that.

---

[*] Commander George Barry Wilson Jr., USN. RMGA was the code designation for some sections of the Bureau of Naval Weapons.

Admiral Meyer: [Laughter] Right. So that's how I got out of the source selection of the Standard missile, although I made Standard missile, and if Standard missile today has a father, it's me.

Paul Stillwell: Well, I encountered Captain Foreman a number of years ago, and he had been in the AA business for a long time. In 1945 he was involved in an experimental task force up at Casco Bay to find ways of dealing with the kamikazes.[*] That task force then led to the Operational Development Force.

Admiral Meyer: Your recall is correct. Or, it's correct as I know it, because I operated in those waters in those years.

Paul Stillwell: We talked last week about why the Surface Missile Project came about to address perceived shortcomings.

Admiral Meyer: Right. Admiral Reich was put in command of the task force, called the Special Navy Task Force for Surface Missile Systems. He was the commander of the task force, and his orders were that he reported to the Secretary of the Navy. This was, I mean, just totally unprecedented. The closest thing to it was SP, or what we later referred to all the time as Polaris.[†]

Now, one of the reasons that Reich knew so much about that and how to go about it is that the deputy in SP was a fellow submariner and a roommate of Admiral Reich at the Naval Academy.

Paul Stillwell: Who was that?

Admiral Meyer: I don't say his name this minute. I never knew him. But because they were such close friends and something called the Special Navy Task Force was stood up, and by the time I reported the next June we were adopting all of SP's procedures and how

---

[*] In the summer of 1945 Vice Admiral Willis A. Lee, Jr., USN, commanded Task Force 69, which conducted anti-kamikaze operational tests in Casco Bay, Maine. Foreman was a member of Lee's staff.
[†] SP – the Special Projects Office was in charge of Polaris development.

they were doing things, particularly in engineering. Our problem was 100 times more complex than their problem, because of different ships, different missiles, different configurations, and so forth and so on. But we quickly put those procedures—I shouldn't say we; the admiral did. And Admiral Reich became a devotee of Vitro Corporation, which had acquired the Kellex Corporation. Kellex primarily gained a teensy bit of fame for its dosimeters and its ability to measure radiation.

This fellow, whose name I'll probably say before we finish, the deputy, was a straight-stick submariner, of course a diesel guy, and he had sailed with Eli. They were buddies, so a lot of our organization rubbed off on us from copying SP. Well, while I was now a commander, I was fresh-caught in Washington, D.C., and it took me a while to understand the inward functionings of the structure around here and how things came about. And that was one of them, and I started really learning a lot from this old man—I call him the old man—Rear Admiral Eli T. Reich. Knew nothing about guided missiles, nothing.

Paul Stillwell: Then how did he get the job?

Admiral Meyer: Well, he got the job because of his chutzpah. In those days, if you were a submariner you topped out at lieutenant commander. And if you'd been good enough you'd get selected for commander, but there was no place for you to go. So then, in that era before nuclear power, you started bleeding over into surface Navy. So the next thing you knew, these surfaced submarine skippers were now out taking command of the destroyers and taking them away from the surface officers, who of course didn't welcome this intrusion at all. And not a small number; a damn big number of them. I don't know how that all got moderated because, I think I mentioned to you before that Arleigh Burke was ComDesLant and he was selected as ComDesLant to be the CNO.

Paul Stillwell: You did cover that.

Admiral Meyer: Okay. And someplace thereafter, as time flew, Red Raborn, who knew nothing about guided missilery, a navigator and a patrol plane pilot actually, he suddenly had this project created called SP.* Well, Red Raborn didn't know anything. That never bothered the Secretary in those days. But command of a cruiser was a major command, and there weren't many of them, and so everybody competed. Well, not many aviators could compete at all, but the submariners were damned good. So they got command of a number of cruisers. Matter of fact, they displaced the surface people.

Paul Stillwell: Pete Galantin came into SP after Raborn; he was a diesel submariner.†

Admiral Meyer: That's affirmative. And they're all kind of clubbish from my viewpoint, in the sense that they all knew each other and had known each other for a long time as a family. I think that they were pretty classy officers, but I don't have anything really to base it on one way or another. I was too young and unacquainted with how they sailed and what they did.

But Eli, mostly because of his war record, managed to get selected to command a cruiser. He had had a tour in BuOrd in Q, so he was a quality man. And he had another subsequent tour in a new OSD staff.‡ So he got to know a lot of appointees one way or another through those years, and it all added up to his—and he was an outspoken person. He was a commanding presence. And when he spoke, people sat up and listened. I admire him very, very much and I learned an awfully lot from him. And that's how he got command. It was just—I don't know if you'd say accidental or his number came up or how you'd say it. But he didn't last long. He got stashed PDQ. And as far as I know he didn't resent it. He started taking command of the task force the first day he was here.

Now, you can imagine how this went over with all the chiefs of the bureaus—BuShips, BuOrd, BuAer, Bureau of Yards and Docks, Bureau of Medicine. Well, wait a minute; the Bureau of Medicine was kind of set aside. BuSandA, Bureau of Supplies and Accounts, aah, they were under SecNav. So he had his fingers in all of these by edict

---

* Rear Admiral William F. Raborn, Jr., USN, was director of the Special Projects Office, which developed the Polaris submarine-launched ballistic missile system. He held the post from 2 December 1955 to 26 February 1962, being promoted to vice admiral in 1960. His Polaris oral history is in the Naval Institute collection.
† Rear Admiral Ignatius J. Galantin, USN, served as director of the Special Projects Office from 26 February 1962 to 16 February 1965. He was an unrestricted line officer as a submariner rather than an engineering duty specialist.
‡ OSD – Office of the Secretary of Defense.

from the Secretary, and he was not welcomed. Nor was he a courting-type person. He didn't spend any time courting anybody. He was from the old school.

When I arrived on the scene in the summer of 1963—it didn't take me long to appreciate there was some hard sledding around. If I was going to get anyplace, I was going to have to develop a circle and a ring of people. And ever since that era, my first tour in the bureau and my first experience at bureaucracy, but from then on I tried to teach officers some fundamentals about that structure.

And, just to state a couple sentences on it, it went along the lines that people are people and they're the same no matter whether they're military people, whether they're civil servants, or whether they work in industry or whether they work in a laboratory. Tonight they'll all have the same aches and pains and the same kind of family problems that you have. So you have to treat them equally and with respect. And I tell them, because most of the officers that I counseled were coming in for their first tour ever in the shore establishment, and I'd say, "Spend a little time, but pick the people you feel harmonious with and that you think know something. Don't worry about the organization." There's nothing that pissed me off more in subsequent years when people would say, "Well, you know, Vitro's supposed to do that," or "Well, I put that APL and they're supposed to get at it; I can't do it." Institutions don't do anything; people do it. And so I'd get on my soapbox, and I'd just start banging people on that.

So, taking a page from the old man, Eli Reich, I traveled a lot. I didn't like it. Travel was hard, and even harder than it is today. But I felt that it had to be done, and therefore I demanded my people do it. When I had first reported in, the captain of the Talos desk, whom I had already known, was Captain Frank Tofalo.[*] But he had this trait of where he would argue with the admiral. And one of the things I was taught early on by Zeke Foreman is, "You'll waste your time arguing with the admiral. Come back to your desk and write him a memo; don't argue with him." Well, it was good advice. Frank always argued with him. So you'd often get sent for, and you'd go in there and there would be Frank Tofalo standing over in the corner. Because when he got pissed off at you, he'd just post you over there in the corner, and you'd just stand there until he got ready to talk to you. [Chuckle]

---

[*] Captain Francis Tofalo, USN.

Paul Stillwell: Would he read the memos?

Admiral Meyer: Yeah, he would read the memos. He'd put little marks on them. He would. He would read the memos.

Paul Stillwell: Do you think that his approach and his personality alienated some people that made it difficult for you to work with them?

Admiral Meyer: Yes. And it sure damaged trust. The bureau chiefs didn't trust him from nothing. They believed him to be wily, and that he would move as a snake when he wanted to get something done. Now, he wasn't crooked or any of those things. He was just clever.

Paul Stillwell: But did he have some kind of a charter that gave him enough clout to sort of ignore a bureau chief?

Admiral Meyer: Far as I know, he could unseat a bureau chief, but I don't believe he ever unseated one, because they knew that he had a direct tie line to the Secretary. And he was pretty close to whoever that Secretary was.

Paul Stillwell: It was Fred Korth when you reported.[*]

Admiral Meyer: Right.

Paul Stillwell: And then Nitze came in at the end of '63.[†]

Admiral Meyer: Yeah. Okay. That's correct. You've got that correct. So it was Nitze. He and Nitze were pretty close. They were pretty good—I don't know whether you'd say friends or not; I was too young and junior to. There was a whole different level of

---

[*] Fred H. Korth served as Secretary of the Navy from 4 January 1962 to 1 November 1963.
[†] Paul H. Nitze served as Secretary of the Navy from 29 November 1963 to 30 June 1967.

respect then than there is now. You may have heard me mention this: You know, we had the GS-16s.* Everybody called the GS-16s "Mister." You didn't refer to a GS-16 by his first name. He was "Mister."

And the selection process—this was my first tour in the bureau—was done out of the field. Virtually everyone that came into headquarters, virtually everyone, came out of depots or shipyards or laboratories, because the laboratories reported to the bureaus. And the way that they got selected was by a board. And usually almost everyone—because the best you could do in the field was maybe GS-12, and that would be rare to get that far. So a board would convene in the bureau to fill the vacancies and they'd be GS-16s. It would be one of the jobs of the GS-16s, to do that. And they would comb through the records and select, and give a slate to whoever needed one as to what their recommendations were, three of them or so. And that was the way the process worked, and a pretty damned good process. I don't believe it had cronyism in it, but it did have a lot of experienced people. You didn't get some jerk into the Bureau of Weapons out of a shipyard someplace. He had to know something. And you had a number of those senior people had their own pets someplace, and they worried about them and the development of them. I don't want to dismiss that. It was my first exposure to it and I thought it was a pretty damned good system. One of the reasons I thought it was good is I didn't know any better; it was the only one I knew. There was no other.

Paul Stillwell: One other question I wanted to follow up on. How did the housing situation resolve itself?

Admiral Meyer: Late in the evening in August we were getting nervous. We were moving further and further down the highway, school was about to open. My roommate in school was an officer by the name of Joseph Talago.†

Paul Stillwell: In what school was that?

---

* GS, for government service, designates a pay grade level within the U.S. Civil Service.
† Commander Joseph Talago Jr., USN, as of 1963.

Admiral Meyer: MIT. He came from Bridgeport, West Virginia, and his daddy and mama operated a tavern there and they were genuine Polish. So in that period of years Joe and I were very close. We went ashore all the time together. And Joe played the accordion. So Joe could get an audience no matter where he went, and that turned out to be a pretty good thing.

We had the address of where the Talagos had lived. They had been transferred out to Ohio, to the new school that had been set up out there for studying management at Wright-Pat.[*] So I said to Margaret, driving around, "Why don't we go drive through this Falls Church place and see if we can look up that house where Talago lived?" Because Talago was my best man, so my wife knew him when they stood up for us in St. Margaret's up in Dorchester, Massachusetts. So we did, we drove up there, and dusk was approaching and there was a big rainstorm, thunderstorm coming up. We knocked on the door. There was a naval officer living there, a commander. And it turned out, of course, he was a surfaced submariner too, and they had rented Talago's house, and they invited us in. It turned out that they gave us a couple drinks and even gave us supper while we were there, our kids and everything. And we bemoaned the housing situation and we were getting desperate. She said, "You know, up here behind us, up in these hills here, there's a big housing project going up. I don't know, you probably can't find anything there or anything available, but it won't hurt for you to look."

Well, that sounded like a decent idea. So after dark we drove through there. It was all clay and mud, it rained like hell. We couldn't tell much, but one thing we did know, it was expensive. So, anyhow, we drove back the next morning in our desperation. We found the salesman's office. He was a retired commander. We walked in, I identified myself, told him we were looking for housing. He said, "Well, I'm sorry, Commander. We just don't have anything right now. But I might as well be upfront with you. You can't afford to live here anyhow. I would not spend my time looking at this if I were you."

"Well," we said, "it sure is pretty housing. Gosh, it's impressive." Just at that time—Coffman and McCaffery were the crack builders in north Virginia—this guy

---

[*] Wright-Patterson Air Force Base, near Dayton, Ohio, was established in 1948 with the merger of Wright Field and Patterson Field. The work done at the base has long been in the engineering and material areas.

McCaffrey walked in, a drinking Irishman. He walked in and said to the salesman, "You know, guess what? That house up there on Midway came back on us last night." Because then they'd buy the house, and they'd wait 8 to 12 months to get in the house, housing was so bad. People always think I'm lying to them; they just never went through the trauma. "So," he said, "we've got to figure out what we're going to do."

The salesman said [chuckle], "Well, you know, Mac, we may have the solution right here in front of us." So he introduced us and we got to talking. He said, "Well, the house is up there on the hill."

We said, "Could we take a look at it?"

He said, "Well, yeah, I'll lead you around."

Well, here we were, sloshing through all this damned clay and mud. The thing that just overwhelmed us, compared to north Virginia, where curbstones were going in, sidewalks were going in, driveways were going in. This was unheard of. And carports. I mean, we knew it was expensive when we saw that, because none of that kind of thing occurred in north Virginia, nothing. Not even in King's Park, which was our limited experience with the Bladeses. So we walked up.

He said, "Well, as far as I'm concerned the house is yours if you want it. But it's going to cost you money."

"Well," I said, "I didn't expect to get it for free."

He said, "I'm telling you, Commander, it will cost you money."

"Well, okay, what will it cost?"

He said, "Well," he said, "if I figure it up, it's going to run you $25,000 and $30,000." Ooh. We'd just sold a house in Monterey before we were transferred there, and we sold that house for $17,000, and it was way overpriced. We made like $6,000 off that house. I looked at my spouse, and she looked at me, and we just almost cried on the spot.

He said, "Not only that, what happened here is this couple waited so long for this house that they broke up. They got a divorce, and they asked me yesterday if I'd take the house back. They had already made some choices in colors, like in the bathrooms and such, and you'll have to take what it is. It's what is."

I said, "Well, I don't know that I'm very choosy at this point." Because it all did really look good. And then we called friends we knew later that day and they said, "Look, if you can get a McCaffery house, you ought to try to take it."

So we went back to the motel and got out all our savings bonds and everything we had and sat down, tried to count out whether we could get enough money to get in there, and whether we could borrow enough money. Certainly couldn't borrow any from my folks, because they didn't have any. And I couldn't borrow any from my uncle, because he didn't have any. So we pondered and pondered that day and finally decided that, well, if we cashed it all in, we could come pretty close. We'd be a few thousand short. We'd have to see if the builder would help us.

So I went back and talked to the builder that afternoon. "Well," he said, "we don't usually do this, but my salesman captain," Watkins [or whatever his name was] spoke awfully highly of you."

I said, "Well, that was nice of him."

He said, "I'll tell you what. I can make you a loan over a few months or so if it would get you over the hump. I don't really have a problem selling the house; it's just that I just don't want to spend a lot of time selling it."

I said, "Well, if you could get us over the hump, we'll buy the house."

The house had a carport, and it had a yard down below it. There was no way to get from the carport down to the back yard. So Margaret had said to me, "You know, you think he would put in a stairs down there?"

So I talked to him, "Mac—"

"Sure, I could put one in for you. It would cost you about $200."

I said, "Well, wait a minute. I don't have $200.00."

He said, "Well, I'll put it on the loan." So he did, he put it in. It's there yet today. The $200.00 was on the house loan, and we spent the next 25 years paying for it. [Laughter] FHA loan, 5¼%, and a half a percent insurance on it.[*] We put up, I forget how many thousand, but it seemed like in a matter of hours we were ready to move in. I mean, we were so sloppy happy.

---

[*] FHA – Federal Housing Administration.

So we started squeezing. It turned out we needed about $5,000. And I had taken a second mortgage on the house in Monterey because the guy couldn't—so I had made an agreement with Mac that I'd give him my second mortgage every month if he would put me up. So that's what I was doing, jiggling funds. And that guy who was an aviator out there was damned loyal to me, and he was very faithful, and McCaffery was very good to me. So he got his money; he didn't suffer anything.

Well, the next thing that became important, when we got over our happiness by the next day, is it took on the order of three months to get a telephone that year in a house. It was that bad. If you're a naval officer, though, I learned from them that you could go over to the Pentagon, and they had a priority system over there depending on what your job was. They'd get you a sheet of paper, and the telephone company worked off that list. So it took us about two weeks to get a telephone. We got one. And after a few months we got several more, but we got one, which was good enough.

But what I wanted to tell you, failed to tell you, dammit. I knew I was never going to get out of that house when we walked in it, because it was August and here was this unheard-of thing of central air-conditioning. I mean, it virtually did not exist then. Once my Irish wife felt that in August, there was no moving her. She'd go in a sleeping bag, she didn't care, as long as she had air-conditioning. And [chuckle] I knew there was no backing out.

But God, were we poor. We were so poor. We had no money. We just barely could scrape, scrape, scrape through. And she got us to scrape through for about three and a half years.

So we got moved into that house. I wanted to dump it. I was going to be transferred, because now I was becoming a big ordnance engineer, and I was going to be transferred to Port Hueneme, California. You know, a possession was even stronger for her than it was for me. It was strong for both of us, because we were both from the Depression. She didn't care. I mean, it was something she had that was tangible. "We're *not* going to sell it. We're going to keep it." Well, we had a couple officers that wanted to rent it. The first one was an aviator, and we rented to them, and they paid us nice rent and we kept the house, and the house kept appreciating. We then went to Port Hueneme and I lived in quarters the first and only time in my life, except for a Quonset hut when we were first married, and I believe I mentioned that—half a Quonset hut. And you could hear all the ablutions and behavior of everybody in the entire Quonset village. There was no damping and no shielding.

Paul Stillwell: Where was the office to which you were commuting from that house? Was that in Main Navy in D.C.?

Admiral Meyer: I was in Munitions. As you will recall, you had Main Navy and you had Munitions.[*] They sat side by side.

Paul Stillwell: On Constitution Avenue.

Admiral Meyer: On Constitution Avenue. Wonderful old buildings. But you really wore yourself out every day in survival and communications. Must have had, I don't know, 3,000 Fedders window air-conditioners in them. Every window had one throughout those buildings, built in World War I. And if you didn't know any better, they were adequate. Except that once you had central air in your house you started to know better now.

So I started riding a bus in from Falls Church and get off down on Constitution. Well, then I worked up a car pool and we had a four-person car pool, and we'd drive in, and because we had four of us we were assigned the mud hole up on a hill where, it was a BuMed place you may be acquainted with; there's still quarters up there. I don't know what else is up there anymore. But on the side of that hill, right where the connector to I-66 and the bridge crossover exist now, in those mud holes up there, if you were a commuter and you had three or four in your car pool you could get a parking spot. If you're less than that, the hell with you. So that's what I did my first tour.

But it was a wonderful experience in several ways. First of all, you were right downtown, or at least you thought you were right downtown. You were in the center of

---

[*] Main Navy was the popular name for the old Navy Department building at 17th Street and Constitution Avenue in Washington, D.C. The building remained in use from its opening in 1918 until the early 1970s, when President Richard Nixon directed that it be demolished. The adjacent Munitions Building was long occupied by the War Department. In 1943, with the opening of the Pentagon, the Army moved out and transferred the Munitions Building to the Navy.

your government, and you felt it. Somehow you just felt it when you walked outside. And every evening the parks were full, playing games of one kind or another, ball games mostly. There was so much intramural activity that goes on. And in that era the armed forces had not yet lost their sense, and so if you were working in Main Navy or in Old Munitions in our kind of business you went out to lunch virtually every day, because that's where you got your business done. Plus, it was so easy. You'd walk out, you'd take a cab, it would cost you a quarter, to take you two or three blocks. Virtually all of those old places have died now, but they were longstanding food pavilions. You'd meet with your industrial partners and have lunch and discuss the seriousness of the work you were trying to do.

Paul Stillwell: What do you mean when you say the armed forces had not lost their sense?

Admiral Meyer: Well, you don't do that today. My God, God forbid, if you accepted a meal from a contractor or from industry. GOD FORBID THAT SOMEBODY ACCEPT A MEAL! Your view is no good; you've been bought! Really? You've been bought for $12.50? How goddamned stupid can people get? And how they have damaged and continue to destroy communications.

You know, it's ironic that at the level of our President—we're always on the ass of our President for not holding face-to-face meetings and communing with other heads of states both here and there. And yet, what is one of the really heinous crimes in DoD—with all of government, but DoD? It's travel cost. It's the amount of money thrown away on travel! The wastefulness of it! Well, Eli taught me—and one of the little tales I wanted to mention earlier and it skipped my mind. I went in to see him one day on a problem. When you went in to see the admiral, usually you might see Tofalo in a corner or one of the others, and Mary Jane Padgett was his secretary. She'd send you in, and she'd tell you how many fingers you had; three fingers, four fingers, or five fingers, that was the time allotted to you.

Paul Stillwell: How many minutes.

Admiral Meyer: Yeah, that many minutes. So you were there to ask him for his support or advice for something. And you wouldn't get through the first sentence. He'd interrupt you. "What kind a work business [phonetic]?" "Commander, have you been there?"

"Well, no, sir. I haven't had a chance yet."

"Has your trusted agent been there?"

"No, sir. We were going to be doing that in a—"

"That's all. You come back when you've seen the thing yourself." He would not talk to you if you had not been there. Well, that was ingrained in all of us, and rightfully so. By God, it made us on-site leaders.

Now, in return for that, in those days, if you were a commander and you had the fire control desk in Terrier, which I had, for example, you were given a book of TRs, transportation requests. You carried that book. You wrote your *own* goddam TR, and you bought your own ticket, and you bought it wherever you had to buy it! And you flew, or train, to wherever you had to. If you were in Long Beach and needed to go someplace else, you were expected to do it, not moan about getting your orders changed or any of those things. You were expected to go *do* it! You were expected every month to get your travel claims in and up to date.

Paul Stillwell: Well, SP had that approach in going to the plants also.

Admiral Meyer: That's where we learned it from in the task force. That's what our admiral expected of us. And we were issued a Hertz rental card, and so when we got to a place we got a Hertz car. And this *bullshit* that was rammed down your throat about, well, you're going to the most expensive and—that's bullshit. A Hertz car doesn't cost any more than anybody else's car, unless you're some transient kid going around.

So he taught us, or attempted to, the value of time, that your time was more important than messing with things that were not going to have contributions to your better performance and efficiency. Did it get you in trouble? Quite a bit, because the jealous bureaucracy could not handle that. As a result, I probably created more whistle-blowing than anything else, almost all of it false, just because of the innate jealousy of people. But that's the way it was.

You know, working in that task force, your tongue would be hanging out, but you would never ever give up, and you would never moan, because you just felt the need for this work. It was just that simple. The admiral endowed you with whatever he could endow you, and in return he expected your performance. It's just that simple.

Paul Stillwell: Did he back you up if there came challenges to what you were doing?

Admiral Meyer: Always. He'd conduct an inquiry. And he may counsel you later: "There really was a better approach to this, Wayne, than what you used." But I don't ever remember that old man chewing my ass out—ever. And yet he was mean, and he was thought of as being mean. But he did protect his people. As a matter of fact, sometimes to a flaw. Because people like that, as am I, you have a tendency to cronyism. And I believe in cronyism. I have counseled my officers. I've developed managers that way, and say, "Look, there's nothing wrong with cronyism. Why shouldn't you use people you know?"

Paul Stillwell: And trust.

Admiral Meyer: Yeah. And you trust them, and you know what their limitations are and what their capabilities are. That's what's important in the people, and you shouldn't let somebody bluff you out of that. Well, does it go wrong now and then? Of course it does. That's what life's all about. But I don't believe it's any different in our profession than anybody else's profession. I think you can ask any priest, and they'll tell you that; it ain't a bit different. So we were treated as adults, and tended to behave as adults.

The other amazing thing about it, in that era. I was a commander, and the respect for a commander throughout industry and the laboratories and the civil service was just phenomenal. It was just phenomenal. In later life I've tried repeatedly—I know I've had a lot of success—I've tried to raise my officers that way, that in our profession here the people want to be led by officers, because they want to trust their officers. They believe in their officers. And so you have no right to double-cross them. You've got to be a straight shooter with them. If you're not going to be, then you're not going to be a decent leader. You're just not going to be. As a matter of fact, you won't last very long. I've tried to imbue that in people, and I believe that you can probably go ask a lot of my progeny who will confirm that, that they have found that to be true.

In those days I could get on a telephone to Great Neck, New York, to Sperry Gyro Company or Ford Instrument, and tell them that I needed this, I needed that. "Yes, sir. Where do you want it, when do you want it?" No screwing around. You didn't have anybody say, "Well, you know, we don't really have a contract on that, Commander, to be able to do that." They believed you were going to take care of it. If you told them to do something, you'd take care of it. Well, trust is a two-way street, and so I expected the same thing. If they told me they were going to do it, I expected them to do it. And, of course, sometimes they'd get tasks they just couldn't get done.

But, you know, your phone would ring all night. The second part of my tour was when we were building this great Terrier fleet and I was, in essence, in charge of it, myself and Lieutenant Commander E. J. Otth.[*] Well, this fleet was scattered all over the United States. We were building the Terrier fleet in eight yards. About half these yards were in the East, so you'd spend most of your day on the telephone with those people. When you got home at night you just started again at the kitchen table, because now you were working on the West Coast yards. It would really piss your wife off; I mean it really would [chuckle]. It would be aggravating. Because it would go on night after night. But it was an effective way to communicate. Worked pretty damn good. We built some incredible ships. And you know what? All of that is what made me the shipbuilder that I became.

It's amazing how uninformed so many people are of what I've done and what I did. I don't believe in running around touting it; I never have. As you can see by my record, I sailed for nearly 20 years off and on. I sailed, I think, in six ships or seven ships. I've done a lot of things on the globe. I've served in both occupations. I was in a war that nobody even knows anything about anymore, and that was the Greek Civil War, which they won, thank goodness, because Truman wanted them to win.

---

[*] Lieutenant Commander Edward J. Otth Jr., USN.

Paul Stillwell: What was the substance of your work on Terrier during that period in the '60s? What were these calls involving?

Admiral Meyer: I came aboard. We'd done a major, major conversion of *Galveston* to semi-active homing and long range, and I had fired—and today I think I fired the longest-range shots ever fired in Talos, and I fired more Taloses than were ever fired, although a couple officers unloaded through the muzzle when they got ready to dispose of Taloses and they kind of tend to think they fired more than anybody. Pow-pow-pow-pow-pow.

When I came on board, the basic guidance had moved from BW, which is beam-rider wing control, to BT, which is beam-rider tail control. And from that came the invention—it all came out of our ordnance plant at Pomona, California, and its forerunner, which was the great General Dynamics plant in San Diego. The building still exists; I don't know who in the hell runs them today. But what was known as homing Terrier was going to be a revolution in getting off of the beam, because now you were going to start the homing way sooner, a lot better accuracy, and working on deck.

The problem with a beam rider is about the lowest you could track or attack was 10 degrees. So, say, *Boston*, *Canberra*, they had a range in the neighborhood of 20 miles and a minimum of 10 degrees elevation. Well, that was a pretty awesome capability, it really was pretty awesome. And it had a PK, a kill power, of maybe .3 or .35 or so, which is overwhelming. The kill power in gunnery, the PK is, you know, .0000000000—forever. I mean, it really pisses me off when these people over here today turn up their goddamn nose when you happen to miss.

And to digress a minute, and that's the reason all those generals were there Wednesday night.

Paul Stillwell: That's when you received the Reagan Award.

Admiral Meyer: When I received the Reagan Award, thank you. But the reason all those generals were there is that Aegis has a record that no one else has in ballistic missile killing. Rempt's leadership in initiation of it—Rempt is not a very good leader once you get outside of piddling around in development research. But I was his counsel and his confidant for a number of years, and he's my son. And he was given an award, I think, Tuesday at lunch for his pioneering ability in ballistic missile defense, and rightly so. Why he has suffered such abuse as Superintendent at the Naval Academy I don't know, but in my little coordinate system I believe it to be unfounded and unfair, of what he was subjected to.[*] Not the Rempt I have worked with for many years.

Anyhow, in going along in that arena when really there was no one in the Navy believed it could be done. Rempt believed it could be done because after I'd spent two or three months screwing around with it and a couple of my old associates, I became convinced that it could be done. But, as you have probably heard by now, my slogan that I invented is "Build a little, test a little, learn a lot." That's the slogan I've tattooed on these people for a quarter-century. "Build a little, test a little," that's what I became known for in my heyday in Aegis. It isn't that I'm a no-risk person, but I'll be damned if I'm going to take a high risk in engineering. Engineering is not a high-risk adventure. If it is, you ain't going to do much engineering.

I've got to tell you, Paul, how irked I get when I see these behavior patterns in several of these shipbuilding programs and in these airplane programs. We're out in engineering of something that we've got no business doing. No automobile manufacturer would ever do it, what we do. No sensible commercial person would ever do what we take on. And it isn't, frankly, because of the opponent, unless it's a very rare occasion. It isn't the opponent; it's because of our constant push push push push push because we want the best, we want the thing that can be imagined, not the thing that can be engineered.

I remember getting kicked around and knocked around in Aegis in my heyday. It started with Dr. Frosch himself, who was Assistant Secretary of the Navy.[†] "Well, this stuff's all obsolete." Of course it is. Anything you can build can be graded as obsolete by the researchers way out on the imaginary axis. Of course it is. But you can't live with the stuff on the imaginary axis.

---

[*] Vice Admiral Rodney P. Rempt, USN, served as Superintendent of the Naval Academy from 1 August 2003 to 8 June 2007. As a rear admiral in the 1990s he was Director, Theater Air Defense and Program Executive Officer, Theater Air Defense.
[†] Robert A. Frosch was Assistant Secretary of the Navy for Research and Development, 1966-73.

I mean, we spent 100 years getting reliable automobiles. You get in your automobile today, and you expect that automobile to do whatever you command it. When it fails to do so, as a matter of fact, you even get your nose out of joint. Oh—battery's dead! Wait a minute, when did you last have a dead battery? Well, I've never had a dead battery. Oh, okay. Oh, you know what? I've got a flat tire on my car! Oh, when did you last have a flat tire? Well, I had one 13 years ago. No kidding. That's a pretty long mean time between failures, especially when you haven't checked it all that time. People forget that.

Paul Stillwell: Were you looking at this longer homing ability to give more versatility to the illuminators to get more targets, since they wouldn't have to stay on a target so long?

Admiral Meyer: There were a couple of reasons, but you're in essence stating an acceptable case. Far and away, throughout the world in missile and air defense the mechanism for killing the target is what we call semi-active homing. In semi-active homing there is a transmitter we call the illuminator sitting on the ground, in our case on a ship, and it's shining on a target, and that energy is being reflected off of the target. Your interceptor, which has been fired with pretty great precision in your fire control equation, is en route up to the target. In our case, our missile is only 13 inches in diameter.*

You can't get a very big transmitter or a very big field of view with a missile that small. I mean, this missile is pretty damned impressive; you can look at it and see it shape-wise over there, but that's a little missile. So you've got to get the missile out to where, when it opens its eyes, it will see what you want it to see, and not see what the opponent wants it to see. So you keep the illuminator off, and for that matter you keep the missile's eyes closed till you get it within, we Missouri boys might call it, within walking distance. So there you are, and now you turn on your illuminator, which shines on the target, and you tell your missile to start looking over there. Well, of course, the missile ain't seeing it sometimes. Oftentimes it's just, wow, just like that. Other times,

---

* This is a reference to the Standard missile 2 (SM-2), the Navy's principal surface-to-air weapon.

okay, so we have a little bitty search pattern within the head of that missile, and that little bitty search pattern starts looking around just a little bit to find it.

If you were to spend a couple hours looking at our data from the last ten years in our ballistic missile work in the Navy, it is just mind-blowing for its precision and its effectiveness and its reliability. No one else can hold a candle to it. The big reason for it—as we often say and I'll say some more later in life but I want to say it now—we killed that spacecraft; we started out killing that spacecraft 30 years ago.[*] That's how we killed that spacecraft. And you've got any number of people going to tell you, well, they could have done the same thing. And you know something? That's B.S. It just ain't correct. And right now I don't think you know anybody older than I or has been in the missile business longer than I in air defense. There ain't no such person left alive, I don't think. There have been some mighty people, and I've worked with a number of them and was led by a number of them, and great admiration I do have for them, but they are unfortunately in the graveyard. I'm it.

The reason you keep the eyes closed, of course, as long as you can is so the enemy can't foil you. Or, for that matter, God can foil you, because weather starts to become a problem, any number of things. Well, if you're way up above the earth, weather then is generally not a problem. But the enemy has all kinds of techniques that can threaten you. I can state categorically that I don't believe he can threaten this missile. Now, he ain't necessarily ever going to tell you, either. But I've got to tell you one thing, I'm going to make him work his ass off to do it. That part I know for sure. He'll have to work his ass off.

So semi-active homing—that's what that's called. Now, you have all these jaybirds pushing hard for active homing today, meaning the missile is carrying its own seeker, it's got its own transmitter, and it's up there. Don't fall for it. Right now our own Air Force is pushing this hard in fighters, that they can do the same thing in killing spacecraft. Take the AMRAAM missile.[†] The AMRAAM missile's about, I think it's 9-some-odd inches. It ain't going to do that. Well, you can contrive situations where

---

[*] On 21 February 2008, the Aegis cruiser *Lake Erie* (CG-70) hit an earth satellite with a modified SM-3 Standard missile. The satellite was by then dead and falling from earth orbit. The interception took place 130 miles above the Pacific Ocean. Meyer discussed the event in a previous interview.
[†] AIM-9 advanced medium-range air-to-air missile (AMRAAM).

perhaps it could, where the fighter got in just a perfect position to launch up just exactly. But boy, oh boy, that is a very, very limited space.

The great capacity of the Aegis, it's the best I've ever done and I don't know of anybody that can outdo me in capacity. I mean, we didn't have any real hesitancy about taking that sucker out.

Paul Stillwell: The spacecraft.

Admiral Meyer: The spacecraft—if we could reach it. I mean, look where we pushed this little missile to. I told you this missile, its ancestor was ten miles in *Boston* and *Canberra*. We pushed it to, what, nearly 300. I mean, that's being pushy. And it made it. Now, would it do that consistently and tempt you to make a general space killer out of it? I don't think so, because it required a controlled trajectory and a controlled operation. Well, we couldn't control the spacecraft. But one thing we knew, we knew that God wasn't going to mess with it, because it was dead as a doornail. So we could count on its behavior to some degree. Except you've got this little bitty homer that's going to home in on it, and you've got this big sucker the size of an automobile and it's tumbling and carrying on and twisting and turning and everything. Are you going to lock on it and home? Beats the hell out of me. But we did, and blew the son of a bitch up. So for a moment at least we were pretty good, really pretty good.

Paul Stillwell: You talked earlier about the traveling with the TRs and the Hertz cars. What did you do during those visits? Where all did you go?

Admiral Meyer: I was again raised, and I'm a big believer in—suppose that you're working at—Raytheon was the first big contract to be in, and Sperry was, and RCA and in recent years now called Lockheed Martin, through about three name changes. But, of course, the Aegis has got millions of parts of it. That missile over there has a couple million parts in it. I mean, if you were to look inside that missile, it would just blow your mind. You'd say: "How do you ever put it together?"

I'll tell you what blows *my* mind, coming out of the gumbo and being raised the way I am, is the reliability we've had out of *Lake Erie*. I think we're up to 11 firings or something like that; all worked perfectly. Well, our design is not that. The theory of our design won't achieve that number. So what that tells you is one of these days God's going to level you off, and you're liable to find you have a string of four failures, because over time reliability *will* catch up with you.

I've said this in speeches. One of the things we *do* know about that missile, which the United States Army occasionally has trouble learning, but we know that if you can get this missile through the land-based test process that we have at Tucson, Arizona, and in Camden, Arkansas, and some of it at White Sands, New Mexico—if it passes we've got virtually 100% confidence that missile will fly, unless some reliability failure occurs. Well, there are a lot of integrated circuits in that missile, thousands of them, and you could have an open circuit someplace that the land-based tests at the round level would never ever get to it. It also may be true that in the firing being done it doesn't matter, because not everything in that missile has to work perfectly all the time. So that's what the laws of reliability are telling you. What they're telling you is in our missile— our missile is what we call a .8, in the jargon. That is to say, it's got a probability about 80%.

Paul Stillwell: As you say, that's a whole lot higher than bullets.

Admiral Meyer: Right [chuckle]. It's a *whole* lot higher than bullets.

Reliability is a funny thing and a tough thing. I mean, you expect your tires to run forever, but they blow out too. And "I don't know why that tire blew out. Why did that tire go out on me like that?" Well, it happens. So that's one part of it.

Paul Stillwell: I'm presuming that there were BuWeps representatives in each of these commercial plants. How much did you rely on them to keep you updated?

Admiral Meyer: They are not widespread, however. But early on I learned—talking about learning, now this sounds stupid for me to say, but a lot of people don't learn it—

that I needed to put reliance on them, and the way I put reliance on them is get them in front of me, and that I keep looking at what they're doing, and quizzing them on it and measuring it. Also, I need to be sure that they become a part of the success. Many people don't do that.

Some things I wanted to say about my heyday—I don't know how it got this way, but I learned about the importance of touring plants. Today we have people that really at most do show and tell, if they do that. But you take that missile over there with its millions of parts. It's being built by several thousand women who do soldering techniques that would blow your mind and my mind. We couldn't be able to do it. And especially when we went into integrated circuits. Well, their performance is pretty damned important. And, as I said, you can't always measure that performance to the degree that you want. If you bought this thing and it didn't work you went in and you bitched to the guy: This thing doesn't work. "Oh, all right, I'll give you a new one. Here you are." And off you go.

Paul Stillwell: You're talking about a tape recorder.

Admiral Meyer: Yeah, tape recorder I'm pointing to. And it's true that we have progressed a long ways in the reliability of elements that we use in these things and in these devices, but none of these things undergo the stress and the strain of the elements we use in weaponry and use in that missile. So I reinstituted in my heyday the technique called award/fee contracts. Now, they've gotten terrible names in our profession because they were unjust, they weren't fair; people have come to believe that. And they were handled so sloppily. I changed all that, because I created degrees of freedom and I was often doing it before everybody realized what I was doing. I'm fond of saying that I never had a single fixed-priced contract. All cost contracts. OOOOOH! People go bananas. God—you're crazy! You can't control contractors that way! And I'm here to tell you that's pure, unadulterated bullshit. You control contractors by your leadership, not by berating them or not by writing specifications or not by threatening them with lawsuits. If that's how much trust you have in your contractors, get rid of them. Go get somebody that you do trust. That's what I do.

Well, pretty soon the people that work for you know that. And pretty soon your officers know it, and pretty soon your civil servants know it. And pretty soon the people in Wisconsin know it. And that when Stillwell comes walking in out of my project they'd better damn well sit up and take notice, and they'd better not have to deal in a lot of B.S. It's just that simple, really. I don't know how I got that leadership, but I got it. I don't know if it's from driving mules or what. It may have come from that.

Paul Stillwell: How would you measure the progress of the Terrier program during that time you were running it in BuWeps?

Admiral Meyer: It saved the Navy. One of the big reasons for my success in Aegis, if I can call it that, is my Terrier experience, and the forerunner was my Talos experience. I don't think I've told you this piece of the story in Terrier; if I did, stop me. Spreen returned from Tuesday morning's staff meeting with the admiral, and he wasn't in a very good frame of mind when he came back, over in old Munitions.* He said, "Commander, get your ass in here, and Otth, you get yours in here too." Otth is an engineering duty officer who had been trashed out of the Bureau of Ships—now called the Naval Sea Systems Command. I said, "Yes, sir, Captain."

Paul Stillwell: What was Spreen's position?

Admiral Meyer: Spreen was the director of the Terrier program in the task force. He was a captain, a very senior one, I might add. He had a deputy who was a GS-16. In my case we called him Uncle Charlie Jekyll behind his back; we called him Mr. Jekyll in front of him. He was, I mean, a *seasoned* civil servant. And then we had some civil servants and officers in that office that reported to the captain, who reported to the admiral. And the admiral had big staffs, and we had our tentacles all around.

Paul Stillwell: So what did Spreen want when he called you in?

---

* Captain Roger E. Spreen, USN.

Admiral Meyer: He said, "You two officers are going to get a plan to introduce the transistor into USS *Leahy*." Well, now, you think about that. *Leahy* was DLG-16, Terrier frigate, and we were going to get a plan to introduce the transistor.[*] I mean, here's like a big leap forward. We've got cabinets the size of that file cabinet over there, I mean we've got several dozens of them in USS *Leahy*, loaded with vacuum tubes. Hundreds of them; well, really, thousands of them when you started counting all the ranger operations. This is mind-boggling. We knew the transistor was coming. Now, the year is mid-'60s. The transistor started showing up on the bench in the mid-'50s. I remind people to stop and knock it off about new technology. It takes a minimum of ten years to apply technology to useful products, and I can show you enough data till you get tired of it. But if you go ask anybody in the automobile industry, anybody that even makes these things, they'll even tell you that. They'll put up this grand scheme of, "Well, we just invented this in February." Well, of course, that's B.S. The back room has been inventing it for the last eight years.

Paul Stillwell: Well, transistor radios came out in the late '50s.

Admiral Meyer: Right. The transistor radios came out in the late '50s, but you couldn't use them for anything else. They weren't fit for what we needed to replace all the triodes in the rangers in our radars. They just weren't capable of it. Bandwidth, reliability, any of those things, or power; they couldn't handle the power.

Paul Stillwell: Did Captain Spreen give you some sort of timeline to achieve this end?

Admiral Meyer: He said, "You're going to do the work, I'm going to raise the money; I want to know from you in a week how much money you think we ought to start with." And we started from there. The plan was to do one ship—wait a minute, we're going to do nine ships. One ship is a nuke and we don't know if we can ever do that. It turned out

---

[*] USS *Leahy* was commissioned 4 August 1962 as a guided missile frigate, DLG-16, the lead ship of her class. She had a standard displacement of 4,650 tons, was 533 feet long, 55 feet in the beam, and had a maximum draft of 26 feet. Her top speed was 33 knots. She was equipped with twin launchers for Terrier missiles, four 3-inch guns, ASROC, and six torpedo tubes. She was reclassified as a guided missile cruiser, CG-16, on 30 June 1975. She served until decommissioned on 1 October 1993 and was scrapped in 2005.

that the whole Terrier fleet was ultimately modernized and converted; this was after I left the project, after I left the task force. All were, as Spreen would say, transistorized.

Well, but what an incredible breakthrough. We made these rangers at Sperry Gyro. The rangers take up about six cabinets in size in the radar, and we reduced those cabinets—now we're down to about three cabinets there. And the whole nature of our heat transfer problem, though, soared. We had less cabinets but, man, transistors are so inefficient that the heat transfer became a hell of a problem in design. You don't think you've got a heat transfer problem here, and you don't, but you wrap that thing up in a blanket, and it won't last more than a couple of days.

We were so cautious. We started in Philadelphia Naval Shipyard, one ship.[*] Went to work the next year and a half trying to get everything in our favor. The captain said, "I'll raise the money, and I'll keep the old man off your back; I want results out of you." Okay.

Well, I had done *Galveston* in Philadelphia yard. I knew a lot of people in Philadelphia shipyard, all not in very good frame of mind on. But we got along pretty well. Lieutenant Commander Dick Albright was the test/evaluation officer in our project, and he'd just been selected for commander.[†] The next day Spreen called him in and he said, "Mr. Albright, you're now Commander Albright. But not only that, you're going to report to Philadelphia, because you are a prospective executive officer in USS *Leahy*, and that's going to be your tour of duty. You're going to sit there and watch that ship. I'm not going to have Meyer come in here every week telling me how it's full of banana peels and everything else. You're going to watch after that."

So we turned everything to our favor. We did something that had never been done before. Now this today sounds—I mean, I might just sound old-fashioned and old-mannish and all those things; yet it's true. Up till that time ordnance equipment did not use connectors. They were all hard-wired, and there were a couple reasons. One is that spaces were invariably so tight, particularly around the fire control switchboards,

---

[*] The *Leahy* arrived at the Philadelphia Naval Shipyard on 27 January 1967 to begin extensive antiair and antisubmarine updates; she was decommissioned 18 February. She was recommissioned 4 May 1968 for testing and departed Philadelphia 18 August 1968.
[†] Lieutenant Commander Richard K. Albright, USN.

there physically was not enough room for connectorized cables, even though we didn't have them, so it didn't matter.

The second was, you lose signal when you go through the connector, and a quarter dB was an important thing in those days. What's happened in these damned things is, we've become totally disrespectful of a decibel in this present life we have. But then we were really respectful of decibels. I mean, you're losing signal, because we're operating on the edge. This thing ain't operating on the edge at all. I mean, it's the most inefficient thing you can buy.

Paul Stillwell: The tape recorder, you're speaking of.

Admiral Meyer: Yeah, the tape recorder I'm pointing to. The little rowdy tape recorder.

So here you are. We said to Spreen, "We've got these new ideas. I got part of them from *Galveston*; you've got to understand this. What we're going to do is we're going to remove all the fire control gear off of USS *Leahy*, and we're going to take it to Great Neck, Long Island, on trailers."

Paul Stillwell: To Sperry.

Admiral Meyer: To Sperry Gyro. "And we're going to modernize and rewire and rebuild that gear with your beloved transistors. And then we're going to put connectors on it all, and we're going to bring it back to the ship so that we can rapidly connect it when we get back there."

Paul Stillwell: Was there a specified yard period for the ship in which this had to be accomplished?

Admiral Meyer: There was. A good question. It was driven by my *Galveston* experience in the very same yard, because *Galveston* took almost twice the time for her conversion. And you would look, and the people would come down and say, "Well, what's the problem?" You know, "What's going on?" Nothing wrong. Here's the problem: Only two people could work in the fire control switchboard. So around the clock the maximum you could get was six people. And it's true; there were no other problems. But trying to do the goddamn wiring in the switchboards broke our back. And in this new age of missilery no one had anticipated that, or the seriousness of it. So Ed Otth and I had this wonderful view we'd put connectors on it all. The shipyards threw a fit. As a matter of fact, Sperry threw a fit.

Paul Stillwell: Why?

Admiral Meyer: The risk. Loss of signal—Sperry's was loss of signal, and the shipyard's was you don't have the room. The room doesn't exist. Well, what if in our scheme we've got a lot smaller number of cables? Or we'll rebuild the ship and we'll get another compartment for it? We did all those things. Well, before we ever started we spent two weeks up in Long Island with Sperry, the yards, Bendix, and a couple other suppliers, and solderers, to try to prove to everybody to accept that technique of putting connectors on. Up to that time no fire control gear had connectors aboard ship. None.

Well, we won that. And it turned out too, of course, as you might expect, whereas Bendix connectors used to be that big around they could now make them this big around.

Paul Stillwell: Maybe 3-inch to a half-inch?

Admiral Meyer: Exactly. I mean, there were breakthroughs all over the place once you got people rolling on it, once you got them behind it all and you got the shipyards to work on it, and you got them working with Sperry, which, God's sake, was unheard of. It was just unheard of that a shipyard would work with the contractor. You get all those people to work. I made Sperry people be posted in Philadelphia. Philadelphia had to send four people up at Great Neck. They were up there some seven months with those guys doing the design. And all those techniques—I'm not a genius, except build a little, test a little, but everything I did in Aegis came out of just what I'm telling you right now. It's as though God had created a movement, and he was pushing me out in front all the time, on leading these techniques. And certainly in hindsight they're not revolutionary, but in real time they were pretty damned upsetting. It's just like changing the shape of a traffic light, pretty upsetting when it starts.

Paul Stillwell: And Commander Albright had a great vested interest in making sure this all came together.

Admiral Meyer: You got it. You got it. [Laughter]. Actually, Spreen was such a good leader. God, he showed us no mercy but encouraged us constantly. And anybody gave us any lip, man, they paid for it. We didn't even have to say anything to Spreen; if he just became aware of it, they paid for it, because he had a lot of power in the whole structure.

Well, that was that revolution. Today people don't know anything else.

I remember the day I finished—to cap this story off—we were going to bring the first fire control system back to the *Leahy* and the shipyard. It was all ready. The spaces were ready. We'd had these walk-throughs, we'd had these drills. About half of our cables were connectorized on only one end, because you couldn't be 100% sure about the length of the cable in the ship design. Well, later on we gained enough experience to know how to connectorize many more of them in the follow ships. But in that first one, about half of them we had connectors on them. But we started that, and that afternoon I believe that the commander of the shipyard just simply dismissed workers and gave them the afternoon off, because thousands came down to watch the lowboys coming in to deliver this fire control system into the ship and land it in one afternoon. In one afternoon it landed!

No turning back. Once we did that, no turning back. It was a revolution. And so people say that I've created several revolutions in my life, which perhaps is true, but that's one I've never ever forgotten. And it sounds so trite. If you haven't done it, what's the big deal here? You don't get what's the big deal.

Paul Stillwell: How long did it take to get it all connected up.

Admiral Meyer: I think we energized it—it was a token energizing—the next day. And then we had the other three systems to bring back yes too. But I mean, it was, like, breathtaking. It was breathtaking! And the goddamn switchboard didn't have to be wired, rewired, checked, rechecked, none of those things. We had all the confidence in the world in the switchboards, and our confidence in coax cables soared, because up to that time we didn't use that much coax in fire control, but now it was carrying signals all over the place once this stupid thing started coming it.

So it was decided to compete the contract for the rest of the ships. The contract for the rest of the ships was awarded to Bath Iron Works, and they commenced work on what was known as the Terrier antiair warfare modernization program, which ultimately became 30 ships.

Well, wait a minute. Years went by. I was long gone. We're down to the last two ships, DLG-10 and DLG-11.

Paul Stillwell: *King* and *Mahan*, I think.

Admiral Meyer: You got it. You're right on. It was decided they were going to be competed. *King* was the first one up at bat, and the contract was awarded to a boatyard in Louisiana.* I was out at Port Hueneme at the time. But the captain had taken his ship and headed to go into this yard for his decommissioning. Actually, we put them out of commission in reserve was the technical term. He sailed in there and he sent an operational immediate to the chief of the Bureau of Ordnance.† It said, "I have arrived at the designated place, but I cannot find the pier which I was instructed to moor to." Of course, all hell broke loose in Washington, D.C. It turned out the next day, of course, there *was* no pier. [Chuckle]. There *wasn't* one. There was going to be a rope walkway out to, and the ship was going to moor to a couple of dolphins. And she'd walk out from

---

* USS *King* (DLG-10) was decommissioned 30 April 1974 for antiair warfare modernization at Boland Marine in New Orleans. She was recommissioned at the Norfolk Naval Shipyard on 17 September 1977, by which time the hull number had been changed to DDG-41.
† BuOrd, the Bureau of Ordnance, existed until 1959, when it was combined with the Bureau of Aeronautics to form the Bureau of Naval Weapons (BuWeps). In 1966 there was a split that separated out the former BuOrd as the Naval Ordnance Systems Command (NavOrd). On 1 July 1974, shortly after the *King* began her modernization, NavOrd was merged with the Naval Ship Systems Command to form the Naval Sea Systems Command (NavSea), which exists to the present.

this little wobbly pier walk onto this walkway out to the ship. That's what a competitive contract got.

Well, it got something else. Seven months later the ship, which was supposed to be done, I believe they had it down to 11 months or 12 months in doing her modernization—the Navy had to send tugs down and tow *King* out, and she was towed back to Norfolk Naval Shipyard, and there that shipyard plus a massive contingent from Bath Iron Works went to work to get *King* back together. You think the Navy ever thanked Bath Iron Works or ever apologized? Zero. I personally wrote a letter of apology to the president of Bath Iron Works for the behavior of the Navy, and I wasn't any longer even associated with it.

Before *Mahan* went in—I can't remember where she went. I don't know whether she went back to Bath or whether she went to Philadelphia or whether she went to Norfolk.[*] But, oh, what lessons this officer had to learn about the behavior of the body politic and its lack of accountability and responsibility. And how the coin could be repeatedly reversed on you. And after that I became a hellion.

So through my years in Aegis, which maybe we'll get to one day, I was a throwaway. No one had any use for me, they didn't want to be around me, and I was intolerant of the processes, because of what I saw in the behavior of our government, and more specifically, my Navy. And how we puff out our chests at the brilliant things we were doing, which turned out to be just not only not brilliant but stupid and very costly, and very damaging, and very destructive of people. We destroyed so many good people in industry, so many good corporation, by our leadership. I at one time thought it was incompetence. I'm not sure it was incompetence at all, but one of the seven capital sins surely fits the situation, as greediness on the part of Navy behavior and wanting to be able to lord over the lowly contractors and to see how bad we could drag their reputation down and destroy their reputations.

That's why I was dragging my feet when I had mentioned to you the other day, when Rear Admiral Mark Woods told me I was to come back and take over the new

---

[*] USS *Mahan* (DLG-11) was modernized at Bath Iron Works from 1973 to 1975.

advanced surface missile systems.[*] Because I knew how it had been formed and I saw what had happened, and I didn't want anything to do with it. It would be nothing but grief and backbreaking. I didn't want it. I was in danger of losing my vocation when I saw how our Navy was inept or refused to look at situations that only it was capable of correcting.

I was born and raised in the gumbo. I was a poor person. I never knew and never had anything. But, God damn it, I learned how to respect people. And if I didn't, my mother and my daddy were standing nearby, and if it needed to be taught again it was taught again. Now, they weren't wild people, they weren't mean people. They were kind and gentle people. But they never let me forget that.

My demands vary on people depending on who you are. This used to really piss off one of my skippers in *Galveston*, in particular, because my behavior was different around through the department of gunnery and deck. He was from the old school, and his view was, well, Paul Stillwell, Wayne Meyer, Schnitzel Mitchell, and so forth are all the same; handle them all the same way. I didn't do that, because I believed that you couldn't get more out of people than they were capable of doing.

And that's why, as years went by, civil servants, I think, came to have such great, I want to say admiration for me, because they did and they have, and today I would guess that I know more civil servants than anybody else in the United States Navy. The retired ones, all the old ones and everything, they never fail to speak to me. And I believe it comes directly from that. I don't know whether "straight-shooter" is the right expression, but they know that there will always be a fair shake. And I came to understand, I tried to raise my officers, that you can't make—well, he's a GS-13 and I ought to be able to get blah-blah-blah-blah out of him. You can't do that. Instead, you've got to know the person and you need to expect from the person what you think he or she is capable of. You aren't always right. You often expect more than they're capable of, and so you learn as you go. And you're not always right in the other direction; you're too dismissing of people who have more ability than you're getting from them.

---

[*] Rear Admiral Mark W. Woods, USN, served as Commander Naval Ordnance Systems Command from May 1969 to July 1972.

Paul Stillwell: And you also find people who are capable of more than they think they are, and leadership brings it out.

Admiral Meyer: You got it. You got it. Leadership brings it out. You put your finger right on it. I mean, it just comes right out. And I've got to tell you, those people in Bureau of Ships and most of Bureau of Ordnance thought I'd never make it, and they didn't want anything to do with it. Nothing. Well, depending on how you look at things, that's good. And another side of it, that's bad. But it turns out that if you keep your cool, sooner or later they come back to you. Sooner or later they start back and say, well, maybe he was right after all.

Paul Stillwell: In a previous interview, you talked about nuclear warheads on some of the missiles. Using a nuclear weapon for antiaircraft sounds like a very heavy approach. I mean, like a sledgehammer to kill a fly.

Admiral Meyer: Well, it is, but the driver was our inability to get sufficient accuracy at long range. When I had the Terrier fire control desk in the special Navy task force, the Navy was ordered to put in nuclear heads for Terrier in its DLGs. Can't say to you the Mark number of that warhead right now because it doesn't come to me. And we did, in fact, load nukes, but they had to be beam riders because we could not guarantee the safety with the homers. So the HTs were never, never converted to carry nukes. Well, this meant that you had to carry the beam rider transmitters and stuff in the system. And we carried them, the warhead.

We had a crisis in submarines, and I may get my years mixed up. We created a serious situation in an attack submarine in San Diego where we ended up mislabeling a couple torpedoes. I've got to think that through. I'm calling this up really deep down about in here in my brain. And the world went ape. It was discovered they had a nuke aboard and they didn't know it. Well, it was later discovered they didn't have a nuke aboard; what they had is a mislabeled warhead aboard. [Chuckle]

And we had a crisis in USS *Dewey*. This was when I was in the task force in the early days,. Mayport had just opened up and—I think this is correct—*Dewey* was home-ported there. And they had a jackass for the gun boss. And they somehow accidentally rammed a beam rider nuke one morning while running the daily system operability test. They rammed the son of a bitch, it went up on the launcher, and it immediately fell off the launcher, and that's where it lay. No one knew what the hell to do.

So finally the SOPA phoned the task force in Washington, D.C., and the admiral was demanding we get a team down there right now. Well, Captain Spreen said, "You're going to lead the team." Aw, I don't know about that. "And Cliff Fawcett [we called him "water faucet," he was a GS-14] and you are going with him." Well, it turned out that in a few minutes the admiral changed that and the admiral said, "Spreen, you're going to lead the team." So I stayed home. They got their ass down there to try to find out what the problem was, and it was in fact bona fide. But the town of Jacksonville almost panicked, and what—I think we call it Mayport today, but I'm not sure it was even a city at that time, I can't recall—they were pretty calm because they had a lot of confidence in the Navy and that the Navy knew what it was doing and such, and by nightfall we had it all straightened up and everything sorted back out. It was a bona fide concern. But it couldn't get armed. It could not be armed.

Paul Stillwell: Well, please talk about the *Leahy*, once she got to sea and tested this new capability.

Admiral Meyer: I'm afraid that we're going to have to quit.

Paul Stillwell: I'll be in suspense for a few weeks, then.

Admiral Meyer: All right, you stay in suspense. We'll stop right there.

Paul Stillwell: All right. Thank you admiral.

Admiral Meyer: I appreciate you, I really do.

Interview Number 9 with Rear Admiral Wayne E. Meyer, U.S. Navy (Retired)
Place: Admiral Meyer's office in Arlington, Virginia
Date: Monday, 12 May 2008

Paul Stillwell: Admiral, last time we talked about the Terrier project and upgrading to transistors at the behest of Captain Spreen. The project was in the Bureau of Naval Weapons from 1963 to '65, and then in September '65 went to the Office of Naval Material. How did your duties and responsibilities change at that point?

Admiral Meyer: They didn't change at all as far as *I* know. I was a commander, and I think it was just a re-accounting of the establishment of the Special Navy Task Force for Surface Missile Systems. It had to do with the reporting structure prior to that time, and I may be wrong, but I think so. Admiral Reich reported directly to the Secretary of the Navy as head of the Special Navy Task Force.

Paul Stillwell: Right. Admiral Reich covered that in some detail in his oral history.

Admiral Meyer: Did he?

Paul Stillwell: He said that he was able to go across bureau lines in order to get what he needed.

Admiral Meyer: It pissed everybody in the world off—really upset the whole world.

Paul Stillwell: Well, did there come a point then when somebody came in and relieved him, so that you reported to a new CO?

Admiral Meyer: There did, but I believe this time that you mention here they were trying to regularize the organization. It was known as the Special Navy Task Force for Surface Missile Systems in the beginning. And then, after many internal struggles, it was reassigned to report through the Chief of Naval Material. And this is the point, I think, that you're talking about. And part of the compromise was the project would report to him, not to the chief of BuWeps. We were billeted in the chief of BuWeps, and our billet accounting was there, but we didn't report to him.

Paul Stillwell: Well, there was a big change in '66 when the bureaus went away and the systems commands came in and reported to this four-star Chief of Naval Material, as opposed to the bureaus reporting to SecNav.[*]

Admiral Meyer: I don't recall unless I sit down and start writing and studying charts exactly that order of battle. Your ability to sort it out is so superb that I can't possibly compete or even dispute what you say. What you have said is correct, but I can't confirm that date or how it came about. And besides, I didn't have that much to do with the front end of the task force anyhow.

Paul Stillwell: Well, the new command was known as Naval Ordnance Systems Command, and BuWeps went away.

Admiral Meyer: Yeah. BuWeps went away and we morphed into Naval Ordnance Systems Command. But that was for housing purposes and accounting purposes. We still continued to report to the Chief of Naval Material. And then Reich left and Admiral Ben Sarver relieved him.[†]

Paul Stillwell: What do you recall about him?

---

[*] BuOrd, the Bureau of Ordnance, existed until 1959, when it was combined with the Bureau of Aeronautics (BuAer) to form the Bureau of Naval Weapons (BuWeps). In 1966 there was a split that separated out the former BuOrd as the Naval Ordnance Systems Command (NavOrd) and essentially the former BuAer became the Navy Air Systems Command (NavAir), which still exists. In 1974 NavOrd was merged with the Naval Ship Systems Command to form the Naval Sea Systems Command (NavSea), which exists to the present.

[†] Rear Admiral Ben W. Sarver, USN, was director of the Surface Missile Systems Project in 1965-66 after relieving Admiral Reich. As a captain, Sarver had commanded USS *Oklahoma City* (CLG-5) in 1960-61. She was one of the World War II light cruisers later converted to carry Talos guided missiles. She was designed to accommodate a numbered fleet staff and thus retained only one forward 6-inch gun turret, compared with two in the *Galveston* in which Meyer served.

Admiral Meyer: He was a wonderful man. He was a gentleman of the old school. He was in fact technically authoritative in the ordnance tradition. Reich was not. Reich was pretty darned brilliant and pretty smart in what you might call material and organization and such, but Reich was not an ordnance person. Sarver was an ordnance person, and he had had command of a cruiser. I always felt he took this post with some trepidation, coming into the wake behind Reich, but you couldn't tell that after a few days. He took over with what I'd say a standard Mark I Navy-type leadership. He provided the model for us, and we all followed the model. And I think that's when the arrogance of the task force started toning down some over time, and it kind of morphed back into the structure.

Reich had picked several very senior civil servants that he had known in his earlier life. One such person was Frank Gilliam. Frank Gilliam was a well-known person. He may have been the most senior civil servant, for all I know, in all the material command, or in the Navy. He was what you would think of in those days as a standard, mind you, Mark I civil servant. He didn't compete with the military. He was there to serve with the military. He was the admiral's deputy, and he did that role.

First of all, he attempted to do what the admiral wanted done, but he also saw that the admiral didn't step on a land mine. And he also worried about raising money. So when Reich suggested to him what ought to be done to raise money, Frank—we called him Gillingham in the back room—Gillingham would take on that task, and he'd run around and solicit from the captains and the commanders. You'd always be tuned in with Frank Gillingham. He never did anything behind your back. He ran around and solicited views of how you thought it ought to be done and what you thought you needed, and such. I assume he's in the graveyard today. I haven't seen him in a long, long time.

Paul Stillwell: But the civil servants provide the continuity and corporate memory as well.

Admiral Meyer: They that did. When the task force was created, he drafted eight or ten—it may have been more—GS-16s out of the structure. Boy, that made the world tremble. And I have told people, and there are people that tend not to believe me, but in those days those GS-16s were called "Mister." And when we officers walked around we called them "Mister." The deputy in the case of Spreen and his predecessor was again a classic civil servant, GS-16, Charlie Jekyll by name. We never called him anything but Mr. Jekyll, except behind his back we called him "Charlie." But they were treated that way, and virtually no one came into the system except through them.

That was the changing of the era; Lyndon Johnson caused those changes to start occurring, and I guess they were on their way from the way we were forming civil service.[*] Frankly, I liked the old way. Virtually all civil servants in the headquarters came out of the field—shipyards, depots, laboratories. So when a civil servant came into headquarters the civil servant knew something.

Paul Stillwell: Sort of a parallel to the naval officers coming in.

Admiral Meyer: You got it. You got it. And they rotated back. As you know, the officers referred to it in the jargon as a "payback tour." When they went to graduate school, they had a payback tour. Well, that wasn't absolute, but it was practiced, and it was a very effective thing to do. And it also created a large group of naval officers who knew something about the materiel establishment. Today it is pathetic. It's just pathetic today, because that kind of rotation/exchange does not occur. As a matter of fact, it's almost rare these days to see one of those officers get a command at sea. It's just rare.

Of course, command has lost, I think, some of its significance or its aura that it had in those days, because in those days working toward command was everything, as it was to me up to when I decided to specialize as an ordnance engineer. That was the hardest decision I ever made. But today there are still a number of officers who focus on command as part of the list of things to do, but it doesn't have that vocational thrust that at one time it had, at all. And it doesn't have that meaning. Command then meant really going to sea and operating as a naval officer in command. Today there are a lot of things that are important, significant. I don't want to sound like I'm denigrating the post, because I personally am one that I never thought that much of command anyhow. I never thought it was the most important thing in the world. Neither did I ever worry about competition. I just knew point blank I was never going to compete with those people,

---

[*] Lyndon B. Johnson served as President of the United States from 22 November 1963 to 20 January 1969.

ever, because the kind of sea duties that I was having was not related to that, and frankly I didn't have the interest in it.

Paul Stillwell: So you had gotten into a specialized track even in your sea duty.

Admiral Meyer: Affirmative. I told you that I had been assigned for the conversion of *Galveston* as their fire control officer, and up to this day I hold the record of having fired more Taloses than any person ever, and those kinds of things. So the aura of being an ordnance person got created, but it was more the aura of a missileer. I didn't hide from that, because I wanted to be a missileer, which is what I eventually became.

Paul Stillwell: What was the status of Typhon during this time when you were in Washington?[*]

Admiral Meyer: Well, to recall, if you want to take a few minutes on that, the admiral created the Special Navy Task Force, and he set up, as he captioned it, four different line offices. There was the Talos office, the Terrier office, the Tartar office, and the Typhon office. Each one of them had a captain and a GS-16. And these captains weren't slugs. If they didn't have some ordnance experience, they didn't get there. I'm trying to think whether they were all post-command, and I think the answer is no. They were really selected on their record rather than on command rotation.

Paul Stillwell: Well, but they'd probably had commands when they were in the commander rank.

Admiral Meyer: They did, off and on. I came back here fat, dumb, and happy and, frankly, I was the world's authority on Talos. I had been led to believe that that's where

---

[*] Typhon was a program conceived in the early 1960s by the Johns Hopkins Applied Physics Laboratory as a means of combating future aircraft and missile threats to the fleet. The system was expected to have close ties to the Naval Tactical Data System. Secretary of Defense Robert McNamara canceled the program in December 1963 because of its high cost.

I'd be, that I would relieve Commander Harmon Penny in the Talos office.* That's where I was confident I was going to go. That was known as the fire control desk. Each one of those structures had a fire control desk, and they had a missile desk, and each of them had a command and control desk. And they had a mixture of civil servants and officers for those desks; they weren't all officers. They were all, I don't want to say handpicked, but they were all carefully picked. You just didn't apply for it and wait for the answer in the mail.

At that time, when I reported in, which would be '63, we had ships in construction in six or eight yards on both coasts. We had them all over, and they were in various stages of undress, and they were highly dependent upon the flow of what in those days was called government-furnished equipment. Of course, all of it is government-furnished equipment. When I took the Aegis, by the way, I had an index of forbidden words, and one of them was GFE and CFE, which are stupid expressions, because the money only comes from one place, period.† [Chuckle]

Then they each had the GS-16, as I said, as a deputy. They had a very senior GS-15 who was what we would call their money man. He was their planner and their budgeter, and he apportioned the people. So this fellow reported to the GS-16 and to the captain, and nominally he had two or three assistants, because he worried about that little cell, say of Terrier, which is the one I—did I tell you how I got assigned to Terrier?

Paul Stillwell: I don't remember specifically.

Admiral Meyer: Well, it's probably a boring story. I reported in in June of 1963. I had been to several meetings of one kind or another that were occurring, but I hadn't reported in yet. Marilyn Smith was a long-standing woman who ran officer detailing in BuWeps. She had checked me in and went through all my assignments and stuff. So she had told me, which I expected, that I was going to relieve Commander Harmon Penny. So I went over into the other wing, and I was walking down to the Talos office feeling pretty good

---

* Commander Harmon C. Penny, USN.
† CFE – contractor-furnished equipment.

about myself, and what happens to me? In those buildings—you were surely in one of those old buildings.

Paul Stillwell: I was in old Main Navy in the late '60s, before it was torn down.

Admiral Meyer: Munitions Building and Main Navy. They were built using drawings from depots, and so they were built as a long shed with wings off it. I think we had nine wings in Munitions. I think there were nine wings in the other one too. And all of the heads, for example, the men's heads, or the women for that matter too, had standard fixtures out of the Navy. For example, all of them had a circular basin with elbow controls so when you went to wash your hands there was this big sink about half the size of this room, and your elbow, you pushed the water on for you to wash your hands in this common bowl. And the towels were set up beside this. So they'd all been built in World War I, and they used standard gear out of Army and Navy.

Paul Stillwell: Are we getting away from Marilyn Smith here?

Admiral Meyer: Yeah. [Laughter] I was reporting in, walking down the hall, and I ran into Admiral Reich. He had got his pince-nez glasses on, and I walked by. He looked up at me, and he said, "Meyer, what are you doing here?" He knew me because he had met me as the gun boss in *Galveston*, and as fire control officer.
 I said, "Admiral, I've just reported in to your task force."
 "Oh?" He said, "Well, where are you going?"
 I said, "Well, I'm on my way down. Marilyn told me I'd be relieving Commander Harmon Penny."
 "Wait a minute," he said, "that doesn't sound right."
 "Well, I know what I was told."
 He said, "Well, wait till I go to the head."
 He came back from the head, and we walked over to his office. His secretary was a lady by the name of Mary Jane Patrick. We walked in, and he was dragging me, and he

said, "Mary Jane, Meyer here tells me that he's going down to relieve Penny." And he said, "That doesn't sound right to me. That doesn't sound correct."

"Admiral, I'll check on it right away." She opened a drawer and whipped out a big book. She went through it and whipped it, whipped it, whipped it. She looked up and smiled at the admiral, and she said, "Admiral, you're right again. We're sending him down to Terrier." She didn't say "You." She said "*We're* sending him down." Lesson 1 for Wayne reporting in: "*We're* sending him down." I rapidly started learning how things worked around there.

So I was going to go down to take the Terrier fire control desk. Well, the reason I was going down to take it is that R. P. "Zeke" Foreman from Hazard, Kentucky, had been selected for captain and had been fleeted up while I was traveling to be the Terrier desk.

Paul Stillwell: Now, we did talk about how he kept you from being hijacked.

Admiral Meyer: Exactly right. Well, so he and I were simpatico from Day One. And so I ended up reporting in to him and the Terrier fire control desk. God's in His Heaven and we moved on.

To cap that piece off, Harmon Penny was relieved by someone walking along the street thanks to McNamara.[*] Now, you're responsible for having asked this question, so you'll get all the answer whether you need it or not. McNamara decided that the Navy and the Army did not need separate missile systems, and here they both were working on advanced systems. He, McNamara, was going to square that away, because he had so much knowledge of what he had learned at Ford Motor Company. And in that process he ordered this project established at Huntsville, Alabama, which was the end of the world. And all that I really knew about it was that that's where the German scientists went that I mentioned to you earlier when they were relocated from White Sands.

Well, the Navy was ordered to not only become part of the joint office but also to assist in staffing it. Seniority of Commander Harmon Penny, who was destined to take command at sea, was such that he was ordered down to take command of this project. That did not set well with Commander Harmon Penny at all. As a matter of fact, I

---

[*] Robert S. McNamara served as Secretary of Defense from 21 January 1961 to 29 February 1968.

believe he was selected for captain just at that time.* So the clock kept ticking and kept going, and Commander Harmon Penny was getting detached, and Commander Carl Kaczmarek had been ordered in and had reported, I believe, to fleet up to relieve Harmon Penny because Kaczmarek had made commander.† About four months or so later, Commander Harmon Penny decided he'd had enough and he retired from the U.S. Navy and went home.‡ I never heard from him again. I don't know where he went, but it was asking too much for him to do.

It was also asking too much for the Navy to do, so ASMS, Advanced Surface Missile System, went limping along, limping along, limping along, while I reported, as I told you, eventually, after the AAW modernization with the frigates this ASMS was still going along. I don't know, it was on its—I can't even remember who they were—I think it was on its fourth captain or something, a captain whose nickname was "Jughead:" Jughead Tazewell.§ Jughead had that project. One of his several helpers was Lieutenant Commander Lowell John Holloway, whom you may know as a retired admiral here, that lives right here in Virginia, who worked for me several times.

Well, time wore on and time wore on. No one could figure out where ASMS was going to go. The Army had said the hell with this, and it split. They named it Patriot and they broke out, split out, and formed their own parabolic course, let a contract with Raytheon, and went to work developing an air defense system.** The Navy was left naked and broke. McNamara disappeared, and escaped accountability, which is what happens in those cases all the time. So we lost our officers, we lost money, we lost organization, we lost everything. And ASMS became a former advanced surface missile system. It was number four in that organization, the line organization.

In the coming years it kept decaying, and, to rush ahead, I got detailed one day by Admiral Mark Woods.†† Called me and told me that, "*We* had a meeting last night, and *we* selected you, Wayne, to be the manager of the new advanced surface missile system.

---

* Penny's date of rank as captain was 1 September 1966.
† Commander Carl C. Kaczmarek, USN; his date of rank as commander was 1 June 1966.
‡ Captain Penny retired from active duty a few years later, in January 1970.
§ Captain John P. Tazewell, USN.
** The MIM-104 Patriot is an Army medium-range surface-to-air missile system manufactured by Raytheon. System development began in 1975, and it was first deployed in 1984.
†† Rear Admiral Mark W. Woods, USN, Commander Naval Ordnance Systems Command.

Paul Stillwell: When was that?

Admiral Meyer: That was in December of 1969.

Paul Stillwell: We've got some ways to go before we get to that [chuckle].

Admiral Meyer: Yeah.

Paul Stillwell: Did Typhon have promise, or was that a victim of the McNamara thing?

Admiral Meyer: Well, it even lost its name. In that whole process, I'm sure you will recall, the test ship was going to be *Norton Sound*, and she was moved to Baltimore.* And Westinghouse, which was in charge of the radar development, was going to undertake, at a private shipyard up there, to do the modifications to her in order to turn her into the test ship for the radar to be landed in her to evaluate its applicability. This radar was a C-band radar, very high powered, so the ship had to have new generators and 400 cycles installed in her and things, and she had to have a launcher. And the radar was what today we'd call had *some* solid state but not much. It just had room after room of spare parts and modules, which are all tube based, and just piles and piles of one of the favorite tubes of that era, which was 6SN7. It was a triode, to work on the signal processor for Typhon. And Typhon just kind of foundered away and foundered away.

 Well, it was finally decided in the middle of this—I may have the story a little bit twisted around—Reich was still in power, and he walked over to testify one day. It was about the money situation in the Congress, and the Congress was asking about how things were going. He said, "Well, we're doing real well in the get-well and everything."

 "Well, how's the advanced system?"

 "Well, it's not doing too well."

---

* USS *Norton Sound* (AV-11) was originally a *Currituck*-class seaplane tender, commissioned 8 January 1945. In 1948 at the Philadelphia Naval Shipyard, she was converted to a mobile missile-launching platform in order to test new guided missiles. She was reclassified AVM-1 on 8 August 1951. On 10 August 1962 she was decommissioned and in November towed to the Maryland Shipbuilding and Drydock Company in Baltimore for modernization. The Typhon weapon control system was installed, including the SPG-59 radar. She was recommissioned 20 June 1964.

And they said, "Well, Admiral, what should we do about it?"

"Well," he said, "I recommend you terminate it, and that you continue the work in the test ship, *Norton Sound*, and take the money saved and reassign that money to me for the get-well program." It so happened it was $76 million, as I remember, which was a big number. And that's how he financed this massive effort of rehabilitating the fleet, including sparing it, training it, and all those things. So he was very clever at that kind of thing. He did an enormous service on it.

But we're going to go off and ponder Typhon. Did we really need it? Well, isn't the world safe? What are we going to waste all that money for? We had this struggle going on on the transistor and whether the transistor was useful or not useful. Had a lot of trouble deciding that. So in fact the introduction of the transistor occurred with me in the modernization effort of the frigates, the DLGs.

Paul Stillwell: You talked about that.

Admiral Meyer: And I talked about that.

Paul Stillwell: Well, so the money for that reprogrammed from Typhon?

Admiral Meyer: I don't know whether you would say it was reprogrammed, but it was sent in lieu of there. Typhon now was a dead duck to be restudied, and the *Norton Sound* was to go out and complete some testing and evaluation—which, by the way, never happened. It all just kind of wilted down. Someplace in there, and here I may have the batting order screwed up, *Norton Sound* wandered off into the South Atlantic and I think she fired two nuclear missiles.* So she was a lady that did a hell of a lot of hidden work for the Navy—necessary, and necessary today, and does not exist today.

The only thing I could inherit when I took over Aegis was *Norton Sound*. I rehabilitated her, because if you look at my life in Aegis what you will find is it's one

---

* In 1958, in Operation Argus, the *Norton Sound* went to the South Atlantic, south of the Falkland Islands, and fired three rockets with low-yield atomic warheads. They detonated at various altitudes. For further details, see the Naval Institute oral histories of Vice Admiral Lloyd M. Mustin, USN (Ret.), and Captain Louis Colbus, USN (Ret.).

rehabilitation after another, including the big engineering site up at Moorestown. I don't think you're planning on coming up next Friday, or maybe you are, to Moorestown, to the renaming of the engineering site up there, the Vice Admiral James H. Doyle Engineering Site, which, I don't know how long it will be there but maybe another 50 years; you don't know. But that's one example of—I took throwaways and transformed them into something.

Paul Stillwell: Admiral Rowden gave Admiral Doyle a lot of credit for the success of Aegis.

Admiral Meyer: No doubt in my mind. I do it repeatedly. I used to say it continually in my speeches. I don't think I would have ever made it without Doyle.[*] I really was worn out at beating down people and beating down the system. Far as I could tell, the Navy had no plan for me. The DoD didn't know what to do. And we rambled along and rambled along, and I just decided, well, that was as good a thing as any for me to keep working on. And when I got called that morning—and I'm skipping ahead—in December of 1970 I was very hesitant. Admiral Woods ran NavOrd then. By that time the SMS task force had faded away, morphed back into the system, because, you know, everything's fixed now and we don't need any special organization anymore, and it can take care of itself. Of course it could. It can't to this day.

I digress. You may be aware of this. About a month ago the Board of Inspection and Survey inspected the Aegis cruiser *Chosin*.

Paul Stillwell: No, I hadn't heard.

Admiral Meyer: Well, and the Aegis destroyer *Stout*—declared both of them unsat.[†] And, as happens in ships, it ain't only one place in a ship that gets unsat. It gets unsat all over. When you inspect a ship, you see how integral it really is, because even the galley is affected by how well the weapons system is run. So this has created, you would hope,

---

[*] Vice Admiral James H. Doyle, Jr., USN, served as Deputy Chief of Naval Operations (Surface Warfare) from August 1975 to September 1980.
[†] "U.S. Navy Finds Glaring Flaws in 2 Surface Ships," *Defense News*, 20 April 2008.

a big firestorm, but it's not. It's going on inside the Navy, and we'll get this fixed. Well they ain't gonna get it fixed! Since there's no organization to fix it.

The CNO has turned it over to Admiral Curtis.[*] I don't know him. He was up there Saturday to the christening, but I didn't get a chance to speak to him. He's the new surface ship fleet commander, which has both oceans. I don't know him, and I don't know what his credentials are. I have no reason to believe he doesn't have decent credentials. But in any event he's got the assignment to square these ships away.

Well, how come the guy he relieved didn't have them squared away? How come the commodores didn't have them squared away? If you read the reports, it just hurts you so badly. The first thing you say is, "Where's the XO? Where's the CO? Where's the commodore? Where in the hell is the admiral?" Ships can't get that way except through gross inattention. And what was sad about it is the ships are still sailing.

You learned in your life naval engineering is a remarkable cult. It is one that receives little credit, and it receives almost *no* credit from the people that it makes possible to sail, namely the rest of the Navy. They don't think very much of naval engineering, only occasionally when something breaks in their ship and somebody magically overnight fixes it. Otherwise they're all bums. Those people over there, they just—you remember Admiral Clark's famed public statements: "I send 40 million a year over there and we don't know where it goes; nobody knows where the money goes."[†] Well, people know where the money goes very easily. As a matter of fact, you can get a thousand people to tell you where the money goes if you want to find out. But I don't know what made him that way. He was totally destructive on the materiel establishment. And he's the one who permitted it, of course, to be dissipated the way it is now.

So today we don't have a materiel establishment. We have outlying camps. We have one in Tennessee, we have a group up in Pennsylvania, we have a big group down in southern Maryland; we have the residues over in the Gun Factory.[‡] We don't have a materiel establishment; one doesn't exist. You know something? It shows it too. If you

---

[*] Vice Admiral D. C. Curtis, USN, Commander Naval Surface Forces/Commander Naval Surface Force Pacific Fleet, 2008-11.
[†] Admiral Vernon E. Clark, USN, served as Chief of Naval Operations from 21 July 2000 to 22 July 2005.
[‡] The Naval Sea Systems Command is now in the Washington Navy Yard, which is on M Street in southeast Washington, D.C. For many years the Navy yard was an industrial facility known as the Naval Gun Factory, and some people still refer to it by that name.

were to sit down on the sixth deck here with me for the last three years you'd see that. You'd see how disconnected the parts are. We've been saying it in our group down there for some time now, two years, they're running on borrowed time. Wham, a month ago she broke open. How do you think that felt to this old sailor?

Paul Stillwell: Terrible.

Admiral Meyer: Terrible! Awful!

Paul Stillwell: So you see a direct cause and effect between this disintegration of the structure and what happened in these ships?

Admiral Meyer: Yes. No doubt in my mind. But I'm not sure that the younger leaders do that. A great advantage of young leadership is that they are not troubled with looking back. And a terrible disadvantage of younger leadership is they're not troubled with looking back. It is an enigma that's gone on since civilization began. Well, I come down because my mentors who raised me, and in my later life it was Spreen and Reich: "Don't ever ignore the old people; pay attention to the old people, because they have been there. Pay attention." I tried to raise all my officers that way, and I tried to raise the civil servants that way. I had modest success. But I see over time the ones where I had success are the ones who are turning out to be pretty darned good leaders. They pay a lot of attention to the older people.

That doesn't occur—like this study I'm on, I may have whined to you before. It's hard for me to see whether anybody cares whether I do this work or not. Now, you can go call them in one at a time and ask them about the significance of what Meyer is doing: "Oh, it's very important. Yes, it's very important. Oh, yes, we value it highly." And we move on. I don't know—well, I do know where that'll actually all end up in the end. We'll end up running out of planning, that's what we'll do. This is the reason today that we can't get a shipbuilding program. We're just running around in circles trying to find one. Do you think we've found one in Destroyer 1000?*

Paul Stillwell: Well, it's been stumbling along for quite a while.

Admiral Meyer: An awful long time. Now, it will be a complete reversal of congressional behavior in my past 50 years if they allow more ships than two to be built until those two have been thoroughly evaluated. That certainly couldn't happen in the old days. Maybe it can happen today, I don't know, but I doubt it.

Paul Stillwell: Well, the littoral combat ship's had a lot of problems as well.†

Admiral Meyer: I could have written the script, but no one wants it, so if no one wants it there isn't much you can do about it. You can get out here and start carrying a banner on a street corner, but that does no good. So that's where I stand on that stuff. There's not many people want to hear it.

You can't help but think that every time you go to a christening if you're in my category. I've not been to every single christening; I've missed about four. But I have been to every single commissioning. Eighty-six ships so far, but every single one. And I plan, with God's help, to make all the rest.‡ And I see the superficiality, and at times I want to blame the materiel establishment because of our inability to articulate their purpose and their value. Our organizational structure anymore does not raise officers with the requisite insight and respect of what's needed. I've said many times the materiel

---

* Guided missile destroyers of the *Zumwalt* (DDG-1000) class are being built to a radical new design that is intended to produce a stealthy, low-profile radar signature. Construction of the *Zumwalt* began in October 2008 at Bath Iron Works, Bath, Maine; the ship is scheduled for delivery to the Navy in 2013. Construction of the *Michael Monsoor* (DDG-1001) began at the Northrop Grumman shipyard (now Hunting Ingalls Industries) in Pascagoula, Mississippi, in September 2009; delivery to the Navy is scheduled for 2014.
† The monohull littoral combat ship is the *Freedom* (LCS-1), built at Marinette, Marine, Marinette, Wisconsin. The keel for LCS-1 was laid 2 June 2005, the hull launched 23 September 2006, and the ship commissioned 8 November 2008. The other version is the trimaran *Independence* (LCS-2). The Navy contract went to General Dynamics in 2003. GD subcontracted the building to the Austal USA shipyard in Mobile, Alabama, an overseas branch of the Australian shipbuilder Austal. The keel for LCS-2 was laid 19 January 2006, the hull launched 30 April 2008, and the ship commissioned 16 January 2010.
‡ The guided missile destroyer *Wayne E. Meyer* (DDG-108) was launched 19 October 2008 at Bath Iron Works. Meyer's wife Anna Mae, as sponsor, christened the ship. The destroyer was delivered to the Navy on 10 July 2009 and commissioned at Philadelphia on 10 October 2009. Admiral Meyer died 1 September 2009, the month before the commissioning.

establishment does not need the operating fleet, but the operating fleet can't work without the materiel establishment. It won't function. It'll be broke in three months without the materiel establishment.

Paul Stillwell: But there wouldn't be a purpose for the materiel establishment if there weren't a fleet.

Admiral Meyer: You got it. But they're the ones that end up making the fleet. So what goes into the design, what goes into the construction, that determines what's a good product. It's not unlike your automobile. Your automobile is what went into it, not what you make it. Now, you can care for it and treat it respectfully, and it will serve you quite well, but you can't make it something it ain't.

Paul Stillwell: Do you think Typhon's demise was the right thing at that point?

Admiral Meyer: I don't know that I thought that in real time. There's no doubt in my mind that it was the right thing. And what I have learned—and again, I'm giving you another dissertation here—is that the outside world, and I think maybe properly so, is really disrespectful of what we call engineering. First of all, the things of value, or what are produced or manufactured or made available, like these things here on the table, we call that production. On the other end, there is discovery. You can't build something that hasn't been discovered. Well, what's between those two things, those two disciplines, that's what I call engineering. Now, that's why you can't put a laboratory in charge of system engineering or those kinds of things, because a laboratory's in essence a research place. Engineering's not a research outfit; it's an application.

At times in my heyday in Aegis, I got upset because the people that I had some admiration and respect for, specifically people like Dr. Frosch, people of that nature, criticized me a great deal about the radar design. Of course, they had no design; they'd never done it in their life. "What we're doing is obsolete. Too old. Superseded." In due course I learned that they don't know what the hell they're talking about. You can't build something that you don't know how to design.

Now, you and I, we could go back to your brother's house in Missouri, and we could tinker and tinker around and put up a new porch, or do new plumbing, more from observation of others than anything else, and we'd fix it one way or another. Our ability to construct a house from start, at least in my case, would be zero, because we don't have any experience. Engineering is a product of experience, and so you learn from it what you can do and you can't do. Well, if you're a researcher, you come out of a laboratory or university: Old fashioned, you're lagging the times, you're way behind. So they'd come up and look at my signal processor. "God, this is old stuff."

I had a signal processor that had to do phenomenal things performance-wise as contrasted to its predecessors. The signal processor for Typhon would not fit in my office spaces. The first signal processor for Aegis was 22 cabinets long. So they would take at least this set of rooms here to fit them, plus water, air, electric. After *Norton Sound* and all our experience, we literally cut that in half. We went to 11 cabinets. Today, 30-some years later, they're building Aegis to be landed in *Meyer* 108, and the superintendent toured Anna Mae and I around Saturday morning.* They're in the process of landing a lot of equipment down the next few months in the ship. But that gear going in there, the signal processor will only be four cabinets. That's what engineering is. That's not research, it's not discovery, it's plod. So I describe it as plod, plod, plod. And you learn by doing.

So repetition has a great deal of importance in that craft because, again, I'm sure you've admired craftsmen all your life. Particularly carpenters always astound me what they can to and know how to do, and I'm so goddamn clumsy I could never do it. Well, you master engineering the same way. And leadership in engineering is the ability to look at the landscape of research and see what's there, and look at what the need is.

How crazy we are in the Navy and in the services, and even in life. We go ask some other group of people, like say in this case OpNav or somebody in the operating force: "Well, what's your need? And, well, we'll go out and do the engineering now." Why would they know? What's the average experience of a person in, say, the Navy operating forces? They may be three years at a time, six years at a time at the most. They know only in general terms, or in specific terms.

---

* This was at Bath Iron Works in Bath, Maine, where the destroyer *Wayne E. Meyer* was then being built.

Example of specific: You can mount the coffeepot in a wardroom in such a way that it virtually consumes the life of the ship's operation because it's so poorly done. You can do that in how you install a console. Or you can do it the other way. Well, you learn how to install a console by some experience and by some examination and some inspection. It takes all those things. You can't throw out a specification and have somebody in Mishawaka or Kansas City know what is needed. I mean, you have trouble knowing it your own self. And then let a contract to say, in the case here, to get specific, to RCA: "By the way, you're going to be accountable for this; you're responsible for this."[*] How in the hell can they be accountable? RCA is not fighting the war, for God's sake. It's the job of the U.S. Navy to fight the war. So the idea that I'll send you a piece of paper and you call me when you've got it complete two years from now is stupid. That's one of the reasons that you get poor products.

Paul Stillwell: But it still seems to me that it's OpNav that establishes the missions, or recognizes them. It's not the materiel establishment that establishes missions for OpNav.

Admiral Meyer: You're absolutely right. Doyle will tell you that is a constant, iterative thing.

Paul Stillwell: Well, it needs to be a partnership.

Admiral Meyer: Doyle will tell you right off, there isn't anybody over there that can describe what the next destroyer ought to look like. They ain't smart enough. It's trial and error. You try to fix flaws. You can issue a decree if you want, like there'll only be 34 men. Well, that's bull. Now, that's a useful objective, but to think that people are so damned smart that you can tell how to fight the ship with 34 people don't know what the hell they're talking about.

So engineering is a constant discovery of itself, and it requires an intimacy, in my view, between the Navy in our case and industry to get a product that is going to have the requisite utilitarian value under a whole broad spectrum of things.

---

[*] RCA was one of the main contractors in the Aegis program.

Well, we have 80-some Aegis ships at sea today. Can you tell me, come even close to telling me what those—it's now noon on Monday—what are those ships doing?

Paul Stillwell: Some are deployed, some are pier side in homeport, some are in shipyards.

Admiral Meyer: And that's a very general statement.

Paul Stillwell: Of course.

Admiral Meyer: They are doing all kinds of different things constantly, including out searching for this couple that disappeared at sea. Including providing the storm assistance. Including, oh, by the way, we have a couple campaigns here, we're fighting a couple skirmishes. Lebanon is threatening another civil war this morning. Well, that goes on and on and on and on. You're not wise enough to predict all those things with mathematical precision. So the designs have to be designs that are adaptive, and they have to be designs that regular people can adapt. You can't or won't have all engineers in the ship.

Now, the MDA has got this gigantic radar, which in my own judgment is useless, on this oil rig, X-band, Raytheon-built, that's something like 500,000 pounds, and it's got it out here as part of the force missile defense for the nation, sailing around.* It's been trying to base it in Adak.† I don't know how much money they've spent to make it safe to base this thing in Adak. It gets under way and it makes a few knots to wherever it's got to go.

It's crewed, of course, by Raytheon engineers by contract. And—well, wait a minute. They operate the radar, don't they? And it's crewed by another group who sails the thing. So you've got this mixed group, carefully separate, and they don't do anything else. They don't do maintenance. They don't even clean up after themselves. They go into port, and somebody else comes in and does all the goddamned work. There's a big

---

* MDA – Missile Defense Agency.
† Adak, Alaska, is in the Aleutians.

difference in a warship design and in those kinds of things, and boy, that really hits home to me.

I get almost exactly the opposite opinion in cruise ships than other people get. Now, I've sailed in about, I think, 12—maybe more than that, but they've all been Holland America, and I'm scared to try any other line because it's so good. But I sail in it, and I said life is really simple when you don't have to put any weapons in the ship. [Chuckle] It's a hell of a lot easier, real simple. But yet they can have the same problems you have every day. Operation of the fire main, fresh water. They don't make their own water. They're never out of port more than three days. First thing they do is pump water aboard when they go in.

They do the maintenance at sea. It almost shocks you to see the little Filipinos or a Pakistani out with a gallon can doing touchup, mostly painting over rust someplace, around the ship. You might see two or three of them on this 65,000-ton ship. And you say, wait a minute. Well, you've got some, even officers, that sail the ship like to say: "Well, look, they don't need people; look how easy this is." Right [chuckle] They don't do a goddamn bit of the maintenance work. It's trivial what's done in the ship. The basic maintenance of the ship—one captain gave me a pretty extended tour—their basic maintenance is two of everything, at least two. They have two of everything. If one goes down, they've got another one. Because they're going to be in port in three days. They don't have to worry about the goddamn stuff working. Well, that's a big difference in designing and building a warship and living in it.

Paul Stillwell: Well, back to NavOrd. You had this period with Terrier under several different overhead structures. How would you measure the progress during that four-year period that you were in Washington? What all was accomplished?

Admiral Meyer: What all I accomplished?

Paul Stillwell: Well, specifically you, yes, and generally the organization in Terrier.

Admiral Meyer: I thought the task force was extraordinary as an outfit for its time. As you know, those kinds of things strike at the right time. And here the Navy's image had undergone attack and assault, and Reich came in with a sledge and started breaking it up and straightening it out, and it didn't bother Reich to piss off everybody in the world. That bothers me, because I'm a long-term person, and what I like to think I mastered in leadership is a different thing. I know how to do that leadership, but I don't practice that kind of leadership.

You know, I was fired by John Lehman the first time in August of 1983.[*] It will soon be 25 years since he fired me. This longest-running shipbuilding program in history, right now, 25 years since I'd been fired. I swear to God you can walk in that shipyard up there, you can walk in the supervisors' spaces, you can look around, you can walk in those ships, you can look at the processes, and every goddamn one of them has managed to sustain themselves. Now, that's what I believe to be a contribution, is what's left behind.

We carried up on the airplane Friday afternoon one of those pictures which, if you're a good boy I'm going to give you one sooner or later, for Captain John Ingram, retired.[†] He had about three tours in Aegis. He was the supervisor of shipbuilding at Bath amongst other things. In my view John Ingram was what I'd call "admiral quality." That is to say, his leadership and—he was an engineering duty officer—his technical prowess were superb. The Navy never saw fit to select him for flag, and the answer can be begged why? Well, they can't select all of them, first of all. Second of all most people, including myself, were realistic. I never expected to be selected for flag. I never made it an objective to be flag.

Paul Stillwell: That's interesting.

Admiral Meyer: Yeah, I never did. That was not my objective. My objective was to do something.

---

[*] John F. Lehman Jr., served as Secretary of the Navy from 5 February 1981 to 10 April 1987.
[†] Among other duties during his career, Captain John Ingram, USN, an engineering duty officer, was supervisor of shipbuilding at Bath, Maine, during the construction of Aegis ships.

Well, John Ingram is my kind of officer. He wasn't even in the Navy when I entered Aegis 30 years ago. Wasn't even in the Navy yet. This is a crackerjack officer, a dedicated officer. You would swear to God that I taught him everything he knows. Well, I did, except it's fourth- and fifth-hand and such, or where he's read it someplace. That's the way he behaves. That's leaving something there, something in place.

If you go look at the 1000 program right now, what you find is even in Raytheon and their godawful behavior with Lockheed and stuff, they're all trying to slip in the back door and get some time up in the CSEDS at Moorestown, because that's where the facilities are and the structure is to do some things they know need to be done.* It's amazing. Those people aren't all stupid down at that level because of the pigheaded goddamn leadership that they have. Well, you're aware that I never tolerated pigheadedness in leadership except by myself. As I always told them, there's only room for one pighead, and that's me. And if they couldn't handle that, they needed to go someplace else. Well, so they all worked and they worried about getting the football over the line. That's what they spent their time on. That's why I don't think that the *Zumwalt* will make it.

Paul Stillwell: That's the "1000" we're referring to.

Admiral Meyer: Right. It will make it. You know why? Because we'll declare it. We'll declare it whether it's worth a damn or not. There isn't any way you can determine it, whether it made it. As long as it doesn't violate Archimedes. There's no way you can tell. It can tell on you.

Paul Stillwell: You're pointing to your gut.

Admiral Meyer: So we think that shipbuilding's in trouble in our Navy, and it is. We're in trouble. But we don't understand what's in trouble. The trouble is officers. The trouble is John Ingrams. Thanks to leadership we've run them away.

---

* CSEDS – Combat System Engineering Development Site, Moorestown, New Jersey, an integral part of the Aegis program.

Up until this present PEO of ships, whatever a PEO is—the PEO is an administrative post.* I'm the sole engineer ever in charge of Aegis. Sole one. Part of it was pigheadedness. Part of it was the determination on the part of the leaders that, well, we'd better put a pighead in it. And the other part is, nobody wanted to touch it because they thought it was a loser. Well, it was never a loser. Now, the 1000 is a loser. And the reason is it's defying too many laws. It's just defying too many laws, and there simply ain't no short cuts. If there's enough money and enough time they'll get by, or they'll leave off a gun, or the launchers can only do certain things. The average person walking by won't know the difference. They won't know the ship can't fight. The fighters will know it can't fight.

Well, does this mean, though, given the two I've described to you, that the whole Aegis fleet is in danger today in its ability to fight? I think it is. So in one sense my 25 years past were all for naught. Yet in another sense it was not all for naught because there are—they're not idolaters; they are respecters and admirers, thousands of them, who remain, and all they really seek is leadership and direction. I mean, Saturday was hard on me because I could hardly walk through the shipyard.

Paul Stillwell: You mean because of your physical condition?

Admiral Meyer: No. Because of the people.

Paul Stillwell: I see.

Admiral Meyer: I mean, I was fired 25 years ago. These people all come around to intercept me, to talk to me. Now, of course, they know it more because that picture right there is staring you right in the eyes as you walk into the little shipyard.

Paul Stillwell: The *Wayne E. Meyer* ship.

---

* PEO – program executive office.

Admiral Meyer: The *Wayne E. Meyer*. But there's another thing. They will stop me, and what they will say to me is, "My dad said to tell you hello." Saturday two guys came up to me and said, "My grandfather wanted to be sure that we told you hello." Well, that's leaving something. Now that stuff is being transferred down to there. Of course, that will run out and play out over time. It'll peter out. But in my mind that's what being effective is for the human race. Now I spent a little time—actually, Anna Mae talked to John Ingram for a while because she brought this signed picture up to him, and he was there. He's there running a little company there in Brunswick, which is on contract with the shipyard to help it in its processes in production and such. John Ingram and his wife are from that area, and they wanted to retire there.

So Ingram is my kind of person. Ingram will leave behind a lot of know-how in young men and women, in the yard, and in the supervisor and the different ones that pass through, of how to do the proper and correct thing. It is what we at one time would refer to as a father-son type profession, because there are not very many books to go read on how to build ships. It just gets passed down and passed down and passed down.

Paul Stillwell: Well, that yard at Bath is famous for the multi-generation employment.

Admiral Meyer: Oh, yeah. Oh, yeah. And they're very proud of it.

Paul Stillwell: Well again, let me ask on this period of '63 to '67, how would you describe your personal accomplishments and contributions?

Admiral Meyer: Step back a notch. I believe that one major accomplishment of mine is that I made Talos work. In my view, in hindsight thinking a long time, it was doomed not to work. Complex, hard, difficult. Now, Talos, as you know, was in combat in Vietnam.[*] Would it have performed without me? One never knows. But the Talos

---

[*] During the Vietnam War the missile was deployed on board the cruisers *Chicago* (CG-11), *Oklahoma City* (CLG-5), and *Long Beach* (CGN-9). It was used to attack North Vietnamese missile sites. In addition, the On 23 May 1968 the *Long Beach* fired two Talos missiles at a MiG fighter at 65 miles. The first knocked the plane down, and the second hit the falling wreckage. In September 1968 a Talos from the *Long Beach* shot down a MiG that was 61 miles away. On 9 May 1972, a Talos from the *Chicago* shot down a MiG during the U.S. mining of Haiphong Harbor, North Vietnam.

performed superbly in the times it was called. That's number-one accomplishment.

Number two accomplishment—it may have flowed from the first; I connect all these things so I get very jabbery about it—is the modernization of the Terrier fleet. Or, as Spreen had ordered me to do, figure out how to get the transistor into those ships. That was significant. It revolutionized what we did in the 3-T ships, and it started moving us out of the conversion—well, conversion is wrong, but the ordalting of what was, and dragging it up to the next era.* So much credit needs to go to Spreen, for which he'd get none. Because, I believe I told you this, when he called in E. J. Otth and myself that morning: "You officers are going to do this; I, Spreen, will raise the money." Spreen raised the money. He never got any thanks for that. Nobody ever recognizes it or understands it. But my genius would have never occurred without that.

Paul Stillwell: How much support and liaison did you have with the Navy electronics organization in developing this package to put in these ships?

Admiral Meyer: Well, I could say damned near zero, and sometimes it seemed that way. But in truth I just took over MacArthur Field on Long Island under Sperry. I made the Philadelphia shipyard move people up there, which they were dead set against, totally opposed. "If you're going to make me move, I quit."

My answer was, "Well, you'll be missed, but quit." They changed their mind.

I'm a strong believer in teambuilding, I'm a strong believer in unification, but only the leader can create that environment. The leader has to do that. And so that program, which was at best to be nine DLG-16s, turned out to be all 30 ships long after I left. That block of ships saved your Navy under protection of the aircraft carriers until Aegis came way late. It's not well understood nor is it written about, of how scared Gorshkov was of Aegis, but I think down here his view was it wouldn't materialize.† And so he prepared his counter forces to take on the AAW modernization, namely in those Terrier ships, which had the basic rangers and the missiles which had been

---

* 3-T – Tartar, Terrier, and Talos. Ordalt – ordnance alteration.
† Admiral of the Fleet of the Soviet Union S. G. Gorshkov served as Commander in Chief of the Soviet Navy from January 1956 to December 1985. He expressed his views in a series of articles on Navies in War and in Peace. They appeared in the book *Red Star Rising at Sea*, published in 1974 by the Naval Institute Press.

transistorized had been introduced into those ships, and they were killers indeed. Matter of fact, I don't know whether you knew Admiral Dick West. You may have met him.

Paul Stillwell: No.

Admiral Meyer: Well, he commanded one of the Terrier ships, and he was sincere in this.* I had trouble getting him stopped because he went around crusading that that converted ship was so good we didn't need Aegis ships. And he crusaded on that, that that ship that he had commanded could kill anything that they put up. Well, and they can, for a time, but the time comes when they can't too. So that was my second thing I left.

Those two things really were my education in how to do Aegis.

Paul Stillwell: How was the contracting set up between the Navy and Sperry to get this new equipment manufactured for the AAW modernization?

Admiral Meyer: Good question. I ended up in an argument with the Admiral Reich. I had said to Spreen, "Look, I'm throwing down the gauntlet. If we can't have freedom of adjusting the money, then I want out. I don't want to be part of it. If you want a fixed-price contract, give *me* a fixed-price contract. I'll do a fixed-price contract, but I ain't going to have anybody working for me on fixed-price contracts." I won it.

When I got to Aegis, they had all these schemes for competition, fixed pricing. I wouldn't have any of it. Well, one problem was, people were scared of me, so that helped. The second was, everybody knew this wasn't going to work and it would be a failure, so why worry about it? My view is, and it is to this day: Form a team, write a structure that you think you can make get your work done, and do it. Ask any officer that worked for me, and any vice president that worked for me—if you got out of your assigned budget your life was miserable. So miserable that generally you were gone.

For a few years we met out at White Oak every June—be just about this time of year—and I'd gather the captains and all the vice presidents and we'd spend three to four

---

* As a captain, Richard D. West, commanded the guided missile cruiser *Leahy* (CG-16) from 1 November 1989 to 23 November 1991.

days out there.* And what we were going to do was apportion the budget for the coming year, which would be this autumn. I treated them all the same. The senior people were the panel. We knew what the amount of money was that we thought we were going to get. And you'd come in. Suppose that you're the vice president and program manager down at Ingalls for the ship.† You'd present your case of what you think your budget ought to be and what it was you thought you had to do. The captains would all present their case.

Because people forget that, if you're going to do a whole ship design and act like a full-spectrum outfit, what that means is it embraces every single appropriation account, every one. I was the only project in the United States Navy, and I think in all the DoD, that embraced every single appropriation account, including personnel accounts, military personnel accounts. So you had all these accounts.

But in my scheme the money had to flow in, it came through, I had to put up the venturi tube of it coming through NavSea 01.‡ Okay. We must befriend NavSea 01. So I mount out a strike, and I make sure that I have got those people working for me. God, it would piss that process off, because every year—I mean, I was the only major project manager for a number of years in NavSea. I was the only flag officer who was a manager.

I may have told you this. We'd have Tuesday morning staff meetings, and I'd go up to the staff meetings because I was an admiral. And I'd sit up there for two hours every Tuesday morning, and I'd listen to this bitching up there at the staff meeting with the chief, the last one of which was Fowler and there were several before him.§ Gooding was there for a long time.** I thought I was doing pretty good in my outfit and things were working pretty good. I'd go up there. *Every* Tuesday it would degrade to Rickover, because there'd be Newport News or New London, either one of which I gave a rat's

---

* Naval Ordnance Laboratory, White Oak, Maryland, in 1974 merged with the Naval Weapons Laboratory to form the Naval Surface Weapons Center.
† Ingalls Shipbuilding, Pascagoula, Mississippi.
‡ NavSea – Naval Sea Systems Command.
§ Vice Admiral Earl B. Fowler, Jr., USN, was Commander Naval Sea Systems Command, 1980 to 1985.
** Rear Admiral Robert C. Gooding, USN, served as Commander Naval Ship Systems Command from 1972 to 1974. As a vice admiral, he served as Commander Naval Sea Systems Command from 1974 to 1976.

toenail about.* But the argument would be over the budgets in the yards and how Rickover was determining it, and Rickover wouldn't take their orders. Dumb me, the first few months I thought, well, I could contribute to this because I had a pretty good plan with my shipbuilder, and it was all working quite well. I found out, of course, all I had to do was just move my lips and they'd all turn and pounce on me. "Yeah, but you don't have to put up with Rickover!" [Chuckle]

Paul Stillwell: Well, I was asking about the contracts for the upgrade. What kind of contracts did you actually execute in that case?

Admiral Meyer: After significant argument, only because Spreen enjoyed it so much—Spreen enjoyed being able to pick an argument with the admiral. He loved it.

Paul Stillwell: And you were giving him ammunition. [Chuckle]

Admiral Meyer: I gave him a cause. And I said, "Well, if we're going to fixed-price Sperry, I want to fixed-price Philadelphia Naval Shipyard too, so your argument to the admiral should be, if we're going to do this work, which we're pioneering, why should the shipyard be excepted in fixed-pricing the contracts?" You can imagine how that went over. I won it all. My view was to treat them all the same.

Paul Stillwell: So did you get a cost-plus?

Admiral Meyer: You got it. I got a cost-plus; that's what I got. And that prevailed even after I left, even in the final parts of the program with Bath, which I believe—I can't remember whether they got award-fee or cost-plus-award-fee or something like that, but prevailed. And people were just amazed that you could operate in a budget. I beat this tom-tom I started out with you on White Oak because, in my scheme only one person had

---

* Hyman G. Rickover was considered the father of the nuclear Navy. He ran the U.S. Navy's nuclear-power program for many years, from 1948 until he eventually left active duty in 1982 with the rank of four-star admiral on the retired list. Rickover Hall at the Naval Academy is named in his honor, as is the nuclear-powered attack submarine *Hyman G. Rickover* (SSN-709), which was commissioned 21 July 1984.

a fixed-price contract; it's me. My fixed-price contract's with Congress. I'm going to tell the Congress what I can do within this amount of money. I ain't going to promise them something on this hand and promise them something else on this hand. That's the way we worked. It lasted for a long time.

John Lehman had trouble with that. Ev Pyatt had trouble with that because they wanted to get their fingers in it.* Well, they finally did when they got rid of me and started bollixing it up. But that process worked just fine.

Paul Stillwell: Well, when you've got a cost-plus, how do you keep it from getting out of hand?

Admiral Meyer: Well, how do you tend to your children? God damn it, somebody's got to pay attention. That's how you keep them from getting out of hand. Don't give me the bullshit that people don't know what things are going to cost. They know exactly what they're going to cost, within reason. Their estimates are pretty darned good. I don't expect them to know any more than I know, but I tell them and I tell those VPs and I tell those captains, and we have these arguments in June: "These are the budgets that I'm giving you, and you're going to operate in the budgets; now you figure out how you're going to get that done." Well, I kept a nominal reserve. In those years I kept about 5% reserve. And I said we're putting this reserve here in this pot for when really bad things do happen and we can bail you out. That's the way I worked.

Never had a *single*, not once in 13 goddamn years did I have a fight with a contractor or did I have a fight *with* a contract or did I have an argument with the Congress. As a matter of fact, the last half of my reign I didn't even have to go to Congress. Rickover went over because it was a bully pulpit for him, but I didn't have to go.

Paul Stillwell: Because you'd established a track record.

---

* Everett A. Pyatt served as Principal Deputy Assistant Secretary of the Navy (Shipbuilding and Logistics), 1981-84, and Assistant Secretary of the Navy (Shipbuilding and Logistics), 1984-89.

Admiral Meyer: Yeah, that's exactly right. And I've tried and tried, and I was effective at preaching to my own officers, "Your word has to mean something. If you tell them over there you're going to do something, you've got to do that. And don't tell them you're going to do something you can't do." I made my contractors that way. Well, what does that mean? That means they trust you. If they don't trust you, how are you ever going to make it work?

We spent a whole era, and John Lehman reinforced it, and we may get back to it again, a whole era creating distrust. You can't do anything with a distrustful outfit. You can't have partnerships that way, for God's sakes. You can't do it. It's too complex. You can't be everyplace every hour of the night and day, and neither can your vice presidents. They're human just like you are. And guess what? They fall into troubles. Every Tuesday morning I'd line them all up and say, "Don't ever forget, we don't build anything. We have to create the environment for our contractors to build it. They're the ones that build it, and our products are determined by them, not by us."

I took me a couple years to convince people of that. I threw people off the program. I just threw them out of the project because they couldn't deal with it. I told them to go someplace else. If they're not prepared to treat the contractor with respect they don't belong there. And some would say, "Well, they don't respect me."

I said, "That's *your* problem, not theirs. You ought to go have a little talk with yourself. If I need to help you, let me know." And it turned out that, of course, the contractors came to trust you. And they're the ones that know when they've got a problem. And if they're scared to tell you, for God's sake, what are you going to do?

I thought, and I think, if you've got a problem you just make sure we all know we've got a problem, because I told them, "I can solve anything, except I'm not going to solve my contract with the Congress. *That* I ain't going to do. I'll cut the project back." And I did.

I mean, here you've got an order to go build a SPY-1 radar.[*] Well, what the hell does that mean? There are 20 million parts in that radar. There are several million parts in that missile. You can't define that with great precision. But what you do, and you

---

[*] The SPY-1 is an integral part of the Aegis system; it is a phased-array radar to detect and track air contacts.

have to manage every week, keep managing the cost and managing the cost, as one element that you manage in the undertaking. And you've got to have your partner with you. I mean, if those people start covering up things because they're scared of you, you've got a big, big problem, because by the time you know it, invariably it's really, really hard to solve it.

Paul Stillwell: And costs more.

Admiral Meyer: Always. If you know it up front—and I did a lot of teaching of project managers through the era and everything, and always tried to get that point across to them: "Wait a minute; there isn't any problem that you've got that can't be solved if you know it, but you can't solve problems you don't know. And the only way you know whether you've got a problem is whether somebody else tells you you've got one. But you can't be everyplace."

You know, this big undertaking like Aegis is all over the United States. It's everyplace. And to this day—and I believe this; I guess it's a point of honor with me, or how I was raised, but I visited plants in the United States that have had Navy contracts for a long time that ain't *never* been visited, before or since.

Paul Stillwell: So I'm guessing you were at Sperry quite a bit during this upgrade of the frigates.

Admiral Meyer: Yes. And I've got to tell you, that has big effects on people. The missile was about to get a bad name before I came on the scene, and the admiral was still pissed off at General Dynamics. So when I became the manager I was worried about the missile and the ability to control it, so I spent two years just redoing the whole structure, really, of one of confidence and trust, making people cut it down to size. And it's not so much that there's a lot of waste. That's a popular myth. Well, do you have any waste at home in your own business?

Paul Stillwell: Of course.

Admiral Meyer: Right, exactly. I mean, that goes on all the time in one form or another. You can wear yourself out every day worrying about picking up flakes of dust on the deck and not do anything.

Now, okay, I'm sorry that I've ground you down. I'm going to introduce you to Admiral Bill Wyatt on the way out, my associate.* And, as I said, another officer whom I respect.

Paul Stillwell: Okay. Well, we'll get to Port Hueneme next time. Thank you.

---

* Rear Admiral William C. Wyatt, USN (Ret.). As a captain he was program manager for the *Spruance* (DD-963)-class destroyer and the first ship program manager for the Aegis cruiser *Ticonderoga* (CG-47). At the time of this interview he was working with Admiral Meyer on a Surface Warfare Study Group chartered by the Chief of Naval Operations.

Interview Number 10 with Rear Admiral Wayne E. Meyer, U.S. Navy (Retired)
Place: Admiral Meyer's office in Arlington, Virginia
Date: Wednesday, 4 June 2008

Paul Stillwell: Admiral, it's great to see you again after some layoff here, and we're ready to resume your career as you moved from Washington and the surface missile program out to Port Hueneme.* How did that new assignment come about?

Admiral Meyer: Admiral Sarver had relieved Admiral Reich as the task force commander by the time that I was willing to be detached. They wanted me to go out in '66, and I refused to do so as long as that officer was out there. Well, how could I refuse? I just protested; that's how.

Paul Stillwell: Which officer?

Admiral Meyer: The guy I was going out to relieve, Paul Roth.† He's in the graveyard now, a so-called iconoclast and a home-wrecker and a station-wrecker—well, a wrecker of about anything you could pick. He was one of Admiral Reich's serious mistakes, in my judgment.

    Finally he was so bad that they got rid of him by about, I'll say November of 1966, and so I accepted orders and I reported in about, I believe February of 1967, to the station. So while Paul Roth was titularly the first chief engineer, he never was one. He just was a gadfly. And you don't know the physical layout out there, but it is still significant. They had taken up residence on the old Seabee base, and there's a big benjo ditch runs down through the middle.‡ The station was housed in buildings that were erected temporarily for the Seabees in World War II. If you're familiar with the Oxnard Plain—

---

* Navy Surface Missile Systems Engineering Station (NSMSES), Port Hueneme, California, which is 55 miles northwest of Los Angeles. Meyer served there from January 1967 to June 1970.
† Captain Paul Roth, USN, a surface warfare officer.
‡ Seabees is the nickname applied to members of the Navy's mobile construction battalions (CBs). A benjo ditch is used for drainage. In some Asian countries it is an open sewer.

Paul Stillwell: No, I'm not.

Admiral Meyer: Well, it is as level as this deck, it is incredible, for maybe, hell, I don't know, 40-50 miles or so. It may be the richest piece of farmland in the United States. The amount of produce grown there just blows the mind.

So what they have is they have built into the whole area big drainage ditches, because when a rain comes there ain't no place for it to go, so they drain it to the ocean. Right through the middle of the station ran one of these big drainage ditches. And when a guy with the Seabee base left the station, the leader of NSMSES abandoned the building that the commanding officer and XO were in, where he is supposed to be, and he went across the benjo ditch and set up his own independent country, and took about 40 souls with him.*

So Admiral Sarver called me in and sent me out there. He gave me three assignments. He said, "The first thing I want you to do is, I want you to rejoin the station and act like you're a member. Secondly, I want you to prosecute the war," because recall at that time, February of '67, the war was really, really heated up. "Thirdly, in prosecuting the war, I want to be sure that we're doing what we were created for there, and that is support the fleet, and support them full blast. Fourthly..."

I don't know whether I told you, Admiral Reich couldn't get the civil servants authorized to create the station, so he solved that. He called up his good friend Augie Augustat. Augie was the president of Western Electric at the time, and he was on the admiral's advisory board. He said, "Augie, I need your help," the story goes.

"What did you need, Admiral?"

"Well, I need some engineers and some logisticians to get the station started." "Yes, sir. We'd be glad to do that." Western Electric and Augie is located down in North Carolina. "How many do you think you need?" He said, "Well, 250 would be about the right starting."

Paul Stillwell: So was he looking at these as contract personnel?

---

* Port Hueneme is also home to the Naval Construction Battalion Center. Seabees is the nickname applied to members of the Navy's mobile construction battalions (CBs).

Admiral Meyer: Right. They were going to go into civil service billets. He was going to create civil service billets out of whole air and post them, and they'd have to move them with their salary. "Well, okay, how long do you want them?"

"I don't know how long I want them, and we have to work out what mix we want, but we need to get this station started and get it started now because there's a war on." So all of that had gone on the previous year by Eli, and he got this monument in motion.

It was pretty incredible. I knew a large number of them, simply from my having built the Terrier fleet and being associated in the task force. And a large number of them were what we used to call field service in the contractors, like Sperry and Northern Ordnance.

Paul Stillwell: What sort of background was he looking for in these personnel?

Admiral Meyer: He in essence wanted field service engineers. He wanted engineers and logisticians, but who had experience in the field.

Paul Stillwell: Had they worked with the fleet by that point?

Admiral Meyer: They had worked with some piece of the fleet. How much they had worked with the fleet was pretty limited, because the fleet was abuilding; it didn't exist. So they were learning along the way. And the facilities ashore were almost zero. When I reported in in 1963—I can wear you out here. That old man, Admiral Reich, was a genius, but here this Navy had built this Terrier fleet and had it coming on, but there was no structure in motion of what to do with this fleet and how to sustain this fleet.

Now, let me digress a minute, I'll just show you why this old sailor gets all upset right now with this bullshit going on over here in things like 1000 and DD(X) and these LCSs, with unproven, untested things one after the other put in motion, to later be discovered as to how to get out of it by somebody else. I've just this morning scanning some of John Young's testimony on that very subject.[*] Now, there's an authority.

---

[*] John J. Young Jr. was Assistant Secretary of the Navy (Research, Development and Acquisitions), 2001 to 2005 and Under Secretary of Defense for Acquisition, Technology and Logistics, 2007 to 2009.

There's a real expert on fleet support, Secretary John Young. He doesn't have the experience of any person you'd pick right here on this deck walking around. That's the level of his knowledge. Well, he's not an ignorant person; he's not a dumb person; that's not my point. My point is, here's a person assigned as Assistant Secretary of the Navy for acquisition that couldn't write a complete sentence on the subject because he doesn't know anything about it. Well, that's not unusual, as you know.

Paul Stillwell: This because of the political aspects of the appointments?

Admiral Meyer: They are political appointments. And the people doing the sorting and appointing don't ever, ever, ever, ever, *ever* worry about execution.

I'm going to digress on the digress. [Laughter] Goldwater-Nichols occurred in the year 1986, I believe.*

Paul Stillwell: Yes, it was.

Admiral Meyer: So I'm some ahead. But remember, the era I'm speaking of is pre-Goldwater-Nichols.

Paul Stillwell: Nineteen sixty-seven.

Admiral Meyer: And those degrees of freedom existed for the people in the line structure to make decisions without interference, always from the political point. As a matter of fact, as long as you honored the political appointees and respected them, you could do just about whatever the hell you wanted done. Now, under Goldwater-Nichols, ten years later, they came in, they thought they had a mandate. *They're* taking charge of acquisition. That's what's going on, the hearings are going on today, this very day, and they went on yesterday. And you've got this guy Levin over there right now, wants to

---

* The Goldwater-Nichols Defense Reorganization Act of 1986 went into effect on 1 October of that year. It mandated a good deal more in the way of joint-service relationships than had been the case up to then. For details, see "DoD Reorganization," *U.S. Naval Institute Proceedings*, May 1987, pages 136-145.

create, stand up yet another czar, who's going to oversee these yahoos in the military to get acquisition squared away. They ain't the problem!

Paul Stillwell: Well, my impression back in the '60s was that McNamara and his people were taking over control of acquisitions along with the systems analysts.

Admiral Meyer: Your impression is a correct one, young officer. It's exactly correct. And it was therefore the forerunner of being able to let a thing like Goldwater-Nichols get started. So *my* Goldwater-Nichols of the era was McNamara, a different horse with a different color, but the same warped type of thinking.

So he sent me out there for those three things plus one more. And that was that [chuckle]. I never worked for Sarver very long, but Sarver was very respectful of me. He had commanded *Oklahoma City*, a Talos ship. And Eli Reich thought one hell of a lot of me, and from there I took my grease. And the final thing he told me was, "Get a plan to get the place converted to civil service." He didn't say get it done; he said get a plan to do it. So that was my assignment.

Paul Stillwell: Would that plan require some congressional approval?

Admiral Meyer: Well, we don't know. At that stage we had no idea. They were being funded by special authorization, as I recall, from the Congress. But just to answer your question, it subsequently turned out it did, in the sense that the Johnson regime is the one that forced it and wanted a plan. They wanted approval of it. The Congress didn't particularly ask for it, but the Johnson administration, Lyndon Johnson being pretty wise, particularly after the murder of Kennedy, pushed and pushed and pushed then to get ourselves back into civil service.

And that was also what I call the liberation years, when all the women were set free too. The Johnson years were the years of the flood of creating all these civil service billets to promote women, jillions of them. And I think most of them are now, maybe, perhaps finally retired. But we got women, and had, in our Navy who are ranked as high as GS-14s, who are really still GS-5s. They've never set foot in a schoolhouse a day.

What did that cause over that period? I'll tell you what it caused. It meant that we had to bring the work down to the leadership, not the leadership up to the work.

So back to Ben Sarver and his orders to me. I didn't have the foggiest idea how in the hell to get the contractors out and how to bring civil service in. I had about that much experience on the subject.

Paul Stillwell: Zero. You made a gesture. [Chuckle]

Admiral Meyer: Yeah, made a gesture, right, with a zero. Thank you. But I knew some pretty wise people back here from my tour of duty here under the admiral, and I learned a lot from Frank Gilliam and those very senior people in government who knew how government functioned.

Paul Stillwell: Was there some inherent advantage in having civil service people in the jobs rather than contractors?

Admiral Meyer: Yes, because it did speak for the government. And secondly, they're way cheaper. Later on, the way I had to get rid of them was through a mandate; I received a mandate. I want to say it came from Johnson; I believe that's correct. Because I believe when Kennedy was murdered I think I was airborne.* I had stopped off in Missouri to visit my parents, I believe, when he was murdered. I had been either out there or here or vice versa, or someplace in that era. He was murdered in '62, would it be?

Paul Stillwell: November '63.

Admiral Meyer: '63, okay. Okay, right, '63, so I was stationed here. And they were trying to get the station thought out. All we had was little pockets of people around, scattered all over. Very few civil service. He started that station out there with, I don't

---

* John F. Kennedy served as President of the United States from 20 January 1960 until he was assassinated on 22 November 1963.

know, 20 civil servants and three officers. It was pathetic. But today it became one of the great in-service engineering structures of this era to support the fleet, and it's one of my great prides.

Now, God is good. Certainly He's been good to me. Because the admiral created that station—I think I told you this—had four captains on it. It was the only station in the whole United States that had four captains. One was the commanding officer, one was the executive officer, one was the director of engineering, and one was the director of integrated logistics. And he very carefully chose these captains. He chose an engineering duty officer of the Naval Academy Class of '37, Ball by name, to be the CO.[*] He chose an unrestricted line officer to be the XO, Captain Mark Woods. Captain Mark Woods was en route to Bath as the prospective commanding officer of USS *Dale*, and the admiral snatched him and ordered him out there, and oh, was he pissed.[†]

Paul Stillwell: I can imagine that. [Laughter]

Admiral Meyer: Oh, he hardly ever got over it until later in life. But he was the XO. This guy Roth I mentioned was appointed as the chief engineer, and some guy out of Ohio, a captain by the name of Bernie McCreery, came to be the Supply Corps officer.[‡] I never heard of him, and he didn't really know anything about our business, but it turned out he was a pretty smooth cookie, and he and I became great friends. And particularly since I didn't shoot golf, and he loved it, and I allowed him to shoot all the golf he wanted.

But that year was a year when the whole new source selection process was in motion in the DoD. I call it the Wright-Pat Heresy, after the Wright-Patterson Air Force Base in Ohio, which created all of this process. It was built around the source selection and engineering development of an offensive ballistic missile. And they created something known as the infamous "work breakdown structure" on how to define a program. And in that world the standpipe for what they called the vehicle, the flight vehicle, ran from here all the way up to the house of the cherubim. All the other pieces

---

[*] Captain Richard E. Ball, USN.
[†] Captain Mark W. Woods, USN.
[‡] Captain Bernard L. McCreery, SC, USN.

of the program were little teensy things that were hardly even points on the chart. And we admire the United States Air Force for their genius? Really? Not me. I wouldn't admire them for two seconds. But God, could they spend money.

Raborn was pretty damned smart.* He knew how to spend money. He knew how to spend it. You ever think about that? I'm sure you have. The CNO took an aviator—and besides that, he's a multi-engine aviator—and put him in charge of Polaris.

The source selection process had been going on, the countdown, for some seven years, really, and Admiral Reich is the one that killed it in the middle; I think I mentioned this to you. And that's how he got money in which to do the 3-T get-well program, $76 million.

Paul Stillwell: Well, with these four captains on the station, what was the charter for supporting the fleet? What was the support role?

Admiral Meyer: Well, remember, the first cult that ever emerged was something called integrated logistics, and that cult was created by a GS-15 in the material command, Chief of Naval Material, by the name of Jim Genovese. He created that cult, and the admiral loved the cult and he promoted it then.

Paul Stillwell: Admiral Reich?

Admiral Meyer: Yes. He promoted it in the SMS, Surface Missile Systems. And so the theory of it ain't bad. As a matter of fact, if people understand it and know how to practice it, it's pretty damned good. But it's an unnatural-type behavior, is the problem, and therefore, as far as I know, Aegis is the only outfit that ever very successfully practiced it.

Paul Stillwell: What do you mean by "unnatural?"

---

* Rear Admiral William F. Raborn, Jr., USN, was director of the Special Projects Office, which developed the Polaris submarine-launched ballistic missile system. He held the post from 1955 to 1962, being promoted to vice admiral in 1960. His Polaris oral history is in the Naval Institute collection.

Admiral Meyer: Well, logistics and engineering, by their nature, are partitioned. They just don't come together, period. You've got all them depot wienies over there, and you've got all them engineers over yonder someplace in Kansas City. That's what I mean. Well, it's even true in the Navy. And so, as a result, all of acquisition invariably was being driven by engineering, not by logistics. That's how all this stuff got born. Suddenly it's on the pier, and nobody knows what the hell to do with it. There's no structure of any kind. None.

I told you that I was assigned to conversion, fire control officer in *Galveston*. Subsequently fleeted up to gun boss. The admiral made a trip out there. We had these ships and no schoolhouse, so at nighttime *Galveston* became the schoolhouse. Daytime, the ship was a test ship. I'm saying this to you for a couple reasons, one being to force me to think a little bit more about it, but also to brag about it, because I was genuinely the leader and genuinely had pretty good degrees of freedom in executing some of it because I was just ahead of the crowd.

All my project management teaching since those days is to try to teach to young project managers: You must be ahead of the crowd. If you're not ahead of the crowd, the crowd's always running you. You *have* to stay ahead. And I can sit down here right now even though I've been away from it for 25 years, I don't even know who they are, but I can tell you in 15 minutes which projects are going to work and which ones ain't going to work, and it's based on that little principle. Because there's a group of people over there in the Gun Factory who wait for their orders. They can wait for a long, long time. Wait a minute, John, why have you—well, nobody ever told us any different.

I often likened project management, as I became the senior applied leader of project management behind Levering and Rickover, as being the most difficult command possible ashore or at sea.[*] Now, at sea we're raised traditionally that we have the courts-martial manual that stands behind us and supports us in authority. In project management you don't have that. In military, and in the courts-martial manual—and I again as part of my teachings—I'm jumping around on you; it might take you a couple days to get me settled back down.

---

[*] In 1957 Captain Levering Smith, USN, became the second technical director in the Special Projects Office on Polaris. As a rear admiral Smith served as director of the Special Projects Office/Strategic Systems Projects Office from 16 February 1965 to 14 November 1977.

Paul Stillwell: I hope not. [Laughter]

Admiral Meyer: Okay. In a ship everybody knows the protocol. The mess cook knows, and the head cleaner. They know who the chief is, the division officer is, the executive officer, all the way up, and that's the old man. Popularly called the old man because it was traditionally the oldest person in the group. So everybody understands that, and there's a lot of commonality in their upbringing, their breeding, their objectives, and all those things.

Take project management, big project. I ain't talking about—we've taken all these little piss-ass things in recent years, in the last 20-25 years, and we've turned everything into a project. If I were running the Navy tomorrow, I've got to tell you, man, I'd slash and burn for about four months, because project after project after project would go down the tubes. And it would either get itself attached to something worthwhile, or poof, it'd be gone.

But here that doesn't exist. And so when I lecture naval officers and civil servants, I talk to them about the seriousness of this and the leadership demands. Here, this is tough leadership. When you're in command of a ship, or even in command of a station, you can issue an order and, yes sir, or yes ma'am, it'll get carried out, or most times it will. Project management—there isn't anybody has to take an order. Who in the hell has to take an order?

Right now in the testimony I was flipping through this morning in the press, where Lockheed is under really, really serious assault, how bad they are, how awful they are, what crimes they've—well, that's pure bullshit. Lockheed's not that way at all. Now, Lockheed Aeronautics in Texas is in some pretty deep serious trouble. That ain't got anything whatsoever to do with Lockheed in New Jersey. Unfortunately, the press doesn't bother to point those little things out. And so here Lockheed is getting its reputation blackened and damaged and kicked around this very day because the joint strike fighter has got itself out of budget.[*] The joint strike fighter has got itself out of budget. That doesn't have anything whatsoever to do with Aegis. Nothing. Zero.

---

[*] The Lockheed Martin F-35 Lightning II is a single-seat, multi-role aircraft that made its first flight in 2006.

Paul Stillwell: Well, can we go back to Port Hueneme?

Admiral Meyer: Okay. We're still there.

Paul Stillwell: What was the support function specifically, vis-à-vis the fleet?

Admiral Meyer: Something called in-service engineering and logistics, neither one of which had any definition whatsoever. I would say that, in hindsight, I made some major contributions in those definitions. And, in hindsight too, I did some things that were not only not major, they were wrong. And I don't mean to imply you can't be 100% right; it's just that that's kind of how the world works, because a person's know-how only goes so far, and experience or mistakes—and that's how you get wise, is making mistakes. So that cult had to emerge. Most people would turn up their nose. Most people would view it as being system technicians.

See, originally they didn't want a single engineer at this station. All they wanted were field techs, like guys that fix televisions.

Paul Stillwell: Whom did they work with in the fleet?

Admiral Meyer: Ships. The ships.

Paul Stillwell: Was this like a central office that would send people out to the ships?

Admiral Meyer: It was when I had it rolling, and that's what it is today. I spent a lot of time on the road communicating with the commodores, the flotilla commanders, and the commanding officers. The admiral had created, and in Terrier we had brought it to a fine art, something called the SQAT, the Ship's Qualification Assistance Team, originally. In those early days, there were no schoolhouses, so the idea was we would assemble a team of coaches and trainers in situ that would get the ship's crew up on the step and its gear on the step and get things functioned. As a reward they would fire so many missiles and get that pride and such, and we'd wave goodbye to them and off they'd go. Well, in six weeks they'd fall apart.

Paul Stillwell: Why was that?

Admiral Meyer: There's no structure. There's no structure that sees after them. I often liken warships to Hertz cars. You can't tell people that your tour of sea duty will be three years and not have 50% turnover every year. You can't achieve a tour of sea duty of three years without that kind of turnover. So in fact it will always run that way. We tend to think, well, it's only the captain and stuff that turn over. One of the reasons they turn the captains over is people can't handle the pace much longer than that. But they also have to create room, because the whole idea in peacetime in our Navy is trying to find out where the leadership is, and the best crucible we have for testing that is command at sea. It ain't a perfect crucible. As a matter of fact, it fails us fairly often. It's failed us today more than ever.

Paul Stillwell: I'm sorry to hear that.

Admiral Meyer: Well, I am too. I am too. But that, as you say, is off the point of Port Hueneme. But you see, my life, I walked in out of Talos into the task force, and I've described that story to you, I know damned good and well I did, with Harmon Penny. And I was stunned that I was not sent to the Talos fire control desk. Instead, I was sent to the Terrier fire control desk. Well, the kindest thing you could say about the Terrier fleet at that stage is that is was FUBAR'd.[*] [Laughter] The DLG-6 class were out trying to sail.[†] The DLG-16 class were in construction.[‡] And the DLG-26 class were on the drawing boards.[§] I mean, man, they were really tick-tick—that's popularly known today

---

[*] FUBAR – "Fouled up beyond all recognition" is the polite translation of this abbreviation.
[†] USS *Farragut* (DLG-6), a guided missile frigate, was commissioned 10 December 1960. In 1975 she was reclassified a guided missile destroyer, DDG-37.
[‡] USS *Leahy* was commissioned 4 August 1962 as a guided missile frigate, DLG-16, the lead ship of her class. She was designated a guided missile cruiser, CG-16 in 1975.
[§] USS *Belknap* (DLG-26), a guided missile frigate, was commissioned 7 November 1964. In 1975 she was reclassified a guided missile cruiser, CG-26.

as the Arleigh Burke fleet, or it was.* Nobody knows who the hell Arleigh Burke is anymore, and that's probably good. But he was the dominating force. People didn't worry too much about Tartar. It was aborning and it was a spin-off out of Terrier. See, there would have been no Tartar without Terrier. So the major missiles were Talos and Terrier, and the Navy decided that Talos upkeep was too hard. Talos is a giant-killer. I always thought it was a bum decision to discard Talos. But the whole purpose is, we had to have a fleet that was going to protect the aircraft carrier no matter what.

Paul Stillwell: When you were in Port Hueneme did you have a plan to try to overcome the shortcoming that the team's good work would last only for a short time? Did you see a way to make it last longer, or permanent?

Admiral Meyer: Yes.

Paul Stillwell: And what was that?

Admiral Meyer: I put a number of things into effect, some that worked, some didn't. Some prevailed and some did not. But to this day, and they just had their 40-some anniversary that they wanted me out, as a matter of fact I think it's this week, to speak, and I had said no because I had this appointment with you, is why I said it. It wasn't quite that way, but—[Chuckle].

What I had to develop was a confidence builder. I mean, I really, really learned so much about leadership, much of it self-taught, and you heard me say there ain't nothing dumber than a self-taught person. But my opportunity to practice leadership and learn leadership of hard problems, I believe, is unsurpassed, as I've reflected on it through the years of what happened to me in the Navy. When I decided to specialize in ordnance engineering, that meant turning down the command of a destroyer, and I remember how difficult that was for me and how badly it hurt me. And occasionally yet, at the age of 82, I wake up pained about that. But frankly, I would have never, never

---

* Admiral Arleigh A. Burke, USN, was Chief of Naval Operations from 1955 to 1961, the period in which these ships were designed and the earliest went into commission.

contributed to the world what I had the opportunity to contribute. Never. Not even close. Which, I'm proud to say, no matter what, some members of the House Armed Services Committee saw fit two weeks ago to nominate me to be promoted.

Paul Stillwell: We talked about the teams that were sent out and had the temporary effect. How did you seek to overcome that?

Admiral Meyer: Well, originally we were building the fleet, introducing all these missiles. It was to be a one-shot thing. We didn't have any schoolhouses, didn't have any of that. Gonna correct all of that, and we're going to do it through this thing called SQATs, ship's qualification assistance teams. "Assistance" was the operative word. These trials would run anywheres from three to eight weeks, depending on the system and depending on the state of the crew. And SQATs would be formed, and I'm the one that institutionalized them, really, because originally we were running them out of the task force back here, and one of the side assignments the admiral gave me is he wanted the station to take custody of them and take them out of headquarters, which was the right thing.

Paul Stillwell: Were they physically set up in Port Hueneme then?

Admiral Meyer: Right. The whole thing was established there.

Paul Stillwell: Did the facility at Port Hueneme serve just the Pacific fleet?

Admiral Meyer: The answer is no. Some people tended to think that, but the station annexed an outfit out of Norfolk that was primarily their radar support group. A Naval Reserve captain by the name of Ted LeFebvre was—well, they made it an attachment to the station, which they didn't like and resented, but they renamed them the detachment of Port Hueneme, of NSMSES, and so we operated now the SQATs out of both places and got them moved out of headquarters.

Well, my schema when I'd started this is I tried to get a lieutenant commander or a senior lieutenant and a GS-14, and my attitude was: Look, if you're going aboard to help a ship or teach the people on the ship, you ought to know more about it than they know.

Paul Stillwell: That stands to reason.

Admiral Meyer: Well, it does, but that's not always true. So in those days, mind you, we didn't have all these modern conveniences you young people have. The next thing I did was, I issued them a telephone credit card. And the next thing I issued them was a Hertz card. And so they had repeat orders. They were based at Port Hueneme or Norfolk, but in the Eli T. Reich way it was inexcusable for you to not take action when it needed to be taken. And those were two important things you needed to take action—one was your ability to use the telephone and the second was your transportation situation. So I solved both of those by a breakthrough of credit cards, so that you didn't have to wrestle or report or do any of those things. You were accountable to *my* controller for your abuse, if you abused those cards.

Now, I detest the expression "waste, fraud, and abuse." That is *bullshit*, and it really irks me that no one in government ever stands up anymore and puts down that kind of behavior and that kind of statement. Just in the paper this week there's some, they want to create a new post to oversee, to get this "waste, fraud, and abuse" squared away. What the hell is "abuse?" What is "waste?" What is "fraud?" I mean, as you know with your own experience, the amount of it in government is hardly even measurable. I mean, you've got to search and search and search and search to find any because it just ain't measurable. And it really pissed me off then by the time I became big Aegis leader of how much time we would spend on the trivial nickel-and-dime things, including the profit margin for the contractors, while pissing away hundreds of millions of dollars!

Paul Stillwell: Well, what did these people do when you sent them out with their credit cards?

Admiral Meyer: Well, they sent them out to solve the problems.

Paul Stillwell: How did they do that?

Admiral Meyer: Sent them aboard to look over the ships, talk to the captain, talk to the gun boss, talk to the sailors. Usually in those days often they were carrying a suitcase full of alterations because we were in the stage of constantly band-aiding the ships.

Paul Stillwell: Did they have a training syllabus as part of this?

Admiral Meyer: Oh, yeah. They had a syllabus approved by me. And the captain got a chance to review it, and it would include firing operations and targeting, and we tried to throw in a little fun for it of cruising or whatever we could get in on the side. And have it also molded in as part of the ship's operation schedule and such. You know, when I had *Galveston* it pissed me off. The attitude that developed in that ship: Well, it's only those missile people back there taking all the time, and the rest of the goddamn ship would be on the forecastle sunbathing. Well, I put a stop to that of any people as I was associated with, starting in *Galveston*, and then when I became chief engineer I stopped it all again. This is serious business, and it's the whole ship's business, just not some little piece of one division or one detachment.

Then I tried to teach the fire control officers and the gunnery officers: "If you've got a problem, you pick up the telephone; we will help." Then I posted agents in critical places—San Diego; we always had ships in Long Beach, not only stationed there but also in the shipyard, and I'd have them posted them there.
(Interruption)

Admiral Meyer: What did I start to say? It was important.

Paul Stillwell: Well, you were talking about the teams that you sent out and also that you had experts in headquarters that could be called on.

Admiral Meyer: No, I went beyond that. I told the officials back here that I thought that we had no choice but to institutionalize it. That we would have to continue it. And to this day, 40 years later, in spite of several times of efforts rising up saying we don't need this, we still do qualification trials and they still belong. And in fact, Mullen decided that the Navy couldn't afford to do—you know, we don't do any training exercises anymore in missiles; we don't fire any missiles.*

Paul Stillwell: I didn't know that.

Admiral Meyer: Well, we haven't fired any for three years. So today you've got COs, gunnery officers, fire control officers that have never seen a missile fired aboard ship. The only place that it's been sustained were the trials associated with the Aegis ships. Now, with it on the downside one wonders over the next five years what's going to happen to the proficiency of our crews. I know what's going to happen. There ain't nobody going to be willing to believe me, but I know what will happen. They'll be downed.

I've told you this, my many years of experience associated with ordnance and gunnery, there's something about a gun. If every day you have to do daily transmission checks, the guns will always work. If you don't, they won't. I don't know why, but that's the way it is. And that's true in missilery; missilery followed gunnery.

Well, of course, so much of it now, over that period of my day from chief engineer to now, has become push-button. You could, in theory at least, fight your ship now without very much knowledge of what's inside of it except knowing the right button to push at the right time. And the computer does a hell of a lot of that, even, for you.

To digress a minute, to jump ahead, for shooting down the spacecraft that window was less than six seconds. Isn't that incredible?

Paul Stillwell: Yes.

---

* Admiral Michael G. Mullen, USN, served as Chief of Naval Operations from 22 July 2005 to 29 September 2007, and then became Chairman of the Joint Chiefs of Staff on 1 October 2007.

Admiral Meyer: It's just incredible. I mean, the global window was six seconds. Well, you can't do a lot of jabbering and carrying on on that. You've got to have her set up. And the truth is, the reason it was assigned to Aegis is that's the only outfit that could do it, that had the requisite automation to be able to take it on. Now, the Chinese shot down, the Air Force satellite, but wait a minute. What did they do? They got their fighters lined up and pointed and waited for the spacecraft to fly in to the pointing of them, when there was F-15s shot down a couple several years ago, which was nothing but a stunt is all that amounted to.[*] What happened here is real. My guess is the Congress is going to demand that the capability be put into the ships. I don't think it should, but that's what's going to happen, in my view.

Back to where we were. Of course, the war was heating up more all the time, and more and more G-ships, or missile ships, were involved in the war in my time.

Paul Stillwell: Were you sending people over to the Western Pacific?

Admiral Meyer: So I've had a steady string of ants over there. And one of the mobile ordnance training units which belonged to ComServPac was based in Sasebo.[†] That's not true. Well, there was one in Sasebo.

Paul Stillwell: There was one in Yokosuka.

Admiral Meyer: Right. But there was one also in the Philippines. And so we formed an alliance with them and integrated our technical forces to be sure we didn't send ships out on the line that hadn't been looked over by adults. Did we do a good job? We'll never know whether we did a good job or not. I think that it was a pretty commendable job that was done.

---

[*] The Air Force's F-15E Strike Eagle multi-role fighter plane is a development of the McDonnell Douglas (now Boeing) F-15 Eagle

[†] ComServPac – Commander Service Force Pacific Fleet.

Paul Stillwell: Well, the *Long Beach* shot down a couple of airplanes around that time.*

Admiral Meyer: That's affirmative.

Paul Stillwell: Something must have been working.

Admiral Meyer: Right. They did that with Taloses. And we had DLG-34, I think it was, "Don't piddle with the *Biddle*," *Biddle*, shot down, I think, with Terrier, Eddie "Three Sticks" Carter in command.† It was as though the only reason he took command was to go out there someplace and sail till he could find a target to shoot at, and once he found one he came home happy. [Laughter] And he got promoted.

Paul Stillwell: He wound up as ComOpTEvFor.‡

Admiral Meyer: You got it. But he was afraid to do any harm with me, since I had protected him. All those guys, interesting enough, because of the way I was detailed, here I had come out of the Talos fleet into the task force, become an ordnance engineer, and became the chief engineer, the key post, of the thriving missile engineering station...

Let me cap that off a minute. This whole source selection process—Captain Bill Arthur was the commanding officer. He'd been CO of *Norton Sound*.§ Well, he was ordered back here by the admiral as the chairman of the source selection evaluation board. Well, it turned out that was over two years to do that. So he was gone practically my entire tour.

---

* On 23 May 1968 the *Long Beach* fired two Talos missiles at a MiG fighter at 65 miles. The first knocked the plane down, and the second hit the falling wreckage. In September 1968 a Talos from the *Long Beach* shot down a MiG that was 61 miles away. For details on this and other aspects of the career of the *Long Beach*, see Malcolm Muir, Jr., *Black Shoes and Blue Water: Surface Warfare in the United States Navy, 1945-1975* (Washington, D.C.: Naval Historical Center, 1996).
† Captain Edward W. Carter III, USN, commanded the guided missile frigate *Biddle* (DLG-34) from July 1972 to August 1974. On 19 July 1972 the *Biddle* was attacked by five MiG fighters. She shot down one with Terrier missiles and was credited with another plane probably destroyed.
‡ As a rear admiral, Carter commanded the Operational Test and Evaluation Force.
§ Captain William A. Arthur, USN, commanded the test ship *Norton Sound* (AVM-1) from June 1964 to June 1965.

Secondly, the XO, Captain Bill Betzer, was there.* Well, Fritz—can't say his name; he was CO of Seal Beach—anyhow, he was off skiing someplace and broke his damned leg, and the chief of NavOrd determined that that place had to be covered with a captain. It was a major load-out point for the war. And so Bill Betzer was snatched right out from over me to go down and be commanding officer at Seal Beach. So here I was now stripped down; Bernie McCreery and myself were the two captains. And so now I was in hog heaven because Bernie McCreery didn't want to run anything; he just wanted me to tell him what to do. So I was everything.

I've talked about some of my major contributions at that station, which perhaps would be an appropriate place to bring them in here. One was the women's head. In the headquarters building, which is there yet, which is, I don't know, 80 years old whatever it is, and my office, the women's head for that end of the building is right inside of the front door and right, in essence, in the lobby. And you could hear every woman pee for half the building. And I made the goddamn crews get in there and get that place insulated so that a woman could go to the head in peace. I tell you, I couldn't do anything wrong from then on. Any woman on that station would make coffee for me. They'd do anything for me because I did that for them.

The second thing I did, which was not nearly as noble, but if you've ever been to the station—

Paul Stillwell: No, I haven't.

Admiral Meyer: Well, it's as flat as this deck, as I told you, and it's got a little separator in the road out there in front of it about this wide . . .

Paul Stillwell: About a yard wide.

Admiral Meyer: . . . which is nothing but sand. Well, I had some palm trees planted in that to put a little decoration in the place. And they're still there to this day. And the

---

* Captain William E. Betzer, USN, became commanding officer of Naval Weapons Station, Seal Beach, California, in July 1971. From 1964 to 1968 he was executive officer of the Naval Ship Missile System Engineering Station (NSMSES), at Port Hueneme.

women's head is still there to this day. So those are two of my major marks at that station, and I'm still known there and I'm recognized as a distinguished alumnus from it. I'm not the only one, distinguished person that served there, but they have plaques around through each building out there that is an Eli Reich/Wayne Meyer plaque. They struck a plaque like about the size of one of these that hangs up there and talks about the two officers who made the major contributions to the station's ancestry, which is kind of nice. There's one in the lobby of every building. There's about 10 or 12 buildings; they've got one in every building, which I hope it's still there because I had to turn them down in order for the meeting here. They wanted me to come out and speak. You know, one of the things they may decide is to remove all them damn plaques.

Paul Stillwell: And they'll blame me.

Admiral Meyer: Well, yeah. That's what I'm going to tell them. [Chuckle]

Paul Stillwell: Now, you said the captain was off on the source selection committee. That was the selection of what system?

Admiral Meyer: Source selection evaluation board.

Paul Stillwell: For what system?

Admiral Meyer: Something called ASMS, Advanced Surface Missile System.

Paul Stillwell: And what did they conclude during that period?

Admiral Meyer: It was a joint system development thanks to McNamara that the United States Army and the United States Navy were to do in concert. Not only that—McNamara decreed that the project office for it ought to be in Huntsville, Alabama. My good and close friend, Commander Harmon Penny, on the list the same year as I was, selected for captain, was ordered down there to be the commanding officer. He went down there; six months later he put his papers in and went home. Said he refused to have anything whatsoever to do with it. And they withdrew his captaincy.* The Navy would not retire him, as you know, without serving a certain amount of limited time. He refused to do it, it was so bad, so awful. And so we had had this divorce. This divorce had now occurred.

(Interruption)

And so Bill Arthur was back here leading us—hell there must have been 200 people at it, and from my viewpoint there was good and there was bad. The good part is there was no one but me running the station. [Chuckle] And associated with that was the war. I mean, I gathered a big name for myself, frankly, and it was not seeking joy or any of those things. It was because I thought that's what the hell the station was for; it was important. I had this steady stream of people into Japan, into the Philippines, and into the country of Vietnam. And I in fact made one secret journey to Vietnam myself during that time, which as far as I know has never been declassified, and I led a team of five officers to do that. The purpose was readiness.

Paul Stillwell: What can you say about that trip in an unclassified fashion?

Admiral Meyer: It came about as a result of the Koreans shooting down an EC-121.†

Paul Stillwell: That was in 1969.

Admiral Meyer: '69. I was getting ready to say I believe that was '69. You took it from me. I think it was about April.

Paul Stillwell: It was exactly April.

---

* Penny retired as a captain in January 1970.
† A U.S. Navy EC-121 electronic reconnaissance aircraft with 31 crewmen on board was shot down 14 April 1969 by North Korean aircraft. The incident took place approximately 90 miles off the coast of North Korea. The entire U.S. crew was lost.

Admiral Meyer: Yeah. Your recall is superb. I'll tell you this part about it. The chiefs had made a decision they were going to strike back, and they were concerned about the readiness of our forces.

Paul Stillwell: There was a large task force in the Sea of Japan.

Admiral Meyer: A *big* task force in the Sea of Japan, commanded by Admiral—little bitty guy. He was aboard *Enterprise*.[*]

Paul Stillwell: So you were over there looking at task force readiness.

Admiral Meyer: The CNO was Admiral Tom Moorer.[†] The SMS project still existed back here and Merrill Homer Sappington had, almost by the same grace that God granted me—I hadn't been selected, of course, then but he was selected as an admiral. He never expected to be promoted or anything. He had that task force. I'm not positive, I think, I don't know, I think he was a classmate of Moorer's.[‡] Anyhow—well, I don't know whether Moorer's dead yet or not.

Paul Stillwell: Yes, he is.

Admiral Meyer: He is? Okay, so they're both dead.
So apparently Moorer had called Sappington and expressing his concern. He was really concerned, and the chiefs were concerned about the readiness and the ability to act, always.

Paul Stillwell: How large a team did you take when you went over?

---

[*] Rear Admiral Malcolm W. Cagle, USN, was at the time Commander Task Force 71/Commander Carrier Division One. Admiral John H. Hyland, USN, who was short in stature, visited the *Enterprise* in his capacity as Commander in Chief Pacific Fleet. Task Force 71 eventually

[†] Admiral Thomas H. Moorer, USN, served as Chief of Naval Operations from 1 August 1967 to 1 July 1970. His oral history is in the Naval Institute collection.

[‡] Sappington was in the Naval Academy class of 1943; Moorer was in the class of 1933. Sappington was project manager for Surface Missile Systems from 1968 to 1972.

Admiral Meyer: Well, so here the word came on Friday, after they'd had these conversations, that I was to field a team of up to six officers, and I could be met by others in different places if appropriate. We didn't know where we were going. At that time, that was the classified piece. And so we got these orders. I believe I had been there two years at that point.

Paul Stillwell: You said you got there in early '67.

Admiral Meyer: Yeah. But I learned an important lesson I put in effect after that. It was: not everybody had their goddamn shots. We had gotten an order from OpNav that we were to have certain shots. Well, from that I put a law into effect that's there to this day that there is to be several hundred people on that station ready to travel anytime, including their shots, civil and military, and that continues, to the best of my knowledge.

So here we were Friday night. The dispensary at the Seabee center hustled up all these strange-ass shots and, of course, by Saturday morning we were sick as dogs. But it didn't matter, because we were in a goddamn jitney and rode to Los Angeles airport. And my orders were that we'd be met at Pearl, and we'd be told what to do then.

So we were, we were met at Honolulu airport, a commander. This was really early Saturday afternoon and we were still just sicker than hell.[*] He said, "Captain, I'd like to let you rest a little bit, but you're not going to rest. We're putting you on a plane and you're going to Guam, and you'll be routed from Guam when you get there." So we were all not feeling too well, but we did.

We got to Guam and the next thing was, well, we're going to route you to the Marine Corps Air Station Iwakuni, Japan. Well, by now we started figuring out what was going on here. And so far no one had given us any instructions. I had a sealed envelope that I could open after I got to Iwakuni.

So then we got on a COD at Iwakuni.[†] We took off on the COD and we started flying south. Hell, we must have flown an hour, and he turned around and started flying in another direction. Well, he flew for, I don't know, 40 minutes or whatever the time

---

[*] The EC-121 was shot down on the previous Monday, 14 April.
[†] COD – carrier on-board delivery, an aircraft configured for carrier takeoffs and landings, dedicated to transporting personnel and cargo between ship and shore.

was, whatever it took, but the next thing we knew we looked down there and we see an aircraft carrier underneath us, which turned out to be *Enterprise*. We were coming in to the *Enterprise*.

We arrived in the midst of everything, and now we were really tired because we'd been up, like, two days now. We get off. The admiral sent the chief of staff down. What's that goddamn admiral's name? Anyhow, he said, "The first thing I'm supposed to find out here, Captain, is why are you here? That's what the admiral told me to find out before I even brought you to his cabin."

I said, "It beats the hell out of me; I have no idea." [Chuckle]

Paul Stillwell: Had you opened your orders in Iwakuni?

Admiral Meyer: As a matter of fact, all they told me to do was report to this—I think Seventh Fleet. I think it was Seventh Fleet.

Paul Stillwell: Well, Bringle *was* Seventh Fleet.[*]

Admiral Meyer: I can't get my names straight. But it was to report to this guy, that's what they said. That's all it said. So I said, "That's it."

"Well," he said, "come on up; we'll see what we can do." So we proceeded immediately to the admiral's cabin, and the admiral continued to be perplexed. The attitude somehow was as though I had something to do with it. Well, as I told you, I had nothing to do with it. I had the least knowledge of anybody.

Well, by that afternoon the air was clearing a little bit. They gave us a bunk to sleep for a few hours and clean up, and the admiral and chief of staff wanted to meet with me again. He said, "Well, all right, here's the situation." I have now talked to the Chairman [that's the first time he had spoken to the Chairman] and I've got a little better idea of what's in mind here."[†]

---

[*] Vice Admiral William F. Bringle, USN, served as Commander Seventh Fleet from 6 November 1967 to 10 March 1970.
[†] General Earle G. Wheeler, USA, served as Chairman of the Joint Chiefs of Staff from 3 July 1964 to 2 July 1970.

Well, the cruiser *Chicago* was in the task force, and there was a bunch of DLGs and such. So he said, "We don't know what we're going to do. We don't know whether we're going to strike or not strike. But the CNO wanted us as ready as we can be, and wanted to check the readiness of the ships and, using your officers to be aboard these ships in case something breaks open." That sounded rational. So he said, "Well, as soon as you all get organized, I'd like to redeploy you to the cruiser *Chicago* and take your officers and put them in different ships, and the first thing to do is have them inspect those ships and then you decide what you want to do next."

I said, "Well, the first thing we don't do, Admiral. We don't inspect ships. We look at them, we'll comment on them, and we'll give you opinion. But one of the things I refuse to do is inspect ships, because that's the road to hell."

"Oh, okay. I accept your judgment" and shifted the words around. So we started heloing off and got dispersed. I don't know how many days we milled around. It seemed to me it approached a week.

You remember the guy that was selected as an admiral and he's dead now, but I'm sure you knew him. He was a cartoonist. He was constantly drawing and sketching. I'm about to say his name in a minute. Here he popped up in the middle of this. He was one of the squad dogs there, and he was just kind of left over, so he and I spent a lot of time trying to understand the operation together because that's where I learn more than anything. And trying to communicate with my other officers was just frightful. But we fiddled and fiddled, and finally it calmed down and things settled down. And then we reassembled in *Enterprise*.

Captain John DeLargy was the CO of *Chicago*.[*] He was pissed that we were sent into his ship. Frankly, it was a good thing we were, because he wouldn't have cut it.

But then, meeting with the admiral, he said, "Look, I've talked to"—whoever in the hell, I don't know whether it was Seventh Fleet or vice versa, Task Force 77 or what; I think it was Seventh Fleet. He said, "Look. After discussing this with him, what we would like for you to do is take your team and go south. We'll get you an airplane."

---

[*] Captain John M. DeLargy, USN, commanded the guided missile cruiser *Chicago* (CG-11) from 9 March 1968 to 19 September 1969.

Paul Stillwell: "Go south" meaning Vietnam?

Admiral Meyer: Yeah. "And inspect our ships. So we'll get you a plane, we'll put you in country, we'll tell you what we want you to do and where we want you to do it, and so forth." That's how I ended up in Vietnam, and more specifically in Danang, or sortied out of Danang, and got back home a couple weeks after that.

Paul Stillwell: What specifically did you do in Vietnam?

Admiral Meyer: We spent our time on two things. One was trying to establish the readiness of the ships, but more specifically talking to the staffs and the officers about how to, if that's come up again, how they could best go about their strike. And, of course, we're withdrawn now totally from North Korea. I mean, that all blew that way and now we're way the hell down in another part of the country. And we finally got out of there, the way I got out of there was on a Coast Guard plane, one of those planes with their big ears, a propeller plane.

Paul Stillwell: C-130?

Admiral Meyer: No, it wasn't that. I want to put a G in it. Christ, you have to fly half a day or longer to get to the Philippines. And so we had a couple days to rest in—what's the air base in Philippines then, the air station?

Paul Stillwell: Cubi Point?

Admiral Meyer: Yeah, Cubi Point. We had a couple days to rest and find our ways back home. And the mission blew away.

Paul Stillwell: Did you go out and do these assist visits on the ships off Vietnam?

Admiral Meyer: All of them. And then, of course, you had to do it by cable, so you had to be dropped by helo and you had to be snatched by helo because those little DLGs didn't have a platform.

Paul Stillwell: What was the state of readiness you found, both in the Sea of Japan and the Gulf of Tonkin?

Admiral Meyer: Well, it wasn't very good. I struggled a long time over whether to release it or not, and I finally reconciled that I guess it didn't matter, but it wasn't very good. On the other hand, based on the experience I had now gained in the previous years, some three or four years now, it was not out of order. And it bugged me and bugged me and bugged me, why couldn't they stay ready? What's the problem?

Now, you know, I'm not sure to this day that I've solved it or understand it. But that experience, combined with my other experiences there, but that specific classified experience led me, it motivated me, on what later became the Aegis design. I didn't know that was going to happen. I just didn't know that was all going to happen. But I reflected later where my motivation came from.

Paul Stillwell: Did you draw any conclusions on why the readiness wasn't what it should be?

Admiral Meyer: I did. And the conclusions aren't very well liked. There isn't anybody that particularly cares for them. It was the inability of the ships, starting right with the skippers, to stay focused on their priorities.

Now, it could be that that's the way life is. So I'll leap ahead here before we close for the day for a couple minutes because, as you know, for over ten years now I took on a task from Captain Peter "Mac" Grant through the next three admirals—it was only going to be three months long—to form a senior advisory team to help them on the killing of ballistic missiles in the ship *Lake Erie*, to not only provide oversight but to provide coaching and direction, because it's an all brand-new experience and such.* Did it right on this deck and in Hawaii. I can't believe I've spent—I'm in my 11th year on it now. It was going to be three months long.

From an earning viewpoint they've paid me well. I've been paid well. I haven't worked for nothing. Haven't gotten rich, but I've been paid well. And I think I've made major, major unsung contributions. I'll give you one particular example.

You know, most people think of fire control gear and the things that I do as being electronic in nature, and it's hard to keep people, even the people involved, thinking in electromechanical nature, not electronic nature. Because fire control, particularly, is highly dependent upon electromechanical systems which have to have a reliability that doesn't exist in very many places, actually. And in these big systems, starting with Talos of how I learned originally—and this is all learned by trial and error, discovery—is that when you don't have no cooling, you ain't got no beer. And in a ship, traditionally, as it emerged, cooling systems, don't you know, they're down in the engineering department. Fire control, that's in the gunnery department. Oh, and by the way, you have to have Type III electrical power, particularly 400-cycle power, and that's down in the electrical engineering department of the engineering department. Well, when you think about it— and it isn't that the people in the early days were dumb, it's just that they had no experience—this approach is doomed to failure, because there's no one accountable, one of the things I started learning in missilery when I went to Fort Bliss, Texas, initially and worked on a Terrier BW-0 team at McGregor Field.†

But then later it kept going up, going up, bigger and bigger. Now, the Talos radar was the highest-powered radar ever put to sea aboard ship. It was fired by big klystrons—they were just almost your size—to generate the power. Giants, on a rotating mount. And they had to have coolant, and a lot of it. Well, that means this water is going up through the rotary joints, all down to carry out heat, coming from down below and everything, in a very complex undertaking with almost no serious design effort applied to it by mechanical people. It was really the engineers kind of there on the spot, who were

---

* Captain Peter McPherson Grant, USN, program director of the Aegis Ballistic Missile Defense Project from 1997 to 2002.
† RIM-2A Terrier BW-0 was a beam-riding, wing-controlled missile, series 0. BW-1 was a more reliable successor, after which came BT-3, which was a beam-riding, tail-controlled missile, series 3, etc.

more electronic than anything else. I learned really, really, really, really tough lessons on that and the criticality and the seriousness of it.

The second I mentioned is electrical power. You could not do what we were doing in Talos, killing an airplane at 120 miles with semi-active illumination of a ten-kilowatt transmitter, the first one that was ever put to sea, unless you could assure that you could deliver the power with the requisite fidelity to produce the proper kind of signal that the missile would home on. I mean, this nation spent a lot of money on it. And to this day we look for other solutions to semi-active homing in killing airplanes. And you know what? All of them are wanting. We keep coming back to the same old thing, they're wanting. It's like: Well, you know, we're going to run our cars without gasoline, and we all end up coming back to it because the other solutions turned out weren't what they're cracked up to be.

Well, so those two things are not only bugaboos, they are disastrous in the readiness of fire control gear. The fire control schools provide almost zero training in those days.

Wayne comes into Aegis—I'm ratcheting ahead on you—I'm progressing with all my knowledge through the years, and in the modernization of the Terrier, the second high-powered transmitters, with something called ASMS, now called Aegis, which replaced the others as high-powered—you realize that today's Aegis transmitters in the ship we're building right here, those radars put out seven million watts of power? Seven million watts! The SPG-49 radars that I worked on, which were absolutely astounding with a tube as tall as you, were half that power. Well, you can't produce that kind of power with one tube. That's why the revolution of the Aegis transmitter is a whole series of tubes. In fact, there are 64 tubes in that radar. They all operate at one-kilowatt power. And the way we integrate up that power and bring it together at the microwave level is how we get seven million watts of power. And we don't kill anybody, and you can walk right up to that radar right there and put your hand on the face of it and it won't hurt you. Pretty amazing. Pretty amazing engineering, for which, of course, you get no credit.

But when I came tramping in to RCA—I'm leaping ahead, but this is just a little tidbit—RCA was not noted for its electromechanical prowess, and I said the first thing we're going to worry about is the cooling system. Who is this man from outer space that tells us this? We know how to build cooling systems. Well, how do you do it? Well, we go buy one. [Laughter] Aha! That's the way you do it. And where do you employ—well, it's true that we've done only shore-based radars and commercial radars, but we know how to do cooling systems. Well, the answer to that young man is: bullshit. That's that answer simply stated.

I put a lot of time on this. I mean, monstrous amounts of time, and money. We spent millions of dollars in Aegis getting fail-safe cooling systems for that radar.

Paul Stillwell: Why don't we get that next time? I've got one final question on Port Hueneme.

Admiral Meyer: Well, you can ask that in a minute. I want to cap that one shot; you shot me off.

Paul Stillwell: All right.

Admiral Meyer: I started out inspecting, down the hall from these fellows, over 20 years later, to examine the readiness of the ships. All this incredible work I had done my whole life. Guess what's down in the goddamn ships.

Paul Stillwell: All the cooling systems?

Admiral Meyer: You got it! [Laughter] You got it. Go to the head of the class. What's your question, your final question?

Paul Stillwell: What connection did you have with the *Norton Sound* when you were in that job at Port Hueneme?

Admiral Meyer: I ran her.

Paul Stillwell: Could you give me more detail on that?

Admiral Meyer: Well, she was administratively under CruDesPac, because nobody knew where to put her.* But for operational purposes she was under the custody of Port Hueneme. She was home-ported at Port Hueneme.

Paul Stillwell: What tests were you doing with her in that period of time?

Admiral Meyer: One big test is the Mark 86 gun fire control system for the 5-inch gun, which was a very advanced fire control system which exists to this day, which I don't believe would have ever worked without *Norton Sound*. The other was the installation of the new Mark 26 launcher into *Norton Sound*.† And I shall give you some stories later on the drama of that undertaking, and moving that old ship, sailing her, to Pascagoula, Mississippi, and sailing her back home successfully with our wonderful sailors, incredible drama. I don't know how many firings we did—I think around 30.

I say it's time to knock off.

Paul Stillwell: Well, that's an interesting note to end on. Thank you, Admiral.

---

* CruDesPac – Cruiser-Destroyer Force Pacific Fleet.
† Mark 26 was the designation of a twin-arm guided missile launcher on a ship's weather deck. It has since been replaced by a vertical launch system from cells inside the ship.

Interview Number 11 with Rear Admiral Wayne E. Meyer, U.S. Navy (Retired)
Place: Admiral Meyer's office in Arlington, Virginia
Date: Tuesday, 17 June 2008

Paul Stillwell: Admiral, we're at the point chronologically where you had the tour out at Port Hueneme and ready to come into Washington and get involved in Aegis, and I guess a couple questions initially—if you could comment on the value of Admiral Withington's committee, and then talk about the status of the program when you arrived.*

Admiral Meyer: When the special Navy task force was born, the popular expression in our Navy was the 4-T's. There were four T's. But rapidly the expression became 3-T's.

Paul Stillwell: The fourth being Typhon?

Admiral Meyer: The fourth being Typhon, and Terrier, Tartar and Talos being the ones not only in development simultaneously but also going into service. A lot of harm was done in many ways by the reformers in those programs, because they demanded a lot of serial operations in engineering as a result of that program which were totally unnecessary and aren't necessary to this day. Polaris has never done it, for example. Minuteman never did it.† The truth is, they tried to solve other flaws by failed leadership. Without leadership it doesn't matter much what the organization is or what kind of program you put together. So the 3-T's, which were meant to introduce our Navy into the new air defense era. When I was a junior officer, virtually every one of my leaders and seniors were terrified about the kamikaze.

Now, I was just reading something yesterday—I can't think even what paper or magazine. But I really got quite pissed off about Nisei Americans writing in letters about their treatment in World War II. I happen to reject that outright as pure bullshit. I

---

* In early 1964 the Navy, specifically the Advanced Surface Missile System (ASMS), sought indications of interest from private industry for project definition. In August of that year, the Navy sought conceptual designs from seven contractors. After the Navy received the proposals, it recalled to active duty Rear Admiral Frederic S. Withington, USN (Ret.), to serve as chairman of the ASMS Assessment Group. Withington had served as Chief of the Bureau of Ordnance from November 1954 to March 1958. His oral history is in the Naval Institute collection.

† Minuteman was a land-based intercontinental ballistic missile under Air Force control.

happened to be present then and I happened to be in our Navy then, too, and I just reject that as pure bullshit. I tell you one thing, the American people didn't have a lot of taste for these people, and in spite of their birthing and their complaints, they never bothered to become citizens until they ended up being forced to become citizens. So I don't have a hell of a lot of sympathy for them. Now, did a few get abused or mistreated as a result of these sweeping policies? That would be true. A number of them did. That would be true.[*]

Paul Stillwell: Well, can we move back to Admiral Withington?

Admiral Meyer: Yeah. Well, so all of these officers came back supporting dragging our Navy into the missile defense era: How are we going to defend against the kamikaze? And so they were for anything. And I made the point earlier to you, I believe, that in the early '50s, I was ordered to Fort Bliss, Texas, to guided missile school for a year, because the Navy saw fit to start getting officers at lieutenant (j.g.) and lieutenant level ready for what was going to happen. Interesting enough, so did the graduate school. Now, the graduate school changes came about primarily, I think, when Arleigh Burke took over, however, which was a few years later. And so the graduate school started grinding out officers, which I attended, in ordnance engineering but was really oriented to guided missilery and to propulsion and guidance and aerodynamics and so forth. And it was a mixed crew of BuAer and BuOrd.

So when I went to Fort Bliss, Texas, there were maybe, I don't know, 75 or 80 or even 100 guided-missile programs in motion in the services, and the new Air Force was just virtually out of control. And one of the Wilsons got so upset that he convinced Dr. Keller to come in to OSD and Dr. Keller, who was president of—I don't think he was one of the founders of Chrysler but he was a very old one—was the president of Chrysler at

---

[*] Shortly after the Japanese attack on Pearl Harbor in December 1941, individuals of Japanese extraction—including those born in the United States—were relocated from the West Coast to inland internment camps. The U.S. Government feared they would sabotage the American war effort. In the 1980s the government paid compensation to the Japanese-Americans because of the relocation.

that time.* Wilson brought him in to try to straighten it out. Dr. Keller created the guided-missile nomenclature.† He was successful at getting OSD to issue an order that it will be used, and that nomenclature is in use to this very day. For example, SAM, meaning surface-to-air missile; SSM, meaning surface-to-surface missile. Those nomenclatures were formed and shaped, and I learned a really important thing as I was— I think I was a lieutenant in that era, that you couldn't get very far in running anything without adequate nomenclature, because people couldn't communicate. You had to have a vocabulary. And so that was an impressive lesson on my life.

He started winnowing all these programs down. He cut the Air Force down to, like, seven or eight programs, and the Navy down to half a dozen programs, and so on. And eventually, then, by the time that the special task force was born in 1962, there formed under that flag the shaping of the Navy's program, in particular the surface-to-air, or some called ship-to-air, missilery. And air-to-air went with that. That was the so-called Eli Reich task force.

Keller supported that discipline, and even though Keller was now gone, his followers had created that discipline in DoD. Eli Reich was no dummy, and he adapted to it just like that. And, as I say, it's here to this day. So we have surface-to-air, we have air-to-air, and so forth and so on. One might think we don't even do gunnery anymore, it's so dominated by missilery.

Paul Stillwell: Well, can we jump to the time that you came to Washington?

Admiral Meyer: Yeah. I'm trying to get there. I was piddling around there, piddling-ass around, and I had a point.

So eventually I landed in the task force and I landed at Port Hueneme. It's significant to my life of how God the Father was ordering my tours around preparing me.

---

* Charles E. Wilson served as Secretary of Defense from 28 January 1953 to 8 October 1957. He was nicknamed "Engine Charlie" because he had previously been chairman of the board of General Motors. Another Charles E. Wilson was chief executive officer of General Electric Corporation in the same era. His nickname was "Electric Charlie."
† Dr. K. T. Keller was director of the Office of Guided Missiles in the Department of Defense, 1950-53, during the administration of President Harry S. Truman. That predated Wilson's service as Secretary of Defense.

I didn't appreciate this till late in life, that I was somehow being prepared, almost vocationally being prepared.

Paul Stillwell: God working through BuPers.

Admiral Meyer: Exactly right. [Laughter] You're right.

Paul Stillwell: Could we come back to Admiral Withington?

Admiral Meyer: Okay. Admiral Withington was a retired chief of the Bureau of Ordnance, which was a very prestigious post in that era.

Paul Stillwell: And an ordnance PG.

Admiral Meyer: And an ordnance PG. And, as you are acquainted, I'm sure, that there were important posts in BuOrd and BuShips, like the chief ballistician and the chief mathematician and things like that. They were key posts that existed, and they reported directly to the chief all the time.

Well, in this reformation of the task force and the crushing together of BuAer and BuOrd it ended up, in essence, no organization. So that the task force became the power center—in our part of the Navy anyhow. Aviation had a hell of a time sorting out their future and where they were going to go. It put aviation on a downhill road to this day. My view is the Navy will never design and build an airplane again, ever. It'll buy its airplanes henceforth through the Air Force or someplace.

Paul Stillwell: The merger that created BuWeps lasted for just seven years, and then it went back to Naval Air and Naval Ordnance Systems Commands.

Admiral Meyer: It did, because Admiral Kidd, who was smarter than all the rest of us put together, he looked at the other services with such great admiration: My brothers in the other services, the Army and the Air Force, have chiefs and systems commands, and that's what we need to solve the Navy's problems.* And that's how we got that, and we have yet to recover from it. We remain in a wounded state and a reduced capacity to this day.† The bureaus were not commands and they never will be commands. It is not an effective command post. They were properly named. We think of bureaus in a derogatory way; there's nothing derogatory about a bureau at all. A bureau is a very effective way to govern democratic people. Nothing wrong with it. But we look at it with our head high.

Paul Stillwell: Well, what value did Admiral Withington bring to this process?

Admiral Meyer: We couldn't get all this mess straightened out—Reich couldn't get it straightened out. So he got the Secretary, who was Nitze, to recall the admiral to active duty, put him in charge of a study, which came to be known as the Withington Study, of what should the future of the Navy be.‡ In one sense, the piece of work I'm on now is finally the follower of that study. Well, it's the fourth derivative or fifth derivative of it. And this study, I'm sorry to report, no one pays any attention to. But those people commanded great prestige, and when they were brought front and center they showed up. You can see around here, no one pays very much attention to me.

So out of that, in our side, he labeled the Typhon to be put back in development. Pieces of Typhon were scheduled into *Norton Sound*. And he labeled the Tartar's development to be pursued because it had not really been prosecuted up till then. This was a breakthrough in a one-stage engine, or a dual-thrust motor, which gave you two stages in one motor. So the Tartar became a little Terrier, a baby Terrier. Hence, hence, destroyers became possible with guided missiles. It's an unsung breakthrough; you don't hear anything about it. We landed Terrier in the destroyer *Gyatt* and we couldn't cut it;

---

* Admiral Isaac C. Kidd, Jr., USN, served as Chief of Naval Material from 1 December 1971 to 18 April 1975—several years after the systems commands were created in 1966.
† In 1985, Secretary of the Navy John Lehman disestablished the Naval Material Command and redistributed functions among the various systems commands. For a summary of the reorganization, see Norman Polmar, "The U.S. Navy: Command Changes," *U.S. Naval Institute Proceedings*, December 1985, pages 156-157.
‡ Paul H. Nitze served as Secretary of the Navy from 29 November 1963 to 30 June 1967.

the ship was just not adequate.* It was not laid out correctly, it was not large enough, it didn't have adequate power, and all those things. So eventually to the *Charles Francis Adams*-class destroyer, which only a few months ago the Aussies put, I think, the last ones out of service.† I believe all the Germans are out of service now, and the Aussies, just I think this past spring, put the last ones out of service.

Paul Stillwell: Well, and that's 40-some years out of those ships.

Admiral Meyer: It's an incredible ship, incredible ship, and people who commanded those ships just loved them. Well, it turned out the DLGs were pretty damned good ships too. They had early little problems with steam and with propulsion, but they overcame them and became really, really good ships, and sleek ships.

Well, I think I covered with you how Reich got the project funded, the task force. He got it out of Typhon, and Typhon was put back on the lab table, and it lay there all those years.‡ But there were fundamentals within the Withington report that kept a-brewing and a-brewing and a-brewing. So after about a five-year period they'd finally bubbled up. And I'm not sure to this day why Reich did it, but Reich was a wily person, as I've told you. Reich thought far more of me than he ever told me. He beat my ass repeatedly but he really—I mean he came right down into the task force and got me whenever he wanted me, starting right in the cruiser *Galveston*. So then it was natural that Woods, who was now chief of NavOrd, it was natural that when they finally decided they were going to do the ASMS, Advanced Surface Missile System, that would now be named Aegis, a name created by one Captain Lewis J. Stecher, the youngest of the Stecher brothers who were captains.§

---

* USS *Gyatt* (DD-712), a *Gearing*-class destroyer, was commissioned 2 July 1945. In 1955-56, at the Boston Naval Shipyard, she was converted to become the world's first guided missile destroyer with a two-rail Terrier missile launcher. She was reclassified DDG-712 on 1 December 1956 and reclassified DDG-1 on 23 May 1957.
† USS *Charles F. Adams* (DDG-2), first of her class, was commissioned 10 September 1960—a few years before the convening of Admiral Withington's assessment group.
‡ Secretary of Defense Robert McNamara cancelled the Typhon program on 27 November 1963, with the exception of continued testing of the SPG-59 radar on board the *Norton Sound*.
§ Rear Admiral Mark W. Woods, USN, served as Commander Naval Ordnance Systems Command from May 1969 to July 1972. Captain Lewis Joseph Stecher Jr., USN. The system was renamed Aegis in December 1969.

The only requirement in the hallowed halls of Dr. Foster, who was DDR&E at that time, the only requirement was it could not have an identity with the 3-T's.[*] We had allowed an outrageous description to emerge of the terrible T's. We'd allowed that to happen, and *no* officer stood up to defend the program. No one! Not even Eli defended it very well. He recovered it and rescued it, but he didn't defend it; he just thought it was a terrible program. Well, it wasn't. By God, it wasn't. To this day it has proven itself time and time again.

Paul Stillwell: Well, Aegis has more of a ring to it than ASMS.

Admiral Meyer: Oh, yes. Yes. Well, through those years—McNamara decreed it—the Navy did not need more than a 50-mile missile. So as the Withington study, and closure was coming on ASMS under what was known as DCP-16, Development Concept Paper 16, which was the mechanism which Foster had introduced to define programs. To this day the Aegis program, if it has any guidance at all, it's DCP-16 Rev 1. I created Rev 1, and that's all those years, now three decades, more than three decades, is what it's been working under. Four decades now.

Paul Stillwell: Was the demise of Typhon, in your view, a wise step? Do you think that was wise to cancel that program?

Admiral Meyer: No, but it was therapeutic.

Paul Stillwell: What do you mean by that?

Admiral Meyer: Well, it was wise in that sense, because it did give the wake-ups calls to the people in the structure that, hey, we're going to have to get a better structure and apply people in a better way if we're going to get anyplace.

---

[*] Dr. John S. Foster, Jr., served as Director of Defense Research and Engineering, 1965-73.

Well, something else helped us, and it was the Egyptians, when they decided to go out one day and sink the Israeli destroyer.* That little thing is what tripped it all, just a little incident. And it took a couple years for it to waken, but it woke up. And that's where I learned, frankly, from that era. The reason we have the shipbuilding—and I'm jumping ahead for a minute—the reason we have it is Reagan.† I never heard of John Lehman.‡ I don't know that Lehman ever heard of him. He was some payoff as the Secretary of the Navy, to the President. Lehman was a schemer, and is a schemer. I should speak of him in the present since he exists, and may very well be back on the scene for all I know. But Lehman knew how to assess plans and run with them.

During that early era, while Reagan was awakening, we were dormant in ASMS.§ But one thing we did—and we stumbled into this, fumbled into it, planning, planning, planning, because I'd had it laid on me in the task force. It wasn't brilliance at all; it was that no one seemed to much care what we did. So we worked on a plan, we worked on a plan. I had about four or five OP-03s before Jim Doyle came along.** And Jim Doyle decided, well we're going to get a shipbuilding plan too. He snatched one Captain Bob Monroe and one Commander Henry Mustin, locked them in a closet, and put them to work.†† He said, "We're gong to get a shipbuilding plan." And that's what they did for two years. And that's how this plan was born, of the ship numbers.

Then I agreed with him that we were going to decide what the character of the ship ought to be. So I had an officer stationed in OP-03. He had an officer who was here in PMS-400, that we had now named it, and when he wasn't here he had our code, but he resided over in the Pentagon.‡‡ And we had this closeness that emerged that has never emerged again, and I don't believe is in any other program except perhaps the

---

* On 21 October 1967, while near the entrance to the Suez Canal, the Israeli destroyer *Elath*, also known as *Eilat*, was sunk by Styx surface-to-surface missiles fired from an Egyptian patrol boat inside the harbor at Port Said, Egypt. The attack killed 59 of the 250 crew members on board the *Elath*.
† Ronald W. Reagan was President of the United States from 1981 to 1989.
‡ John F. Lehman Jr., served as Secretary of the Navy from 5 February 1981 to 10 April 1987.
§ The keel for the first Aegis-equipped ship, the cruiser *Ticonderoga* (CG-47) was laid on 21 January 1980. Reagan became President a year later, 20 January 1981.
** Vice Admiral James H. Doyle, Jr., USN, served as Deputy Chief of Naval Operations (Surface Warfare) from August 1975 to September 1980.
†† Captain Robert R. Monroe, USN; Captain Henry C. Mustin, USN. Both eventually retired as vice admirals.
‡‡ In 1977 the Aegis Shipbuilding Program Office was established within the Naval Sea Systems Command and designated as PMS-400.

submariners. The submariners follow their senior leader. It's a big difference. Surface Navy doesn't do that.

So that step started formulating the characterization of these ships and the numbers of these ships.

Paul Stillwell: Well, the character had been established. The *Ticonderoga* was already well on her way by the time Lehman became Secretary.

Admiral Meyer: Only, really, in advanced engineering. But the point was, we had a plan and Lehman took the plan. He went to Reagan with it and he came back with a 600-ship program, of which these ships ultimately came to 27 cruisers. It just so happened that's the way the numbers worked out for protection of the aircraft carriers and the amphibious fleets. So it was three for the amphibious fleets and the other 24, two per strike group. That's how you got 27. And then they came out with the number of 50, or thereabouts, for destroyers. That's how those were born.

Paul Stillwell: Well, can we go back to 1970, please, when you were coming in from Port Hueneme. What was your role in the Aegis organization at that point, after God and BuPers had sent you there?

Admiral Meyer: I reported in to the special Navy task force, or its residues, now called the surface missile system project. It no longer reported in to chief of NavMat; it reported now to chief of NavOrd, but had additional duty to NavMat. And then-Captain Merrill Homer Sappington became the commander of it, the manager. So I reported in back here to Captain Merrill Homer Sappington, and I reported in to be the captain of ASMS. That's what I reported in to, now named Aegis. So I think four still remained. There was Tartar, Talos, Terrier, and ASMS, now called Aegis. But this Typhon was undergoing a name change, or a mutation, that was going to become the point defense outfit, or self-defense outfit.

Well, the flag list came out that subsequent year. Sappington already had his papers in, was going home. The flag list came out, and Sappington was on it.[*] It had been intended for me to fleet up to relieve him; that was his plan. Well, it was decided for him to remain there for most of a year, which he did, and that I would ultimately fleet up, which gave me one more year to kind of solidify organizationally what was to go on.

Well, in the meantime there was a lot of turmoil in the systems commands. The last chief of the NavOrd was Spreen, and it was crushed into NavSea.[†]

Paul Stillwell: That happened in '74 when that merger took place.

Admiral Meyer: Yeah, okay. I need you for all of your beautiful chronological recalls.

So we piddled that year—are we going to kill it or are we going to keep it? Are we going to kill it? Going to keep it? Going to kill it? It was off, on, off, on, off, on. In truth I was its savior and its salvager. The program as it stood was not salvageable. So myself and whoever wanted to follow me, we just reformed the program on a table like this, redid it and restructured it. And I got RCA behind me and Computer Sciences behind me.

Paul Stillwell: Did you have to redo the contracts with RCA?

Admiral Meyer: We just polished it up a little bit and went at it. Because, interesting enough, John Flaherty was the contracting officer, and John Flaherty had grown up under me in my first tour.[‡] He thought I was going to be a big shot, and so he wanted to tie himself to me, so John Flaherty wanted to please me. John Flaherty's in the graveyard now, but by God he was good, and he raised a crew behind him that were good, and I had the advantage of those even after he got promoted on up to higher places and stuff. So I had the good fortune the whole rest of my time in the Navy of really top-drawer contracting officers.

---

[*] Sappington's date of rank as rear admiral was 1 July 1972.
[†] Rear Admiral Roger E. Spreen, USN, was Commander Naval Ordnance Systems Command, 1972-74.
[‡] John Flaherty, a civilian, was a contracting officer in Naval Sea Systems Command, later moved to the Naval Material Command.

Now, what do I mean by that? I mean I'm talking about contracting officers who want to work to get something done, not to work for themselves. The longstanding traditional problem with contracting outfits is they work for themselves. They don't work for a project. People are always stunned that the contracting officers weren't in my project. Well, they weren't. Only SP had enough power to have its own contracting officers, and only Rickover had enough power to do that. Didn't anybody else in the Navy have that power.

Paul Stillwell: Why was RCA amenable to go along with your changes? How did it help RCA?

Admiral Meyer: I knew Bill Goodwin for a number of years.[*] He was the Aegis manager. He was the same age I was. He had been a radio technician in the war and then he'd gone to school, worked for Bendix, transferred to RCA. And he was the one in fact captured this contract. And as a result 30 Rockefeller had no choice except to promote him, I guess, and they did.[†] They made him Aegis, and in the first years of Aegis the RCA annual report would not even recognize us or mention it. It was anti-war. Thirty Rockefeller Center wanted nothing to do with it.

Paul Stillwell: Well, the whole country was that way at the time.

Admiral Meyer: Yeah, they wanted nothing to do with it. So in essence RCA didn't want the program. What there was, though, was a little band of brothers and sisters that wanted the program.

Paul Stillwell: Was Bill Goodwin their leader?

Admiral Meyer: He led that group, and Bill Goodwin believed in me, and I believed in Bill Goodwin. And so we just defied the goddamn world. We just took them on. And

---

[*] William V. Goodwin worked for RCA from 1959 to 1987. He was vice president of the Missile and Surface Radar Division from 1978 to 1987.
[†] RCA's corporate headquarters were at 30 Rockefeller Plaza in New York City.

the first thing I did was trash the terms that they had in the contracts, and I turned the contract into a cost-plus-award-fee contract, and I started handling it that way, that every four months we'd make a decision on an award fee. They loved it, and I loved it. And I brought in award-fee contracts in our Navy—or brought them back, I should say. The reason they didn't exist in the Navy is they had a terrible name. The reason they had a terrible name is the government just so abused industry with them and beat industry so badly that industry wouldn't sign such contracts. RCA signed the contract with me, and the terms were—I just might mention that—in the R&D contracts they could earn up to 15 cents.* I guaranteed them a profit. I guaranteed them three cents. They couldn't go below three cents. But they could earn up to 15. They never earned 15. They earned anywheres from 10 to 12, someplace in that vicinity.

Paul Stillwell: You're talking about that many cents on a dollar.

Admiral Meyer: Yeah, in profit. And I mean just good profit, no-strings-attached profit. Well, it was too good in the early years. We had to learn how to hide it a little bit, because Bill Goodwin wasn't about to give it to those bastards at 30 Rockefeller. [Laughter] So we had to think about how to secrete this money. So in the union which we formed between the government, the Navy, and he, that's how we got all our new development work started. And that's how we've been able to move the Aegis into this incredible, this *incredible* digital age. The signal processor in Aegis today is two cabinets, pretty damned big cabinets. But the Typhon cabinets were some 40 cabinets in the signal processor; they would not fit in these spaces here.

Paul Stillwell: Well, you needed a good-sized ship to support Typhon.

Admiral Meyer: I needed a massive ship. A minimum is a cruiser. Well, to take the first Aegis to sea we had 24 cabinets in the sig processor alone, just the signal processor. By the time we went to *Norton Sound*, we were now down to 14 cabinets. This is what good engineering does for you, Paul. You can't get these yo-yos around this place to

---

* R&D – research and development.

understand that, that the way you get better products is through better engineering. And it really pisses me off. GE's slogan for a long time was "GE brings good things to life," and they violate their own slogans, because they get so profit oriented that they forget how you earn money.

So Bill came off the rocks, and I had come off the rocks and we were hard workers, and we were determined. I want to say we both believed, we believed that the situation was really serious. This was before 1970, and we believed that a serious situation was aborning. And we believed that we might be the only outfit that really appreciated the headlong rush of the digital into shipboard things. It's true that SP had adopted a lot of the digit into its specialized systems. But we now were finding ourselves having to adopt it in a broad shipboard basis, and we took it on. We adopted the principle that we'd do our experimenting and research in the laboratory. It was primarily APL.[*] We would do our engineering in industry, and it was primarily RCA. It was RCA-led. That's an important principle. Today none of these programs are sorted out that way. Right now the 1000, for example, it's all mixed in one gunnysack. And what are you going to get when it comes out? You're going to get ground bran.

I've mentioned to you in this relatively short boring period three significant learnings that I underwent while in a leadership position that made me what I am, but made the program what it is. We decided from day one we were going to do the best to do it right, and so we took all—you should have been with me at our first major review after seven years of adopting what I call the Wright-Pat, for Wright-Patterson, new theology of how to write specs and how to write requirements. And we had our first review, we had a massive overflow of several hundred people, but the books had to be brought in by carts, cart after cartful of books that we were expected to look at and review. I fixed that the first day. Put them over in that room and you don't take them out until we call for them. We never looked at them again. We just started over.

Paul Stillwell: What kind of feedback did you get from OSD and the General Accounting Office to this contract that you made with RCA?

---

[*] APL – the Applied Physics Lab of Johns Hopkins University.

Admiral Meyer: Well, some of it wasn't good. [Chuckle] But they also got a little scared, because—I didn't think I had started out to do this, but somehow I did—I developed some pretty darn good relations with congressional staffs, and the reason was there were people in those staffs that truly believed that we were in trouble from this cruise missile and we needed to get hot on it.[*] And I could tell you some of their names to this day, the staffs. One was Hy Fine, who couldn't even say the multiplication tables but his Jewish mind was so good, and he trusted in me so much that what he said was going to be done was done.[†] And he started teaching me. "Captain," he said, "I'm going to teach you how Congress works."

Paul Stillwell: What staff was he on?

Admiral Meyer: Well, let's see. Hy Fine was on the Armed Services. He exerted an extraordinary amount of respect, though, throughout the whole congressional staff. It wasn't the size it is today, of course. I mean, there was only a few hundred then. But he was well, well respected, Hy Fine was. But he was a money man. But the important thing was those people had to believe in you, and if they believed in you, you got it. Now, Tony Battista became a big supporter. I don't know whether you ever knew Tony Battista.[‡]

Paul Stillwell: No; I've heard of him.

Admiral Meyer: Tony Battista had started as a civil servant down at Dahlgren and, since I'd known him for some time I knew how to pronounce his name. Very few people did. They called him "Batteesta," and he detested that.

Paul Stillwell: Like the Cuban dictator.[§]

---

[*] This is another reference to the Egyptian Styx missile sinking the Israeli destroyer *Elath* in 1967.
[†] Hyman Fine, a member of the professional staff of the Senate Armed Services Committee.
[‡] Anthony R. Battista, a member of the professional staff of the House Armed Services Committee.
[§] Fulgencio Batista was the dictator and military leader who was President of Cuba from 10 October 1940 to 10 October 1944 and from 10 March 1952 to 1 January 1959. His government was overthrown by rebels under the leadership of Fidel Castro.

Admiral Meyer: Yeah. He detested that name. But I called him Battista, and every time I showed up he'd just beam. Every time I showed up I'd be sitting over there in a back row, and somebody would be under Tony's fire and he'd say—he had the R&D subcommittee on Armed Forces—he'd say, "Well, have you asked Captain Meyer about this?" Some subject I didn't know anything about. Well, that really changes the respect level on you.

So the importance of having them with you not only was critical, but I'm a big ground truth man. I strongly believe in it. I just believe the truth won't hurt you, and if it will hurt you then you haven't handled it well someplace. I don't mean to go out and stand on the street corner. I told my people repeatedly we're not going to go out on the street corner and commit hara-kari.[*] That's not being truthful; that's being hara-kari. But we must frame the truth the way that the people who get it can understand it. You can't go give some learned goddamn lecture on a Fourier transform to people in Congress that can't understand it. You can't get anyplace that way. So you've got to reframe that in a way that they grasp it.

And I remember this one day—a little sea story. In those days Commander George Meinig—he was a commander then; he's a retired admiral now.[†] But George was with me as one of my technical directors; we were over there testifying. And Strom Thurmond was sitting up there, and they were quizzing away and trying to understand.[‡] So George was trying to explain to Strom how Phalanx worked under control of the Aegis and the radar, and he couldn't get it.[§] Finally George got up from his chair alongside me and walked up and started talking to him, and finally Thurmond said, "Oh, I get it. That's just like you lead to shoot a rabbit, isn't it?"

George said, "Senator, you've got it. That's just the way it is."

Paul Stillwell: Frame it so they can understand it.

---

[*] Hara-kiri, also known as seppuku, is Japanese ritual suicide.
[†] Commander George R. Meinig Jr., USN, an ordnance engineering duty officer.
[‡] J. Strom Thurmond, who represented South Carolina at different times as both a Democrat and Republican, served in the Senate from 7 November 1956 to 3 January 2003.
[§] The Vulcan/Phalanx close-in weapon system includes a tracking radar and six-barrel rapid-fire Gatling gun for use against incoming antiship missiles. The system entered the fleet in 1980.

Admiral Meyer: You've got to frame it so he could understand it.

We came under assault in the same committee another time on why we would not use the Army Patriot in Aegis. And I mean the pressure was on heavy now.

Paul Stillwell: What period was that?

Admiral Meyer: Well, I know what time of the year, but I don't know whether I can tell you which year, but you'll know. Because it was on St. Joseph's Day. St. Joseph's Day is March 19.[*] We were over there testifying, and I had not gone out for a firing operation in *Norton Sound*, a big countermeasures operation. Commander Bob Beers had gone out to be out there because I had to stay back here to get ready.[†] But Bob flew all night to be back here off the ship to be able to report at this hearing. But this guy from Indiana was a big Patriot person, and he was a big anti-Aegis person.

Paul Stillwell: Birch Bayh?

Admiral Meyer: Birch Bayh.[‡] Thank you. And he was determined that we were wasting money, and what we ought to do is kill this thing and put Patriot in it. I can't remember who the chairman was. Anyhow, they invited him to come over and participate, which he did. He got up and he started asking his questions, and he was obviously ill prepared.

Paul Stillwell: You're saying Birch Bayh was ill prepared?

Admiral Meyer: It was Birch Bayh, I'm pretty sure. So he was kind of standing on the side in the hearing room on the steps there asking his questions and a big thunderstorm came up while we were there. St. Joseph's Day. So I was keeping control of the conversation and Tony Battista was sitting back enjoying the show while it was going on, because he knew I was going to win.

---

[*] The year was 1975.
[†] Commander Robert C. Beers, USN, an ordnance engineering duty officer.
[‡] Birch E. Bayh, a Democrat from Indiana, served in the Senate from 3 January 1963 to 3 January 1981.

Paul Stillwell: And Bayh was hassling you about whether it would work in ill weather.

Admiral Meyer: Right. Exactly right. [Chuckle] So you know about the famous thunderclap.

Paul Stillwell: Well, I just read about it last night. [Laughter]

Admiral Meyer: Oh, you did? Oh. So right in the middle of this, and Bob Beers was back there now and he was sitting behind me, was this monstrous thunderclap right over the building. Just a monster. You know how the lightning comes and you wait and God the Father speaks at you? And for just a couple seconds everybody was stunned. They were just stunned, and just looked at each other. And finally this guy said, "It's all right, Captain, don't do it again. I won't ask you any more questions." And that ended that. [Laughter] Well, that story made it all the way back over here before I ever got here, about that day. That was an incredible day. We really had something that day.

Paul Stillwell: Well, back to OSD and the GAO. Did they bless your new contracts with RCA? Did they challenge them?

Admiral Meyer: Well, by now I had pretty good congressional support. And by now I had pretty good support, and a lot of it came from Jim Doyle, out of the Bureau of the Budget, out of BuBud. And so they were constantly in a tug of war of their own. The truth is, they never did bless them and they never did un-bless them either; they just got to where they tolerated it.

Paul Stillwell: Well, that was sufficient.

Admiral Meyer: Yeah, that was good enough for me. That's what I tell my troops. And they say, "Did you win it, Captain?"

"We won it. It's ours." I've said repeatedly, I've never lost a nickel. In my 13 years of leading Aegis I never lost a nickel. I always got the money. And I thought that

that was something pretty significant, since people all around you lose money repeatedly. You take even nicks if nothing else, little hits. I never lost any.

The other thing that never happened in Aegis: The Aegis never had an overrun. Never. They didn't have it after I left. Now, why didn't we have an overrun?

Paul Stillwell: Well, that was my next question. You've already anticipated it.

Admiral Meyer: Well, I usually draw three routes up on this blackboard in running a program. And there's no room up there. But there are three lanes on this highway. The two outriggers—one lane is the temporal schedule, the time schedule. The other lane is the fiscal schedule, how much time do you have, how many dollars do you have? The center lane is the technical lane. Well, the technical lane is where you're trying to get to, in performance. But you know, damned few managers guard the others.

Right now, right now on the F-35 they're ignoring the center lane.[*] That airplane's in overrun right now. The F-22 is in overrun. Well, the Air Force has this massive lobby structure to overcome overruns, but I don't believe in them in the first place. What I believe in is trying to do what you've been funded to do in the time you've been given to do it. So what you have on those three lanes constantly as the manager is keeping those lanes apace with each other. It sounds simple, and it's easy to say. Of course, it's hard to execute. And one of the reasons it's hard to execute is that managers make mistakes in tracking the technical program. They'll have a four-month review or a six-month review or something like that, and by the time they see it, it's too late. They can't do anything about it. It's out of control. They've lost it. Now they're in a situation where they've got to go tell somebody they're in trouble. "Well, we've got a problem here, yeah, but wait a minute; we can work our way out of this." "Yeah, we're six weeks behind, but we can overcome; we've got a plan here to overcome." You never, never overcome schedule, dollars or time. When it's gone, it's gone. You can't overcome. This day passes tonight and it's gone; we can't get it back. Whatever money you run up for bills today occurs, and tomorrow can't affect it. You owe it, period.

---

[*] The Lockheed Martin F-35 Lightning II is a joint strike fighter under development.

Those sound simple, but they're a state of mind and behavior. It's not beating on people or banging on people; it's creating a state of mind and it's trying to make every person feel some responsibility for operating in the structure we've got. Well, how in the hell are they going to do that if they don't know your structure?

Now I'll start right at the top. And they do it to this day. In my day there was a habit of when you were sent for at the Pentagon, only the officer went. Sometimes he would take one junior officer with him, and go over there and resolve issues of one kind or another. And they'd come back home, and of course now it would be a quarter to 6:00 and everybody's gone. And by the time you got around the news the next day, half your people are spread out and gone someplace else. Civil servants were never on board.

Now, this wasn't my brilliance at all, I want to tell you. It's because of the way I was raised, goddammit. Because people are people. I've never met a lousy civil servant, just like I've never met a lousy officer. I've met some that ain't very good, but I'll tell you there are some damned fine ones. And I had a structure, believe it or not—now remember, I reported in—now that I think about it—it was this very week, I think, in 1970, June. Over Fourth of July weekend I had my first budget crisis, and that Saturday I had to call in a whole bunch of people, officers and civil servants, to figure out how we were going to address this issue, because this is my first slash and burn. It turns out, in those buildings over there, in the middle building, in those days, the air-conditioning was run on Saturday until 12:00 o'clock.

Paul Stillwell: Was this in the Munitions Building?

Admiral Meyer: No, no. No, I'm talking about NC-2.

Paul Stillwell: Oh, in Crystal City.

Admiral Meyer: Crystal City. The reason it was on till noon on Saturday is Rickover paid for it to keep it running, because these sons of bitches who signed the contracts for these buildings decided no, we didn't need air-conditioning. No, nobody works on Saturdays. Well, there's a hell of a lot of people work on Saturday, including in this building right here. I mean, you'd come in here on Saturday in Techmatics and Anteon, this whole deck would be full of people. So it is the genius of detached contractoring who sign these stupid contracts. So we'd only have air-conditioning on Saturday until noon. And, of course, in July it only took a half hour for it to get hotter than hell.

I was very apologetic that afternoon, and the civil servants felt it. They came to me that night, and they said, "Look, don't worry about that; let's just worry about whether you're going to get the job done." Because already the budget was under slash. Already the budget was under assault.

Paul Stillwell: By whom?

Admiral Meyer: I want to say it was the House staff but whom I didn't know. That's what I want to say it was. As I recollect it had something like $80-some million in it, which was a big number in those days, and they already are going to slash about $20 million out of it. Because there were a lot of people didn't want Aegis, a hell of a lot of them. It's also why I learned—that's an era when I starting learning who you pay attention to. So when a guy like Hy Fine or Charlie Cromwell tells you, "Don't worry about it, Captain," I quit worrying about it.* Because I learned where the power sources are in the structure.

Paul Stillwell: So how did you respond to this particular crisis? What was the result?

Admiral Meyer: We slammed a paper in on Monday to OpNav. But I started learning my lessons real, real quick. That paper would take forever, so I realized that I had to be like the FBI; I had to develop other sources. I had to get that paper over in the hands of people I didn't yet know. I'd only reported in. So I had to take the word of one of my civil servants.

I learned another important thing, and I learned it in the next few years, and it's why you need to know people, why you need to listen to people. I have no idea what you did this weekend, what you did last week, or who you even associated with. But the

---

* Charles H. Cromwell, a member of the professional staff of the Senate Armed Services Committee.

knowledge that people have you never know is there if you don't try to pull it out. It's amazing what civil servants know. Nobody ever asks them. But what's more important is who they live around and who they live with. So all of a sudden you'll find you've got a GS-13 that lives alongside a staffer, out someplace in Virginia or out someplace in Maryland. All of a sudden you discover this. That's never volunteered until you start scratching. Or—"Well, you know, Captain, you know, I know Charlie; you know, would that be any help if I talked to Charlie about this?"

I said, "Well, what do you think we ought to talk about?"

"Well, whatever data you think I ought to talk to him about." So pretty soon you've got these networks forming.

Paul Stillwell: Did people start volunteering this kind of information?

Admiral Meyer: When they start believing in you. When they start believing in you, I found. Man, I tell you, those are my wonderful years. I never ever had a civil servant refuse to work or refuse to come when I asked for it. Not once. Never. I had to discipline a couple civil servants in my 13 years. I had to do the same with some officers. But it was rare indeed. So the performance of people kind of stunned me. One way it went up is I wouldn't go to the Pentagon without dragging two or three of them with me. I've said to them when I get back, and said "I want you all to go over there and hear the torture I get. You take some of it for a while." [Laughter] "And start learning how we've got to respond."

I found out there's nothing worse. You have civil servants work their ass off writing point papers for you or putting something together, and you don't even use the goddamn stuff. You don't even use it.

Paul Stillwell: That's frustrating.

Admiral Meyer: Yeah. "I can't use that; it's trash." Well, what do you expect? You've got a man trying to write a paper about something he doesn't know anything about. Once you go put his nose in it, he loses that option. The whole thing starts changing then. And all things start coming forward, people you don't even expect to come forward. I mean, you'll have clerical people start volunteering things to you that you never expect. That's what makes teams; that's what makes organizations, because people start believing in their success and they start believing in their permanency.

Now, leap ahead for a couple minutes. The demise of Aegis today has been very, very traumatic for a lot of people, because now there are thousands of people who have never known anything else. Today, when I go to Moorestown to visit, sons and daughters will find me. I had a granddaughter seek me out last time I was up to tell me that her grandfather worked for me there. So they recruited them into the structure, and a lot of them went on to become engineers of some kind or something.

And since my first introduction to Moorestown, by the way, back before Aegis, back in the early '60s, there's something about the place. There is the Italian-Jewish mixture of people in that area that go to the schools, like Stevens, a top engineering school, and other engineering schools around them nearby.* Some of them go as day students, and they get good basic educations. And there's just something about that class of people and their ethic. I have to say it really overwhelmed me in the early days. Pretty soon you get so you expect it. Then the leaders that follow you think, well, what's wrong with that? You know? They forget to even bother to thank the people or recognize the people. So in my time I created all kinds of things that I thought were useful to people to just put a little excitement into it.

We had an Aegis flag that we awarded. We had Aegis excellence awards. You could get them as individuals, get them as a team, or get them as a unit. And if you got it as a unit you could fly the Aegis—for example, out at Port Hueneme the station flies the Aegis flag because it was given to them as an award for their unit performance in the program. Well, it does mean something to people. It's *bullshit* that it doesn't mean anything. It *does* create pride.

What is kind of hard on you, and you've got to be careful how you resent it, is because others pretty soon start trying to emulate you, and they don't have the ability to

---

* Stevens Institute of Technology, Hoboken, New Jersey.

copy you. For example, Tomahawk tried to copy, not very successfully.* But the Aegis movement was a great movement.

Well, pretty soon—this is long after I was fired—the goddamn Aegis people became arrogant sons of bitches. Now, why is that? It's because the leadership didn't know any better. The leadership became arrogant, that's why. So the better you're doing in leadership, the more humble you have to be with people, your behavior. But that doesn't mean you stop making decisions. You've got to make them. And in all the counseling sessions I have and in the training of leaders I've always said, "Make the decision. If you're wrong, change it." That is the important thing. You've got to be right 51% of the time, or pretty soon people will get nervous about you.

Paul Stillwell: And better if it's higher than that. [Chuckle]

Admiral Meyer: It'd be a lot better. But people will follow you if they know you're a good decision-maker and you're timely on it. They can't stand deferred decisions. They can't handle that. And yet there are many things where decisions ought to be deferred, should be postponed; otherwise they get made prematurely. I learned all of that, but I must say, without a hell of a lot of administrative help from a leadership viewpoint.

Having said that, I had people associated with me or mentored me who would do anything I wanted done. I think part of it was vested in: My success meant success at a greater level. Roger Elmore Spreen, admiral, in the graveyard, was a mentor that I've told you about.

Paul Stillwell: Yes.

Admiral Meyer: Who was often hard to deal in. When he was chief over there he lived in Holloway's house, which is over on 26th Street right here in Aurora, and he would call

---

* Tomahawk is a long-range cruise missile that entered the fleet in the early 1980s, capable of delivering either conventional or nuclear warheads. Originally conceived to have both antiship and land-attack versions, the antiship type is no longer in service. The original guidance system relied on the missile matching its course with the terrain below its path. Navigation now is guided by satellite.

me down about 4:30 or a quarter to 5:00 and he'd say, "Have you got your work all done?"

I said, "No, I don't have."

"Well, I'll give you 30 minutes to get it done."

He'd get on the phone and he'd say, "Jan, I just told Wayne to call Margaret and asked them to come on by for supper, if that's all right with you."

Of course, what did she have to say? [Chuckle] She'd say, "Oh, that would be great." So he'd tell me to go home, pick up Margaret—in his mind we lived way out in the country in Falls Church—and come over to their house. We'd run through a whole quart of whiskey that night. He would argue with me and argue with me until I was worn out.

Paul Stillwell: Did this happen frequently?

Admiral Meyer: Well, often enough. It would happen every four weeks or so. And the women would go off in another room, lie down and go to sleep, go to bed, while he just sat there and argued with me. He loved to argue. Well, he loved to find somebody could argue with him, and he thought a great deal of me.

Paul Stillwell: You were worth arguing with.

Admiral Meyer: You're right. [Laughter] But he would reform the whole Navy for me. He would move whatever had to be moved for my success. And one of the ways he admired me, he detested Ike Kidd.[*] I think he was Ike's plebe. I think Spreen was Class of '43.

Paul Stillwell: Kidd was '42.

---

[*] Admiral Isaac C. Kidd, Jr., USN, served as Chief of Naval Material from 1 December 1971 to 18 April 1975. Spreen was his subordinate as Commander Naval Ordnance Systems Command, 1972-74.

Admiral Meyer: Right. And so I think that he never had any use for Ike Kidd. Well, of course, I didn't either; he was an asshole. But I learned a long time ago that you've got to get along with assholes. And when I served under Spreen in the task force Ike was First Fleet, and so he was always creating trouble for the task force, and it was mostly Terrier.* Spreen wouldn't go to see him. He'd put my ass on an airplane to go out there and handle it. And, of course, Ike would throw my ass out after about 30 minutes and I'd come on back home, but it would cool off. But he always admired me on how I handled Ike Kidd. [Chuckle]

Paul Stillwell: Well, you were talking about decision-making. It sounds as if you're saying there's an art to not making it too soon but making it soon enough.

Admiral Meyer: Right. You've got to make it soon enough, and credibly enough. It's like raising your kids. You can't give your kids more than they can handle, so as a parent you've got to know how to deal in them at different ages or on different subjects. That's the mark of a top parent versus a not-so-top parent. Well, that follows over in leadership. But the big thing is their belief, in my mind, at least I think it is. I mean, even Rickover kept books on me throughout that era because I'd have big meetings. I believed in big assemblies, and the reason is somebody was always attacking our budget, and I wanted all the people to always be sure that that was my responsibility. They needed to do their job and I would try to do my job. *My* job was protecting the budget, but I couldn't do that without their performance. It couldn't be done. So they believed that.

Paul Stillwell: Was Rickover involved because he wanted Aegis in nuclear-powered hulls?

Admiral Meyer: Oh, yes. And I'm one of the few people that could get along with Rickover. I don't know why.

---

* Vice Admiral Isaac C. Kidd, Jr., USN, served as Commander First Fleet from 30 September 1969 to 1 August 1970.

Paul Stillwell: What was your technique?

Admiral Meyer: [Chuckle] You know, in the beginning of this reorganization I mentioned earlier I was still—see, I was always in NavSea. I was the only flag officer that was a project manager, and I was the only one that was left; the rest of them were in the materiel establishment, NavMat. So I'd go over to the staff meeting every Tuesday morning. The first one was Gooding—he was the first chief—and on down the line.[*] And I kept the chiefs always cut in. I made a point to make sure they knew what was going on in my big project, because the big project was resented by a lot of people within the structure. They'd just as soon it would go away. And yet I fed a lot of money into NavSea, piles of money into NavSea, both to ship design and in the combat systems. I mean, big buck, big bucks.

Norman Polmar has always said he's going to write a book. Of course, he's always said a lot of things that he's never done.

Paul Stillwell: Well, he's written a lot of books, though.[†]

Admiral Meyer: He's written a lot of books, but he ain't written one about me yet. He said he's going to. But his claim, that he kept reminding me of, is I did it in the system. Now, I never thought much about that till Norman kept making a point of it. Rickover did it clear out of the system. Levering was specially empowered. I did it in the system. I stayed right there in NavSea. And, you know, in the end I like to think that my way was the right way, because it left something behind me that the others did not leave.

One thing today is we have a continuing operating fleet that's functional, even though you cannot find a single Aegis label in the phone book. If you were to get out the phone books right now you won't find the word "Aegis" anyplace. Not a one.

Paul Stillwell: That's curious.

---

[*] Rear Admiral Robert C. Gooding, USN, served as Commander Naval Ship Systems Command from 1972 to 1974. As a vice admiral, he served as Commander Naval Sea Systems Command from 1974 to 1976.

[†] Norman Polmar has been author or coauthor of dozens of books on naval subjects. He is the editor/compiler of several editions of *Ships and Aircraft of the U.S. Fleet*, published periodically by the Naval Institute Press. He was formerly editor of the U.S. section of *Jane's Fighting Ships*.

Admiral Meyer: Yeah. They couldn't wait till I got out. They couldn't wait to get rid of it. Before the patient's even dead. Because we still have, I think it's seven ships to build, seven ships to be completed yet.

So, where does that pick up on the point I wanted to make?

Paul Stillwell: Well you were talking about working within the system.

Admiral Meyer: Within the system, right. So I always tried to do it within Sea 01, which is the planners and programmers, the money people. Guess what—they worry about getting my goddamn money. Guess what—we always invited their people to any of our major reviews, our major shows and tells. We always invited them to send somebody. They never forget it. And I typically invite those guys over there, George Main, whom I knew very well, who got GS-99, to—okay, send your little people, send one of them so they get some feel for what goes on around them and stuff.* Which they did, and they always welcomed. And my view was, "George, if you don't have the travel money for them, I'll pay for it." And I would. Well, of course they get the idea then that you're just loaded with bucks; you've got all the money and everything, which of course is not true at all. What is true is how you handle it and where you direct it and how you spend it.

But that matter of working in the system leaves behind you some residue that will endure. It doesn't follow that it's going to be perfect; I don't mean that. But it will endure. It won't have to be rediscovery and rediscovery.

In LCS I believe there's going to be a lot of rediscovery, a hell of a lot of it to be re-found before it's done. You'll be able to write about ten issues of the *Institute Proceedings*, as a result of trying to build those ships, my view.

So that way, too, you develop support of those people around through the system that you may never need, but when the day comes you need them, you need them. May only need them once. And they're the little people. People overlook the little people or push them aside, don't pay enough attention to the little people. And I learned a lot about that in dealing with women, because it was in my era—it's what I refer to as the Lyndon Johnson era—where he set everybody free. Everybody was set free. So I didn't have the

---

* George Main, a civilian, was the head of cost estimating in Naval Sea Systems Command.

billets. Now, it's funny, I could get all the women I wanted, but nobody'd give me any billets. So what did I take? I took upward mobilities.

I just, a few weeks ago, went to retirement of, I think, the last one. She retired as a GS-16. She started with me as GS-5. Now, some of them, I'm sorry to say, as a result of watering down our civil service, they're still GS-6s. They didn't reach GS-16 capability at all. That I resent. I resent what we did in the name of quotas, and what we have done. We, as a result, have really watered down our civil service.

Paul Stillwell: Grade creep.

Admiral Meyer: Grade creep and ability. So people tend to direct things in a way they know how to do things. So you could see it develop in these buildings around here, in such things as configuration management, configuration control, and abstract things, because people could learn how to do that by shuffling pieces of paper around. It didn't have anything to do with what the hell the product was. They could let out their little contracts, and they could get a little group of people to follow them and carry on and just keep going, and have a whole career that way, including their grade creep. Over time that waters down your whole structure. Over time it really, really gets infiltrated, and it's experience that disappears.

First time I served in the bureau, they still had the rules in effect that the only way you could serve in headquarters was having served in the field. So every person, every civil servant came into headquarters came from the field. From a shipyard, a depot, or a station, or some such. And every one that came in was board selected. So my first time the GS-16s did the board selections. I tell people this and they look at me, they look at me and they smile and unbelievable to me. But I was a commander in my first tour in the Bureau. We called GS-16s "Mr." And when a GS-16 walked by we braced up, because they were not only above us, they were quite a bit above us. They were deputies to the captains. And your behavior mattered. So I've never forgotten that kind of upbringing right there, of how significant that was. We, of course, don't have it now. Johnson set them all free and we threw standards out the window and threw discipline out the window when Johnson put all these hiring practices into effect. So not only did we want to promote women and promote blacks, we wanted it done *now*. We wanted it done now. Never mind that you want a development program or structure. *Now*. So that's how it happened and, of course, the civil service never recovered from it professionally. Never.

Let's take a break a minute.

[End of interview]

Interview Number 12 with Rear Admiral Wayne E. Meyer, U.S. Navy (Retired)
Place: Admiral Meyer's office in Crystal City, Arlington, Virginia
Date: Friday, 11 July 2008

Paul Stillwell: Admiral, your staff provided me with a timeline here, and in November 1970 it reports on an "end-of-the-world" speech that you made to answer criticisms of the CAM study from the Center for Naval Analyses.[*] What was the "end-of-the-world" speech?

Admiral Meyer: Well, it's been so long that I haven't thought about it in so long, I've got to do a little fumbling of recall. I'll work up to it.

Recall that I finally reported in reluctantly in June of 1970, and the process was not too certain what my assignment was except, well, the admiral says you're to take over ASMS. At that time the surface missile system project existed in principle. Now, it had, over the years since it was created, which would have been '62 or thereabouts, but over that eight-year period or so, it had migrated from an admiral commanding a task force reporting directly to the Secretary of the Navy to that admiral eventually being relieved by another admiral who it was decided, well, he could report to the Chief of Naval Material instead of the Secretary of the Navy.

Paul Stillwell: Right. We covered that. That was in the reorganization.

Admiral Meyer: I realize, but I'm just trying to get down to about November; I'm talking about myself.

The first crisis I recall did occur in July, and I believe I said someplace in my words that I had to call July 4 weekend action meetings with the people in the project.

Paul Stillwell: Well, you talked about that and the air-conditioning.

---

[*] CAM – "Countering the Antiship Missile."

Admiral Meyer: Yeah, and I vowed it would never happen again. And it didn't. It hasn't. But it didn't abolish the threat. Every half a dozen weeks there was a new breakout on the threat. Much of that attack was led by people that somehow you just felt ought to know better, or did know better.

Paul Stillwell: What was the motivation for the attack?

Admiral Meyer: A question, a damned good question, which the British would refer to as an imponderable [chuckle], because there were several mixed motivations, and I can't tell you exactly which one it was. There, of course, was a lot of jealousy left in that structure.

Paul Stillwell: Who were the attackers?

Admiral Meyer: This process had gone on for years to the killing of Typhon, whether it was going to reemerge, and whether we're going to do this fixed-array radar, and how it was going to be put back together. And one thing that was certain, it could not be named a "T"!

Paul Stillwell: We covered that as well.

Admiral Meyer: We covered that part. Well, this kind of behavior went on for months, I should say years. People in the Center for Naval Analyses, for one institution. Periodically the IDA institution would stick its head up.[*] And these institutions were pretty damned good at covering their tracks, or not exposing themselves, because they would take on some item that was, frankly, irrelevant to the issues at the moment. They were significant in an abstract way but not relevant at the moment. And I believe it was mostly driven by, I'd say jealousy. I don't believe it was driven by the losers. I honestly don't believe we had sore losers, because in fact Raytheon ended up a winner, General Dynamics ended up a winner, Hughes ended up a winner. Boeing, which frankly was not a winner to start with, ended up a non-winner.

---

[*] Institute for Defense Analyses.

Paul Stillwell: RCA ended up a winner.

Admiral Meyer: And RCA ended up a winner, although RCA was not yet heavily involved in the SMS up to that time. It was on the fringe.

Paul Stillwell: Was the Defense Science Board part of this array of attackers?

Admiral Meyer: My recall from that era is not good enough to say. There were so many internecine couplings between various board and panels and such. Charlie DiBona had become the director of CNA.[*] Which year did Zumwalt come to power?[†]

Paul Stillwell: Nineteen seventy, this same year.

Admiral Meyer: Same year. Charlie DiBona had now become the director, and somehow Charlie DiBona was all-brilliant, an ex-lieutenant commander. Where he got this brilliance I don't know. God perhaps secretly disclosed it to him out on a desert one time. But he somehow could speak no wrong. And it wasn't only the CNO that believed that, Zumwalt, but there were a lot of others, although they may have been just lackeys of the CNO too.

Paul Stillwell: Well, DiBona had been in the OP-96 shop and gotten a good reputation there, and worked with the OSD people in systems analysis.

Admiral Meyer: And they were in the process of being born. The call to systems analysis was emerging, and they had created these new careers. And frankly, those careers were endangered. The truth was, they were so endangered they finally broke down, they finally collapsed. You don't see any systems analysis going on anymore in

---

[*] Charles J. DiBona stood second of the 681 graduates in the Naval Academy class of 1956 and subsequently studied as a Rhodes Scholar. In 1967, as a lieutenant commander, he resigned from active duty and became chief executive officer of the Center for Naval Analyses. He served in that capacity from 1967 to 1973. Subsequently he headed the American Petroleum Institute.

[†] Admiral Elmo R. Zumwalt Jr., USN, served as Chief of Naval Operations, 1 July 1970 to 29 June 1974.

programs like Patriot or programs like Aegis. On the other hand, you see a hell of a lot of money peed away week after week after week in the name of analysis.

There's nothing that irked you more in that era and the coming decade after that, irked *me* anyhow—I was a captain and, of course, I was usually, if I wasn't the mark over in the program center then one of my officers was. You'd go in there. I asked you before, I think, whether you were acquainted with that room. I think it's still there. There's a big long table. It would take, hell, I don't know, 30 people at it. And whoever was leading the meeting would be down at this end, and the goat would be tethered way up on a 3-inch-high stage on the other end, and all the straphangers would be around the back. And these officers would come in.

The meeting would be called like 1500 or some gracious time, and they would all march in, and they'd have ribbons from here to here, ribbons all over the place, officer after officer after officer. And, of course, they insisted on having this big pile of paper out in front of them before the presentation, which is something I refused to do. I just categorically refused to do it. Well, rather than constantly fight I put out a pro forma piece—it didn't have anything to do with what we were going to speak—because I just got tired of arguing on it. But my view is, if you're going to publish it, why in the hell are you calling a meeting? So they would look there while they were sitting there. The next thing you'd look around, they were all asleep. They'd all take a nap. Well, I decided that process wasn't too important.

But invariably the outfits, many of them led by Charlie DiBona and that crowd, started gaining power. They'd be in the back of the room, and they would interrupt and start blaring out their questions. Well, I wasn't running the meetings. I was a peon, really, when you think about it. I was just the goat. And they would just get off on these parabolic courses. "Why don't you use the Patriot? What's wrong with the Patriot radar? Well, how did you get S-band? S-band's not the right frequency." Well, the Navy, and the nation actually, had already spent over a decade on frequency selection and visited every frequency that could be visited, and S-band became the compromise. The truth is there is no perfect frequency for anything. It's always a compromise. And in this case it was getting the search you wanted with the amount of weight you could handle, plus the height you could tolerate in a ship. I set a lot of those coordinates because it turned out they really hadn't been set.

For example, I set the one that the base of our array shall be a minimum of 40 feet above the waterline. That had not been set. People just sat around and argued all the time about it. So I just passed a law one day. It turned out nobody gave a damn.

I set another law. This might not seem significant but it has been. Had to do with the missile, and it had to do with the fast Fourier transform design and the processing in the seeker. We had one on the bench, and I had taken a look at it. We had never had it in the air, and we were doing firings that were working up because by now I inherited the missile because it was broke; it was bankrupt. And I was working my way up to something called the fast Fourier transform, which was—that process was totally revolutionary then. It's generally in use today. I mean, there ain't no missile, I don't think, built without fast Fourier transform, which is a frequency domain instead of a time domain. That's what it fundamentally is.

Also, I want to say the name of the admiral who was looked upon as the authority and expert in evasive countermeasures in the airplanes, particularly the—

Paul Stillwell: Julian Lake.

Admiral Meyer: Thank you. Julian Lake.* Julian Lake came to me one day, and it took me a while to figure out what was bothering him, because he just kept prancing around, pawing like an old cow trying to find her calf in a pasture. And what was bothering him is, he had gone taking a look at the work we were doing on the fast Fourier transform and he was scared because—Julian was pretty smart in a backhanded way. Julian knew that if we were doing it, it would only be a matter of time till the opponents would be doing it. And when that seeker came into the opponent's missiles they didn't know how to handle it. They didn't know how to kill a missile with a fast-Fourier-transform seeker. Truth is, we don't really know how to kill them yet today very easily. But this is what was bothering Julian. And I said, "Well, I don't have anything to"—he and I got along. As a

---

* Rear Admiral Julian S. Lake, USN, was a naval aviator who specialized in electronic warfare. From 1973 to 1975 he was Vice Commander Naval Electronics Systems Command (NavElex). In 1975-76 he commanded NavElex.

matter of fact, from that we became pretty good friends. But I didn't really have anything to contribute to him to the solution, because I had no interest in it, first of all.

Paul Stillwell: You sort of helped define the problem.

Admiral Meyer: Yeah, right. [Chuckle] And 40 years later I don't have the foggiest idea of where that is today, where we stand on defense against those kinds of threats. I think we don't consider those kinds of missiles as threatening against our airplanes as we then did. We just seem to fly our airplanes around today as though nobody's ever going to attack them. That's my take from these campaigns we run. It may be sour grapes, too.

Anyhow, when I left the stable where was I headed with this boring tale?

Paul Stillwell: Well, you were talking about these transforms and frequency instead of time.

One of the other events that's noted here for 1970 is a mockup of the CIC for the DLGN-38.*

Admiral Meyer: Right.

Paul Stillwell: And the genesis of the combat system evaluation lab at APL. Was the *Virginia*-class DLGN the original vehicle for Aegis? Was that the intention?

Admiral Meyer: It was a grand pronouncement by those who were going to have no responsibility, accountability, or anything else to do with it, in order to get on with program approvals. Recollect that era is going along, we had something called DX, DXG, and DXGN, and the theory was that what became the -38 ancestry was the DXGN, renumbered by one of the CNOs to CGN.

In the meantime, Rickover, not being in a very tolerant mood—and I didn't blame him—he had to do something about his engineering teams. So he went to the Congress

---

* DLGN-38 was the original designation for a nuclear-powered guided missile frigate that became the USS *Virginia*. In 1975 she was redesignated CGN-38, nuclear-powered cruiser. the ship was commissioned 11 September 1976.

and got them to lay down *California*.* Nobody knew what to arm *California* with. "Well, we're certainly not going to arm it with that stinking Terrier." So she was armed with Tartar. Well, time passed, time passed, it happened again. So the next thing he did is, he went and got *South Carolina*, which was number 37.†

Paul Stillwell: She was the sister of *California*.

Admiral Meyer: Yeah, which filled in the empty spots in the engineering world of nukes, primarily. And we had these kind of bastardized systems which we're putting into them. I believe I'm correct that we still had the Mark 13 launchers then; we had not introduced the 26 launcher, because the 26 launcher was not proofed enough to bring it into shipbuilding. Today we're not bothered by that.‡ Proving is not a requirement; just do it. That seems to be the idea. Well, those people—it's easy to do that if you've never had to be accountable for it or never gotten hurt.

As I wander around in that, I'm trying to work my way to that autumn as the new budget was being worked up and the crisis was emerging. A number of 128 million sticks in my mind, which was kind of the initial allotment of dollars we had, which I took and judiciously spread to RCA and others, and I ran the Raytheon contract and the Computer Sciences contract through RCA. The other contracts I kept either in the project or, really more properly, in what was later called NavOrd. I can't recall what it was called at that time.

Paul Stillwell: Well, you covered that contracting process last time.

Admiral Meyer: Okay. Well, pretty soon you had these pencil pushers who decided, well, Aegis was going to cost too much money, it was too complicated. Zumwalt never

---

* USS *California* (DLGN-36), nuclear-powered guided missile commissioned 16 February 1974, redesignated cruiser (CGN-36) in June 1975.
† USS *South Carolina* (DLGN-37), nuclear-powered guided missile commissioned 25 January 1975, redesignated cruiser (CGN-36) in June 1975.
‡ The Mark 13 and Mark 26 guided missile launchers projected above the ship's deck, rotated through various azimuths horizontally, and contained twin arms, or "rails," that launched the missiles. Since then the above-deck launchers have been done away. Now missiles are often fired directly from storage cells within the ship's hull—a vertical-launch system. Some rail launchers still exist.

liked it. Went through that part. They'd calculate how many millions of dollars it would take every day to stoke the radar and how many tubes you had to have in stock, and on and on and on. So the end-of-the-world speech came in getting ready for the subsequent budget, or came to be billed as the end-of-the-world speech, because of course we had no physical things to show. So it was easy to assault you in thin air, and that's all they had to assault you with.

At the same time the threat was pretty damned serious. I mean, plenty serious. And all the officers who were back from the war hadn't died yet. They were JOs, but they still remembered the kamikazes. In 1970 it was still pressing on them. They were at the end of their rope almost; they were about to go down. But they knew damned good and well that something had to be done, and it had to start with the radar and with reaction time.

We've talked about the Withington study and the Israeli destroyer being sunk by the Styx missile. And out of that flowed what came to be called the five cornerstones of Aegis. They were the operational cornerstones that the Aegis system had to be targeted to meet. One was reaction time, one was firepower, one was resistance to countermeasures, one was reliability, or availability actually, and one was coverage. I might have them out of order, but the gist of them is all that's critical here. And they had numbers attached to them.

For example, firepower came to be defined as X. Well, what did that mean? What it meant is you had to have the capacity to have X number of salvos airborne. Well, the doctrine up to then, we went through that era, were dual-round salvos, so that meant in order to have X missiles in the air, you had to have half of X in dual-round salvos. You had to be pretty damned fast with the illuminator designs we had, and such. And we could achieve it. You could see on paper we could achieve it. You could see it in the modeling. It was achievable. Whether it's executable beats the hell out of me.

But later I'll say this—and I think that year was, I don't know, it was the mid-70s—our demos in *Norton Sound* were good enough for OpTEvFor, and they were good enough for OSD, because there we engaged two targets at the same time, and the rest we simulated them simultaneously. They really were impressed and awed. As a matter of fact, I was myself, because by then we were in the lifeboat. We had come through the end of the world, we were out in the River Styx, and I kept assembling these people and telling them, "Wait a minute; make sure you've got your lifejacket secured, because we're not out of this thing. The world's after us. We're going to need more money and more money and more money."

Paul Stillwell: So you saw the program as in definite jeopardy at that point.

Admiral Meyer: Yes, it was. Yes, it was threatened repeatedly.

So I had to start from the beginning building confidence in people. One example was Tony Battista.

Paul Stillwell: Right. You discussed him last time, too.

Admiral Meyer: I did, right. There are other examples all around. And I tried to get one strong believer in every institution that I had to work with, the labs, the corporations, and such, so that there was at least one disciple that I felt I could rely on. It wasn't necessarily the head person. Matter of fact, more often than not it was not the head person. But it was almost—you know, it was like a religious fervor. You had to believe.

That's different than Patriot, and I think God was good in dissipating McNamara and the demand that the Army and the Navy build one system and both use it, because the needs, the operations, are dramatically different. But if you never built anything, it's hard to tell somebody that and get them to accept it, especially if they want to put the money someplace else.

You've never, as far as I know, worked directly in this business. Believe me, that process is capable of drumming up and dreaming up anything to take your money. And they always have a voice, and they always have no accountability. And I, in my day of developing project managers, I've always told them, "If you don't have the stomach and you don't have the stamina, get out; it'll just destroy you. Get away from it. And by the way, make sure your spouse can handle it, because she's going to undergo a lot of torture." It is really arduous duty.

Breaker, I'm jumping now for a moment; I'll be right back. Two weeks ago I agreed to take on an examination of the DDG-1000. That captain at one time had been selected by me as a junior officer along with a couple others for potential meat in the Aegis project when they were junior officers. I was fired by John Lehman before that ever had come to pass, but they did all end up working in Aegis. Today one of them—you may know him—is Captain Fred Parker, retired. He built the FFG, and he was my aide for a while when I was trashed to ComNavSea.[*] The other is Sean Stackley, who is in the process of being confirmed as Assistant Secretary of the Navy.[†] And the other is Jim Syring, who is the captain that commands the DDG-1000 program.[‡] So these officers, these rescue officers and firefighters, all come out of Aegis.

That's the way LPD-17 had to be salvaged.[§] Well, there's nothing wrong with that in one sense. That's where the meat was; that's where the good people were. But a lot of them lost their vocation when they got reassigned. They got assigned to things that they viewed to be losers, and they left. Today, to the best of my knowledge, the LPD-17 is still not operable worth a damn, years after she having been put in commission. She has got so many Tinkertoys in her, she's got so many random type organization processes with the Marine Corps, she's got no stability.

Well, so I started to stick my nose—what I'm saying now is proprietary. By the time you print it won't be proprietary in anything. I decided that I was going to try to help this officer, Jim Syring, if he wanted it. So I had him over here about two weeks ago. He is the kind of officer—those officers are so damaged. God, they're damaged. I came out here to meet him when she told me he was here. He had three others with him, two of them from the Pentagon. I said, "Look, Jim, I was just going to have a sit-down meeting with you."

"Well, this is the way it is, Admiral." And I thought, if they can't behave [phonetic] with their own mind, for God's sake, what has come over us? I know what's

---

[*] He was Lieutenant Commander Frederick H. Parker, USN, while serving with Admiral Meyer.
[†] Sean J. Stackley on 28 July 2008 became Assistant Secretary of the Navy (Research, Development and Acquisition).
[‡] Captain James D. Syring, USN, program manager for the *Zumwalt* (DDG-1000). Subsequent to this interview he was selected for flag rank in 2010. In 2012 he was promoted to vice admiral and now serves as Director, Missile Defense Agency, Office of the Secretary of Defense.
[§] USS *San Diego* (LPD-17) is the lead ship of a class of amphibious transport docks. She was commissioned 14 January 2006 and took a few years before getting problems ironed out.

come over us; it's Goldwater-Nichols, that's what's come over us. That's exactly what's come over us. It's simple manifestation of it right here in my lobby. So I went in and had a meeting with him, which turned out to last three hours and I made them all sit right here in reception [chuckle] while I met with Syring.

I was trying to get him to lay out for me what *his* appraisal was and *his* assessment. It didn't take me long to figure out that he didn't have a friend in the world. It took me about an hour to, I'd say, have him get over his fear. I would expect that you know who he was dealing with. I'd warned him ahead of time, I said, "You come here, you're coming here at risk; you keep that in mind, young captain. It's risk."

"Well," he said, "Admiral, I need help." "Okay, it's good enough for me. Just understand you're in a high-risk movement here." So we spent those three hours.

Earlier this week we spent another three hours here in this building. Of course, here he came, dragging a bunch of officers with him. I said I can't help you till I know what the program is. I don't know anything about the program. Charlie Hamilton did not see fit to ask me a single question, share anything with me, or seek any knowledge whatsoever associated with the programs.* Well, who was the loser? I wasn't the loser. Take it from me, Charlie Hamilton was the loser. Charlie Hamilton could have been a winner. He just got too damned stuck up. He did himself in. I don't know what politico over there pushed him through the knothole to promote him, but I believe that was an unsound promotion.

Well, Goddard was one of those three that I told you that I had collected early on to raise, actually out at Carderock.† Goddard and Corky Graham—I don't know whether you know him, you probably do—and Jimmy Baskerville.‡ They were lieutenants. They were EDOs. They had attended the top schools. One's from MIT, I can't remember whether one was from Shoemaker, and the other was from Michigan.

---

* Rear Admiral Charles S. Hamilton, USN. He became program manager for the never-built arsenal ship in 1996. From 1998 to 2000 he was in the Program Executive Office (PEO) Theater Surface Combatants. From 2000 to 2002 he was PEO for Surface Strike. In 2002-03 he was Deputy PEO for Ships, and from 2003 to 2007 he was PEO for Ships. His tenure ended because of cost overruns on the littoral combat ship.
† Lieutenant Charles H. Goddard, USN, who received a master's degree from MIT. He eventually became a rear admiral.
‡ Lieutenant Clark Graham, USN, and Lieutenant James E. Baskerville, USN, both engineering duty officers.

Paul Stillwell: We're getting kind of far afield. Can we get back to 1970? [Laughter]

Admiral Meyer: Well, I'm still at 1970. That's where I am. You think I'm far afield.

Paul Stillwell: Charlie Hamilton wasn't in 1970 [chuckle].*

Admiral Meyer: Well, he was! He was!

Paul Stillwell: Well, he had another name then.

Admiral Meyer: They keep lasting and lasting and lasting. But you asked me a question about November of '70, and if you don't understand the goddamn history I'm just wasting your time. So if you want to move on, we'll just move on.

Paul Stillwell: All right. When did we get into the mockup at Moorestown and developing that facility?

Admiral Meyer: We had built, or modeling something called Engineering Development Model 1, starting the program. That was a new expression. It was an Air Force expression, and the whole program was modeled after what I call the Wright-Patterson heresy. The whole DoD had been twisted and re-formed process-wise to these ideas coming out of Wright-Patterson, which were in the main based on the strategic missile programs.

For example, you'd get a work breakdown structure for the, I think it was the Minuteman then; I can't recall. But you'd get that work breakdown structure on a map that you'd unroll on this table, and it would go from one end to the other and it would consist of standpipes. On this end would be the standpipe that started at that end and went off the top on this end, labeled "The Flight Vehicle." "Flight Vehicle," whatever the hell that is. Then the rest of them, there would be, hell, 20-25, I call them side lobes,

---

* Hamilton was commissioned in 1974. He served on board surface combatants for several years before getting into the ship-acquisition side of the Navy.

modules of the other parts of the program. The second one would be maybe that high, and you got to the end down there you'd need a magnifying glass to see what it was. That was their idea of a project. Well, you sure as hell can't do what I did with that approach. That's like saying the radar is all that's important, and we'll do it well. Matter of fact, it would be: Only the transmitter's important. We'll do it all there, and the rest of you, you can latch on the best you know how.

So I just trashed that whole goddamn process in the summer of 1970. And, who became my good friend, Bill Goodwin—I'd known Bill Goodwin a long time; he'd been in the Navy as a petty officer in the war. He'd got out and he'd gone to Villanova, I believe it was, and he'd gone to work at Bendix. He worked as an engineer. He was pretty damned good. He was, identically my age, and he was a patriot and he thought that way. How fortunate I was that God caused Bill Goodwin to be made the project manager at RCA to lead that team. Well, when that team started, all he was, he was one of the marketers. He worked his ass off. They worked themselves for, I don't know, five years longer. Bill led those teams, and they captured the contract. Well, my goodness, what was the corporation to do? It finally decided they may have to make him a vice president, which they did that year.

By the way, that year and the subsequent year and the subsequent year, I think it was up to three years, RCA put out its annual report and did not have one word in it on the Aegis program. At that time RCA was quartered at 30 Rockefeller Center. Those were: "We don't want to touch anything with war in it. We don't want anything to do with war." Well, the sons of bitches would take the money, but "we don't want anything to do with it. We sit over here in this lofty structure in the Tower of Babel in Rockefeller Center, and Aegis is, you know, it's not...." Well, Bill Goodwin got told very early on: "You don't bring in the amount of money that one Elvis Presley record does." Well, it turned out that that was bullshit. It turned out it's the biggest, longest running, safe program that the corporation has ever had, it and its successors, in spite of the butchering that occurred through there when it went through General Electric. But it went through General Electric, it went through Martin Marietta, and it settled finally at Lockheed.

The establishment of it, somebody will get around to writing that book. Joe Threston has written some pretty good parts to it. He started as a youngster out of school in the program in system engineering, and it turned out—well, system engineering didn't exist then, but it turned out he had a natural knack for that kind of thinking. And so he retired from RCA, or whatever its name was, as the general manager at Moorestown. He and, by the way, my guess is no less than 100 people—it may be many more than that—retired several times over as millionaires because of me. Because of me. Some of them understand it; some of them just turn up their noses.

Paul Stillwell: Well, where did the development of that Moorestown facility fit into this sequence?

Admiral Meyer: Well, you're going to get there, but very slow.

Bill and I had made a decision that we were going to mockup, mockup, mockup, mockup, because we didn't know where we were going, and there wasn't anybody, frankly, who was capable of telling us. So we started out with garden hose and plywood, and we got an empty room up at Moorestown, and we got ourselves a couple craftsmen. We started laying out with a garden hose and plywood what we thought the CIC would look like.

Well, then we decided the computer center was very critical also. And also the signal processor was very critical. So those were critical spaces that we decided we had to pay attention to all the time. The big reason is, the signal processor was going to be high in the ship, and we had to fight—they were architectural balance in weight.

Paul Stillwell: Ship stability.

Admiral Meyer: Yeah. And, of course, Patriot doesn't even know what that means. So right there tells you why we should never touch Patriot.

Through the years we learned a lot about it. And a couple valued captains retired, who were naval architects, which Bill hired and they became advisors in our team. They became pretty damned good in helping us. What I knew about shipbuilding was related to conversion of *Galveston*, and sailing. But it turned I knew about as much as anybody else when you get right down to it. You just had to pay attention to Archimedes. No matter what shape you took on, Archimedes still ruled.*

So we built that up, and we fumbled around, and we did a lot of what you might call human factors stuff. We went out to the basement at APL and we built another one where we were able to put some hardware in it. We were trying to figure out the consoles. When we started, for example, and I walked in on the program in the middle of 1970, it called for brand-new consoles, it called for brand-new missiles, and it called for brand-new launchers. No kidding. I've seen this movie now several times. Right now it's called DDG-1000. The DDG-1000 trashed everything that was Aegis-labeled. Trashed it! Right in the eyes of the American people. The billions being spent is not possible to spend in the shipbuilding that was advertised. It's being spent in development. Will it make it? That's another song that I don't want to get off too far on.

But Bill and I learned rapidly on that we'd better face reality and fit reality, and not get on the imaginary axis. That's why you can't get *Zumwalt*.

We started learning very quickly that, really, warship design and shipbuilding is empirical. It's not analytical. It's what at one time would be referred to as a father-son-type craft.

Paul Stillwell: So did you have these mockups at both APL and Moorestown developing simultaneously?

Admiral Meyer: No, no, no, no. The mockup at APL was an advanced one compared to what we made up there. But I had both people heavily involved. I wouldn't operate without a team. I'm totally intolerant of separatism. I won't put up with it. I had an index of forbidden words that came out about circa 1971, I'd say, or so, that I forbade to be used. One of them were the pronouns: "We, they, us, them." All the goddamn civil servants would just infuriate me in a meeting and stand up and talk about "they," the contractors. And you'd go to a review someplace and somebody would stand up in industry and start talking, "Well, they—well, we needed that and we couldn't get it out of

---

* Archimedes, an ancient Greek physicist, developed the principle that a body immersed in a fluid has a buoyant force equal to the weight of the fluid it displaces.

Dahlgren." Or "We didn't get...." Well, I knocked that bullshit off. By the way, in the process I fired about half a dozen people because they couldn't get with it. I learned this and, I mean, it's so obvious to me afterwards anyhow. You can't play football that way. Just watch on Sunday. You can tell on Sunday how integrated the defense is with the offense. And guess what, when they ain't, they lose, they're losers. I mean, if your head coach is one that pays no attention to both of them, you've got a loser.

So we learned as we went along. Everybody was equal. I have to say, I've said it about myself, I take great pride in this, and I get very braggadocio on it. And no one will ever decorate me for it. Well, maybe they will, but I decorated myself right in here because I know I'm doing the right thing. Because I learned from my teachers and my grandmother and my mother and my daddy to do the right thing, frankly, and that's where it came from.

So in a meeting I didn't care who you were. I was totally uninterested in what was in the contract. My interest is whether we had our eye on where we were going to go. That started the evening star syndrome. In that whole era every meeting room had an evening star posted in it so that people never lose focus on where they're heading.

Paul Stillwell: But the contracts have to lead to that guiding star.

Admiral Meyer: Oh, yeah. But I had another item. The Navy's contracting officer was a fellow by the name of John Flaherty. Before that I'd known him casually. He had worked in BuShips contracts for a long time.

Paul Stillwell: You mentioned him last time too.

Admiral Meyer: Okay. Well, he's in the graveyard now. And he started out training and developing a group which survive to this day, some of them. And similarly we had a contracting officer at Moorestown by the name of Pete Dwyer. You couldn't be more Irish that Pete Dwyer. But they got along like this. But what was important: Every meeting that I held up there in that control room, they had to be present, and they really would get a sore ass because they had nothing to speak, but I put them on the front row.

And my favorite [chuckle]—my favorite said we'd knock off at 5:30 or so, and my announcement would be, "Well, the rest of us are going to go party, but you two guys are going to go get recorded and shaped what we've decided today so tomorrow we can review it and approve it." And we did it as we went.

Every few months they'd issue a change order and they'd balance the books. Pete would get $12.00 here, John would get $9.00 there, and we kept those books in balance. Never let them get out of balance. Never. I don't believe that people have learned that today. Matter of fact, I know they haven't. We never let them get out. That didn't mean you wouldn't have arguments. You'd have people, you know, that had their little pet rocks someplace, that RCA wasn't doing this, or Raytheon wasn't doing that. Or you'd get out of Raytheon: Well, you know, we were promised this out of APL or promised that. You had all those things. I mean you had the sibling arguments going on. That didn't eliminate them, but what it did is it kept you up to date. When somebody asked me the status of the program, I knew what the goddamn status was. I knew what it was. And if there was going to be any lying done, I told everybody that ever associated with me, "*I'm* the one that's going to do the lying; if I catch any of you in a lie you're off the program."

Paul Stillwell: Did you have charts laid out comparable to the PERT charts in the Polaris program, with timelines and milestones?[*]

Admiral Meyer: We tried to. The first major meeting at Moorestown occurred in January 1970. I was still at Port Hueneme. I hadn't been detached yet; I was going to be detached about March. I came back to participate in that program review because Captain Jughead Tazewell was running the program, and he was going home.[†] So I came back, and it was a very disturbing review. Jughead was very, very proud of what he had done. And what they had done is they had complied. They had followed the process. It

---

[*] PERT – Program Evaluation Review Technique, a system of milestones for tracking the progress of a program against its schedule.
[†] Captain John P. Tazewell, USN, was program manager for Advanced Surface Missile System (ASMS)/Aegis from 1967 to 1970.

was a cost contract, but they followed the process and they had specifications and they were all patterned—

See, at that time, remember, we didn't have things like Fort Belvoir or any of those things, in that era.* The first school started to teach anybody or develop anybody was in my first tour in the bureau in the mid-'60s. I believe that's right. And in that tour the Navy would send commanders, sometimes lieutenant commanders. They had this six-week school out at Wright-Patterson Air Force Base, and they'd send them out there. In theory they'd be taught contracts, specifications, and all those kinds of things. I never went. I never went to Belvoir either. What I did do is, the Navy, BuOrd, had a program in those ratty-ass little buildings over in Anacostia that were surviving from the war that were cooled with 10-inch fans around and broken chairs. They ran several schools over there. They ran two-day schools, five-day schools.

For example, when you reported in to the bureau in those days, you went to a two-day school over there which tried to teach you a little about indoctrination to the organization, and BuOrd and BuShips and Bureau of Yards and Docks, and how that all fit and stuff. And then when you came in as project management was starting to take hold. I was right in the beginning; I mean I was in the beginning of this, so in essence we were pioneering it. They created a five-day course, and then they created a ten-day course, which was to teach you some basics and fundamentals about contracts, about specifications, including general specs and such, and they were pretty good, but they were superficial. And the teachers weren't the experts of the world.

But I tell you, you could learn just about all you needed to know in those few days, because those few days couldn't piddle around with a lot of parabolic excursions, which is done down at Belvoir over 26 weeks or 40 weeks that these students do. And today I don't believe there's a single piece of evidence that can show that that school has contributed one thing to effective procurement and acquisition.

If you read the stuff coming out of the Congress today or the bitching coming out of the writers and such, you can close your eyes and transport yourself back to 1970. It's as though none of this ever existed. So several times in my heyday I attended meetings I

---

* The Defense Systems Management College (DSMC) is at Fort Belvoir, Virginia. It is co-located with the Defense Acquisition University (DAU).

thought were significant. The senior managers would be called for a seminar or symposium. Three or four of them occurred up at Harvard, to discuss all these business practices. Well, it turned out that isn't what they wanted at all. What they wanted was to jam down your throat what their goddamn idea was on how it ought to be done. And in the main these were unwashed people in military programs, and I wouldn't have none of it. And to this day I tell my officers, "If you're going to make mistakes, don't make mine; you go make your own, goddammit, but pox on you if you fail to hear me and fail to see the mistakes I made. That's bad. There's no need for you to repeat the mistakes. There are plenty to be made without repeating them."

Were you going to ask a question?

Paul Stillwell: How far in the future did your timeline extend? How far ahead was that guiding star, as you projected forward from 1970-71?

Admiral Meyer: I'd say I was well into my second year before we had streamlined the program to where all of us understood it. I was a captain; I had three commanders. Let's see, one was an EDO, one was a URL, and one was something else.* They'd gone to graduate school, and I thought they were pretty damned sharp. In ensuing years I learned some hard lessons. Not a single one of them made flag. It turns out that what you do in that world doesn't matter a tinker's damn unless you're somebody's goddamn pet. I tell you, I have had *hundreds* of officers who worked for me, top of the line, not a one of them promoted. Not a single one. Well, we've been promoting 30-35 officers to admiral for as long as I've been in the Navy every year. Go get the list out this year and look at it. You can't find them. So we whine and carry on about, you know, we need to fix acquisition, we need to do something about leadership. You're goddamn right we need to! We need to think about promoting the right people.

Take this officer Sam Perez. I don't know whether you know him.

Paul Stillwell: No, I don't.

---

* EDO – engineering duty officer; URL – unrestricted line officer.

Admiral Meyer: Well, Sam Perez, who had worked for me, he was a crack officer. He's an unrestricted officer. He was selected this year for flag.[*] As a matter of fact, Monday he is being frocked over in the hall of heroes in the Pentagon. And where is he going? He's going down to be the deputy for that jerk Stavridis down in the Southern Command, or whatever it is they do down there.[†] Been running the goddamn Navy for 50 years without all those commands. Now all of a sudden we've got to have them all. And so there's an officer who has extraordinary qualifications, the first being leadership. That's what we need for acquisition is, first, is officers who have demonstrated leadership capacity. Now, I've given this lecture a number of times, and you're going to get it again. If you've got to get it piece by piece, that's the way it is.

You know, it's often thought of that the toughest job, and referred to continually even in the *Proceedings*, the most lonely post in the world, is commanding officer of a major ship. And the responsibility is heavy. Well, that's all true, except it ain't the most lonely post, and it *ain't* the heaviest responsibility. You can cause, as a captain, for our biggest attack carrier to be sunk, and at most you'll lose 5,000 souls. You can screw up a major program and you don't know how many people you'll kill over the next 30 years. That's the difference. This responsibility has never been accepted. It's just not accepted. It's thought of in terms of administrative effort, not in command effort. Just not thought that way at all.

I believe that effective project management in a major undertaking is 100 times harder than command at sea. Think about this, say in a cruiser, commanding a cruiser. Even the mess cook knows who the boss is. The mess cook knows who his chief is. The head cleaners know who the exec is. Everybody understands the hierarchy. It is a pyramid, and it's understood, and it's time tested. And periodically it has flaws, but everybody understands it. And I'll guarantee you there's not a single person in that ship with 400 souls that doesn't know who the captain is and who the exec is.

That's different in major project management. You don't know who's in charge of you. You don't know from week to week what the program is, you don't know what the attitudes are. There are so many factions and so many variations. Think how

---

[*] Rear Admiral Samuel Perez Jr., USN.
[†] Admiral James G. Stavridis, USN, served as Commander U.S. Southern Command from 19 October 2006 to 25 June 2009.

homogeneous the people are, even though they're all God's creatures and they're all made in the eyes of God, the people in a cruiser are still not heterogeneous. But they have so much homogeneity compared to, say, the Aegis project with their thousands of people. You don't even know who they are.

Paul Stillwell: But don't you think that the thousands of people in Aegis knew who you were?

Admiral Meyer: Damn right.

Paul Stillwell: All right. [Chuckle]

Admiral Meyer: Now, that's why you see those ball caps in there.* That's where the ball caps came from. That's the difference. And I just got nauseating here a couple nights ago, as I said to Anna Mae: "You know, what we're coming down to is this only major fleet built since World War II save the undertaking of the 963s, which didn't survive, and the attempt in the FFGs which did not survive."†

Paul Stillwell: You're talking about surface ships.

Admiral Meyer: Yeah, I'm talking about surface ships. Well, it's true in submarines too. I mean, we're spending more money on submarines now than we've ever spent. You know, it's hard for me to figure out how we spent a billion dollars apiece on the Tridents for so-called conversion. I mean, how do you spend a billion dollars in a submarine for a conversion, that's supposed to be a missile ship to start with?‡ They do. They got away

---

* Meyer's office was filled with baseball caps bearing the names of the dozens of Aegis cruisers and destroyers that had gone into service.
† USS *Spruance* (DD-963), lead ship of her class of 31 destroyers, was commissioned 20 September 1975. The Navy eventually built 51 guided missile frigates of the *Oliver Hazard Perry* (FFG-7) class. The first of them was commissioned in December 1977.
‡ USS *Ohio* (SSBN-726) was originally commissioned 11 November 1981, armed with Trident ballistic nuclear missiles for the role of strategic deterrence. From 2003 to 2006 she was converted to fire Tomahawk and Harpoon cruise missiles and reclassified SSGN-726. Sister ships also converted to the new role were the *Michigan* (SSGN-727), *Florida* (SSGN-728), and *Georgia* (SSGN-729).

with it. Will they keep getting away with it? They ain't got no Giambastiani anymore.[*] Giambastiani served for a long time in those critical positions, and he built the submarine fleet, and they'll be able to coast on it for a long, long time too.

I'm sorry to say that I don't believe that'll be true in the surface fleet. We started out already with this division. Go get out the phone book; I defy you right now. Get the phone books out, and I defy you to find the word Aegis anyplace in the phone books. Anyplace! I defy you to. Even a hint of it, you can't find it. It's amazing how the opponents and the enemies have spent trying to destroy any sense of camaraderie, any sense of togetherness, any sense of enthusiasm or excitement. It's the backhanded side of jealousy.

I've lectured project managers right there in your chair, and I've said to them, "If you're not prepared for that kind of treatment and that kind of behavior, you'd better look around for something else to do, because it will tear you up, especially if you come from the kind of code that I came from in the gumbo in Missouri, where I generally believed people to be honest, believed them to be hardworking, believed them to be fair, and believed them to have the drive of some important accomplishment in their life." If it's not material, it's religious, or some other walk that we have in life. But it just turns out the world ain't that way, at least. I've got to tell you, that was a hard lesson for me still. That was really, really hard learning for me.

Paul Stillwell: Well, we all get that one at some point in the road.

Admiral Meyer: I'd say it was really hard learning for me to find out what goddamn dunderheads existed in the engineering duty officer corps, but they're not nearly as bad as what exists in the line Navy. One of the officers that worked for me one time, Peyton Randolph Wise III, had a saying I've never forgotten. One day he said it—it's a trite statement. He said, "You know, the trouble with naval officers is every one of them work for themselves." You have to mull that over for a while. You have to think about it for a while. We *raise* them that way. We raise them to be appointed to be commanding

---

[*] Admiral Edmund P. Giambastiani Jr., USN, was Vice Chairman of the Joint Chiefs of Staff from 12 August 2005 to 27 July 2007.

officers and to think for themselves. We *raise* them to do it. I don't know whether that's the right way or not.

Now, I'm going to run out of steam here because I'm getting tired, but I want to finish one piece for your own information. I don't mind if you don't record it at this stage.

Paul Stillwell: Well, let's turn it off then.

Admiral Meyer: Okay.

Interview Number 13 with Rear Admiral Wayne E. Meyer, U.S. Navy (Retired)
Place: Admiral Meyer's office in Crystal City, Arlington, Virginia
Date: Wednesday, 16 July 2008

Paul Stillwell: Admiral, last time we talked about the early stages of Aegis, and you talked about the mockups that involved garden hoses and layouts, developing Moorestown, and APL. And one time earlier you described this as sort of a Venturi tube that we go through to describe the beginning of Aegis. So could you talk about going forward from, say, 1970-71, and getting it beyond that stage?

Admiral Meyer: All right. Last time you had brought me to the point of, at the beginning, the end-of-the-world speech.

Paul Stillwell: Right.

Admiral Meyer: And it turned out to be the first of many end-of-the-world speeches that, at least in that era, one had to give to preserve a major program. I'm talking about major undertakings. Today, across the armed forces, God, I don't know how many hundred programs we've got. We need about ten, and we've got hundreds of them. But this was a bona fide, genuine, major program, and the first engineering development contract was $200 and some-odd million, which was considered to be a giant.

Well, it was awarded, I recollect, in December of 1969. I had reported in here in June of 1970. I had gone to several meetings up in Moorestown and other places in that interim of six months. But then we started getting serious. Well, by November we were in crisis.

The nature of the crisis was several-fold. The people who originally wanted Aegis no longer seemed to want Aegis. Secondly, when they had to now do the subsequent year's budget: "Oh, well, we didn't understand that would be that." Well it, of course, was plain as day for several years. So we just had one familial crisis after another. And most of this, as you appreciate from your years, comes down to squabbling over the money. There's so much allotted, and by the end of the year it's a constant harangue of who's going to get what, where, and who going to—and, in truth, it is a bona fide democracy. It's very hard to make decisions that stick.

I have said several times in my life, "If you don't believe this is a democracy you ought to be a major project manager for several years, and you'll find out that everyone believes in his democratic right to criticize, and it doesn't matter whether it's schedule, operational, or technical. It just simply doesn't matter." Everyone feels qualified to speak, just like my late wife used to do in front of the television every Sunday with the Redskins. So you develop—I don't want to say an ignorance of that because you can't spend your time pissing people off. If you do, you don't get anywhere.

Paul Stillwell: On the other hand, you cannot respond to every criticism either.

Admiral Meyer: Good point. You cannot. So you're always struggling with what is critical and what's not critical.

And in that same era another important thing I learned that I've later used through the years in training my civil servants and training my officers and my vice presidents: "Don't ever forget, you don't know who the customer is. The customer is always shifting on you." The abstract expression "It's the Navy" is just like nothing. There are 500,000 people in the Navy. Or saying it's the Congress; well, there are 500 of them. So you have to be constantly alert to what you might call the *du jour* client or *du jour* customer, or one who may become a significant player somewhere down the highway. I learned all of that—I don't want to say the hard way. Matter of fact, I learned it probably the easy way.

One person that I had known for some time was a fellow by the name of Tony Battista.

Paul Stillwell: Right, you did talk about him.

Admiral Meyer: And I've mentioned him. Well, I want to say a couple more words about him. As far as I know, Tony still lives down in Fredericksburg. He had started at Dahlgren as an engineer of some kind and then went over into the congressional staff and went on the R&D subcommittee staff in the House. And since I'd known him for a long time and since he had an abiding interest in the importance of missile defense and air defense, he and I became pretty good associates, pretty good friends in the coming years. And so I had come to understand Tony and his—the ego that exists in everybody, but his existed in a unique way also. It got so after the second year I could take Tony's word. He was there quite a long time. So I just quit fighting the problem. If Tony told me something was going to get done, I believed it.

Similarly there were two in the Senate—Charlie Cromwell and Hy Fine were on the Armed Services staff. They were old-timers there. And I learned in that year, with associations with them, that I could take their word. Now, in hindsight I believe that came about because they decided they could take *my* word. It wasn't the other way around. They decided they could believe me. And I just learned that there's nothing more important than that in steering and managing a big controversial program—and a big program by nature is controversial.

I mean, look at the Iraq situation if you listened the last few days. You just want to throw up when you listen to what's being said by some of those people about: "We don't belong in Iraq, Bush got us into an unapproved war, and lied to us, and on and on and on."* Of course, that's all bullshit. It really isn't correct at all. It is that they're just simply rewriting it to suit their own purpose, and the political structure will do that, and it's going to do that. I mean, you saw evidence of it yesterday on the tube if you had a chance to watch them. I stayed home and I watched both of them in their speeches.

Paul Stillwell: Did you develop that kind of relationship with some of the members of Congress in addition to these staffers?

Admiral Meyer: Yes and no. It was a limited relationship, because I am not by my nature, growing up in the gumbo and going to Wharton School, one who goes and seeks out the President or some other top person. I almost never do. But what did happen to me is, those staffers whom I developed a relationship with made sure that their principals

---

* In 2003 President George W. Bush initiated war against Iran with bomb and missile strikes and invasion by ground forces. The war went on for years. In 2010 the United States withdrew its last combat troops.

knew who I was and what I was doing, and I could count on them. They knew it. And so they admired me, they respected me, and they supported me. So in that sense I did develop relations with a number of them, a half a dozen of them. For example, Ike Skelton, who is from Missouri, but he's not in my district and he's never been on any of the committees, the direct subcommittees that I worked with, but Ike was one of these who—Tony had known Ike Skelton fairly well—I didn't—and so he became a great booster of mine.* Those kinds of people.

You don't need 600 of them, but you do need some that you can count on. Because once you start understanding the Congress and how it works, almost every piece of legislation, every appropriation, every authorization is done by just a handful of people. Really, only a handful of people do it. It appears that there's a full body, and under the rules and, frankly, under our democratic behavior, the full institution does vote and support things, but most of them have little knowledge. I mean, when you think about what each of those principals is exposed to every day, you couldn't get those papers in my office, there's so much of them, that they have to learn and have to master. So they have to take word, they have to trust people, and the ones that they can repeatedly trust, they're never a problem for them.

But that doesn't mean that trickery will substitute. I, in working with them, tried to develop experiments, data, and repeat behavior in a way that would impress on them the seriousness of what we were doing and how significant it was, and how important it was to get a fleet that was armed that met the numbers that the five operational cornerstones called for in the development of the system. That was important. And, of course, you never knew until after the last dog was killed whether your budget survived or not. You never knew that. But when it came back over to the Department there aren't very many would even contest it once it had been approved or come back over. It's still the case that power protects power and so forth.

Paul Stillwell: But also you were building success on success, so that would make them more confident for going forward in subsequent years.

---

* Isaac Newton Skelton IV, a Democrat from Missouri, served in the House of Representatives from 3 January 1977 to 3 January 2011.

Admiral Meyer: Hold on one second while I get a prop for you.

Admiral Meyer: This radar is the highest-powered radar we have ever put to sea until this last experimental one we're using now, built by Raytheon for ballistic missile defense. The Aegis radars, as you see them in these ships today, put out something like seven million watts peak power. The highest-powered radar before that in our ships was four million watts, in the Terrier fire control systems. Now, the specification on the radar is four million watts, but engineering through the quarter-century has brought those radars to the place where they put out this incredible amount of power. There were any number of fears—how are we going to handle all this power aboard ship? How can this possibly be? This is unsafe, it's unreliable, it's un-anything you can think of, with this incredible thing.

We had two power tubes in development, and the idea was to have a whole series of power tubes of low wattage, in fact at 1,000 watts each, one kilowatt, and gang them up within the array, and going out the array would be this massive amount of power, but inside the array no place would this kind of power exist. It wouldn't exist. As a matter of fact, this radar today with that kind of power is so safe you could walk up and put your hand right on the face of this radar. You could stand right in front of it. There is nothing unsafe about it for a human. We disperse the power. That's an incredible design that, every time I look at it I say to myself it's "his master's voice" speaking.* It is the true RCA of when I was a child.

Now, they didn't do it singlehandedly, of course, and frankly I'm not sure we'd ever have gotten there without someone like myself, who just said, "To hell with it; we're not going to take any prisoners. If we know what we're going, I'm going to lead you. But if I lead, you damn well better follow, because I'm not about to get out there by myself. And I will see that the money is raised." I learned all this in those first few months, although a lot of my prowess was stored from Eli Reich and Roger Elmore Spreen, my two mentors; I just didn't appreciate it yet, that I would be able to do it.

---

* For many years the motto for the Radio Corporation of America was "His Master's Voice," which included a picture of a dog named Nipper faithfully attentive to the horn of a gramophone record player.

We had to raise unprecedented amounts of money in regular programs, and we weren't one of these gigantic nuclear programs or any of those things, who just spend hundreds of millions of dollars. None of that was allotted when we started. So by November, in formulating the next budget, we were in crisis, and a crew of people were in the position of saying, "Well, it's going to take a long time to develop this, it's going to take a lot of effort, why don't we cut these budgets back and kind of dribble them along." That was the attitude and that's what had to be fought off.

Paul Stillwell: You talked before about the guiding star on the horizon that you were moving for. In the early '70s did you have a timetable for when you would get to that star?

Admiral Meyer: We had attached to that star in those days. Very early on, I think no later than ' 71, somewhere in there, we created the slogan: "Aegis to sea, Aegis to sea, Aegis to sea." And while the original big engineering development contract, Air Force style, called for three big engineering development models and a brand-new missile and a brand-new launcher, none of those were meant to be, because when you finally had to sober up and get around to reconciling the money and stuff, it couldn't be done. Furthermore, it turned out it *could* be done, if you had the right kind of team and the right kind of attitude and the right kind of products.

And so we decided every bloody week to undertake it. I called it "lifeboat behavior." We're all in this lifeboat, and we've got the option of trying to save ourselves or saying the hell with it. And I may have mentioned to you, I've said it on several occasions, and I brag about it, I've never had anybody with me that wasn't a volunteer. I just refused to have a civil servant or an officer or a vice president in those days that was not a volunteer. I didn't want anybody else. First of all, they had to believe. Second of all, they were in many respects risking their future if they failed, we failed. I'm proud to say that many, many of them went on to great successful undertakings as a result of the outcome, but it sure didn't look that way.

We had two power tubes, one with an outfit called S-F-D in New Jersey, and one was the California group for power tubes; I can't say right now who it is.[*] And that was the introduction of what came to be known as the introduction of the crossed-field amplifier as a new power tube. It was a tube smaller than this table, much smaller. Actually, it was a 40-pound tube, so one man could handle it. And we got the design down to where each array had 32 power tubes. So two arrays had 64. So four arrays in a ship had 128 power tubes, is how we massed all that power.

We had what we referred to in those days as a trombone section in the deckhouse. If you went and looked in our deckhouse we had this. It would just blow your mind. This was the frequency of S-band, around 3,000 megacycles. And the waveguide for 3,000 megacycles in horizontal is about that wide.[†]

Paul Stillwell: Four inches, maybe.

Admiral Meyer: Yeah, about four inches. And it's about 2 inches vertically. Well, we decided that we could get by with half-height waveguide, so we could use, like, less than 2-inch waveguide but still needed the 4 inches to put this waveguide all together. We went to work with big mockups up at Moorestown, because the physical layout was a challenge, a real challenge. How to gang this stuff all together and get it to come out and focus and hit a spot on the array. Magic numbers on this radar, they are all digital: 16, 32, 64, 128. These are all digital numbers, all the powers of two, and for the first time we were doing in a radar design this effort of ganging this power up out of these one-kilowatt tubes and bringing it all together and making it come in phase and focus on you out at 220 miles, and get a detection. It's stunning. It was just mind-blowing. It is amazing what we have contributed, actually, to the field of engineering in high-powered microwave since then. Patriot was alongside us, but they weren't dealing in high power. AWACS was alongside us, but they weren't dealing in high power either.[‡] And AWACS was not dealing in fixed arrays.

---

[*] S-F-D Laboratories, Union, New Jersey.
[†] A waveguide is a structure that carries electro-magnetic waves from the source to different parts of a ship.
[‡] AWACS – airborne warning and control system. This is an aerial look-down radar and tracking system carried on board the Air Force's E-3 Sentry, a modified Boeing 707 airliner with a rotating radome on top.

So the heart of the arrays was this thing here. This is called a ferrite phase shifter. Today we don't use them anymore. We use digital phase shifters.

Paul Stillwell: It's about 6 or 7 inches long, maybe.

Admiral Meyer: Right, and maybe weighs half a pound. Each radar in a cruiser has got 16,000 of these in the radar, and 2,000 more for the countermeasures piece, so there are 18,000 of these little mothers in each radar. So right away you're told that, boy, one of the important things on this is not only its cost but its reliability. And we designed them so that they're installed in nests. And we originally, because we had so much pressure from the purists and the theorists, that we could sample and determine every single one of these on-line, as to whether it was functioning or not functioning. We don't do that anymore. Of course, it turned out to not be important then. We operated for several years in *Norton Sound* with one array which was about better than 4,000 of these, and as far as I know we never had a failure the whole time. They were that good. We put a lot of time on it. We put a hell of a lot of effort on it. The materials in this came from a little outfit up in the Catoctin Mountains here in Maryland. And RCA and Raytheon together, we engineered this thing. The first one of these cost us something like $700.00 apiece. When we got through, by the time we were building Serial 1, we were making them at $40.00 apiece. That's how much engineering we accomplished.

We chose to have these assembled at that little place, and some of them finally completed in RCA itself—worked closely to supervise it. And I regularly made trips to these places because these things, you can see, originally were pretty darned dainty. They called for a lot of dexterity and skill in their assembly and putting them together. It really was mostly women, far and away women. We had hundreds of them. Their performance really, really mattered. And the rejection rate was very, very costly. We spent a lot of time on that.

We went, on this thing, in the next two years we went from an acceptance rate of something like 40% till by the end we were 98% off the production line.

Paul Stillwell: How did you achieve that?

Admiral Meyer: Well, I told those women it was because of them. But I had engineers in the production department, manufacturing department. I had women in the engineering department—I had them all mixed in there. Put them in a gunnysack and shake them every day. I had sailors with them *every bloody day*!

I started with two officers and seven sailors at Moorestown when we opened the doors, and I had a couple rules on that. Number one, they had to come in the front door. Number two, they had to wear their uniforms, so that people never forgot what they're doing. And if you watch the Lockheed Martin slogan today—you know, in their big ads like in the *Post* and stuff just this weekend—their biggest slogan for a number of years now: "We never forget who we're working for." Well, I think that this in recent years came from Captain (retired) Fred Moosally, who had worked for me in another era, and they ended up adopting that slogan for the whole Lockheed Corporation—not the RCA one but the whole Lockheed structure.[*]

So this thing has any number of parts, and they've really knocked the hell out of its cost. Making processes to be able to constantly check it turned out to be unnecessary. We did a lot of unnecessary things. Fear helps a person a lot, because we knew that if we failed they were coming after us; they were going to kill us. These are known as ferrite phase shifters. Well, today in the latest one we're using what are called digital phase shifters, so they're a little lighter weight that this. I don't know what they cost today when they make them. I think we have the same numbers in them. These phase shifters will be there when you and I are in the graveyard. Incredible, just incredible.

And so you look in the back of the array, the radar, there's nothing to see. You look there and say, "Well, wait a minute, what am I looking at?" Because all you see are the panels that are over all of this, and it's all hooked together. And you look up above you, and you see all of this waveguide running around, or what we call the trombones—they're all running around up there—which pipe all this stuff together in its use.

When I took over, there were three engineering development models. By the end-of-the-world speech, there was one. Number two got cancelled before the contract was ever let, and that was to develop a missile. Number three was to refine EDM-1, so

---

[*] Captain Fred P. Moosally, USN (Ret.), served from 2002 to 2010 as president of Lockheed Martin's MS2 division, involved with the Navy's *Freedom* (LCS-1)-class littoral combat ships and the Coast Guard's Integrated Deepwater System.

number three was to be what you may call pre-production billing.* Never happened. One unit was to go to Desert Ship at White Sands, New Mexico, for long-range testing. Never happened.

Norton Sound did become available. *Norton Sound*, when I walked in the door, was in a private shipyard in Baltimore. She had parts of the Typhon program in her. She was going to be the designated ship for Aegis.

Paul Stillwell: Did she still have that big Typhon dome at that moment?

Admiral Meyer: She did. So I got my arms around that, which was not an easy thing to do—but I didn't have any money with it either. One of the things I found, and you've heard me say this, when something's bankrupt you can get custody of it anytime. Stuff that's out of money, anybody will give it to you. But if you're not experienced, you never know what you're picking up. It's like going to yard sales; if you're not experienced you'll just get a truckload of junk.

But we got *Norton Sound* back, sent her down to Long Beach shipyard, undertook supervision directly for what the yard was to do to prepare her for a partial deckhouse to put in this one array, and another array was to be a fake array. We didn't have enough money for two. We got one in.

Set her up and started operating her, and she was operating with the new UYK-7 computers, which were specced, by the way, at 25 hours. We've got UYK-7 computers today around through the Aegis fleet that have never failed. They've got hundreds of thousand of hours on them. The UYK-43 came out of Sperry's engineering simultaneously, a smaller computer, which we adopted also into Aegis, so we have those two basic computers to this day. Computer failure is not an issue. You never hear anything about it. Our opponents, right on the congressional floor, would talk about how we had so many computer programs and everything that the system couldn't possibly be made to work with any length of time. The Aegis system being down is very unusual indeed.

---

* EDM – engineering development model.

An expression emerged then that I have never really cared for, but it's descriptive: something called "graceful degradation." All our designs, first of all, depended on good components. They depended on careful assembly. They depended on rigorous, exhausting testing. All those things were vital, and review, review, review, review. I never worked for Rickover, but I've been around him and associated with him for a long time, and I took a lot of pages out of his behavior. And similarly Levering Smith, whom I idolized as an engineer. So I never worked for either one, but I sure learned a lot from watching them in action.

Well, we finally achieved critical mass maybe by '73 or '74, somewhere in there. The Navy had sold this program even before I arrived by bragging that they had no ship, because the Congress had just beaten the life out of them for committing ships to systems that hadn't been engineered or hadn't been built yet. So we were in the meantime building *California*, *South Carolina*, and the tail end of the Terrier fleet and such.

So now that went on; that was good for three years. So I would go over, and they'd say, "All right, we hear you, Captain, we hear you, Captain; what's your plan?"

"Well, my plan is to do this, do—"

"Well, what's your plan in shipbuilding? What's your plan?" I just kept getting beaten up and beaten up and beaten up. And I discovered again how fickle the whole democracy structure is and how it just jumps around to various kinds of things. So this meant I had to develop a plan. Since I couldn't get one out of the Navy, I got into it myself. Guess what—there wasn't anybody that would stop me. But, of course, I'm stealing the money, in essence, out of the Aegis program. Nobody would stop me, and yet they didn't want to be identified with it either.

Paul Stillwell: Well, two of the things that were looked at as candidates for Aegis were the *Virginia* class and a conversion of *Long Beach*. Were those in your horizon?[*]

---

[*] The Navy had four nuclear-powered cruisers of the *Virginia* (CGN-38) class. The *Virginia* was commissioned in 1976 and decommissioned in 1994. The last ship of the class, *Arkansas* (CGN-41), was commissioned in 1980 and decommissioned in 1998. The Navy budget for fiscal year 1978 included funding for components for an Aegis-equipped version of the class, beginning with CGN-42, but construction plans were cancelled in 1979. *Long Beach* (CGN-9) was equipped with Talos and Terrier.

Admiral Meyer: Oh, yeah, they were. [Chuckle] I mean, we studied them ad nauseam. Originally, *Virginia* was the designated class.

Paul Stillwell: And the Moorestown facility sort of looks like what that would have been with Aegis.

Admiral Meyer: Right. I mean, I was just beat to pieces on it. You can even find models of *Virginia* around here someplace. The same way, since we had no ship—well, why don't we convert *Long Beach*? I've never forgotten, we spent a whole Sunday in Admiral Frank Price's office, who was OP-03 at the time.*

Paul Stillwell: And had commanded *Long Beach*.

Admiral Meyer: And he had had command of *Long Beach*. So he had a picture about this size hung in the office over there, maybe three by four or so, a little bigger. I had Commander Bob Beers with me. And what Price was making us do was redesigning *Long Beach* on that picture. Spent all Sunday afternoon trying to mark up that picture with a grease pencil—it had glass on it like that one—of what she might look like. Well, we pulled something off of Skyhook, or whatever we call it. It saved the program for several months. It turned out to not be a serious contender in the end. But there just was no ship you could pick that we didn't study.

And then there was one year—I forget which year that was now—Rickover caused the Congress to pass a law that all ships of the surface combatant forces had to be nuclear-propelled. And so that was really driving us into the water because you had this big movement that, well, why don't we take the 963s and use them?† At that time NavShips was split up into ship engineering centers. It's biggest, the design one, was located in Hyattsville.‡ And they developed proof that there was no way that the Aegis

---

* Vice Admiral Frank H. Price Jr., USN, served as Deputy Chief of Naval Operations (Surface Warfare) from July 1974 to August 1975. As a captain, Price had commanded the nuclear-powered cruiser *Long Beach* (CGN-9) from September 1963 to August 1966.
† USS *Spruance* (DD-963), lead ship of a class of destroyers, was commissioned 20 September 1975. Her hull design later became the one used for the *Ticonderoga* (CG-47)-class Aegis cruisers.
‡ Naval Ship Engineering Center, Hyattsville, Maryland.

could be landed in a *Spruance*. It was too big and too heavy, both, to be able to install it in there.

The tale I'm about to tell I believe occurred about 1973. There was a fellow by the name Dr. J. J. McMullen. I didn't know him. Bill Goodwin didn't know him. But one of the senior vice presidents at RCA knew him. And so Bill called me up, and he said, "You know, what do you think about us having a meeting or something with this guy McMullen? Because he's got all these grandi-ass ideas on how to make ships out of blue haze and everything." Okay, so why don't we go have supper with him? And we did. It was a February, as I recollect.

J. J. McMullen—it's worth knowing a couple minutes of his history.*

Paul Stillwell: I've met him. He went up through the Navy as a commander and then started his own company.

Admiral Meyer: Right. He graduated from the Naval Academy, and he became an engineering duty officer. He was selected by the Navy to go to the University of Zurich. I believe he was the first officer to get an education in gas turbines, and he had to go to the university in Switzerland to get it, and that's where he got his PhD. He's a pretty impressive guy. Amongst other things, his father owned a whole tug structure of New York City. So the tug fleet—I don't know whether it's totally the tug fleet, but a giant piece of it. He grew up not poor, but he grew up on the waterfronts, and his father ended up kind of willing that stuff to him, which he sold because he didn't have the interest in it. But he had an abiding interest in trying to build something.

Well, he got involved in the Middle East. And so he built them a couple dry docks, and he got to know the Saudis pretty well, and he got to know the Iranians pretty well from his constantly traveling. I don't know how much money he made. He never worried about how much he made, and I never worried about how much he ever spent on me, because money was not an issue with him.

---

* Midshipman John J. McMullen, USN, was commissioned with the Naval Academy class of 1940. He served on active duty until he resigned in December 1957 as a commander. That same year he founded John J. McMullen Associates, a naval architecture and marine engineering firm.

As a result of his association with us he caused to be created the J. J. McMullen Company, the designers. They still exist right here as part of the naval architectural structure around here.

Anyhow, McMullen said, "Look, if you're going to do something in the Navy, you're going to have to move out and do it yourself. And I'd like to try and help you." Sounded good to us. So he said, "What do you think the characteristics ought to be?"

I said, "Well, first of all, we don't believe that we can fit in anything under about 5,000 ton, and that would be a real struggle." We couldn't get the power out that we wanted at that size. So we settled 6,000 tons.

Paul Stillwell: And stability was probably a concern as well.

Admiral Meyer: Well, it came to the next, and it said, not only is it not big enough, but we've got to worry about we've got a lot of topside weight, and we have to learn how to handle that topside weight and provide the stability. Okay. So Bill Goodwin and I said, "Look, we want a minimum of one 5-inch gun on this ship. We're not going to be party to a warship that doesn't have a gun on it."

Now here I was in a situation, totally estranged from NavSEC at Hyattsville, totally estranged from all the ship designers, who constantly were telling us it couldn't be done, it couldn't be done. And the combination of Zumwalt and the others were so desperate for where could they steal money, and Vietnam, of course, was bleeding everybody dry. And so it's funny how very few people give a rat's toenail about the threat. Nobody seemed to care about the threat.

So we kept futzing around, futzing around, futzing around, and finally we decided by late February—because J. J. had talked to a couple of his designers in New York, including George Sawyer.[*] George Sawyer worked for him at that time. And they had quarters in the, you know, the two buildings that got destroyed...

Paul Stillwell: World Trade Center.

---

[*] George Sawyer served as Assistant Secretary of the Navy (Shipbuilding and Logistics), 1981-83.

Admiral Meyer: Yeah, World Trade Center.[*] They were in the World Trade Center on, as I recollect it was the 40th deck. So J. J. said, "Well, come on up, you all get a group, come up here and let's talk about it to them." It's the only time I was ever in the World Trade Center, and I was awed. Because they mostly did design work for yachts and things like that, and pleasure boats, powerboats. So they had—it wasn't a whole deck but they had a big, big area.

So McMullen took us out to some incredible restaurant in the city. I don't even recall the address, but it's called, I think, The Indian Company, or something or other. Anyhow, Bill and I, who aren't big splashers past meat and potatoes, we went out and had a big lunch that day. We allowed McMullen put on the dog. I'm trying to think of the name of the fellow who was McMullen's lead architect. His name was George somebody. God, he was a brilliant fellow, but not a Navy person. He was not a Navy person. He really was a yacht designer.

Well, they decided after they finished that—I want to say this number but I ain't sure it's the correct number. McMullen said, "Look, I talked to my people last night," a week later. He said, "I think that we could try to get you a design, but we've got to have some money. We've got to have something to go on." Well, we don't have a lot of free money. So we agreed Bill would go to RCA, which was in 30 Rockefeller Center, and Bill would get $20 million out of them. And I would find a way to get $20 million out of this program down here. We'd put up $40 million.

So McMullen said, "Well, that's pretty good. We ought to be able to get something with that amount of money. But if you don't get somebody to supervise it you can't get anything done." So, okay. We decided that the right person was Commander Bob Beers, who worked for me, and a couple engineers that worked for Bill Goodwin at RCA Moorestown, and a couple engineers that we knew who were retired from the naval design and architectural persuasion that would be under the custody of Beers. And we sent Beers and his team up there and we gave them a ground rule: my birthday is the 21st day of April; whatever you're going to do, you're going to be done by the 21st day of April, that's your target.

---

[*] On 11 September 2001 terrorists deliberately flew hijacked commercial aircraft into the twin towers of the World Trade Center at the tip of Manhattan in New York and destroyed both buildings.

Well, we reviewed them. I was there twice, and reviewed them fairly regularly in those few weeks. And finally the 20th, they said, "Captain, we think we've got something."

Paul Stillwell: What year was that April 20?

Admiral Meyer: I was afraid you would ask that. I want to say it was '75. They said, "So we think that we can meet the numbers," but remember, this is all on paper. Good enough. So they brought down here these sketches and a drawing of something called the "DG," with a 5-inch gun sticking out there and a whole superstructure that was the Aegis. It was just a big radar with a little piss-ant mast pole stuck atop it. And their estimate was somewhere approaching 6,000 tons.

Paul Stillwell: Did it look like the *Spruance* class?

Admiral Meyer: Well, it did in a traditional ship sense, yes. The answer is yes. And it would be propelled by turbines. But those were really paper things. They brought it down here. Goodwin and I wrapped it up under my arm, and I went to the Pentagon and flung it down.

Paul Stillwell: Was this now the 21st that you went?

Admiral Meyer: Well, I took that day off. [Laughter] But it was a day or two after that.

Paul Stillwell: Okay.

Admiral Meyer: We plopped it down. Well, of course, it was electric. And it took only about 30 minutes for the word to travel throughout Crystal City, throughout Hyattsville, all over, of what I had now done. That it *could* be done, and it *could* be done in 6,000 tons.

Paul Stillwell: Whom did you present it to?

Admiral Meyer: I presented it to, we called him—it doesn't sound very good, but he's in the graveyard now—he was called Frank "Horseapple" Price.

Paul Stillwell: So he was still OP-03 at the time.

Admiral Meyer: I believe he was. I don't think he'd been relieved yet.

And so this terrified the system so much that about, I'd guess someplace in May, NavSea people showed up over in OpNav and OP-03, and guess what? And NavMat still existed. "Well, you know, we've restudied this thing, and it turns out that with all the weight reduction Aegis had undergone"—which had been none—"it can be installed and landed, we believe, in a *Spruance*. Now, it'll take ballast, you've got to understand. You've got to understand, Admiral, have to put ballast, got to understand, have to put ballast in it, have to have ballast in it." And everything. But it could be done.

So we went from impossible to, well, it could be, to enthusiasm. So we broke their back. And we took our DG and we stuck it in the file cabinet, and there it resides to this day. And left it there. And we got ourselves a restart that, in fact, we could do a *Spruance*. It was not exactly a *Spruance* we started with, but that wasn't what we started. We started because, remember, the Ayatollah class fell in.[*] Those ships were significantly better designs than a basic *Spruance*, as you might expect. So we chose that, and that's how we proceeded.

Well, it turned out—I will come back to this about four months from now when you're getting to the end, but—when *Ticonderoga* finally went on trial she had, as I remember, 120 tons of ballast in her as a result of what's called the inclining experiment, which is done at a pier with the ship to measure what her stability numbers are.

Paul Stillwell: Metacentric height.

---

[*] Four ships of the DXG variant were ordered for delivery to Iran. After that country's government fell to the Ayatollah Ruhollah Khomeini in 1979, the ships were completed for the U.S. Navy. The USS *Kidd* (DDG-993) and her three sisters went into commission in 1981 and 1982.

Admiral Meyer: Exactly. And her KG.* Well, we had never stopped. In *Yorktown* that number went down to about half, I think, around 60 ton. In *Vincennes*, which was number three, I believe the number was around 40.

Paul Stillwell: Was this because of weight reduction topside?

Admiral Meyer: Yeah. It was because of our general engineering effort. We just kept plugging away at it, plugging away and plugging away, and then measuring it and seeing what happened. Well, it shows you the way you solve problems is with engineering. I mean, I'm a strong, strong believer that you don't solve problems with technology; you solve them with engineering. And you get teams of men focused on what it is they need to do. That's how you get problems solved in design, whether you're building ships, tanks, or buildings. You've got to get focused on what you need to do.

Now, that sounds trite and bombastic, but I guarantee you, Paul, that in our Navy today, easily a half of these programs are not focused that way at all. It may be a much bigger number. There's very few focused on that. All of them are focused on the cost numbers, every one of them. Well, cost is important, but it isn't the only thing that's important. There are a lot of other things that are important.

That set of years, of the early '70s, was very fiery and very threatening to me and to the project and to people in it. And how hostile people were. God, they were hostile.

Paul Stillwell: For what reason? Because you were getting the money that they wanted?

Admiral Meyer: I don't know that I'll ever know. You can't help but come to believe it was you or somebody serving with you. I spent a lot of time on that, a real lot of time. And, of course, I could develop a complex—I may even *have* developed one, thinking: "The hostility is so great that it must be me." But I said to someone about a month or so ago who had come calling in my office: that bulkhead in there with 85 ball caps on it reflects me, and there is no other person anyplace anywhere can make that statement. Nowhere. Not even Hyman G. Rickover could do that.

---

* KG – center of gravity.

I developed sayings in my speeches and talks; no one every disputed me or sassed me, but I would bring up the seven capital sins. And I'm always reminding people that the seven capital sins are always operable. And, as a matter of fact, there's a lot of universality in those seven capital sins throughout all of the great cults of the world. They, of course, are propagated by the Vatican, but virtually all Protestants believe the seven capital sins, virtually all the Jews do, and I think a lot of Islamism contains the seven capital sins. As a matter of fact, Islamism contains them far more viciously than Christianity does. And I believe Buddhism contains a lot of them. So there's not anything startling about that. It's just that as human beings we don't stop to think very often, if at all, beyond the catechism stage about the seven capital sins and what they are. But they define the general behavior pattern of a human, and what free will means. And it used to be Jesuits talked a lot about them. You just don't hear any talks like that anymore.

Paul Stillwell: How was this hostility toward you expressed?

Admiral Meyer: Well, a couple ways. One was that there would be subtleties appear in some of the testimony, not directly made. As a matter of fact, you had to be able to read a great deal to find out what was left out of the testimony on the surface Navy. I've made no secret about it—Zumwalt did not want this fleet; he was anti-Aegis. He was anti-Aegis from day one.

Paul Stillwell: What was the reason for his antipathy toward it?

Admiral Meyer: He had this perception that it was too expensive, too complex, took too many people, and it would take too long to get it. He didn't have anything in its favor. Well, I have to say point blank if I were naming a fleet I would have never named a fleet after Zumwalt. I served under him; I served directly under him. I watched his behavior pattern, just as I watched the behavior pattern of John Lehman.

Paul Stillwell: Where was the direct connection that you had with Zumwalt?

Admiral Meyer: None, but he was the CNO. Goldwater-Nichols, remember, did not exist.

Paul Stillwell: Right.

Admiral Meyer: But my protection was Worth Bagley. He brought Worth Bagley in to be OP—I think it would be -08 today; at that time it was OP-090.*

Paul Stillwell: Well, he ran the budget shop, and then he was director of program planning.

Admiral Meyer: Right. And he was a very wise officer. He had a brother, an older brother, that I barely knew, Dave Bagley.† I believe Dave Bagley's dead; I don't think Worth is.

Paul Stillwell: You're right on both counts.

Admiral Meyer: My office was always on a corner, it seemed like, but in my early days of Aegis it was on the tenth deck of Building 2 over there, so I'd face and look right this direction.‡ But I kept the name Worth Bagley up on the blackboard, because I always said that if I were going to have a vote on naming an Aegis ship I'd name it *Worth Bagley*. Worth Bagley, as far as I know, never sought, nor did he ever—

(Interruption)

Admiral Meyer: So the reason I got along great with Zumwalt—and I could talk from now till suppertime about it, but it was Worth Bagley. Worth Bagley knew exactly how to handle him. I've told you the story of me and Worth Bagley, have I not?

---

* Vice Admiral Worth H. Bagley, USN, served as the Navy's Director of Program planning from May 1971 to April 1973. He and his brother David were close confidants to Admiral Zumwalt.
† Vice Admiral David H. Bagley, USN, served as Chief of Naval Personnel from 1 February 1972 to 10 April 1975.
‡ National Center 2 (NC-2) in Crystal City, Arlington, Virginia.

Paul Stillwell: I don't recall it.

Admiral Meyer: Well, do you want it recorded?

Paul Stillwell: Sure.

Admiral Meyer: I told you, I believe, that I'd been ordered out to Port Hueneme to be the chief engineer, and the admiral had given me a set of instructions. Right at the peak of the war, 1967. At the same time Worth Bagley got orders to command the cruiser *Canberra*.[*] She was in Long Beach shipyard. In that era I had about, before I went out there, or when I came back, actually, three or four assignments. I came back as the Aegis manager, became the SMS manager, became Director of Surface Warfare, all those things, when I came back from Port Hueneme. Well, before I went to Port Hueneme out of the task force, and then while I was out there, we had these thrusts going on of what the hell were we going to do about cruise missiles. And there were all kinds of frantic things and shenanigans going on of how to, you know, get a quick fix for something for which there was no quick fix. So everybody's getting their own invention on how to kill cruise missiles.

Worth Bagley, being hyperactive, was ordered to take command of *Canberra*. *Canberra* was in Long Beach shipyard. He wanted to hurry up and get her out of there because he wanted to get to Vietnam. He didn't want a crippled ship, either. So, as hyperactives are wont to do, they find themselves a fire controlman or two in their ship who say: "Well, you know, Captain, we know how to solve that; we can kill those missiles."

"Oh, okay lads, let's go at it." So the next thing you know—recall those ships had the SPQ-5A radars on them, and Terrier missiles, and did well to shoot, period. So they were going to redesign the fire control system and the missile system to kill cruise missiles.

---

[*] Captain Worth H. Bagley, USN, served as commanding officer of the guided missile heavy cruiser *Canberra* (CAG-2) from 23 November 1968 to 20 September 1969.

One day—this is a sea story—I got a phone call from Worth. He'd been in command down there about three months or so. "Wayne, I need your help." Well, I knew it was coming because I kept a regular engineer stationed down at Long Beach shipyard in the war years, because we were doing so many things to the ships before they sailed, so I expected it. He said, "I need your help to get the ship straightened out so we can get to sea."

"Well, Worth, let me think about it."

Paul Stillwell: Did you know him prior to that?

Admiral Meyer: Yes, I knew him, though casually. I'd never served with him.

Paul Stillwell: But you were in a job at Port Hueneme where you were in a position to help him.

Admiral Meyer: Right. Now I could get that ship back together. So I called him back the next day and I said, "Look, you all have got several things kind of screwed up, and my data are that you're estranged from the shipyard. You've got everybody in the shipyard pissed off at you and your behavior. And I can't help under those circumstances. But if you'll follow my ground rules I'll do my very best to help."

"Wayne, I need your help, I need your help."

I don't know whether you ever personally knew Worth.

Paul Stillwell: I interviewed him a number of years ago.*

Admiral Meyer: He's very persuasive. Worth could never take "No" for an answer. He's very persuasive. Which is why Rickover had him.

So I put together a team, with an officer in charge of them, went down there with instructions, try to get the ship glued back together, and getting her so she could do as

---

* Admiral Bagley's recollections in the Naval Institute oral history collection are contained in a volume from officers who served with Admiral Zumwalt.

best she could what she was supposed to do. Besides that, she had her 8-inch guns on there. Well, they did. They went back down there in the next five, six weeks. They got the ship put back together, and Worth got out of the shipyard and got to the war.

Worth Bagley never forgot that, never forgot it. So when he became Zumwalt's lackey and his protector, he came to support me. Well, I couldn't pester him, you know, 12 times a day. The man was so overloaded there was no way he could get to it. So when I pestered him it had to be very well thought out in what to do.

He called me up—I may have my years mixed up here. That era is such a loaded, exciting era. I didn't tell you this, I guess. He said, "Wayne, the boss is on the warpath. He wants to kill something, and the Aegis is the nearest thing he's got to kill because that's where the money is, and he's after it."

I said, "Well, what do you want to do?"

He said, "Well, we've got to show him something. My experience has been that you turn him around by letting him get exposed to something real, and he can't resist it."

I said, "Well, in town all we've got is the stuff we have out at the Applied Physics Laboratory." We had a number of experiments going on out there which were forerunners to get into the engineering development at Moorestown.

Paul Stillwell: This was at APL, at Laurel, Maryland.

Admiral Meyer: APL, Applied Physics Laboratory. At APL, Laurel, Maryland. I said, "The stuff we have there is mostly experimental things we've worked on before we let the contract."

He said, "You've got to do something. He's on the warpath, we've got to try to stop him."

So, "Okay, let me get back to you in an hour."

I got hold of my commanders and my deputy, and George Luke, my best man at APL, and said, "We've got to do something and do something now. I will deliver the CNO; what are you going to do?" We cobbled up this goddamn plan that we would say to Bagley: "You get the CNO out here by helo at first light, and we will show him some things down in the basement of the lab and let him see that, and it will take less than an hour, the whole thing."

He said, "That sounds good. Let's do that. I'll have him there tomorrow morning." Well, of course we were up all night worried about what the hell we were going to do. We had a technician out at APL who had been the chief fire controlman for Zumwalt when Zumwalt commanded the DLG *Dewey*.[*]

So the next morning it just barely was daylight, allowed them to leave the Pentagon. They got out, I met them out on the sward and there we were going along. And, of course, you get wet clear to your hips, the dew was so damned heavy—and met the helo, along with the director, and we were all lined up. Zumwalt came up. Worth didn't come, because Worth didn't want a part of it. The CNO came off of there, plodding off with two or three aides behind him. Everybody was scrambling to keep up, and Zumwalt going a mile a minute. Didn't want to ride in a car. Walked up the hill and everything to get to the lab. Well, I was running to keep up.

We got up there, and we headed down into the cellar, which is down two decks, to start showing him around these different places. People were standing around, and very pleased and proud the CNO had come to visit. And so guess what—standing there in the middle was the chief fire controlman. Zumwalt said, "Chief, what are you doing here?"

"Well, Admiral, I work here now; I work for this."

"Chief," he said, "have you got anything to do with this Aegis?"

He said, "Yes, sir. That's where I'm working."

"Well," he said, "is it going to work?"

The chief pondered for a minute. He said, "You know, Admiral, I think it will."

"Well," he said, "that's good to know." Turned around and walked out!
[Laughter]

Paul Stillwell: That's a great story.

---

[*] Commander Elmo R. Zumwalt Jr., USN, served as commanding officer of the guided missile frigate *Dewey* (DLG-6) from 7 December 1959 to 15 July 1961. The *Dewey* was the Navy's first DLG, and Zumwalt was her first skipper.

Admiral Meyer: Walked out and got on the goddamn airplane and flew back. Worth called me later that day and said, "Don't know what you did, but you saved the day." [Laughter] It was unbelievable. Like a salvage operation. We damn near knighted the chief later, and he said, "Well, I just told him the truth."

But that didn't mean I'd become a big buddy of Zumwalt's, but Zumwalt stopped attacking. He stopped the attack. That was someplace there in the end-of-the-world era; I don't know where exactly it was. But from then on I generally did not lose any money. Of course, Model 2 was gone, Model 3 was gone, and I was clinging to *Norton Sound* to keep her going and such. But in those years of Zumwalt I never had a problem. Never.

I haven't talked to Worth Bagley in a number of years. As far as I know, he had no continuing interest in Aegis or, for that matter, in fleet operations. I honestly don't know what this really fruitful, productive man did out in La Jolla—I believe that's where he lives—all these years. I've not seen anything to come out of his cultivated and learned mind.

Paul Stillwell: He and Zumwalt used to write a newspaper column that ran regularly for a while.

Admiral Meyer: They did.

Paul Stillwell: I haven't seen anything recently.

Admiral Meyer: They did, but that was a relatively short period.

Paul Stillwell: Right.

Admiral Meyer: And it was not regular either. It was sporadic.
One of my heroes.
In talking to incoming project managers, civil servants, I'm constantly reminding them that you're moving into an era, a position, where you do not know who the client is

for a long period. So be careful who you smart off to. They may be your boss, and simply because they don't know anything about it doesn't mean that it can't happen.

I had her look up for me the dates of Jim Doyle, and the rest of your time on this we'll cycle in and out of Jim Doyle.

Paul Stillwell: I interviewed Vice Admiral Bill Rowden, and he gave Admiral Doyle great credit for support of Aegis.

Admiral Meyer: I give him overwhelming credit. I've said in many of my speeches that he's the reason we have Aegis. And he served as OP-03 from '75 to 1980, and he made the difference. The Navy ignored him. He's a shy person anyhow. He's a Navy junior; many Navy juniors are very shy. His dad was the commander at Inchon.*

I was commissioned in February of 1946 and originally was placed at the tail end of '45 in the great book, but then when I became a regular officer—the reserves weren't in the great book at that time yet; they were in another book. But you opened the book, I found out that I was ahead of the Naval Academy class of '46, not at the tail of '45.

Now, discrimination always exists in some manner in humans, and I get tired of hearing about it. And I particularly get tired of hearing about it from the black people in how they were treated and where I came from. And, of course, anybody that looks at any history at all knows that discrimination has existed for thousands of years and continues to, and will always. But I can't say that that really bothered me in the end. I know what I am. I know what I did. I know how many officers worked for me for the benefit of them, and I know the officers that worked for me for the importance of the Navy and the nation. There's a difference in those officers. All officers aren't the same. Think about the officers you know who spend their time worrying about their next tour of duty, and whether it's career enhancing or not. I can genuinely say that I never did that. Now, I don't want to get too bombastic. I think the reason is I was too dumb to know better. It never occurred to me you had to do that.

---

* On 15 September 1950, U.S. troops under the command of General of the Army Douglas MacArthur made an amphibious landing at Inchon, the port for Seoul, South Korea. The surprise landing, 150 miles behind enemy lines, temporarily turned the tide of war in favor of United Nations forces. Rear Admiral James H. Doyle, USN, was Commander Task Force 90 for the seaborne aspects of the invasion.

I've told you my daddy was a humble man. He went to the sixth grade. He was born a farmer and he died a farmer. And he lived through the Depression with his four kids, the youngest of which was born in 1931, a wife, and a mother-in-law, and he raised them all in spite of losing everything he owned. He and his woman, my mother, somehow imbued in us a knowledge of right and wrong that stuck with all four of us. I'm sorry to say that the other three are all in the graveyard.

The significance of that is, even though I left home this month, the first week in July in 1943, to never return, 17 years old by two months, having enlisted on the 12th day of May, three weeks after my 17th birthday, they were scared to death, but they did not hold back on signing the papers for me to enlist in the U.S. Navy. Well, not everybody came out of that kind of stock and not everybody got imbued with some kind of shyness or a form of humbleness, which is not humbleness at all, as a result of that kind of growing up.

Paul Stillwell: Were you trying to make a point there about relative seniority of yourself and Admiral Doyle?

Admiral Meyer: Oh. Not particularly, but it's worth an observation. Doyle was commissioned in June of 1946. I think he's listed on the register as the Class of '47.

Paul Stillwell: Yes.

Admiral Meyer: I was commissioned in February, and that's the way I'm listed. Zumwalt was senior to us and everything, as was Holloway, who was a wonderful CNO.

Paul Stillwell: And Worth Bagley was a classmate of Doyle.

Admiral Meyer: Right, that's correct. And so it seemed to me we were very harmonious, and so was Hayward when Tom Hayward later came to office.[*] That was a harmonious

---

[*] Admiral Thomas B. Hayward, USN, served as Chief of Naval Operations from 1 July 1978 to 30 June 1982. His oral history is in the Naval Institute collection.

little era. It didn't seem like very long. But I told a person the other day on this present situation, because they're holding hearings in the Senate today, right now, on the confirmation of the replacement for Assistant Secretary, and people might think, well, that's only a few months; well, you can do a lot in a few months if you're in the right place. That's true here. That little band, which were close to being the same year group, carried through and swam through all of that white water in that era.

The other thing that you learn from all that, which is trite, and I've made this pronouncement several times, is year groups tend to move together through our Navy, so they tend to know each other all their life, whether they're an admiral or whether they're an ensign or someplace in between. They tend to know each other. I mean, Mike Mullen's got a lot of classmates and chums of his year group that know him well, and he's the number-one officer in the country.[*] And so it's not a spoils system. People tend, or I've always encouraged people, to try to surround yourself first with somebody you know. If you know them it's much to your advantage. Now, if you know them and dislike them or don't admire them, I wouldn't get them. But why in the hell go find strangers. But the truth is, most of the officers that I ended up with in Aegis were strangers in my beginning. I didn't know them.

But, here I'm working today, to beat that horse to death, on this stuff for Roughead.[†] Well, hell, I was an admiral before most of these people even entered the Navy. I don't have any problem with their seniority or what they do, particularly. It's never bothered me. I think it's because of the way I was brought up, the way I was raised. There's probably a lot of people that bothers, and I couldn't care two cents about it.

What I do care about is some of the—I don't know whether they're injustices or not. I don't believe that you can prevent discrimination, but you can argue against injustices. It's hard for me today to find any black people, for example, that have been treated unjustly. There was a time when that was not true. And I can get pretty damned wise and pretty damned smart when I engage in conversation with those. They aren't the

---

[*] Admiral Michael G. Mullen, USN, served as Chief of Naval Operations from 22 July 2005 to 29 September 2007, and then became Chairman of the Joint Chiefs of Staff on 1 October 2007.

[†] Admiral Gary Roughead, USN, has served as Chief of Naval Operations from 29 September 2007 to 23 September 2011. He was the first officer to command both an Aegis destroyer, USS *Barry* (DDG-52), and an Aegis cruiser, USS *Port Royal* (CG-73).

only people that grew up with no goddamn toilet. They aren't the only people that grew up with no running water. You're looking at one right here. I never knew what running water was, or a toilet, till I was in the Navy, or till I went to my grandmother's downtown. So this bullshit of disadvantage is just generally not acceptable to me to people who don't often want to plan their way out.

One of my more enjoyable times, I think, was when I was executive officer in USS *Strickland*, because I was a lieutenant (senior grade) and that era, which was, I guess it would be the mid-'50s, had a lot of reserve officers who came out of Reserve ROTC at Harvard or Yale, out of the preppy schools, who somehow thought that they were above everybody else. And my ship, which was a radar picket, tended—of course, BuPers had to man that ship, or officer it, they looked for people that weren't assignable someplace else, so I got a lot of them, a lot of them. Well, I'm pleased to say that I reformed a number of them. And a number of them, I put them in their place. Whether they all went on to be great or not, I don't know. I can shout off almost every one of the names of those officers that worked for me when I was XO and they were ensigns, and some of them I've often wondered where the hell they ever went or what they're doing.

There's only one of them that I thought had any moxie, really, and he was not out of a preppy school, but he was an Irishman, came out of the Boston area, and he had decided he wanted to be a schoolteacher, so he had studied math a great deal. But he was serving off his service which, I forget, I can't remember whether it was three years at that time or four years, what the service was, requirement.

They were never slackers as far as I was concerned. They often looked at me of how stupid I was for being in the regular Navy. They never said it, they just looked it, they radiated it to you, of: "You're so smart, why would you be stupid to stay in the regular Navy?" I've often wondered what they did with their lives, and my guess is, not very much. They might have piled up money on one side after another after another, maybe. I didn't keep up with them. I just didn't have the motivation to.

I went through, in the middle of that project and the founding of it, in the middle of it I went through probably a downer on it, but I entered with great enthusiasm and I left until that jerk Lehman fired me. I was there 13 years, and I was just as enthusiastic the day I was fired as I was when I started. As were my people. I always prided myself on not having fired people, because, I don't know, I just was somehow raised in the goodness of God.

Well, Missouri has always been kind of a forward-looking state, as you know. And in that era the public school buses—we lived five miles out of town but we lived on what was known in those days as a farm-to-market road, it was a gravel road—turned around right in the driveway. It was the end of its route, where we lived. We couldn't ride the bus. We weren't allowed to ride the bus because we were going to another school. The next year, the subsequent year, the state changed the law. We could ride the bus if we paid ten cents apiece. I don't know where in the hell my folks found the money, forty cents a day, two dollars a week. I don't know where they found it. But that year they paid ten cents for us to ride the bus.

The subsequent year the legislature ruled that any child could ride the bus providing the bus did not have to go substantially out of its route. God, what forward-looking. At that time, in that era, Episcopalians had a school in Brunswick and the Lutherans had a school. Well, they long since fell by the way—so's the Catholic school now; it fell after I went in the Navy. But what a pity that the public school bus drove right by the Catholic school and the Lutheran school every damn morning and every evening—kids couldn't ride the bus. Well, that kind of thing passed along its way and they lived through that and they learned how to deal in discrimination, and I don't remember people in that era bitching and moaning about their lot in life. They just knew it and accepted it. Today you can hardly turn on the TV without somebody wanting to get paid because of their situation they generate. What a different attitude.

I have to say that all that taught a lot to me. I don't know whether it was deliberate or how it came about, but it taught me a lot.

Paul Stillwell: Well, Admiral, I think it's time for your next appointment here.

Admiral Meyer: Is it? All right, well.

Paul Stillwell: See you next week.

Interview Number 14 with Rear Admiral Wayne E. Meyer, U.S. Navy (Retired)
Place: Admiral Meyer's office in Crystal City, Arlington, Virginia
Date: Monday, 21 July 2008

Paul Stillwell: Well, we're back at it, Admiral. A topic that I wanted to pursue is that in a previous interview you talked about Admiral Rickover and getting a law through Congress that major surface warships would be nuclear powered. How, then, were you able to get a gas-turbine-powered ship for Aegis?

Admiral Meyer: Well, I'll answer your question provided you allot me five minutes.

Paul Stillwell: All right.

Admiral Meyer: To talk about last night's TV program. And it's apropos of nothing except it's timely. I received a notice that the History Channel for the next two to three months is running an hour program on shooting down the errant satellite.[*] I don't know whether you saw it or not.

Paul Stillwell: No, I didn't.

Admiral Meyer: Well, it's on several more times. It is a pretty good program in many respects.

One of the things that's bothersome to me about it, and I have taken it up with all my successors and I'm going to redo it again and again and again—there's not one goddamn word mentioned in the 50-some-minute program of how we got there from here. It was as though it occurred Friday morning before we went out to do it. *Nowhere* did Admiral Hicks, that other admiral, that general or the other people, nowhere—and I'm surprised, frankly, at the announcers and the crafter of the programs in the History

---

[*] On 21 February 2008, the Aegis cruiser *Lake Erie* (CG-70) hit an earth satellite with a modified SM-3 Standard missile. The satellite was by then dead and falling from earth orbit. The interception took place 130 miles above the Pacific Ocean.

Channel—nowhere did he mention where Aegis came from.[*] How long did it take to get to that night? Getting to that night never got mentioned, not once, by the present incumbents, by the present people in command and in charge, not one damned person. The captain of the ship spoke; he didn't mention it. Different people in the project spoke, didn't mention it. Different industrial officials spoke. None of them made any mention of how they got here. It's as though the tooth fairy came a week ago Friday and left it on our doorstep.

And so what an opportunity has been missed for the public to grasp and understand how long and how difficult such things come to pass. And that is the reason that this program is so enduring. The really enduring programs—as I said, I modeled the two you-know-whos: Rickover and Levering Smith.[†] Well, their programs are enduring and the Aegis program is enduring. And it may undergo several name changes. My guess is it's going to. My prediction is that the 1000 destroyer—my prediction—will morph out and somehow merge into Aegis.[‡] I just don't know how that will be done, but that's how I feel.

I say it simply based on 60 years at it. So it was an excellent program; on the other hand I'm a little irked that the makers of that program didn't bother to get some advisory service or a critical review. I told you that not once but many times Admiral Reich, Admiral Roger Elmore Spreen, beat my ass unmercifully about paying attention to your elders. "Watch your elders. *They* know what has happened, and they are the reason you're there." Nothing contained in the program on that. Nothing. Zero. As a matter of fact, nothing contained in the program on the Aegis fleet, the fact that it is the dominating fleet in our Navy today. Nothing. Just nothing.

I was stunned at how much they filled up 50 minutes with it. It may have had a lot of mother-son interest and father-daughter interest because there were some nice shots

---

[*] Rear Admiral Alan B. Hicks, USN, Program Director, Aegis Ballistic Missile Defense System.
[†] Rear Admiral Levering Smith, USN, served as director of the Special Projects Office/Strategic Systems Projects Office from 16 February 1965 to 14 November 1977.
[‡] Guided missile destroyers of the *Zumwalt* (DDG-1000) class are being built to a radical new design that is intended to produce a stealthy, low-profile radar signature. Construction of the *Zumwalt* began in October 2008 at Bath Iron Works, Bath, Maine; the ship is scheduled for delivery to the Navy in 2013. Construction of the *Michael Monsoor* (DDG-1001) began at the Northrop Grumman shipyard (now Hunting Ingalls Industries) in Pascagoula, Mississippi, in September 2009; delivery to the Navy is scheduled for 2014.

of the sailors and the ship and stuff like that. I don't want to take from that. But in truth, while it was an excellent tape, it missed a grand opportunity, and of course the opportunity will never come back again. It won't be recovered.

That's all, thank you. Next subject.

Paul Stillwell: All right. Back to Admiral Rickover and the law about nuclear power. How were you able to get gas-turbine-powered hulls for Aegis?

Admiral Meyer: The debate became national, and it simmered and went on for, I don't know, maybe four years or something like that, off and on, on the utility of nuclear power, the cost of nuclear power. You've heard all the songs on nuclear power that the anti-nuclear-power people bring up. They were all developed in that era besides.

My own view is the Navy committed a serious error. Now, my excuse is: I wasn't asked.

Paul Stillwell: What was the Navy's error?

Admiral Meyer: The Navy's plan was to do both. Recall, out of the DX/DXG/DXGN programs, DX morphed into DD-963, DXG didn't morph anyplace except into the Ayatollahs.* And the DXGN morphed into DLG-38, *Virginia* class. Wasn't a bad plan. Funny how it got itself executed, and it indicated once again that there often is not very much concern about the arming of our ships. Not very much. And yet we know it's critical, we know it's important, we know it's absolutely vital to win, but somehow it's just assumed it will occur. And it's even true inside the Navy.

Look at the *Zumwalt*s right now. We're arming that ship with stuff that's a half century old. Now, it so happens it's damned good stuff because there's virtually nothing there that I personally didn't have a hand in in its development and stuff, or directing it or leading it or some such. But the designers of that class, the perpetrators of it, turned up their nose. Nothing from Aegis is to carry forward; it's to be all new. All new! Well,

---

* Four ships of the DXG variant were ordered for delivery to Iran. After that country's government fell to the Ayatollah Ruhollah Khomeini in 1979, the ships were completed for the U.S. Navy. The USS *Kidd* (DDG-993) and her three sisters went into commission in 1981 and 1982.

we'll see. We'll see how it comes out. Kiss a piggy. The ships ought to already be at sea, but they're not, and that's today's crisis, you know. Today's crisis is: What's the shipbuilding program? Did I generate the crisis? I don't think so. I think those piddlers generated this crisis because they couldn't hear.

What's your next question? Get me on track again.

Paul Stillwell: All right. You said that it was the Navy's error to plan for both nuclear and gas turbine. Are you pleased that Aegis wound up only in gas-turbine hulls?

Admiral Meyer: Not particularly. I didn't fight it as a manager, because I had my plate full every place I turned. But as a professional naval officer I didn't agree with it. I didn't agree with it at all. And I still don't agree with it. I don't agree that we demand, insist, that our attack carriers all over the globe be nuclear propelled, and we give them no escorts, no accompaniment, that are nuclear propelled. Instead, they've got to act as the tanker and the oiler for its escorts. Oh, really? Yeah, they do. They're acting as the interim oilers you might say. So on Wednesdays they refuel the escorts, and maybe every other week, in a safe environment, the oiler comes sailing by and they all refuel.

If you watched the Vietnam era—and I'm not that acquainted with the campaigns in the Middle East but some form of it occurred; I had a lot of acquaintanceship with the Vietnam campaign—they would set those supply ships, *Mars*, *Sacramento*, and the different ones, they would set them on a course generally northeast and they'd put out a signal—under way, 12 knots, or whatever it is. You take your ship, you go rendezvous someplace on that line, and I'll take my ship, I'll refuel on that line. Well, when she turns around and comes back, hell, I'll be back refueling again, maybe. That was the plan. Was it a good plan? If there's no submarine threat. If there were no missile threat at that range. In that era they were generally out of range of cruise missiles and, for that matter, ballistic missiles. So most of the ocean was a sanctuary.

And we now have two generations of naval officers, including our senior leaders, including some retireds, who somehow believe that our oceans will always be sanctuaries. I look today at the admirals and even the junior officers, and I'm not jealous of them, I just comment on the change of attitudes and times. Because we've got senior officers and even senior petty officers today participate in all these campaigns. They've got ribbons from here to here. At the end of the war Nimitz had one row.[*] My generation generally felt like really big shots when they got to an overflow from the one row, that they were pretty good. So my point is the times changed, the whole attitude changed. I don't know that it's wrong. Maybe I'm just being smart-ass, but it certainly changed the reason for the awarding of them. And today I don't know, I suppose the time is about here when we'll develop something that's even greater than the Distinguished Service Medal. Looks like to me we going there, because we're giving out Distinguished Service Medals all over the place.

I was awarded a Distinguished Service Medal by Admiral Jack Williams, surfaced submariner.[†] He was the Chief of Naval Material. His civilian deputy was Dr. Jim Colvard.[‡] I don't know who went off and did this because I was—just one day I was called to an assembly over to the theater in Crystal City, which had been closed for lack of interest and off and on, particularly the Navy, would rent it for assemblies. I was called over there, and my late wife was present. Can't remember whether any of my children were. But a number of people had been called out, including Admiral Williams, and he called me over kind of—I wouldn't say in the middle of my tour, because I had the post 13 years. In any event, they awarded me the Distinguished Service Medal. Well, I just damned near fainted on the spot. I just fainted. I couldn't handle it. I didn't even know what to do with it or what to say about it, because I'd never seen it done before.

One thing I did know. I do know that Admiral Williams, who is in the graveyard now, was an incredible leader. He was a wonderful officer, a really thoughtful person on performance. I never served with him except in that kind of post. Before that he was Deputy CinCPacFlt.[§] In any event, my late wife and I were on a trip out to Hawaii for some reason or other and we stayed at Makalapa. Jack Williams had arranged a dinner for us the evening we were there with maybe 20-25 people, in his quarters. He didn't

---

[*] Fleet Admiral Chester W. Nimitz, USN, served as Commander in Chief Pacific Fleet and Pacific Ocean Areas, 1941-45.
[†] Admiral John G. Williams, Jr., USN, served as Chief of Naval Material, 1 July 1981 to 31 July 1983.
[‡] Dr. James Colvard, a civilian who was technical director at the Naval Surface Weapons Center Dahlgren and later deputy to Admiral Williams.
[§] As a vice admiral, Williams served as deputy and chief of staff to Commander in Chief Pacific Fleet.

really know me. He was just that thoughtful. He thought I was doing something incredible for the United States Navy and he wanted to let it be known. And he so said that in a couple of remarks he made that night. What an officer. What a leader.

Paul Stillwell: I've heard good things about him from other people as well.

Admiral Meyer: It is a pity that there aren't more of Jack Williams in the world. It is a pity.

Well, so, how did I feel on nuclear power? I felt, professionally, the Navy's main battle force ought to be nuclear.

Paul Stillwell: Did you feel that Aegis should be exclusively on nuclear-powered ships?

Admiral Meyer: No. I never have. Because the threat is not exclusive. As I told you in an earlier talk, we had the popular myths of the day, of Aegis is too big, too complex, too heavy to be able to get in any useful ships. Well, of course, every single one of our allies today have Aegis in what you and I would class, in another era, as destroyer escorts. So you can generate any kind of myth you want to generate if you don't want to do something. And that was the situation we were in there.

But my calling, my vocation, was to get our fleet armed. By good fortune I had a heavy hand in my development periods of preparing the Navy to deal in the cruise missile. I've probably done more than any other person. And the motivation came from my leaders, and my following the war in the Pacific. When the Japanese struck in 1941, I was only 17 years old at the time, but my mates and I believed there would be no turning back. And 17-year-olds aren't all that thoughtful. They don't have that wide a bandwidth. So it was our view we would go to war. The real reason that we'd go to war is Roosevelt had said the war would be very long, and no matter how you wanted to cut it we were the ready reserve for officers. That's why he created the program, because he believed it was a very long war and that he'd better do something about education. And with education that's how you got officers.

Today you note that that's become a secondary issue in the officer corps. We don't worry very much about it anymore. As a matter of fact, we've gone through a whole era where we've just filled our whole officer corps up with limited duty officers. Whenever we'd find a good petty officer, we'd hang shoulder boards on him. Well, that's still going on to a large degree. I bitch to everyone I could get to stop and listen to me about how that is a bad thing for the long-term Navy, really bad thing.

Well, how's it been solved? I'm digressing on you again, but how? I'll tell you how it's been solved. It's been solved with that goddamn computer. I tore it out of the paper yesterday, I didn't bring it in, how you could get your master's degree. You could get your master's degree in any subject you wanted to get it in. Be offered online. Now, how can that be? How can you be an educated person and a leader with that kind of an education? And yet we're succumbing to it. We're accepting it. People say, "Well, you don't understand. We still have professors." As a matter of fact, the advertisement was you'll be taught the same courses that are taught in campus, and have the identical type of professors. Do you believe that? I don't believe that for one minute. But we'll accept it.

Jim Colvard and I have talked a great deal about this; the time is upon us already—is how do we evaluate the academic stature of an officer today or of a person today, because of the ease in which you can get degrees? Because, of course, I mean, we went through—we have hundreds of women over in the ancestors of NavSea, BuOrd and stuff, went off and got BS degrees. Well, the derogatory expression was that the degree was in basket weaving. It wasn't basket weaving, but it wasn't something very hard. And almost all of it was thanks to the computer and Thursday night sessions.

So our education, in my view, needs—I've bitched to Colvard; he's the only one I can get to listen to me—needs some thoughtful people to think through: What are today's standards, or what should they be, for an academically educated person? Because I tell you, those degrees are no longer the answer. They're no longer valid. 'Tis a pity. There are many schools, many institutions where they're damned valid, but there are a lot of them where they have no validity at all. You can come here and get a job in government today, never set foot in a schoolhouse. Take yourself right to the top.

On the matter of nuclear power.

Paul Stillwell: Well, I thought you said it was an error for the Navy to plan for both nuclear and gas turbine, but later you said that it was useful to have both, so I'm trying to find where the error was.

Admiral Meyer: The error was to kill the nuclear-powered Aegis ships.

Paul Stillwell: All right.

Admiral Meyer: And, as far as I can tell, they didn't have a lot of help. You're constantly in competition for money; everybody knows that. And so the submariners have made it a divinely revealed commandment that we shall have no diesel submarines.

Paul Stillwell: Well, do you recall who it was that made the decision that Aegis would not go into nuclear-powered hulls?

Admiral Meyer: I don't think you could run a specific person up on the meat hook on that decision. I think it just came from the admixture of people that, by the time that Goldwater-Nichols started creeping in by 1987 and so on, the people who felt one way or another about it, the officer corps, didn't much care anymore. And that's true to this day. The present generation, I don't know of anybody in this generation that much cares.
  See, in my generation, recall, submariners peaked out at lieutenant commander. Virtually all submarine commands were lieutenant commanders. There was no place else for them to go. What happened, they started leaking over into the rest of the Navy, so by the late '50s the destroyer forces were filling up with submariners, in command. They were surfaced, but they made commander, and as a commander they could command destroyers. So that creeping kept occurring. Well, every time one of them was put in, another surface guy was not put in someplace in the competition process. So it went on and on.
  Today I don't know how it works. I think we managed to sustain a large enough submarine fleet today, which is all nuclear, that by now—I'm speaking, goodness, 50 years have passed, of the whole adjustment of officer development. So that the

submariners tend to match what the submarine opportunity is. And, no matter what anybody says, we do have a pretty damned big fleet of submarines.

Paul Stillwell: Well, and it's now a captain's billet to command some of the big ones.

Admiral Meyer: You betcha. You betcha. And, of course, in the creation of these Tridents—and I think it certainly was the right thing to do, or for that matter the boomers—creating these dual crews we've created these command opportunities all over the place that didn't exist. So the whole Navy shifted and changed. The submarine fleet today is pretty big, biggest in the world as far as I know, and it doesn't operate on a shoestring. Their officers are good, they're well developed, and they're well developed ashore and afloat.

Paul Stillwell: We talked last time about *Norton Sound* getting one real array and one for show. Please talk about how that ship worked out in practice. The tests were going on in 1975, and there were some hits. That had to be a big step forward.

Admiral Meyer: Well, the second array was not so much for show as it was we put a blank over it, because the design was a reflection of what our view of the deckhouse had to be in the combat ship. So that meant that it was either two eyes—and at that time, as I recollect, we were shaping the eyes like this.

Paul Stillwell: Angled in.

Admiral Meyer: Yeah, angled in. I don't believe it was exactly 45 degrees but it was someplace in that neighborhood. Now, when you look at the 963s when we did this creative work—don't get any credit anymore but it was damned creative then; couldn't be done. But we decided that we could fit those arrays, still hew to our design, still hew to that design, but we rotated them. And the reason we did was the massive effect that gas turbines had. The gas turbines have such large intakes and such large exhausts that we just wrapped around them. So we didn't relocate any of that stuff. So that's why you see the boxy shape of the cruisers. In hindsight it may be a hell of a lot better design, frankly, than the destroyers.

Paul Stillwell: Why do you say that?

Admiral Meyer: I don't know. I'm probably prejudiced. As I've told you, I sailed when I was executive officer and senior fighter director in USS *Strickland*, radar picket, and these cruisers very much modeled on *Strickland*, which was a baby Aegis, because the *Strickland* displaced between 1,600 and 1,700 tons, taken from a DE design, and here the whole CIC structure was just kind of wrapped around her so she looked like a box. And those ships had a big sail area. They were, in fact, quite stable. They met all of the rigid, conservative naval engineering requirements of the United States. But when one of them would roll, and they invariably would roll into the trough, oh, they'd get there and you'd just think you'd never would come out.

Paul Stillwell: Back to *Norton Sound*—what do you remember about those early missile-firing tests?

Admiral Meyer: There was the one that was going to be conducted that was in conflict with congressional testimony. And I was not going to be present for it.

We were going out to fire the first Standard missile at sea.[*] We had the Mark 26 launcher.[†] In theory we could unload that launcher in 60-65 seconds if you could fill it up. I had a conflict on testifying, and the ship had to get under way in order to get out in position. It isn't clear to me how Admiral Woods found this out, but he was now the commander of cruisers and destroyers, Pacific Fleet, San Diego.[‡] I think he learned it

---

[*] The first firing of the SM-1 missile at sea with the Aegis system was from *Norton Sound* on 16 May 1974.
[†] The Mark 13 and Mark 26 guided missile launchers projected above the ship's deck, rotated through various azimuths horizontally, and contained twin arms, or "rails," that launched the missiles. Since then the above-deck launchers have largely been done away. Now missiles are fired directly from storage cells within the ship's hull—a vertical-launch system.
[‡] Rear Admiral Mark W. Woods, USN, Commander Cruiser-Destroyer Force Pacific Fleet.

from the ship's captain, because the ship was really under his opcon.* So he phoned me up and said, "What is the problem?"

"Well," I said, "I can't make it. It's too much of a conflict and the operation's got to go on."

"Well," he said, "tell me how to solve it. It's too important for you not to be there."

So he called me back. He got somebody working. He called me, he said, "Look, I can have *Bainbridge* available to rendezvous with you at Long Beach. As soon as your testimony's over, you get out there and get transport from the airport down to *Bainbridge*. They'll pick you up and they'll take you out to *Norton Sound*." Sounded good to me. Okay, we'll do that. And we did!

Well, there were a couple, as the saying goes, of hairy-chested things to occur. We put out—and, of course, that whole country is mostly haze out there—and eventually found *Norton Sound*. It was decided that the best way to transfer me was to put me in the whaleboat of *Bainbridge* and have me go over and come up a Jacob's ladder.† I don't know whether you'll recall *Norton Sound* but she was seaplane tender, so she had massive, massive freeboard.

Paul Stillwell: Lot of sail area.‡ [Chuckle]

Admiral Meyer: Just goes everywhere, the sail area. And she had these cargo hatches about halfway down, which were for the whole matter of airplane tending. Not to worry. We got under way, went over there to do that. And, of course, you get under there. I had done this several times in my life. As a matter of fact, I had done it several times in Vietnam. But I had never done this when you look up and you can't even see the *end* of the Jacob's ladder. So I life-jacketed, lines sent down, put around me and stuff, and so they were ready for me to go on up. The countdown was going fine. I was just about to clear the boat when a breaker came by and took the boat right out from under me. I had

---

* Opcon – operational control.
† A Jacob's ladder is a portable ladder with wooden rungs; the sides are made of rope or wire. It is slung over the side of a ship when used, rolled up when stored while not in use.
‡ "Sail area" is a term for a ship's vertical surfaces on which the wind exerts force.

grabbed the Jacob's ladder and I was clinging on, and they had a line around me. A boatswain's mate that must have been 12 feet tall came down out of that cargo hatch, clear down that goddamn ladder, came out of there and got me, and demanded that I hold his legs. And eventually they got me up and we landed on the deck up there, and both of us lay there for the next 15 minutes or so, just totally exhausted. That may have been the closest to drowning I've ever been. But that was my experience, and I got to see the firing.

Paul Stillwell: Please describe the firing.

Admiral Meyer: Beautiful. Only one word, just beautiful. Just incredible. I don't know whether you ever knew Mr. Will Willoughby?

Paul Stillwell: No.

Admiral Meyer: Mr. Willoughby, in the graveyard now, but I'd known him casually. He was in NASA, and he was hired by Admiral Kidd to come over into the material establishment, to get us squared away like NASA.* That was the idea. Well, Willoughby knew nothing whatsoever about Navy business, but he was a reliability person, and he was reliability, reliability, reliability, reliability, so I used him a lot. I mean, he became a great advantage to me in the ensuing times. Well, he could never partake of the ecstasy of a firing success. He just couldn't handle that.

Paul Stillwell: What do you mean, he couldn't take it?

Admiral Meyer: It had no meaning to him. So, I don't know whether it was that firing or the next one, in the session after I got back and I was describing the operation and such

---

* William J. Willoughby was head of reliability and safety for the National Aeronautics and Space Administration during the Apollo moon landing program. He later became Director, Reliability, Maintainability and Quality Assurance, Office of the Assistant Secretary of the Navy (Shipbuilding and Logistics).

and how it went on, and Willoughby finally interrupted and said, "Aw, c'mon, Captain." He said, "That's just another ho-hum firing. That's all that was."

I never said another word to him at that meeting, and I virtually never spoke to him except when I had to, for his remaining active duty, because that just hurt me so bad, and it hurt all our people and all our team, that a success didn't mean anything to him.

Paul Stillwell: And a real milestone to the program.

Admiral Meyer: Oh, because every firing, as you know, in this kind of engineering development *every* firing is a milestone, no matter what anybody tells you. Every one is, or you wouldn't be doing it. So it just was another ho-hum firing.

Paul Stillwell: How were you able to benefit from his reliability knowledge, even when he had that attitude?

Admiral Meyer: Well, I let him travel around through the project. Interesting enough, he spent almost no time on the radar. He had virtually no interest in the computers. It was only the missile that he had interest in. In his NASA-developed mind, somehow the missile was the only thing that was important. The rest of it was secondary and tertiary. Which, of course, is not true in our craft. And so I would send him around to General Dynamics, and he'd go to RCA, and he could give lectures off the top of his head, very academic and very professional and applied, that none of us were capable of. He just had that much experience. And he'd talk about the mathematical theory of reliability and how you came by it. So that's how I used him. I just kept him on the move, and every now and then I'd write a note to the admiral pointing out how much help Mr. Willoughby had contributed the last three weeks in speaking to our people and talking to them about where to go.

Paul Stillwell: This is to Admiral Kidd.

Admiral Meyer: Yeah. And in fact the next one did introduce a lot of institutions which we weren't acquainted with, where we had a lot of theorists on reliability and design because they were related to NASA.[*] The NASA designs had to be man-rated if they were going to carry a man. And so I adapted a lot of that stuff into this undertaking and these missiles. In fact, the Standard Missile, which is now over a half a century old, I'm one of the forebears of that missile and its borning. I was a commander, selected for captain, at its borning. It was to be a missile with high reliability tactically. Its reliability was to be so high that it was to have a single-shot kill of .6. And so our doctrinal salvo was around a two. You could fire one round, but a round of two would get you about .83 or something like that, reliability-wise. I've only a couple times in my life ever fired a dual-shot salvo, and really it was to establish the benchmark of what the performance was, but there was no time, really, when we needed it in the engineering work.

So we adapted a lot of his thinking on that. So I talked to everybody about man-rating, which I had not the foggiest idea of what I was talking about. I'd go around in that big ordnance plant at Pomona, California, operated by General Dynamics. I'd walk around on that floor because now I had Standard Missile 2. As a matter of fact, all of Standard Missile, which went bankrupt, had been given to me. It was under the Aegis, so to speak, but it was all bankrupt. I had to raise the money.

I ended up hiring a fellow by the name of Ed Libby.[†] Hired him as a civil servant, GS-14. He came in to the project to take over the direction and the leadership of the Standard Missile. And Ed Libby whined and moaned and carried on me, "Captain, I don't know anything about the missile."

"All right, Libby, here's your big opportunity to show me how fast you can learn."

Well, he turned out to be a wonderful leader. He'd come out of NASA, and he got over his initial fear. NASA and, I think, he was with General Electric, I can't remember what, but he turned out to be a wonderful leader, especially when I assigned an officer to him, because he was a nitpicker. And so if he had an officer to provide the leadership and direction he was really good at nitpicking. He could just wear them out.

---

[*] Admiral Frederick H. Michaelis, USN, served as Chief of Naval Material from 18 April 1975 to 1 August 1978. His oral history is in the Naval Institute collection.
[†] Edward Libby was a civil servant in the Naval Sea Systems Command and the Aegis Project Office.

Willoughby loved this. He loved it. Well, a nitpicker means a lot in engineering if you want to get reliability.

So I'd go walking through those production lines down where I'd assemble all of those women, talk to them about the significance of what they were doing, how important it was. And, of course, we were still in Vietnam. And they would assemble in groups to listen to me. I talked to them about reliability, but I talked to them really about their sons. When that missile came out of that plant out there, that missile underwent acceptance and it went to the magazines. I said, "Whether that missile works or not is dependent on you, not dependent on me, dependent on you."

Then I have made a breakthrough, simultaneous in that era, of taking women to sea.* So it was almost like contests, because they either elected someone to go or their superiors would appoint someone, but it was people out of the production floor and stuff like that. When there was a firing at *Norton Sound*, and sometimes when we had one in Terrier that was at the Pacific Missile Range, I'd get them aboard so they could see it. Boy.

Paul Stillwell: And this planted the thought that you want a reliable missile protecting your son when he's at sea.

Admiral Meyer: You got it. Or, by the way, your grandson, because a number of them had grandsons in the Navy. Big, big thing. No one else can make that statement. I don't know how I got like that but, boy, it's a winner. And you know something—and you heard on the TV last night—I forget the number of missiles we've fired; we've fired 30-some in the ballistic missile defense thing here. We've had two failures. That's one hell of a far cry from the design. The theoretical design is not nearly that.

Well, how do you overcome it? I'll tell you how you overcome it. You overcome it by good assembly, good manufacture, good components—you overcome it by all of those things, and people who care and who worry about it. I had many cases of that. And it occurred too at Moorestown. Cases would emerge of people would be at home or

---

* The women Admiral Meyer discussed in this context were civilians who worked in Aegis program offices and contractor plants. He arranged for them to go aboard ship to observe tests.

be off on leave, and they'd come traipsing back and get ahold of their superiors because something was bothering them and they'd been thinking about it—there have been a few cases where they thought about it for weeks—that something's wrong with that process. The process is not good enough. That process needs to get fixed for the reliability that the admiral kept talking about. Well, hell, we had to pounce on it. I mean, they kept smocks for me in all these manufacturing plants, with gold stripes on them, for me to wear around when I talked to their people. So it was like I was bringing something down from God the Father.

Paul Stillwell: Did you have a specific procedure to encourage them to bring those concerns forward?

Admiral Meyer: Well, I did it in a backhanded way: "It's your missile. It's as good as you make it." It's amazing how people get that. And I created that environment with the vice presidents and the foremen.

Now, some factories don't operate that way, and I'll tell you why. Virtually all the foremen of the world running those kinds of things are measured by their schedule. So if they have to get eight widgets, they've got to get eight widgets. If they've got to get nine bolts to glue onto the widgets they've got to get nine. That's the measurement process. I killed that goddamn measurement process. It doesn't sound magical, it sounds soupy, but I said, "Look, we're going to do it right; just going to do it right. If you don't think it's right, we will stand behind you. And don't worry about whether you're wrong or not, worry about whether you think it's right."

Well, I had another big thing supporting me in that era, and it was the Japanese, because the Japanese had created all this myth of how great they were and how every person in Japan on a production line, every person was empowered to stop the line.

Paul Stillwell: This is Dr. Deming's philosophy.

Admiral Meyer: Exactly. Deming was roaming around through there, and they'd raised them all, and they were all empowered to stop the line.* Well, I wasn't prepared to sign up 100% to any of that, but I was prepared to create the image and have it carry, and it did; it carried forward a lot.

The other thing we did—this is particularly on the missile but we did it also at Moorestown in making these damned phase shifters and such. We brought the production women into what we called the experimental factory. We had an engineering factory, and we had an experimental factory, and that's where we experimented on how to assemble stuff, or how to do integrated circuits and so forth.

But what was worse, I created the problem that: "By the way, engineers, you're going to go to the production floor and you're going to serve some time there, and you're going to find out with your own eyeballs how much difficulty these women are having. [Because it's mostly women.] You're going to sit there and watch that." That's a powerful movement, really powerful, if they believe you're behind them. But almost all of them are running on: the measurement is cost. Well, the old George Main thing out of BuShips—she costs what she costs—is what I believe, and frankly I don't believe it costs a damn bit more. Rather, what's important is attitude. Attitude's important. And the best things in the world won't amount to anything if the attitudes of the people putting it together aren't right.

Well, and I've seen it in ships, and perhaps you have too. Sailors can take a dog aboard ship. If they like it, it's their dog, and don't you try to take it off. You can have a really shining, shining parakeet there; if they don't like it, it doesn't matter. Well, that's true also in this kind of production.

There is a good deal of grunt work in it, but so you need a little creativity in doing it. You need plans to develop little cells of people that rotate around, change their work habits, and stuff like that. But most of them, I have to say, seem so obvious in hindsight. They often do not seem obvious at all in foresight. Because when we went over to the Fourier-transform-type design in the seeker in this missile we had to have really skilled women in those early days to be able to do this solder work. So we brought those women

---

* Dr. W. Edwards Deming (1900-93) was an American statistician who was credited with improving industrial production during World War II. He helped Japan recover from the effects of the war and later improved productivity there. He fostered the total quality management concept.

in, as I say, to the engineering factory. We taught them. We created a certificating process. Maud, if you've got a certificate at this level, you've got—it didn't matter much what it was—ten cents an hour or something. Recognition matters. You get to this level, well, you get two bits an hour more, and so forth, because you're certified here. It makes a big difference on people.

We tend to turn up our nose. People that never had to do it or be with it turn up their nose about that smallsy kind of stuff. It doesn't matter what it does, it is important to people. It's true that it sounds trivial, but it's trivial things that make life—

(Interruption)

Paul Stillwell: We just had a break for lunch and brought up a couple topics that we want to include in the discussion, and one would be your evaluation of the Boeing team and General Dynamics team and how they would have worked out with Aegis.

Admiral Meyer: When the engineering development contract was finally let in December of 1969, after years and years—at one time there were some 27 teams of bidders, winnowed down to nine, and eventually winnowed down to three. One team was led by RCA, one team was led by Boeing, one team was led by General Dynamics. Well, they had signed up. Their team members weren't incompetent. Every team member they had, those three, had significant competence and may be the best in the nation in some particular piece of the undertaking. But since the undertaking as a whole was not yet very well described, then, of course, the parts couldn't be very well described either.

I believe I had told you someplace back there that my commanding officer out at Port Hueneme in the final countdown had been selected to chair the source selection evaluation board by the admiral.[*] He had come from commanding *Norton Sound*. And it turned out that a major part of my tour he was not even physically present. He was back here all the time. We had an executive officer, who was a captain. He had been yanked out of the station. The station had four captains, the only naval station that I know of that had four captains: CO, XO, director of logistics, and director of engineering. Well, the

---

[*] This individual was Captain William A. Arthur, USN.

only non-line officer, the only staff officer, was the director of logistics; he was a supply corps officer, and a pretty damned competent one, but he had nothing whatsoever to do with the surface Navy. So when the CO was spending all his time here—

Paul Stillwell: I wanted to get you to speculate on how Aegis would have turned out if Boeing or General Dynamics had wound up with the contract.

Admiral Meyer: Well, I'll speculate, with the caveat that I would expect you in all your experience to edit it. If I'm too derogatory or too bombastic, it's not my intention. I'm enthusiastic. And frankly, I don't know of any other person you could go to today to conduct such a question and get an answer, because there are no such people. I'm virtually the only one alive.

It got winnowed down, as I was saying, about sometime in the year 1969, as I recollect, to three teams that I mentioned. And they were determined to try to get this selection done by Christmas of 1969, that was their target. Well, the team at Moorestown, RCA, was led by a fellow by the name of Bill Goodwin.

I'll come back to that in a minute; let me ask you one other question. Do you dig the expression DCP, development concept paper?

Paul Stillwell: No, I'm not familiar with that.

Admiral Meyer: Well, Johnny Foster was the chief of DDR&E in those days, a great, great leader, a great man.* But he passed a rule that the only engineering development programs he was going to work on would have to be worked on on the basis of what was called a development concept paper, DCP. And it could not be more than 20 pages long. So this immediately meant in that era that you had to learn how to write sideways, crossways, backwards, and all up and down, and you had to be very, very careful, with little bitty words, to get the information in there that everybody was demanding be put in it. Because what had made these programs so big, of course, is all the people in our democracy who were demanding something be put in them.

---

* Dr. John S. Foster, Jr., served as Director of Defense Research and Engineering, 1965-73.

Well, we have something called Development Concept Paper 16. The ASMS, now called Aegis, is run under that paper. That paper was updated once, about ten years later—revision 1—after the contract was let. To my knowledge, it is the sole governing document of Aegis today. It is the statement of requirements. It's the statement of the performance it has to have. And while there are specifications and such exist, they're translated directly out of that DCP.

So we had this development concept paper. It had been signed off. And one of the things it had in it was a new missile. Just like in the *Zumwalt*s, it had about new everything. But then they had to start sobering up, and Johnny Foster probably made them sober up more than anybody. He was a big R&D, national, international, R&D person, sobered them up. So they sobered up on the launcher to the Mark 26 launcher. And in December, two weeks before Christmas, they were having this go-to-hell meeting over there one night in Foster's office. His aide was Captain Lew Stecher, the youngest of the Stecher brothers, both of whom retired as captains. Lew was a surface sailor; Bob was a submariner. Both pretty damned good officers. Both had been to graduate school and those kinds of things, so they had a big rounded education ashore and afloat.

I don't know whether they had a hundred people, I don't know how many they had, but they were up till like 8:00 o'clock that night. And the budgets would not match the program. And the determination was made by whatever that council or panel was that was meeting with Foster as its chair that they had to be brought into line. Well, it happened, it happened that the amount of money needed to bring them into line was the amount of money budgeted in there for the missile. So it was decided to strike the missile, at 8:00 o'clock at night, take the missile out. And Captain Lew Stecher, standing in the background, quickly wrote a phrase into one of the sentences of the DCP-16, and the phrase said, "The interceptor shall be Standard Missile with mid-course guidance." The deal was closed and the team was selected, and far and away the dominating team was the radar proposed by RCA team.

Well, there's a couple reasons. First of all, RCA was a good radar house. It had no experience at sea. Secondly, it was very reliable. It had Raytheon on its team, who was pretty damned good and such. And the surface missile system project office for over a half a decade had spent a lot of money at Moorestown and RCA to develop and introduce digital processing. And had even gone so far as to ship the infamous SPG-55B Ser 67 to Moorestown to be set up and put into operation for RCA to study, SPG-55B being the fire control radar for the Terrier ships. So they were pretty alert and had a pretty good leg up from that work. Boeing was out in the cold.

Oh, the missile person on the team, the RCA team, was Bendix. Good outfit. Designed and built Talos, amongst other things. Good. But now they were out in the cold.

The one losing team, which General Dynamics Pomona was moaning and moaning and carrying on, well, they weren't out in the cold. As a matter of fact, they'd just been brought into gobs of money with almost no responsibility because Standard Missile, or some derivative thereof, had to be the ammunition, and General Dynamics the only people that knew how to do it. So they were salvaged. Well, that meant all their team—amongst other people were Hughes and I can't recall who else—they were all thrown away.

Boeing was out in the cold because they had these big grand and glorious command-and-control screens and stuff, literally Star-Wars-type design, but nothing underneath it. But the good thing they had going for them was they had contracted—Sperry Gyro was on their team, who was the Talos and Terrier designers in fire control for the Navy. So they were the only good piece of that if you think about it, from my viewpoint. They were out in the dust.

So there was joy and there was no joy.

Bill Goodwin, whom I knew quite well through the years, associated with, same age as I was, and Bob—I'm trying to say his name in a minute here, in General Dynamics, whom I also knew quite well, I'd been associated with for a number of years. Well, I thought I'd done pretty good when I had finally been assigned and reported back here in January. I got the two of them together and asked them whether they wanted to play ball or whether they just wanted to argue. Well, what they really wanted, frankly—and both of them are in the graveyard now—what they really wanted out of me was assurance that I was going to be on the job.

Paul Stillwell: Why was there any question of that?

Admiral Meyer: Things, like always, tended to flip around and snip around and flip around and jump around, even as late as January, and as late as the end-of-the-world speech by November of that year. You had somebody running around with big fire axes wanting to cut down the program, cut all the fire hoses, and spray water everyplace. So there was some question. Survival was serious, really serious. We just toughed it out.

But the problem was, see, that Standard Missile had no money, so money for the missile was left as an exercise to the reader. The missile didn't belong to me as a manager. It belonged to what was—I think NavOrd was its name at that time. Well, in a go-to-hell drag-out over there I agreed one day to take the missile. And Ed Libby was going to be in charge of this missile, and I wanted all the people in NavOrd to be responsible to me for the missile. I'd allot money through them, they'd vote on it and everything, but I was going to be in charge of the missile. If I'm going to take it, I'm going to take it. I'm going to take not only the Aegis version, but the Terrier version and the Tartar version, so I'm going to drive them all with commonality. Well, they all capitulated because none of them had any money.

Well, people who've been in this business for a while know it takes a minimum of three years to raise any money in the whole appropriation process. So for the first three years I was behind the eight ball. So I had to shift moneys around and manipulate them. But always the missile was behind the radar, from day one, and the reason was the money flow was mismatched. And so in those early days we started out with Standard Missile 1, because we agreed—Bob and Bill Goodwin and who became my close friend, a fellow by the name of George Luke that I've mentioned to you, from the Applied Physics Laboratory. He's in the graveyard too. He had been one of the leaders in the late Typhon program. We all agreed at supper that we had to go make the design fit Standard Missile 1, because we had no idea when we were going to have any missile that we could fire that would exploit the radar's ability. We just didn't know, because we didn't have the money raised.

Paul Stillwell: But you also had some flexibility, or had to have, in order to accommodate a later version.

Admiral Meyer: Yes, but we also had to be pretty good at, I don't want to say juggling money. We had to be pretty good at how we rotated money, moved money around. And what that mostly means is you've got to have a one-A team who's smarter than the rest. It's just like winning football. And that's when I started my famous cry that they still use here 25 years after I retired, is that "If six of you know what you want, you can win it in this town." That's what this democratic process is. If you can get half a dozen people that know what is needed and if you don't give it up, you'll win. But oh, boy, does it take a lot of stamina. It takes a lot of energy. And it takes a lot of dedication.

It doesn't matter whether they're officers or civil servants. What matters really is that there's a mix. And a couple really good vice presidents. So you've got to have those people working as a group. We did. And by maybe the fourth or fifth year, my money flow was pretty damned good. Well, one of the reasons it was good is I finally got my arms around all of it, where I was getting it into control and I was causing what was going in to the Congress to be impacted too. So we were never rich, but we were okay.

Paul Stillwell: One of the other topics we talked about at lunch when the tape recorder wasn't running was the impact on the families of individuals who were involved in the Aegis program.

Admiral Meyer: That was an era of upheaval in American society. We're fond of blaming it on the Vietnam War, but I doubt that that was the reason. And it stemmed from the movement that Lyndon Johnson put into effect, particularly in government, where everybody was set free. It's my first tour in Washington, and that was the mid-'60s. And so all of a sudden we were being demanded to promote women right and left. It simply didn't matter whether they had credentials, they were to be promoted. Well, in my early days I just couldn't get the Navy to allocate civil service billets to me of the requisite rank for me to be able to hire people I needed. I was heavily dependent on APL and on Vitro, RCA Service Company, and those people.

I jumped on the female movement, because you could hire women. These women were generally—some were at GS-4 level but most of them were GS-5, GS-6s. You could hire them. You could start with -7s, start promoting them. All they had to do was get a *plan* to educate. Not get educated, get a *plan* to. It's a big difference. So I started letting women into the system.

We started having a lot of socials in Aegis. Virtually I think every one of these women is today retired; I can't think of one that's still active. A couple rose all the way to GS-16 eventually. Their education wasn't any better than it was when they started. But a number of them went on to do really, really contributory work because what I call the Wright-Patterson syndrome of the United States Air Force in procurement and acquisition practices. The whole matter of configuration management, configuration control, and paper exploded. And, frankly, women thrived on this and were great contributors, to be able to do it and get someplace with it.

Now, that's all kind of run its course today in one sense. Ratcheting ahead a little bit—John Lehman came by. He was going to be part of this whole freedom movement. And as it moved along—I regret to say I've dropped the point I was going to make. It'll come back to me. Somehow it got dumped out of my register just as I was sliding through it.

Paul Stillwell: Well, earlier you said there was a considerable divorce rate in the families of Aegis people.

Admiral Meyer: You could see it developing, especially in this big project where the organization of my project was a card you carried in your shirt pocket and a listing of the telephone numbers. Everybody I had was a volunteer, and I took people who wanted to work for me, or wanted to work on the project. That's about the only thing I promised them. Some made great careers. Some moved on. Some were misfits, some were crackerjacks. You got all kinds over time.

What the hell's wrong here? I dropped the digit again that I was going to.

Paul Stillwell: We were talking about the divorce rate.

Admiral Meyer: Yeah, divorce rate. Right. Thank you for getting me back to it.

There were these great social movements, direct fallout of the Vietnam War. The peak of the Vietnam War was when I was chief engineer out at Port Hueneme. I'd not yet reported; I was just reporting. But it was exploding all over, of middle-aged people more so than young people. What was to me stunning was the number of officers that got divorces. Now, I think that if you went through the numbers statistically it'd probably turn out that that it was just like the rest of our society. But, boy, it sure didn't seem to me in real time to be that way. And I'll never know how guilty I am, as a result, of causing it, because I was raised by those two other admirals—"Get your ass on the road."*

Paul Stillwell: So by instituting that same approach yourself later, maybe there was a tie-in between your subordinates' travel and their divorces.

Admiral Meyer: I always think that there is, because I didn't make people travel who didn't want to travel, but I made sure people understood that part of their duty was travel. Just from that simple expression, of being there. And I have always been plagued by the thought of, did that create a lot of the divorces? I don't know that. Over time there were a few intermarriages, but I think that happens of any separation that was going to occur, the next marriage tends to be from someone you know or you've met or associated with, or have something in common with.

Paul Stillwell: By intermarriage you mean between two people in the program?

Admiral Meyer: Right. People who spend a lot of time together. And in fact some of the women were divorced, a number of the women, and as I was fleeting them up they were younger. And so I've always wondered, ethically, about whether I did a wrong thing or not. I ain't losing sleep about it, but it still occurs to me. I'd find another solution the next time. On the other hand, people don't worry about it today. People travel, shack up as they please, unshack when they please, or ignore it as they please. It's

---

* This is a reference to a topic discussed in a previous interview—that Admiral Reich wanted his subordinates to make in-person visits to the various contractors who were manufacturing missiles and other components for the antiair systems.

a different culture, this generation. Because that was the culture of having been set free, so everybody's participating in this culture. What developed these attitudes beats the hell out of me, what developed them.

All those officers have gone on and done well in employment or coming by material things, because they were good officers, I mean from a leadership viewpoint and such. Whether I had any responsibility—well, I think I did—of teaching them that, because I spent a lot of time teaching officers and teaching people because I decided that your success would stem from that teaching. There was no way I could do otherwise. So when I traveled I took a large body of people with me. When I held project reviews I had large numbers of people. I believe I covered some of this with you. I was out at Pomona, for example, there might be 150-200 people in a review. They'd built an auditorium out there to just be able to hold program reviews. So it was an opportunity for me to deliver the program. So I'd give the program review, and I would end it up at the end of what my expectations were for the next four months and where I thought the problems were. My approach to problem solving is to get everybody working on it.

Now, it's true that Reich taught me a lot of that, of getting a lot of people working on it. There's some risk when you do that, because you get a lot of Brownian movement going on, and people run into each other in a passageway someplace and suddenly discover both of them are working on the same problem. But they quickly overcome that and solve it and they start working together.

So that was my technique. I never believed in hiding it. I felt they needed to know my situation. On the other hand, they needed to know it in terms that I thought they could comprehend or understand. There's no need for me to give them problems which exceed their bandwidth. On the contrary, what I tried to give them is where their performance mattered in my being a winner.

And I believe I told you this, because I had to line them up repeatedly and I'd tell them there is only one person in this outfit's got a fixed-price contract, and that's me. I've got a fixed-price contract with the United States Congress. All of you have cost contracts. But that doesn't mean that you can operate out of budget. I've got a fixed-price contract, so Paul, if you overspend your 50 million then guess what—I'm going to have to take some of Anna Mae's 50 million away from her, because I've got a fixed price.

I have never once told the Congress that I needed more money for what I promised to do. I raised a lot of money in Congress. I raised hundreds of millions of dollars, but it was for new undertaking, because in that era, recollect how fast the world was moving. The transistor introduction was in runaway. The whole transistor issue was just completely over everybody's heads. This nation spent billions on things in its social life and in its personal lives they never got anything for, in non-working TVs and any number of other things. We spent millions, and probably billions, in weapons of war, because in truth we just didn't know how to deal in them. Had to be learned.

Well, this program came out ahead; the Aegis program came out as a model. And while I've been reviewing the *Zumwalt* program a little bit for several days here recently, and while it's hard to get admission, what you find is the techniques introduced into Aegis, pioneered into them, are being used in those programs. Now, there are a few who, in an effort to curry your favor, say, "Well, we're doing it just like you did it, Admiral." Well, of course, they don't have the foggiest idea whether that's true or not.

The other point is that whatever processes there are tend to be adapted by people who are trying to do something, and they don't have the foggiest idea how those processes came about or where they came from. But almost all of the testing operations today, the firing operations in the surface Navy, the development processes, most all of them came out of the flow of the Aegis from its beginning.

Again, one of the reasons is it was viewed to be highly successful to the point of jealousy. And so there were people determined they were going to emulate it, or even out-emulate it, so they were going to out-Aegis Aegis, [chuckle] if you follow my thought. So it did a lot of good for our Navy. And today it's interesting, that has generally passed. But I've got to tell you right now, flat out, the *Zumwalt* program would be running wide open if those officers would have adapted the leadership principles that they have been exposed to. I know they would have. They threw them away, and they got some unproven that are losers, or turning out to be losers.

Paul Stillwell: We talked earlier about alternative hulls for the Aegis. One thing that was a prospect for a while was the so-called strike cruiser.* What do you remember about that?

Admiral Meyer: Few people recall that *Long Beach* is the only new cruiser laid down by this nation since World War II. And that *Long Beach* was holed for ballistic missiles.†

Paul Stillwell: You're right. Few people know that.

Admiral Meyer: They are. And they were thought of as strike missiles. And strike missiles in the sense they're going to strike on land, not particularly strike other ships. But few people know that. And few people appreciate that when we did the conversion and modernization of the three CGs, *Albany*, *Columbus*, and *Chicago*, that they also were holed. And they had Talos in them and they had, for their self-protection, Tartar. Those ships were powerful ships, they were wonderful ships, but never rose even close to their potential. I have gotten pig-headed enough in recent years that they could have if they'd just had the leadership. And frankly, that's the reason I interrupted myself to go talk to Dr. Colvard at the moment, because he and I are working on the thing with the Secretary concerning the leadership issues of the *Zumwalt*s and others right now, including the Aegis modernization. And how's that going to happen? Well, it sure as hell ain't going to happen by: "Let's see, let's look at the list, where's that—bring in that list of contemporary admirals on active duty; let's go through them and let's see if we can find one in here who—let's see, oh, here's one, Smith; what's wrong with Smith?"
    "Well, I don't know anything about him, Admiral, I don't know."
    "Well, he'll probably be all right."

---

* The strike cruiser (CSGN) was a concept that almost came to fruition in the Ford Administration in the mid-1970s. It was to be a nuclear-powered cruiser, armed with surface-to-surface missiles, surface-to-air missiles, an 8-inch gun, and intended for independent operations, as opposed to being part of a carrier screen. See Norman Friedman, *U.S. Cruisers: An Illustrated Design History* (Annapolis: Naval Institute Press, 1984), pages 419-442, and *Jane's Fighting Ships: 1976-77*, page 572.
† In the late 1950s there was a plan to install Polaris missiles in the nuclear cruiser *Long Beach* (CGN-9), but the plan was never executed. For details, see the Naval Institute oral histories of Commander Paul H. Backus, USN (Ret.), and Vice Admiral William P. Mack, USN (Ret.).

Now, is that their fault? It's not their fault. Who will pay that penalty? I don't know, and neither do you. It may be that no one will, but the issue is certainly begged as: What if you're wrong? Which was another one of my constant crusades to my VPs and my captains. You must always keep going through the drill: What if you're wrong? Make the decisions. I was intolerant of not making decisions. I would not accept that answer. And you could go interview some of these older captains and find out if they really wanted to get an ass-chewing was to say, "Well, we needed this decided, Meyer, but you weren't here. That was the worst ass-chewing they ever got." Now, I didn't mind them using that as an escape clause and said: "Well, you've got a good point here, Stillwell, but, you know, Meyer likes to approve that type stuff and look at it and so forth, so I'm not going to decide that." That's all right as an answer, because that's a strategy that you've got in mind that you want to exercise. That's different than backing away from a decision. In this second case maybe you ain't so sure about the correctness of the decision, or maybe it is you just don't want to do it right now. So, as I've told them repeatedly, you can blame me repeatedly, but you'd better damn well have a strategy on why you're doing that because you're not going to be with me if you refuse to make decisions.

Reich and Spreen both rubbed that onto me till I was sore, all the way back to when I was commander. Make it.

Paul Stillwell: Do you think that the strike cruiser would have been an appropriate platform for Aegis?

Admiral Meyer: Well, it would have been no platform without Aegis. Turn the coin around. The strike cruiser had several problems of its own. It's got the same problems we're going to have with trying to get the new cruiser started now. In my judgment the new cruiser will not get started without gross change in attitude, and it won't because the so-called bells and whistles operations take over. Be a $10 billion ship, and you won't have a ship, and particularly with Goldwater-Nichols. It allows everybody in the world except naval officers to vote on it. If you want to hold naval officers accountable, make them vote on it. That's my view.

I think the nation needs a capital ship right now. What is the nation's capital ship?

Paul Stillwell: Probably a submarine now.

Admiral Meyer: Yeah. Yeah. We're spending on the order of, I think it's a billion-plus on these Tridents and their conversions. We've spent outlandish numbers on them. But it's always stuck in me the speech that Arleigh Burke gave out at graduate school, in King Auditorium one day when he got asked the question, and he answered, "I don't know how our Navy does 'presence' with submarines. I, Burke, am not anti-submarine, but presence is an extraordinary dimension of naval forces, and you have to be able to project a presence, which a submarine cannot."

Paul Stillwell: That people can see [chuckle].

Admiral Meyer: They've got to be able to see it. And we tell the incident—I forget what island was acting up in the Caribbean. USS *Leahy*, DLG-16, the first one that had been completed in that class, was down in the Caribbean in exercises. Some island was acting up down there. It may have been Haiti, I'm not sure, but it doesn't matter. But in any event they had come into harbor and they had loaded the TSAMs, the training surface-to-air missiles, on their forward launcher, two rails, to test the system with. Loaded them. That very day calm came over the island. That is a manifestation of what naval power does, and that's what presence does. So the people there ashore didn't know what's under there. No need to tell them, either, till the right time.

Paul Stillwell: You talked last time about the great support from Admiral Doyle. Do you have a number of specific examples on that and how he helped the program?

Admiral Meyer: Well, I think he still holds the record of having served the longest time of any, what we used to call the Op-Deps, but surface warfare. Some five years he served. That of itself was significant.

The second piece that was significant is before he—let's see, when he was selected for vice admiral—I believe this is correct—he was sent out to command Third Fleet.* Third Fleet was based in Pearl Harbor. First Fleet was based in San Diego. And just as there was no Fourth Fleet in the Atlantic, the Second Fleet, who had responsibility for doctrinal matters, so did Third Fleet have some.

Doyle's foresight in looking at it is, where is the doctrine for the laying and handling of surface-to-air missiles? And, by the way, at the time we had surface-to-surface missiles too, primarily Regulus.† And we had nukes on all of them. What kind of doctrine have we got? So he set to work on a lot of doctrinal effort with his officers. He had a pretty good-sized staff. In those days they had a lot of officers on that staff. Well, up till then I honestly didn't know him very well. I never knew him as a JO. But it came time to figure out what the layout was going to be for the design of the CIC and the bridge. "Oh, by the way—yes, well yes, well, wait a minute; we do want a commodore's space. Oh, no, we don't need a—there's not going to be a flag, not for an admiral."

Paul Stillwell: Are you talking about the design of *Ticonderoga*?

Admiral Meyer: I am. I'm talking about the design of those cruisers. "By the way, it's got to be able to take a commodore, though." And so how are we going to do this? Bill Goodwin and I and my officers are all looking around trying to figure out. Well, everybody, of course, in that era is worried about PIRAZ station, in Vietnam.‡ I had already learned in Terrier. Now I was learning in spades, that you must be careful in designs about falling victim, or becoming enamored, with what the operating fleet's du jour problem was. Instead you need to concentrate on a design that could have adapted to that problem, or been made to fit it. And so there's a lot of pressure on me to just build a big PIRAZ station in the Tico. We weren't sure how to do that.

---

* Vice Admiral James H. Doyle Jr., USN, was Commander Third Fleet from August 1974 to July 1975.
† The Regulus I surface-to-surface missile was removed from active service in August 1964, long before Admiral Doyle commanded the Third Fleet.
‡ The NTDS-based system was called positive identification radar advisory zone, almost always known by the acronym PIRAZ. For details, see Garette E. Lockee, "PIRAZ," *U.S. Naval Institute Proceedings*, April 1969, pages 143-146. The article includes a photo of an NTDS console.

Now, we didn't have Jimmy Doyle yet, although he was getting close. Jimmy Doyle's people out at Third Fleet developed the warfare concept of coordination. So it had AAW coordination, ASuW coordination, and ASW coordination.* So these three fundamental warfares were developed by them, and they had to be coordinated. Well, up till that time in the Terrier fleet our ships could fight in what I came to call "or" modes. For example, the DLG-26 design, *Belknap*s, the ASROC used the same launcher as did Terrier or Standard.† So that ship could fight in the ASW mode *or* the anti-air mode *or* the surface mode—read guns. They all had a transition from one warfare to another.

So what we set out to do in that warfare—and nobody was very smart on it. It was based, really on your own experiences. But Doyle and Third Fleet got behind us foursquare of how were we going to integrate those warfares. So it was not going to be an "or" ship; it was going to be an "and" ship. So you could lay ASROC or torpedoes at the same time that you were defending against a cruise missile attack, and so forth. So that is a theological change that has occurred that, frankly, has never been well understood or grasped in the ability to fight these ships. These officers—by now we have hundreds of them in this fleet of Aegis ships, who commanded these ships, that no longer appreciate how hard it was or how adept you had to be at waging battle before you got in an Aegis ship, because we've got officers now that have never served in any ship except Aegis ships. Or they were so young they didn't appreciate it.

That is an unsung contribution of Jimmy Doyle. And he brought that constantly. What he did is he kept ratifying what we were doing, or we kept soliciting his opinions. He never ordered us to do anything that I can remember, but he talked to us about this or that. Frankly, he's kind of a shy person to start with. He's very shy. And so I think he was very shy of engineering. He was a little scared of it; it was a world he was not acquainted with. He himself has said in any number of occasions, "I never understood the materiel establishment until I retired from the Navy." That's a significant observation if you think about that. Said it a number of times, that we need to be doing a much better

---

* AAW – antiair warfare; ASuW – antisurface warfare; ASW – antisubmarine warfare.
† USS *Belknap* was commissioned 7 November 1964 as a guided missile frigate, DLG-26, the lead ship of her class. She had a standard displacement of 7,930 tons, was 547 feet long, 55 feet in the beam, and had a maximum draft of 29 feet. Her top speed was 33 knots. She was equipped with twin launchers for Terrier missiles, one 5-inch gun, ASROC (antisubmarine rocket), and six torpedo tubes. She was reclassified as a guided missile cruiser, CG-26, on 30 June 1975.

job of getting this insight and appreciation of the significance of the materiel establishment if you're going to have an effective Navy, operational Navy.

Well, so those were major hidden contributions.

Another major contribution is he was really instrumental in locking Captain Rapid Robert Monroe, who later went on also to become a vice admiral who was OpTEvFor, amongst other things—he was a captain then—and the commander, Mustin, Henry Mustin, of the Mustin collection, and Mustin went on to become an admiral too, a vice admiral, in due course. He picked them. He had them in OP-03. Well, they tried not to be in OP-03, but he was slicker than they were. And at that time my ex-deputy, one W. H. Rowden—he had been my deputy—left me to command the heavy cruiser *Columbus*, and returned from there to become the deputy to, now, Doyle. So, man, I had this connectivity that there's nobody ever gotten it—submariners may have it; nobody else ever got it. I had the same kind of connectivity with Donald Pete Roane, who became admiral, whose 15 minutes of fame was the *Mayaguez* incident.* He was the on-scene commander at *Mayaguez*.†

Bill Rowden—I may have told you this tale—is fond of telling a little tale. One day there was some assistant secretary or something up in OSD that was demanding and pressing on Doyle's admirals that they were going to change their process. They were going to do it this way and that's the way it was going to be. So he was telling Doyle, and Doyle said, "Well, how about getting him down here?" So Rowden finally tracked this guy down, got him the next day, and brought him in to Doyle's office. He sat there and Doyle, frown on his face, listened to him and everything, and he talked and talked about how this had to get corrected and that had to get squared away and looked at him and talked about it.

Finally Doyle said to him, "Well, Mr. Jones, we're not going to do it that way. Now, if you have any question about that, you can call the Chief of Naval Operations." And that was the end of it. I mean, it was beautiful. Rowden is fond of telling that tale of

---

* On 12 May 1975 a gunboat of the Cambodian Communist regime, the Khmer Rouge, fired upon and seized the American containership *Mayaguez* while she was en route from Hong Kong to Sattahip, Thailand. On 15 May U.S. military forces executed a crew rescue operation directed at Koh Tang Island, 34 miles off the Cambodian mainland. In the meantime, the Cambodians had released the *Mayaguez* crew and left the ship herself unguarded. In the rescue attack on Koh Tang, a number of U.S. servicemen were killed or wounded. For details, see *U.S. Naval Institute Proceedings*, November 1976, pages 93-111.
† Captain Donald P. Roane, USN, Commander Destroyer Squadron 23 from June 1974 to October 1976.

how old Doyle, just in his legalistic mind just clipped him off, cut him right off, head to heels.

There was another thing about Doyle, is once he believed in you, he was almost unforgiving to others. So there was a little piece almost like Zumwalt in him, but Zumwalt had these negative pieces in him. But Doyle decided early on that the future of the Navy was Aegis, and if he didn't get it built it wasn't going to get built. Well, the admirals had cycled in and out of there one after the other and stuff, and their view was, "Well, Aegis is just one project amongst many we've got over here, and we've got all these decisions to make, and all these things are important." Well, Doyle would not accept that. Doyle would not just pass a bucket full of money to me, but he would ask for guidance from my officers and my vice presidents on what they thought ought to be done, and he would cut and shape what we suggested, to try to make it fit. Well, of course, there always were losers in the process, and they weren't very happy.

That's when Doyle and I did something that has, I don't believe ever been done since and never been done before. We set up the process of OP-355, which was exclusively Aegis and Standard Missile under him over there.* Those officers attended all our staff meetings, participated in all our reviews right up with us. And in return my deputy, which in that era was later-Admiral Pete Roane, went to everything over there. And so we set up a communications mechanism that's never been bested. Of course, Goldwater-Nichols argues against such a communications mechanism. And I remind all of them, including Secretary Winter, I said, "You want to keep in mind here that what I say when I talk about my genius is pre-Goldwater-Nichols. Everything I did is pre-Goldwater-Nichols. Because I'm not sure that you could do what I did under Goldwater-Nichols."† Well, I believe you can now, because everything tends to run its course and Goldwater-Nichols has run its course.

You want a prediction from me?

Paul Stillwell: Sure.

---

* OP-335 was the Aegis sponsor in OpNav.
† Donald C. Winter served as Secretary of the Navy from 3 January 2006 to 13 March 2009. He was Secretary at the time of this interview.

Admiral Meyer: All right. Well, I believe that before this year is finished, the concept of PEOs will be dead and that the bureaus will be reborn.* Now, they may have a different name, I don't know, but they will return to their tradition of: I've got a vice admiral over here and he's going to be in charge of something and I'm not going to have shipbuilding scattered all over town. I don't know how the Secretary's going to overcome this whole matter of his Navy scattered all over the country. See, they say, "Oh, that's not a problem, you know, we communicate regularly with our e-mail." Bullshit. The great strength of the Navy traditionally has been its centralization in Washington, D.C. That's its great strength. Just like the United States Air Force has managed its great strength—oh, has it?—between Wright-Pat and the Air Force base out here at the edge of town, Andrews. Well, they ain't done too well at keeping those two together. The Army, they've got no strengths.

Well, what did that guy, Clark, let happen here?† Just look at what happened. He scattered the Navy all over the country. Can you tell me today where the Bureau of Supplies and Accounts is?

Paul Stillwell: No.

Admiral Meyer: No, you can't. Well, I'll tell you. There's two of them. They ain't even in the same state.‡

Do you know where, we used to call them BuDocks, Bureau of Yards and Docks, is?§

Paul Stillwell: Well, I'm going to guess the Washington Navy Yard.

Admiral Meyer: Washington Navy Yard? No way. They have down here at the end of Shirley Highway—you don't hear that word anymore—but they have a rutty-ass building

---

* PEO – program executive officer.
† Admiral Vernon E. Clark, USN, served as Chief of Naval Operations from 21 July 2000 to 22 July 2005.
‡ What used to be the Bureau of Supplies and Accounts (BuSandA) later became the Naval Supply Systems Command, located in Mechanicsburg, Pennsylvania.
§ The old Bureau of Yards and Docks became the Naval Facilities Engineering Command in 1966, and in 2003 it was re-established as the Navy Installations Command.

down there, a piece of the Hoffman Building, and they're located there, one cantonment, but they're scattered all over the United States.

Do you know where BuPers is?[*]

Paul Stillwell: Tennessee.

Admiral Meyer: Really? Why don't you walk over to the Pentagon and see how many BuPers are over there? Oh, by the way, why don't you go over to the Ridge and see how many BuPers-ers are still over there? We've abandoned that goddamn building, and yet the building's totally occupied, with Marines, with the Navy, and with the Missile Defense Agency.

Paul Stillwell: The Arlington Annex.[†]

Admiral Meyer: Yeah. So the truth is there's no organizational integrity in the structure. It's none at all. If the people are living apart all the time they're always going to have problems.

What I learned in the Navy a long time ago, which in the beginning I wouldn't believe when I was an ensign, I thought how stupid can people be? But we always made fun of the Atlantic Navy and the Pacific Navy and how different they were. Well, there are good and solid reasons why they're different, and thank God they remain different. There's no need that those two fleets be the same. And so for a long time we said, "Well, you know, they can't even operate together." Well, my question is, well, why the hell should they? Why do they need to?

Well, it turns out today, particularly the Aegis fleet, because it's the thing I corrected—they can't, and I proved it. It's when we did the cooperative engagement capability, that communications thing that came out of APL. I use your radar data and you use my radar data. So we ran two cruisers over to Kauai, sailed them here from

---

[*] BuPers – Bureau of Naval Personnel.
[†] The Arlington Annex is a large, multi-wing building near the Pentagon and the Arlington National Cemetery. It contains the headquarters of the Marine Corps and for many years had the Bureau of Naval Personnel also.

Norfolk, and two out of the Pacific. They met up over there in ten minutes. They were operating just fine, as though they had operated all their life in the same outfit. So that's bullshit, is what it is. Well, you may have some faulty designs, or did have. You ain't got any anymore.

So there's a lot of nonsense runs around in our man's Navy, as big as it is. Of course, Roughead ain't asked me for any further advice, but one of the pieces I gave him immediately was to get a plan to get his Navy put back together organizationally. I said, "Now, you can't get it done. It's liable to take four to six CNOs to do it. But somebody better start on it." As far as I know, he didn't bite on it.

So they're getting so—every night I wonder, how long do they set with their foot up, they get home. Because they've all moved into goddamn quarters over there at the Gun Factory or up on the hill. It really bothers me. We've got all our admirals no longer associated with society. We've now given them all these crowded comforts within the compounds. They're not rich quarters, but they ain't poor either. But the worst part is they've got nothing whatsoever to do with our society. *Nothing.* They're out of touch with the world. And they might even smile, you know, about nunneries and priories, but that's what they are. So tonight when 5:00 o'clock comes, or 6:00 o'clock comes, what do you think they're doing over there? Well, they're having a cocktail hour. Who do they meet? They meet the same goddamn people every night, that's who they meet. I don't like that. I'm dead set against it. And I have had opportunities to move into quarters, finally, since I got back here, although no one gives a damn about people in materials, and I refused to do it. But my guess is the new chief of NavSea will move into quarters unless he's got a long-established home.* He takes over next week or the week after.

Paul Stillwell: Well, we talked earlier about the impact of Aegis on families. What was it on your immediate family? How well did your wife and children accommodate to your pace?

---

* Vice Admiral Kevin M. McCoy, USN, has served as Commander Naval Sea Systems Command from August 2008 to the present.

Admiral Meyer: I'd say it was a strain. And yet I don't think you'd find a more dedicated woman to the Navy than my late wife, and her feelings about the Navy. Now, she would get emotional about what I had done for the Navy and the inability of the Navy to understand that.

But I attributed that really to nature. It's hard on you, and you can't offset it simply by more association or more closeness. You can ameliorate it, but you can't offset it. And the reason you can't is you can't get it off your mind. And it is another fundamental difference between major project management if you're doing it correctly, and command of a major ship. Command of a major ship, even on the edge of battle, is a relatively short period in your life. Today I don't think tours are more than two years. They had them as low there at times as 12 months and 18 months because the backup was so big. So most couplings can survive that long. Some can't.

The other thing is that it becomes hard to really know your kids, because when you're at sea you're gone. We're seeing a lot of bullshit now concerning Iraq, and we've brought a lot of this bullshit on ourselves. You know, letting women with three kids as a corporal or a sergeant is our fault. We generated a stupid-ass problem when we knew it wouldn't work. We keep trying to convince ourselves we can make that work, and it isn't working, and we're just going to be loaded in problems post-Iraq. Piles of them. But those aren't the kind of problems I'm talking about.

When you're at sea, you set up an adaptation because you generally know that it's going to be a—it's a finite period, and so you set standards to adapt to it and adjust to it. That isn't true for major project management. And today it's worse than ever. We have given our project managers today so many degrees of freedom that I honestly don't know how they effectively lead. As a matter of fact, I don't think they do. So today it would be very hard for me to defend many of the posts of major project management today to be a military, a general or an admiral. It would be very hard for me to do that. Because there are plenty of people can do what that expectation is today. The reason we have military in there is because of the significance of the cause and the importance of it, and to bring close experience of what the output is to be.

It is a lonely life if you accept the principle I just said, taught to me by Reich and Spreen, if you've been there. I don't know how I could ever be President. I don't know how anybody can be President very long. If you look at George Bush, look at how he's aged. He might think he hasn't, but you and I can look at him and see how he's—what is he now, going into his eighth year, snowy white, totally snow white, his hair, and in his mind, really.

Well, the truth is he doesn't have to make any hard decisions. What he has to be able to do is stand the beatings. Project managers don't have to stand beatings as much as they have to make hard decisions. Because you've got to get some age on you before you understand that your decisions are genuinely affecting lives, some of which are not even born yet, and how they're to wage the skirmish or the battle or the operation they get in.

Paul Stillwell: What would be an example of a hard decision you made in Aegis?

Admiral Meyer: How powerful the radar ought to be. What frequency it ought to be. Whether the manpower level is sufficient. I don't think the manpower level is sufficient to this day in those destroyers. I think they're drained way down.

I confess that many of the hard decisions I overcame in another way, and it is: Offset them by my ability or my assistants' ability to raise money because they are good products. I've often said that warships are not unlike a Hertz car, as far as maintenance is concerned. You can operate these destroyers a damned long time with just superficial attention. Well, even superficial attention may be worse than no attention. It may cause them to go downhill faster. How can you be sure that the captain understands when his ship can't fight? I've never solved that.

Paul Stillwell: It's a hard thing for a captain to accept.

Admiral Meyer: It is, because he never accumulates enough knowledge either to accept it. The closest I came to it, which might sound like a total misfit, I came close to it pretty damned—I touched it when I was an ensign but it was many years before I understood it, in the Eastern Mediterranean. The closest I came to it when I had grown up is when I was chief engineer at Port Hueneme, when the war was in runaway and every week was unpredictable, the outcome. And whether I was doing the right thing or not.

As I told Admiral Woods why I didn't want to be ordered out—I had a steady stream of ants back and forth to the Western Pacific to Vietnam—couldn't go in there myself—and the Philippines and Subic Bay. I had people stationed there, and I had parts stored at different places because it is wrong to come to believe that those sailors, of themselves, the way they're rotated in and out, can ever master their gear. And this was Tartar, Terrier, and Talos. The closest people ever mastered it is Talos because that's where the senior people were, in the cruisers. *Oklahoma City, Long Beach.*

Oh. I have served as the chairman of the senior advisory team to the Aegis project office in BMD, now under MDA. What a mess they are. But I served there because I was asked by the managers, the first one being Captain Peter "Mac" Grant. And so now that's gone on for about 12 years. And the difficult thing is that if you're going to go into an operation today in one of our ships, what we do, yet, is we send a team in to check things out, because we want to be sure that we have things operating correctly before we run this test or this trial that we're going to do. Well, the fleet commander has virtually committed *Lake Erie* full time through those years out at Pearl Harbor, which just wears the ass out of everybody else, to get out there. And so we minimized it there.

But that ain't true in the destroyers. And I read the reports. They send a team in, say, to the destroyer *Decatur*. She's going to participate in some jazzed-up missile exercise with *Lake Erie*. So they go in and they look, and you read the reports. The coolers aren't working correctly. The high voltage power supplies are all out of tolerance. And you say to yourself, "I've worked my ass off for a lifetime in the design of those things. I have beat myself to pieces to try to fail-safe those things. And I know damned good and well they're good elements. I know they'll work well if they just get a little bit of attention. Not genius attention, not exhausting, tiring attention, just a little bit." And yet you go into a ship like *Decatur* and you find out that you can't conduct the exercises you want to conduct because she's not at 100%.

Well, part of the problem is this. That's all right most days in the fleet because these ships can fight at 50%, the Aegis is that good. Fight better than anything ahead of them. But they can't fight at spec because they ain't that good. You can't be 50% and still fight at spec.

On the other hand we modified the specs a lot. The original spec, for example, on the radar the peak power's 4 megawatts, 4 million watts. Today those radars regularly put out 7½ million watts when they're properly tuned. Well, maybe it's us, I don't know.

Anna Mae and I just bought a new Cadillac, paid 53,000 and some odd dollars for it. That sure as hell ain't no el cheapo number where I come from. You know, in lease it's about 900 and some odd dollars a month. Will that thing run forever? The answer is, no, it won't. Is it a good design? Well, I think so. It's got some little piss-ant things wrong with it. But you could analog that to the Aegis. That's true in the Aegis design. I mean, the Aegis design is the longest running program in history. We're up to, what, 112 or so in the numbers. This system right here is Serial 100, right here on this board, that's going into 108.[*] That's a lot of Aegises, and that's not counting the ones bought by the allies.

So what gives here? Does it mean we can't ever get ahead? I don't know. I don't know that answer. As the British would say, that's an imponderable. And maybe we ought to shut down for the day on that.

Paul Stillwell: All right. I'll ponder the imponderable for a week.

Admiral Meyer: Will you do that? And think up some more questions.

Paul Stillwell: All right, I'll see you in a week. Thank you, Admiral.

---

[*] USS *Wayne E. Meyer* (DDG-108).

Interview Number 15 with Rear Admiral Wayne E. Meyer, U.S. Navy (Retired)
Place: Admiral Meyer's office in Crystal City, Arlington, Virginia
Date: Monday, 28 July 2008

Paul Stillwell: Hello, Admiral. We're moving along. I've got some highlights of the year 1977. In March of that year there were technical characterization contracts to Bath, General Dynamics, and Ingalls. In April Aegis became the first system to engage two targets simultaneously. In May Congress authorized the first Aegis ship, DDG-47, and also that month CSEDS was commissioned and PMS-400 was established. What do you remember about that period and the momentum that was obviously building?

Admiral Meyer: Well, I want to say a short word, because you triggered me on the nature of the shipbuilding contracts. We insisted, and were approved to the top, that our contracts would be cost contracts. And what the future contracts would be was left as an exercise to the reader, unresolved. So we fulfilled and met the demands of the leadership of a competitive contract, knowing full well that it was a cost contract, and my intention was that it would remain a cost contract. And in the back of my mind, I was thinking in terms of three shipyards, a shipyard on each coast—Gulf, Pacific, and Atlantic.

Now, I was thinking in those terms for several reasons. In my youth I observed that when we built ships we tried to build them fast. Shipyards can only build a little handful at a time, in spite of what is claimed at Ingalls and what will be claimed for the LCS.[*] That's one point.

The other point is, I kept saying to all my superiors and everything, "Look, these shipyards are our shipyards. Just because we have a civilian in command of them, an industrial person, doesn't mean that they aren't ours."

Paul Stillwell: What do you mean by "ours"?

Admiral Meyer: Well, they have no other work. Now, if you kind of grew up in ordnance you didn't have any problem understanding that, or either in aviation, because

---

[*] LCS – littoral combat ship.

the Navy's always had a lot of what are called Naval Industrial Reserve Ordnance Plants, and aviation is patterned after that. For example, Pomona, California, was owned by the Navy as a NIROP, Naval Industrial Reserve Ordnance Plant. The Navy put originally substantially its own money in there, and substantially instrumented it and fed it, and then contracted General Dynamics to operate and run it. The big plant where we're at now in Tucson, Arizona, was originally founded and operated by Hughes, and it built air-to-air missiles—Sparrow, primarily, in the beginning, and such, and later years AMRAAM, what's referred to as the air-to-air missile that is the in-service missile today on our fighters.[*] 'Tis a bad thing we've drifted away from that as an approach in recent years, and I don't want to get derailed here in a discussion about it, but it's one of the many things that damaged our profession and the integrity of it.

But anyhow, I said that we weren't going to have any bidders that didn't have any idea how to build a ship. And we were going to make that determination before we issued you a package.

Paul Stillwell: Did you see any likely candidates on the Pacific Coast?

Admiral Meyer: Yes. We thought that Todd, Seattle, which would need some bootstrapping, but stood the best chance of being able to do this ship. And I had made a trip out there and looked at the place. While Todd had about seven or eight shipyards of different sizes, what I call Seattle yard was the most adult-type yard for military work. And they were building FFGs up there, you remember. The FFG-7 fleet, they were one of the three shipbuilders.[†]

We let in one other bidder, because for social reasons, political reasons, and because the leadership wanted it. So we had Ingalls, we had Todd, we had Bath, and we had General Dynamics Fore River, Quincy. And we started out.

Well, we hardly executed any paper before Todd decided it was beyond them. They backed out. Shortly thereafter Bath backed out, that it appeared to call for more

---

[*] AIM-9 advanced medium-range air-to-air missile (AMRAAM).
[†] The Navy eventually built 51 guided missile frigates of the *Oliver Hazard Perry* (FFG-7) class. The first of them was commissioned in December 1977.

engineering and more manpower than they could handle. So this got the bidding pretty quickly down to Ingalls and to General Dynamics in Quincy.

Paul Stillwell: Had you settled on the *Spruance*-type hull by then?

Admiral Meyer: We settled on a *Spruance*-like hull. We never did settle on the *Spruance* hull. Never settled on the *Spruance* hull, in spite of the popular claims made by some of these assholes who talk about all they did was land a deckhouse on a *Spruance*. Not true. And if you want I'll say a couple words about that.

One of the big things we did—well, let me finish this part. Remind me to get back to it, and a big advantage I had.

We got down to the two bidders, and there really was no contest. Well, depended on how you looked at it. Quincy wrote an incredible proposal, really well done. And the reason it was well done is they went to Pomona and they got a couple crackerjacks, older people out there, one fellow by the name of Clancy McCabe. He'd been with Pomona ever since it began. I'd known him a long, long time. Good man, and a good writer and a good observer. I mean, he'd get people in this room and sit down with his pencil and tablet and start outlining as he made everybody talk, and then they'd end up with their work assignments. And he'd review it and it'd get rejected, and he'd review it again. Really, I mean, genuinely good. He headed that proposal. To this day it's the best proposal I've ever read. And I mean it was a thick one.

Paul Stillwell: Six or eight inches, maybe.

Admiral Meyer: Say. And they had a lot of, you know sub-submissions.

Well, Ingalls came in, and it was as though they got part of the night crew and a couple guys standing around on leave, and put the thing together. Grammar poor, English poor. Their attitude just came through loud and clear: "We've got it knocked." Well, here was the situation. They *did* have it knocked, so what's a person to do? Down here we didn't think we were so damned stupid as to think that we'd walk out on the sidewalk and could get somebody that never built ships to put this together, when at that time the biggest non-nuke shipyard in America was Ingalls.

Well, wait a minute. They were in the process of getting rid of their nukes. See, they were nukes on the west bank, and they had so damned many fights with Rickover that finally, when the last leadership came in: "Hell with this. We're getting out of it. We're not going to put up with him." Well, Rickover ran around the rest of his life taking credit for getting rid of them, but the truth is it happened in the other direction. Same result. And it was a wise thing on their part, because in that yard in subsequent years they built boxcars, they built oil rigs, they are a major Gulf repair outfit for big rigs that get in trouble out there. They've got a big business in that. So they developed a whole new business as a result of that changing times and the pressure on them too.

Everybody in Washington wanted a hand in the selection of the shipbuilder.

Paul Stillwell: Did that include Congress?

Admiral Meyer: Well, they were continually briefed on it. They were up to date.

Finally the day came when the announcement was made that Ingalls had been selected. I believe I'm speaking of the year '77 or '78.[*] It's right about in there. And, I mean, the clock had not turned one revolution before the Navy came under massive, fiery assault from Kennedy of Massachusetts and O'Neill.[†] He was the Speaker, recall, at that time, but he was a normal man. O'Neill was a pretty well-mannered person. And amongst other things he liked Reagan, he befriended him, and he was also, he listened. Kennedy has never developed any sense whatsoever—this is Ted Kennedy—has none today, on anything. Just listen to any speech he makes. So he got this staff of all these 24-, 25-, 28-year-old kids to start retorting and starting attack. Well, I looked around for someone to go with me over there because immediately they started holding hearings. Guess what?

---

[*] In September 1978 the contract for the detailed design and construction of DDG-47 was awarded to the Ingalls Shipbuilding Division of Litton Industries. In January 1980 the ship's designation was changed to CG-47, guided missile cruiser.

[†] Edward M. Kennedy, brother of President John F. Kennedy, was a Democrat from Massachusetts. He served in the Senate from 3 January 1963 until his death on 25 August 2009. Thomas P. O'Neill, Jr., a Democrat from Massachusetts, served in the House of Representatives from 3 January 1953 to 3 January 1987. He was Speaker of the House from 1977 to 1986.

Paul Stillwell: You couldn't find anybody.

Admiral Meyer: I couldn't find anybody. [Chuckle] I couldn't even find anybody out of the materiel establishment. They wouldn't touch me with a ten-foot pole. I could go...by...myself.

So for around three months I ground them down and ground them down. It's something I've always been deep down—I've never said much about it—proud of. And I have to say that the Aegis team, or what became the Aegis team, of industry and government formed together professionally, and we just wore them out. The truth was they were amateurs. But you know how hard it is in our society to wear out an amateur. It can really get tiresome, in its way. You know, you've got a stubborn kid that doesn't want to do something it can exhaust you. [Chuckle]

Paul Stillwell: What was the basis for picking in favor of Ingalls, who had the night-crew proposal, versus McCabe's proposal for General Dynamics?

Admiral Meyer: Well, number one, New England was deserving of the work, just categorically. Number two, their bid was competitive. The truth is, their bid was, I believe, a few dollars even—I can't recall now, even under or even over Ingalls bid. But they were a wash. It was as though they had copied each other. On the other hand, my team had put out a hell of a lot of data ahead of time of what we thought the thing should cost, what our estimates were, so they all knew our numbers. We had no secrets. They knew our numbers, and they hewed pretty closely to the numbers. They genuinely hewed to the numbers.

So we had an argument, albeit flimsy, that Ingalls was the low bidder. But we had an overwhelming argument on experience and on know-how. And the promise was they would all be competed.

Paul Stillwell: Ship by ship.

Admiral Meyer: Ship by ship. In the future they'd be competed. Well, General Dynamics was not that stupid. They decided they just weren't going to burn out their engine on this.

Now, if you've got the time and want it on this tape—in that whole process of working up to that there's a Greek by the name of Taki Veliotis.*

Paul Stillwell: He was with General Dynamics.

Admiral Meyer: He was with General Dynamics. He'd been hired by General Dynamics. I don't know whether you ever met him.

Paul Stillwell: I did.

Admiral Meyer: Tall fellow.

Paul Stillwell: Up in Quincy.

Admiral Meyer: Yeah. He was put in charge of that yard to try to clean it up—he'd had some other piece—and to try to clean it up and make it go.

Paul Stillwell: They were building the LNG tankers at that point.†

Admiral Meyer: Ah, you got it. Affirmative. So the reason I got involved with him is to try and understand that LNG process and what they were doing. They were building piece parts of it, and they were doing some down in Charleston and some pieces, had rented some ground over in Quonset and such like that. So I got to looking into their techniques, which I personally thought were pretty good. They were rebellious, but they

---

* Panagiotis Takis Veliotis was born and educated in Greece. He was with Davie Shipbuilding in Quebec, Canada, from 1953 to 1972. From 1973 to 1977 he was general manager of the General Dynamics shipbuilding yard in Quincy, Massachusetts, then became general manager of the Electric Boat Division of General Dynamics in 1977.
† LNG – liquefied natural gas.

weren't too rebellious. They had their head and their feet on the ground yet. So I didn't deny their processes; what I denied was their experience.

I don't know whether they lost their hat, ass, and overcoat on those LNGs or not. I don't know. I think they probably came out ahead. And I think they came out ahead enough that the yard tended to survive, as far as I know, to this day, in the commercial business. But in essence they were out of the military business, period. They just couldn't cut it.

Taki had a really tough thing happen to him along in the middle of that process someplace. His brother's son had come over here to work for the summer in the shipyard. And one day he was working on a crane there, and the crane tipped. I can't remember now whether it tipped completely over. In any event, it killed this boy. And Taki underwent a really, really tough change. Not only was it his nephew, but he felt some accountability at its being his brother's boy and such, and Taki never again, in my view, recovered his stamina and robustness of leadership, even when he later went down to, you know, to do the other yard.

Paul Stillwell: He went to Electric Boat and got into a fight with Rickover.[*]

Admiral Meyer: Right. And I personally believe he saved that company. But I may be the only person that thinks that. Because they didn't have any use for him internally, and the Navy didn't have any use for him. He was a ruthless son of a bitch, but he was really a tempered one when he was down there, as compared to how he in the beginning was. But he was a man that thought he could do anything, and that boy being killed had a big effect on Taki. I think Taki died, I'm not sure. He retired, and I think he may have returned to the old country, I don't know.[†]

Paul Stillwell: He did leave the United States, yes.

---

[*] For details see Patrick Tyler, *Running Critical: The Silent War, Rickover, and General Dynamics* (New York: Harper & Row, 1986).
[†] In 1983 Veliotis went back to Greece, shortly before he would have been indicted by the United States for taking kickbacks from a sub-contractor.

Admiral Meyer: Yeah. Well, that's that tale.

So we forked our way through it with Kennedy and his crowd. And it's funny, and I knew it would happen, after the initial set-to, which lasted maybe three hours or four hours, Kennedy never showed up again. But a couple guys had been empowered to keep calling meetings and calling meetings and they, I think, thought they would grind us down. I really think their strategy was that we'd cut a piece off of the pie for them to have. We weren't going to do it. So we just finally wore them down and they dissipated.

Paul Stillwell: We should make the connection that the Quincy yard was in Kennedy's state.

Admiral Meyer: Right. Massachusetts. Sorry. Get it in the record. And it was also in O'Neill's state, but he was more rational about the thing.

Then the other thing that happened—because shipbuilding was in a—I mean, we think we've got a train wreck today in shipbuilding. Hell, we don't have a train wreck in shipbuilding. We don't have shipbuilding contracts out of control today. We don't have them. We did in those days. We had all the competitive-bid fixed-price contracts, and they were categorically out of control.

Paul Stillwell: And the shipyards were trying to make it up through claims.

Admiral Meyer: Right. They had no other option, because the government would give them no attention. They simply had no other option. And so they worked at it. I knew a number of people, really good, smart professionals, that were hired by Litton, who just were experts in that subject, to help them in preparing their claims on the LHA and on the first destroyers.*

Paul Stillwell: *Spruance* class.

---

* LHA is the designation of a type of amphibious assault ship. The first of the type, USS *Tarawa* (LHA-1), was commissioned 29 May 1976. The builder was Litton/Ingalls.

Admiral Meyer: Yeah. Recollect the *Spruance* class. They bought a whole package of 30 destroyers, I believe that's right.

Paul Stillwell: Total Package Procurement, they called it.

Admiral Meyer: Total Package—$85 million a ship. They never even came close. Never even came close. I mean, it was like missed 300% or 400%. Well, the way that they originally, the government, kept trying to solve it was by disarming the ship. That's what attracted me to the ship. The ship work going on I thought was pretty darned good. I just thought it was pretty good. But here we were building 8,500-ton ships and all they had on them was two 5-inch guns and a sonar. They were disarmed. So that's what got me started on it, because I figured I was way, way up the ladder with a ship put together, and offering that ship was a better thing than starting from scratch.

I just recently told the captain who is running the *Zumwalt*s about that experience. I found that you're always better off offering and working on what you've got than starting from the ground up. Automobile companies have learned that time and time again. They've learned it repeatedly. The most classic of all is Saturn. I don't know whether General Motors has made any money *yet* out of Saturn, and they've been at it for 25 years. They went years and years and years building Saturns at a loss, and the determination was, almost like *Zumwalt*s, by the way: "We're not going to put anything in it out of those Chevrolets; there'll be no parts in there out of Detroit." That's how Saturn was built. Funny, isn't it, how people get those ideas? It's funny how those lessons don't get learned. It's funny how they get repeated and repeated. It's amazing.*

Paul Stillwell: Did the Iranian version of the *Spruance*s figure in your calculations?

Admiral Meyer: Good question, but I'm going to give a flaky answer. [Chuckle] Here the U.S. Navy snatched them and took them over. They had been bought by the Shah,

---

* The Saturn Corporation was established in 1985 as a subsidiary of General Motors. New production ended in 2009, and the corporation went out of business.

and I'd had a hand in it.[*] They were to be armed as missile ships, in essence what we would call Tartar ships, but Standard missile. They were to have the Mark 26 launchers in them. And they were going to be really, really powerful; so powerful in my view that our nation could label them perhaps as light cruisers, and if need be get on with them.

I don't think we did any flimflam on the Iranians. I think what we did is we tried to cater to their wants. They wanted the best.

Paul Stillwell: And were willing to pay for it.

Admiral Meyer: They were willing to pay for it. And then they fell into political crossfires, and the Shah could not be found. I had spent a good deal of time with the Vice CNO of the Iranian navy, who had come to talk to me several times about my views on arming that ship. Because you recall I mentioned the two earlier ones for Iran, *Babr* and *Palang*. I believe I mentioned them to you.

Paul Stillwell: I don't recall it specifically, no.

Admiral Meyer: Well, may I take a minute?

Paul Stillwell: Sure.

Admiral Meyer: We're not going to get very far down the highway.

If you go through my career in that era, backing up a little bit, you seem to have pretty good intelligence there. I was ordered back here, just to get the technicalities, from Port Hueneme to be the weapons system manager for the new ASMS, now called Aegis. It had a code within the SMS project of 403. It had a captain, a GS-16, the whole series of people under it. The contract was awarded in December. I attended my first meeting in January. I reported in back here in the subsequent June, for the program. Well, in the meantime, reorganizations were occurring on a biweekly basis through NavMat and the

---

[*] Mohammad Reza Pahlavi (1919-1980) became Shah of Iran (or Persia, as it was then known) in 1941 and held office until his regime was ousted in 1979 by the Ayatollah Khomeini.

problems that were related to shipbuilding—or perceived ones. If we had no real problems, we made up problems. So we're just slam-dunking everybody.

Over the next, say, three to four years, to me the real objective of Admiral Kidd, the late Admiral Kidd, was to destroy Naval ordnance.[*] Just that simple. 'Tis a pity, after all it had done for him in his professional life. 'Tis a pity.

You will recall, I'm sure, the story of how he got there. I don't know whether it's true; I think it is. Zumwalt put him there, remember. And Zumwalt said, or is quoted as having said—and I believe Kidd, I can't remember whether he was still at Sixth Fleet or not—but Zumwalt said, "He did so much bitching about how the materiel in the Navy was so bad, I decided what I'd do is put him there to fix it." And that's how he got ordered there. Or that's a popular story.

In the very beginning we had a bicameral structure in the Navy. Material establishment reported to the Secretary, the CNO reported to him. Then we went through this change where the Chief of Naval Material also reported to the CNO, and that's the era I was in.

Paul Stillwell: Where did these two Iranian ships come in that you mentioned?

Admiral Meyer: The two, *Babr* and *Palang*. Well, by default I was ordered also to take the surface missile system project, about the second year I was back here or so or the disintegrating surface missile system project. The whole thing was coming to pieces. An officer by the name of Captain Merrill Homer Sappington was the manager when I reported back here, so I reported to him. A determination was made that I would relieve him, because this whole thing was disintegrating. Talos, Terrier, Tartar, all scattered. The so-called "G" Fleet, or Arleigh Burke fleet, was in essence built, and maybe we didn't need all this management, but we did. So amongst other thing we reorganized—not we, others reorganized the Bureau of Ordnance into the Naval Ordnance Systems Command, and created in it was a structure called director of surface warfare.

I don't know whether it's in your notes, but I was appointed the director of surface warfare. I served in that post for around three years, but had all these other

---

[*] Admiral Isaac C. Kidd, Jr., USN, served as Chief of Naval Material, 1 December 1971 to 18 April 1975.

assignments. I had Aegis, I had the surface missile system project, which hadn't been decommissioned. And in fact I had three desks over there, on the ninth deck and on the tenth deck. So I cycled back and forth on those desks, and then I had me a desk at Moorestown, because I had to spend a lot of time up there worrying about getting this thing on the track.

You had asked me a question and I started out to answer and all I did was blabber.

Paul Stillwell: The Iranian ships, *Babr* and the *Palang*.

Admiral Meyer: Oh, the Iranian ships. Okay.

So there was a captain who ran the Tartar operations by the name of Randall Wayne Young. There was a captain who ran the Terrier operations by the name of Donald Pete Roane. Donald Pete Roane later, after the disintegration, went on to become my deputy, and later on was selected as an admiral and rose to his 15 minutes of fame as the on-scene commander in the *Mayaguez* incident. A crackerjack officer, a crackerjack operator. He lives to this day in Virginia. His son is in the Aegis Navy today.

But I do not say this in a negative way—he was such a crackerjack officer in the years he was my deputy I had all the confidence in the world for Pete Roane. He was well respected, well known, hard worker, professional people liked him. So when I was fired by the Secretary—I'm ratcheting ahead now to my 13th year—I had remaining only two hours to nominate someone to relieve me, so I threw the name of Admiral Donald Pete Roane in, and they were so anxious to get rid of me, the institution, that it stuck.

As far as I know, Pete Roane was never consulted or anything else, and he was really a little out of touch with the structure at the time. He had been through two or three changes of duty. But anyhow it turned out he only stayed there less than two years as my relief, maybe one year, because he had no stomach for what I had put up with and the life that I had to lead to get this thing going.[*] Here was an officer with ribbons from here up to here, maybe 6 inches of them, crackerjack, and a smart officer, technically ept. Graduate, one that I loved like a son. He just didn't want it. He's lived happily ever after, I guess, down on the Eastern Shore someplace, or down by Yorktown.

---

[*] Rear Admiral Roane was the Aegis Shipbuilding Project Manager from 1983 to 1985.

Well, back to where we were, as I drift around here in elliptical orbit.

Randall Wayne Young had gotten a number of things going as the Tartar manager, because the allies were all interested in Tartar ships, you'll recall. We built a lot of ships for our allies. Built a lot of them in Bath as the *Charles Francis Adams*-class destroyers, or modified in some way or other. Damned good, powerful ships. If you talk to the Germans today or you talk to the Aussies they will tell you what incredible ships those ships were—their staying power, their fighting power. They really loved those ships. I think the Aussies have decommissioned their last one too.[*]

Paul Stillwell: I read that recently, I believe.

Admiral Meyer: Yeah, I think they've all gone their way now. They were just wonderful ships.

Well, Randall Wayne Young had his fingers in all those things and he had gotten involved somehow with the FMS and the Iranians.[†] And, of course, the Shah was walking down the street buying everything he saw, including, he wanted something that could kill missiles. Money was no object, and he wanted it now. The grubby people of the industrial base—and I don't think that they were wrong, particularly—convinced him that we could take the Mark 25 radar that was a long, long-time fire control radar in our destroyers. When I entered operations, the basic fire control radar was the Mark 12 and the Mark 22. Well, the new radar that replaced it is the Mark 25, which is a parabolic dish. It's a Westinghouse design with a magnetron, really good radar—Westinghouse right up here at Baltimore. So that went on the Mark 37 directors. You've probably seen it many times, maybe even served with it for all that matter, because, hell, there may still be some in operation.

Anyhow, we had two recently decommissioned destroyers in the reserve fleet up at Philadelphia. The Iranians looked at that. We had done some calculations, primarily by General Dynamics at Pomona. We had in fact fired a Standard missile out of a box on

---

[*] HMAS *Perth* (D-41) ended her active service in 2001 and was sunk in 2005 to serve as a dive wreck.
[†] FMS –foreign military sales.

the deck of a destroyer and proved that it could be guided—what it needed was homing—with the Mark 25 radar. Didn't have much range, but it could be done.

The Vice CNO of Iran—I can't remember for sure now about the CNO—they had sons in the Naval Academy. I think I told you they were going to the Naval Academy, and I mentioned to you in an earlier meeting about Dr. John J. McMullen.

Paul Stillwell: Yes.

Admiral Meyer: Dr. John, retired commander, and he was the connector to those because for a long time he was on the board of visitors or administrators or whatever it is at the Naval Academy, and so he was the mechanism by which they got into the academy. Because he had built one of the shipyards over there, forget which country now, but he got to know a lot of the people. That's how this whole thing got itself in motion.

We going to be able to put—I can't remember now whether it was eight missiles or four missiles—on the decks of those ships. Not only that; the Shah wanted an airplane. Off came Mount 53 and on went a hangar, put in those ships. Their Iranian/Persian names were *Babr* and *Palang*.[*] Their officers and crews were just tops, the best that Iran had. I got to socialize with them. I got to know the captains quite well in that era of helping them. The time was approaching now and the Naval Ordnance Systems Command was drawing its last breath, thanks to Admiral Kidd, and Admiral Spreen was the commander of the Naval Ordnance Systems Command of that time when they were headed to their home.[†] And in talking to Spreen, which I did almost every night I was here, I said, "You know, Admiral, we need to get scared about sending these two old ships with these totally inexperienced crews on their way around the world with no escorts. I mean, I just view that to be unsafe."

(Interruption for change of tape)

---

[*] The *Babr*, former USS *Zellars* (DD-777) was commissioned in the Iranian Navy in 1973 and the *Palang*, former USS *Stormes* (DD-780) in 1972.
[†] Rear Admiral Roger E. Spreen, USN, served as Commander Naval Ordnance Systems Command from 1972 to 1974.

Admiral Meyer: Well, for your purpose these came right in the middle of my major duty, which was still Aegis and the disintegrating surface missile systems project, and the disintegrating materiel establishment.

Paul Stillwell: What was the solution on not escorting these ships?

Admiral Meyer: We got an escort. Spreen agreed with me. Spreen was well enough known in the operating forces, and he talked to them and told them this was a poor thing for us to do. It wasn't an escort the whole way; they were handed off in a relay-type operation.

Now, did I tell you about their missile firings when they got home?

Paul Stillwell: No.

Admiral Meyer: Well, we took those ships under my counsel and advice, in essence under me, and sent them to Puerto Rico, because again I said to Spreen, "You know, we at least need to test these ships and see if they can fire, for goodness sake. Because these are all handmade, custom made, off the back of a suitcase. The way we're going to maintain these ships are with General Dynamics field engineers. But we need to find out if they can really fire them."

"You're right."

Paul Stillwell: Especially to satisfy the customer.

Admiral Meyer: Yeah. So he got ahold of one of his deputies. I said, "The problem is, I don't have my hands on any missiles."

He said, "Well, we'll find some." Well, it turned out that we were making some modifications to the Standard Missile's fuze at that time that, by golly, needed some evaluation at sea. So the right and proper thing to do was take four of those fuzes and test them to be sure that what we have done would be proper. Sounded good.

So we set that all up. They put on the range. One of the *dumbest* things that we've ever done in the Navy is do away with the Roosevelt Roads missile range.[*] I know the officer that did it, and I still write him strident notes. But we set that all up and the missiles, set up the teams, that these two young crews would do this test firing under our supervision, two missiles out of each of their ships, those old destroyers.

Along the way a couple of things happened. One is, we sent them in to San Juan for liberty when they first arrived, before they went over to Roosevelt Roads. They were off on liberty, and they moored at the big State Pier down there. When I was a junior officer we'd moor there quite frequently for liberty. We don't do that so much anymore as far as I know. Doesn't anybody even go to San Juan anymore. But, you know, the climate was good, the food was good, the whiskey was good, and the women were good. I mean, it had everything for a sailor.

Well, they went in there, moored, and had liberty. Their sailors coming back that night to one of the destroyers, they were walking back, walking along in kind of semi-darkness approaching the pier, and a goddamn car ran over one and killed him. What a sad, sad situation we had. I wanted to send an escort with the body back to Persia, but the embassy here said they didn't feel it was necessary. They accepted it, and they understood, and they appreciated what the Americans felt about that. Sent the body back, but it surely brought a pall over everything.

They went out and, of course, they fired these four missiles and bang, bang, bang, bang, just blowing the goddamn drones right out of the sky. They weren't difficult shots, but as far as I'm concerned anything with that rig we had would be difficult, but they did it.

We sent them on their way. Made them lay out some liberty en route. They went through Panama. We had them escorted to this end, had them picked up on the other end. Brought them to San Diego for a day or two, and then skipped them across the Pacific to Pearl and to Guam and on the way around. It took them, hell, I don't know, six weeks or so, but they got there safely.

---

[*] U.S. Naval Station Roosevelt Roads was located at the eastern edge of Puerto Rico. Its land mass consisted of 31,000 acres: 8,600 acres on the island of Puerto Rico and 22,400 acres on Vieques Island, seven and one half miles southeast of the main station. The facility was completed in 1943, and Roosevelt Roads was commissioned as a U.S. Naval Operations Base. It served as both a training facility and base for Navy ships until being closed in 2004.

Well, the reason I pick up on this personally is what they thought of me. I came to have great admiration for them, as sailors and professionals, and the same way with the Vice Chief, who had come and visited me several times. And he had a captain stationed over here as his agent. As a matter of fact, he lived out in Maryland. And I got pretty friendly with the captain.

Their number-one objective was to put on a demonstration for the Shah. And this was going to be their real pride.

Paul Stillwell: Did the Iranians buy a group of missiles to equip these ships?

Admiral Meyer: Yes. And that's when the Iranians commissioned a new naval base. There's a port which I've never been to by the name of Bandar-Abbas, which is right down on the—as you enter the straits, I believe, which they had a couple of commercial ships home-ported in down there, and I think they had a couple of their local ships. That's where they were going to home-port those two destroyers.

I've known what they were up to, and so I again got Spreen all fumed up, so I gave him one of my officers at that time, Commander Bart Dalla Mura, who'd been selected for captain and who was very creative at getting things done. I said, "Look, we need to get somebody to go over there and see what the hell this place is, how it's laid out."

"I agree," he said, "send him over there" to go find out where in the hell Bandar-Abbas was and see how well it was equipped to deal with these ships and handle these ships. So he did. He was over there, I don't know, a couple months off and on. 'Twas a stroke of genius on my part. They came to think that Bart Dalla Mura could do no wrong, and it was true he could.[*] He was well enough informed, he knew exactly where he had to go to get his hands on something to get those ships functional. God's in His heaven, and all is right with the world.

This captain caused the invitation to me from the CNO, for me to come to witness their firings for the Shah. I didn't tell you this?

---

[*] Commander Bart M. Dalla Mura Jr., USN, an ordnance engineering specialist.

Paul Stillwell: No.

Admiral Meyer: Okay. They were going to put on a firing exhibition, and it was going to be for the Shah, and our CNO, Holloway, was going to attend.* And they wanted me to be part of it. Well, I thought it was a pretty nice opportunity. They were going to buy the ticket, pay all the expenses, do all that. So we counted down as we were getting ready, and Bart was over in country and getting things shaped in.

On a Friday night I was to leave out of Dulles, about 2000, as I recollect. I was at home, all packed up and everything. About 4:00 o'clock I took a call from Pentagon, OP-36. I think that's what it was at that time. I was told that my trip is cancelled, and I would not go. "Is there a reason?" I asked.

"Well, no, there is no reason, at the moment." I was really hurt, was really taken aback. That reason has not emerged to this day. I just have no idea what caused that.

Paul Stillwell: Did Admiral Holloway go?

Admiral Meyer: Admiral Holloway went. I mean, they almost canonized Holloway over there. They virtually canonized him. They had him out in the ship, they lifted him around by boat, and I can't remember whether he was lifted by helo or not. My own view was I wasn't going to fly on a goddamn helo in and out of those ships. I thought it was pretty hazardous.

But in any event they were just so excited, so enraptured at what they had accomplished and what they had done, and it was an incredible thing. I've never known to this day what happened that wiped me completely off the face of the earth and, for that matter, I have no idea whatever happened to those ships. No idea. Because the house kept coming to pieces and fell down. I would presume *Babr* and *Palang* are sunk or moored someplace in a junkyard. I don't know. And the four ships shortly became abandoned, the idea of them, the whole thing was abandoned.† As I recollect, some

---

* Admiral James L. Holloway III, USN, served as Chief of Naval Operations, 29 June 1974 to 1 July 1978.
† Four ships of the DXG variant were ordered for delivery to Iran. After that country's government fell to the Ayatollah Ruhollah Khomeini in 1979, the ships were completed for the U.S. Navy. The USS *Kidd* (DDG-993) and her three sisters went into commission in 1981 and 1982.

F-14s had been delivered; the rest were cancelled.* I think some patrol planes never made it. I forget.

Paul Stillwell: I know the F-14s did.

Admiral Meyer: Right. So everything started falling in. The revolution occurred.

Paul Stillwell: And then the hostages were taken later that year.†

Admiral Meyer: Okay. But 'twas a sad thing, besides a disappointing thing to me. I was very interested in it, and I was so impressed with their officers and their sailors, and I thought what a blessed country we have where we're not yet—maybe we did at one time, but we're not yet treating our officers and our sailors like dirt, slapping them and throwing them around and ignoring them. I've often wondered whatever happened to those officers. I think they probably were trashed in the revolution. I've never heard from a single one.

Philadelphia Naval Shipyard did that work, and they did a wonderful job. Contrary to much of the chatter you hear, or used to hear at least, all the time, I've always had pretty damned good service with Navy yards. They've always treated me all right. So when I heard people bitch about them you start to wonder, well, wait a minute. Who's the problem here? Now, you don't hear about it anymore because, first of all there aren't that many yards; second of all, conceptually the overhaul cycles are way different than what they were 40 years ago or 50 years ago, probably to our loss. And the whole mother yard concept kind of went to the dogs. See, the real mother yard, the design yard for the Aegis cruisers is Ingalls, and Bath is the destroyer yard. Not a Navy yard for a very simple reason: There simply was no capability to do it. No capability to do it. So you said to me, well why do you call them "our yards"? My word was, they *are* our yards.

---

* Grumman F-14 Tomcat fighters first entered U.S. training squadrons in late 1972. In 1976 they were exported to Iran, the only foreign customer for the F-14. Some are still in Iranian service.
† When the Shah left Iran in January 1979, the Ayatollah Ruhollah Khomeini seized power and declared the nation to be an Islamic republic. On 4 November 1979 Iranian militants seized the U.S. embassy in Teheran and took the staff members there as hostages. The hostages were ultimately released on 20 January 1981.

Paul Stillwell: By default.

Admiral Meyer: By default. And I said we ought to treat them that way. And when Weinberger asked me, that's what I told him.[*] Both of those yards were absentee owned. For a long time we didn't even know who the hell owned Bath. But my point, then—I forget what year was the Weinberger study that he caused to be made. In my view, that study, those yards can go there. I made several trips to Beverly Hills concerning Ingalls.[†] They didn't give a rat's toenail about this shipyard. All they cared is what the hell were the monthly reports and the quarterly reports.

Paul Stillwell: That was the Litton headquarters in Beverly Hills.

Admiral Meyer: The Litton headquarters in Beverly Hills, which, by the way, were quite something indeed. Tex Thornton's quarters were quite impressive.[‡]

So they had bought them originally, you'll recall, all these yards had been sold to aerospace, and they'd been sold for tax sense. That's how these yards were disposed of. Well, now we went through a whole cycle where they started buying the yards back because they were now profitable. Who do you think made them profitable?

Paul Stillwell: Aegis.

Admiral Meyer: You're goddamn right. And how much credit do you think we get?

Paul Stillwell: Well, I don't know. What would you say?

Admiral Meyer: I would say that it's hard to measure. You really have trouble measuring it.

(Interruption)

---

[*] Caspar W. Weinberger served as Secretary of Defense from 21 January 1981 to 23 November 1987.
[†] At the time Ingalls was part of Litton Industries, headquarters in Beverly Hills, California.
[‡] Charles B. "Tex" Thornton was the founder and chief executive officer of Litton Industries.

Paul Stillwell: As we resume, what was the effect of the creation of PMS-400? What was that designed to accomplish?

Admiral Meyer: I say this as though I'm bitter, but I don't know whether I am. And it may sound arrogant, and I don't know if that's true either. But instead I did search for a solution, trial-and-error solution I might add, to better do what I interpreted to be my assignment. If you went to look for an appointing order for Aegis today, PMS-400, I don't even know whether you can find one. You probably can, but it's not very explicit. It just kind of says go build these ships, cooperate with the rest of the Navy, use those things, report to whoever you report to, Assistant Secretary.

Paul Stillwell: Did it change anything?

Admiral Meyer: It changed a lot, but what it changed is what I—I used it as my authority to go change things.

Paul Stillwell: Like a hunting license?

Admiral Meyer: Whenever the question would be posed, "Well, why are you doing that, Captain? How are you doing that?"
"Well, that's what my charter says." And no one ever was willing to put the time to do the research to understand whether it was in the charter or not.

Paul Stillwell: Did you initiate the process to create that charter?

Admiral Meyer: The answer is yes, in a backhanded way. I told you I had all these assignments. And this disintegration associated with the perception that shipbuilding had gone to hell—everybody was in the courthouse someplace, everybody was suing everybody and countersuing, and they organizationally were disintegrating. So it gave me the opportunity to do some things that I thought needed alignment to be more effective. Now, if you had asked me to prove it, I couldn't have done it. I can prove it in hindsight.

I am trying to recall what year I got James H. Doyle. You're good at that.

Paul Stillwell: He became OP-03 in 1975.

Admiral Meyer: Seventy-five, right. Project managers used to come to me for instruction and guidance and such and test ideas; none of them do that anymore. Now, I think there are a couple reasons why they don't do it. One is that they don't know me anymore. The whole officer corps is a year-group corps, and you just keep moving all your life in that shuffle, and so you've got commanders in the Navy today that weren't even in the Navy the day I was forced into retirement. Because I have been retired approaching 25 years. Well, I was fired 25 years ago from Aegis. So isn't anybody there that was even active working, hardly, when I was removed.

And I get this often. I've said this several times, but I'll repeat it anyhow to make sure you don't ever lose it. Last week we were up to a program review at Moorestown, and I go to different meetings. I'm generally still invited and respected and allowed to participate even though I offer repeatedly: "If you don't want me, just tell me." I believe that I'm generally wanted as long as I don't go overkill. And I want to tell you first why I think I'm wanted. There no longer are people of age with my experience, learning, and such, who go around to the young and talk to them in a levelheaded manner about their engineering, their design, their programs, or what they're doing.

Let me tell you an example of that. Just don't let me drift too far. This thing called "open architecture," which I'm sure you've heard of.

Paul Stillwell: No.

Admiral Meyer: Well, we've got this madness on to do something called "open architecture." One of the present active-duty admirals is madly executing it because an Assistant Secretary of the Navy had said, "Well, it's really, really, really the thing, and will get away from being strapped together and locked in with the Aegis-type architecture, where every time you go to make a change in the system design—and you constantly have to do that all your life—well, it's a major, major effort." But with open architecture you don't have that problem. Really? Well, you *do* have that goddamn problem and there ain't no architecture that overcomes that problem. But we've convinced ourselves of that.

Now, just for a moment, a system in the ship, no matter where you want to dice it or sort it out, is composed—it's a major discovery we made in Aegis—it's composed of computer programs, equipment, and people. What I've said here is trite, or sounds trite. To my knowledge, the first people that ever discovered it is the Aegis program, and the Aegis program discovered it roughly ten years after we'd been in existence. And Bill Goodwin, the Aegis vice president, now in the graveyard, contributed to that discovery along with me. We came to call that technique—we didn't know we were discovering this—we called it functions, flow, diagrams, and descriptions. "F-squared, D-squared." We were having some iced tea one night at one of the iced-tea places nearby, and what kept bugging us all the time in our decision-making, which I've tried to teach—I'm sorry to say the present people aren't doing this, but all that time we kept always bugging ourselves: "What if we're wrong? We've made a decision; what if it's wrong?"

Paul Stillwell: About what year was the iced-tea meeting?

Admiral Meyer: Which year? It would be just right in this very era, the '75-'77-type era, somewheres along in there.

Bill Goodwin kind of thought this out, because we had a couple old guys up there in engineering, and they were kind of clerkish in their behavior. But what we did was, we put them in a room which was maybe twice the size of this room, and they were asked to describe the system on the bulkhead in this room, the Aegis system, the Mark 7 system. Over here is a goes-inna, and over here is a goes-outa—now, this is not the ship, mind you, this is the system, which is going to dominate the ship—and see if we can write that down.

They started out trying to do it and, of course, no one wanted anything to do with it. Bill and I had to just virtually order and beat the hell of them; we had to threaten people, to get with this and help. To get these, what I've said are functional flow diagrams laid up. Get those laid up.

So the idea was to take a function that comes in and test its flow all the way to the output. It turned out in that particular design of that day there were some 11 major parts to the design, and so three of the bulkheads were covered in these function/flow charts. And everyplace in them that there was a junction, a junction with a function, we had to make a determination whether a computer program or a piece of equipment or a human being was in charge of that junction.

These guys worked on this about three months. You walked in, and Bill and I called them our "measles charts." They had two bulkheads full of all these goddamn red pins, where they could not get the answer on these junctions. No one seemed to know what it was. For a year we fought and argued and fought and argued getting those down. We made great progress for about four months. Then we got to some of the really, really toughies. It was the most brilliant thing we ever did. It was the most brilliant thing we ever did.

Now we had a table that was maybe twice this size in that room, and the engineers and different ones—and we didn't care where you came from, it didn't matter—had to come in. We called it our meditation room. And they had to sit down at table, and they had to reconcile that junction—Raytheon, RCA, Computer Sciences, Dahlgren, to name some of the more famous ones. General Dynamics off and on. They would sit and they'd all get in an argument at the table of what came in that junction and what was supposed to come out of that junction. Because, of course, engineers, like everybody else, tend to compartment whatever piece they're going to work on.

The summation was an astounding thing, so simple in statement, so mind-boggling in execution.

Paul Stillwell: What would be an example of one of these functions that went from input to output?

Admiral Meyer: Well, usually it was a waveform signal, and that signal would be determined by what its timing structure was and its magnitude, and nominally the signals were spoken of in terms of a voltage wave or a current wave. And since much of the system was digital they were really, really spikes. But you couldn't work with spikes. It's odd, in the digital world you have to still convert them to sine waves and cosine waves to understand flow, because you can't understand flow in spikes, in spite of what people tell you.

Then it's just like you're going to get up to walk out of this space to go out and see "Speedball" out there, and you've got to go through that door.* And you get over there, and all of a sudden you kick something and say, "Well, wait a minute; what's in the way here? I can't get out this door." Well, of course not, you damned fool; there's a wire and a fence across there. Oh. Well, I just want to get through there. Snip! And go on by. And generally that's the way you solve a lot of problems.

They, up till then, mostly were treated as interface diagrams, and that was an important step forward. You're sitting on one side, and I'm sitting on the other side, and so you and I had to make sure we were compatible because you're going to hook up your gidgets to my gidgets. Well, there's one thing we virtually *never* worried about in design in the early days of transitioning. And in real early days it didn't matter. But once you were half mixed in digital and analog, and also you need the high speed, it really did matter, and that's time. The fixed quantity in such a design, the dynamics of such a design as a warship design, the fixed quantity, is time. One second has 1,043 milliseconds in it, is the digital expression for it. Actually, in life, analog, a second is 1,000 milliseconds, but actually digital is a few more than that, which always clutters things up. It turns out you can't ignore them in high-speed systems. They've got to work in parallel and work simultaneously. Much of the designs, commercially, can ignore it.

Let's take for example, suppose right now you get up and you want to go down to the bank. You say, I've got to get hold of Burke & Herbert; I want to do a deposit.† I've got to turn in my payment, or something or other. So you go over there up to the window. "May I help you," blah blah blah. You put it in and you stand there and they— so pretty soon you say to the clerk, "Hey, is there a problem?" "No, we don't have any problem; we've got to wait for the computer. It's just the computer here. Pretty soon.

---

* "Speedball" was Admiral Meyer's nickname for his receptionist, Charlene Yang.
† Burke & Herbert is a bank with many branches in Northern Virignia.

Pretty soon, Mr. Stillwell. Oh, here it is now, here's the answer." Well, see, you can't do—

(Change of tape)

Paul Stillwell: We were talking about milliseconds and junctions.

Admiral Meyer: So, you've got a lot of things that are running in parallel instead of series, and in parallelism it's like many, many cars arriving at an intersection. If you don't have a plan in the intersection, guess what? You're going to have one damned big crash. And there ain't going to be no intersection after that, because it'll be crashed.

Paul Stillwell: And when you've got a threat coming in you don't have time to wait for the bank's computer.

Admiral Meyer: No, you do not. You don't have time. That technique is not a practical technique in this, and that is where much of my revolution came from. It is doing it in real time. A lot of people talk about this. You've got any number of people today who, of course, claim to have invented real-time programming and real-time design, and I don't care, because that was the era the revolution was occurring, and in my world it was occurring in AWACS, it was occurring in Aegis, it was occurring in Patriot, and it was occurring in Trident, because they were the people that needed to deal in real-time high speed. Oh, wait a minute. None of those things I ticked off were full systems in the sense that Aegis was going from start to finish, kill the damned target. So of all of them the Aegis was walking on their bed and their mattress, learning from them, but yet had a lot more complicated one when it came to timing. Timing is what's important.

In our early days of design we learned that we had to have at every review, we had timing charts posted on how many milliseconds we had at different places in the design. Because it was, I would say it did not even take weeks. By the first summer of 1971 we were in crisis, because we understood already we had created timing problems that we didn't appreciate were going to occur. Fortunately we very rapidly understood it was going to happen. Because heretofore getting things done simultaneously or nearly simultaneously, and being able to react not only simultaneously but instantly, and able to move around to what the situation was dynamically, we just hadn't done before.

So we did create a revolution. We created a real revolution. I do a damned poor job at trying to articulate that revolution, and there are a lot of people who will say, "Oh, we did that too. That's not unique to Aegis; we did that too." Not quite. They did it in single-function flows and far simpler and slower dynamic situations than we had to deal in.

So we did cross over into the green mountain patches and the gardens from out of the deserts heretofore, and we brought a lot of learning and a lot of knowhow into engineering and applied design. Paren: I can go into a review today and say the *Zumwalt*s or another advanced system or purports to be an advanced system, and you can see the building blocks that flowed from those days which made what they're doing possible. Now, just like kids going to school, many, many of them have not the foggiest idea where their building blocks came from. They have no idea how they were born. Some of them even think they discovered them themselves. But generally, as you know, that's not true.

Much of this discovery in modern functional design came right out of Aegis because we were real-time. The bank is not a real-time thing. You go to get your airplane ticket, that's not a real-time thing. Hardly anything commercially is real-time. And where is the spring in that equation? What is the absorber or the damper in that equation? Well, it's the human. So, well, if it's going to take this much time to read the check by an optical reader, okay, you just accept it. Or if it's got to double-check the curlicues on an S someplace, who absorbs that? You do. You're the one that stands at the window and waits. In our work that won't work. Or, put another way, you're going to get killed or get hit. That's a fundamental difference.

A problem I've had since day one in ballistic missile defense, and with the organizations involved including the present one, is their own backgrounds. There's virtually no one in the Missile Defense Agency who has the appreciation of a warship so complex, must accomplish so many different kinds of things, many of them simultaneously, randomly, and—and house the human. You can't find many instruments of war that have to house the human for 30 years. Like there ain't none. Now a tank, for example, may go on to a mission or a trip for three hours, four hours, eight hours, that's it. An airplane similarly. So the human had to be housed or taken care of for a relatively short period. Here it's forever, from the day the commissioning pennant goes up till the day the commissioning pennant comes down. That nominal value's 25 or 30 years. And in there all the dimensions of life have to be accounted for simultaneously.

Here you and I are in an airplane or the tank, and we're headed out and we're carrying out a mission and everything. "Hey, Skipper, Skipper, we're running a little low on drinking water over here."

"All right. All of you conserve water; save the water. No more water without permission," so forth, "till we get back in. Let's say we'll be back in in two and a quarter hours." That's not true in this life. Your plan has to work indefinitely, and it has to work simultaneously. You have to be able to make water all the time in the ship. You have to be able to feed people every bloody day.

I'm sure you've read many articles in magazines and, I think, probably written some about life, for example, in an aircraft carrier. And how does an aircraft carrier function?

Paul Stillwell: Like a city.

Admiral Meyer: There's a really good article. It's several years old now, maybe eight or ten years old. I don't know whether I have it in my keepsakes or not. You may have read it. Can't remember whether it appeared in *Technology Review* or where it was, which is the alumni magazine at MIT, but it's written by a couple guys who spent several weeks in an aircraft carrier. What they set out to do was understand air control and the national/international implications of air control on land. It turned out when they finished that they decided it couldn't be explained. It just could not be synthesized to an explanation. Logic did not prevail in that aircraft carrier. Their conclusions were they learned to function by, what's the word, not trial and error, but learned to function over time. Aircraft carriers started in the '30s, so they're 80 years old or better. And it's all constant trial and error of learning how to do it and how to handle it. I'm sure you've stood on aircraft carriers and watched them. I've never served in one, but I've stood on them, and particularly out in the Gulf of Tonkin and on station—you know, what's the air control station out there?

Paul Stillwell: Yankee Station.*

Admiral Meyer: Yeah, Yankee Station. And I just tell you, you go up there and stand in the sponson in, say, *Kitty Hawk* or *Constellation*, which is a couple I visited fairly regularly because they had Terrier batteries in them. You stand in there. If you stand there as an observer, you're scared to death. It just scares you to death when you see what's going on. And yet all those people, hundreds of them, are doing it constantly with almost no mouth. Signals, color coding, practice, ability to adjust it, stop it. How many people do we kill in an aircraft carrier?

Paul Stillwell: Well, very small compared to the population.

Admiral Meyer: Damn small. Damn small. As a matter of fact, we still pay pretty significant flight pay and pretty significant combat pay in carriers for an era that no longer exists. Well, really, they deserve the money today because they have to work every bloody day, 19 or 20 hours. Pretty soon that gets old. Well, I'll put it another way: *You* get old. You can't handle it anymore.

Paul Stillwell: Wonder if we could come back to PMS-400.

Admiral Meyer: We're coming back to it, but slowly. But you're the one that led me off, you remember.

So the question was, how—I want to say, and I say this in hindsight, but I also decided it in real sight, that there wasn't anybody going to tell me what to do. They were

---

* During the initial stages of involvement in the Vietnam War, the U.S. Navy maintained aircraft carriers on two stations based on Civil War designations—Yankee Station off North Vietnam and Dixie Station off South Vietnam. The latter, which began on 16 May 1965, was dropped 15 months later once airfields were available ashore in South Vietnam.

going to beat me unmercifully, people were going to bitch, criticize, and carry on. It's kind of like—sometimes I think of it as criticizing and bitching about the opera singer and how bad her arias are. But you can't sing them and you can't do them, nobody else can do it. So you've just got to blow that away.

An officer who had become a good friend of mine through the years by the name of Edward J. Otth, who had worked with me back in Terrier—he was an engineering duty officer.

Paul Stillwell: You talked about him in regard to the upgrade program.

Admiral Meyer: You got it, underneath Spreen. He was a lieutenant commander, and I was a commander. Well, time wore on and I became the Aegis manager, he became the manager sent over to do the FFG-7s, as a captain, and he absolutely detested that. He did not believe in the FFG-7, but he was ordered to go do it, and so like a good sailor he went and did it. Well, in due course, he was selected for admiral. And someplace in there— now, I think 1975 is the year I was selected for admiral, I believe it is. As I remember, I was notified like in, I want to say January of '75, but I don't know if that's exact, but someplace in that vicinity. Ed Otth was a couple years behind me. But in that era he had been moved around, and he had been shuffled over to NavMat staff as special assistant for shipbuilding. What it meant is he had no job. So he'd wander around, we'd have lunch a day or two a week, and we talked about this and, "How are we going to do this, Wayne? How are we going to go about this?"

So every evening we'd get on the blackboard, and we'd start drawing things on the blackboard about different structures and what were the strengths and what were the weaknesses. I've never liked the expression "total ship system engineering." I've never liked that expression, because I do not believe a ship is a total system mathematically. Yet a ship is a system from the captain's viewpoint. He's got to fight and operate the ship every minute every day. So it's a real dichotomy when you think about this, of the structure. But mathematically, or even engineering-wise, it's not. So ships operate, Aegis ships, mostly by—I almost said the word I've been fishing for, but operated by trial and error. I'm the one that created the expression originally: "Build a little, test a little, learn a lot." Now, that's an expression that's used almost universally today by many people that have no idea what it means. Yet they will still take on bites that are so big that they think they know the risks; they have no idea what the risk is, it's too big an undertaking. Or they do not have it fractionated enough to be able to understand what the risk is. So I'm a big believer in build a little, test a little, see what you've got, add to it, do it again, and add to it, do it again, till finally one day you decide: "Well, I'm done." That's how you do a ship.

Paul Stillwell: Is "incremental" the word you're looking for?

Admiral Meyer: Did I think of it?

Paul Stillwell: No, no. You said you were searching for the word to describe this process. I wondered if "incremental" is the word you were searching for.

Admiral Meyer: No, it's not, but it's a try. You keep at it. (Laughter) I'll tell you in a minute. It's still a discovery-type word.

So Ed Otth and I spent a lot of time, but no one anyplace seemed to care much whether we existed or not. So we would periodically run over and talk to the chief for an hour or two till we'd worn him down. He'd dismiss us and throw us out Chief of NavSea—and send us off, figuring that we were probably harmless.

Well, Ed Otth went to work writing a charter for a new organization. And we kept looking at, well, something to be said for how you code it and how you put it together. Well, we decided that we were on a precipice here between NavSea and NavOrd, NavElex and, let's see. One bureau used the 300 codes, one used the 200 codes, I think NavElex, and the other used 400 codes. Well, we decided it turned out the 100 codes were not used. So we said, well, we're going to be one of each. And that's how we came at 400. It's just that simple.

I never told you the story of how Aegis got the nomenclature of Mark 7. You probably, I guess, maybe don't want to know it, but I'll put it in here just for the hell of it.

Did you ever follow the program "Dragnet," or are you too young to know it?*

Paul Stillwell: No, I certainly remember that. Mark VII Productions.

Admiral Meyer: Mark—you got it! You jumped right on it.

Paul Stillwell: There was a hammer coming down on an anvil.

Admiral Meyer: That's exactly right. In our early days Bill Goodwin and I were having some iced tea at lunch about how the—by the way, I can't teach people this. They won't learn it. You cannot be successful in system design without nomenclature, and the reason is you don't have any way to communicate. There are fundamental flaws right now in the *Zumwalt* program; they don't have any nomenclature. I looked at another program a couple weeks ago. Can't communicate. They're describing them with a collection of words, and all of them different.

The best structure that ever got thought of, wouldn't you know, by the United States Army and the United States Navy, was Mark numbers. Well, we always—in the Navy it's "Mk." In the Army it's always "M." M-16, M-12, and such. But you know, when you use that number, right away the entire Army knows what it is you're saying, and you can find it in a book what it means. It's described by bounds. And we decided that had to be done. Up till then it was being referred to as the Aegis or ASMS or Advanced System, or any number of other things. He and I got to talking about that on our second iced tea, I think, and bang—Mark 7 and the anvil. That's how it was born. We gave it that nomenclature.

Paul Stillwell: And you equated Aegis to the hammer?

Admiral Meyer: You got it exactly right. [Laughter] You got it right.

---

* "Dragnet" was a very popular television program in the 1950s. It starred actor Jack Webb as Sergeant Joe Friday, a Los Angeles police detective.

Paul Stillwell: I remember that would come on at the end of each program and there'd be a resounding clang as the hammer struck.

Admiral Meyer: You know, I pick up a rerun every week or so on Direct TV of "Dragnet." And their stories are just as good as they ever were, simple-minded, but they've still got that anvil on at the end. [Chuckle] "This is a Mark 7 production." So there you are. We started building from there.

Well, Ed Otth and I put all that together and tested it out on a few of our friends and associates, and some didn't care for it, some thought it was too hokey, others would get a little excited about it if you got the right people and they'd sit—you had to give them a little time to reflect on the significance of what you were doing.

Well, we went up to the chief. Well, he allowed as how he didn't care. So a charter was signed out then, a new one, that was appointing me from—you know, I may be wrong here, because I was the weapons system manager, I then became director of surface warfare, I became director of integration, I became several things. But somewhere in there we put a piece of paper out that announced it as PMS-400, a unique structure. Now, of course, we've had copiers all over the place since then, because there is a -500, there's a -600. It's amazing how people will turn up their nose and snarl at you and grind—that's been the story of Aegis, jealousy. But you know what? They'll copy it. That's what they'll do. Because they want some of it too. It's the nature of the human. If they see something that's gaining attention or having some success, they'll glop onto it.

Well, enough of that. We set that up, went through, then we pushed through the whole charter and we got—you know, right now I can't remember who the hell signed it. I believe I am right that it was signed by the chief of NavSea.*

And then it's like everything else. You just start using it and pretty soon everybody's using it. And pretty soon it's everybody.

Paul Stillwell: That gave you more of an identity, the Mark 7 and the PMS-400.

---

*PMS-400 was chartered in June 1977.

Admiral Meyer: Yes, and it created an attitude. It created a house of order. It created a town. And people started forming around it, being a part of it. And I was reaching in my pocket for my telephone card, but they're in my office someplace. As we advanced we kept trying to figure out how to keep communicating. Now, let me again skip a block.

Norman Polmar's always said he's going to write about this, but he never has. Polmar claims that I'm the only person that developed and led a major program in the system. He likens me to Rickover and to Levering Smith and others who had to break out of the system to get it done. Well, I didn't and, I don't know, I don't want to sound smug. I don't know why I didn't. I guess I just kind of felt I couldn't, so we stayed right where we were. As I tell project managers today, "Don't worry about who you report to. Matter of fact, report to everybody. Just decide what it is you're going to do and start doing it. And in a couple weeks it'll be that way, because that's the way the system works."

We tend to think this is a very formalized system, very structured, very rigid; nothing to that at all. That's nonsense. So we just kept kind of trotting along. Ed Otth helped me. I can't remember when Ed Otth went home. We had kind of drifted apart. He helped me a lot in thinking about shipbuilding.

Oh, the telephone card. If you worked for Aegis you got an Aegis code, and you used that code or you didn't work for Aegis. Now, Norm Polmar's point on me working in the system is what I did. One of my big supporting outfits was Sea-06. Another was Sea-05. 05 is the design outfit; 06 is where all the weapons were, all the systems, radars, sonars, stuff like that, all the ordnance. So my set of cards, 3x5's, which a girl that worked for me learned how to stylize this, and I could flip them out. And in there I had the phone numbers of everybody and what your code was. So I had people at Dahlgren that worked for me, I had people at Crane that worked for me, Hueneme, Pentagon, so forth. The day I got fired by John Lehman there were something like only 86 people in the project, but the world thought it was a gigantic project. And it was. It had between 300 and 400 people. They just weren't attached to the body. They had an Aegis code, though, and boy, they guarded it religiously. It was a badge of honor.

A lot of those things are still practiced today. And, again, I think it comes back to be, it was discovery on my part, not brilliance on my part. And when I say discovery, what are the things that make people tick? Why do people work on things? Why do people do their damnedest to overcome obstacles? Well, most of the time it's the challenge. It's the challenge. And there's some kind of excitement and fulfillment that comes to a person who's able to do that. You hear people talk about drudge work. Well, in Aegis you never had anything that would meet the definition of drudgery, ever. You were constantly moving, adjusting, examining, looking at it, and people felt as though they had a lot of freedom when in fact they didn't. But they felt they did.

Paul Stillwell: But that's useful, if you can create the perception that they do.

Admiral Meyer: You got it. You got it. And that is a dimension of leadership that I don't know how I got it. I just got it, and I have watched others who never get it, and others who get it in the middle someplace. But once people feel empowered it's really rare for one to overstep his or her bounds. That's really rare.

Paul Stillwell: Well, let's go back to the Aegis milestones.

Admiral Meyer: Let's go back to the Aegis milestones.

Paul Stillwell: One in early '78 was that the SPY-1 was tracking targets at CSEDS. How had CSEDS matured to that point?

Admiral Meyer: Well, we crossed through the first crossover on tracking, I believe it was '73, on my birthday, where the Aegis radar did its first tracking ever, at 0200 in the morning. As I remember it, it was—I think it was late February—it was colder than hell.

Paul Stillwell: Where was that done?

Admiral Meyer: That was done in a little hut that still exists up there on—they call them campuses these days—still exists there near the plant, where we had put up this piece of radar, the piece of radar that we were going to ship to *Norton Sound*. Which of itself is an incredible operation, revolutionary, totally revolutionary. We had built it in the plant, we had set it up and structured it into this little bitty hut, one face, face two simulated, everything running.* We ran some amazing things for us if you've been a sailor for a long time. I mean, you just can't imagine how tears come to your eyes after years and years of plodding and trying to figure out in the sea whether it's a target or not, and here coming across these beautiful scopes was this incredible radar. We have this airplane coming across their track, tracking right across there, tracker right with it. This is just mind-blowing as we see it. That night was a night that hundreds of people cried who saw it. That's '73.

Then I believe—did I talk to you about how CSEDS was born?

Paul Stillwell: I don't think so.

Admiral Meyer: I'll be damned. I didn't dream all this.

Later in life—I forget what year. Let's see, if you take 30 years off of two years ago, that would be what year?

Paul Stillwell: 1976.

Admiral Meyer: '76, okay. That would be about it. You know, there was a great big gigantic radar built there on that place under the custody of the United States Air Force, and it was a supplemental tracker for the national defense.

Paul Stillwell: The NORAD system.†

Admiral Meyer: I believe it was part of the NORAD system. Let's say it was. It's good enough for that now. In any event, Bill and I frankly—one of the things in a big program like this, the way they used to be funded, you had to keep staying ahead: Where's the next tranche of money going to come from? Where's it going to come from? Because as

---

* The land-based test site was a deck house with the system enclosed.
† The North American Air Defense Command (NORAD), an Air Force command based in Colorado Springs, was responsible for detecting and attacking Soviet bombers headed toward the United States.

I've said repeatedly and I tell project managers, "You're the only person can raise the money. None of your warfares can raise the money. Your vice presidents can't. You can demand they all perform, you have that right, but you don't have the right if you don't raise the money. That's your unique job."

So he and I were having a glass of iced tea at Rancocas Inn, there by Rancocas Creek a couple miles up from the plant, and wondering just what kind of a story are we going to talk about to get this next thing to functioning. And Max Lehrer, a good friend of ours, was the general manager at the plant at Moorestown, and Max was totally financial-oriented.[*] That's all he could—he could only talk in terms of dollars and cents. But he was so good to me and to Bill because we had now dominated the plant, and he understood that the success of the plant depended on us. And we were all pretty good friends.

So we were driving back from Rancocas Inn and were talking and Max said, "You know, the Air Force has just declared this place here surplus, this radar station." Oh? Talked about it for a minute. He said, "Yes, it turns out that we own the land and everything and we have a lease with the Air Force for 99 years to support it and sustain it, but it's populated by a captain, Air Force captain, and sergeants, and about a 40-person crew. Also, the Service Company RCA generally provides service to this station for maintenance and repair and all that kind of stuff, and we've been told that they're going to take that down and they're going to abandon, and the terms of the lease were something like a dollar a year or something, and they have alerted us that it will be coming back to us."

I looked at Bill, Bill looked at me, and we got to thinking there. I don't know whether you've ever walked around in the place, but it abuts a Holstein dairy farm, Mr. Winter's dairy farm. Got to thinking about that: "Hey, God is good; here's an opportunity." Well, that afternoon we got so excited.

Max said, "Oh, y'all are all wet.

And we kept saying, "Max, you don't understand us Aegis people. We're going to figure out a way here how to rescue this." So I got an officer and a GS-14, put them in charge of this, gather data, our usual research, get some facts, find out what's going on.

---

[*] Max Lehrer had previously worked as a budget expert in the Defense Department.

And, sure enough, they wanted to get rid of it and didn't know how. Well, to me it's obvious. Why don't we give them a plan?

We started out doing this, and by now Doyle was available, but he was brand spanking new, and we hooked onto him just like that. He didn't know what he was getting hooked—we did a number on him. We did a real number on him. They all looked at it, oh, what are the legal aspects? On and on, hand-wringing. How are we going to get permission to operate with this high power? And on and on and on. People kept thinking all kinds of reasons not to do it. Well, we told Doyle, "We need some money. Put money in and let's create this engineering development site. You want a whole ship? We'll work on a whole ship."

Well, almost overnight it came to be dubbed the cruiser in the cornfield.[*] And the Air Force was so tickled to death that they said, hey, we'll tear this all down, we'll clean it all up, we'll take it all away, and it won't cost you anything. I mean, we about passed out. We thought we really ripped them off. [Laughter]

Paul Stillwell: And it was a good deal for them, too.

Admiral Meyer: Oh, it was. They didn't know how to solve the problem. And so here we figured all this out in the months ahead and the next year we structured it all, did some redesigning work. And the thing is, they had a foundation in there went all the way to China, so we didn't have to worry about pouring concrete or anything like that. And this radar antenna, I went under—I mean, it's a gigantic goddamn thing, as tall as this building as you walk around in it.

So we went to work on it, went to work on it, shaping it up, drew it approximately the plans of the cruiser.

Paul Stillwell: That is the superstructure.

---

[*] The building that houses the facility is in the shape of what would have been the superstructure of a nuclear-powered Aegis cruiser if one had been built.

Admiral Meyer: Superstructure, right. And, by the way, underneath the spaces to be underneath there too. We formed them, structured them, but also structured them so we had space to train and to test and to engineer and train. Doyle said, "Well, we'll get more sailors, I'll get you a couple more officers, and on and on and on." So we went from good to really good, and so on. Everything's really blossomed. And we got a line item in the budget.

These big programs like this, you have to constantly be getting something new in there for the Congress and the OSD. That's part of your promotional aspect. You don't lie to them, but you can't keep bringing back the same stuff. People tire of it. So we were just going like gangbusters. The state of New Jersey was really happy; here they were, Aegis was now implanted, RCA was going to be there forever. And we went over, we sent a delegation to Mr. Winter to be sure—because we felt that if he just said one word we'd be dead; the environmentalists would kill us.

Paul Stillwell: What was Winter's capacity?

Admiral Meyer: Well, he's the one that had a dairy farm.

Paul Stillwell: Ah.

Admiral Meyer: And we were scared to death if people would tell him this radar's going to affect his milk cows, and all the trouble. So we spent a lot of time with Mr. Winter. Well, it turned out he and his two sons were wonderful. They believed us, they trusted us, and in all those years we've never had one day problem, not once. Well, any number of people have had trouble trying to operate radars. We had a lot of trouble trying to operate there at CSEDS; we had the SPS-49 radar also, which is our big search radar that goes with it. This is a low-frequency radar, at about 1,100 megacycles. Well, it can create interference in TVs. I mean, it's just a natural phenomenon of the frequencies it's run at. But we had a license, we complied with everything. We operated only at certain hours. And people who filed a complaint, we sent crews to go to your house to see if there were a set of filters that we could put in the house to help you. We had one old lady that never gave up. She hasn't given up to this day. All these years she's constantly harassing; it doesn't matter whether it's on or not.

But it's turned out to be a wonderful relationship. The way we handled it we put a commander there. I got a commander to be OinC.* Bill Goodwin said, "Okay, we'll have a deputy OinC and that will be an RCA person, and they will have charge of everybody that comes in there." And that's the way we've always run it. We've never had a problem with it. We've had as many as, I think, around 75 sailors resident. We berthed a lot of them over at New Jersey, McGuire Air Force Base.† Then we finally got authority to rent a hotel for them. I think we've still got some of them in a motel. They can choose to live that way. A lot of them are married these days so they don't want to live that way. But it's worked out just fine. All of industry, the labs and everybody, can come and do today their system work, get their tests, get the imprimatur of the RCA senior engineers on what it is they propose to do, and it's really worked out well.

I think you know, to digress a minute, I'm the chairman of a little company called Mikros.

Paul Stillwell: I did not know that.

Admiral Meyer: Well, its office is right here. It's based up at Fort Washington, Pennsylvania. I've been with them for a number of years for various things, primarily with the Link 16 and Link 11 before that. We did a lot of work in data links. But today we have a couple little different inventions, one of which is a test machine to rapidly check and test the operability of the radar, Aegis radar, which we invented, which we invented, and General Electric had not invented. Well, Lockheed has taken us right aboard. We have relationships with Lockheed. They take our gear in there and they'll test it for you and rig it and tell you how to do it and stuff, so they're all—it really works well. And, as you know, PMS-400 has a captain who commands the whole structure up there, the whole, what we call the tech rep. And the CSEDS part is commanded by a commander who reports to the captain. They all understand how to function; they've

---

* OinC – officer in charge.
† McGuire Air Force Base is adjacent to the Army's Fort Dix near Wrightstown, New Jersey.

never had a fight. Never have the Navy or the owners ever had an argument or a fight. Had a lot of good stuff.

In the heyday, OpTEvFor was raising the living hell, as was the OSD, about testing, stuff not having been tested. You know, all of Aegis was tested right out of there. And it got the endorsement out of all the testers, right out of there.

Then we did some follow-up on *Norton Sound* where we could do a couple different things that we couldn't do close by up there. For example, we couldn't drop chaff up there. But we operate the big jammers up there, we work closely with the FAA stations and got permission.* They had to do it between three and four at night, to run all these trials. I mean, we've done it for ten years, of running all these jammers and everything with airplanes flying in and such.

I mean, it's been a marvelous story of how—you'd think that people would come to it and maybe want to learn from it or copy it. "We don't want to touch it; it's Aegis." Well, it turns out that a lot of them are coming back to Aegis now because they like our facilities. [Chuckle] It turns out when they have to start out getting these facilities on their own it's a lot harder than they thought it was, both in finding the people and the money and such. And then just licenses to operate. See, you can't operate there without a license. All those radars have to have a license. Every time you energize one of them you have to have permission of FAA to run them. That all worked out; it all works just fine. We have it manned around the clock; never closed. It's been a grand thing, and as far as I know it'll be there forever, is the present plan on it.

Paul Stillwell: Well, you mentioned it's designed to look like the cruiser.

Admiral Meyer: Yes.

Paul Stillwell: Ironically, the CGN-42 was cancelled in '78. What were the factors of its cancellation?

Admiral Meyer: I'd say lack of interest.

---

* FAA – Federal Aviation Administration.

Paul Stillwell: Was cost part of the consideration?

Admiral Meyer: It was, but it became an issue when they didn't want to do anything. I think what happened is the whole process was just tired. It can only deal in so many variables going on all at the same time, as could I, so it just got tired of it. We did a lot of studies on the cruiser *Long Beach*, modernizing her, converting her, and on and on and on. And those things, all of them just wore you out, they consumed so much of your time. And the Congress tired of it. They just went on to other things. You know, the Congress in many respects is just kind of like shepherds. They just keep grazing and grazing on, grazing on. Pretty soon they get far enough away they no longer have an interest in it. Or they can't connect it to anything for their constituents.

The whole shipbuilding issue right now is for constituency, and that is a valid concern. And I have said repeatedly, and part of all of my effort is: "We must worry about the constituency. You just can't suddenly call Ingalls and say, hey, by the way, Thursday morning I'm going to send three ships down there; can you handle them?" That isn't the way it works. "By the way, Bath, we want to make a square bow instead of a pointed bow, and I would like to have the design on Friday." Things don't work that way.

Well, at the review last week I was sitting there and I just— we sit in what's called a control room, which is a horseshoe table up front, and the place holds maybe 100 or 120 people. And then we have a room atop that that holds another 100 people and they watch it through scopes, cameras and stuff. But I looked around there, and I swear to goodness—I was trying to spot somebody that I would recognize that had been at Moorestown longer than I had been. I couldn't find one. They've all retired. Many of them have died, of course. But it's been so long. I mean, it literally is the longest running program that can be cited. And I mean *genuinely* long running, and it's not been done with disruptions, it's been continuous. So you've got an age group of people who've never known any other job. You've got people there that are not there now but when we started in 1970 they—well, you know, we've captured this big contract now; it's called, well, you pronounce it "ay-jis" or "ee-jis." We've got this big contract and people look at it and the engineers, and in those days we had draftsmen, and they kind of viewed this whole thing as, you know, as a four- or five- or six-year undertaking as a project. And their entire career was there. All their promotions, their children, and everything. It all occurred in that plant. So it is genuine.

In the very early days after I got there we had a strike within the draftsmen for a few days. Never had a strike otherwise. Never, in that whole plant. And the quality I will put against anybody in the world. And one of the reasons is attention. Attention on the part of the leadership and the corporation, but it was attention on my part and I've tried to get my followers to pay attention, but I'm sure they're not. But every time I went up there, almost every month, for review or anything, I went through a piece of the production areas, which is where we populated the arrays, that's where we built the signal processor. A lot of the gear is built outside, a hell of a lot of it. And Raytheon builds the transmitters and stuff. Raytheon builds a lot of this gear, which at times really irks me that they failed to—they somehow think that only RCA is recognized, you know, as an Aegis group. Well, I recognize them, but they themselves reject it.

So that family of industrial contractors has been together this incredible period. That plant was out in soybean fields in 1970, sat out there. It was quite a distance from out of the towns, from Moorestown and such. I said to Anna Mae the other day when we were driving away from there, "You can hardly get here anymore." By now it has big shopping centers, big housing centers, a gigantic Wegmans grocery store just opened recently that's only 100 yards from the plant. And it's really getting populated though.

It's going to have some heavy weather ahead because it's hard to get planning in the government and in the armed forces for long-term support for such teams. It's hard to get that done. But I will have done my part, and I would say that the leaders up at Moorestown will have done their part.

I have always been treated very respectfully there, and we never have had a one up there that's not a patriot. They've all been very professional people, very people oriented, very anxious to do the right thing.

Paul Stillwell: One of the other milestones for that year, '78, was awarding the production contract to RCA.

You're looking at your watch.

Admiral Meyer: I'm looking at my watch...

Paul Stillwell: Okay [chuckle].

Admiral Meyer: ...and I'm going through a motion.

Paul Stillwell: [Laughter] And that motion means that we've talked enough for today.

Admiral Meyer: Yeah, I believe you have about worn me out for today.

Paul Stillwell: Okay. Thanks, Admiral.

Admiral Meyer: Well, thank you. I appreciate your patience.

Interview Number 16 with Rear Admiral Wayne E. Meyer, U.S. Navy (Retired)
Place: Admiral Meyer's office in Crystal City, Arlington, Virginia
Date: Friday, 15 August 2008

Paul Stillwell: Well, in our sequence on Aegis we were up to 1978, and two major milestones of that year were the awarding of the production contract to RCA and the contract for detail design and construction of DDG-47 to Ingalls Shipbuilding. So this was getting the project closer and closer to reality.

Admiral Meyer: So, 30 years ago.

Paul Stillwell: That's right.

Admiral Meyer: Right. And so working on, 1983 we commissioned Tico.[*] And I've always said in this business in recent years a good planning number to get a ship is five years. It takes five years before—and then you don't always make it in five years time, depending on the administrative processes.

At that time, you will recall, or you may recall, as my civil servant Bob Hill would say, we'd been through shipbuilding crises, of which I was in the middle of, really, in not building any ships.

Paul Stillwell: Well, there was that huge backlog of claims that was creating a lot of animosity with the industry.

Admiral Meyer: Exactly, and a lot of turmoil. Not only animosity but turmoil. So it was difficult to get the engineering process settled down. It's hard to get focused on it. And the people at Mississippi, I feel for them in two different ways. On one hand I think that

---

[*] The first of the Aegis cruisers to join the fleet was the USS *Ticonderoga* (CG-47), commissioned 22 January 1983. The ship was originally classified as a guided missile destroyer, DDG-47, and later reclassified as a cruiser. She had a full-load displacement of 9,800 tons, was 567 feet long, 55 feet in the beam, and had a maximum draft of 34 feet. Her top speed was 32.5 knots. She was armed with two twin launchers for Standard SM-2 missiles, two 5-inch guns, ASROC, Harpoon missiles, Vulcan/Phalanx close-in weapon system, and two torpedo tubes.

Litton's a big boy.* But it turned out the Navy was not a very big mature outfit at all. Had they had any maturity they would have never awarded that contract that way.

As an aside for a moment, she may have told you that I'm spending all day Tuesday I think it is, or part of the day, with this SecNav panel that's been put together with George Sawyer chairing it on acquisition and shipbuilding.† Well, in many respects we've made little progress. It's said, I read someplace, that the reason history repeats itself is people don't change. As you get older and you read some of the great stories of the Bible, the Old Testament in particular, all they really are are stories of people, and they're repeating themselves in some form generally on the planet today. Different words, a little different behavior pattern, social pattern, but the thrust of them is still the same; it hasn't changed.

Paul Stillwell: When you said that the Navy should not have awarded that contract to Ingalls, are you talking about the *Spruance* class?‡

Admiral Meyer: I am. And they let themselves get bludgeoned into the so-called total package, full package award, embarking on something on which they had no data at all. There wasn't anybody knew what the ship was going to cost. And when they started out in those ships—one of the things—again, I've had talks with this Secretary on it. I don't know why people can't get it through their heads. If you're going to fixed-price something it has to be pretty simple and straightforward. It can't be some flaky-type invention that's going to have to occur, the outcome of which is not known. And yet, for example, he has decreed in shipbuilding here recently—I believe I've talked him out of it, because I stuck my nose into it. Matter of fact, he was decreeing the first ships were going to be fixed price. Remember when he blew up on LCS and stuff? Well, he backed away and, well, after the first ships they would be fixed price. Well, he's going to find out that doesn't work either. As a matter of fact, I learned some fairly hard things in that

---

* The Litton/Ingalls shipyard in Pascagoula, Mississippi.
† George Sawyer served as Assistant Secretary of the Navy (Shipbuilding and Logistics), 1981-83.
‡ USS *Spruance* (DD-963), lead ship of the class, was commissioned 20 September 1975. LHA is the designation of a type of amphibious assault ship. The first of the type, USS *Tarawa* (LHA-1), was commissioned 29 May 1976. Ships of both classes were included in a program called Total Package Procurement, which was initiated in the 1960s by Secretary of Defense Robert S. McNamara.

15-year undertaking which I don't think George Sawyer's panel is going to particularly care for tomorrow, or Tuesday. But I don't believe in fixed-price contracting.

Paul Stillwell: Well, you mentioned that before.

Admiral Meyer: I did. I have mentioned it to you. I don't believe in it. And the reason I don't believe in it is you just ain't smart enough to do it. The period is too long, the undertaking is too complex. It has too many unknowns, and too many things that you have no control over. Well, I want to be able to say Tuesday, and I think I'm right, but I'm going to have a double check made again on Monday: "Here is the Aegis program, over three decades old. There's not a single claim pending anyplace today, anywhere. There never has been."

When I took over the missile there was one claim, the missile itself, at Pomona, but it was a carryover from before me, and ain't been one since. And so everyplace in my time I trashed fixed-price contracts. I don't know whether that's one of the reasons for my being relieved by the Secretary or not, because I'm not sure that the reasons I was relieved were that mature or substantive. But if I had my way, we'd never build a ship again fixed price.

Well, wait a minute. Immediately—well, how're you going to control the cost? And my point is, "Well, what the hell's that got to do with it?" Fixed-pricing it doesn't control the cost. People think that, that somehow that controls the cost.

I'll think of an incident that broke out last week on—oh, McCullough's testimony.* Matter of fact, I may have mentioned to you, I've got to write him a letter. I congratulated him on his testimony a couple weeks ago, and then after I read some of it I'm withdrawing it because he said, "Well, you know, in Aegis that's all under the control of Lockheed, and there it was run under Lockheed and the project and so no, we don't have fixed prices there." Well, that's pure unadulterated BS. Now, here's a three-star admiral that doesn't seem to know any better. And he also said, "Well, the

---

* Vice Admiral Bernard J. "Barry" McCullough III, USN, testified 31 July 2008 to a House subcommittee on behalf of the air-defense capabilities of the *Zumwalt* (DDG-1000)-class destroyer. He later backtracked, saying that the ship would not be capable of area air defense. McCullough was then Deputy Chief of Naval Operations for Integration of Resources and Capabilities.

reason for that is it was all Lockheed closed systems." There's not a single transistor in all of Aegis that's proprietary, not a single one, zero. And yet here he made that statement, that somehow closed systems and proprietary systems are synonymous. Well, they're not at all. I had closed systems, and I had them for a damned simple reason. I was not going to let every Tom, Dick, and Harry mess around in the design. And by the way, in my judgment, we're headed for really heavy weather in the coming years, which will be my point that I'll leave this panel on Tuesday. And it is this open architecture, on which we have zero experience. We've not done anything big with open architecture, and it is permissive of anybody who wants to delve in the design to delve in it. Well, who's going to be accountable? Who's responsible for it?

Paul Stillwell: But I imagine you like the part of his testimony where he said to cut back five *Zumwalt*s and build eight more Aegis ships.

Admiral Meyer: There's a tendency to think that the project manager is in the pocket of the contractor. In my 50 years, I've never seen a project manager in the pocket of the contractor. As a matter of fact, I happen to think that our industrial base in the United States is pretty damned good, and it's pretty moral and it's pretty upright and it's pretty patriotic. That happens to be my opinion. And it's amazing the number of people that go into the Pentagon that don't think that's true. It's even amazing the number of political appointees that go into government that don't think it's true. And you wonder, well where in the world did these people come from? What cave did they crawl out of? Because that's not true in the people I've been around.

Now, getting on my soapbox further here, and I believe I've said this to you before, because I've railed at my civil servants and my officers every Tuesday morning staff meeting, and I railed at my vice presidents. But my officers and civil servants: "Don't ever forget your contractors are only as good as you are. You am their asymptote. We forget that. We am their asymptote." That's why we need well-qualified officers and well-qualified civil servants. It's a caveat emptor world. We have to be able to speak in terms of what we think the nation needs. Lockheed Martin is not responsible for articles of war. They're not responsible for battle. *We* are responsible for battle.

Paul Stillwell: What is asymptote?

Admiral Meyer: Oh, asymptote? That's a mathematical expression that in exponentials, as they're climbing up like that they reach, they level off, when out in infinity is the only place they have a finite value. Infinity, finite, opposites. Well, so in that series, that expanded series, the terms—you know, you get out to —well, take pi, for example, the mathematical expression pi, 3.1416. Well, people have calculated it out to, I don't know, 50,000 terms or so, and of course they cannot find the end but the number gets smaller and smaller. That's called the asymptote. You can theoretically calculate the asymptote, but you can't ever reach it.

Paul Stillwell: Well, getting back to these contracts, you said it was a mistake for the Navy to go with Litton on the *Spruance* Class. Did you have any misgivings about a contract with Litton for the *Ticonderoga*?

Admiral Meyer: Zero.

Paul Stillwell: What had made the change?

Admiral Meyer: That's a valid question, and I don't want to windbag it too much. I know that one of the changes is there had been some significant changes in leadership throughout Litton, and Litton generally had lost interest in shipbuilding. Recollect that the way this originally came about is that the aerospace companies bought shipyards as loss leaders. So Litton bought one, General Dynamics bought one, the...

Paul Stillwell: Tenneco bought Newport News.

Admiral Meyer: Yeah, that's it. Tenneco bought one. None of them knowing anything about it, but they bought them as loss leaders because a shipyard was not known to ever make any money, so they were good tax sinks.

Paul Stillwell: I think it was a flooring company that bought Bath, wasn't it?

Admiral Meyer: Who?

Paul Stillwell: A flooring company, something unrelated.*

Admiral Meyer: Well, for quite a while we didn't know who it was. They kept it secret. They did it through Prudential and kept it secret.†

Paul Stillwell: Well, that would seem to decrease your sense of confidence, if they weren't really interested in the business per se.

Admiral Meyer: Well, it's a good point. I made two trips to Beverly Hills, and one, Tex Thornton was still alive. And I made it as clear as I could that I planned to run the contract and that I planned for Ingalls to do whatever it was I wanted done. They were just tickled to death to get rid of it. [Laughter] Their accountants didn't want anything to do with it. They were tickled to death to shed it. Never heard from them again. As a matter of fact, whenever we'd have ceremonies down there in those days, guess who would show up. My buddy, Admiral Tom Hayward, retired.‡ Because he was on the board at Litton, so he always showed up as the board's rep. Nobody else had any interest.

And when we christened *Ticonderoga*, just a little sea story—Tom Hayward really got pissed off at me then, but he was still on active duty. And the reason he did was kind of simple. We had picked Armed Forces Day for the christening, a Saturday. Well, it so happened the aviators were having their big annual bash down in, I think it was Dallas as I recall, so they were all gathered down there for a three-day free-for-all. Nancy Reagan was the sponsor and she threw a fit toward the end because our big scheme—and Tex Thornton's the one that did it for us, so I'm ratcheting ahead here a

---

* In 1968 Bath Iron Works merged with Congoleum-Nairn, Inc., a flooring producer.
† This was a separate deal, a leveraged buyout in the early 1980s.
‡ Admiral Thomas B. Hayward, USN, served as Chief of Naval Operations from 1 July 1978 to 30 June 1982. His oral history is in the Naval Institute collection.

couple years—but our scheme was, as we sat and drank iced tea one night at Miss Molly's, of how to do this, was—"Okay, why don't we get the First Lady to be the sponsor [which we did], and if we're that good why don't we get the President for the speaker?"

Mr. Erb, a great leader I mentioned to you, the late Mr. Erb, said he believed he could get that done, because the Reagans were great friends with Tex Thornton.[*] He said, "I'm getting along pretty good with Tex Thornton, because I'm profitable at this shipyard." Sounded logical to us. So why don't you do that?

So Tex Thornton slid into the White House one night at some social and asked her to take this on and the President to take it on, which they had kind of agreed to. I forget the calendar right not but in there somewhere is where the President had been shot, the Pope had been shot someplace along in those couple years...

Paul Stillwell: It was 1981.[†]

Admiral Meyer: ...and by now Nancy was trying to back out from the christening. So [chuckle] it was kind of funny. Wouldn't let her back out. Pressure on her just kept her going, but she's a kind of nervous person anyhow. But she was successful, at not having the President speak. She wouldn't hear of it. So Weinberger, who was away with the troops in Europe on an Armed Forces Day mission, got recalled by the President to come and be the speaker at Nancy's ship.[‡] Because the Weinbergers were very close to them also. Well, when he got called back this meant that the CNO decided he'd better be present, and this is why the CNO was not too happy. He was a little hung over, as a matter of fact. I've never forgotten it because I was in the car with him, and he was really unhappy about having to leave their affairs in Dallas because, as you know, he's mostly a Pacific Sailor. He didn't care much about the rest of the world. And so he

---

[*] Captain Leonard Erb, USN (Ret.), a retried nuclear submariner, was president Ingalls Shipbuilding Division in Pascagoula, Mississippi.
[†] On 30 March 1981, President Ronald W. Reagan was shot in an assassination attempt.
[‡] Mrs. Reagan christened the ship on 16 May 1981. Caspar W. Weinberger served as Secretary of Defense from 21 January 1981 to 23 November 1987.

blamed this all on me, of getting these dates bollixed up. Of course, I didn't give a damn whether they ever had a convention or not in naval aviation.

Well, we pulled it off. I think that I figured out what got me relieved.* It took me quite a while, maybe damn near two years. I may not have even figured it out till after I was relieved. And it was that incident.

Paul Stillwell: But Hayward was gone by then.

Admiral Meyer: I didn't go through the Secretary of the Navy. And the reason I didn't do it is I didn't know any better. Because everything I have done I learned the hard way, including shipbuilding. A lot of people think I don't know anything about shipbuilding. I've got to tell you, I know a thousand times more about shipbuilding than the people who are on duty here today, including engineering duty officers. But I had broken into that clubbish structure, and they broke away.

Later years they came back because I led them and drew them back, and they finally understood that if they wanted to be in their profession they'd better get on board because there's going to be more than three ships. And now, as we point out, it's over three decades' worth of ships. That made a big difference in their behavior. But in those days times were hard, and I just thought as a natural course, well, I had this opportunity with Mr. Erb and my own presidents and here, well, we'll just go out and get it done. That's the natural way. Nobody ever helped me in any of this undertaking. It's a wrong thing. I never knew it. I never knew I did such a dumb thing. Nothing was ever said to me. That's why it took me so long to understand what I'd done. But he got even.

Paul Stillwell: You could also draw the parallel, though, that Lehman had knocked Rickover out after a long period and maybe he wanted another scalp.†

Admiral Meyer: Well, depends on what pew you were sitting in, is what that depends on.

---

* This is a reference to Meyer being removed as Aegis program manager in 1983 by Secretary of the Navy John Lehman. By then Admiral James D. Watkins, USN, was Chief of Naval Operations.
† In March 1982, Admiral Kinnaird R. McKee, USN, succeeded Admiral Rickover as Director of the Naval Nuclear Propulsion Program.

Paul Stillwell: Well, you mentioned Len Erb. We haven't talked much about him. What are your recollections of the working relationship with him?

Admiral Meyer: Len Erb was a professional. He was a professional naval officer, Naval Academy graduate, had been a boomer. And he had only had a modicum of sailing in surface ships as a JO, because in those days you had to sail for a little bit. But he is one of the finest leaders I have ever been associated with. There's a lot of ooh and aah; the Navy was kind of opposed to him going there, but he was maybe like the fourth or fifth in command of the yard in two or three years, so my view was, well, he certainly couldn't be any worse then the ones that they'd brought in there, and every one of them ended up getting fired.

Len Erb was a strong leader but a patient listening leader, and he brought discipline into that yard. He and I formed a relationship which was a disciplined relationship. I don't want to say he did everything that I wanted done, but he heard me and what I thought ought to be done and he understood it, he tried to get it done. Late in our relationship, as time passed, he had the saying that, "It was Wayne Meyer turned this shipyard around; Wayne Meyer made this shipyard America's yard." And in my speeches I kept correcting that. That's not true. It was Len Erb that did that.

Now, it is true too, I created the environment. I don't think it could have been done without me. I created the environment. Erb understood it and he took it.

Paul Stillwell: How would you articulate that environment?

Admiral Meyer: Well, first of all we started treating the people like they were professionals. And when we'd hold meetings, I told you Rickover would even keep book on me. Hell, they had to build a new hall down there just to house the people in the early days. We started out holding meetings in the LaFont Hotel because they didn't have anyplace to hold a meeting. Well, why was that? Did we need all those people? No, we didn't need all those people. Oh, wait a minute. How are you ever going to teach them anything if you don't ever talk to them? So, as Erb and I agreed, I spent in those kind of meetings I did a lot of talking, a hell of a lot of talking. So I made sure the people on the deck plates understood that there was a new broom around here, and it was a professional broom, and if it's shoddy work, you're gone. Or the old expression—your ass is grass. Which is understood in Mississippi. That was the situation here.

Well, it took a while. The first year Len Erb and I spent a lot of time walking that yard. He and I walked that yard. Matter of fact, he's the first president that walked that yard repeatedly, and I may be the first manager, although Bill Wyatt, who was the guy came in on the 963s, did a lot of yard walking.[*] As a matter of fact, Bill Wyatt and I learned a lot. I mean, Bill Wyatt taught me a lot of mechanics associated with shipyard stuff. And Lisanby, who was the supervisor of shipbuilding down there and also had the LHAs—it was rare, kind of, when he walked the yard.[†] He spent a lot of social time.

But we walked the yard, and we went down into those places and we talked to all those foremen and tried to understand what they thought their problems were or such. And well, of course, in this adventure that they'd been on, 30 ships fixed price at $85 million apiece, never even approximately achieved. So the company took a bath and the Navy took a bath, but so did the ships take a bath. We ended up building 8,500-ton ships without any armament in them. Two 5-inch guns and a sonar. So they in truth didn't know any better within the yard. There was only a modest handful of what you'd call professional shipbuilders. They'd been recruited all over the coast, bums most of them.

They tell the stories down there—in their heyday they needed to build up to nearly 15,000 people to run the yard and they'd hire these people that were 100 to 150 miles away. They'd commute every day. And if they didn't, they'd sleep in their car. Take a bath once a week. And they'd talk about how many paychecks—they'd hire people and they'd have paychecks—never picked up. They'd quit before they ever got to the first pay period. They were just really trash of the earth, which were the only people available. Now, in the eyes of God they were all humans, but in the eyes of professional shipbuilders, that they were not.

Paul Stillwell: Well, what was the solution to that? How did you go about getting a trained, competent work force?

---

[*] Captain William C. Wyatt III, USN, *Spruance*-class program manager and supervisor of shipbuilding at Pascagoula.
[†] Captain James W. Lisanby, USN, became supervisor of shipbuilding at Pascagoula in 1970.

Admiral Meyer: Well, it started with the two leaders, and it started with our demands. Erb sent a few VPs walking. They thought it ought to be done a different way and Erb didn't think so, and that was that. He didn't maliciously or publicly castigate or fire them, he just, *puk*, that's it. And so in the main the people that relieved them were people that were fleeted up. And Erb's relief was a guy by the name of Jerry St. Pé. Jerry St. Pé had studied industrial engineering and he, in fact, was the public affairs in the yard.

He eventually fleeted up to be the president.[*] It turned out Jerry St. Pé made a hell of a good leader, and I'll tell you why, because Jerry St. Pé wasn't worth nothing, but Jerry St. Pé was a fantastic observer of Erb and Meyer. He paid attention, and he had those couple years or three years under it that he really paid attention. And so they reached the point where I couldn't do any wrong, because Erb had told St. Pé whatever I needed I was to have, because time was important. And like, in those days, trying to travel just wore your ass out. I tried like hell to lease an airplane because we had Bath on stream, we had Pomona, we had Pascagoula and stuff, and I'm a big believer in being on site.[†] I mean, that's my style. I was raised that way. I've told you how if you appeared before Admiral Reich to ask him or discuss a problem with him that's the first question he asked you, and if you hadn't been there that was it. You just, *puk*, wasted your time.

Paul Stillwell: No credibility.

Admiral Meyer: None at all. I was raised that way. So we were on-scene people, and we had a lot of what I call "milking-stool sessions" with the people down on the deck plates. And they had a lot of different kinds of women who, you know, maybe had been to the third grade or someplace, they just hadn't done much, and they didn't have much skill. Well, what are you going to do? You either teach them some skill or get rid of them, which is what we did. And we took some of them, and we made them pretty damned good people. Cleaned them up, polished them up. They opened little schools there with the yard to help you get through grade school and different, like grammar school and such that operated at night for them.

---

[*] Jerry St. Pé was president of Ingalls Shipbuilding from 1985 to 2001.
[†] Bath Iron Works in Bath, Maine, became the second shipyard to build Aegis cruisers. The first of the Bath-built ships of the class was the *Thomas S. Gates*, for which construction began in 1984.

Then Erb cleaned house. The yard couldn't work 15,000 people. They couldn't work 11,000 people. He finally decided that about 9,500 or so was a pretty good body count. And my view to Erb was, "Look, let's run the yard the right way and let the schedule form from that, not the other way around." And the people who had come there, well, we got all this work and everything, we need 15,000 people to get it done. Well, sure, you get 15,000 people, and if 12,000 of them are monkeys you can't get very far.

So the truth is they said the yard couldn't function, because the yard was an automated yard, built out of whole cloth, just as flat as this deck here. They said, well, it couldn't function with the Aegis fleet. We had one ship. One. Before I could hold my first meeting—I think I mentioned this to you—I got down there, the production officer was already cutting steel. We didn't even have a design. So I said, "Why are you doing that?"

"Well, I've got to put the people to work." So it took a whole—

Paul Stillwell: Culture shift.

Admiral Meyer: Yeah. Significantly. From a continuous process to a discontinuous process. And the discontinuous process is one ship. We finally got *Yorktown*, but one of the reforms was that we were going to put a year between ships, first and second ship, skip a year. Well, that's a dumb idea, but I couldn't control it; that's what was done. So it meant that you had a gap forever. You never overcame the gap. Because skills migrate along, and if you're going to have any kind of a semi-continuous process you've got to be able to accommodate the skills.

Well, automobile companies do. Right. What do they do? Thank God for their unions, that's what they do. They furlough them. They don't fire them, they furlough them, and the unions see that they get some kind of decent paycheck while they're furloughed. We weren't in that kind of situation. At the shipyard, these geniuses thought that you building airplanes or building cars or building ships—all the same thing. Well, it *ain't* all the same thing, not by a long shot. That's why we call it construction. And I just shiver every time somebody talks about—like right now we talk about, well, get the

DDG-51 production line going. You don't have a production line in shipbuilding. What you have is you have construction, not production.

So in every ship I tell people—the ship you went to Saturday, that was the first ship where some 68% of the sailors in that ship—

Paul Stillwell: The *Sterett*.*

Admiral Meyer: Yeah, people forget that. That's their first ship, the first time they ever sailed was coming down Kennebunkport River.

Paul Stillwell: Are you talking about the crew or the builders?

Admiral Meyer: I'm talking about the crew. So I don't believe in this "first ship" baloney. Every ship is the first ship. So every ship is custom made, and we ought to approach the crew that way. It's their ship. And, you know, I left a lot of things that will be unsung for which I have a certain amount of pride, and it's the kind of stuff that just stuck.

When people take pride in their product—I remember in my day when I was on the Terrier desk and we were building the Terrier ships. God damn, the arguments and fights between ship's force and the shipyards, just awful, just terrible. It's just like constant cussing and yelling and fighting with people and calling them every name you could think of and how incompetent they were, how bad they were. Well, there was something to be said for it, because the shipyard people are dirty damn people if you let them be dirty.

The first overhaul I ever did was in my first destroyer in the Brooklyn Navy Yard. And in those days you didn't move off the ship. You stayed in the ship, and it's in winter, and you go around through the ship, the trash, the garbage that they'd leave around in your ship would really just upset you. Well, Erb and I became intolerant of

---

* On 9 August 2008 the interviewer attended the commissioning of the *Arleigh Burke*-class destroyer *Sterett* (DDG-104) in Baltimore, Maryland.

that kind of behavior. We just didn't accept it. And that radiates down. It doesn't take long before the whole attitude changes.

And I think I told you that after about a year and a half or so Erb caused to put up big billboards on Highway 10, one on each side of Pascagoula, about America's shipyard and Aegis ships built here. Those two billboards had an incredible effect on people and their behavior and their pride, which they did not have. I gave them speeches all the time.

Now, remember, I'm talking to you pre-Goldwater/Nichols, which all these people on Tuesday will have trouble understanding. I'm the one that pioneered and led award fees in contracts. I led cost contracts, and they were award-fee contracts. Now, I started off day one with my contracts; I started off RCA that way. I lined them all up and I said, "I'm going to guarantee you a profit. There's nobody going to lose money here. But you're going to do the job. That's what you have to do in return." And I stuck to my word, and I raised my officers and I raised my civil servants: "Look, if you give your word to industry, goddamnit, you keep it, you stick to your word." I mean, we were, and we still are, we're frivolous in government in our behavior with industry, really frivolous. They don't trust us, and rightly so.

And, of course, after I was forced out of the Navy I really discovered this. One of the first jobs I worked on was a task to help a group at General Electric bid a contract, review their bid and see how they were doing on it and everything. I was absolutely appalled. The attitude just left me cold. I'd sat on a number of source selection boards, evaluation boards. I had been chairman of source selection advisory councils. I'd done billions of dollars worth of work. And I couldn't believe how those people who were working to put this bid together, how they distrusted the government, that it was totally dishonest, that they couldn't take their word. And they sat there to plot to figure out how they were going to get around them. As a matter of fact I never completed the job; I finally left it. I could not work under the circumstances.

Paul Stillwell: I want to address one point you made and that was about the shipyard workers who commuted for dozens of miles. Was there any effort to build up the housing in the area to attract better qualified people?

Admiral Meyer: It was a different culture. It was what you and I would call trailer house country.

Paul Stillwell: You talked about Ingalls building the shipyard there at Pascagoula from scratch for the *Spruance* class. How much benefit did you have by the time *Ticonderoga* came along from the learning curve from the *Spruance* class? You weren't starting from scratch this time.

Admiral Meyer: There was a supermarket in Pascagoula. It had gone broke and shut down. It was mostly because of the completion of the *Spruances* and the LHAs. Well, we rented that abandoned building and put together an integrated team from all over the country. We got all the ship's drawings of the 963s and the 993s, which had had a lot of upgrade put in them correcting the flaws. We got those all out.

Paul Stillwell: And they had more of a weapon system too.

Admiral Meyer: Oh, yeah, exactly. They had a Tartar weapon system. But material-wise they were much better ships. So we laid those all out, put our teams to work. My GS-15, Joe Maurelli, my architect, and naval engineer went down there. We spent a year just marking up those drawings, just like creating one big shipalt is what it amounted to, all through the ship.* And it was a cooperative adventure. Where there were things that could be fixed, we we're going to fix them.

And we were going to do all this in a budget, so we laid out a budget. Some things we didn't undertake. But we created, with that approach—and some, of course, flowed out of the Shah's money, but we in essence created the *Ticonderoga* class, a whole new ship, really. It was a whole new ship, built on the bones of those others.

Paul Stillwell: But there had to be some nucleus of experience in the shipyard itself.

---

* Shipalt – an alteration to a ship.

Admiral Meyer: Oh, yes, all kinds of it, but it was lacking in the kind of quality we wanted. So again it was an educational and a cultural process, and part of the motion was America's Yard, and getting people to start to build their pride over it. And that's when—I already had award fees up at Moorestown. The shipyard was absolutely terrified of an award-fee structure. It was all brand new, never been used, they didn't know how it was going to work.

Well, I just take a second to talk about that structure. People thought, well, you're just dealing with a cost contract; the contractor can get away with anything. That, again, is more BS. And I lined them all up and I said, "Look, there's one person that's got a fixed-price contract and that's me. I've got a fixed-price contract to the Congress. And we're going to operate on what I tell the Congress I need, and if they appropriate the money I said we need, that's what we're going to build the ship out of."

The other thing I said as I started anew is, "I'm going to guarantee you a profit. I'm not going to have anybody that works for me that doesn't make a profit, because I don't see how a company can function that's not earning money. That's mandatory. Now, if you can't cut the mustard, then you're going to have to find some other customer because you ain't going to work for me if you can't cut the mustard. But as long as you work for me and you get the product, you're going to earn a profit."

So we ended up setting a base up which ran for several years. Oh, it frosted John Lehman something fearful when he got his hands into it, but he didn't affect it. I guarantee you three cents, so you've got three cents on the bottom. If you were doing engineering work and stuff you could earn up to 15 cents. If you were doing what you'd say production-type work, or assembly-type work, you could earn up to 12 cents. The first three I guaranteed. Three from twelve is nine, so there's nine points that you can strive for. And I had a set of rules how you'd go about getting it.

Paul Stillwell: Was it on the basis of efficiency?

Admiral Meyer: One of the things was efficiency, but the real thing was quality, the basis of quality, and doing it within the budget and doing it on time, all those things. And it can be done. I've told people it's inexcusable that these contracts get out of control.

Just not excusable, that they're in overruns. Well, does that mean I'm that good? No. But there's a requirement: There must be some leadership. Well, how can you do it and that guy down the street can't do it? Because he's trying to make something that he thinks the specifications is calling for or that he has ordered, and they don't want to pay any attention, and the next thing you know he's in an irreversible process. He can't withdraw it. We started out day one with the thought in mind that we're going to operate within this budget and this allocation. And in that era when I started setting that thing up—it took me a couple of years to get it functioning—every captain I had and every vice president I had operated on a budget.

Every February for about four years we'd have these big meetings out at White Oak ordnance laboratory. And that would be the tentative allocation for the coming year. Every vice president, every captain would come before my tribunals, which everybody else was a member of, and they'd argue their case. So the VP and program manager down at Ingalls, for example, he'd argue his case of how much money he needed. Well, he needed a pretty damned big piece of it. Same way at Moorestown. They'd argue their case to my tribunal, which was known to last a week, of what they thought they needed. And then when we finished we'd tote that all up and see how we were doing, and we'd go give them tentative marks. And then I kept the reserves. All reserves belonged to me.

We'd meet again in June, and they'd become final. So, say, this past June, you would know what your money was to be starting this 1 October, and that was the money given to you and you were expected to operate within that money. I'm not interested in how much you're going to overspend, because you're not going to overspend. Instead, what you're going to tell me is: "Wait a minute, Admiral, it turns out that we're just not cutting it; we can't operate in that budget, we've got to have an adjustment. Okay, then we'll come to the tribunal and we'll all sit down and reason together. We've either got to take something out or we've got to put more money in."

Well, that's perfectly logical, and it's massive. By then, see, I'm up to billions of dollars, and I'm in every single appropriations account that the Navy has, every one. So it is a big movement, overseen with a small amount of people within the project proper. I had less than a hundred people. Matter of fact, the day I left there were something like 86 people in the project.

Paul Stillwell: In PMS-400?

Admiral Meyer: In PMS-400. That project, before it got disassembled by my followers, had as much as 450 people in it. And today award fees in many places have bad names because the industry doesn't think they're fair. Well, they are fair if they're done correctly, but it takes mature people in government and it take mature people in industry. We've got to sit down here and decide whether that's a good job you've got there or not a good job.

Now, you and I both can decide whether it's a good job or not. Just because you are at Ingalls and I'm in the Naval Sea Systems Command doesn't mean that we have uncommon views of what's a good job. It doesn't mean that at all, not if you're a professional person. That's my point. Now, it might turn out it's going to cost more than we thought it was going to cost. Okay, we're going to take something out. Or, as I did in June each year, I'd start allocating the reserves. Paul, that's a logical argument, the stuff you've run up against, this strike out in Wisconsin and so forth, okay. So you'd get a little booster.

The other thing we did in that era—I learned this, I didn't learn it myself; it's because I had some really wise counselors. You need to pay attention to COLA and things like cost-of-living adjustments and inflation corrections. So you'd pick up some change along the way that would almost be handed to you by the feds; they'd almost demand you take it. At first, if you're a straight-stick person you don't want any of that welfare stuff. Well, I learned that PDQ. I'll take whatever you're throwing out. And we used it well.

Paul Stillwell: Who was the arbiter who decided where that profit fell between three cents and 12 cents?

Admiral Meyer: You're looking at him. [Laughter]

Paul Stillwell: What were the benchmarks you used to measure? I mean, quality, for example. How did you measure quality?

Admiral Meyer: Well, we had some generalities written into the contract, but we sat down and defined them amongst ourselves with the leaders in the project and the leaders in industry of what we considered. And I had these award-fee boards. We'd hold hearings. And a hearing generally would take at least one day for the contractor, the awardee, to present his case of what he thought he had done in responding to it. And then we'd go get all the different people of government and other people in industry. For example, when we were looking at the Standard missile we'd call in what's now Lockheed, call them in and say, "Well, what do you think? Are they servicing you well? Do you think they're doing a good job?" I mean, we got everybody's opinion, and you'd get all this mixed opinion. And it took, I'd say it took maybe the first year to get people's confidence and not be scared to just say what they felt.

Well, it was the same way with the shipyard. But we did another thing, because people like to think they do things good. So pretty soon they will start going out of their way, in Mississippi, to make sure they're doing what Moorestown thinks it needs, and vice versa, because they know sooner or later the old man is going to be asking the question.

When I first starting learning it was in engineering design reviews. Nominally, the way they were conducted in those days is the representative of industry, let's say RCA at the time, would present this portion of a design review to a board or to the senior people, and then some person from government would come up and say, "Well, they haven't done this, they haven't done that, this is in the spec, that's in there, they haven't done it that way at all, they haven't gone about that." And then you'd sit there and listen to arguments for hours. Bill Goodwin and I in the early days, of pioneering decided we were just not going to put up with that bullshit, so he and I ran these reviews and sat and listened to them and we hit upon something. We decided that the two of them would have to present the review.

Paul Stillwell: Which two do you mean?

Admiral Meyer: The government guy and the industry guy. Aha! Now they've got to decide who they're going to fight with.

Paul Stillwell: Would this be the supervisor of shipbuilding at the yard as the government representative?

Admiral Meyer: No. No, it would be right out of my project office, right out of my project office. Well, not normally, would it be. Or it would be out of—see, much of my support came out of NavShips, now called NavSea, and NavOrd. Much of it came out of there.

And so pretty soon they've got to decide who they're going to fight with. It's kind of like fighting with your brother. Are you going to take on your parents or are you going to take him on? Which one are you going to have a fight with? Well, most people are not going to choose to fight their parents. They'd rather go off in the woodshed and argue themselves to pieces on it. And I encouraged them, but wait a minute—"When you guys get through arguing, if you come back here and you lay out before Bill Goodwin and I what you think the issues are, we'll try to help adjudicate those. But you must sort out the issues first. I'm not going to sit here and do you goddamn debates for you." It was a big learning process and a teaching process and a maturing process and a confidence process, all those things.

Paul Stillwell: Well, and probably it also taught them to negotiate so they didn't have something imposed on them.

Admiral Meyer: You got it. You got it. They decided, "Hey, wait a minute, we'd better just be a little careful here, Paul, because they're liable to ram something down our throat we don't want." And people are still people, no matter who they work for or where they work, and they're just as wise as the next people. Because most of them in this process have to be in cahoots in some manner, in some agreement, because the money flowing from the top flows to both their advantages. It's not uniquely RCA's or uniquely Sea-06 or anything like that. Actually, it got so it was a lot of fun.

Now, I want to go cap that off a minute. Normally, after the program reviews, Moorestown, Pomona, then Pascagoula, it'd take three to four days. And the last day, at least half of the day would be devoted to the board meeting, which I was the chairman, to determine what that fee would be, that nine cents. I had a rule that just sent delirium tremens through the government, and it was that my president was going to sit in on the board's proceedings. Now, he was not going to vote on his own award fee.

Paul Stillwell: What do you mean? What president?

Admiral Meyer: Well, in the case of RCA it was Bill Goodwin.

Paul Stillwell: Okay.

Admiral Meyer: In the case of Mississippi it was Len Erb. They were going to sit in on our proceedings of the board. It was very simple. I kept saying, "Hey, wait a minute. There's no use of us sitting around here listening to all these people bitching about how Ingalls is not performing and we don't even have the general manager here to hear it. We ought to have him sitting right here." And by the way, that has a big effect on the supervisor of shipbuilding too, because pretty soon he gets his own socks together. So we'd have him sit with the board, and they'd have to decide again who they're going to argue with. Whether they're going to be brothers, or whether they're just going to sand piss in each other's shoe all day. I tell you, that's really good team building. I brag about it. I learned it accidentally. Maybe there are other people that think they're so brilliant that they already knew it, but I'd never seen it practiced. It ain't practiced to this day.

Well, we'd work on that award fee till whenever it was an hour and 20 minutes to the airport so we needed to be finished by then, which was my escape plan. [Laughter] We would finally come to a number, and I would stand up at the end. All the different people would be called back in, the foremen, the leaders, and stuff, and I'd try to sum up the comments of the board and what was thought and such, to put just a little bit of drama in it so that just at the end I could announce—on the spot I announced the number and the letter, the letter and the number.

Paul Stillwell: Is this a letter grade?

Admiral Meyer: Yeah, A-student, B-student, C-student, just like in school. A couple things that come from that. I'd announce those and, *poooh*, I'd whoosh out the door. One of the officers would be driving me or something, and off to the airport I'd go. I'd walk down the passage; every door, I'd look around, there were people standing with their heads sticking out, watching out, everyplace you looked. Hundreds of them ganged up waiting to get the signal and stuff. You know, that stuff would be posted in the plant before I ever got to the airport, people were that interested.

Paul Stillwell: Well, that was their bread and butter.

Admiral Meyer: It subsequently turned out what they cared about was the letter grade.

Paul Stillwell: Well, that's interesting.

Admiral Meyer: Yeah. They didn't care what the number was. They wanted to know whether you thought they were a C student or an A student; that was their interest. Because there was no one in the process got any of the money. Well, pretty soon the general managers got a little wiser; they'd make little handouts, they'd do handouts to just almost gift checks—I encouraged them to do it—to people that they thought that this quarter had done a phenomenal job. Give them $100.00, what the hell. Makes people feel good and doesn't cost the company that much. Give it to them. So it was a good process. And I want to stress this. The difference was, people cared what you thought about them. They cared what you thought about them.

Well, we had other things that we had created early on, Bill Goodwin and I. Started at RCA. There were Aegis excellence awards, including for individuals, including for groups of individuals who had done some particular job that was really good, was complimentary. And we created an Aegis excellence flag system, that you could fly the Aegis flag at your flagpole if it was awarded to you by the project manager.

There's an outfit I am not sure you even know where they are—St. Inigoes, Maryland, there's an outfit to do our radios. Aegis is the first goddamn shipbuilding program that ever had working radios when they were landed in the ships, hooked up.

They came out of St. Inigoes, Maryland. It's the leftover residues from the runways down there. And it was under the supervision of what today would be called SpaWar, in those days known as NavElex, Naval Electronics Systems Command.[*] It was a big deal to people down in the South, particularly. And they got something like—before I got fired I think they got something like ten stars, gold stars, on their flag. And they'd get old Steny Hoyer every time to come down and hand it out.[†] He and I'd go down there, and I'd make the announcements and such, and old Steny would just beam and talk about how wonderful the people were and everything. Goddamn, they'd just go night and day to make sure their gear was put together. Because we did it in industry and government. We did it all over. You could fly the Aegis flag if it was awarded to you.

Paul Stillwell: There was a counterpart of that in World War II, the Army-Navy E that manufacturers could win.

Admiral Meyer: That's where I started forming up these ideas. I formed them up at NASA, different places; the assholes that followed me didn't believe in it, the leaders. "Waste of money, don't need that kind of thing, waste of money. If you've got to that, if you've got to do that, then what kind of people are they?" Well, I tell you what they are; they're people that need a little excitement in their life, and it always stirs them up.

Paul Stillwell: Well, and everybody likes a pat on the back.

Admiral Meyer: You're damn right they do. You're damn right people do. And they like to think that the leader cares what they're doing. They know the leader can't come and spend a week with them. Even if it's just ten minutes, it's important to people. And if they get a couple words about what they're doing is important. And I'd always give them those words about the gear—was their son, daughter, niece, nephew, brother, or friend next door, you didn't know who they were, that you didn't know who was going to use their gear, or how well it had to work.

---

[*] SpaWar – Space and Naval Warfare Systems Command.
[†] Steny H. Hoyer, a Democrat from Maryland, has served in the U.S. House of Representatives from 19 May 1981 to the present.

Paul Stillwell: Same approach you used with the people building the missiles.

Admiral Meyer: You got it exactly, same approach. People call it whatever they want to call it, but goddamn it, it worked and it worked well, and there ain't no program ever existed like it in the Navy, and I'm not sure there is going to be another one this century that will be like that one at all. And you saw only a little bitty teensy piece of it Saturday night, and I'm not sure you saw one of the better ones, because we've had some wonderful shows.

Paul Stillwell: Ship commissionings.

Admiral Meyer: Wonderful commissionings and presentations, just wonderful ones.

Paul Stillwell: You talked about all these millions and millions of dollars flowing through. Who was your money manager in the program?

Admiral Meyer: For a long time my civil servant was a fellow by the name of Billy Love.[*] He's retired now. I had recruited him, actually, out of Vitro. He didn't really know anything about money, but he was a problem solver. And we're in that era where you couldn't get people.

I briefly mentioned this to you earlier on in another session, that I call them having been set free. This was when all the women were liberated, and upward mobility programs were created. And so with just a little effort you could get all of the so-called upward-mobility people, or women, that you wanted. The problem was, virtually none of them had any skills. And there was some percentage, some level, who had the potential to be skillful and some whose potential was not all that great, and some, just like always happens, thought that, well, here's a gravy train for me to jump on and I'm going to get on it. So at one time in the project, percentage-wise I probably had more women than any other project anywhere. And people get jealous. But one of the reasons I had them is I couldn't get the structure to let me hire others. Secondly, I could be very choosy of the

---

[*] Billy G. Love, supervisory budget analyst for Aegis shipbuilding, PMS-400.

ones I brought in who were ambitious or wanted to be ambitious, and I could start them from the beginning with some pretty stern measures. And if they cut the mustard, okay, and if they didn't, that was bad. Today, as we speak here in 2008, I can't think of any of them left on active duty now, but quite a large number of women went on to become GS-12. Some became senior executives, GS-16s and such. So it was a good program to me in many respects.

Now, one of the things I resented about it—there's a couple of things, but one was there weren't many of them that thought they had to go to school. So I was hiring them at a GS-5 or a GS-6. Well, they want to be GS-12, but they don't want to upgrade themselves to be that. So that was one of the tough parts about the thing.

And it was that similar way in experience. I've told you several times how much I believe in experience. As I grew up and learned in this business, you've got to go get your experience on the road; you can't get it sitting here in an office in Washington, D.C. If you're going to be with me, you're going to travel and you're going to get out there and start learning.

Paul Stillwell: Did Billy Love operate by raising red flags for you if there were aberrations in the cash flow that was expected?

Admiral Meyer: Okay, there's a subject I was getting to, as usual very windy-like. We worked hard and played hard in that project. And it is very aggravated by several things. One is I felt people had to be on the scene; in fact demanded it. I mentioned to you, I believe in one of the earlier tapes of that era where divorce rates were just out of control in the country and it was happening in naval officers. Naval officers were getting divorced all over the place there for several years. Billy Love was a great teacher, and he could take a woman who had no skill at all and, I tell you, by suppertime tonight he would have her keeping books. And so an expression emerged which I detested and don't like, called "Billy's girls." Because we could hire them, we could get them. A number of them, we upgraded them eventually. I mean, they learned so much they got recruited by other projects, which in a way was good for us because that meant that we were spreading out and accumulating help, because in a big project you're always needing help from different places.

The have-nots are always coming after you. We're taught this at church, that the have-nots become very resentful if you have money. They become very resentful if you're doing well. I've had even admirals say to me, *admirals* that I've known a long, long time say, "Well, you know, Wayne, I could have done what you did if I'd had all of the money you had."

I'd say, "Well, Harry, why the hell didn't you?" Because the truth is that's BS. They couldn't have, because they didn't have the determination, the fire, the know-how, nor did they understand what had to be done. I did. I admit that it was all a learning experience for me, and in those kinds of things you virtually never get a chance to repeat it, but I did, and we raised an incredible group of professionals out of almost nothing.

I don't know that I've shown you the wallet card that we had made for communication within the project. I must do that the next time. I don't have one on me right now, but I think I have one. But one of the girls that worked for Billy and for Bob Gray, she's the one, she created a set of 3x5 cards like an accordion. I carried the entire program in my shirt pocket, the whole program. I drove the people in Congress crazy, particularly the staffers, because they were constantly after me where they could get a copy, and the answer is "I don't think so."

Paul Stillwell: What was on the cards?

Admiral Meyer: The whole program. What the budgets were, what the structures were, who the people were, the telephone numbers, the code numbers, all those things. You could ask me a question about how many tubes were in such-and-such and I'll—[flipping sound] "Thirty-two." [Flipping sound] That's the answer. So that astounded people, it just astounded them, of how that connectivity occurred within that project.

Then I had established something I came to call the area commanders. Now, again, that's not revolutionary. But every place of interest I set up an officer, and that officer reported to me. Of course, my big places were—oh, okay, Moorestown. I created a massive place at Moorestown with all that business commanded by a captain. Well, I already had one in Mississippi; I co-opted him. I dual-hatted him, the supervisor, to be my area commander. I put the test officers under him. I furnished the test officers.

Paul Stillwell: Now, these would be Navy captains, I presume.

Admiral Meyer: In this case we're talking about Navy captains. Occasionally civilians, but mostly Navy captains or commanders. And the same way with the field stations of the nation. So I had a communications network, and some of these things I learned off of Rickover and stuff like that, but each of them had to file a report with me every week. Well, you get these reports and so here: "Well, you know, we don't have this done, that didn't get done, this didn't get done." So all I had to do was put about two question marks on it and send it to the captain responsible in the project, with question marks, and let it go at that. The next thing you know he'd come slamming into my office and say, "Well, why the hell doesn't he ask me? Why don't you ask me?" I said, "Well, (A) you didn't tell me, (B) if he needs to ask you I assume you'll tell him to ask you." Well, pretty soon they got smarter. [Laughter] So they had to decide who in the hell they were going to fight with.

Paul Stillwell: And solve it before it got to your level.

Admiral Meyer: You got it. You exactly got it. So it brought this coherence and cohesiveness amongst people, and they started exchanging notes. The other thing it did is it caused them to start communicating with the general managers and presidents and such in their area of command, so that they didn't look so goddamn stupid. Because I'd ask a question from the RCA person and get one answer and ask the question from my tech rep and get another answer. I'd say, "I ain't going to work with two answers; you people go figure out what the goddamn answer is and come back and tell me what the answer is. I'm not going to sit around and solve these things."

Well, pretty soon they started learning their lesson—whose lip are they going to put up with? It was just that simple. So they'd start learning how to communicate, and they'd learn how to sort out their bona fide differences, of where they disagreed. They had disagreements. As a matter of fact they had a lot of them. But a lot of them turned out they could solve themselves. Some they couldn't, and some were pretty major. I urged them all the time of how important disagreements were, because after all the products we were building are pretty damned important to the nation, and we want to be sure we're doing the proper thing and the right thing. No one's got a lock on know-how and a lock on talent. And that's just kind of the way it went on.

Well, Billy's girls, Billy trained—God, he trained a lot of people in the project. A guy by the name of Bob Gray that I mentioned to you—you've met him, I think, down in the war room, he's been with me a long, long time. He's a civil servant, and he became my planner so he was with me a number of years as my planner. I think I took him all the way from GS-9 to GS-14. After I left he went out and started a business. Joe Maurelli, GS-15, he went out. These guys went out and started their own businesses to support NavSea or something like that. All of them have done real well in business, because they knew how to run a business. From working with me they knew how to get things done; they knew how to go about it.

So that was just a lot of it. We were, you know, a take-no-prisoner-type operation. If something was wrong, we'd just mount out a task force and go fix it. And I taught them all that we generally won't make it by hiding things; we need to get them out on the table, but that doesn't mean getting them out on the newspaper. But we need to get them out in front of us to understand what it is we're working on.

I learned here it's important to stay ahead of the law. You've got to keep ahead. You need to stay ahead, because a democracy-type structure runs on whispering campaigns and gossip. And I have said in many of my speeches: "If you don't believe this is a democracy, become a major project manager for a while, because everybody in this town believes they know more about shipbuilding, right now, than you do. Believe me, that's the way it is." Well, your only option is either to get out or get ahead and be ahead of what they're after. Because many of them just set out to—it's as though they're self-appointed auditors—they set out to see if they can destroy you.

I tell you one of the most terrible things we have in government is the auditing process. It is so wasteful, it is so dishonest, and it's dishonesty on the part of the auditors and that whole process.

Paul Stillwell: You're talking about the GAO?*

Admiral Meyer: Well, that ain't the only one. That's one of them, one of several. Of course, the Congress has it own investigative staffs. They're not as active today as they once were. So there's plenty of these investigators. Our government is just full of them, and they are so wasteful and they contribute so little. The problem is they're hardly ever constructive. If you get a useful point out of them it's almost accidental.

Paul Stillwell: Is there a "gotcha" mentality?

Admiral Meyer: It's a "gotcha" mentality. Now, let me digress a minute. The chief engineer, the admiral sent me out there, his newly created station, his pride and joy, and I don't know how I learned it, from the officers and the civil servants: "Look, we are not going to be an auditing outfit, and if I catch one of you behaving that way you're off my case, you're not here. We're *not* going to go into a ship and go down and tell the type commander what's wrong with his ship. We're not going to do that. And you tell any of your friends at the TyComs or the fleets, if they want that kind of work they can come to me and I'll decide, but you're not to do it." Well, that created an attitude of coaching, and it created an attitude in the crews too, and the officers, so they'd get so they'd get on the phone and call an engineer up there and ask a question they had, or a petty officer would, because that fear would evaporate on them. Now, when I had captains ask me if we would take a look at his ship and give him an assessment, we'd do that. We'd do that, and hopefully it would be constructive.†

Now, I'm going to mail to you the two InSurv reports on USS *Stout* and USS *Chosin* of last April. You'll see when you read them why this makes this old sailor so ill, who built this beautiful fleet, who led it, who's created an incredible thing in our Navy, and the performance in those two ships, it really causes you to cringe. They had their five-year inspection, and if you read the report and if it just said, well, you know, this department's got these problems, or something's screwed up—but it's the entire ship in

---

* GAO – General Accounting Office, since changed on 7 July 2004 to Government Accountability Office.
† This paragraph refers to Meyer's service from 1967 to 1970 at the Navy Surface Missile Systems Engineering Station (NSMSES), Port Hueneme, California

both cases. Not only that, there's an accompanying letter with them from the admiral that's in charge of these things—Curtis by name, I think it is; I don't know him.

Paul Stillwell: Curtis is the surface type commander.*

Admiral Meyer: Right. I think that's who it is. Saying, well, it's not their fault. The things in these two reports are so grievous that you could not serve one day in these ships, with your experience, and not see them, they are so self-evident. And you say to yourself, what's wrong here? What's happened? I don't believe the officers have been relieved, as is common in my Navy, and sometimes wrongly so. But the ones that I hand you, you'll find I have a note on them "third read." I've read them three times. The first copies ever issued by me were issued yesterday. They're not classified or anything, but they are so awful. And they're not rabid; they're pretty objective. And just ordinary day-to-day things is what's bothersome. What's happened in my Navy here? I don't know.

Now, I got off on that tangent. Where did I leave from?

Paul Stillwell: Well, one thing I'm still trying to get at was the communication link between you and Billy Love. How often, what was the substance of it?

Admiral Meyer: Yeah. Well, I've been giving it to you for the last 30 minutes. [Laughter] You must not be getting it.

I hired him as a GS-13 and finally made him a -14, but he, I don't know, I talked to him 15 times a day or something. I did the allocation myself with my captains and my deputies. He didn't do these allocations. I'd tell him the kind of problem I wanted to solve, and I'd say, "Billy, I want y'all to see if you could lay out something for us to have a meeting on," and have him do that.

The other thing I was hell on is, we're not going to do anything illegal. You don't have to do illegal things, not if you've got the experience. There's plenty of ways to solve problems legally, and I believe in that.

---

* Vice Admiral Derwood C. Curtis, USN, Commander Naval Surface Forces and Commander Naval Surface Force Pacific Fleet at the time of the interview.

And furthermore, as I said to you earlier, I don't believe in going in the hole. That's unsat to me. A ship is a complicated—look at this thing right here on this poster board. Do you have any idea what that costs?

Paul Stillwell: Hundreds of millions.

Admiral Meyer: Yeah. There's no one knows what that costs. You don't know what that costs. Nobody is that smart. Well, that takes pretty damned good leadership, doesn't it? That takes awfully good leadership to get this ship put together for you to see what you saw last Saturday in *Sterett*. And yet here I'll show you the report from a ship that's only a few years old, that is a sister ship of *Sterett*—really sad.

Well, we did have an intimate coupling with Billy and I held, as I told you, the reserves. I gave the captains their money, and I made sure that we gave the vice presidents their money and our area commanders. Everybody had a little budget for me because I believed that everybody ought to have a little budget of at least semi-discretionary money, of money that he or she could adapt, see fit to whatever the situation was, because I wasn't smart enough to determine that and neither was anybody else. I've never had anybody let me down on it. Never. I've never had a vice president let me down. I've never had a person in industry let me down on it. Never. I think that one of the reasons is that they were pretty confident that they'd only get to let you down once, and they understood that because we're professionals. They stayed that way.

And Billy understood that he had to serve those captains. And I, again, Tuesday mornings—the captains run this business. The GS-15s, their deputies, are just what the name says, their deputies. They carry out and execute the business that the two of them agree to do. That's the way I want it run. If you've got a problem, I want to know about it. I want you to write me a note. And you need to understand that I'm a very curious person, and I am by nature a very curious person, and I can walk down on the deck plates and I can ask more questions in ten minutes than you could answer in two weeks, I guarantee you that. And invariably, of course, there's no one on the deck plates going to tell you he doesn't know. He's going to give you an answer. [Chuckle] And most of the time it won't be right. But it gives you a feel for how he sees the world, and he hardly ever sees it the way you see it.

Paul Stillwell: Well, let's say you had a specific area and some budget that was consistently coming over the amount that you expected. How would you address that with Billy?

Admiral Meyer: That's a fair question, and I don't want to sound too smug as to say that, well, I never had that happen. I like to think that the February-June processes were pretty leveling. But the way I addressed it is, I believe in participation, so if we've got an area that we consistently seem to have problems with, I'd convene this caucus, and we just sit down and let the blood run out on the table till we see if we can understand the situation and what's causing it. I don't start with the people being incompetent, although I had some incompetent people. Or there's another way to put it: Some people are more competent than other people. So you can't excuse incompetence, but people have to get the feeling that if they're in trouble there's some chance that they can overcome.

You know what I think part of the problem is today, as I see it here in the last few months and everything? Goldwater-Nichols, which is a leaderless-type structure, it's got all those officers and those civil servants, they don't know who they can rely on. They don't have anybody they can trust. They don't know who to rely on. One thing they do know, there's virtually no one going to help them.

Well, they've coasted for 25 years. That's what Aegis did, this long-running program which brought order out of chaos of the 963s and the LHAs. I mean, in that day when I entered it there wasn't a single shipbuilding program that wasn't in the courthouse. They were all in the courthouse. I told my contractors, "Anybody that takes me in the courthouse is not going to be working for me, because I'm just not going to spend time on that subject." All you ever get out of the courthouse is a solution unsatisfactory to both parties. Ask anybody that's ever gotten a divorce. So you don't have to be in a courthouse. It is an expression of the failure of leadership.

Paul Stillwell: It's a counterproductive use of time.

Admiral Meyer: It sure is, and boy, it burns it something fearfully. So I believe in resolving it yourself. I don't believe in hiding it; neither do I believe in printing it, but I believe you've got to get it out on the table with your mates. And I'm a strong believer in the vice presidents and, in my case, the captains. I'm a strong believer in whatever your top structure is—in my case it was vice presidents and captains—and their opinions and their experience. Because every one of them brings something unique to the table, so you need to try to integrate up that.

I think I mentioned this to you before. It took me a long time to learn this, and I have always used the expression that God will help. And in this business you don't ever want to forget God will help you. At the same time, the devil won't help you. Don't ever forget that. So watch for it and use the opportunity when it occurs. I told you that we believed in a lot of socials. I'm still on the Billy Love case, by the way. As a matter of fact, we even had a number of parties at Billy Love's house. Billy Love lived with his French wife, Mimi, down in La Plata. To go down there for a party was a hell of a challenge for people, both from a driving viewpoint in the middle of the night—

Paul Stillwell: Especially getting home [chuckle].

Admiral Meyer: Yeah. But we believe pretty strongly about socializing, and I have never, never, ever, ever believed, nor do I believe today, about this separation of church and state when it comes to your industrial base, your contractors, and your project. I don't believe in it. I said wait a minute, how're you going to get things done if you don't fraternize? How do you expect to get things done? I mean, right now, where was our own President last week?

Paul Stillwell: China.

Admiral Meyer: Exactly, and by our publically stated enemy, sitting right in his goddamn front room. So I believe in that. I think that's important in humanity, that that is the fundamental way that things break—I mean, if you listen to Judge Judy, listen to anybody, listen to the divorce cases and everything, what's wrong?* Well, the communications broke down. Invariably that's what the answer is. I'm a strong believer against it. So we can start writing rules till the cows come home about no association, no fraternization, no socializing. You know, Anna Mae tells me she thinks—I don't know, but she says—you know, there weren't many people there Saturday.

Paul Stillwell: At the commissioning of the *Sterett*.

Admiral Meyer: At the commissioning of the ship. She believes it's because of these directives been put out over here as a result of the one admiral we have allegedly in trouble right this minute, and the directives have been put out about associating and fraternizing. I mean, there are inspectors right now going around for the last three years trying to find out who all the people were who attended Aegis commissionings and Aegis christenings and such. Isn't that something? What kind of a people are we if we've gotten that way?

Paul Stillwell: Well, I read the new *Newsweek*, which praised Bush for going to the Olympics and talking to the Chinese for creating a communication channel.†

Admiral Meyer: Right [chuckle]. Yes. I don't understand this in our behavior. Hell, this is not even childlike in behavior. It's really the behavior of the devil in that kind of thing. So I don't believe in it.

Paul Stillwell: You painted an excellent picture of the relationship with Pascagoula during the production process. Could we get a comparable picture relating to Moorestown and the administration of the RCA part of it?

Admiral Meyer: If you would have been up with me the last two days at Moorestown I think you'd have been conveniently [phonetic] surprised. One of our top managers up

---

* "Judge Judy" is the title of a syndicated television program that resolves civil lawsuits.
† George W. Bush served as President of the United States from 20 January 2001 to 20 January 2009.

there, vice president, Joe Rappisi, had been promoted about three months ago to run the new division of Sippican that they had acquired. And so Orlando Carvalho, who is the plant manager and president up there at Moorestown was taking this time to get Joe's replacement.[*] Well, she has arrived. Her name is Lisa Callahan.[†] She's maybe, I don't know, someplace in her 40s. She's got two subteen children and a husband. And she is an engineer and she's out of their Orlando division in Florida, working in simulations and such. But she had started in Manassas out here, and so they wanted to work their way back to this part of the country. She had had a lot of her development in submarine fire control in her younger life. Well, I'm one of Orlando's major consultants, and I have been ever since he became the general manager there, so he wanted me to give a little hand in her shakedown.

And so on the night before last Orlando and I went out and had supper with her. And we had the standard New Jersey Italiano supper and such. As I chatted her up and thought about her and how she was going to fit in, I decided that my quick study of her is she's going to fit pretty damned good, because I happen to think Orlando is a pretty damned good leader and a pretty incisive person. He's Portuguese by upbringing, and he's a good engineer, and I think his instincts are really good. And frankly, I'm really concerned about him. I'm afraid I'll lose him because I think he's going to get promoted, and get promoted away from Moorestown. It'll be a tragic loss.

But those two days, if you'd been sitting there with me in their new conference room they just opened, gathered around in these chairs, and you listened to the speakers, I would guess that you would have not been more than 50% correct if I asked you to identify where that person is from that's on the stage. Or where do you think that person works? You'd be wrong every time. That's what 30 years of integration has done between government, General Dynamics, Computer Sciences, Raytheon, and all of that structure. That's how glued together they are. It just simply overwhelms the Missile Defense Agency. The Aegis ballistic missile defense effort, which I am a consultant in, which has helped our government in what's called the MDA, which is the agency of DoD, this outfit is head and shoulders above the other services and above other parts of it.

---

[*] Orlando P. Carvalho, president and general manager of marine systems and sensors for Lockheed Martin at Moorestown.
[†] Lisa Callahan, vice president, Lockheed Martin, Moorestown, New Jersey.

I mean, here's the rundown of the incredible things that the Aegis fleet does. It included what took everybody's breath away here in February when the people of the cruiser *Lake Erie* shot the spacecraft out of the ether. Things that couldn't be done, couldn't be done, couldn't be done, couldn't be done—oh, well, we've done it, one after the other after the other after the other. The Aegis is nothing like it was a quarter century ago. Every week it's kept itself up to date. Every week it's dealing in the—you know why? Because in the particular structure of air defense, or missile defense, your opponent determines the time and location. You don't. So you can't work on a problem that doesn't exist. You got to wait till there *is* a problem. You can't shoot down a missile that ain't been built. The Iranians keep trying to scare us and maybe they are, we don't know. At least I don't know. Why are they keep throwing out this—well, they keep trying to scare us. They know darn good and well how good we are. Not that stupid.

If you look at the integration of government, the tech rep up there and the CSEDS, or the cruiser in the cornfield or whatever you choose to call it, or now the James Doyle Engineering place, it runs around the clock. It's seven days a week. It's doing so much testing and so many things to do that the number of different kinds of people that come in there on a given day, some of them you never even heard of. Because some company is here which has some piece of work they're doing for Lockheed or for the Navy or some such that's going to be a modification to a piece of Aegis and it's here being evaluated with our sailors and officers there and civil servants, and Lockheed Martin people, all as a body. And so, as I said to Lisa, I said what I think will set you back is you're going to see a degree of intimacy that you've not seen before in your career, and neither have I. These people know each other so well and know each other's capabilities and capacities so well that they know exactly what has to be done given a set of circumstances. That's real football, man, that's real football.

Now, have I burned you out for today?

Paul Stillwell: No, but have you burned yourself out?

Admiral Meyer: Well, I'm getting close. I'm getting close.

Interview Number 17 with Rear Admiral Wayne E. Meyer, U.S. Navy (Retired)
Place: Admiral Meyer's office in Arlington, Virginia
Date: Wednesday, 25 February 2009

Paul Stillwell: Admiral, it's great to see you again after a delay of a few months.

Admiral Meyer: Well, I feel actually embarrassed. And then I have to say that these women let this sneak up on me this time, because I frankly didn't know that it was programmed today. But I've been out of bed for a couple days, so I'm a little behind in my manners and my behavior. Where do you think we are?

Paul Stillwell: Well, one big event that happened since our last visit was the christening of *Wayne E. Meyer* in Bath, Maine.[*] Could you talk about that, please?

Admiral Meyer: All right. It was not only a rare event, it was a very nice event, I thought. It was done well by the president of Bath, and may have been his last official undertaking, I don't know. I think he's retiring this month or next month.

Paul Stillwell: Is this Mr. Shipway?[†]

Admiral Meyer: Yeah. Which I'm sorry to see. I think he has done a wonderful job in that shipyard. I don't believe in mandatory retirements; I never have. I think you ought to instead evaluate the person for the leadership provided, and he has been an exceptional leader, in my view.

Paul Stillwell: What characteristics about him made him that way?

---

[*] Admiral Meyer's wife Anna Mae Meyer christened the Aegis destroyer *Wayne E. Meyer* (DDG-108) on 18 October 2008.
[†] Rear Admiral John F. "Dugan" Shipway, USN (Ret.), retired as president of Bath Iron Works on 31 March 2009. He had served in the position since 2003.

Admiral Meyer: Well, I've known him for a long, long time, but I can't say I ever served with him. He served around headquarters a lot of times while I was here, and he's of the submarine persuasion. But as I watched him emerge up at that shipyard I saw his leadership in action. You walk around that shipyard with him, it was obvious what the people think of him. Many of them called him by his name. He called a lot of people by their names, women and men. But there was no doubt that he was held in respect in that yard, no doubt at all. And he gave it. It was just that simple. I guess it's your upbringing more than anything else that starts you off and makes you that way. And whoever replaces him will have some pretty heavy boots to fill up. So that's my feeling on him.

Paul Stillwell: What do you recall about the ceremony in October?

Admiral Meyer: Well, I was standing up on the platform with the CNO, and Anna Mae and all of her following went down those few steps.[*] I don't know how far away you were; don't know how close you were.

Paul Stillwell: No, I was not there.

Admiral Meyer: Oh, you weren't there. Oh, I'm sorry about that.

She was maybe as far as from here to the far bulkhead, 20 feet. I was standing up there alongside the CNO and the two senators, and we had some pretty good cross-chat.

Paul Stillwell: Susan Collins and Olympia Snowe.

Admiral Meyer: Olympia Snowe and Susan Collins, and Admiral Roughead. Originally I had invited Admiral Mullen, and he ended up being preempted.[†] And so the Secretary, rather than take the assignment—which, I don't know, I kind of didn't like this—yanked the CNO home. The CNO and his wife were taking a couple days' vacation in Venice

---

[*] Admiral Gary Roughead, USN, has served as Chief of Naval Operations from 29 September 2007 to 23 September 2011.
[†] Admiral Michael G. Mullen, USN, served as Chairman of the Joint Chiefs of Staff from 1 October 2007 to 30 September 2011. He had commanded the Aegis cruiser *Yorktown* (CG-48).

when they were over there for a big meeting there someplace, and they got yanked out of that and brought home for this affair. If a christening is ever routine this one is, because we've done a lot of them and a lot of this kind of ship. It's very rare that the CNO is there, or the Secretary for that matter, rare that either one attend. So I felt quite honored by it and quite moved by it. And I don't know who did that. I don't know whether Mullen did it or the Secretary did it or both of them did it, but I took it anyhow.

And Anna Mae, of course, performed quite well. There's a few pictures around here someplace; you've probably seen them all.

Paul Stillwell: Yes. What sort of emotional reaction did you have to that event?

Admiral Meyer: Well, I don't know whether it was draining off of me by then or whether it had built. I notice here that what the women have done in essence is put these pictures up on the board here that reflect that, and also over here is when the CNO came to Moorestown and signed off on the 100th Aegis, which is also a little bit unusual, you think about that.[*] That's Mullen. And here is the captain and his crew. So frankly, all I could do is walk around and cry. I don't know whether you actually cry; tears just flow out of your eyes all the time. That was my reaction all that day. You can see it the way I kept my head down more than I usually keep it down. That's the way it was.

Paul Stillwell: It's a long way from Brunswick, Missouri.

Admiral Meyer: It is a hell of a long ways from Brunswick. And I did have there, by the way, which was a pleasant surprise to me and I liked it— I believe I told you earlier that I have one surviving uncle up in his 90s, and that's it. But my cousins, who were born after I went in the Navy, from Brunswick, decided that they were going to attend, and that included the widow of one of my cousins. And so they made a little trip out of it by coming—I think they drove up through New York and up into Maine, and then they spent a couple days at this affair, and of course they had a wonderful time. That old hotel is a

---

[*] The *Wayne E. Meyer* was the 100th Aegis ship delivered to the Navy.

wonderful place to stay. It's a great place to stay; it takes a little money to stay there but still pretty nice.

And they probably put on the best sponsor's dinner of any I've ever attended. Except it was pretty small, but it's the best one I've ever attended. It makes you feel the class. I've attended some pretty darned big sponsor's dinners, and down when Pascagoula was holding them generally they had to put up a tent, usually, to handle them all. They'd have big crowds at the sponsor's dinner. So it was emotional to me.

Now, there's a secondary point. I don't know whether I'd want it to appear in the recorded record. My late wife, Margaret, was the sponsor of *Lake Erie*. And *Lake Erie* was launched up at Bath down the rail. And it subsequently turned out to have been her last public appearance. She was launched in July and she died in October. I don't know how many officers have had two wives who were sponsors, but it may be, you know, some footnote, like about Appendix 13 in the book. [Chuckle]

Paul Stillwell: Very few, if any, others, I would think.

Admiral Meyer: I would think so too. I can't recall any. I can't recall a single one. So unusual in that respect, which I really don't like to make a public point of, because there's my daughter and my daughter-in-law, and my stepdaughter are all there with Anna Mae, so she had all three of them shaped up.

Paul Stillwell: Well, back to the timeline we were pursuing before. You talked about the construction of *Ticonderoga* and working with Len Erb and with Moorestown. One of the things that didn't come to fruition was the nuclear-powered version, CGN-42. What led to its cancellation?

Admiral Meyer: Well, one thing about it, I didn't have to take a position, even though I was the centerpiece. I don't recall right now who I testified before, nor do I even recall whether Rickover was part of it or not. I don't think so. But I allowed as how I had no position, when I was asked. And so from then on I was never asked about it. You will recall that Ingalls, our shipbuilder then, had also been a submarine builder until they and

Rickover came to a big parting of the way and Rickover put them out of business, and they've been out of the submarine business ever since. So he had no love for that shipyard. And then the other shipyard never built a nuclear ship anyhow. So the only really viable candidate available would be Newport News, who had built the -38s and such. And, I don't know, we didn't keep any of the -38s, so it's not apparent to me that we, as an entity, thought very much of them.[*] They were damned good ships from a general ship viewpoint; they just didn't have the weapons system in them.

Paul Stillwell: And they had an expensive power plant.

Admiral Meyer: Right, but they had what we would call Tartar. And I think generally it was an anti-Aegis movement.

Paul Stillwell: Did you feel disappointment at the time not to get a nuclear hull in the program?

Admiral Meyer: I thought it was the wrong choice for the Navy, and I so stated it to a number of officials. But I wasn't prepared, either, to go get on the stump on it. I wasn't going to crusade for it.

Paul Stillwell: You thought cancellation was the wrong choice?

Admiral Meyer: Yeah, cancelling the nuke was the wrong choice. It was the wrong choice. There will be a day when our progeny will criticize us for that, for not having those ships in operation. And they would have been incredibly armed.

You are aware that we put in quite a bit of study work and engineering work on *Long Beach*, but there was so much anti-*Long Beach* that you couldn't get it in motion.

Paul Stillwell: Well, and you would have been dealing with a 25-year-old hull as well.

---

[*] The Navy had four cruisers of the *Virginia* (CGN-38) class. The *Virginia* was commissioned in 1976 and decommissioned in 1994. The last ship of the class, *Arkansas* (CGN-41), was commissioned in 1980 and decommissioned in 1998.

Admiral Meyer: That'd be true. But my view was, in those days we still felt that—I kept asking the naval leaders, you know, what is our capital ship? What do we want for the capital ship? We took the destroyers and starting calling them DLGs, and then now we took them and we started calling them cruisers. So is that our capital ship? It's what it looks like, and it's what it'll look like where you and I are concerned. And certainly this administration isn't going to get very concerned about it one way or another as far as I can tell. As a matter of fact, there's just not much interest right now in shipbuilding or in construction of the Navy, I think the general viewpoint being, everything's satisfactory. Which it's not.

Of course, that's how you get in these ups and downs, is you can't—Jimmy Doyle and I spent ten years trying to establish a steadiness to the structure, and so that every year you built three on this end and you took three off that end, and over time that would give each ship a life of 25 or 30 years, which was about right. But without somebody to carry the water you just can't get the political process mentally adapted to that, nor the political process, for that matter.

Just look at the leaders right now in our DoD and in State. You've got to search a long way to find a disciple for shipbuilding, or for that matter for potent offensive armed forces. They don't believe in it, and I think the reason they don't believe in it is they've had too good a life. Life's been real good to most people of middle age here today, except those who have lost their boys someplace, or in some cases their girls.

Paul Stillwell: You mentioned last time that you set up a system of area commanders in various locations that wrote you a weekly letter, and you mentioned that that was something that Admiral Rickover had done. Were there other techniques of his that you adapted to the Aegis program?

Admiral Meyer: Well, I tell you, the biggest one I did, which I was predisposed to do when I decided I could get away with it because of Rickover, was to take charge. Now, my relationship with Levering Smith was somewhat different. He was not a very aggressive person. He was really an engineer, not particularly focused on building submarines, so he was able to adapt himself to whoever came along. But there's no doubt in my mind that effective shipbuilding requires effective leaders. Just no doubt in my mind on that. And it requires some with some experience.

We are in danger right now of falling back to where we've fallen several times in my life, and that is that shipbuilding is an administrative process, not an engineering process. Design and construction of warships is unique to warships. We're in danger of that. We believe that we can contract with just about anybody to do it, and we've convinced ourselves—without throwing rocks, not meant to throw rocks—that we can go up and take some little yard up in Wisconsin and take an industrial outfit, and of course they can build a ship. And we have let contracts to build many of them. These are the LCSs.[*] And we've lost no time at praising how great they are and how wonderful they are. And I say to myself, "Wait a minute, how did they get wonderful, and how great are they? Where did that come from, that no such things existed?" So, what will happen in seven or eight years is we'll have to take on one big program to get those ships armed and get them ready to fight, or we'll throw in the towel on them, you don't know which one.

It sounds trite, but what I learned from Rickover is you've got to take charge.

Paul Stillwell: Well, my understanding was that Levering Smith and Raborn and the Special Projects people deliberately built a wall so that Rickover would not get into their business, so that there were two different things, the shipbuilding and the weapons system.

Admiral Meyer: In one sense they could do so. And the reason is, those submarines were single-purpose ships. And I used to draw right on this blackboard right here, and I could see it when I was on active duty. There's three parts to that submarine, and you could put a bulkhead between them. The forward part was the SHAPM or the shipbuilding manager's part; the after part, the propulsion, was Rickover's part; and the middle part, the weapons, were SP's part, and they damn near have an infinite impedance between the three of them.

---

[*] The monohull littoral combat ship is the *Freedom* (LCS-1), built at Marinette, Marine, Marinette, Wisconsin. The keel for LCS-1 was laid 2 June 2005, the hull launched 23 September 2006, and the ship commissioned 8 November 2008

And they could make it work, in my view, on several counts. One is, they had a lot of money. They had a lot of money. They could cover a lot of mistakes. And in that era there were a lot of mistakes to be covered, a lot of them. Whether they'll ever get published beats the hell out of me, and I'm not qualified to write on them.

Secondly, they had national priority, so they had money. They didn't have any problem fighting for money.

Thirdly, they had a core of the Navy, namely the submariners, that they could draw on, and they had Rickover behind them. The submarine force without Rickover was bona-fide-ly the silent service; it was a nothing. I remember these admirals all being born in that era. That's when the 39-, 40-, 42-year-old admirals were christened, because we've got to be fair, we've got to be fair in promotions, and so we ended up promoting an awful lot of them, who in my day wouldn't even have had their command yet.

So did they all work out? I don't believe they all worked out at all. But do we ever assess that? I don't think so. I'm not even sure historians are capable of it, not in any detail. I tell you, we got a mess of them ordered into what is now the Naval Sea Systems Command, materiel establishment, because the operating Navy didn't have any place for them. I didn't think they could cut it. Good technicians. Their record says as submariners they performed that task quite well, and they managed to create the image that being a submariner is very hard indeed. And, God love them, they created it and they sustained it. I wonder how hard it really is. God, the Navy spent a lot of money on them, taking care of them, looking after families, creature comforts in ships. I make observations about them; I don't criticize them. I say God love them.

And, frankly, I tried some of that stuff in these Aegis ships. I had to upgrade them, and I had to fight for the dollars, but I fought and argued for better living conditions and a better social life in these ships, certainly far better than I had in the 20 years I sailed.

Paul Stillwell: On the *Ticonderoga*, what do you remember about the completion of the ship, and then the trials as she got into operations?

Admiral Meyer: When?

Paul Stillwell: She was commissioned in '83.

Admiral Meyer: '83, right.

Paul Stillwell: I'm interested in your recollections of the first operations and the trials she went through.*

Admiral Meyer: I had created something called the "Milestones of Eight," which was to be the proofing of these ships. And I generally got agreement out of people, and I particularly got it out of Doyle and those kind. The eighth milestone was the first deployment. And my schema—and it's really from my experience—was, okay, the project will keep custody of that ship, we'll take her through construction, we'll put her through shakedown, put her through her trials, and, *and*, we'll accompany her on her first cruise, and we will see that we will be a full-service outfit. That was my idea.

Well, you can imagine that the crusty shipbuilders weren't in favor of that at all. And, interesting enough, neither was the rest of the Navy. They thought it was just a waste of money. But they could spend the rest of their life bitching about what was wrong in the ships, but they wouldn't authorize you to, literally, spend your time trying to chase the gremlins out of the ship. We think that somehow a computer can do all this designing.

One of the things I got thrown at me many, many times in those years was, well, the automobile industry doesn't have any problems with that. They don't have any troubles. Well, of course, that's BS; they've got troubles running out their ears. Second of all, I believe when they only sell three cars a year they'd have troubles, and a lot of them. Third of all, the complexity of a warship doesn't even approximate the complexity of the design or the building of an automobile. So I don't put up with that nonsense. I don't sign up to it.

Early on I spent some time looking at the automobile industry, and frankly I decided I just wasn't going to learn anything there. It was just going to burn up my time because their objective was completely different than mine.

---

* Sea trials for the *Ticonderoga* were in May, August, and November of 1982.

I created these milestones. Milestone Eight was the certification on my part that the ship was ready for war. And it was my view that the best way to find out if she's ready for war is send her on a cruise.

Now, when I was a JO, and it was true we were building very few ships—*Forrest Sherman*, *John Paul Jones*, and the DLs—so there were just a handful, and they were generally under the custody of the type commander but more specifically DesLant. And recall I had a tour on DesLant in the late '50s and I learned a lot. Usually those ships were built, the ones I remember best, were built at Bath, sent to Boston for what was called fitting out, where they might spend a year or longer getting fitted out at the Boston Navy Yard. And then they'd sail to Newport, would be their beginning homeport. Virtually no schools. Of course, the production run was not either—you had to be a pretty good thinker to realize you had to have training and schools when you're only doing two or three ships a year. You had to do a lot of thinking about that.

Paul Stillwell: Did you have any hand in picking Captain Guilbault as first skipper of the *Ticonderoga*?[*]

Admiral Meyer: I did, but it was more related to Jim Doyle than it was to me, although he and I discussed it at great length. We talked at great length about it.

Paul Stillwell: What factors led to his selection?

Admiral Meyer: Well, they weren't necessarily the right ones. Actually, Doyle knew Guilbault pretty well. I think he sailed with him. I'm trying to think whether he sailed with him or not. Doyle had sailed in *Bainbridge*.[†] I can't remember. And Guilbault served a tour in OpNav, and his performance was not that remarkable. As a matter of fact, he was just the kind of officer, frankly, that I don't like in OpNav, or for that matter do I like in headquarters, because all they're prepared to do is bitch about what *you're*

---

[*] Captain Roland G. Guilbault, USN, commanded the guided missile cruiser *Ticonderoga* (CG-47) from the ship's commissioning on 22 January 1983 to 19 January 1985.
[†] Captain James H. Doyle Jr., USN, commanded the guided missile frigate *Bainbridge* (DLGN-25) from 17 December 1966 to 30 August 1970. Guilbault had been in the commissioning crew of the *Bainbridge*.

doing. No one's prepared to pick up a shovel and do something. And so that's one of the reasons, I think, that I got so alienated, a big reason, because I finally learned to make it perfectly clear, "The day you came to me is the day you're going to work for me, and you're going to do it the Navy way. It's not going to be arbitrary, but we're going to do it correctly and we're not going to put schemes into effect that are unproven. We're not going to do that."

Look right now what we're doing with these schemes with Lockheed and others in building these LCSs. We're double-crewing them, do them in a shipyard with zero experience. I don't know how much money we're throwing at making infrastructures. Neither am I aware of any admiral who's got any damned experience whatsoever associated with that kind of undertaking in those ships. Now, you think that's all going to work out okay? I don't think it's going to work out okay. Do you think it'll ever become a big issue? No. Some historian may pick up on it. Your grandson may pick up on it or someone like that who's doing the requisite research, and say, "Wait a minute, isn't there something missing here? Is there something wrong with this approach?"

I tell you another thing about shipbuilding. As a matter of fact this is true even of weaponry. I founded the Aegis project, as you know...

Paul Stillwell: Yes.

Admiral Meyer: ...when I was assigned in December 1969, and I was there the next 13 years when Secretary Lehman fired me without even the courtesy of "Good job," or anything else. That was a contrast to the courtesies I got from people who in the main are dead now. I mentioned earlier, for example, Admiral Jack Williams, who was a submariner.[*]

Paul Stillwell: Chief of Naval Material at one point.

---

[*] Admiral John G. Williams, Jr., USN, served as Chief of Naval Material, 1 July 1981 to 31 July 1983.

Admiral Meyer: Exactly, the Chief of Naval Material. What a leader. I never knew him before. What a wonderful person, a really, really good, thoughtful leader and person. And he always worried about whether the materiel establishment was trying to help me.

Paul Stillwell: Well, you said that part of your charter with *Ticonderoga* was certifying her as ready for war. What was involved in that process?

Admiral Meyer: I'm the one that insisted for the first time that proofing and firing of weapons had to be part of it, and part of the trials. Of course, the institution was aghast to think that we could have trials that would occur in three different places, and not all done in one place and one thing. They couldn't conjure up the fact that we might fire missiles there and guns there and do fleet exercises there as part of it.

You're good at this, so you can probably figure out what year this was. We finally got her shaped up, and part of my check-off was, as I say, my acceptance on her was to go through a deployment.[*] Guilbault had made arrangements, and I had agreed with him and ratified them, that she would make a stop—we were going to send her to the Mediterranean, and she'd make a stop at Portsmouth, because one of his English friends, they had agreed to have her make a show stop. As happened, you know the kinds of things, of course war broke out while she was involved in that, so she no more than got to Portsmouth the second day—she had broken off from the task force she was with to go. She was called into the Mediterranean, pulled right up on the line at Lebanon, and that was the incident that occurred when Lieutenant Goodman was shot down.[†]

So she drove up on that line. She was in the *Independence* battle group, I think. The ship tracked that airplane in defilade all the way down to the ground. They dead reckoned the whole one-third, or whatever it was, of her trajectory, but they knew where she was just like that. The Sixth Fleet people couldn't believe it. They couldn't believe it, but they couldn't disprove it either. Hundreds of people boarded the ship to see what

---

[*] The *Ticonderoga*'s first deployment to the Sixth Fleet in the Mediterranean began in October 1983.
[†] On 4 December 1983, the aircraft carriers *Independence* (CV-62) and *John F. Kennedy* (CV-67) launched a 28-plane strike against Syrian antiaircraft positions in Lebanon. A-7 and A-6 attack planes were shot down. The pilot of the A-7 was rescued. The A-6 pilot, Lieutenant Mark A. Lange, USN, was killed; his bombardier/-navigator, Lieutenant Mark O. Goodman, Jr., USN, was captured. Goodman was released early in 1984.

the radar was and what it was doing and what the pictures were. They couldn't believe it. That really turned Aegis around.

Paul Stillwell: The battle group commander was Jerry Tuttle, who has a lot of experience and knowledge in electronics, so that would tie in.[*]

Admiral Meyer: You know, that was the last time we ever had any trouble at getting Aegis ships. Except we had her loaded with all the SM-2 ammunition we had. Watkins, I believe, was the CNO.

Paul Stillwell: Yes, he was.

Admiral Meyer: Yeah, you're right. She had gotten in a fight and gotten in an argument. She came out of the Med, she was diverted to the Caribbean, to Puerto Rico, and on Good Friday she unloaded her magazine. We had, almost overnight, assembled every target we had out of Point Mugu and out of Puerto Rico, because the CNO had somehow gotten himself backed into this goddamn turkey shoot. So it's going to prove that it couldn't cut it. Now, mind you, they'd just come out of the Med and had this experience. They were all whipped up, and here they were headed home for leave, for holiday leave, and diverted. [Snap] Diverted like that. They drove up on the line, and it wasn't long till they came home because they took out every target that came.[†] Cleaned the goddamn sky. Couldn't conduct any operations the rest of the year.

    Well, that just kind of wore the whole process down. The whole process, after that, lost interest in attacking Aegis. And so the next thing you knew we had a winner. We had to get rid of that guy Meyer, though. It's still not clear why, but we did.

Paul Stillwell: Did you ever get any explanation? You're shaking your head no.

---

[*] Rear Admiral Jerry O. Tuttle, USN, served as Commander Carrier Group Two from April 1983 to August 1984. He was concurrently Commander Task Force 60, the Sixth Fleet Battle Force. During this operation he was embarked in the aircraft carrier *John F. Kennedy* (CV-67).
[†] In April 1984 the *Ticonderoga* had a successful firepower demonstration to complete her operational evaluation.

Admiral Meyer: Right, I'm shaking my head no. I doubt I ever will.[*] Matter of fact, the person involved may be so ignorant that he doesn't even understand what he did.

Paul Stillwell: By that do you mean Lehman?[†]

Admiral Meyer: Yeah. He's so power-mad, but that's what happens when you give inept people a lot of power. I often think today I'd like to march his ass right into my office and look at those ball caps.

I set out to try to change things with the Aegis fleet. And it's true that God was with me, because I always say, "God is good." The reason I could change it is the Aegis destroyer became a capital ship, and ironically it was something that Arleigh Burke couldn't stand. He couldn't stand the thought of that ship being a capital ship and not being a small boy. So I believe I personally had a great deal of effect on the profiles not only of the officers but also the petty officers that went into that ship.

Despite the success of Aegis, I was fired by John Lehman, who amongst other things knew so much more about ship design and shipbuilding than I knew, and he told me so.[‡]

My downfall consisted of a couple petty things but one significant thing. The significant thing, my downfall, was he and I got in a disagreement on the design of the destroyer.[§] I thought that I would win this hands down. I was doomed to discover how dumb I really am, just like my dad said, because I could not imagine after all my sailing days and the experience I had in the modernization in the Terrier fleet and such, and then the first fire control officer in *Galveston*, which was the first Talos cruiser, I couldn't believe that there was any officer who thought that a warship didn't need a helicopter. I mean, I had grown up with all that experience.

---

[*] Though he said in this interview that he did not know why he was relieved in 1983 as Aegis program manager, Admiral Meyer had offered some speculation in a previous interview. That section from the earlier interview has been inserted here for the sake of continuity.

[†] John F. Lehman Jr., served as Secretary of the Navy from 5 February 1981 to 10 April 1987.

[‡] On 1 September 1983, Rear Admiral Donald P. Roane, USN, relieved Admiral Meyer as Aegis Shipbuilding project manager.

[§] This is a reference to the *Arleigh Burke* (DDG-51) class of Aegis destroyers. The first ship of the class was commissioned 4 July 1991.

I was surrounded in a number of people who I thought had similar experience. They were officers at the OpDep level, specifically OP-03 and others not unlike him.[*] And when it came to determine the number—I've never forgotten this day; I'm adrift here a minute, but I've never forgotten it. We were at a meeting over there in the infamous PEC, Program Evaluation Center, in those days had charts hanging all over. And we'd had a pretty stormy meeting with the Secretary as the focal point and all the sundry admirals. I was the only person who was what you'd call a working stiff. I was a flag officer at the time. I was a flag officer, and they all seemed to have forgotten that. But I was also the project manager, and I'd had my views presented at that long table in the PEC, and Lehman was sitting down at the end receiving them.

After they finished, they went into discussion with about, I don't know, eight or ten senior people left. I couldn't believe the breakdown of senior officers. I thought I was a senior officer. I couldn't believe their breakdown. "Yes, sir, Mr. Secretary, what you say there makes a lot of sense." "Yes, sir." "Yes, sir, Mr. Secretary, maybe it ought to be done that way." "Yes, sir, we can do it that way." When they finished, that destroyer was stripped.

Lehman said, "Well, I don't think it needs a helicopter."

"Well, you're right. We can get helicopters from other places."

I've never forgotten that pathetic day. It was really hard on me. From then on I knew my days were numbered someplace, because I discovered that I couldn't trust my brothers. I thought they were sailors, and I thought what I was doing was what I thought was for the good of sailors. And I couldn't believe how they would break down at that level, but they did.

Why did it happen? Well, there are a number of things you never get too old for. One is you never get too old to fall in love. Another is you never get too old to be stunned by people's opinions or attitudes that you thought you knew for all those years. I can't say that I have actually gotten over it yet. Now, there are a lot of officers feel sorry for me. There are a lot of them running around with a—I don't know that it's a guilt complex, but I've never talked to any of them about it. But what it says to me from all of

---

[*] Vice Admiral Robert L. Walters, USN, served as Deputy Chief of Naval Operations (Surface Warfare) from June 1981 to September 1984.

them—quite a number of them were promoted to vice admirals. What it says to me is they all feel guilty. Well, I'll be damned if I'm going to grant them absolution. I ain't going to go off and argue with them. I'm not going to put them to death. But neither am I going to grant them absolution.

So where did we get to? We got to the seventh ship. All of a sudden we discovered we had no airplane on the ship! All of a sudden the goddamned ship's got to be rebuilt! All of a sudden we've got to spend hundreds of millions of dollars redoing the ship! Well, we didn't even yet get to a doghouse for the airplane. We had to yet do that in another step, of millions of dollars! For which no political appointee is held accountable except by historians.

Paul Stillwell: Roger.

Admiral Meyer: That's what you are.

Paul Stillwell: Yes, sir.

Admiral Meyer: And it turns out, as I'm sure you appreciate, that it doesn't matter a rat's toenail what historians think, because most of the people involved are in the graveyard, and the harm and the damage they did will be of only passing academic interest. We will say sometimes, well, we rediscovered that lesson. Did we? We don't rediscover the lessons. What we choose to do is ignore them in the first place.

Right now—you know, you ain't got time to do this today, but I can talk to you for three days on shipbuilding, maybe longer, because I'm telling you flat-ass, you don't know anybody alive that knows more about shipbuilding than I know.

Paul Stillwell: So I've come to the right place.

Admiral Meyer: Yeah, you've come to the right place. You don't know anybody. I've had more experience than anybody you can mention that's alive. And if you can find someone active in that business you can't find them except the three or four that I have in my little team down here, working on the Meyer 2 study.

I told Delores Etter, a longstanding friend of mine, the first day she moved into office, "Delores, I'm giving you a piece of advice, and I won't give it to you again," and I didn't.[*] "What will bring you down is shipbuilding, and it will bring you down because everyone is an authority on that subject without any know-how or experience. And it doesn't matter whether they're military, civil, or political." All humans are regularized in that sense.

I don't know why that is. I don't know why it's that way in shipbuilding, but it is. And yet shipbuilding's the whole heart of our Navy. There is no Navy without ships. It's the whole heart of our Navy. And you'd think that we would be concerned as hell out of our graduate school about how we're teaching and raising officers. Instead we're busy as hell teaching them national security and other socially acceptable things, which are important in their context and their compartment. It isn't that they're unimportant, it is that *they* don't make a navy. Ships are what make a navy. Without ships there is no navy. Why do we say we're the greatest navy in the world? Why doesn't Sri Lanka declare itself as the greatest navy in the world? Well, it's very simple; they have no ships.

Why are the Japanese so admiring of us? One is their ancestry, and the other is seeing us in action, that they understand they're not a great nation if they don't have a great navy. They understand that. And I've got to tell—maybe it's happened to you, I don't know, but I've got to tell you if you've had any of my experiences, it brings tears to your eyes to watch the Japanese in action. You'd swear to God if you closed your eyes you're seeing the American bluejacket, they emulate you so much. They do their darnedest to be just like us. It's incredible that in, I'd say I guess two generations, depending on how you count, in two generations we've turned that all around in their behavior pattern. As a matter of fact, may have turned it around so much that we have difficulty getting them to face their obligations as a great nation and as a great leader.

---

[*] Delores M. Etter served as Deputy Under Secretary of Defense for Science and Technology from 1998 to 2001 and as Assistant Secretary of the Navy (Research, Development and Acquisitions) from 2005 to 2007.

But I think back to that era. I don't know how to document that piece. There's a couple reasons why I don't know. One is, I go unstable when I start talking about it very long. Second is, there is no one else who has undergone the specific experience or suffering which I personally underwent.

I think I told you about the Secretary of the Navy Winter looking at those Aegis ball caps in my office.[*]

Paul Stillwell: I think so.

Admiral Meyer: And how that awed him. Lehman doesn't have the insight to even grasp it. Only thing I ever saw in Lehman was Lehman. He sure had a great ability to fool people that weren't around him very long.

I think I told you a story about him. See, after he had had me removed, it came time we were going to commission *Yorktown*.[†] And arrangements had been made that we let Secretary Lehman seize the initiative. She would be commissioned in Yorktown at that little teensy pier, which you have to be very, very careful how you load the ship of *Yorktown*'s size to bring her in to the pier because there ain't much water. But Miss Mary, Mary and Nick's Restaurant, was the sponsor of *Yorktown*.[‡] This was a Lehman innovation. And so that's how it all came about, and all the officers in those years—I don't know whether it is today, but in those years an officer or a sailor could never pay for a meal in Nick's Restaurant in Yorktown, never. Always free, whatever they wanted. She loved sailors and Aegis people.[§]

So I was supposed to be on the platform on the ship, even though I had now been fired. What happened is that July 4, of course, was hotter than hell. I sat down on the front row right underneath the platform. I sat down in the audience. I sat alongside Mrs. Lehman. Well, wait a minute, I sat alongside her kid, because she had expectations that I wasn't about to do, and that was look after one of her kids. So I put up with her kids that

---

[*] Donald C. Winter served as Secretary of the Navy from 3 January 2006 to 13 March 2009. He was Secretary at the time of this interview.
[†] The second Aegis cruiser, USS *Yorktown* (CG-48) was commissioned 4 July 1984.
[‡] The sponsor was Mary Mathews, co-owner of Nick's Seafood Pavilion in Yorktown.
[§] Mary Mathews died in September 1998. Hurricane Isabel in 2003 damaged the restaurant, which was subsequently demolished.

whole ceremony, and they went through it. I don't know what that officer—I think you probably know him, the officer who was in command. One of the Andersons.* At that time I had three Andersons. Once I had four Andersons in the project. But he decided he was going to cater to the Secretary, so that's why I was sitting down with the audience. It's the only Aegis ship I've ever, ever sat in the audience in her commissioning. I've been present at all commissionings, and that's the only one that I wasn't on the platform. Thank you, John Lehman.

So I look upon that, frankly, Paul, as, in the breast I know what I did. You can conduct a poll of, well, wait a minute, who's John Lehman? What'd he do? What has he done for our Navy? You can't find anybody who will even know that, or know the man's name, because he didn't leave the Navy anything. Well, I can truthfully say that he left my shipbuilding program, because it was the only one that existed when he took office. He's a great thief. And when he saw that we had a shipbuilding plan—and by the way, that shipbuilding plan came out of some of the men that you've seen here in my war room down here right now; they were very young then and so was I, but we were in eclipse and that's what we worked on that winter was the shipbuilding plan, because we figured that rescue would come, we just didn't know where or how. It came from John Lehman. In his desire to be a big shot he went over and talked to Reagan. And, of course, I'm fabricating this conversation. But in the process convinced Reagan that his naval initiative ought to be to build the Aegis fleet. That pushed it over the hump. Never again, never again was the fleet in question. We're still building it today. To me that's just amazing.

Paul Stillwell: Did you ever talk to Secretary Lehman after the firing?

Admiral Meyer: Nope. He never bothered. One of the ships we commissioned—I thought it was in Norfolk and I can't remember now, but the CO concerned was pretty goddamned stupid anyhow, I think. He got Lehman to be his speaker, I don't know, half a dozen years ago. I sat right beside him on the platform. He spoke. All he ever did

---

* Captain Carl A. Anderson, USN, commanded the *Yorktown* from 4 July 1984 to 27 June 1986.

when he walked off was nod his head. I have been honored at every one of those commissionings by the other people involved, but not by John Lehman.

So there's a way to look at it. And it is, if you set your mind that you're going to do something and you concentrate on it hard enough, you get it done. Now, if it was a great thing, you'll leave a great thing. If it wasn't a great thing, you won't leave a great thing. I happen to think that my associates and myself rebuilt our Navy. Today our Navy is overpowering to whoever wants to take it on. And while we press forward to keep it modernized and to keep it updated, which I believe is an important thing to do, it nevertheless can today, I believe with extraordinary confidence, outfight any navy in the world and any navy anticipated. I don't believe there will be a navy for a long time that will challenge the U.S. Navy.

Because I think it was the Goodman shoot-down, I don't know, but somehow from then on—and I knew the aviators of that era, particularly Bob Dunn and a couple of those guys like that who became good supporters and were good thinkers.* And so the attack carrier and the cruisers became a natural fit for mutual protection, and they became—I think that once the aviators understood the great strength of those cruisers I don't think they ever worried about their safety again in those attack carriers. They downloaded their fighters and they uploaded their attack planes, and I don't even know what the mix is today in an attack carrier. [Chuckle] There may be no standard mix, I don't know what it is.

Paul Stillwell: Well, they now have the dual-purpose planes that can do both, the F/A-18s.†

---

* Vice Admiral Robert F. Dunn, USN, served as Commander Naval Air Force Atlantic Fleet from 8 December 1983 to 23 December 1986. He later served as Deputy Chief of Naval Operations (Air Warfare) from 15 January 1987 to 25 May 1989. The title changed from Deputy to Chief to Assistant Chief on 1 October 1987. His oral history is in the Naval Institute collection.

† The F/A-18 Hornet, originally built by McDonnell Douglas, is a jet aircraft capable of both fighter and attack roles. It first entered operational service with VFA-125, a fleet readiness squadron, in May 1980. The F/A-18C model has a wingspan of 37 feet, 6 inches; length, 56 feet; gross weight of 36,710 pounds in the fighter version and 49,224 pounds in the attack version; top speed of 1,190 miles per hour. It replaced the F-4 Phantom and A-7 Corsair in fleet units.

Admiral Meyer: Right. Meaning they can't do either one very well. [Laughter] That's what that means. You know how short-legged the F/A-18 is.

Paul Stillwell: Yes.

Admiral Meyer: And it can do, like you say, both good things, as long as you take the short leg. Can we get away with it? Well, we are. We've kept the peace for a long time. Will the F-35 provide the substitute?[*] I don't know. I don't even know what its status is today; I haven't kept up with it too well.

Paul Stillwell: I don't either. But going back to the trials and certification, I'm presuming that you had a PMS-400 representative, or more than one, on board the *Ticonderoga*.

Admiral Meyer: Oh, I wouldn't have it any other way. I wouldn't have it any other way. The early ships I sent all hands. One reason was that I can't stand having people in the project that don't know their product, so I made them go. I'm the one that pioneered women at sea. As a matter of fact, you can go ask my spouse, Anna Mae, right now. She's one of the first women that ever went to sea, and it's because back in my heyday in *Norton Sound* she and Adelaide Madsen, I was able to get authority to have them go to sea for a firing. She was selected up at Moorestown, and Adelaide Madsen was in the project for me, a civil servant.[†] She was selected in the project, and those were the two that went to witness a firing, the first ones that ever saw a firing, aboard *Norton Sound*. So I pioneered that kind of thing for them because I'm a strong believer of that. Well, that's a manifestation of your leadership, and I've sent a lot of women to sea in those days. For example, I sent a number out of the production places—Moorestown and Raytheon and such—and I had them elect their own. They generally had an election of who would get to go. So I have gewgaws around here someplace or at home of all those

---

[*] The F-35 Lightning II joint strike fighter is under development as a stealth aircraft.
[†] Adelaide M. Madsen was a senior systems analyst and special assistant to Meyer in his role as project manager for Aegis.

women, all gave me a little thing, sewed me a little something, or give me a little pin thing or something because it just awed them.

Paul Stillwell: What kind of reports were you getting back from your representatives as the *Ticonderoga* was going through these trials?

Admiral Meyer: Well, in a way the trial was almost an afterthought, because we had done the workup and the preparations so well. I mean that they all just kind of merged in with each other. And we had developed extraordinarily good relationships with the OpTEvFors, to get over the goddamn hostility. Because I went down to Norfolk and I talked—I can't even remember who was in command at the time, and I had said that, "I'm not going to run a hostile operation. I'm not going to have it. If you want to help me, I'd really appreciate it. If you don't want to help, then you can just get the hell out of the way."

I think he's an aviator, and he said, "That's fair enough," and that's what he did. And no longer, no longer are our data suspect. I'm not sure the data before me on any of the programs are suspect, I don't know. I'm sure there was some, but a lot of it was made up, too. Data are data, and I went on a crusade in that era. I don't care who collects the data; it's immaterial who collects it, because data are data. They're facts. It's immaterial how it's collected or who collected it, except for, usually, the timing marks, because dynamic data needs timing marks on it for you to be able to read it. So by the end of Tico, OpTEvFor got so that they just took whatever we gave them because they trusted us.

Paul Stillwell: Did they have that kind of credibility?

Admiral Meyer: Right. And never can I recall since then, never has there been a single incident in OpTEvFor, which up till then was goddamn near hostile. People like Eddie

Carter and those who commanded just created hostility throughout our Navy, destructive hostility.*

Paul Stillwell: One of the concerns that came out in the media at the time was that the *Ticonderoga* had stability problems, or top-heaviness. How would you address that?

Admiral Meyer: Well, I think I surprise people. People underrate me, and have underrated me. The dumber people are, the more careful you've got to be with them. So when those started coming up, I started asking them, "Well, where's your data? What do you base it on? What is your data?" And invariably they had to back down. Invariably they were dealing in hearsay. They were just running around.

And the other thing I did, I never had a meeting in that project in the 13 years that I was in it, that OpTEvFor and InSurv was not welcome to attend. Never. I had the kind of relations, actually, with the officers both in InSurv and in OpTEvFor that they always had an officer there. Occasionally a civilian. And it was on my account that they had one there. Because I had made it clear to them in the beginning that I don't deal in hearsay. If I'm doing engineering here, engineering's not a hearsay thing. What are the data?

We had a saying that we used in those days, and a fellow by the name of Ralph Hawes, my friend and associate, a retired president and vice president from General Dynamics, and grew up with me in missilery, is: "In this business you've got to look at all the data all the time." Now that sounds trite. It doesn't sound like any big deal. But that usually isn't what happens. Matter of fact, OpTEvFor is even guilty of that, until I had taught them differently. And certainly InSurv would do these fly-bys and never— you know, they'd just pick some fly-by-night piece of data they picked up on deck someplace and never bother to look at it. Well, I never maintained we were perfect, but what I did maintain is we were honest. And that's the way I had expected to be treated, is to be treated honestly. And I want to see what you base your comments on. What are they based on? Well, of course, they'd usually get put down.

---

* Rear Admiral Edward W. Carter III, USN, became Commander Operational Test and Evaluation Force in August 1982.

Hearsay is a powerful thing. It's our form of government. Our whole congressional structure operates on hearsay. So I just sit there at the table and take data and take data and take data and take data till you can get to the bottom of it. And pretty soon people do their homework.

Paul Stillwell: Did you have any concerns about the stability?

Admiral Meyer: Of the ship? Of course I do. How can you be a shipbuilder and not be concerned about the stability? That's not an analytical thing.

Paul Stillwell: But did you think those charges were unfair?

Admiral Meyer: Totally. They were created by opponents, the whispering campaign.

Paul Stillwell: For political reasons?

Admiral Meyer: And people missing an opportunity to keep their mouth shut. I always told my people all those years, and I've always told auditors, visitors, inquirers, "You can go anyplace in my project you want to go. You can talk to anybody you want to talk to. But you must go through the front door. If you don't go through the project manager, you're not welcome. And I will be with you or I won't be with you. If you don't want me, say so. But I will not have sneaking around and that kind of carrying-on." Well, after a couple times I busted that. It didn't take me more than a year for people to get that goddamn message.

Paul Stillwell: Who was trying to sneak around?

Admiral Meyer: Well, one of them that was related to a lot of them were the congressional people. And you know some of them. And one in that era was one of my good friends was Tony Battista. I've known Tony Battista a long time, came out of Dahlgren. And he's one of these guys that can take three letters out of the alphabet and create a whole alphabet. Well, pretty soon he got so he never called me to testify unless he wanted to show something off. I don't know what Tony does today besides work on old cars, but I made him a believer. I finally got him convinced, I think, because I'd known him a long time, that he didn't have to behave that way.

But the seven capital sins are always working. They're always operable. So you've always got greed, lust, jealousy, and those sins are always functional. And you're often dealing in the haves and have-nots. And so you have to learn to put up with that. Now, I tried to keep my area commanders informed. I trusted them. I authorized them to speak for me. And if they said something that they weren't sure of, they'd better damn well get their skirt cleaned up real quick, because I wasn't about to let people come into the middle of my project and start busting it open. And that's a popular habit in this town, it was in the era. Today people got so they don't even care anymore. They don't care anymore as far as I can tell. Nobody cares about overruns anymore. They don't care about overruns in dollars, they don't care about overruns in schedules. Just, nobody cares. And I care. It's intolerant to me. I won't accept it, and I didn't accept it. If I'm going to operate out of budget, I want to know I'm operating out of budget, and I ain't going to do it secretively. Because how in the hell are you going to make up a billion-dollar budget to build a warship that you don't have the foggiest idea what it is you're going to do in it yet?

(Interruption for change of tape)

Admiral Meyer: Will you be there for the commissioning?

Paul Stillwell: When will that be?

Admiral Meyer: It'll be in October.

Paul Stillwell: Well, I hope so.

Admiral Meyer: It'll be Philadelphia. The date's not yet set.*

Paul Stillwell: Well, we were talking about the critics of Aegis and *Ticonderoga*. Did you have any speculation on what the motives were, what people had to gain by that?

Admiral Meyer: Well, I was transferred to the "Cat-licker" school in the fifth grade when we moved from the gumbo to clay country.

Paul Stillwell: And what's the tie between your Catholic education and the Aegis program?

Admiral Meyer: Well, I believe the tie was in leadership. The Aegis presented, I guess you'd say the opportunity to not only be a leader but to be a creative leader. Programs were in different states of undress all over the place. Project management was ill-y thought of. And Aegis was right up there because it was too big, too expensive, too complicated, and it'd never make it. I could wear you out from now till supper on the downfalls of Aegis and how we didn't need it. Today I think of that often.

Paul Stillwell: Was this by people who thought the money should be better spent elsewhere?

Admiral Meyer: Or they should have a hand in it, which is why I referred to the seven capital sins. If you take the seven capital sins and the Ten Commandments as a group, in one little hand you can pretty well sum up all the evil side of the human race. Jealousy was always a strong one, no matter what people say. I mean, jealousy starts before you ever go to school. It starts before you can even talk, because jealousy sets in naturally with a baby. And greed. All those sins set in because all a baby wants is me. Me, me, me, me, me, me, me. So somehow—I don't know how that got imbued in me.

---

* USS *Wayne E. Meyer* (DDG-108) was commissioned at Penn's Landing in Philadelphia 10 October 2009. Sadly, Admiral Meyer did not live long enough to attend. He died the previous month, 1 September.

Paul Stillwell: Moving back to Aegis, what do you remember about the transition from the traditional twin-armed launcher to vertical launch systems?

Admiral Meyer: Well, a couple things are stuck on me that I never talk about anymore, and I never realized at the time. There'd have been no vertical launcher without me. I'm the one that generated the launcher. Now, no one has ever given me the credit on it. As a matter of fact, they deliberately and determinedly went off and got nomenclature for that launcher so to be totally unrelated and unidentified to Aegis, and yet its only application was Aegis. But by then I got so I didn't worry about it, one of the reasons being is it had no home unless it got me for a home. And in fact it had to undergo a good deal of reengineering and design after I inherited it.

I think I mentioned to you once that you can get all the programs you want that don't have any money, and all the authority you want for things that have no money. So the new launcher—my objection to that launcher in the beginning was it was not going through engineering, and therefore I refused to adapt it into Aegis. And so it was decided I hated the launcher and that I was against it, and no one would take my word. And the reason was because I didn't invent it, that was their reason, which is totally untrue.

Paul Stillwell: Who did invent it?

Admiral Meyer: That's the problem. A couple people sat down at a table someplace and started fiddling-ass around and went back on a bench and started putting it together out at General Dynamics Pomona without any fundamental engineering in it. That was the problem. And in the meantime the Navy had no school for the rail launchers, the Mark 26 launchers; I had to invent one. Mark 26 was given to me as an Aegis element. Well, it turned out then I had to go get money and I had to go get an engineering structure and create a school. I created a school up in Minneapolis to send the fire controlmen to school, gunner's mates actually, to understand the launcher.

It finally turned out that OpTEvFor got their foot in the way and ruled that unless the vertical launcher went through proper operational testing it was a no-go. No one knew how to do that because they had no money. So I stepped forward and I listed the conditions that were necessary for me to take it over and bail it out. That's how I got the launcher.

Paul Stillwell: What were your conditions?

Admiral Meyer: The biggest one is it had to be under me. I wasn't about to have it floating around someplace else. Because the geniuses of the launcher were saying, "Oh, well, wait a minute, it doesn't have to be identified, that has no relation." You know, there's infinite impedance; well, of course it's not. Now, you can fire other kinds of missiles out of that launcher that don't require that close identity, because the matching impedance is not that important. For example, Tomahawks. The goddamn engineering in the Tomahawk and the launcher is all in its can, so if the can fits in the launcher, fine, you don't have a problem with it. I mean, we've fired them off of the decks of ships, we've fired them off all kinds of places, the Tomahawks.

So those things have long since been forgotten. The managers, after the family manager, all came under me finally, because the biggest reason is they had no home, and I was an admiral and they were all captains so they, frankly, came to me because they knew if I would sign up to their product the product would make it. Because as I've told people repeatedly, why in the hell do we want to sign up to stuff we don't intend to use? I was fired 25 years ago by John Lehman, 1983—to this day there are officers, retired, civil servants not yet retired but they were just, you know, learners then, who remember me, recall me, talk to me, ask me about stuff. And what they will do is: "Admiral do you remember when that happened?" Of course, I don't remember and I'm not sure they do. I think it's, you know, a lot of second-orders things are brought up. But it nevertheless makes a man feel good.

And I had some of it last week. I looked around in that big conference room up there last week at Moorestown and I decided, well, I probably have been there longer than anybody in the entire room, including the company. There's no one in the company there when I started there in 1970. So believe that that continuity is key to a program and that experience is key to it, and only a few programs make it, really. Only a handful.

Paul Stillwell: What did you do to vertical launching system to develop it, once you got it into your organization?

Admiral Meyer: First thing I did is go get a goddamn budget established for it. So the first thing you've got to do is get a fundraising group and get that started. Then I got an engineering group and I said, "Okay, all right, we're going to do this launcher, guess what. We're going to take the launcher to sea."

"Well, you don't have to do that; it's all done." This launcher goes to sea. I'm not about to put it in a fleet of ships without adequate testing. I'm going to do that, said I'm going to do it in *Norton Sound*. "How we going to do that? Oh, it's going to cost a lot of money. Oh, how you going to do that?" Well, do you want it or not?

Norton Sound was home-ported at Port Hueneme, and I put together a team. I mean, I had, I tell you by then I had GS-15s and -14s that were so competent, and I had commanders and captains that were really competent. They really got competent. And I think they all, like others, had a lot of trouble at home because they were on the road all the time. But we put this group together and we just said, okay, we're going to do a launcher change-out. Now let that be our goal. Let's get on the blackboard and figure out what's got to be done to do that. "Well, you don't need that; that's all been done." No, it hasn't been done at all. A defined launcher didn't even exist. All that existed was a box. And Lockheed at Florida had fired a couple out of a box.

Paul Stillwell: What did you learn from the tests on *Norton Sound*?

Admiral Meyer: Well, I did something that couldn't be done. Okay, where are we going to build the ship with the first launcher at? Well, I said, aren't we going to build it in the Aegis yard? The only Aegis yard we had at that time was...

Paul Stillwell: Ingalls.

Admiral Meyer: Ingalls.* And our contractor is Lockheed Martin in Florida, whom I didn't know very well, but I'd not had very good luck with either, because they were not ordnance people. So why don't we send *Norton Sound* to Ingalls Shipyard to install the launcher? "Oh, she can go right down here at Long Beach. It can be done right down here at Long Beach. Don't have to move anybody, displace anybody."

I said, "I'll ask the question again—why don't we send her to Ingalls? And why don't we get people learning how to do it in *Norton Sound*? And that way we'll build a team, we'll finally get it done in Long Beach but we won't leave anything behind us either."

Well, they finally got over the shudder of it because it turned out—because I knew from the beginning I was going to pay for it if it was going to be done. There wasn't any of those yahoos going to pay for it. Matter of fact, my project made money on it, because they were so damned pleased. You know, bureaucracy is like everything else; it's just people. But they were so pleased that somebody else was going to take this responsibility and take it over that they'd do everything they could to help raise their share. Well, all I'd do is make their share 25% higher, put a markup on it, so we made a little money. And we taught the shipyard how to do it. We left an investment in the shipyard.

And some other interesting things happened in that trip. I'm the first one that took women in the Aegis program to sea.

Paul Stillwell: Well, you did mention that.

Admiral Meyer: Yeah, took them to sea in *Norton Sound*. And we had a number of black people in the ship. So I talked to Mr. Erb, he was the general manager down there, and the superintendent, and said, okay, we're going to do this. We've got this all approved. Now let's get a plan that we can make it work. We're bringing women in a combat ship, we're going to shut her down because she's not going to be active in the

---

* In the spring of 1981, a pre-production version of the vertical-launch system was installed aboard the test ship *Norton Sound* (AVM-1) at Ingalls Shipbuilding in Pascagoula, Mississippi.

shipyard. It's the first time it's been done down here. And then we've got a lot of black people in Pascagoula, Mississippi. That doesn't go over, necessarily, very good.

All right, so they put together teams, and they went to work on it. God, it was an incredible experience. They mobilized the town of Pascagoula to welcome the women and to welcome the crew from California. So for the three months they were down there they had a whole set of activities and programs and things—the city, the Navy, and Ingalls—for these people. We didn't have one single, solitary incident. Not one occurred. Now, was that accidental? Beats the hell out of me but I know it didn't happen, and I know it happens out of a lot of people. It worked out wonderfully.

And getting her installed. We sailed her from there, we sailed with the Ingalls people. We just sailed with already an integrated crew to take her to sea and start testing her and checking her out. Everybody was integrated; it wasn't some new outfit that came along or anything like that. And it really was an excellent experience. It was applied engineering at its best. And the people, once they made up their mind they were going to do it, it was incredible what they'd do. It was really something. It's a long sail around there from California for an old ship that at best makes 17 knots, mostly makes 13 knots. It's a long dragged-out—there's no air conditioning in the ship. None. Didn't have a single incident. None. Zero, swabo [phonetic]. The women loved it. They got to go someplace and do something. Never got taken advantage of. It all worked out quite well.

Paul Stillwell: What were the engineering aspects involved in that that you had to master?

Admiral Meyer: The biggest thing was the power and the physical fit. I had decreed that the launcher had to physically fit in the same place that the Mark 26 fit. Well, it didn't, so that had to be mastered. That sounds trivial. Well, they could master it in old *Norton Sound*, where you could cut a hole wherever the hell you wanted to cut a hole and stuff till you got a fit.

The electrical power, it turned out, was not all that challenging. It took a little more power, but it didn't take it in the big doses that the Mark 26 took it, so when you averaged it all out it took less power, because you're firing one rail out of this thing with all the rest of the stuff not moving. That Mark 26, she is a powerful monster, but goddamn you really get a surge out of her when she goes.

I always like it when people think it was a piece of cake after they're done. What that means is that they did good work; that's what it means. They did their homework. So they had their inspection teams, their acceptance teams, they knew how to do it the Aegis way. And they either do it that way or they ain't going to do it. And so the outsiders found out, and pretty soon you start finding that stuff being adapted throughout the Navy. If you go look at building ships up there in that little bitty shipyard, right now those LCSs, what you're going to find is a lot of Aegis procedures adapted from people who were learning them when they were very young. That ain't all good because they don't necessarily have this kind of bandwidth when they were learning before, but it's better than nothing.

Paul Stillwell: You're holding your hands three feet apart.

Admiral Meyer: Right. [Chuckle]

Paul Stillwell: How did the tests go in *Norton Sound* once you fired the missiles?

Admiral Meyer: You didn't even get a hiccup. Never got a misfire, not a thing. Never had a misfire, nothing. I think we had one operator error someplace where some fellow decided he knew more than his teachers. But it was as though the launcher had always been there. It's amazing. It's simply astounding.

Now, we have not had to carry atomic missiles in those launchers yet. That may have been very, very difficult. We designed the launchers so that there are modular in their design. There are six cell modules, with the thought that we would have to have nuclear capability. My guess is the day will come when they will have to have that, and whether it'll be a problem beats the hell out of me. But I remember what a hell of a job it was in a Mark 26, and before we put it into the cruisers I made us proof it in *Norton Sound* so we knew what the hell we were doing. I'm a big believer in proofing; I'm a strong believer in proofing. Because you just aren't smart enough to conjure up all the things that need to be conjured up for a complex undertaking, just not. And your organization is always kind of, not disheveled, but hardly ever do you have a very tightly knitted organization in shipbuilding or those kind of undertakings. You have people that cycle in and cycle out, cycle in and cycle out, and if you don't have a core group that's absolutely got their fingers on things you're searching for trouble. Then, if you let people get in an argument over, well, was that contractor or government, that's where you start coming to pieces. And I just declared all of it Aegis, and that was that. So the launcher became Aegis. And today when you talk to people they think of that launcher as the Aegis launcher, although we've got the launchers all over the place besides the Aegis ships, but they think of it as the Aegis launcher.

We did something I didn't agree with. We demanded that—this was after me—the launcher be competed. So we had Lockheed building it, we had Northern building it. And the reason was, "We're going to show those Northern Ordnance people, we're going to show them they didn't get their bid down." See, I was intolerant of that kind of thing in my day, but most programs are run that way. We bid them on what they cost, not on whether they're going to perform. Almost all of them, then, we get pissed off at the contractors because the contractors are trying to respond to what it is we want. Well, we get what we teach them; that's what we get. And that may be one of the reasons that the undertaking by Lockheed was so successful up in that little shipyard. I haven't seen any data, but from what I've read it was quite an impressive drill. However, I don't think there's a single piece of standard gear in that ship.

Paul Stillwell: You're talking about the LCS?

Admiral Meyer: Yes. Now, does that mean that standard gear is no longer important? I happen to believe that it is, but it may just be because I'm an old-timer. Because I remember how critical and important it was when I was a youngster. But it runs off of people today; they don't think about it.

An example are the consoles in Aegis. Bill Goodwin, the RCA Aegis manager, and I, after many, many sessions with our senior people, both civil servants and officers and industry, we decided that we would drive the design for the UYA-4 console, which was the console going into the DLGN-38 class and such, and that way we would drive the design that didn't fit us the way we wanted it fit but it would be a standard design. And what we would do is we'd just OrdAlt.* So we had what we called the Aegis OrdAlt that went on it, or the Aegis hat, which we added onto it so that it would. But it was common, it was common in parts, it was common in schools, it was common in the sailors. And so when the sailors saw one they started recognizing things that they had seen where they came from.

That's so important that we overlook and don't pay any attention to, how important commonality is. We forget that the statistical age is 20.6 in those ships. That's the statistical—and it never changes. And the captain in, bona-fide-ly the old man. And he's nominally, say, 38 or 39 years old. He may even be a couple years younger than that, and he is the old man. Well, it's easy to forget what the mechanism is that fights that gear when you do it all the time ashore, or say you're at Moorestown. It's easy to slip through your fingers. That's why I make people go out and sail on ships and get themselves refreshed, and be sure they come to understand what the heck it is. That's why I've kept that big unit at Moorestown. I'm surprised that it hasn't been under attack, frankly, the past three or four years because it's got quite a few people. It's got a commanding officer that's a captain, top-drawer engineering captain, up there at Moorestown. He's just like that with Orlando Carvalho, who is the general manager at Lockheed up there.

Paul Stillwell: You've got your two fingers right together.

Admiral Meyer: Right together. They're just like that the way they do things. Now, do you think they sit around and fight? No, they don't. They sit around and solve and resolve.

---

* OrdAlt – ordnance alteration.

Paul Stillwell: Well, Deborah would probably be happy if we'd end it on that note for today.*

Admiral Meyer: If you don't mind.

Paul Stillwell: All right, and I'll look forward to seeing you next week. Thank you.

---

* Deborah Geanuleas was Admiral Meyer's executive assistant in the company he ran at the time of the oral history interviews.

Interview Number 18 with Rear Admiral Wayne E. Meyer, U.S. Navy (Retired)
Place: Admiral Meyer's office in Crystal City, Arlington, Virginia
Date: Thursday, 12 March 2009

Paul Stillwell: Admiral, good afternoon. When we talked last time, you mentioned that you had a rare distinction in that two different wives of yours had christened ships, been sponsors. What we haven't really talked about was the passing of your first wife, and then how you came to get acquainted and to marry Anna Mae.[*]

Admiral Meyer: Well, the more I think about it, the more I think it's significant, and at the same time I just—again, I don't want to offend anybody, including their memories. But we put what sometimes is now referred to by the nickname USS Rancocas, which is CSEDS at Moorestown—put her in commission with Admiral Jimmy Doyle as the speaker, and my late wife was going to be the sponsor. We ran it as a ship ceremony. And Bill Goodwin's wife and my wife were going to be the cosponsors. Margaret, of course, had become an Aegis zealot, because it turned out that the whole second half of her life, just like mine, was Aegis, night and day, week after week after week. And if you are going to successfully run a big program, there's no solution except be on the road.

Paul Stillwell: So it sounds as if she was very supportive during that time.

Admiral Meyer: She was very supportive of me in the Navy. She was Irish, so there was some danger of anybody that picked on her husband which she disagreed with, because she had no compunctions about taking them under fire, and she'd get their ass hauled in, in her own Irish way, if they said something bad about him.

Paul Stillwell: Do you remember any examples of that?

---

[*] Margaret Garvey Meyer died in October 1992.

Admiral Meyer: I do, but I don't know whether I should bring them up. Of course, one big one is John Lehman.

Paul Stillwell: That's understandable

Admiral Meyer: Yeah. But I can get some more.

Let me deviate here a minute because I woke up thinking about this in the middle of the night. I may have mentioned this to you before. It had to do with Admiral Worth Bagley and the effect he had on me and what it meant to me. He carried a lot of Zumwalt's trash for him, and he defended Zumwalt quite well, I thought. And while I knew Worth off and on, and knew him casually, I never actually served with him except in Washington.

When I became the chief engineer out at Port Hueneme he, Worth Bagley, got himself ordered to command of *Canberra*.

Paul Stillwell: You did talk about that.

Admiral Meyer: Okay, popularly referred to as "Cranberry." Okay, I won't repeat it then. But it is a story that had significant impact on my whole behavior and my subsequent development of my life, was Worth Bagley. I often think of him, and yet I've never gotten in touch with him. But only last night I woke up again in the middle of the night thinking of him, and, by God, if he's able I'm going to want him to come to commissioning of the DDG-108 in October. And I told you, I believe, in that little tale that I kept on my blackboard in my office over there for several years that the first Aegis ship should be named Bagley, because Worth Bagley is the underground reason why we have a Navy. Now, I'm the reason except I didn't have the capacity or the capability or the pull, nor was I located properly, but Worth Bagley had such consummate faith in me, and it was genuine and Worth Bagley *did* have it. And as far as I know, he's never gotten any credit, he's never sought any credit, and never have I seen Worth do anything for personal credit. But he had a hell of an effect on our Navy, big effect, unsung effect. That story's over, then; let's move on. Where were we?

Paul Stillwell: Well, that raises a question: How did the name *Ticonderoga* get attached to the first Aegis ship?

Admiral Meyer: Well, I didn't have anything to do with it. It was a complete surprise to me. And I don't know that I can even clarify it today. But there was a movement by several outfits, associations, wanting to get the first name. The aircraft carrier *Ticonderoga*'s group was fairly active at that time.[*]

Paul Stillwell: This would be the group of former crew members of the aircraft carrier?

Admiral Meyer: It would be. The "Big T" Association was the name of it. It still is the Big T Association, except there is no Big T now, and they're having trouble getting themselves reborn with Aegis *Ticonderoga* being decommissioned and the carrier gone, so here they are, they're holding an empty sack. And the younger people, of course, have little interest in the thing. You've got to get a lot older as a vet before you start getting interested in that kind of stuff. So I don't know whether it'll revive itself after the cruiser Tico or not.

Paul Stillwell: Well then, back to Anna Mae. How did that relationship develop?

Admiral Meyer: I'd known her for a number of years. I had first met her early in Aegis because she worked in the presentations group. She was a young girl there. She had started at RCA in—I think she was 19. She had helped Bill Goodwin really capture the contract. And Bill Goodwin would not have any of his presentation work done except by Anna Mae. Every slide he ever used, every chart he ever used, Anna Mae had to do it and approve it. And she was a nit and a real pain in the ass and all the others, but the boss wanted it that way. And Goodwin finally willed her to me and said that I could employ her whatever way I needed, because Goodwin and I saw alike that a big program like this needs to keep itself sold.

---

[*] USS *Ticonderoga* (CV-14) was an *Essex*-class aircraft carrier, originally commissioned in 1944. She was eventually decommissioned in 1973 and sold in 1975 to be scrapped.

Paul Stillwell: Was she then living in New Jersey?

Admiral Meyer: Yes, she was. She lived right there in Cherry Hill, and she worked at Moorestown, with about, I don't know, 12 or 14 other people in there. She was not the boss by a long shot. She eventually became the boss. But as far as viewgraphs and that kind of material, she was a perfectionist, which could be a pain in the ass at times because you didn't have the time to mess with it. But it also paid off because the Aegis became known by its presentations. You could find people all over the country who'd say, "That's an Aegis slide." They'd recognize it as an Aegis chart, because it somehow had that artistic mark on it that went with it.

Paul Stillwell: These would be photo slides before PowerPoint came along.

Admiral Meyer: Yes, many drawn by hand. God, they spent night after night after night doing this stuff. Bill Goodwin told them it was important, and therefore it *was* important and they did it. And we went to, I don't know, a couple dozen symposia. We participated in a big national radar symposium each year that was held in different parts of the country. And our materials always overwhelmed the audience. They always wanted to get it and look at it and study it. And, of course, about half of it was classified so you had a lot of trouble trying to distribute it. But it was top-drawer material. And that continued, became its mark till this day of PowerPoint now where all you get is trash. And I mean really trash.

You and I can go to a program review tomorrow up at Moorestown, and they'll start putting the charts up at the horseshoe table, and I'll just start throwing up. They'll have misspelled words on them, they'll be poorly colored, they'll be a goddamn mess. And they will be what people tend to do when they make their own charts; they put everything they know on the chart. Why is that? Because of PowerPoint, so people make their own charts now. So you get a presentation, their chart's made by the person that's going to give the presentation. Think about this. That person is talking to himself. [Laughter] See, he's not talking to you. He's not talking to the audience at all. And he loses impact, and he loses it and he loses it and he loses it, and he doesn't know why. His answer is, "Well, I tried hard." Yeah, but he tried hard on the wrong thing.

The hardest thing I've found through the years is to get men to sit down ahead of time if they're giving a presentation and try to block it out what it is they want to get across, and *then* start making the charts and thinking about the charts, not the other way around. Oh, let's go in the file cabinet over there and see what we've got and see if we can make a presentation out of it; that's what most people do today.

So back off that subject. Presentations have lost their meaning, and therefore your ability to, I'll say market in its nicest sense, your ability to market disappeared with it. Because they don't have any meaning, they have no effect upon people. When you put up some drawing from the radar and people look at it you don't get any Aw's and Gees, ah—used to get it all the time. You'd put something up and people just, man, they couldn't believe it, what you said this radar was going to do and what it could do. That's not projected anymore.

Paul Stillwell: How did your social relationship with Anna Mae develop?

Admiral Meyer: Well, because she worked for Goodwin and because he put her on Aegis it just happened. It went along, it went along, it was a working relationship, and it was that way for those years. She was some younger than I. And then it got so that when we had major presentations Goodwin always wanted her, so he always dragged her along. So Goodwin and I—for example, we went to 30 Rockefeller Center several times when RCA was based there, and I mean this was with the biggies. You know, for two years the annual report at RCA didn't even mention Aegis, they were so anti-military. Well, Goodwin and I just assaulted 30 Rockefeller something furious. And one year we took Jim Doyle up there with us, and then we really assaulted them. They never let it happen again. But they never, up till then, never ever featured Aegis. Well, in recent times then they started featuring it. Well, today even Lockheed features a lot of Aegis in their annual reports. And for RCA it was a big program.

Paul Stillwell: Well, at some point your relationship with Anna Mae went beyond just that she was supporting the Aegis program.

Admiral Meyer: It did. I got to know her pretty well from just messing around. She had separated from her husband.[*] She had a child, and then Margaret died in '92.

Paul Stillwell: Your first wife had christened *Lake Erie*.

Admiral Meyer: She christened *Lake Erie* in '91, and '92 was when she died. So it just kind of picked up and kind of picked up, and that's the way it finally worked out. I think we've been married three years or four years now, which was a damn good thing for me.

Paul Stillwell: Why do you say that?

Admiral Meyer: Well, because I would say she's a wonderful wife, at least for someone like me. And so we get along really, really, really well, and I enjoy her. I really enjoy her. And my kids like her. I was very nervous about that. My kids are adults, but I was very nervous about what impact that would have and what effect, and it's turned out that I think they genuinely like her quite well.

Paul Stillwell: Great.

Admiral Meyer: And, as you know, or may know, that's 98% of living decently. So let's move to another subject.

Paul Stillwell: Well, you touched last time on going into second sourcing. Ingalls had been the shipbuilder when the program started. How did Bath then get involved?

Admiral Meyer: Originally, when it was demanded that we compete the ship, I didn't want to compete it at all. Matter of fact, I don't believe in competition.

---

[*] At the time her name was Anna Mae Seixas.

Paul Stillwell: Where did the demand come from?

Admiral Meyer: From what I call the know-nothings. It came from all those people who, frankly, were only interested in their own district.

So when it was determined that the base would be the 963 and then the 993 and we would evolve out of that, and in spite of NavSEC and NavSea the system *would* fit in that hull design and that ship, it *would* fit in spite of what they said in NavSEC, out at Hyattsville at that time. And it's fit there ever since; it's never tipped over once. And so I'm not a big believer in change. If you've got a group that's doing what it is you want done, then I don't believe in changing it. So I thought that Ingalls was doing a pretty damned good job, and my friend at that time, Captain Bill Wyatt, now Admiral Bill Wyatt, engineering duty officer and presently serves on my team here working on the CNO project, he was running the 963 project and the 993s, and I thought it was run pretty damned good.[*] So I thought what we could do is just morph right in there and not go start teaching some group that knew nothing about it how in the hell to build a ship, and worse yet how to build the Aegis.

We don't run our Navy that way. We don't run our Army that way. The Army, as you know, is in a very big pissing contest right now for the lack of competition, and they've got this competition going on in their major combat system, that it went to Boeing, and are they paying. They're paying and they're paying and they're paying and they're paying. Now, Boeing knows about that much—show a quarter of an inch between two fingers—knows about that much about ship design and shipbuilding. Well, we were prepared to let them in the business. I wasn't prepared to do it. Matter of fact, I threatened to quit. If we did that, I wasn't going to be part of it. I wanted the contract directed to Ingalls. I couldn't win it. I had no support.

Well, why didn't I have any support? There's a couple reasons. One is, it was Meyer. The institution didn't want anything to do with Meyer. That was one problem. And so that—damn, I lost my trend of thought here; where was I going?

---

[*] The Surface Warfare Capabilities Study-21 was being led by Admiral Meyer at the time of these oral history interviews. The study was done by Meyer's company in response to tasking from Chief of Naval Operations Michael Mullen and Chief of Naval Operations Gary Roughead.

Paul Stillwell: We were talking about moving into second source and people who had objections.

Admiral Meyer: Yes. Well, we were talking first about building the first source. I mean, I hadn't got the first source built yet. It wasn't foregone it would be Ingalls at all. We had a whole pile in the Navy didn't want Ingalls to have anything to do with it.

Paul Stillwell: But that would seem the logical one if you're developing it on the *Spruance* hull.*

Admiral Meyer: Well, you would hope so, wouldn't you?

Paul Stillwell: Yes.

Admiral Meyer: You would hope so. It's like saying we're going to Marinette, Wisconsin, to build the next attack aircraft carrier. Well, we can do those stupid damned things; we do them repeatedly, and we're always stunned at the outcome, that we've got a mess. Well, shunt that aside.

    I got off scatterbrained there again.

Paul Stillwell: Well, how did you get Bath up to speed with all the things that had been learned at Ingalls?

Admiral Meyer: Well, wait a minute. We're not *to* Bath yet. We're a long ways from Bath. My view was, I believe in a team. I don't believe in competition; I've told you that. I have *never* had a good outcome from competition in a half a century at it, never! And the reason is it's the behavior of human beings. When you start competing every member of your ball team, pretty soon you ain't got no ball team. And when they start playing as a team, guess what—you'll win the games. That's true here.

---

* Ingalls had built the *Spruance* class.

I couldn't win that, so I relented and agreed to it, and in order to get my concurrence they gave me a good deal of leeway. So here we set up this competition for Tico, which was to include Ingalls, General Dynamics in Massachusetts, Bath, and Todd Shipbuilding, and it was going to be Todd Seattle. Well, the dust had not yet settled when Todd Seattle decided they didn't want anything to do with it and backed out. Then—I'm trying to think who backed out next, but next or third Bath backed out, decided they weren't up to the task. So when the dust settled here was General Dynamics, for God's sake, which had no qualifications whatsoever, still was the bidder along with Ingalls. Well, that was hardly a contest.

So we ran it. We spent well over a year doing what the goddamn institution wanted. And, of course, you know, to run one of those things you piss away a lot of the taxpayers' money. Not a few hundred dollars, you piss away *millions* of dollars. And what's even worse is lost effort, because those people are all working on things that you're not going to do, not going to use. That's the really, really bad part, is the lost effort. Because we get this idea in the nation that all these qualified people exist to do things. They don't. How many qualified outfits exist to build an automobile? Not very damned many. How many exist to build a ship? Not very damned many. How many exist to build an icebox? Not very damned many. And so you get these stupid ideas of where we'll compete it and we'll get all these outfits involved. Well, I don't want anything to do with a company who joins that kind of competition, that doesn't have any qualifications. I mean, as a shareholder I don't want to own them, because they're stupid. That's a stupid management that's got the reasoning that somehow, well, anybody can build a ship. Right!

So when all the dust settled all we had left was General Dynamics and Ingalls. And putting General Dynamics aside was harder than you think, in the sense that it didn't matter what your opinion was, you couldn't just throw them out. "Oh, well, General Dynamics, look at everything they've built. They've built these great big gas tankers." Really, yeah, that really fits this warship fine. Taki Veliotis. Well, I finally convinced Taki Veliotis that he should not be wasting his money on this. Because that's what they're doing, they're wasting their money on it that they ought to be putting someplace else.

So in essence it was a hands-down Ingalls thing. We went through the motions. And, of course, all the people that pushed for this, when it was all over who had to go see Ted Kennedy?

Paul Stillwell: You. You're pointing to yourself.

Admiral Meyer: Yeah, I'm pointing to myself. All those geniuses, not a goddamn one of them showed up.

Paul Stillwell: Because Veliotis's shipyard was in Quincy, Massachusetts.

Admiral Meyer: Right. So there you are. It's a lesson learned, relearned, learned, relearned, and relearned. Anyhow, we went down there to Pascagoula, took over the LaFont Hotel, and started to remake Ingalls, and we turned them into a pretty damned good shipyard. They had a lot of difficulty understanding quality was the name of the game. They had real troubles with that. Why? Because they'd been dealing with these fixed-price contracts. And we're so goddamned stupid in this country that we think that you can make fixed-price contracts and quality harmonious.

Paul Stillwell: You've covered that.

Admiral Meyer: I've covered that. And you can't do that. You just can't do that. So time passed and that's where we are.

Paul Stillwell: Now, how did Bath get up to speed then to be able to build the ships?

Admiral Meyer: A lot of money. A lot of money. Now, I'm probably going to say some things here that I've never said before. I have trouble accepting the disintegration of teams. I'm just the kind of person that believes a team will last forever. And yet I could see Ingalls disintegrating. The older people drifting away, finding something else to do. I could see it going downhill. And so I decided that we were best off inviting Bath, and we cobbled up whatever competition had to be cobbled up, which was none, but inviting Bath in.

And we laid on several requirements in that whole process. Ingalls had to send people to Moorestown. Bath had to send people to Moorestown. They had to reside on the same deck, and they had to figure out what the challenge was on this ship. So after about a year or so we started shaping a team of people that communicated with each other instead of cutting their throats.

Paul Stillwell: Well, Bath probably also had to send some people to Pascagoula, didn't it?

Admiral Meyer: Oh, yeah, but not nearly as many as they had to send to Moorestown. But it worked out okay. Made it work out. One of the reasons is, of course, I put a lot of attention on it. I mean, I put a lot of officers and a lot of civil servants on the job, which is another thing people do. They go let these multi-hundred-million-dollar contracts, and put two GS-13s, totally laboring beyond their capacity both physically and mentally, to undertake the task. And damned little attention and damned little support.

You can't write the specifications to build a warship. You can summarize them. You can estimate them. You've got to write them every day. I mean, the millions of parts that go into a ship. And while you're doing five years—really, it's about an eight-year cycle on a warship, and in eight years it's amazing the number of companies in the United States go out of business for one reason or another. And all these things you have some dependence on. Some you can find an easy solution to. But you may have a place where you need hexagonal bolts and the hexagonal-bolt guy is out of business. So it ain't cut and dried at all. You don't just look around in the paper and see if you can pick up somebody else. That stuff can kill you, really kill you. It's little things that kill you in shipbuilding, just like everything else. It's little things. When these big shipbuilders get in trouble they don't get in trouble from them, they get in trouble from all the little people that they've had to take on that aren't able to rise to type-A quality.

(Interruption)

Paul Stillwell: Well, we're just back from a break and I got a note that, from last time, you wanted to talk about sea trials in the Gulf of Mexico and cutting Z's in the water at 32 knots. What ship was that?

Admiral Meyer: There is a chapter unto itself about *Ticonderoga* being unstable to the point where she'd tip over. I never confirmed exactly where that came from, but I'm pretty sure where it came from, and of course it came from people who knew not whereof they spoke, people determined to punch a hole in Aegis. Because that whole story is a shameful story that I'm loath to spend a lot of time repeating, wherein the official Navy position had been determined that Aegis could not be landed in the *Spruance*-class destroyer, which forced me to do my own calculations. And from it all I learned how untrustworthy that process could be when it wanted to be.

There really was no danger at all as long as you obeyed the fundamental laws of weights and balances. If you ignored the buoyancy laws and Archimedes' laws, guess what—the ship will tip over given the right circumstances. The implication being that these jerks didn't know what they were doing, and they'd put such a ship to sea. So something happened which I had a rule against in my project. It never happened again, but it happened once. My position in the years that I was the project manager, some 15-20 years, was investigators could go wherever they wanted to go. They could ask whatever questions they wanted to ask. But they had to go through the front door of the project.

Paul Stillwell: You mentioned that last time.

Admiral Meyer: I mentioned that. And the guidance to all my people, far and wide, throughout industry and in government, is: "Look, you answer the questions that you think you're qualified to answer. And you get asked a question by some jerk walking down the street that you don't know the answer, just say, 'That's out of my bailiwick, I don't know that answer,' and walk off. You don't have to answer it." But, of course, people have a habit of doing it for a couple reasons. One is they want to appear smart. And two is, they don't want to appear stupid. But it always happens. So the rumors started chasing themselves in circles, that just as we had predicted, this ship is overweight. I know where it started, and it came out of the soul of Hyattsville, out of disgruntled people who got it started. I know where it got started. And who were bent on pointing out that this ship would not have adequate safety margins, the Aegis would be defying them, both in stability and in weight control.

Well, of course, the opponents were fond of pulling my chain because they had all these communication channels, and the world believed me to be a novice in shipbuilding. The only place I was a novice at is I had never been assigned to *build* a ship before, but I'd associated in a lot of shipbuilding, including overhauls in shipyards and other things in shipyards and stuff, so to assert that I didn't know anything was their downfall.

Well, time wore on, time wore on, and so people kept generating these stories of we had this mammoth, monstrous deckhouse would sit atop the superstructure, and that it'd tip over. That's how it kept building itself up and building itself up. Well, I ignored it in the beginning. It was so damned stupid that it wasn't worth getting in a discussion or an argument on, because the people who made an issue of it simply were so ill informed that you'd waste your time talking to them.

Well, over time it didn't stop, and it managed, of course, the way they solved this—and that was an era where I learned another thing, and that is never underestimate, *never* underestimate the power of junior civil servants, and particularly civil servants in the field. Never, in this business. Here you and I sit here this afternoon—I am no longer in charge of anything, but in another era there are civil servants all over the nation associated in some form or another in that big shipbuilding program. It was a billion-dollar undertaking in the beginning, a monster, the biggest ever. And so people were perfectly willing to spread whatever dope they wanted to spread. And if they didn't think that they were being treated fairly, they'd just take over.

Paul Stillwell: So did you decide to use the sea trials as a way to quiet those critics?

Admiral Meyer: I did. I did. And, just kind of for the record—I believe I'm correct—we've never had a surface ship go to sea since World War II that didn't have ballast.

Why is that? Well, it's because of all the gear we have topside.* We have so much electronic gear. And the solution's very simple. You ballast it out. And what effect does it have? Well, it has the same effect on you as you have when you've got a belly of your own. It might slow you down. But you might have a ship that's ballasted that, instead of making 32.16 knots, now it can make 32.14 knots or something. It's like it ain't no big deal as long as it's within sensible region. And things that work in your favor, of course, were these big launchers, of putting in these Mark 26 launchers, which go all the way to the keel, so they really assist in weight balance. Does it slow the ship down? Well, I've never heard anybody bitch about it being slowed down or everything; it runs just about the same speed as every other ship. I mean, there ain't very often you run the entire fleet at 32.62 knots, not very often. But that was the thing.

Are you acquainted with the investigators? I don't know whether they even have them anymore, but the appropriations committees had these investigation teams on various programs.

Paul Stillwell: No, I don't know specifically.

Admiral Meyer: They may no longer exist. They were ad hoc teams. They'd borrow three people from the FBI and four people from some other investigative outfit. They'd go all over the country and put together these ad hoc teams and put them to work investigating these programs. And, of course, you had a case here of the deaf leading the blind, and not being encumbered with any data, nor particularly did they worry about the truth of the data. And sometimes it took you a long time to identify who they were. And, as I say, I had a rule. My rule was—repeatedly I've said it—you can have anything, because what I do is a matter for the public, but you go through the front door. Well, these guys, of course, they didn't have to go through the front door, they thought, so they'll start sneaking around and wending their way in. Well, one time they got in the shipyard. It never happened again, though, because, again, I had rules to all the people that worked for me in the industry. I'm not operating closed doors, but you're not to let

---

* Weight high in a ship can make it less stable; the remedy is to put ballast weight low in the ship to counteract the topside weight.

anybody in, goddamn it, without appropriate authority and appropriate permission. And then they can go wherever they want to go, but they're going to follow the rules, or otherwise we'll go clear to the top.

Paul Stillwell: Did the sea trials achieve your objective in quieting the critics?

Admiral Meyer: Oh, totally. Totally, the short answer is. The ship is going to tip over, it won't make—well, Mr. Len Erb—I've mentioned him to you before—

Paul Stillwell: Yes.

Admiral Meyer: He and I won. So we went out on this trial, what we call Trial Alfa, modeled after the submarines. And so we, because of the matter of the day, everybody bitching about this ship and its dangers and everything, we decided that we were going to change our process a little bit, and on this sea trial we were going to open this ship up. Our whole team, from Ingalls and all the participants, felt that they had the ship together pretty damned well. Well, they should be, because we had virtually all the propulsion and much of the hull patterned after the *Spruance*s. I mean, we didn't have somebody we just found on a street corner someplace. And their view was, "Admiral, you can open her up; it's ready to be opened up." So Erb and I decided, by God, we're going to open her up. And to prove it further we had lifelines rigged on the gun deck, which is back on the fantail where the Harpoon launcher is and the gun, we had holding lines, safety lines.[*] Mr. Erb and I went back there with our jackets on in the Gulf of Mexico. We stood on the fantail and sent the order to the bridge, "Open her up, maneuver the ship as hard as you can maneuver her."

Well, I've got to tell you, when they start slamming that rudder, you slam that goddamn rudder from 25 degrees to 25 degrees, I mean, and you're on that fantail, man, you're standing like this.

---

[*] Harpoon is an antiship missile with a range of approximately 75-80 nautical miles. It can be fired from surface ships, submarines, and aircraft.

Paul Stillwell: At an angle.

Admiral Meyer: Yeah, a big angle, right, a big angle [chuckle]. So you do hang onto the lifeline because you're standing at an angle and, of course, the seawater is washing up around you all the way from back in your own wake backfiring on you. So we told them, "Turn her loose, and if she goes down we'll go down too." Well, of course, it was beautiful, just beautiful. We had two helos up. As a matter of fact I had, God rest his soul, my buddy Ned Beach.* And I'm trying to think who in the hell his sidekick was all the time with him. But we made sure they got pictures.†

I mean, if you've seen any of those pictures they are beautiful to behold. They are so pretty, as we're cutting those Z's or slamming that rudder back and forth, just slamming the hell out of it. You'd never do that in real life unless you were really in danger. And, of course, as you might expect, everything in naval engineering is way overdesigned. I mean, there's real safety margins in everything we do, so it was a nothing, was just a nothing.

Well, of course, those assholes, when they get embarrassed they'll never apologize. They go off and try to find something else. But I have to say this: That whole program was never bothered again, ever, on anything, ever again. So I really did embarrass the bastards, as they well should have been. Did any of them get fired? Not a one. Not a one got fired, to my knowledge, for their own incompetence. Here are these powerful satraps who were prepared to tell you how incompetent you were, but no one was willing to admit *their* incompetence. So that's that story, in a ten-minute version.

Paul Stillwell: What was Ned Beach's role in that process?

Admiral Meyer: Curiosity. He was a friend of mine, and he was such a lovable person that I involved him every time I had a chance because he loved to be involved.

---

* Captain Edward L. "Ned" Beach, Jr., USN, wrote a number of books, most notably the submarine novel *Run Silent, Run Deep*. For a profile of Beach, see *Naval History*, Summer 1988, pages 62-64.
† Edward L. Beach (writer) and Fred J. Maroon (photographer), *Keepers of the Sea* (Annapolis: Naval Institute Press, 1983).

Paul Stillwell: Well, and he could help spread the word, as well.

Admiral Meyer: Oh, yeah. He spread the word and he could walk around and say a few things that were very, very helpful indeed. I mean, I used it all. I wasn't on the turnip truck yesterday. Been on there a long time. So Ned was a great friend of mine and a great person.

Paul Stillwell: Well, I agree with those assessments. Please talk, then, about the transition of bringing along the DDG-51 class. There you had a lower profile as far as superstructure, and also you were not building on a previous hull.[*]

Admiral Meyer: I wasn't particularly happy with the -51 design, but, as you know, during the process Lehman removed me. I know I'm right, but it doesn't matter whether I'm right. The design is all right, but I believe it could have been better.

Paul Stillwell: In what ways?

Admiral Meyer: I believe the ship could ride a lot better than she does. I've only sailed in the ship two or three times a little way, and she's not a rough rider. If you came out of the old destroyer Navy, she rides beautifully. She does not ride as good as the cruiser. In my view she could ride better, but of course we'll never know because it has become a proven hull design that's well accepted. And I don't want to sound like I'm critical of it because I'm not. It's just that I felt that we didn't do our best.

Paul Stillwell: Well, it's an interesting irony that your name appears on the stern of one of those ships.

---

[*] For details on the hull design factors, see Paul Stillwell, "Designing the *Arleigh Burke*'s Hull," *Naval History*, August 2010, page 6.

Admiral Meyer: Isn't it? It really is. [Laughter] You know, I said that one night to Anna Mae, that's really an interesting irony that my name is stuck on there, and none of those assholes have their names stuck on it.

Paul Stillwell: What organization produced the design for the -51?

Admiral Meyer: Well, it started out to be a totally integral design, which is what I wanted, and we rented a couple decks over in Building 1, Airport Plaza 1—I think it's Airport Plaza, the farthest one down—and we set up the teams there that included the shipbuilders, included now called Lockheed, and all the key people, and we put Captain Jerry Fee in command of the whole structure, a crackerjack engineering duty officer.[*] He worked for me, and it always made me feel bad that he never got promoted because he was just such a good officer. And he led that motley crew into a pretty damned tight interval down there. And so they ripped their shirts off when they came in the door, and they started worrying about that design and not worrying about whether they were from Ingalls or whether they were from Bath or anyplace else. So Jerry is another one of those unsung heroes. There are a lot of unsung heroes in that undertaking, a lot of them.

Paul Stillwell: Well, you're getting a chance to sing about them here rather than leaving them unsung.

Admiral Meyer: Yeah, right, I am getting a chance to mention them. Captain Jerry Fee was another one that made unsung contributions, a good leader. But there's something else. I believe, and I may be wrong, and so I don't like to say it too strongly. I believe my leadership really brought out the leadership of those officers. These were good officers, I mean crackerjack officers. They were all volunteers; I didn't have a single officer that wasn't a volunteer for me. But I don't know whether it was my extra ability, something that befell me, or how I got that way. I don't know that. And I say it a little braggadocio because I've thought about it a lot, and at times it bothers me.

---

[*] Captain Jerome J. Fee, USN.

I don't know whether I told you the story about my incident in high school with Miss Florence Puckett.

Paul Stillwell: Very likely you did.

Admiral Meyer: Yeah, I probably did, my English teacher. In giving my first speech at the American Legion oratorical contest—I was a junior, and it stuck with me all these years, and the subsequent Florence Pucketts. And somehow, I don't know whether it's being loudmouthed or whether I speak plainly, I don't know what the trait is in me, but one thing I do know: It's there. I know it's there, because I know that people will follow me. I've *never* had anybody tell me they won't do something, not once in my life.

Paul Stillwell: That is remarkable.

Admiral Meyer: I never have. And on the contrary, it's the other way around. "We can do it, Captain. We can do it." So I know there's something there, and as I say it's something that's hard to brag about it. You can't brag about it at all, but I know it's there. And I know it, too, by the way they'll cluster around me. And I know by the hundreds of people that found a way to work for me. And I first started noticing it in women, because in my heyday as I started this project was what I call the freedom years. It's when Lyndon Johnson set the women free, and the blacks had already been set free. So I went through a whole long era where I could hire any woman I wanted to hire. I just couldn't get a man. Well, I learned a lot about women and about leadership with them, and also I think I taught them a lot, and that word spread.

Paul Stillwell: Well, success breeds success. People want to be a part of a going enterprise.

Admiral Meyer: Well, you got it, that's exactly right. And so those women spread that word more than men, even, about: "Well, why don't you go get a job with Meyer?" And it was in the era where, you know, they were all—we've got, I mean there are hundreds of women in our part of the government that are way over their head, been promoted way over their head, in my view. But they didn't promote themselves; somebody else promoted them. And a lot of it was driven by a quota or perceived quotas. And, frankly, I didn't much care whether you were over your head or not. What I cared about is whether you were willing to follow orders and whether you were willing to learn. That's what I cared about. Because when I say "loyal people" I don't mean people in adoration; I'm talking about people who have a sense of duty to you as their leader. And, I tell you, I could count on them every time.

And it was amazing the amount of, we used to call it scuttlebutt in the Navy; I guess we don't call it anything anymore. But there'd be a leave period or they'd go someplace, and they'd come back in and say, "You know, Captain, you ought to hear what I heard last Saturday night."

"Well, sit down, young lady, and tell me about it." And it's amazing how that stuff would flow into you, which put you above the rest. It put you above them and kept you above them.

Well, that works in industry too. So people wanted to be on the team, they wanted to be part of it. I mean, everybody wants to be a winner, even if you're under fire, even when you're getting the hell criticized out of you. People recognize a winner when they see one. They still want to be a part of it if it's a good one.

So 'twas a golden era, a golden era, and it's interesting that I followed Anna Mae all the way through that and I'd known her all those years, and then ended up, the way God created things, married to her in the end. It was an interesting thing how that all came out.

Paul Stillwell: God has interesting plans for people.

Admiral Meyer: He surely does. So I have not had to grieve, and I have not had to feel bad or any of those things. And I have not had to fight with my children or any of those kinds of things, or anybody else for that matter.

It's interesting to this day. Now, I was fired in 1983 by John Lehman, so that's 25 years ago?

Paul Stillwell: Going on 26.

Admiral Meyer: Well, to this day people recognize Anna Mae from having been originally associated in the Aegis and growing up in Aegis, and being part of the Aegis. It's true that they're getting awfully young now, and they may recognize her by hearsay more than any other. But you've got men walking around this deck who have known her quite a while as a result of Aegis. So it was a protective thing for me and sometimes a tearful thing. But I think the goods are better than the bads.

Paul Stillwell: Did you have a hand in picking Admiral Roane as your successor?

Admiral Meyer: Yes and no. The Secretary wanted me gone so fast, I had about two hours if I wanted to nominate someone.

Paul Stillwell: How did you get the word that you had to leave the job?

Admiral Meyer: You know, that's a darned good question. I wonder if I know that answer today. I wonder if in hindsight I know that answer. I don't mean to evade the truth, I'm not trying to, but it could be that I just smelled it. If I didn't name someone, somebody else was going to get named, because I smelt it coming. Because John Lehman and I—I mean, we'd come to a point and I had no use for the man. But the point that we'd come to was the subsequent two years, which really was my downfall because he fired me out of there, then I was on a contract which had a couple years to run, and he wasn't too—I'm making this up—he wasn't too sure of his own power, really, to get rid of me.* I was eligible to retire if I wanted to, but I'm not sure he thought I could, or that he had the power to get it done. I think he was scared of my perceived power, which I did not have, but by God I had a lot of it and I had it in Congress, and I can't recall where I ever overused it. I had a lot of it in both houses.

---

* Meyer served in NavSea-06 from 1983 to 1985, then retired from active duty.

Paul Stillwell: Well, you said "yes and no" as far as being able to name a successor. What part did you contribute?

Admiral Meyer: Well, I thought this was coming here, and one afternoon, wham, my—goddamn, I just can't think of the circumstances, but I remember being asked if I had a recommended relief and I said, "Yes, he's sitting right here alongside me, and his name is Pete Roane." And I never even asked Pete Roane, and I'm not sure to this day that Pete Roane has agreed to that. It turns out that—and again, I don't want this to be derogatory, because Pete Roane was an incredible warrior and Pete Roane worked for me, I think three times. Most people don't know it, Pete Roane wore ribbons from here to here. He may have been in a era where he was the most decorated officer in the Navy, at least in the surface Navy. His last claim to fame was the *Mayaguez* incident.

Paul Stillwell: He was a DesRon commander in that.

Admiral Meyer: Exactly. Exactly. Well, he was a wonderful officer. It turned out, something that I guess I didn't want to accept, and it was that he had no stomach for leadership. He was an incredible deputy. I think you know he was a Navy junior.

Paul Stillwell: I did not know that.

Admiral Meyer: I believe I'm right. He was born, I think, in Oklahoma, in McAlester, I think. But he was just a superb officer, superb leader, and people loved him for his leadership abilities. But he loved being number two, and somehow I didn't know that. Somehow I just didn't know that. But he loved to be that, and I had no qualms about walking away from the office if I wanted to go someplace, because as long as I was there he had run that place any way that it needed to be run and what I wanted to be run, and he'd keep a little running record. And I never, one minute, felt left out of anything. But it turned out that once he was cut adrift he didn't last two years; he got himself out of there real quick. And I could see it happening to him. I could see it on his face every time I ran into him, that his stomach was breaking up on him, and of course dealing with that goddamn John Lehman was enough to break anybody up.

And then I had, you know, my blows with John Lehman. After Lehman fired me into Sea-06, which was the director of systems....

Paul Stillwell: Deputy Commander for Weapons and Combat Systems; I looked it up.

Admiral Meyer: Yeah, that's right. From 1983 to '85. And there is where I was till he, Lehman, could get rid of me. And so I could sit there, and I don't know that Pete Roane said ten words to me in the two years. He and Bill Rowden were my two greatest officers, I think, and Dick Albright.[*] I mean, I had some just wonderful deputies. But the batting average on flag was not that high. Rorie made flag.[†] Roane made flag. Dick Albright you may not have even known; he was a wonderful officer that worked with me in Terrier. He's retired down in the Carolinas now someplace.

Paul Stillwell: What was the focus of your job in this new role?

Admiral Meyer: Well, I was Sea-06, which was combat systems, and Lehman couldn't stand me by the second year, because I overhauled the whole damned place, and it turned out he didn't want that place doing anything. He didn't know what it was. He sent me there because it was a dead end, it was someplace out in the wilderness, as a way to get rid of me without him being accused of mistreating me. He didn't know what he was doing. At the end of the second year he knew.

Paul Stillwell: Well, what specifically were you doing?

Admiral Meyer: Well, because I re-inspired the officers, the captains. I mustered all those captains and I was pointblank with them, because there was at that time in

---

[*] Captain William H. Rowden, USN; Commander Richard K. Albright, USN.
[†] Rear Admiral Conrad J. Rorie, USN.

Sea-06—I had relieved Dempster Jackson.[*] There was maybe, hell, I don't know, there may have been 30 captains in Sea-06, and there were two or three admirals. I mustered them all, and I said, "Look, I want you to understand the straight story on me; I want there to be no bones about you understanding that I was fired. I'm not going to cover it up; I want you to understand it. I'm not going to brag about it, but I want you to understand it. And if you don't want to work for me, say so now or write me a note and we'll change it. You don't have to. I don't want anybody working for me that doesn't want to work for me, not a person."

I never did get a note.

(Interruption)

Paul Stillwell: You were talking about people, whether they wanted to work for you or not.

Admiral Meyer: Yeah, right. I've always had that habit. I don't want people working for me that don't want to work for me. I just make it right up front. And I'm not going to hold it against you; if you don't want to do it, that's fine with me, because I'm a hard driver, and if you don't want to work for me I don't believe a person should be abused that way. If you hard drive people that don't want to do it, they don't belong there.

Paul Stillwell: Did any leave.

Admiral Meyer: I never had a one. Never had a one. Never. Well, you had some jerks say, well, they were afraid to. I don't believe that. There've got to be one or two who ain't afraid.

But Pete Roane was such a top officer, and I nominated him in the little time I had to nominate him because, as far as I could tell the Secretary didn't care as long as he got rid of me. Hell, he would have put a mess cook there, but he wanted me moved.

I think Rowden may have been OP-03 at the time, I can't recall.

---

[*] Rear Admiral Dempster K. Jackson, USN.

Paul Stillwell: I think he was the commander of Military Sealift Command at that time.

Admiral Meyer: It could be.

Paul Stillwell: He went from there to NavSea in '85.[*]

Admiral Meyer: He got trashed.

Paul Stillwell: He had been the Sixth Fleet commander before that.

Admiral Meyer: Right. See, if you go track all of that whole process, if you look at the EDO admirals of my genre, I'm the only one that did not get promoted to vice admiral. Lehman promoted all the others—Fowler and the other two. He never promoted me. Matter of fact, I think I told you that Worth Bagley was responsible for my promotion. Did I tell you this?

Paul Stillwell: No.

Admiral Meyer: I never expected to be promoted.

Paul Stillwell: Now, are you talking to two stars or three?

Admiral Meyer: Two. I never got promoted to three stars, though I never expected to be. And when that board was convened it turned out that Worth was sent in there to be the president of the board. He was the Vice Chief at the time.[†] Worth Bagley never forgot what I did for him when I saved his ass as commanding officer. And I remember late that Friday night, it must have been on the order of 10:00 o'clock, Worth Bagley called me up, because in those days the board met and adjourned the second Friday, when they got

---

[*] Vice Admiral William H. Rowden, USN, served as Commander Naval Sea Systems Command from 1985 to 1988.
[†] Admiral Worth H. Bagley, USN, served as Vice Chief of Naval Operations from 5 June 1974 to 30 June 1975. The selection board picked Meyer in January 1975 for flag rank. His date of rank as a rear admiral was 1 July 1975.

their ten days in, the regulatory ten days. He said, "Wayne, I just wanted you to know that you're on the list." And I cried like a baby. I couldn't believe it.

I subsequently learned, but I don't have it documented but I have no reason to believe it's not correct because it came out of him: Not a single EDO voted for my promotion. And, as you know, those boards, unrestricted line, those boards must have a minimum of three officers if there are three officers. So in the line board three unrestricted lines are displaced and three restricted lines are put on in their place for the promotion of restricted lines. [Chuckle] He didn't tell me that night, but he told me that later, he said, "You ought to know that not a single EDO voted for you."

I said, "Well, thank you for confirming what I already knew." [Chuckle]

Paul Stillwell: Well, what were the changes you made in Sea-06?

Admiral Meyer: Woke them up.

Paul Stillwell: Specifically. [Laughter]

Admiral Meyer: Well, you're going to stir my memory. See, at that time we had ASW, AAW, Surface W, we had Harpoon, Tomahawks, we had all of those, and all they needed was leadership. I mean, they had the top ordnance officers of the Navy, the top line officers of the Navy, and hell, there was just a whole damn pile of them. There were more of them then in 06 than I think there is in the whole damn bunch today. And I'd say two-thirds of those officers were from relatively fresh sea duty, so they were a pleasure to lead because I knew a hell of a lot more than they knew, and they came to believe that.

The other thing they came to believe is that I'd speak up to the Secretary. That's what I warned them on the very first day, "I might not be here very long, but I want you to understand what my view is and what my policies are, and I will support you, I will back you, but don't count on me on the Secretary because I don't agree with it." Well, not a one of them walked away, as I said. But having said that, it did calm down.

There's one place it did not calm down. It didn't keep him from destroying Standard missile. He destroyed Standard missile, he insisted it was going to be thrown on the auction block, demanded that it be thrown, and it was. I don't know that you can say that it's recovered yet. One thing we know is that beautiful organization that the Navy had devoted years to building, General Dynamics, in Pomona, was now gone forever. And I guess that what saved the Navy is that it ended up finally being resident in Tucson.

(Interruption for change of tape)

Paul Stillwell: You talked about destroying the organization.

Admiral Meyer: Oh, right. The officers wouldn't prevent it, and the reason they wouldn't prevent it is they couldn't count on the Secretary supporting them. They could have stopped this destruction of this organization with General Dynamics to Hughes to Raytheon. They wouldn't do it because they couldn't count on the Secretary, and I couldn't blame them—I was no longer part of their problem—because their basic authority had been displaced by the Secretary. So the whole thing went to Hughes in Tucson.

Now, I only had a casual knowledge of Hughes Tucson, and it was a good outfit but it was the Navy's air-to-air missile they'd built, the Phoenix.[*] And so they didn't last long. As a matter of fact it ended up just being kind of a matter of time before they were snuffed out by Raytheon, and then the whole damned thing became very confused because Raytheon had no structure at all in that part of the country.

I guess we've recovered. You never know. You never know whether your war reserve is all right or not, you just never know. I have to say this—we've had some pretty damned good shooting in Standard missile through the years. Their reliability has been incredible. And so this means that Tucson is a pretty darned good outfit. It's got an admixture of some General Dynamics blood in it, some Hughes blood, but Raytheon's flag is on the door. And Standard missile is just a little handful of what they do anymore. I mean it's in the minority by a long shot. They're just kind of a, you know, a custom

---

[*] The AIM-54 Phoenix was a long-range (more than 100 miles) air-to-air missile developed for use with the F-14 Tomcat fighter.

shop for whatever you call for. You need ten of these or five of those, and I'll make them. So Standard missile no longer dominates the theme because, particularly with Mullen taking over and deciding the Navy couldn't afford it, we stopped firing Standard missiles. Hell, we haven't fired Standard Missiles for several years now except as part of the qualification trials done in Aegis. So all of the doctrines that we had established on the surveillance of ordnance and such have been set aside and not been executed now for seven, eight years.

We've got to assume the ordnance is good, because, in truth they can't build a cheap missile. Those teams don't know how to build a cheap missile. The integrated circuits and everything they do are tops. You can't build a cheap integrated circuit in our missilery. So, you know, providing the environment is kept correct they could last 50 years or more. I have to say this, the Navy has no plan whatever for ammunition that I know of. Zero, today. How much war could we handle with what we've got? I don't know. Thirty minutes or an hour. We ain't got a hell of a lot. I think we still cross-deck ammo, but I don't know.

Paul Stillwell: That's a pessimistic view.

Admiral Meyer: Yes. It really is pessimistic. And worse yet, it's double pessimistic because you can't find anybody very worried about it. No hand wringers that's concerned about it. And we might go on for a hundred years with peace, I don't know, and not have a problem.

How will that sense or reflection of readiness come back in our Navy? Who's going to be the charger on a white horse ride in?

Paul Stillwell: It will depend on the external threat.

Admiral Meyer: Right. And men are liable to die in the process. And this time there'll be women die too. I think all we've got to do is kill a few more women and I think we will get an awakening in our Navy not heretofore seen. We just haven't hurt nor killed enough women yet to cause the society to wake up to it. And maybe I'm wrong. I'm just an old man. I'm going to cross another threshold here in a couple weeks, and I could be just wrong.* Maybe we don't have that kind of respect for womanhood anymore that we had at one time. We just could not bear the thought of sending young girls running across the battlefield; we just couldn't bear that thought. Today it's maybe old hat for all I know. I don't have any feel for it.

Paul Stillwell: Well, I've been surprised there's not been more reaction to the casualties in Iraq.

Admiral Meyer: Right, exactly, yeah. Hell, I don't know, we may have a Navy that can't fight. Well, wait a minute, it may not have to fight, in the sense that older people think it has to fight. It may *be* pushbutton. I don't know whether you've seen any of these articles about how you've got these goddamn majors and Air Force captains sitting up in Nevada doing the targeting operations over in Iraq and everything. There have been some pretty stiff articles written on that and I couldn't agree with them more. I don't see how in the hell you can take two captains which are maybe 26 years old sitting in Nevada, and they are doing the targeting and the planning in Iraq on what you're going to strike. I don't see it. But that's what we're doing.

And we've got another team, I read it this weekend I think, there's another team that runs around issuing apologies. You may have seen that. Because when we hurt civilians we've got a team that's running around now apologizing for hurting or harming a civilian.

Paul Stillwell: No, I hadn't heard that.

Admiral Meyer: I don't know if that's a Mullen innovation or not.† I hope it's not, but it may very well be, because Mullen is a little soft, and it may be his innovation to keep calmness around the house, to do that.

---

* Admiral Meyer's 83rd birthday was on 21 April 2009.
† Admiral Michael G. Mullen, USN, served as Chairman of the Joint Chiefs of Staff from 1 October 2007 to 30 September 2011.

Paul Stillwell: What was your relationship to Admiral Fowler when you were in that weapons job?*

Admiral Meyer: You know, I've known, I've followed him for a long, long time. He was a graduate of Georgia Tech, and a V-12-er. And in the earlier years I always got along with him pretty fine. He was electronics by specialty, so forth. But, frankly—he's in the graveyard now, so I don't suppose it matters—he and Gardinaker [phonetic] both, they were big buddies, and he became braggadocio about his being promoted, becoming the chief. He became too braggadocio for me about how he had held Lehman at bay. And I finally said to him one night, I said, "Well, Earl, I don't see it that way. I never saw you hold him at bay." I said, "I'm not criticizing you because I'm not in your shoes, but neither have I seen you ever hold him at bay." He let me do what I wanted to do.

Paul Stillwell: You had autonomy in that job.

Admiral Meyer: In essence I had autonomy, right. And I guess the way it kind of worked out is, I took care of OpNav and he took care of the secretariat, the way it kind of worked out. Because he had Jim Webber—I don't know whether you ever knew Jim Webber.† Jim Webber kind of took care of the submariners, and he did it pretty good. And so I took care of OP-03 because they all knew me and they all trusted me. They didn't trust Earl Fowler.

Paul Stillwell: That was Admiral Walters and then Admiral Metcalf.‡

Admiral Meyer: Right. Right. And, of course, Walters had—I can't remember whether he directly worked for me or not, he worked with me. And then Metcalf and I were associated together. And I finally—you know, when the Secretary trashed me, I still

---

* Vice Admiral Earl B. Fowler, Jr., USN, served as Commander Naval Sea Systems Command from 1980 to 1985. Admiral Meyer reported to him from 1983 until 1985.
† Rear Admiral James H. Webber, USN, Vice Commander Naval Sea Systems Command.
‡ Vice Admiral Robert L. Walters, USN, served as Deputy Chief of Naval Operations (Surface Warfare) from June 1981 to September 1984. Vice Admiral Joseph Metcalf III, USN, was Deputy Chief of Naval Operations (Surface Warfare) from September 1984 to December 1987.

wish I had not put in for retirement. I didn't have to retire, I was on a contract, but my officers convinced me to do it, so I applied for retirement about a year early on the contract.

Paul Stillwell: What were the arguments of those who persuaded you to do that?

Admiral Meyer: Well, they wanted me to go down standing tall, so that's what they wanted, and I finally relented on that. And in the end it doesn't matter because there may not be three people left in the world who even remember or recall the circumstances or how it was done. On the other hand, 'tis a pity how records don't get recorded very well of actual events and actual happenings. But that's what I did, I put in for it and, God, it got snapped up in about three hours. It got approved, like, real fast.

The vice chief at the time was Jim Busey.[*] I had been put in exile. I called Building 5 over here the "exile building," because all the people had been trashed by the Secretary, starting with Willoughby on down, all of them.[†] They were in exile in that building, and that's where I was. Well, I took about 15 people and we all went into that building in exile, and we were there for approaching a year. And they sat there and pondered each day or thought about evil things to do.

So Jim Busey came over to see me in exile after my papers were in. He came over one day to see me and he said, "Wayne, I just want to tell you that the Secretary said that he would not be available to speak at your retirement date." We'd picked a date then.

I said, "Well, I didn't have in mind that he was going to speak."

And he said, "Well, the CNO's not available either."

So I said, "Well, why am I not surprised?"

But he said, "I'll speak at your retirement if you want."

"Well, that's nice of you, Jim, but don't worry about it. Don't worry about it. Maybe I'll speak at my own." And that's the last time I saw Jim Busey.

---

[*] Admiral James B. Busey IV, USN, served as Vice Chief of Naval Operations from 1985 to 1987.
[†] William Willoughby was a reliability expert who had come from NASA.

Well, what I really did is, I'd dug Joe Metcaif out of a couple holes himself. I couldn't dig him out of the goddamn rifle hole, he dug that, which I had nothing to do with, he and the Secretary. So I called him up and I said, "How'd you like to speak at my retirement?"

He said, "Well, I'd be honored."

I said, "Wait a minute; you might want to think about this a little while."

He said, "Well, I've thought about it. I'd be honored." So that's how Joe Metcalf became the speaker.

Some of my relatives came from Missouri to see it. We had it in the sail loft above the museum in the Navy Yard. I want to say it was the eighth of December or something like that. It might have been the fifth of December. It was somewhere in there. It was cold outside, anyhow. So that's when we did it.

And we had a motley collection. Most of them cried, and that was that.

Paul Stillwell: Well, I suspect that there were very few officers still on active duty at that point who had been commissioned in 1946.[*]

Admiral Meyer: Like there was zero. Right, like there was zero, none at all. And by that time I didn't much care whether they were on active duty or not. But a lot of the young officers came, which pleased me greatly. A lot of them came. As a matter of fact, the sail loft was full, it was jammed full, it was standing room. And civil servants, a lot of civil servants came. And industry. Industry doesn't much go to those affairs, a handful, but a lot did here in this case. I don't know if it was out of pity or to see what I was going to say or what. And the truth is I didn't say anything. I just thanked the Navy for the opportunities that had been given me, and how blessed I was and fortunate I was that I was able to exercise those opportunities and that I was able to create a fleet.

Before we close this thing in the next couple years we're going to talk about that fleet, because you're going to have to search your history over there in Annapolis for a pretty long time to find out a person who has had more to do with numbers of

---

[*] Admiral William J. Crowe, Jr., USN, served as Chairman of the Joint Chiefs of Staff from 1 October 1985 to 30 September 1989. He was in the Naval Academy class of 1947, which was commissioned in June 1946.

shipbuilding, warships, than me.* There's 85 ball caps in there now.† Today, this year, as you know, we're in such a fix, the Congress is so disgusted with us, that they put three Aegis ships in the budget, even though the Navy kept crying no, no, no, we don't need them, we don't want them. Well, do it anyhow, because we couldn't produce a shipbuilding plan.

One thing the Congress did know is, this thing called the DDG-1000 was not an adequate substitute. And one of the things I learned in all those years of dealing with them and associating with them in the body politic: It's clumsy, it's slow, even to the point of stupidity at times, but it eventually corrects itself. Winston Churchill had a couple sayings associated with democracy and how it functions, and it's true here from my days of being associated with it of how, as a society, we tend to go on and we tend to do the right things, albeit it making a lot of missteps on the road to rightness. Not on the road to righteousness but on the road to rightness and correctness.

And so if I don't shut down Miss Deb will come in here and probably tow you out. [Laughter] Thank you for your patience again today.‡

Paul Stillwell: Thank you, sir.

Post-retirement addendum follows, transplanted from a previous interview:

Admiral Meyer: Come 1985, Wayne is fired by John Lehman the second time and goes home. Comes 1986, and one day Captain John Joseph Donegan Jr. comes walking into my space right here. "Admiral, I need your help."

"What do you need?"

"I have been reassigned to the ballistic missile outfit." What had happened is Weinberger and the President and the general, Abe Abrahamson, who was a buddy of the

---

* Sadly, the plans to discuss Admiral Meyer's post-active duty career did not come to fruition because of his declining health and death. The story below about ballistic missile defense has been moved to this location for the sake of chronological continuity. He actually told the story as a jump-ahead in an earlier interview.
† In Meyer's office in his company housed in Crystal City he had a display of baseball caps embroidered with the name of each Aegis-equipped ship.
‡ Sadly, because of the admiral's deteriorating health, this was the final interview. The plan had been to do further ones to cover his post-active duty career.

President's, said that each service was ordered to provide ten officers to Abrahamson to populate the, whatever the hell it was then called, the ballistic missile defense outfit.*

Paul Stillwell: Strategic Defense Initiative.†

Admiral Meyer: It didn't hold that name very long.

Paul Stillwell: Well, it was also called "Star Wars" for a while.

Admiral Meyer: Yeah. It didn't hold that first name very long. And he was partly billeted over on K Street and scattered around, and finally they put him in the goddamn bus station in the Pentagon.‡ Scattered all over the place. Well, about a year after that these agreements that had been made, they checked and Abe said, "Well, you know, Mr. Secretary...." It turned out the Air Force produced its ten officers in about three days. The Army produced its ten officers in about three months. The Navy had yet to produce an officer, and over a year had passed. Watkins was pissed—I believe it was Watkins—and so he ordered it done, like *now*.§

Well, John Joseph Donegan had been selected for captain, and he had planned and was intended to be the new technical director in Aegis. Overnight he was no longer the technical director. His ass was yanked, and he was ordered to SDI, and he went over and reported in and he came back over here and he, "Admiral, you can't believe what I've just seen. You can't believe it. You've *gotta* help me." And he got on this very blackboard and started trying to draw the structure, and it turned out he couldn't. And that's how I got started in ballistic missile defense, that very way. I believe I'm correct;

---

*Caspar W. Weinberger served as Secretary of Defense from 21 January 1981 to 23 November 1987. Lieutenant General James A. Abrahamson, USAF, became director of the Strategic Defense Initiative in 1984.
† The Strategic Defense Initiative (SDI), was President Ronald Reagan's proposal for a space-based system to protect the United States from nuclear missiles. The system never came into being, primarily because of the end of the Cold War.
‡ The Ballistic Missile Defense organization was housed in a part of the Pentagon that was formerly the bus terminal.
§ Admiral James D. Watkins, USN, was Chief of Naval Operations from 1 July 1982 to 30 June 1986.

the year was '87, I think. I think it was '87. I could be off a year or so. But that's how I got started. John Joseph Donegan.

I said, "I've got too many other things I'm doing."

"Oh, you've got to help me," he said. And he said, "I'm going to pay you. Don't worry about it; I'll pay you." He said, "I've got to have help. I can't do this." So eventually I served on the national advisory committee for the BMDAC, Ballistic Missile Defense Advisory Committee. I served on it for ten years. I was a member seven years and then I was the chairman for the last three years before—what the hell's the last Air Force general? Kadish.[*] He disbanded it. He is one of these kinds of people didn't think he needed any advice, and so he got rid of it. When I first joined it, it had all the biggies on it. Well, pretty soon they thinned out. Like, you know, who was out at Livermore, Dr.... He's the strategic defense guy.[†]

Paul Stillwell: I don't know.

Admiral Meyer: He's dead now. Yeah, you do know. He's dead now. He's famous for—he's a gadfly. And he spoke directly to the President. But he's back, '95 or '96 he died, he lived so long. Actually, I thought he was a pretty nice fellow, but all he wanted is he just wanted his way. So he was the original chairman of it, for Abe. Time passed, and that's how I ended up there.

Anyway, I ended up serving on that committee and stuff. It turned out, of course, myself and Gene Fox, and Gene Fox was still on active duty as the deputy. And Dr. Julian Davidson, who lives in Alabama, and I'd known him because he was an Army civil servant for a long time. He was their main authority on radar, is how I knew him. He was a smart guy. He and I were the only two people on the goddamn committee, which had about 30 people, that had the foggiest idea what the fire control equation was or what had to be done in order to execute one of these operations. The rest of them were on there for their image.

---

[*] Lieutenant General Ronald T. Kadish, USAF, was director of the Missile Defense Agency from 2002 to 2004.
[†] This is probably a reference to Dr. Edward Teller.

Well, that went on for a long time, and then I watched the drama unfold. As I say, I told you how many years I was on it. I'll be damned, I thought that I had revisited the 1950s, between the Air Force and the Navy. By the way, it turned out the Navy was generally correct. The Air Force was generally wrong. They were wrong in the '50s, and they were wrong here again. Their understanding of warfare and their view of warfare is just tainted badly. I told Gene Fox one day, I mean, I said, "I feel like I've been reverted to being a senior grade lieutenant, because of the discussions I hear going on here and what people are saying." And these are all at least grandsons of the originals. I'm finished with that. That was my closer.*

---

* Up to the time of his death, reported his associate Troy Kimmel, Admiral Meyer served as chairman of the Navy theater-wide ballistic missile defense senior advisory team. The body was later called the Aegis BMD senior advisory team after the project name was changed around 2002. It was a group of retired senior program managers, flag officers, and senior government retirees who advised the program manager.

Launched in 1969, the U.S. Naval Institute's award-winning oral history program is among the oldest in the country. Used in combination with documentary sources, oral histories offer a richer understanding of naval history through candid recollections and explanations rarely entered into contemporary records. In addition, they help depict the atmosphere of a particular event or era in a manner not available in official documents.

The nonprofit Naval Institute accomplishes its history projects through contributed funds and gratefully accepts tax-deductible gifts of all sizes for this purpose. This support allows the Institute to preserve the life experiences of today's service men and women so they may enlighten and inspire future generations.

For information about opportunities to underwrite Naval Institute oral history projects, please contact the Naval Institute Foundation at 291 Wood Road, Annapolis, Maryland 21402; by phone at (410) 295-1054; or by e-mail at foundation@usni.org.

Index to the Oral History of
Rear Admiral Wayne E. Meyer, U.S. Navy (Retired)

AJ Savage
Carrier-based aircraft used for nuclear weapons training in the 1950s, 185

Abrahamson, Lieutenant General James A., USAF
In the 1980s was director of the Strategic Defense Initiative organization, 641-642

Acapulco, Mexico
Visited in August 1962 by the guided missile cruiser *Galveston* (CLG-3), 254-256

Adak, Alaska
The Missile Defense Agency operates radar-equipped platforms in Adak, 324-325

Advanced Surface Missile System (ASMS)
Proposals for the forerunner of Aegis were studied in 1964 by a group under Rear Admiral Frederic Withington, 370-374
Source selection in the late 1960s, 358, 469-470
In December 1969 was renamed Aegis, 375

Aegis Combat System
Proposals for the system, then known as Advanced Surface Missile System (ASMS) were studied in 1964 by a group under Rear Admiral Frederic Withington, 370
Source selection in the late 1960s, 358
Renamed from ASMS in December 1969, 375, 399
Criticism from the Center for Naval Analyses (CNA) in 1970, 399-402
Program steps in the early to mid-1970s, 399-440
Within the Naval Sea Systems Command, PMS-400 managed the Aegis shipbuilding program from 1977 onward, 377-378, 513-560
Long-time role of the Combat System Engineering Development Site (CSEDS), 176-180, 391, 466-467, 472, 527-535
Meyer's views in 2007-08 on training and leadership of Aegis personnel, 123-124, 244-245, 286-289, 303-304, 336, 347, 391-392, 413-414, 418-419, 466-468, 477, 480, 545-546, 550-572, 626-627
Value of visiting contractor plants that produce missile, radar, and fire control components, plus shipyards, 293-294, 336, 545-547, 557-560
Funding and contracts involved in the Aegis program, 294, 331-334, 379-384, 387-390, 427, 436, 473-474, 477-478, 493-498, 539-540, 546, 550-557, 560-569
Decisions in the 1970s not to create nuclear-powered Aegis ships or strike cruisers, 454-459, 479-480, 533-534, 576-578
Divorce rate for individuals in the Aegis program, 475-477
In 1977 Congress authorized the first Aegis ship, which became the guided missile cruiser *Ticonderoga* (CG-47), 493

Hull forms of the *Spruance* (DD-963) and *Kidd* DDG-993) classes were used in the 1970s in developing *Ticonderoga* (CG-47)-class cruisers, 101-102, 433-440, 501-502, 614-619

Contention in the early 1980s over whether Aegis ships should have helicopters, 586-588

Secretary of the Navy John Lehman removed Meyer from the Aegis program in 1983, 326, 408, 450-451, 514, 526, 539, 544, 583-592, 600, 609, 627-631

In the 1980s Aegis missile-firing ships moved from twin-arm rail launchers to vertical launching systems, 599-605

Meyer's assessment of the program's place in naval history, 172, 639-640

In February 2008 the Aegis cruiser *Lake Erie* (CG-70) shot down a satellite in space with a modified SM-3 Standard missile, 168, 174-182, 291-293, 354-355, 365-366, 452-454

Attempts in the 2000s to move from Aegis to "open architecture," 514-515

Air Force, U.S.

Strategic Air Command (SAC) relationship with the Navy's nuclear weapons school in the 1950s, 193

Measures in the mid-1950s to provide warning of the approach of Soviet bombers, 198-200

Involvement in the mid-1960s in the source selection process for new equipment, 344-345, 469

In the 1970s turned over a NORAD site at Moorestown, New Jersey, for use by the Navy, 528-529

Alaska

The Missile Defense Agency operates radar-equipped platforms in Adak, 324-325

Albright, Commander Richard K., USN (USNA, 1953)

In the late 1960s monitored the modernization of the guided missile frigate *Leahy* (DLG-16) prior to becoming the ship's executive officer, 297-300, 630

Alcohol

Drinking to celebrate Meyer's commissioning in Kansas in 1946, 76-77

Medicinal alcohol served in the late 1940s to members of the crew of the destroyer *Goodrich* (DD-831), 109

Ammunition

Storage of 6-inch ammunition for light cruisers on board the destroyer tender *Sierra* (AD-18) in the early 1950s, 157

Meyer insisted that the guided missile cruiser *Ticonderoga* (CG-47) have ammo on board during trials in the early 1980s, 265

Anderson, Captain Carl A., USN

Served 1984-86 as the first commanding officer of the guided missile cruiser *Yorktown* (CG-48), 590-591

Antiair Warfare

In the late 1940s the destroyer *Goodrich* (DD-831) served as a radar picket destroyer, 97-100, 102-104

Mission of the Distant Early Warning Line in the mid-1950s to warn of Soviet bombers, 198-200

Talos missiles on board the guided missile cruiser *Galveston* (CLG-3) in the early 1960s, 196, 241-244, 250-251, 256-263, 269, 288

Work in the 1960s of the Special Navy Task Force for Surface Missile Systems, later called the Surface Missile Systems Project Office, 249, 269-278, 283-330, 338

In the 1980s Aegis missile-firing ships moved from twin-arm rail launchers to vertical launching systems, 599-605

Anti-Missile Defense

In the 1990s Rear Admiral Rodney Rempt was Director, Theater Air Defense, 288-289

In Meyer's view, the AIM-9 AMRAAM has limited capability in missile defense, 291-292

The Missile Defense Agency operates radar-equipped platforms in Alaska, 324

U.S. missile-defense programs in the 1980s and afterward, 640-643

In February 2008 the Aegis cruiser *Lake Erie* (CG-70) shot down a satellite in space with a modified SM-3 Standard missile, 168, 174-182, 291-293, 354-355, 365-366, 452-454

Meyer served on the Ballistic Missile Defense Advisory Committee, 642-643

Arleigh Burke (DDG-51)-Class Destroyers

Design of the in the 1980s, 624-625

Army, U.S.

Sent troops ashore in the northern area of Japan in the late 1940s, 141-142

Fort Bliss, Texas, was the site of joint-service Guided Missile School in the early 1950s, 162-170, 371

Rocket and missile testing at White Sands Missile Range and Redstone Arsenal in the 1950s, 164-165, 182-183

Arthur, Captain William A., USN (USNA, 1942)

Commanded the test ship *Norton Sound* (AVM-1), 1964-65, 356

In the late 1960s was involved in a source selection board while on temporary duty from the Navy Surface Missile Systems Engineering Station, Port Hueneme, 356-359, 469

Ashworth, Captain Frederick L., USN (USNA, 1933)

Involvement with nuclear weapons in the 1940s and 1950s, 185, 193-194

Atkinson, Ensign Edward C., USN (USNA, 1946)

In the late 1940s served in the destroyer *Goodrich* (DD-831), 92-93, 101, 104-105

Atlantic Barrier (BarLant)
    Patrols in the mid-1950s to detect Soviet bombers, 199-201

Awards, Naval
    Meyer's view on the awarding of medals to naval personnel over the years, 456
    In the early 1980s Meyer received the Distinguished Service Medal for his role in Aegis, 456-457

Babr
    Former U.S. destroyer *Zellars* (DD-777), sold to Iran in 1972, 502-511

Backman, Captain Fred M.
    As Commander Pacific Missile Range, Barking Sands, modernized the facility, 174

Bagley, Vice Admiral Worth H., USN (USNA, 1947)
    Commanded the missile cruiser *Canberra* (CAG-2), 1968-69, 442-444, 609
    As the Navy's Director of Program Planning in the early 1970s, arranged for CNO Elmo Zumwalt to visit the Aegis program at Johns Hopkins Applied Physics Laboratory, 441-446, 609
    In 1975, as Vice Chief of Naval Operations, headed a selection board that chose Meyer for rear admiral, 632-633

Baird, Commander Leonard J., USN (USNA, 1935)
    In the late 1940s commanded the destroyer *Goodrich* (DD-831), 94-96, 104-105, 108-110, 115, 117-121

Ball, Captain Richard E., USN (USNA, 1937)
    In the mid-1960s served as commanding officer of the Navy Surface Missile Systems Engineering Station, Port Hueneme, 344

Ballentine, Vice Admiral John J., USN (USNA, 1918)
    Served 1949-51 as Commander Sixth Fleet, 159
    Wife's entertaining habits, 159

Bath Iron Works, Bath, Maine
    In the 1960s and 1970s did modernization work to guided missile frigates, 301-302
    Corporate ownership, 512
    In the late 1970s dropped out of bidding for the guided missile cruiser *Ticonderoga* (CG-47), 494-495, 616
    In the 1980s became a second source for Aegis ships, 613-618
    Built the guided missile destroyer *Wayne E. Meyer* (DDG-108), 2007-09, 322, 328-329, 573-574

Battista, Anthony R.
    Congressional staff member involved with the Aegis program in the 1970s, 383-385, 423-425, 596-597

Bayh, Senator Birch E.
In 1975 questioned the capability of the Aegis system in bad weather, 385-386

Beach, Captain Edward L., USN (Ret.) (USNA, 1939)
Went on the sea trials of the guided missile cruiser *Ticonderoga* (CG-47) in 1982 in preparation for writing the book *Keepers of the Sea*, 623-624

Beers, Commander Robert C., USN
Aegis program staff member who accompanied Meyer to congressional testimony in the 1970s, 385-386, 433, 436

Berude, Lieutenant (junior grade) John B., USN
In the late 1940s served in the light cruiser *Springfield* (CL-66), 145

Betzer, Captain William E., USN (USNA, 1942)
In the early 1970s was executive officer of the Navy Surface Missile Systems Engineering Station, Port Hueneme, 357

***Biddle*, USS (DLG-34)**
Frigate that in 1972 shot down a MiG fighter in Vietnam with a Terrier missile, 356

Bird, Commander Horace V., USN (USNA, 1933)
In the late 1940s served in the Bureau of Naval Personnel and later as executive officer of the light cruiser *Springfield* (CL-66), 126-127

Blades, Commander Lawrence Todd, (USNA, 1952)
Served in the 1960s in the cruisers *Long Beach* (CGN-9) and *Galveston* (CLG-3) and in the Surface Missile Systems Project, 269-271, 280

Boland Marine, New Orleans, Louisiana
Incomplete modernization work on the guided missile frigate *King* (DLG-10) in the mid-1970s, 301-302

Budgetary Issues
Funding and contracts involved in the Aegis program, 294, 331-334, 379-384, 387-390, 427, 473-474, 493-498, 539-540, 546, 550-557, 560-569

Bureau of Naval Personnel (BuPers)
In the post-World War II period, reserve officers augmented to the regular Navy, 121-125

Bureau of Naval Weapons (BuWeps)
Formed in 1959 by combining the Bureau of Ordnance and the Bureau of Aeronautics, 225

Work in the early 1960s of the Special Navy Task Force for Surface Missile Systems, later called the Surface Missile Systems Project Office, 249, 269-278, 310-311, 283-330, 338

In the mid-1960s had headquarters in the Munitions Building on Constitution Avenue in Washington, D.C., 283-284, 312

Burke, Admiral Arleigh A., USN (USNA, 1923)
Commanded the Atlantic Fleet Destroyer Force (DesLant) in 1955, 212
During his tenure as Chief of Naval Operations, 1955-61, the Navy made great technological changes, 223, 247, 350, 481
Views on professional capability of naval officers, 123-124
Views on Aegis destroyers, 125

Busey, Admiral James B. IV, USN
Served as Vice Chief of Naval Operations, 1985-87, 638

Cagle, Rear Admiral Malcolm W., USN (USNA, 1941)
Commanded a task force in the Sea of Japan after North Koreans shot down a U.S. EC-121 intelligence plane in April 1969, 360-363

Campbell, Ensign William R. Jr., USN (USNA, 1945)
Served in the late 1940s on board the destroyer *Goodrich* (DD-831), 104-105

***Canberra*, USS (CAG-2)**
Limited range of Terrier in the late 1950s-early 1960s, 288, 292
Problems with Terrier missile performance in 1961, 248-249
Repairs at the Long Beach Naval Shipyard in the late 1960s, 442-444

Carter, Captain Edward W. III, USN (USNA, 1951)
Commanded the guided missile frigate *Biddle* (DLG-34), 1972-74, 356
Commanded the Operational Test and Evaluation Force in the early 1980s, 594-595

Carvalho, Orlando P.
General manager of marine systems and sensors for Lockheed Martin at Moorestown, New Jersey in the 2000s, 571, 606

Center for Naval Analyses (CNA)
Criticism of the ASMS/Aegis program around 1970, 399-401

***Charles F. Adams* (DDG-2)-Class Destroyers**
Served the Navy well for many years, 375

Chelsea, Massachusetts, Naval Hospital
Birthplace in 1950 of Meyer's daughter Paula, 151-152, 158, 189

Chicago, USS (CG-11)
: Took station in the Sea of Japan after North Koreans shot down an EC-121 intelligence aircraft in April 1969, 363

China
: Visited by the light cruiser *Springfield* (CL-66) in 1948-49, 141-146

Chosin, USS (CG-65)
: Problems with material condition observed in 2008 inspection, 317-318, 565-566

Civil Service
: Civil servants who worked in the Navy's Surface Missile Systems Project in the 1960s, 308-309, 311-313, 397-398
: In the late 1960s replaced contractor personnel at the Navy Surface Missile Systems Engineering Station, Port Hueneme, 339-344
: Advent in the 1960s of large numbers of women into Civil Service, 342-343, 396-398, 474-475, 560-562, 616-627

Clark, Admiral Vernon E., USN
: Dispersal of Navy offices during his tenure as CNO, 2000-05, 318-319, 486-487

Collins, Captain John T., USN (USNA, 1946)
: Served in the destroyer *Goodrich* (DD-831) in the late 1940s, later was involved in the *Spruance* (DD-963)-class program, 101-102

Columbus, USS (CG-12)
: Armed with Talos missiles in the 1960s and 1970s, 266-267

Colvard, Dr. James
: Involvement over the years with missile systems, 456, 479

Combat System Engineering Development Site (CSEDS), Moorestown, New Jersey
: Long-time development location for the Aegis system, 176-180, 317, 391, 410-415, 422, 428-430, 466-468, 472, 527-535, 552-553, 562-563, 570-572, 600, 611-612

Commercial Ships
: Meyer's observations on the difference between Navy warships and commercial cruise ships, 325

Communications
: Radio on board the destroyer *Goodrich* (DD-831) in the late 1940s, 103-104
: Increased radio capability on board the radar picket destroyer escort *Strickland* (DER-324) in the mid-1950s, 204-206
: Quality radio communication in Aegis ships from the 1980s onward, 558-559

Computers
Meyer's views on computers, including the fact that he didn't use one himself, 234-236
At the Naval Postgraduate School in the late 1950s, 235
Reduction in size of signal processors in missile-equipped ships from the 1960s, onward, 322, 381-382
Computers in Aegis-equipped ships, 431, 517-520
Meyer's disdain in 2008 for on-line college education, 458

Congress, U.S.
Relationship with Meyer and the Aegis program, 315, 334-335, 383-386, 423-425, 432-433, 477-478, 596-597, 617
Admiral Elmo Zumwalt's testimony on Aegis in the early 1970s, 440
In 1977 authorized the first Aegis ship, which became the guided missile cruiser *Ticonderoga* (CG-47), 493
Ted Kennedy and Tip O'Neill complained that the shipyard in Quincy, Massachusetts, did not get the *Ticonderoga* contract, 496-500, 617
Effect of the 1986 Goldwater-Nichols Defense Reorganization Act on Navy material acquisition, 341-342, 485
In 2008 some members nominated Meyer for promotion, 351

Contracts
Funding and contracts involved in the Aegis program, 294, 331-334, 379-384, 477-478.493-498, 539-540, 546, 550-557, 560-569

Cotten, Captain John H., USN (USNA, 1935)
Commanded the guided missile cruiser *Galveston* (CLG-3), 1961-62, 243

Crenshaw, Captain Russell S., Jr., USN (USNA, 1941)
Commanded the destroyer *Forrest Sherman* (DD-931) from 1955 to 1957, 213-217

CSEDS
See: Combat System Engineering Development Site (CSEDS), Moorestown, New Jersey

Curtis, Vice Admiral D.C., USN (USNA, 1976)
Served as Commander Naval Surface Forces, 2008-11, 318

Dalla Mura, Commander Bart M., USN (USNA, 1954)
In the early 1970s helped the Iranian Navy set up a base at Bandar Abbas, 509-510

Daniel, Rear Admiral John C., USN (USNA, 1924)
Commanded Destroyer Force Atlantic Fleet (DesLant), 1955-58, 209, 217-218

Davisville, Rhode Island, Naval Construction Battalion Center
In the late 1940s was the temporary home of Destroyer Division 142, 106-108

Defense Department
Took control of the shore patrol and military police in San Francisco in the late 1940s, 90-91
Dr. K. T. Keller served from 1950 to 1953 as director of the Office of Guided Missiles in the Defense Department, 371-372
In the 1950s ran a nuclear weapons training course at Sandia Base, 184

Defense Systems Management College, Fort Belvoir, Virginia
Role in training acquisition professionals in the 2000s, 416

DeLargy, Captain John M., USN (USNA, 1944)
Commanded the guided missile cruiser *Chicago* (CG-11) from 9 March 1968 to 19 September 1969, 363

Destroyer Force Atlantic Fleet (DesLant)
Based at Newport, Rhode Island, in the 1940s-50s, 108, 120-121, 209-218

DePrez, Lieutenant Richard J., USN (USNA, 1944)
Aviator who was involved in nuclear weapons training in the mid-1950s, 185

Dewey, USS (DLG-14)
In the mid-1960s had problems with a nuclear-capable Terrier missile, 304-305

DiBona, Charles J., (USNA, 1956)
In the early 1970s was CEO of the Center for Naval Analyses, which criticized Aegis, 401-402

Distant Early Warning (DEW)
In the mid-1950s Navy ships provided a seaward extension of the warning line against Soviet bombers, 198-200

Donegan, Captain John Joseph Jr., USN (USNA, 1963)
In the 1980s was involved in ballistic missile defense, 640-642

Doyle, Vice Admiral James H., Jr., USN (USNA, 1947)
Served as Commander Third Fleet, 1974-75, 482-483
As DCNO (Surface Warfare) in the late 1970s, provided strong support for the Aegis combat system, 177, 317, 323, 377, 447-448, 481, 483-485, 530-531, 578, 581-582
The Combat System Engineering Development Site (CSEDS) in Moorestown, New Jersey, is named in his honor, 317, 608

Draper, Dr. C. Stark
As a professor at the Massachusetts Institute of Technology in the 1940s and 1960s, 239

Drones
P-2 Neptune drone version used as a target for missile firings in the early 1960s, 251-252

Dunn, Vice Admiral Robert F., USN (USNA, 1951)
As DCNO (Air Warfare) in the mid-1980s was a supporter of Aegis-equipped escort ships for aircraft carriers, 592

EC-121 Warning Star
Large gathering of U.S. warships in the Sea of Japan after North Korea shot down an EC-121 intelligence aircraft in April 1969, 241, 359-363

Electronic Warfare
Role of the Naval Electronics Systems Command in the 1970s in connection with Aegis, 403-404

Enlisted Personnel
Fleet sailors volunteered for V-12 training in World War II to get out of shipboard duty, 69-71
On board the destroyer *Goodrich* (DD-831) in the late 1940s, 100-101, 105, 109-110, 113-114, 118
Meyer's view on enlisted personnel becoming limited duty officers, 123

***Enterprise*, USS (CVAN-65)**
Took station in the Sea of Japan after North Koreans shot down an EC-121 intelligence aircraft in April 1969, 360-363

Erb, Captain Leonard, USN (Ret.) (USNA, 1942)
As president of Ingalls Shipbuilding at Pascagoula when the guided missile cruiser *Ticonderoga* (CG-47) was built in the early 1980s, 265, 543-550, 557, 602

F2H Banshee
Nuclear weapons delivery methods in the 1950s, 192

F8F Bearcat
Tests near the Grumman plant in the late 1940s, 118-119

Fee, Captain Jerome J., USN (USNA, 1960)
In the 1980s was involved in the design of the *Arleigh Burke* (DDG-51)-class destroyers, 624-625

Fine, Hyman
Congressional staff member involved with the Aegis program in the 1970s, 383, 424

Fire Control

System on board the guided missile cruiser *Galveston* (CLG-3) in the early 1960s, 251-253, 258-260

For Terrier missiles in the mid-1960s, 287-293, 295-296

In 1967-68 the Philadelphia Naval Shipyard did an upgrade to the fire control system of the guided missile frigate *Leahy* (DLG-16), 295-301, 330-333, 349-350

Upgrade work on subsequent ships in the 1960s-70s, 301-302, 330, 349-350

Cooling systems for radars on board guided missile ships, 366-367

For Standard missiles in the 2000s, 290-291

Flaherty, John

Naval Sea Systems Command civilian involved in Aegis contracting, 379-380, 414-415

Foreman, Captain Robert P., USN (USNA, 1944)

In the early 1960s served on the Special Navy Task Force for Surface Missile Systems, 271-272, 313

First commanding officer of the guided missile frigate *Wainwright* (DLG-28) in 1966, 271

Forrestal, James V.

As Secretary of Defense, visited the Mediterranean in 1948, 114-115

Forrest Sherman, USS (DD-931)

Destroyer that experienced an oil spill at Newport, Rhode Island, in the mid-1950s, 213-217

Fort Belvoir, Virginia

Site of the Defense Systems Management College and the Defense Acquisition University in the 2000s, 416

Fort Bliss, Texas

Site of joint-service Guided Missile School in the early 1950s, 162-170, 371

Foster, Lieutenant Commander Charles F., USN

Served in the late 1940s as chief engineer of the light cruiser *Springfield* (CL-66), 128, 131

Foster, Dr. John S. Jr.

As Director of Defense Research and Engineering, laid down a requirement for the Aegis combat system, 376, 470-471

Fowler, Vice Admiral Earl B. Jr., USN

Remained on active duty for nearly 40 years after being commissioned through the V-12 training program in 1946, 61

Served as Commander Naval Sea Systems Command, 1980-85, 332, 632, 637

Freedom, USS (LCS-1)
Littoral combat ship built in Marinette, Michigan, commissioned in 2008, 579, 320

Frosch, Dr. Robert A.
As Assistant Secretary of the Navy (Research and Development) in the mid-1960s, view on obsolescence, 289, 321

Galveston, Texas
The guided missile cruiser *Galveston* (CLG-3) visited the city in August 1962, 254-256

Galveston, USS (CLG-3)
Talos missiles on board in the early 1960s, 196, 241-244, 250-251, 256-263, 269, 288
Missile testing in the Caribbean in early 1961, 242-244, 250
Shipyard period at Philadelphia, 1961-62, 243, 250-254, 298-299
Transit to new homeport in San Diego, July-August 1963, 253-256, 264
Pacific operations in 1962-63, 256-264, 269
As a training platform for guided missile personnel in the early 1960s, 346

General Dynamics Corporation
In the late 1970s the shipyard in Quincy, Massachusetts bid unsuccessfully on construction of the guided missile cruiser *Ticonderoga* (CG-47), 495-500, 616
Construction of liquefied natural gas tankers in the late 1970s, 498-499
In the mid-1980s the Standard missile was shifted from General Dynamics to Hughes and later Raytheon, 633-635

General Line School, Monterey, California
In the mid-1950s was used for training former Naval Reserve officers, 187-190

Germany
Former German scientists worked in U.S. rocket and missile development programs in the early 1950s, 163-168, 182-183

Giambastiani, Admiral Edmund P. Jr., USN (USNA, 1970)
Provided senior leadership to the Navy's submarine community prior to his retirement in 2007, 420

Gibson, Dr. Ralph E.
Director from 1948 to 1969 of the Johns Hopkins Applied Physics Laboratory, 271

Gilliam, Frank
Civil servant who worked in the Navy's Surface Missile Systems Project in the 1960s, 308

Goldwater-Nichols Defense Reorganization Act
　Effect of this 1986 law on Navy material acquisition, 341-342, 485

Goodrich, USS (DD-831)
　Home-ported in the Newport, Rhode Island, area in the late 1940s, 91-97, 105-108, 120-121
　In the late 1940s served as a radar picket destroyer, 97-100, 102-104, 118-119
　Enlisted crew members, 100-101, 105, 109-110, 113-114, 116-118
　Differences between regulars and reservists in the crew, 99-102
　Deployment to the Mediterranean in 1948, 109-118
　Operations in the Atlantic in the late 1940s, 118-119, 258

Goodwin, William V.
　Spent many years in the Missile and Surface Radar Division of the RCA Corporation, 1978-87, 380-382, 411-412, 434-436, 469-473, 515, 528-529, 532, 557-558, 562-563, 570-572, 605-606, 608-612

Gorshkov, Admiral Sergei G.
　Meyer's view that this Soviet Navy Commander in Chief was apprehensive in the 1980s about Aegis-equipped ships, 330-331

Grant, Captain Peter McPherson III, USN (USNA, 1976)
　Served as program director of the Aegis Ballistic Missile Defense Project, 1997-2002, 175-176, 180, 365-366, 491

Gray, Robert E.
　Civil servant who worked for many years in the Aegis program, 562-564

Great Britain
　Involved in the administration of Trieste in 1948, 112, 115-116

Guilbault, Captain Roland G., USN
　Served as first commanding officer of the guided missile cruiser *Ticonderoga* (CG-47), 1983-85, 582-584

Gunnery-Naval
　The guided missile cruiser *Galveston* (CLG-3) fired 5-inch and 6-inch guns in the early 1960s, 256, 260
　Vietnam shore bombardment by cruiser *Oklahoma City* (CLG-6), 258

Guy, Commander Robert S. USN
　As a detailer at the Bureau of Naval Personnel around 1960, 240

Hack, Commander John A., USN (USNA, 1935)
　In the early 1950s served as executive officer of the destroyer tender *Sierra* (AD-18), 154-155

Hamilton, Rear Admiral Charles S., USN
    Role in various ship acquisition programs in the 1990s and 2000s, 409-410

Hayward, Admiral Thomas B., USN (Ret.) (USNA, 1948)
    Attended the christening of the guided missile cruiser *Ticonderoga* (CG-47) in 1981, 542-544
    After retirement from active duty was on the board of Litton Industries, 542

Helicopters
    Contention in the early 1980s over whether Aegis ships should have helicopters, 586-588

Herrmann, Rear Admiral Ernest E., USN (USNA, 1919)
    Served in the late 1940s as Commander Cruiser Division 17 and in the early 1950s as superintendent of the Naval Postgraduate School, 126-127, 142-143, 146-147

Hicks, Rear Admiral Alan B. "Brad," USN
    Served from 2005 to 2009 as Program Director, Aegis Ballistic Missile Defense, 175-178, 452

Holloway, Admiral James L. III, USN (Ret.) (USNA, 1943)
    As CNO in the mid-1970s visited the Iranian Navy, 510-511

Holmberg, Rear Admiral Paul A., USN (USNA, 1939)
    Grew up in Brunswick, Missouri, before entering the Navy, 122

Hunters Point Naval Shipyard, San Francisco, California
    In 1949 inactivated the light cruiser *Springfield* (CL-66), 134, 148-150

Ingalls Shipbuilding, Pascagoula, Mississippi
    Corporate ownership by Litton, 512, 542-543
    Built nuclear submarines from the 1950s to the 1970s, 576-577
    Construction of destroyers and amphibious assault ships in the 1970s, 537-538, 541
    Built *Ticonderoga* (CG-47)-class guided missile cruisers in the 1980s, 265-266, 495-498, 537-538, 541-557, 616
    In 1981 installed vertical-launch missile tubes in the test ship *Norton Sound* (AVM-1), 601-605

Ingram, Captain John, USN (Ret.)
    Engineering duty specialist who was involved in the Aegis shipbuilding program, 326-327

Iranian Navy
    In the early 1970s bought two former U.S. destroyers and commissioned them as the *Babr* and *Palang*, 502-511

Four guided missile destroyers ordered by Iran wound up in the U.S. Navy in the early 1980s as the *Kidd* (DDG-993) class, 501-502

Israel
Officially established as a nation in 1948, 110

Italy
The destroyer *Goodrich* (DD-831) visited Venice in 1948, 111-116
Contested election in April 1948, 112-113

Japan
Meyer's views on Japanese Americans who were interned during World War II, 370-371
Desolate nation visited by U.S. warships in 1948-49, 141-142, 144, 148

Johns Hopkins Applied Physics Laboratory
In the 1950s worked on the development of the Navy's three T's missiles, 170-171
Auditorium named for nuclear weapons pioneer William S. Parsons, 194-195
Long-time role in the Aegis combat system, 176-177, 413, 444-446
Visited by CNO Elmo Zumwalt in the early 1970s, 444-446

Johnson, Rear Admiral Felix L., USN (Ret.) (USNA, 1920)
Served as first commanding officer of the light cruiser *Springfield* (CL-66) when she was commissioned in 1944, 120-121
Served 1948-49 as Commander Destroyer Force Atlantic Fleet, 107, 109, 120-121

Johnson, President Lyndon B.
Connection in the 1960s with civil service personnel for the Navy Surface Missile Systems Engineering Station, Port Hueneme, 342, 397

Joyce, Captain Gerald P., USN (USNA, 1937)
Commanded the guided missile cruiser *Galveston* (CLG-3), 1962-63, 242-243, 253-256

Kansas, University of, Lawrence, Kansas
Naval Reserve officer training site during World War II, 61-77, 84-88
NROTC program initiated shortly after World War II ended, 74-78

Keen, Lieutenant Commander Timothy J.
Served in the early 1960s on board the guided missile cruiser *Canberra* (CAG-2) and on the Special Navy Task Force for Surface Missile Systems, 250

Keller, Dr. K. T.
Served from 1950 to 1953 as director of the Office of Guided Missiles in the Defense Department, 371-372

Kennedy, Senator Edward M.
Around 1970 complained that the shipyard in Quincy, Massachusetts, did not get the *Ticonderoga* (CG-47) contract, 496-500, 617

Kennedy, President John F.
Made a visit to Atlantic Fleet warships in April 1962, 248-249

Kidd, Admiral Isaac C. Jr., USN (Ret.) (USNA, 1942)
Served as Chief of Naval Material, 1971-75, 393-394, 503, 506

Kidd **(DDG-993)-Class Destroyers**
Originally designed for the Iranian Navy, they entered the U.S. Navy in the early 1980s, 501-502, 510-511

Korea, North
Large gathering of U.S. warships in the Sea of Japan after North Korea shot down an EC-121 intelligence aircraft in April 1969, 241, 359-363

Korth, Fred H.
As Secretary of the Navy in the early 1960s when the Navy had problems with surface missile performance, 248-249, 277

Lake, Rear Admiral Julian S., USN
In the 1950s was involved in methods for nuclear weapons delivery with the F2H Banshee, 192
In the 1970s, as Vice Commander Naval Electronics Systems Command, worked with Meyer on Aegis, 403-404

Lake Erie, **USS (CG-70)**
The sponsor was Admiral Meyer's first wife, Margaret, 174, 576, 613
In February 2008 shot down a satellite in space with a modified SM-3 Standard missile, 168, 174-182, 291-293, 354-355, 365-366, 452-454

Leahy, **USS (DLG-16)**
Problems with Terrier missiles in the 1960s, 272
In 1967-68 underwent an upgrade to her fire control system at Philadelphia Naval Shipyard, 295-301, 330-333, 349-350
Naval presence mission in the Caribbean, 481

Leave and Liberty
For sailors in the Kansas City area during World War II, 86-88
In Shanghai, China, in 1948-49, 143-144

Lehman, John F., Jr.
Meyer's assessment of his performance as Secretary of the Navy in the early 1980s, 335, 377-378, 440, 552, 586, 590-592, 628-630

Removed Meyer from the Aegis program in 1983, 326, 408, 450-451, 514, 526, 539, 544, 583-592, 600, 609, 627-631
Relationship with Meyer in the 1983-85 period, 633-634, 637-638, 640

Lehrer, Max
In the 1970s managed an RCA plant in Moorestown, New Jersey, 529-530

Libby, Edward
Civil servant who worked in the Aegis project office in the 1970s, 465

Lockheed Martin Corporation
The involvement of the corporation and its predecessors in the Aegis program over the years, 292, 327, 347, 411, 429-430, 532, 539-540, 555, 572, 583, 601-602, 605-606, 612, 625
Problems in the late 2000s with development of the F-35 Lightning, 347, 387

***Long Beach*, USS (CGN-9)**
Meyer's assessment of the ship's performance, 267
In 1968 shot down two MiG fighters with Talos missiles in Vietnam, 356
In the mid-1970s was considered a candidate for the Aegis combat system, 432-433, 534, 577-578

Long Beach Naval Shipyard
Repairs to the missile cruiser *Canberra* (CAG-2), in the late 1960s, 442-444

Longmuir, Ensign Edward B., Supply Corps, USN (USNA, 1947)
In the late 1940s served in the destroyer *Goodrich* (DD-831), 116

Loprete, Captain Joseph E., USMC
In the late 1940s commanded the Marine detachment on board the light cruiser *Springfield* (CL-66), 147-148

Love, Billy G.
Long-time civil service budget analyst for the Aegis shipbuilding program, PMS-400, 560-569

Madsen, Adelaide M.
Systems analyst and special assistant to Meyer in the Aegis program, 593

Main, George
Civil servant who worked in the Aegis program, 396

Marvinsmith, Commander Harry, USN
Served at nuclear weapons training school at Norfolk in the mid-1950s, 187

Massachusetts Institute of Technology (MIT), Cambridge, Massachusetts
Postgraduate education for naval officers shortly after World War II, 79-84, 89
Postgraduate education for naval officers in the early 1960s, 225-240

Mathews, Mary
Served as sponsor of the Aegis cruiser *Yorktown* (CG-48), which was commissioned in July 1984, 500-501

Mayport, Florida, Naval Station
In the mid-1960s the guided missile frigate *Dewey* (DLG-14) had problems with a nuclear-capable Terrier missile while in Mayport, 304-305

McCullough, Vice Admiral Bernard J. III, USN (USNA, 1975)
Testimony to Congress in 2008 on Aegis ships, 539-540

McCreery, Captain Bernard L., SC, USN
In the mid-1960s served as supply officer of the Navy Surface Missile Systems Engineering Station, Port Hueneme, 344, 357

McMullen, Commander John J., USN (USNA, 1940)
Top-notch naval engineer who received specialized training in Switzerland, later left the service in 1957 and founded his own company, 244-246, 434, 506-507
Worked with the Aegis program to provide a modified *Spruance* (DD-963) hull for the *Ticonderoga* CG-47), 434-436

McNamara, Robert S.
As Secretary of Defense in the 1960s had a large impact on acquisition of equipment, 313-314, 342, 358, 376, 407

Medical Problems
Venereal disease in Italy in 1948 when the destroyer *Goodrich* (DD-831) visited Venice, 113-114
Meyer had a brief case of vertigo in 1948, 117-118
Food poisoning for the crew of the guided missile cruiser *Galveston* (CLG-3) in 1962, 255-256

Mediterranean Sea
In 1948 the destroyer *Goodrich* (DD-831) deployed to the area, 108-118
In 1950 the destroyer tender *Sierra* (AD-18) deployed to the Med, 152-156, 158-160

Mexico
The Meyers went to Juarez for entertainment in the early 1950s, 163-164
The guided missile cruiser *Galveston* (CLG-3) visited Acapulco in 1962, 254-256

Metcalf, Vice Admiral Joseph III, USN (USNA, 1951)
>Served 1984-87 as Deputy CNO (Surface Warfare), spoke at Meyer's 1985 retirement, 637-639

Meyer, Rear Admiral Wayne E., USN (Ret.)
>Parents, 2-12, 15-20, 22, 27-30, 32-34, 41-45, 50-51, 63, 75-76, 96, 138-140, 198, 448
>Siblings, 3-4, 12-13, 18-19, 27-30, 35-40, 43-45, 55-56, 75-76, 139-140
>First wife Margaret, 43, 45, 136-140, 150-152, 158-164, 169, 174, 189-191, 270, 279-282, 287, 393, 423, 488-489, 576, 608, 613
>Second wife Anna Mae, 5, 20, 40, 169, 182, 235-236, 322, 492, 570, 573-576, 593, 608-613, 627-628
>Children, 158, 160, 189-190, 236, 270, 419, 488-489, 613
>Youth in Missouri, 1920s-40s, 1-65, 96-97, 197-198, 450-451, 626
>Received college education and a Naval Reserve commission through the V-12 Program, 1943-46, 60-77, 84-88, 96
>Postgraduate study at the Massachusetts Institute of Technology, 1946-47, 78-84, 89, 136-137
>First shipboard duty was in the destroyer *Goodrich* (DD-831), 1947-48, 92-125, 258
>In 1948 augmented from the Naval Reserve to the regular Navy, 121-125
>In 1948-49 served in the light cruiser *Springfield* (CL-66), 90-91, 120-121, 125-150
>Served 1950-51 on board the destroyer tender *Sierra* (AD-18), 42-43, 151-160
>In 1951-52 attended Guided Missile School at Fort Bliss, Texas, 160-170, 182-183
>From 1952 to 1954 taught in nuclear weapons school, 184-187, 191-197
>In 1954-55 was a student at General Line School, Monterey, California, 187-190
>In 1955-56 served as executive officer of the radar picket destroyer escort *Strickland* (DER-324), 197-209, 450, 461
>Served 1956-58 on the staff of Commander Destroyer Force Atlantic Fleet (DesLant), 209-218
>Attended the Naval Postgraduate School at Monterey, 1958-60, 219-225, 228
>Further postgraduate work at the Massachusetts Institute of Technology, 1960-61, 225-240
>Served 1961-63 as fire control officer in the guided missile cruiser *Galveston* (CLG-3), 133, 241-244, 250-266, 269-270
>Served 1963-67 in the Surface Missile Systems Project, 269-330, 338, 349-350
>In 1967-70, served at the Navy Surface Missile Systems Engineering Station (NSMSES), Port Hueneme, California, 282-283, 338-369, 442-443, 565
>Served 1970-83 in the Advanced Surface Missile System (ASMS), which became Aegis, 370-628
>Served 1983-85 as NavSea-06, Deputy Commander for Weapons and Combat Systems, Naval Sea Systems Command, 630-639
>Post-1985 activities in the area of ballistic missile defense, 640-643

Midway, **USS (CVB-41)**
>Deployment to the Mediterranean in 1948, 110-111, 117-118

Missiles
    Multi-service Guided Missile School at Fort Bliss, Texas, and White Sands, New Mexico, in the early 1950s, 161-170, 182-183
    The Lark was an unsuccessful Army missile in the 1950s, 163
    Convair developed the Atlas rocket for the Air Force in the 1950s, 165-166
    Navy's use of surface-to-surface Regulus missiles in the 1950s, 261
    Talos missiles on board the guided missile cruiser *Galveston* (CLG-3) in the early 1960s, 196, 241-244, 250-251, 256-263, 269, 288
    Difficulty with Terrier missiles in the early 1960s, 248-249, 272
    Role in the 1960s of the Special Navy Task Force for Surface Missile Systems, later called the Surface Missile Systems Project Office, 249, 269-278, 283-330, 338
    In 1963 the *Galveston* hit a surface ship with Talos, 262-263, 269
    The Typhon surface-to-air missile program was canceled in 1963 because of its high cost, 310-311, 315-316, 321-322, 374-376
    Role of the Special Navy Task Force for Surface Missile Systems in supervising the construction of Terrier-equipped warships in the mid-1960s and upgrading capability, 285-291, 295-302, 313, 330-333, 349-350
    In the mid-1960s some Terrier missiles had nuclear warheads, 304-305
    Support for missile-equipped surface ships in the late 1960s-early 1970s through ship's qualification assistance teams (SQAT), 339-340, 348-354, 359
    In 1968 the cruiser *Long Beach* (CGN-9) shot down two MiG fighters with Talos missiles in Vietnam, 356
    In 1969 Meyer took a team to assess missile capabilities of ships operating off Vietnam, 364-365
    The Patriot missile was a candidate for Navy use in the early 1970s, 400-401, 407
    Aegis program steps in the early 1970s, 399-410
    In 1972 the frigate *Biddle* (DLG-34) shot down a MiG fighter in Vietnam with a Terrier missile, 356
    In the mid-1980s the Standard missile was shifted from General Dynamics to Hughes, 633-635
    In the 1980s Aegis missile-firing ships moved from twin-arm rail launchers to vertical launching systems, 599-605
    In February 2008 the Aegis cruiser *Lake Erie* (CG-70) shot down a satellite in space with a modified SM-3 Standard missile, 168, 174-182, 291-293, 354-355, 365-366, 452-454
    In Meyer's view, the AIM-9 AMRAAM has limited capability in missile defense, 291-292

Missile Defense Agency, U.S.
    Operates radar-equipped platforms in Alaska, 324

Moosbrugger, Captain Frederick, USN (USNA, 1923)
    In 1948-49 commanded the light cruiser *Springfield* (CL-66), 127, 134-135, 147

Mullen, Admiral Michael G., USN (USNA, 1968)
As Chief of Naval Operations, 2005-07, 124, 354, 449, 635
Chairman of the Join Chiefs of Staff, 2007-11, 574-575, 636

Naval Construction Battalion Center, Port Hueneme, California
In the late 1960s co-located with the Navy Surface Missile Systems Engineering Station, 338-339

Naval Postgraduate School, Monterey, California
Ordnance curriculum in the school in the late 1950s, 219-225, 228, 238
No nuclear submariners in ordnance studies in the late 1950s, 224-225
Scarce computer availability in the late 1950s, 235

Naval Reserve, U.S.
V-12 officer training program at the University of Kansas during World War II, 60-77, 96
Differences between regulars and reservists in the crew of the destroyer *Goodrich* (DD-831) in the late 1940s, 99-101
Reserve officers on board the radar picket destroyer escort *Strickland* (DER-324) in the mid-1950s, 206-208, 450

Naval Reserve Officer Training Corps (NROTC)
Established at the University of Kansas shortly after World War II, 74-78
NROTC-trained reserve officers on board the radar picket destroyer escort *Strickland* (DER-324) in the mid-1950s, 206-208

Naval Sea Systems Command (NavSea)
PMS-400 managed the Aegis shipbuilding program from 1977 onward, 377-378, 395-396, 513-630
Meyer served 1983-85 as NavSea-06, Deputy Commander for Weapons and Combat Systems, Naval Sea Systems Command, 630-639

Naval Ship Engineering Center, Hyattsville, Maryland
Expressed doubt in the mid-1970s on the Aegis combat system fitting into a *Spruance* (DD-963)-class hull, 433-437, 614-616

Navigation
During Atlantic Barrier (BarLant) patrols in the mid-1950s, 201

Navy Surface Missile Systems Engineering Station, Port Hueneme, California
Buildup in the late 1960-early 1970s, including conversion from contractor personnel to civil servants, 338-343, 469-470
Support for missile-equipped surface ships in the late 1960-early 1970s through ship's qualification assistance teams (SQAT), 339-340, 348-359, 491, 565
Physical upgrades to the facility in the late 1960s, 357-358

Newport, Rhode Island
    Homeport for the ships of Destroyer Division 142 in the late 1940s, 91-97, 105-108, 120-121
    Homeport for the radar picket destroyer escort *Strickland* (DER-324) in the mid-1950s, 200-201, 209
    In the 1940s-50s the destroyer tender *Yosemite* (AD-19) was based in Newport as flagship for ComDesLant, 108, 120-121, 209
    Construction of new piers in the 1950s, 211-214
    Large oil spill by the destroyer *Forrest Sherman* (DD-931) in the mid-1950s, 213-217

News Media
    Capper's Weekly served farm families in the 1930s, 53
    Radio reports of damage at Pearl Harbor in December 1941, 57-58
    Coverage of an oil spill in Newport, Rhode Island, in the mid-1950s, 216

Nitze, Paul H.
    As Secretary of the Navy, 1963-67, involvement with guided missiles, 277-278, 374

Noble, Lieutenant Thomas I., USN (USNA, 1950)
    As a graduate student at Massachusetts Institute of Technology in the early 1960s, 226-228

***Norton Sound*, USS (AVM-1)**
    Test ship that for many years supported Navy guided missile programs, 315-317, 356, 368-369, 374-375, 381, 406-407, 431, 460-466, 527-528, 533, 601-605

NROTC
    See: Naval Reserve Officer Training Corps (NROTC)

Nuclear Power
    Decision in the 1970s not to create nuclear-powered Aegis ships, 454-459, 533-534, 576-578

Nuclear Weapons
    Training in the mid-1950s at Sandia Base and Norfolk, 184-187, 191-196
    Carrier-based AJ Savage aircraft were equipped to carry bombs in the 1950s, 185-186
    Nuclear-equipped Talos missiles on board the guided missile cruiser *Galveston* (CLG-3) in the early 1960s, 196, 261
    In the mid-1960s some Terrier missiles had nuclear warheads, 304-305
    Tactical weapons removed from U.S. warships in the early 1990s, 196

Odening, Captain Robert E., USN (USNA, 1935)
    In the late 1950s was in charge of the ordnance curriculum at the Naval Postgraduate School, 219-220

Oil Pollution
　　Large oil spill in Newport, Rhode Island, by the destroyer *Forrest Sherman* (DD-931) in the mid-1950s, 213-217

***Oklahoma City*, USS (CLG-5)**
　　Operations during the 1960s, including the Vietnam War, 257-258

Olathe (Kansas) Naval Air Station
　　During World War II, served as a receiving station for trainees going to the V-12 program, 65

Operational Test and Evaluation Force (OPTEVFOR), Norfolk, Virginia
　　Relationship with the Aegis program in the 1980s, 594-600

Otth, Rear Admiral Edward J. Jr., USN (USNA, 1949)
　　In the mid-1960s worked on the Terrier missile desk in the Bureau of Naval Weapons, 287, 295, 522
　　Ran the program for *Oliver Hazard Perry* (FFG-7)-class frigates in the 1970s, 522
　　In the 1970s aided Meyer in developing the structure of the Aegis program, 522-526

P-2 Neptune
　　Drone version used as a target for missile firings in the early 1960s, 251

Pacific Missile Range, Barking Sands, Hawaii
　　Role in tracking missiles fired from Aegis ships in the 1990s and 2000s, 174-175

Paige, Rear Admiral Kathleen K., USN
　　Served from 2003 to 2005 as Program Director, Aegis Ballistic Missile Defense, 175-176

Palang
　　Former U.S. destroyer *Stormes* (DD-780), sold to Iran in 1972, 502-511

Parramore, Lieutenant Commander Douglas G., USN
　　Commanded the radar picket destroyer escort *Strickland* (DER-324) in the mid-1950s, 202

Patriot Missile
　　Candidate for Navy use in the early 1970s, 400-401, 407

***Pasadena*, USS (CL-65)**
　　In the autumn of 1948 deployed to the Far East, 140, 146-147

Pay and Allowances
　　For students in the V-12 training program during World War II, 86

Penny, Captain Harmon C., USN (USNA, 1946)
　　In the 1960s served in the Surface Missile Systems Project Office, later served with the Advanced Surface Missile System (ASMS) officer in Huntsville, Alabama, 311-314, 349, 358-359

Perez Jr., Rear Admiral Samuel Jr., USN (USNA, 1980)
　　Aegis-experienced officer who served in the late 2000s in the Southern Command, 418

Philadelphia Naval Shipyard
　　Conversion of the light cruiser *Galveston* (CL-93) in the late 1950s to become a guided missile ship, CLG-3, 246
　　Upgrade work on the *Galveston* in 1961-62, 243, 250-254, 298-299
　　In 1967-68 did an upgrade to the fire control system of the guided missile frigate *Leahy* (DLG-16), 295-301, 330-333, 349-350
　　In the early 1970s converted two old U.S. destroyers to missile ships for Iran, 502-511

Pond, Commander Robert M., USN
　　In the early 1960s served as executive officer of the guided missile cruiser *Galveston* (CLG-3), 254, 256

Port Lyautey, Morocco, Naval Air Station
　　Storage point for nuclear weapons in the mid-1950s, 185-186

Price, Vice Admiral Frank H., USN (USNA, 1941)
　　Served as OP-03, Deputy CNO (Surface Warfare) in 1974-75, 433, 438

Promotion of Officers
　　In January 1975 a Navy board selected Meyer for rear admiral, 632-633

Propulsion Plants
　　Diesel plant in the radar picket destroyer escort *Strickland* (DER-324) in the mid-1950s, 197-198, 204

Quonset Point, Rhode Island, Naval Air Station
　　Operations in the late 1940s, 103, 106-107

Raborn, Vice Admiral William F., Jr., USN (USNA, 1928)
　　Ran the Navy's Special Projects Office from 1965 to 1962, 274-275, 345

Racial Issues
　　Discrimination against African Americans has diminished over the years, 449-450

Radar

In the late 1940s the destroyer *Goodrich* (DD-831) served as a radar picket destroyer, 97-100, 102-104, 115

On board the light cruiser *Springfield* (CL-66) in the late 1940s, 129-130

Height-finding radar on board the radar picket destroyer escort *Strickland* (DER-324) in the mid-1950s, 200

The Navy developed the SPG-49 radar for the Talos missile in the 1950s, 163, 252, 367

Teaching about radars in the Naval Postgraduate School in the late 1950s, 223-224

On board the missile test ship *Norton Sound* (AVM-1) in the early 1960s, 315

Cooling systems and power requirements for radars on board guided missile ships, 366-367

Used with the Patriot missile in the 1970s, 402-403

SPY-1 radar in Aegis-equipped ships, 335-336, 403, 426-430, 460, 490, 527-528

At the Combat System Engineering Development Site (CSEDS) in Moorestown, New Jersey, 531-532

The Missile Defense Agency operates radar-equipped platforms in Adak, 324-325

On board the guided missile cruiser *Ticonderoga* (CG-47) in 1983-84, 584-585

Radio

On board the destroyer *Goodrich* (DD-831) in the late 1940s, 103-104

Increased capability on board the radar picket destroyer escort *Strickland* (DER-324) in the mid-1950s, 204-206

Quality radio communication in Aegis ships from the 1980s onward, 558-559

Rawls, Lieutenant (junior grade) Elbert S. Jr., USN (USNA, 1945)

Served on board the destroyer *Goodrich* (DD-831) in the late 1940s, 94, 105

RCA Corporation

Role in building combat systems for Aegis cruisers and destroyers, 323, 367-368, 380-383, 401, 405, 411-412, 426, 429-430, 436, 469-474, 527-535, 550, 555-558, 605-606, 612

Reagan, Nancy

The First Lady christened the guided missile cruiser *Ticonderoga* (CG-47) in 1981, 542-543

Reagan, President Ronald W.

Backing for a strong defense program in the early 1980s, 377

Victim of assassination attempt in 1981, 543

Redstone Arsenal, Huntsville, Alabama

Rocket and missile development in the 1950-60ss, 182, 313

Regulus Missile

Missile on board surface warships and submarines in the 1950s, 263

Reich, Rear Admiral Eli T., USN (USNA, 1935)
Commanded the guided missile cruiser *Canberra* (CAG-2), 248-249
Ran the Navy's Special Task Force for Surface Missile Systems/Surface Missile Systems Project the 1960s, 242, 246-249, 257, 268-269, 272-277, 284-286, 306-308, 312, 315-316, 331, 338-342, 345-346, 352, 358, 371-375, 426, 453

Religion
Meyer's upbringing in the Catholic Church and school, 1920s-30s, 10, 19-34, 40, 48-49, 52-58, 451

Rempt, Rear Admiral Rodney P., USN (USNA, 1966)
In the 1990s was Director, Theater Air Defense, 288-289

Rickover, Vice Admiral Hyman G., USN (USNA, 1922)
Meyer contends that Rickover kept nuclear submariners out of the Naval Postgraduate School in the late 1950s, 224-225
Relationship with the Polaris ballistic missile submarine program, 579-580
Relationship with shipbuilders in the 1970s-80s, 332-333, 439, 496, 499, 576-677
Testimony to Congress, 334
Possible connection to Aegis if put aboard a nuclear-powered ship, 394, 404-405, 433, 453, 576-577

Roane, Rear Admiral Donald P., USN (USNA, 1952)
Commanded Destroyer Squadron 23, 1974-76, 484, 504, 629
Served as Meyer's deputy in the Aegis program and later headed it himself from 1983 to 1985, 504, 628-631

Rockets
Convair developed the Atlas for the Air Force in the 1950s, 165-166

Rook, Captain Eugene C., USN (USNA, 1924)
Commanded the destroyer tender *Sierra* (AD-18), 1949-50, 154-156, 158

Roosevelt, President Franklin D.
Reaction to the Japanese attack on Pearl Harbor in December 1941, 58
Role in connection with the Navy's V-12 training program in World War II, 60-61, 69, 72

Roosevelt Roads Naval Station, Puerto Rico
Missile range used for testing in the early 1970s, 507-508

Roth, Captain Paul, USN
Served in the mid-1960s at the Navy Surface Missile Systems Engineering Station, Port Hueneme, 338

Roughhead, Admiral Gary, USN (USNA, 1973)
Served as Chief of Naval Operations, 2007-11, 488, 574-575

Rowden, Captain William H., USN (USNA, 1952)
Commanded the guided missile cruiser *Columbus* (CG-12), 1973-74, then became Deputy OP-03, 266-267, 484-485
Served as Meyer's deputy in the Aegis program, 630
From 1985 to 1988 served as Commander Naval Sea Systems Command, 632-633

Rudden, Captain Thomas J., Jr., USN (USNA, 1939)
Commanded the guided missile cruiser *Galveston* (CLG-3) in 1963-64, 257

SC-1 Seahawk
Operated from the light cruiser *Springfield* (CL-66) in the late 1940s, 129-130, 150

St. Pé, Jerry
Was president of Ingalls Shipbuilding at Pascagoula from 1985 to 2001 after having been in public relations, 547

Sanden, Lieutenant Oscar E. Jr., USN
As a student at the Naval Postgraduate School in the late 1950s, 227

Sandia Base, New Mexico
Defense Department facility that was the site of nuclear weapons training in the mid-1950s, 184

San Diego, California
Homeport for the guided missile cruiser *Galveston* (CLG-3) in the early 1960s, 254-257

San Francisco, California
Shore patrol and military police in the late 1940s, 90-91
In 1949 the light cruiser *Springfield* (CL-66) went into the Hunters Point Naval Shipyard for decommissioning, 90-91, 134

Sappington, Rear Admiral Homer M. Sappington, USN (USNA, 1943)
Served 1968-72 as Director, Surface Missile Systems Project, 360, 378-379, 503

Sarver, Rear Admiral Ben W., Jr., USN (USNA, 1935)
Served 1965-66 as Director, Surface Missile Systems Project, 307-308, 338-339, 342-343

Sawyer, George
In 2008 chaired a SecNav panel on shipbuilding, 538-539

Security
    Clearances for those involved in nuclear weapons work in the 1950s, 194-195

Selection Boards
    In January 1975 a Navy board selected Meyer for rear admiral, 632-633

Semmes, Captain Benedict, J., Jr., USN (USNA, 1934)
    Served on the ComDesLant staff in the mid-1950s, 209-210, 212, 217-218

Shaffer, Captain J. Nevin, USN (USNA, 1935)
    Served on the ComDesLant staff in the mid-1950s, 209, 212, 217-218

Shanghai, China
    Visited by the light cruiser *Springfield* (CL-66) in 1948-49, 141-146

Shaw, Milton
    In 1961 made a critical report about the performance of surface missile systems, 248-249

Shipbuilding
    Construction of Aegis ships at Bath Iron Works, 1980s and later, 322, 328-329, 512, 613-614
    Construction of Aegis ships at Ingalls, 1980s and later, 265-266, 537-538, 541-557
    Meyer's warning in the 1990s to friend Delores Etter that shipbuilding would bring her down, 589
    In 2008 George Sawyer chaired a SecNav panel on shipbuilding, 538-539

Ship Design
    Hull forms of the *Spruance* (DD-963) and *Kidd* DDG-993) classes were used in the 1970s in developing *Ticonderoga* (CG-47)-class cruisers, 101-102, 433-440, 501-502, 551-552, 614-619
    Contention in the early 1980s over whether Aegis ships should have helicopters, 586-588
    Design of the *Arleigh Burke* (DDG-51)-class destroyers in the 1980s, 624-625

Shipway, Rear Admiral John F. "Dugan," USN (Ret.)
    Served as president of Bath Iron Works from 2003 to 2009, 573-574

Shore Patrol
    In San Francisco in the late 1940s, 90-91

***Sierra*, USS (AD-18)**
    Operations off the East Coast in the early 1950s, 151-158, 160
    Deployments to the Mediterranean in 1950-51, 152-156, 158-160
    Storage of 6-inch ammunition for light cruisers, 157

Sixth Fleet, U.S.
    In 1950 the destroyer tender *Sierra* (AD-18) deployed to the Med, 152-156, 158-160
    Role of the guided missile cruiser *Ticonderoga* (CG-47) in December 1983, 584-585

Smith, Rear Admiral Levering, USN (USNA, 1932)
    Served for many years in the Navy's ballistic missile submarine programs, 346, 395, 432, 453, 526, 578-579

Skelton, Isaac Newton IV "Ike"
    Congressman who was a strong supporter of the Aegis program, 425

Slaughter, Commander John S., USN (USNA, 1937)
    In 1948-49 served in several leadership positions on board the light cruiser *Springfield* (CL-66), 128-130, 132, 134-135, 136, 145, 148-149

Sonar
    In 1948 the destroyer *Goodrich* (DD-831) tested thermal gradients in the Mediterranean, 108-109

Soviet Union
    In the mid-1950s Navy ships and aircraft provided a seaward extension of the warning line against Soviet bombers, 198-209

Space
    In February 2008 the Aegis cruiser *Lake Erie* (CG-70) shot down a satellite in space with a modified SM-3 Standard missile, 168, 174-182, 291-293, 354-355, 365-366, 452-454

Sperry Rand Corporation
    Work on behalf of Navy missile fire control programs in the 1960s, 252, 287, 292, 298-299, 330-333, 336, 472

Spreen, Captain Roger E., USN (USNA, 1943)
    In the mid-1960s headed the Terrier missile program for the Surface Missile Systems Project, 295-300, 305, 330-333, 426, 453, 522
    Served 1972-74 as Commander Naval Ordnance Systems Command, 379, 392-394, 506-508

***Springfield*, USS (CL-66)**
    Commissioned in 1944 with Captain Felix Johnson in command, 120-121
    Operations around California in 1948-49, 125-130
    Electronic equipment on board in the late 1940s, 128-134
    Enlisted personnel on board in 1948-49, 132-134
    Deployment to the Western Pacific in 1948-49, 140-148

In 1949 went into the Hunters Point Naval Shipyard for decommissioning, 134-136, 148-150

In the late 1950s-early 1960s was converted to a guided missile ship, CLG-7, 148-149

Spruance (DD-963)-Class Destroyers

Approved in the late 1960s under the program of Total Package Procurement, 500-501, 537-538, 541

Hull form used in the 1970s in developing *Ticonderoga* (CG-47)-class cruisers, 101-102, 433-440, 501-502, 614-619

Standard Missile

Source selection for the missile in the mid-1960s, 271-273

Funding for in the 1970s, 473-474, 477-478

Used on board two former U.S. destroyers sold to Iran in the early 1970s, 502-510

Test firing from the *Norton Sound* (AVM-1) in 1974, 461-465

In the mid-1980s the Standard missile was shifted from General Dynamics to Hughes, 633-635

Fire control of in the 2000s, 290-291

In February 2008 the Aegis cruiser *Lake Erie* (CG-70) shot down a satellite in space with a modified SM-3 Standard missile, 168, 174-182, 291-293, 354-355, 365-366, 452-454

Stansfield, Lieutenant Richard J., USN

In the early 1950s received training in guided missiles and nuclear weapons, 164, 184

Stavridis, Admiral James G., USN (USNA, 1976)

Served 2006-2009 as Commander U.S. Southern Command, 418

Stecher, Captain Lewis Joseph Jr., USN (USNA, 1942)

In 1969 created the name "Aegis" for the Advanced Surface Missile System (ASMS), 375, 471

Sterett, USS (DDG-104)

Aegis destroyer commissioned in 2008, 549, 567

Stout, USS (DDG-55)

Problems with material condition observed in 2008 inspection, 317-318, 565-566

Strategic Air Command (SAC)

Relationship with the Navy's nuclear weapons school in the 1950s, 193

Strickland, USS (DER-324)

Mission in the mid-1950s to warn of Soviet bombers as part of the seaward extension of the Distant Early Warning Line, 198-209

Diesel propulsion plant in the mid-1950s, 197-198, 204
NROTC-trained reserve officers on board the ship in the mid-1950s, 206-208, 450

Surface Missile Systems Project
Created in 1962 as the Special Navy Task Force for Surface Missile Systems, renamed in 1963, 249, 269-278, 283-330, 338
In September 1965 moved from the Bureau of Naval Weapons to the Office of Naval Material, 306
Role of senior civil servants in the 1960s, 308-309

Syring, Vice Admiral James D., USN (USNA, 1985)
In the late 2000s headed the DDG-1000 program, later became director of the Missile Defense Agency, 408-409, 501

Talago, Commander Joseph Jr., USN
Postgraduate study at the Massachusetts Institute of Technology, 1946-47, 80, 279
Stationed in the Washington area in the early 1960s, 278-279

Talos Missile
On board the guided missile cruiser *Galveston* (CLG-3) in the early 1960s, 196, 241-244, 250-251, 256-263, 266, 269, 288
In 1963 the *Galveston* hit a surface ship with Talos, 262-263, 269
Talos desk in the Special Navy Task Force for Surface Missile Systems in the mid-1960s, 276
In 1968 the cruiser *Long Beach* (CGN-9) shot down two MiG fighters with Talos missiles in Vietnam, 356

Tazewell, Captain John P., USN (USNA, 1943)
Served in the 1960s in the ASMS/Aegis program, 314, 415-416

Teeter, Lieutenant Commander Phillip H., USN
In the late 1940s was executive officer of the destroyer *Goodrich* (DD-831), 94-96, 98, 105, 109, 113, 119-123

Terrier Missile
Difficulty with Terrier missile performance in the early 1960s, 248-249, 272
Work of the Special Navy Task Force for Surface Missile Systems in supervising the construction and upgrading of Terrier-equipped warships in the mid-1960s, 285-291, 330-333, 349-350
Mid-1960s introduction of transistors in the Terrier fire control system, 295-296
In the mid-1960s some Terrier missiles had nuclear warheads, 304-305
In 1972 the frigate *Biddle* (DLG-34) shot down a MiG fighter in Vietnam with a Terrier, 356

Thurmond, Senator J. Strom

In the 1970s received an explanation of the Vulcan/Phalanx close-in weapon system, 384

Ticonderoga USS (CG-47)
Authorized by Congress in 1977, 493
Competition for the shipbuilding contract, 494-495
The name honored the former aircraft carrier *Ticonderoga* (CV-14), 610
Construction in the early 1980s, commissioning in 1983, 537, 542-543, 580-581
Sea trials for the ship in 1982, 265, 438, 581-584, 619-623
Mediterranean deployment in 1983-84, 584-585
Firepower demonstration in April 1984, 585

Ticonderoga (CG-47)-Class Cruisers
Hull form of the *Spruance* (DD-963)-class destroyer used in the 1970s in developing *Ticonderoga* (CG-47)-class cruisers, 101-102, 433-440, 495, 501-502, 551-552, 614-619
Less amount of ballast needed for later ships in the class, 439
No on-board quarters for flag officers, 482
In 1977 Congress authorized the first Aegis ship, which became the guided missile cruiser *Ticonderoga* (CG-47), 493
Concerns in the early 1980s about the stability of the ships of the class, 595-596, 619-623

Todd Shipyards
In the late 1970s dropped out of bidding for the guided missile cruiser *Ticonderoga* (CG-47), 494-495

Tofalo, Captain Francis, USN (USNA, 1942)
Ran the Talos desk in the Special Navy Task Force for Surface Missile Systems in the mid-1960s, 276, 284

Trieste
While under tripartite administration in 1948, the destroyer *Goodrich* (DD-831) sat offshore for possible evacuation or shore bombardment, 111-112, 115

Tsingtao, China
Visited by the light cruiser *Springfield* (CL-66) in 1948-49, 141, 145-146

Typhon Missile
Surface-to-air missile program canceled in 1963 because of its high cost, 310-311, 315, 321, 374-376, 431

V-12 Program
Naval Reserve officer training program at the University of Kansas during World War II, 60-77, 96

Veliotis, P. Takis
    In the 1970s was general manager of the General Dynamics shipyard at Quincy, Massachusetts, 498-499, 616

Venereal Disease
    In Italy in 1948 when the destroyer *Goodrich* (DD-831) visited Venice, 113-114

Venice, Italy
    Visited by the destroyer *Goodrich* (DD-831) in 1948, 111-114

Vickery, Commander Hugh B., USN (USNA, 1940)
    In the late 1950s, while in OpNav, sponsored the ordnance training at the Naval Postgraduate School, 220

Vietnam War
    Shore bombardment by cruiser *Oklahoma City* (CLG-6), 258
    Involvement of the Navy Surface Missile Systems Engineering Station, Port Hueneme, 339-340
    In 1968 the cruiser *Long Beach* (CGN-9) shot down two MiG fighters with Talos missiles in Vietnam, 356
    In 1969 Meyer took a team to assess missile capabilities of ships operating off Vietnam, 364-365, 520-521
    In 1972 the frigate *Biddle* (DLG-34) shot down a MiG fighter in Vietnam with a Terrier, 356
    PIRAZ role for NTDS ships, 482

***Virginia* (CGN-38)-Class Cruisers**
    In the 1970s later ships of the type were considered for Aegis combat systems but not built, 404, 432-433, 454-459

von Braun, Dr. Wernher
    Work in U.S. rocket development programs in the 1950s, 164-168, 182-183

WV Warning Star
    Role in the Atlantic Barrier (BarLant) patrols in the mid-1950s to detect Soviet bombers, 199-201, 204-205

Wadleigh, Captain John R., USN (USNA, 1937)
    Commanded an escort squadron in the mid-1950s, 210
    Served on the ComDesLant staff in the mid-1950s, 211, 218

***Wainwright*, USS (DLG-28)**
    Commissioning of in January 1966, 271

***Wayne E. Meyer*, USS (DDG-108)**
    Aegis destroyer built at Bath Iron Works, 2007-09, 322, 328-329, 573-576
    Commissioned at Philadelphia in October 2009, 597-598, 609

Weather
    The radar picket destroyer escort *Strickland* (DER-324) encountered high seas during North Atlantic patrols in the mid-1950s, 202-203
    A damaging hurricane hit Newport, Rhode Island, in the mid-1950s, 211-212

Webber, Rear Admiral James H., USN (USNA, 1949)
    Served as Vice Commander, Naval Sea Systems Command in the mid-1980s, 637

West, Captain Richard D., USN
    Commanded the guided missile cruiser *Leahy* (CG-16) from 1989 to 1991, said that Aegis was unnecessary, 331

White Sands Missile Range, New Mexico
    The location for missile testing was chosen because of granite formations, 164-165, 182-183

Williams, Admiral John G. Jr, USN (USNA, 1947)
    In the early 1980s, as Chief of Naval Material, awarded Meyer a Distinguished Service Medal and hosted a dinner for him, 456-457, 583-584

Willoughby, William
    Former National Aeronautics and Space Administration official who taught reliability to Aegis personnel, 463-466, 638

Wilson, Commander George Barry, USN
    Served in the early 1960s in the Special Navy Task Force for Surface Missile Systems, 271-272

Winter, Donald C.
    Served as Secretary of the Navy, 2006-09, 485-486

Wise, Lieutenant Peyton Randolph II, USN (USNA, 1953)
    Served in the guided missile cruiser *Galveston* (CLG-3) in the early 1960s, 244, 420

Withington, Rear Admiral Frederic S., USN (Ret.) (USNA, 1923)
    In 1964 chaired a group to assess proposals for the Advanced Surface Missile System (ASMS), 370-374

Women
    Advent in the 1960s of large numbers of women into Civil Service, 342-343, 396-398, 474-475, 560-562, 626-627
    Role of women in assembling components of the Aegis SPY-1 radar and missile components in the 1970s and beyond, 430, 468-469
    Civilian women from the Aegis program went to sea on trials in the 1970s and 1980s, 593-594

Navy women served in the missile test ship *Norton Sound* (AVM-1) in the 1980s, 602-603

In the 2000s women are increasingly exposed to combat threats, 635-636

Woods, Rear Admiral Mark W., USN (USNA, 1942)
In the late 1950s, while in OpNav, sponsored the ordnance training at the Naval Postgraduate School, 220
In the mid-1960s served as executive officer of the Navy Surface Missile Systems Engineering Station, Port Hueneme, 344
Served 1969-72 as Commander Naval Ordnance Systems Command, 302-303, 314-317, 375
In the early 1970s as Commander Cruiser-Destroyer Force Pacific Fleet, 461-462

Woods, Radio Electrician Norman G., USN
Served on board the light cruiser *Springfield* (CL-66) in the late 1940s, 129-134, 149

World Trade Center, New York City
Suite of offices for John J, Mullen Company, 244-246

Wyatt, Rear Admiral William C. III, USN (USNA, 1952)
Served around 1970 as *Spruance* (DD-963) program manager, 546, 614
In the 2000s worked with Meyer's company on a surface warfare study, 614

Yorktown, **USS (CG-48)**
Commissioning of in July 1984 at Yorktown, Virginia, 590-591

Yosemite, **USS (AD-19)**
In the 1940s-50s was based in Newport, Rhode Island as flagship for ComDesLant, 108, 120-121, 209

Youman, Lieutenant Commander, USN
Commanded the radar picket destroyer escort *Strickland* (DER-324) in the mid-1950s, 201-202

Young, John J. Jr.
Served as Under Secretary of Defense for Acquisition, Technology and Logistics, 2007 to 2009, 340-341

Yugoslavia
Involved in the Trieste situation in 1948, 111-112, 115

Zeni, Lieutenant Levio E., USN (USNA, 1946)
Served on the ComDesLant staff in the mid-1950s, 212

Zumwalt, Admiral Elmo R., Jr., USN (USNA, 1943)

As CNO in the early 1970s, stance toward the Aegis program, 401, 405-406, 440-446, 485

Relationship with Admiral Ike Kidd, 503

Zumwalt **(DDG-1000)-Class Destroyers**
Under construction in the late 2000s, 171. 319-320, 327, 340, 408-409, 453-455, 478-479, 501. 524, 540, 640